Essentials of Marketing Analytics

Joseph F. Hair, Jr.
University of South Alabama

Dana E. Harrison
East Tennessee State University

Haya Ajjan
Elon University

Mc
Graw
Hill

ESSENTIALS OF MARKETING ANALYTICS, FIRST EDITION

Published by McGraw Hill LLC, 1325 Avenue of the Americas, New York, NY 10121. Copyright ©2022 by McGraw Hill LLC. All rights reserved. Printed in the United States of America. No part of this publication may be reproduced or distributed in any form or by any means, or stored in a database or retrieval system, without the prior written consent of McGraw Hill LLC, including, but not limited to, in any network or other electronic storage or transmission, or broadcast for distance learning.

Some ancillaries, including electronic and print components, may not be available to customers outside the United States.

This book is printed on acid-free paper.

1 2 3 4 5 6 7 8 9 LWI 26 25 24 23 22 21

ISBN 978-1-264-26360-8 (bound edition)
MHID 1-264-26360-0 (bound edition)
ISBN 978-1-264-26364-6 (loose-leaf edition)
MHID 1-264-26364-3 (loose-leaf edition)

Portfolio Director: *Laura Hurst Spell*
Marketing Manager: *Nicole Young*
Content Project Managers: *Harvey Yep (Core)/Emily Windelborn (Assessment)*
Buyer: *Susan K. Culbertson*
Design: *Beth Blech*
Content Licensing Specialist: *Lorraine Buczek*
Cover Image: *Ico Maker/Shutterstock*
Compositor: *Aptara®, Inc.*

All credits appearing on page or at the end of the book are considered to be an extension of the copyright page.

Library of Congress Cataloging-in-Publication Data
Names: Hair, Joseph F., Jr., 1944- author. | Harrison, Dana E., author. |
   Ajjan, Haya, author.
Title: Essentials of marketing analytics, 1e / Joseph F. Hair, Jr.,
   University of South Alabama, Dana E. Harrison, East Tennessee State
   University, Haya Ajjan, Elon University.
Description: 1 Edition. | Dubuque : McGraw Hill Education, 2021. | Includes
   index.
Identifiers: LCCN 2020054554 (print) | LCCN 2020054555 (ebook) | ISBN
   9781264263608 (hardcover) | ISBN 9781264263646 (spiral bound) | ISBN
   9781260597745 (hardcover) | ISBN 9781264263639 (ebook) | ISBN
   9781264263653 (ebook other)
Subjects: LCSH: Marketing research—Juvenile literature. |
   Marketing—Juvenile literature.
Classification: LCC HF5415.2 .H265 2021 (print) | LCC HF5415.2 (ebook) |
   DDC 658.8/3—dc23
LC record available at https://lccn.loc.gov/2020054554
LC ebook record available at https://lccn.loc.gov/2020054555

The Internet addresses listed in the text were accurate at the time of publication. The inclusion of a website does not indicate an endorsement by the authors or McGraw Hill LLC, and McGraw Hill LLC does not guarantee the accuracy of the information presented at these sites.

mheducation.com/highered

Dedication

To my wife Dale, our son Joe III, his wife Kerrie, and grandsons Joe IV and Declan.
—*Joseph F. Hair, Jr., Mobile, Alabama*

To my husband John, and our children Mason and Faith, for your enduring patience, love, and support.
—*Dana E. Harrison, Johnson City, Tennessee*

To Najwa, Mahdi, Alexander, and Julian for making it all worthwhile.
—*Haya Ajjan, Elon, North Carolina*

About the Authors

Joe F. Hair, Jr. is Professor of Marketing, Cleverdon Chair of Business, and Director of the PhD degree program in the Mitchell College of Business, at the University of South Alabama. In 2018 and 2019, he was recognized by Clarivate Analytics as being in the top 1 percent globally of all Business and Economics professors. He was selected for the award based on citations of his research and scholarly accomplishments, which for his career exceed 240,000. Google Scholar ranks him #1 globally in the categories of Marketing, Multivariate Data Analysis, and Structural Equation Modeling. Joe formerly held the Copeland Endowed Chair of Entrepreneurship at Louisiana State University. He has published more than 75 editions of his books, including market leaders *Multivariate Data Analysis*, 8th edition, Cengage Learning, UK, 2019, which has been cited more than 130,000 times; *Essentials of Marketing Research*, 5th edition, McGraw-Hill/Irwin, 2020; *MKTG*, 13th edition, Cengage, 2021, used at over 500 universities globally; *A Primer in Partial Least Squared Structural Equation Modeling* (PLS-SEM), 3rd edition forthcoming, Sage, 2021; and *Essentials of Business Research Methods*, 4th edition, Taylor & Francis, 2020. In addition to publishing numerous refereed articles in academic journals such as *Journal of Marketing Research*, *Journal of Academy of Marketing Science*, *Journal of Business/Chicago*, *Journal of Advertising Research*, and *Journal of Retailing*, he has presented executive education and management training programs for numerous companies, has been retained as a consultant and expert witness for a wide variety of firms, and is frequently an invited speaker on research methods and multivariate analysis. He is a Distinguished Fellow of the Academy of Marketing Science and the Society for Marketing Advances, and he has served as president of the Academy of Marketing Sciences, the Society for Marketing Advances, the Southern Marketing Association, the Association for Healthcare Research, the Southwestern Marketing Association, and the American Institute for Decision Sciences, Southeast Section. Professor Hair was recognized by the Academy of Marketing Science with its Outstanding Marketing Teaching Excellence Award, and the Louisiana State University Entrepreneurship Institute under his leadership was recognized nationally by *Entrepreneur Magazine* as one of the top 12 programs in the United States.

Dana Eckerle Harrison is an Assistant Professor of Marketing and the Stanley P. Williams Faculty Fellow at East Tennessee State University. Prior to her work in academia, Dana spent many years assisting software companies in the areas of marketing and sales management. She teaches marketing research, analytics, digital marketing and strategy courses at the undergraduate and graduate level. Her scholarly research has been published in journals such as the *Journal of Business Research*, the *Journal of Product and Brand Management* and the *Journal of Marketing Theory and Practice*. Her research focuses on the intersection between customer relationship management, business ethics, data quality and governance, and marketing analytics methods. Dana is a co-author on the *Essentials of Marketing Research*, 5th edition, McGraw-Hill/Irwin, 2020. She currently serves as an Associate Editor for the *Journal of Marketing Theory and Practice,* as well as on the Editorial Review Board for the *Journal of Business Research* and *Journal of Marketing Education.* Dana continues to be an active member of prominent marketing organizations. She has presented and led panel discussions at conferences such as the Academy of Marketing Science, American Marketing Association, INFORMS Society for Marketing Science, and the Society for Marketing Advances, regarding topics such as Artificial Intelligence and business ethics, social network analysis, sales management, the impact of analytics techniques and technology on marketing education and practice, the emergence of Blockchain in marketing, and information governance. Furthermore, she has offered certificate programs on marketing analytics and currently serves as the Proceedings Editor for the Society of Marketing Advances and the Director of Technology and Data Management for the Academy of Marketing Science.

Haya Ajjan is an Associate Professor of Management Information Systems, the Sheldon and Christine Gordon Professor in Entrepreneurship, and the Director of the Center for Organizational Analytics at Elon University. Haya joined Elon in 2010 and teaches data analytics courses in the Love School of Business' undergraduate business, MBA, and M.S. in Business Analytics programs. She was instrumental in developing the business analytics undergraduate major and the M.S. in Business Analytics program. Her research focuses on better understanding the impact of technology use on individuals, groups, and organizations, and she has been published in journals such as *Journal of Business Research*, *Communications of the Association for Information Systems, European Journal of Operations Research, Business Horizons* and *Journal of Marketing Theory and Practice.* She currently serves as an Associate Editor for the *Journal of Marketing Education.* Her commitment to infusing technology and innovation into the curriculum resulted in her appointment as Faculty Fellow for Innovation and Assistant to Elon University President Constance Ledoux Book. She also serves as a project lead for Elon's participation in Apple's Everyone Can Code initiative. Ajjan received the Love School of Business Dean's Awards for Scholarship and Service and was named Top 50 Undergraduate Business Professors in the United States by Poets & Quants. During her tenure at Elon, she founded the Center for Organizational Analytics, Elon NEXT for professional advancement and continuing education studies, and the Elon Innovation Council. She teaches a certificate program on marketing analytics for the Academy of Marketing Science and currently serves as a program co-chair for the AIS Special Interest Group in Decision Support and Analytics.

Preface

We developed this new book with enthusiasm and great optimism. Marketing analytics is an exciting field to study, and there are numerous emerging opportunities for students at the undergraduate level, and particularly at the master's level. We live in a global, highly competitive, rapidly changing world that is increasingly influenced by digital data, expanded analytical capabilities, information technology, social media, artificial intelligence, and many other recent developments. We believe this book will become the premier source for new and essential knowledge in data analytics, particularly for situations related to decision making that can benefit from marketing analytics, which is likely 80 percent of all challenges faced by organizations.

Many of you have been asking us to write this book, and we are confident you will be pleased it is now available. This first edition of *Essentials of Marketing Analytics* was written to meet the needs of you, our customers. The text is concise, highly readable, and value-priced, yet it delivers the basic knowledge needed for an introductory text on marketing analytics. We provide you and your students with an exciting, up-to-date text and an extensive supplement package. In the following sections, we summarize what you will find when you examine—and we hope, adopt—the first edition of *Essentials of Marketing Analytics*.

Innovative Features of the Book

The past decade or so has witnessed an explosion in data, particularly digital data—so much so that we are in what has been named the era of Big Data! The emergence of literally huge amounts of data has led to the need to develop methods of identifying the underlying patterns in data so they can be used to solve marketing problems. At the same time, marketing professionals, like others, are quite busy. To solve this problem, software has been developed that enables marketers to drill down into the large amount of data available, identify relationships, and visually present the results in a manner that creates marketing knowledge.

Our book introduces students to several of the most popular analytics software tools, such as Tableau and Python. In addition, students will learn social network analysis, web analytics, automated machine learning, neural networks, cognitive analytics, and natural language processing. No other book available provides such comprehensive coverage of these topics to students. As a professor, therefore, you can choose to cover all methods to familiarize your students with the various analysis possibilities. Or, you can select specific methods and drill down into a limited number of approaches that are consistent with your course objectives.

The starting point in learning marketing analytics is to understand the marketing problem. For example, is the ultimate objective of an analytics approach to create awareness through social media, develop an effective message strategy, persuade customers to purchase your product or service in a highly competitive market, or overcome a service quality crisis situation? The second step in the marketing analytics process is becoming familiar with what data is available and whether the data can be directly used to solve marketing problems. One type, structured data, can be used directly because the format of the data has a clearly defined structure and is often made up of numbers stored in rows and columns. Examples include analyzing the click-through sequence on websites, the time of day or day of the week a purchase was made, and how much was paid for the purchase. The other type of data, unstructured, cannot be directly analyzed because it includes text, images, video, or sensor data that does not have a consistent format. Before unstructured data can be used, it is extracted and categorized so it can be statistically analyzed. For example, online videos, visual images, and website postings can be coded into numbers or categories before being used with analytical methods. The challenge of managing different data types is a major obstacle to working with marketing analytics, because an estimated 80 percent of the emerging data is unstructured. We discuss the fundamentals of analytics, data management, data exploration and data visualization in applying marketing analytics in Chapters 1 through 4 of this book.

Marketing analytics methods can be categorized into two groups: supervised and unsupervised learning. Supervised learning methods are applied when the available data includes a target (outcome) variable that is already identified in a historical dataset. For example, a target variable could be purchase versus non-purchase, or to post on a website or to not post. When a target variable is available, the objective is often to see if other variables in the dataset can predict the target variable. In contrast, unsupervised learning does not have an identified target variable. Thus, the goal of unsupervised learning is to examine the underlying structure and distribution in the data to discover patterns. The three most popular supervised learning methods—multiple regression, neural networks, and Automated Machine Learning—are explained in Chapters 5, 6, and 7. Moreover, to enhance student analytical skills, case studies for each of these chapters enable students to complete an exercise using all three of these methods with real-world data.

Unsupervised learning methods are covered in Chapters 8 and 9. These methods are applied to explore relationships that may exist when no target variable is available and patterns in the data are unknown. Cluster analysis, for example, works by learning the underlying structure of the data to identify distinct groups in the dataset. In contrast, market basket analysis discovers associations among items in a "shopping basket." These associations can help companies develop marketing strategies by gaining insights into which items are frequently purchased together by customers.

The final three chapters are devoted to emerging analytical methods. They include natural language processing, social network analysis, and web analytics. Chapter 10 provides an overview of two increasingly popular analytical methods being used in marketing—topic modeling and sentiment analysis. The implementation of methods like topic modeling and Vader Sentiment are explained in a step-by-step approach. Social network analysis, covered in Chapter 11, identifies relationships, influencers, information dissemination patterns, and behaviors among connections in a network. One approach to social network analysis, Polinode, analyzes the web of connections that link people to one another, presents the results visually, and can identify influencers on social media sites. Finally, in Chapter 12, we cover the latest developments in web analytics and introduce a retailer website analysis example using the Google Analytics platform.

As part of the "applied" emphasis of our text, *Essentials of Marketing Analytics* has three pedagogical features that are very helpful to students' practical understanding of the topics. One is the Practitioner Corner that features an industry expert who has applied the method explained in that chapter. The practitioner summarizes an applied example using the method and also poses questions for discussion. Thus, students can truly see how marketing analytics is being used to improve decision making. A second pedagogical feature is chapter case studies. Students gain hands-on experience with step-by-step case studies using datasets representing a variety of marketing scenarios. A third pedagogical feature is the variety of analytical software introduced in the book to familiarize the students with the marketing analyst's toolbox.

As noted earlier, analytics is rapidly changing the face of marketing, and the authors have experience with, and a strong interest in, the issues associated with data analysis. Other texts on marketing analytics—and there are very few—have limited coverage of the field of analytics. In contrast, our text has extensive coverage of all the most important analytical methods available.

Pedagogy

Many marketing analytics texts are readable. An important question, however, is whether or not students can comprehend the topics they are reading about. This book offers a wealth of pedagogical features, all aimed at enhancing students' comprehension of the material. In addition—and probably most importantly—the authors are not only knowledgeable about the field but also experienced in writing at a level that can easily be understood by students. Our past textbook publishing success is clearly evident in this book and the case studies illustrating analytical methods use real datasets.

The following is a list of the major pedagogical elements in this book:

Learning Objectives. Each chapter begins with a clear set of Learning Objectives that students can use to assess their expectations for and understanding of the chapter, in view of the nature and importance of the chapter material.

Practitioner Corner. Each chapter includes an interesting, relevant example of a real-world business situation that illustrates the focus and significance of the chapter material. For example, Chapter 6 features insights on neural network analysis from Stephen Brobst, the Chief Technology Officer at Teradata Corporation. In Chapter 7, Elpida Ormanidou, the VP of Advanced Analytics and Insights at Starbucks, shares lessons learned from the use of Automated Machine Learning in her work.

Key Terms. These are boldfaced in the text, listed at the end of the chapters, and included in the comprehensive Glossary at the end of the book.

Discussion and Review Questions. The Discussion and Review Questions are carefully designed to enhance the learning process and to encourage application of the concepts learned in the chapter to actual marketing decision-making situations. There are five or six questions in each chapter directly related to clarifying the understanding of concepts and methods introduced in the chapters, and particularly to apply them to solve practical marketing and customer behavior problems. Finally, the questions provide students with opportunities to enhance their marketing analytics applications and interpretative skills, and to explore how their knowledge of analytics can enhance their career success.

Critical Thinking and Marketing Applications. The critical thinking and marketing applications exercises are carefully designed to enhance the self-learning process and to encourage application of the concepts learned in the chapters to real business decision-making situations. There are two or three questions in each chapter directly related to the analytical methods and designed to provide students with opportunities to enhance their analytical and interpretative skills.

Supplements

An extensive and rich ancillary package accompanies the text. The following is a brief description of materials in the Connect Instructor Resources:

Instructor's Resources. Specially prepared Instructor's Manual and electronic Test Bank and PowerPoint slide presentations provide an easy transition for instructors teaching with the book the first time. In addition, there are many other support materials to build upon the notes and teaching enhancement materials available. Finally, a wealth of extra student projects, real-life examples, and datasets are available as additional classroom resources.

Datasets. Ten datasets are available, which can be used to solve the case studies in the chapters.

An additional resource available for use with the text is described next:

Analytical Software. Many software providers offer academic licenses at low or no-cost for faculty and students. The analytical software used in the textbook provides a real-life experience for students in identifying and understanding relationships in data. These powerful software tools enable students to apply many of the tools they will need to know when searching for jobs.

Acknowledgments

The authors took the lead in preparing the first edition of the most comprehensive book in the field of marketing analytics. But many other people must be given credit for their significant contributions in bringing our vision to reality. We thank our colleagues in academia and industry for their helpful insights over many years on numerous research topics:

Pia Albinsson
Appalachian State

Chad Autry
University of Tennessee

Barry Babin
University of Mississippi

Nichol Beacham
University of Alabama–Birmingham

James Blair
Eastern Kentucky University

Mike Brady
Florida State University

Angeline Close Scheinbaum
Clemson University

Vicki Crittenden
Boston College

Amit Deokar
University of Massachusetts Lowell

Diane Edmondson
Middle Tennessee State University

Keith Ferguson
Michigan State University

O.C. Ferrell
Auburn University

Prachi Gala
Elon University

Susan Geringer
California State University-Fresno

Anne Gottfried
University of Southern Mississippi

Gohar F. Khan
University of Waikato

Ciara Heavin
Cork University

Jennifer Henderson
Louisiana State University

Bryan Hochstein
The University of Alabama

Phillip Holmes
Pensacola Christian College

Chris Hopkins
Auburn University

Lucas Hopkins
Florida State University

Matt Howard
University of South Alabama

Astrid Keel
University of LaVerne

Scott Keller
University of West Florida

April Kemp
Southeast Louisiana University

Kacy Kim
Bryant University

Anjala Krishen
University of Nevada

Amanda Ledet
Louisiana State University

Britton Leggett
University of South Alabama

Marianne Loes
University of South Alabama

Bryan Lukas
University of Manchester

Greg Marshall
Stetson University

Lucy Matthews
Middle Tennessee State University

Chris Meyers
Texas A&M University, Commerce

Adam Merkle
University of South Alabama

Adam Mills
Loyola University-New Orleans

Dena Mitchell
Troy University

Zach Moore
University of Louisiana-Monroe

Allona Murray
University of Southern Mississippi

Stephanie Noble
University of Tennessee

Obinna Obilo
Central Michigan University

Janna Parker
James Madison University

Mike Peasley
Middle Tennessee State University

Lou Pelton
University of North Texas

Maria Petrescu
ICN Business School-Campus Artem

Torsten Pieper
University of North Carolina-Charlotte

Michael Polonsky
Deakin University

Kelly Price-Rhea
East Tennessee State University

Mary Pritchett Harrison
Birmingham-Southern College

Charlie Ragland
Indiana University

Melanie Richards
East Tennessee State University

Christian Ringle
Hamburg University of Technology

Jeff Risher
Southeastern Oklahoma State University

Wendy Ritz
Florida State University

Marko Sarstedt
Otto-von-Guericke University, Magdeburg, Germany

Justin Scott
Pensacola Christian College

Emory Serviss
Auburn University

Stefan Sleep
Kennesaw State University

Donna Smith
Ryerson University

Goran Svensson
University of Oslo

Raghu Tadepalli
Elon University

Drew Thoeni
University of North Florida

Gail Tom
California State University-Sacramento

Ron Tsang
University of South Alabama

Steve Vitucci
University of Central Texas

Alvin Williams
University of South Alabama

David Williams
Dalton State University

Our sincere thanks to the analytics industry experts who contributed to the *Practitioner Corner* of each chapter:

Stephen Brobst
Teradata

Nikola Cuculovski
22squared

William Disch
DataRobot

Peter Drewes
Lockheed Martin

Jasmine Jones
MetLife

Theresa Kushner
data.world

Kaitlin Marvin
Progressive Insurance

Aran Moultrop
Alteryx

Elpida Ormanidou
Starbucks

Jessica Owens
Ntara

Marc Smith
Social Media Research Foundation

Jim Sterne
Digital Analytics Association

Rob Taylor
SAS

Our sincere thanks also go to the helpful reviewers who made suggestions and shared their ideas for the first edition:

George Bernard
Seminole State University

Ali Besharat
University of South Florida

Julie Blose
College of Charleston

Jennifer Burton
University of Tampa

Mark Case
Florida Gulf Coast University

Nikola Cuculovski
22squared

Bill Disch
DataRobot

Chris Hopkins
Auburn University

Chris Huseman
Liberty University

Kacy Kim
Bryant University

Judy Ma
California State University-East Bay

Maria Petrescu
ICN Business School

Emily J. Plant
University of Montana

Jeffrey Risher
Southeastern Oklahoma University

Gail Tom
California State University-Sacramento

Gina Tran
Florida Gulf Coast University

Tuo Wang
Kent State University

Finally, we would like to thank our editors and advisors at McGraw-Hill Education. Thanks go to Laura Hurst Spell, associate portfolio manager; Meredith Fossel, executive portfolio manager; Allison Marker, product coordinator; Nicole Young, marketing manager; and Sarah Blasco, developmental editor. We also are grateful to our professional production team: Harvey Yep, project manager; Beth Blech, designer; Mark Christianson, program manager; and Emily Windelborn, assessments project manager.

Joseph F. Hair, Jr.
Dana E. Harrison
Haya Ajjan

Students: Get Learning that Fits You

Effective tools for efficient studying

Connect is designed to make you more productive with simple, flexible, intuitive tools that maximize your study time and meet your individual learning needs. Get learning that works for you with Connect.

Study anytime, anywhere

Download the free ReadAnywhere app and access your online eBook or SmartBook 2.0 assignments when it's convenient, even if you're offline. And since the app automatically syncs with your eBook and SmartBook 2.0 assignments in Connect, all of your work is available every time you open it. Find out more at **www.mheducation.com/readanywhere**

> *"I really liked this app—it made it easy to study when you don't have your textbook in front of you."*
>
> - Jordan Cunningham, Eastern Washington University

Calendar: owattaphotos/Getty Images

Everything you need in one place

Your Connect course has everything you need—whether reading on your digital eBook or completing assignments for class, Connect makes it easy to get your work done.

Learning for everyone

McGraw Hill works directly with Accessibility Services Departments and faculty to meet the learning needs of all students. Please contact your Accessibility Services Office and ask them to email accessibility@mheducation.com, or visit **www.mheducation.com/about/accessibility** for more information.

Top: Jenner Images/Getty Images, Left: Hero Images/Getty Images, Right: Hero Images/Getty Images

Brief Table of Contents

CONTENTS

PART

1

Overview of Marketing Analytics and Data Management

1 Introduction to Marketing Analytics

LEARNING OBJECTIVES

1.1 Discuss marketing analytics.

1.2 Discuss how to identify the right business problem.

1.3 Identify and compare different data sources.

1.4 Describe different data types.

1.5 Explain the difference between predictors and target variables.

1.6 Differentiate between supervised and unsupervised modeling.

1.7 Investigate the 7-step marketing analytics process.

1.8 Explain the value of learning marketing analytics.

alphaspirit/Shutterstock

1.1 Introduction to Marketing Analytics

A primary responsibility of marketing is to properly manage the wants and needs of customers. This can be accomplished through strategic decisions about products, pricing, distribution, and communications that are based on insights from marketing analytics. This chapter will introduce you to the exciting possibilities of marketing analytics, which companies are increasingly using to satisfy customers and maintain a competitive advantage.

Have you ever wondered how Hotels.com, Spotify, or Stitch Fix obtain and provide the information customers want so fast? As examples, consider the three situations below:

- **How does Expedia, Orbitz, or Hotels.com determine the price to quote when you are shopping for a hotel room?** Prices of hotel rooms are frequently updated based on demand, seasonality, day of the week, time of the day, and even the type of technology being used to find accommodations. For instance, Orbitz Worldwide Inc. knows that Mac computer users spend as much as 30 percent more a night on hotels, so Orbitz shows its Mac customers different travel options, and sometimes even more expensive rooms than Windows users.[1]

- **How does Spotify know what songs to suggest for you?** From user-generated playlists, listener preferences, and advanced data analytics, Spotify, an audio streaming platform, can build collections of music their listeners enjoy and help users find their new favorite music.[2]

- **How does Stitch Fix achieve the highest-ever rate of purchased items per "Fix" for its female customers?** Stitch Fix is only 7 years old and in 2018, it generated $1.2 billion in sales. Their stylists work closely with the analytics algorithm suggestions, and then match results with the customer's style. Over time, the analytics algorithm learns and continuously becomes more accurate when making clothing suggestions, stocking decisions, packing at the warehouse, and shipping.[3]

In the rest of this chapter, we describe and explain an analytics framework, the relevant marketing analytics concepts, and industry best practices. Building on this foundation, you will continue to work through practical exercises and develop the mindset of a marketing analyst.

Marketing Analytics Defined

Marketing analytics uses data, statistics, mathematics, and technology to solve marketing business problems. It involves modeling and software to drive marketing decision making. Not long ago, marketing analytics was a highly specialized field for individuals who had in-depth knowledge of mathematical modeling, computer programming, and specialized software packages. Today, however, the availability of large amounts of data, improvements in analytics techniques, substantial increases in computer processing power, and affordability have made marketing analytics more practical and available to a much larger audience. To survive, companies increasingly need to differentiate products and services, optimize processes, and understand the drivers for business performance, and marketing analytics can help them to do that.

Marketing analytics is one of the fastest growing fields of analytics applications. This growth can be attributed to the increase in user-generated data from social media (e.g., Instagram, Facebook, Twitter), mobile applications (e.g., weather, text, maps), and multiple search and shopping channels now accessible by customers (e.g., phone, in-store, online). Marketers can use insights from analytics to increase company performance through various marketing capabilities such as pricing, product development, channel management, marketing communications, and selling. Restaurants are even beginning to apply marketing analytics to optimize the selection of new locations. For example, the restaurant chain Roy Rogers Franchise Co. uses advanced analytics to expand into new markets, determine their next site locations, and forecast sales.[4] Their machine learning platform integrates internal and external data to ensure restaurant locations match the needs and wants of the geographical area. Internal data such as the current location of stores, sales, and competitor locations are integrated with external data such as demographics, traffic near the store, and social media activity (e.g., geo-tagged posts) to gain a more holistic view of the site potential.

Marketing analytics is increasingly being applied in numerous industries and functional departments, and the impact and benefits are evident. Exhibit 1-1 compares the interest in marketing analytics to analytics use in other business functions. Results are measured based on the search volume for the word "Marketing Analytics" using Google Trends from 2004 to 2020 (estimated). The search for marketing analytics has been consistently higher than other fields, with financial analytics, HR analytics, and supply chain analytics being much lower.

Exhibit 1-1 Google Search Trends for the Terms Marketing Analytics, Supply Chain Analytics, Financial Analytics, and HR Analytics (2020 estimated)

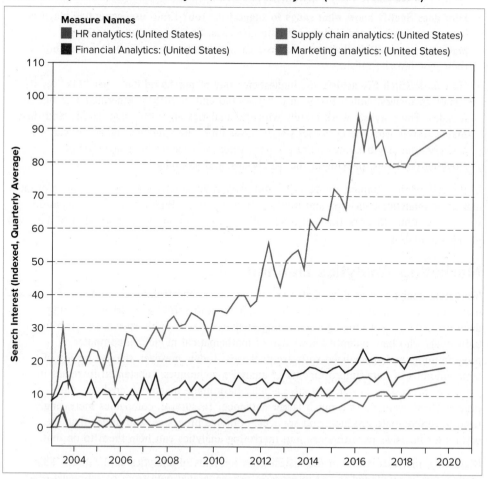

Source: Google Trends.

A large amount of marketing data exists, which explains the interest in learning more about the area. A lack of marketing analytics skills, however, has left many companies in a situation described as "data rich but information poor." Until recently, many organizations were making decisions based upon intuition or opinion versus data-driven knowledge. Data analytics techniques provide an excellent opportunity to bridge the gap between information and insights.

As technology continues to improve and dominate innovative processes, analytics will become a ubiquitous part of everything we do. To prepare you for this, we explain how to creatively approach a problem, comprehend the essence of communication and collaboration, understand key elements of project management, and complete a successful project. These skills are the most critical in the age of data analytics.

Analytics Levels and Their Impact on Competitive Advantage

Analytics involves techniques as simple as descriptive statistics and visualization, as well as more advanced predictive modeling, prescriptive, and newly emerging artificial intelligence (AI) and cognitive analytics. As organizations adopt more advanced techniques (i.e., predictive, prescriptive, and AI methods), higher data management maturity is required to achieve a competitive advantage, as depicted in Exhibit 1-2.

Exhibit 1-2 The Competitive Advantage of Marketing Analytics

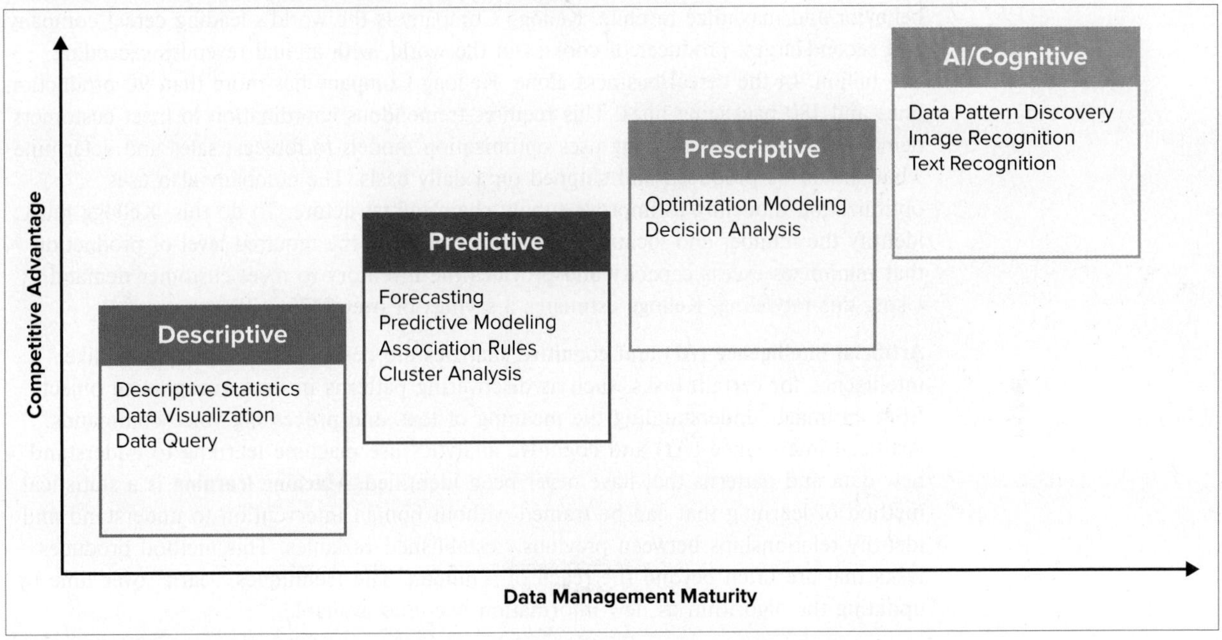

Source: Adapted from SAS.

Descriptive analytics are a set of techniques used to explain or quantify the past. Several examples of descriptive analytics include: data queries, visual reports, and descriptive statistics (e.g., mean, mode, median, variance, standard deviation). This type of information is essential to summarize questions related to how many and how often situations occur. For example, how many customers use a mobile app each day, and how often do they visit a website within the same month? Customer needs and motivations are not always understood, but these fundamental insights provide a foundation for marketers to explore what is fueling the behavior. Descriptive analysis can be especially helpful when marketers collect data from a survey. Retailers such as Dick's Sporting Goods and Dunkin' survey customers in return for a coupon code or free product following a recent experience. The survey questions focus on capturing whether customers feel stores maintained correct levels of stock or were satisfied with the purchase experience. Overall averages and trends resulting from this technique can be beneficial in reinforcing existing practices and determining how the company might improve the customer's experience moving forward.

Predictive analytics is used to build models based on the past to explain the future. Mathematical models examine historical data to predict new values, needs, and opportunities. For example, historical customer sales data can be used to predict future sales. You might recall when Target predicted a teen girl was pregnant before her father was aware.[5] How does this happen? Target Corporation collected data from customer purchases and used predictive modeling to classify customers as "pregnant" or "not pregnant." Customers identified as pregnant based on their purchases were then sent sales promotions for early pregnancy to capitalize on a significant revenue stream. Zillow, an online real estate database and analytics platform, also develops predictive models from publicly available city housing data. Zillow predicts a "Zestimate" or value for every home based on over 100 predictors for each of the 100 million homes in its database.[6]

Prescriptive analytics identifies the best optimal course of action or decision. Consider, for example, how UPS efficiently maps drivers through a city using optimized routes that reduce the number of left turns, or how airlines maintain productivity, reduce costs, and increase customer satisfaction by optimizing flight and crew scheduling. Price optimization, also a growing e-commerce practice, is used by Amazon to develop pricing strategies and remain competitive in the retail industry. In fact, the company has reported changing prices more than 2.5 million times a day[7] to influence customer behavior and maximize revenue. Kellogg Company is the world's leading cereal company and second-largest producer of cookies in the world, with annual revenues exceeding $14 billion. In the cereal business alone, Kellogg Company has more than 90 production lines and 180 packaging lines. This requires tremendous coordination to meet customers' demand at a low cost. Kellogg uses optimization models to forecast sales and determine what should be produced and shipped on a daily basis. The company also uses optimization modeling to improve supply chain infrastructure. To do this, Kellogg must identify the number and location of plants to produce the required level of production that minimizes excess capacity and provides the inventory to meet customer demand. Using this modeling, Kellogg estimates a savings of over $475 million a year.[8]

Artificial intelligence (AI) and **cognitive analytics** are designed to mimic human-like intelligence for certain tasks, such as discovering patterns in data, recognizing objects from an image, understanding the meaning of text, and processing voice commands. Artificial intelligence (AI) and cognitive analytics use machine learning to understand new data and patterns that have never been identified. **Machine learning** is a statistical method of learning that can be trained without human intervention to understand and identify relationships between previously established variables. This method produces tasks that are often beyond the reach of a human. The techniques "learn" over time by updating the algorithm as new information becomes available.

Using technology powered by AI, Olay, a Procter & Gamble skincare line, has doubled its sales conversion rate.[9] Olay encourages customers to upload personal photos to an app where it uses image recognition to identify the age of skin and then recommends specific products. This process can be completed in the convenience and privacy of a customer's home on their computer or mobile device, so customers know what they want before arriving at the store. Mtailor, an online clothing retailer, also uses customer images to create a customized clothing fit. The customer uses an app that measures 17 different points to develop a personalized fit and recommended size. In fact, Mtailor claims their method is more accurate than a professional tailor. In the case of Olay and Mtailor, AI engages the customer to obtain data and then produce personalized recommendations for products.

Indeed, today's AI technology enables almost any company to augment or complement human capabilities in developing customer solutions. Hitachi, a Japanese multinational conglomerate, is using AI named "H" to discover patterns that typically go undetected by humans. The H process generates customer solutions and selects the best options to

Courtesy of Ian Tuttle

Theresa Kushner, partner in Business Data Leadership, comes with over 20 years of experience in deploying predictive analytics at IBM, Cisco, VMware, and Dell. She is an accomplished, Business-Centric Executive and Board Advisor who understands data and leads companies through transformations in the midst of rapid technology, regulatory issues, and market disruptions. Theresa has expertise harnessing data analytics and company and customer information to lower costs and contribute multi-billion dollar growth for publicly traded, technology leaders. She has co-authored two books: *Managing Your Business Data from Chaos to Confidence* and *B2B Data Driven Marketing: Sources, Uses, Results.*

Q *The Wall Street Journal* **recently reported that automotive companies were struggling with the use of artificial intelligence.[10] Barriers to adoption included "difficulties in implementation technology, limited data for algorithmic training, a shortage of talent in data science, and uncertainty about the return on investment." Theresa, from your perspective, how can companies address these problems prior to pursuing AI?**

A To begin with, I think that all traditional companies are having trouble making the transition to an environment where AI and machine learning are applied effortlessly because they haven't relooked at their strategy and made room for this kind of transformation. For example, an automotive company obtains over 8 billion records a day from its automobiles, but what to do with those records is not always thoughtfully planned against a strategy. Let's just assume that someone in engineering thinks it's a smart idea to track whenever a seat belt is buckled. That immediately helps with safety standards and you can get some great data off that click. However, the remainder of the engineering staff may be looking at several other events that could be just as telling about the safety of the car and driver. Are those events planned with the seatbelt click or without considering it at all?

The holistic approach of data management and how it relates to a strategy is very difficult for companies like GM or any of the car manufacturers, because they did not begin with the end in mind. They are improvising the use of AI as they go along. All the problems mentioned—such as difficulties in implementation, limited data for algorithmic training, and even the shortage of trained personnel—can be traced back to a company not articulating how AI/Machine Learning supports their strategy. If the strategy were there, the companies had a strategy connected to their data, and they would have no problem articulating a return on investment.

Continued to next page

improve operations at call centers, retail sales, financing alternatives, warehouse management, and similar tasks.[11] Applications like "H" can easily automate and improve customer interactions to increase sales and, ultimately, customer loyalty.

1.2 Defining the Right Business Problems

Marketing analysts face complex challenges in today's data-intensive and competitive business environment. They are often confronted with multiple courses of action that must be completed quickly. Evaluating these alternatives and choosing the best action forward is at the heart of decision analysis. But one of the most important initial steps in the marketing analytics journey is defining the right business problem to pursue. A successful understanding of business problems requires deep knowledge of the customers' journey, from how they search to where they purchase, and how satisfied they are with products and services. Problem identification helps to uncover strategic business opportunities. Business initiatives that improve market share, establish a better relationship with the customer, or position the enterprise to take advantage of innovation are a few business strategies that can be supported by an analytical approach.

One of the most critical steps in the analytics process is to start with an understanding of the real business question the data needs to address. Knowing the right business question leads to smarter decisions that drive impact.

Continued from previous page

PRACTITIONER CORNER

Theresa Kushner | Advisory Board Member at data.world and Partner at Business Data Leadership

Q **What are the greatest challenges facing analysts when attempting to define the business problem?**

A The biggest challenge facing analysts when attempting to define the business problem is their innate way of thinking. Analysts have a very structured way of thinking about problems, but business problems are not always structured, especially in marketing and sales, where relationships play a part in the success of most actions. The challenge usually begins when the teams are defining the problem, and it begins at a very basic level. Ensuring that everyone understands what needs to happen, how it will happen, who will be responsible for it happening— these are key decisions that must be made by all involved in the analysis *before* it begins.

Q **What is the impact of inaccurately defining the business problem prior to undertaking an analytics project?**

A I've seen too many "problems" given to analysts to analyze that weren't carefully thought through. For example, a marketing manager commissions an algorithm to predict which customers will buy the new product to be made available next quarter. He doesn't tell the analyst how the information will be used. He just wants a "list." The analyst assumes that the "list" will be used with the inside sales team and develops a ranked list of customers that might be in the market. But the marketing manager really wanted a "list" of potential customers who might be willing to beta test the new product. The difference between success and failure of this analytic project depends on how thoroughly the problem is discussed and how vetted the solution is for its applicability to the problem.

Continued to page 13

How do you arrive at the right business problem? The process begins by understanding the intent and business considerations behind the question. Consider you are working at a retailer that was once the largest in the country, but it recently filed for bankruptcy. The marketing executive calls you to her office and explains that large investments were made specifically to develop mobile applications. Unfortunately, visitors are registering for an account, but then not using it for purchases. The executive asks you to determine how to entice those first-time users back to the mobile application, because the company was relying upon this technology to make them competitive again. At this point, is the underlying business problem evident? A better understanding of the business problem can be gained through interviews with business stakeholders. Conversations that more broadly discuss problems facing the company are likely to uncover more relevant issues. During your initial conversation with the marketing executive, she explains that the threat of competition from Amazon, Target, and Walmart continues to rise and profits are falling. Moreover, the company's brick-and-mortar locations are outdated, rely on obsolete technology, and are experiencing declining foot traffic and low levels of customer satisfaction. It is apparent the company should not limit the investigation to attracting new customers, and should expand it to encompass how to retain loyal customers. If you were to proceed with the original project and focus only on returning visitors to the mobile application, it would mean overlooking important relationships, and stakeholders would criticize your limited analytics approach. Thus, marketers must incorporate relevant stakeholder inputs through discovery methods to collectively understand the business problem and align projects to achieve business objectives.

MARKETING ANALYTICS EXTRAS

A good analytics approach must engage stakeholders in determining project requirements. Marketing analysts must seek cooperation from appropriate stakeholders in the project outcome. These stakeholders may include customers, employees, suppliers, and subject matter experts. Collection of feedback related to the business problem could occur via interviews, observation, surveys, and brainstorming sessions.

Discovery begins in asking the traditional six discovery questions: What, who, where, when, why, and how. Exhibit 1-3 provides samples of discovery questions and how they might be useful when considering the business problem.

Exhibit 1-3 Asking the Right Questions to Identify the Right Business Problem

BUSINESS CONSIDERATION	SAMPLE QUESTION
Context	What happened?
	What is the current problem we are trying to solve?
	What is the potential opportunity?
	Why is there an interest in solving this particular problem?
	What is the business doing to mitigate or solve the problem?
	What efforts have been made in the past?
	How has this problem evolved over time?
Impacted unit	Where did this problem happen?
	What divisions are impacted by this problem?
	When did it take place?
Root-cause analysis	What might have caused this?
	What do you think continues to drive this problem?
Timeline	When do decisions need to be made?
	What is the optimal timeline for reaching milestones along the way?

Continued on next page

Continued from previous page

Stakeholder	Who is asking for the analysis?
	Who are the executives interested in the results of the analysis?
	Who will be impacted by the analysis and subsequent recommendations?
	Who will carry out the analysis?
	What financial or emotional interest is involved from stakeholders? Is it positive or negative?
Expected impact	What are the actions to take based on the analysis?
	What support will end users have?
	What is the anticipated ROI from solving this problem?
	What are the ethical implications of the analysis?

Source: Adapted from Tony de Bree, "8 Questions Every Business Analyst Should Ask," *Modern Analyst,* http://www.modernanalyst.com/Resources/Articles/tabid/115/ID/179/8-Questions-EveryBusiness-Analyst-Should-Ask.aspx; and Piyanka Jain and Puneet Sharma. *Behind every good decision: How anyone can use business analytics to turn data into profitable insight* (AMACOM, 2014).

In an effort to define the right business problem, it can be useful to follow the SMART analytics principles. The **SMART principles** can be used as a goal-setting technique.[12] The acronym stands for specific, measurable, attainable, relevant, and timely (see Exhibit 1-4). First, the project's goals should be specific and clearly defined. Second, the project should be trackable and the outcomes measurable. For example, One SMART analytics goal could be to determine changes to the mobile application that will most efficiently increase returning visitors by 10 percent on a quarter-by-quarter basis compared to the same quarter last year. If data related to returning mobile application visitors is unavailable, it would be necessary to develop a project to obtain the data. The new goal would reflect the data acquisition and be stated as follows: "By the end of 6 months after the mobile application data has been collected, the data will be analyzed to determine the most efficient app changes to increase returning visitors by 10 percent on a quarter-by-quarter basis compared to the same quarter last year." Third, project goals should be reasonable to achieve. Fourth, the project should solve the analytics problem and align with the business objectives. Fifth, the project should be completed in a timely manner. Developing sound goals and objectives allows the analyst to monitor the project's progress, ensure it remains on track, gain visibility among stakeholders, and verify that everyone is on the same page.

Exhibit 1-4 SMART Principles

S	M	A	R	T
Specific	Measurable	Achievable	Relevant	Timely
The goal should be clearly defined.	Progress of the goal should be trackable and have a measurable outcome.	The goal should be reasonable to accomplish.	The goals should solve the analytics problem and align with business objectives.	A timeframe to successfully complete the analytics project should be determined.

Following the SMART analytics goal-setting technique is important. But equally important is examining the potential success of the analytics project and whether it makes a valuable impact. To do so, the opinions of the most powerful stakeholders should be included when developing project goals and success measures, as well as in evaluating the results.

When the SMART analytics goals are identified, it is time to focus on understanding the data requirements. Let's begin by taking a closer look at data sources.

1.3 Data Sources

Data sources consist of both primary and secondary data. **Primary data** is collected for a specific purpose. Companies conduct surveys, focus groups, interviews, observations, and experiments to address problems or answer distinct questions. For instance, Walmart and other companies are now observing customers in real-time through facial recognition software. The objective is to detect customers that are unhappy or need further assistance while shopping and, in turn, have an employee respond to their needs.[13] These observations provide primary data to achieve a specific objective.

In contrast, **secondary data** relies on existing data that has been collected for another purpose. While secondary data might not address specific or current problems, it could be useful in formulating ideas about how to ask the right questions or to design future data collection initiatives. At the same time, internal and external secondary data sources can be useful in exploring current business questions. Sources of secondary data include:

- *Public datasets:* Google launched Google Dataset Search in 2018 to enable scientists, analysts, and data enthusiasts to find data that is important for their work. Each dataset has a description and a discussion of the problem the dataset can address. Google Dataset Search includes data from NASA, NOAA, Harvard's Dataverse, GitHub, Kaggle, and other sources.

- *Online sites:* Online browsing behavior, purchase history, and social media chatter have become increasingly popular sources of data. As one example, food safety is a common concern in the restaurant industry. The third-largest fast-food chain in the United States, Chick-fil-A, is now exploring social media content to identify words or phrases often associated with food safety issues.[14] This data and analytics are used to produce results that are quickly made available to managers on a corporate dashboard to make local decisions. Managers also review the results of website postings and identify individual customers to contact. The objective is to eventually make selected information available on GitHub, a software development platform where creators can share programming insights at no cost.

- *Mobile data:* Most mobile applications track data so companies create more effective marketing strategies. As consumers have increasingly adopted mobile applications, companies like restaurants and clothing retailers have developed mobile apps that record customer purchase behaviors and geographic locations. Aki Technologies, for example, a mobile advertising company, offers a platform that companies can use to track mobile phone activity and then develop customer segments based on certain behaviors.[15] The data is then used to engage customers through personalized advertising campaigns or messages that increase store traffic.

- *Channel partners:* Multiple companies often operate within a distribution channel. The companies, referred to as channel partners, include suppliers, wholesalers, distributors, or retailers. Each member of the channel collects data unique to their business, but the data frequently provides value to other partners in the channel. In the fast-paced retail environment, where customers can purchase and receive products through same-day delivery services, brick-and-mortar retailers are increasingly concerned with maintaining the correct levels of inventory. Walmart strives to meet the needs and wants of customers by collecting data that enables them to always have products in stock for purchase. To reduce the time involved in restocking products, they are now sharing inventory data with suppliers and other channel partners.[16] They expect suppliers will be better prepared to restock products at the right time at the right location.

- *Commercial brokers:* Companies collecting and selling both public and private data to a wide range of customers have emerged in recent years. Acxiom is one example of a consumer data broker. In a typical year, the company aggregates and sells over 10,000 types of data, including socioeconomic status, health interests, and political views on more than 2.5 billion consumers.[17] Companies purchase this data to create customer profiles that can be used to target a wide variety of target segments.

- *Corporate information:* In this era of big data, many companies constantly collect and store data ranging from general business transactions to customer exchanges with accounting, finance, sales, customer service, and marketing. For example, customer service interactions are useful when the marketing department wants to better understand product quality, customer satisfaction, and loyalty. Integrating data across functional areas enables companies to better understand customer interactions based on a more holistic view of transactions.

- *Government sources:* This is an important source of secondary data collected by local, state, and federal government agencies. More than 200,000 datasets are searchable by topic on Data.gov (see Exhibit 1-5), including the following data sources, which are directly applicable to marketing analysts:

  - The U.S. Census Bureau is part of the U.S. Department of Commerce data. It includes data related to the population, economy, housing, and geography.
  - Consumer complaint data provides customer sentiments about financial products and services.
  - Demographic statistics by ZIP code, gender, ethnicity, and citizenship.
  - Fruit and vegetable prices for over 153 commonly consumed products are available from the Department of Agriculture.
  - ZIP code data showing tax return data by state and ZIP code level.

Exhibit 1-5 U.S. Government's Dataset Topics

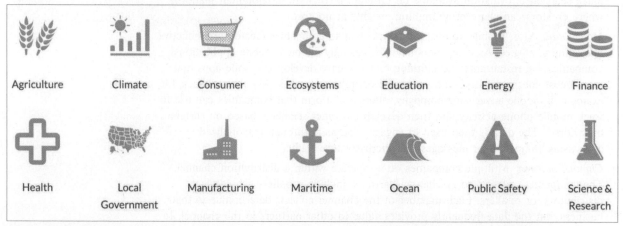

Source: Data.gov.

1.4 Data Types

Types of Data

Data is facts and figures collected, organized, and presented for analysis and interpretation. Data is available in two main forms: structured and unstructured.

Structured Data **Structured data** is made up of records that are organized in rows and columns. This type of data can be stored in a database or spreadsheet format. It includes numbers, dates, and text strings that are stored in a clearly defined structure. The data is easy to access and analyze using descriptive, predictive, prescriptive, and AI data analytics techniques.

Unstructured Data **Unstructured data** includes text, images, videos, and sensor data. The data does not have a predefined structure and does not fit well into a table format (within rows and columns). Examples of this type of data include voice recording from customer service calls, text, images, video recording, social media conversations, and the Internet of Things sensor data. Unstructured data could benefit from advanced analytics techniques such as AI to prepare and analyze. When possible, unstructured data is converted to a structured format prior to analysis. The number of companies collecting unstructured data has increased substantially as technology has advanced to efficiently support manipulation and exploration of this data type.

Both structured and unstructured data are important in executing marketing analytics. As noted, structured and unstructured data come in different formats and measurement types.

Continued from page 8

PRACTITIONER CORNER

Theresa Kushner | Advisory Board Member at data.world and Partner at Business Data Leadership

Q How are companies using both unstructured and structured data in solving business problems?

A Companies started combining unstructured and structured data to better understand their customers. Companies like Cisco Systems and Dell Technologies combine unstructured data from conversations on their support sites with structured data about their individual customer accounts.

Q What technologies have facilitated the integration and use of both data types?

A Graph databases have greatly improved the combination of these kinds of data structures. But users who understand how to implement these technologies are still lagging.

Q How do you see this evolving over the next 5 years?

A In the next 5 years, we should see more and more of the combination of these data structures aided by AI and machine learning.

Continued to page 21

Data Measurement

Data measurement can be categorized in a variety of ways based on the type and means for collection (see Exhibit 1-6). The two main types of data measurement most often explored in the remaining chapters are numerical and categorical (see Exhibit 1-7).

Exhibit 1-6 Data Measurement Definitions and Examples

DATA MEASUREMENT TYPE	DEFINITION	EXAMPLE
Discrete	Is measured as whole numbers: 1, 2, 3, . . .	Number of items purchased on a website
Continuous	Includes values with decimals: 1, 1.4, 2, 2.5, 3.75, . . .	Amount of time spent on a website
Binary	Has only two values	Yes/No, True/False
Nominal	Consists of characteristics that have no meaningful order	Marital Status, Country of Origin
Ordinal	Represents rank order	Ranking products/services in order of preference
Interval	Has fixed interval between data points	Degrees Fahrenheit
Ratio	Has a true zero point	Product Sales, Age

Exhibit 1-7 Types of Data Measurement

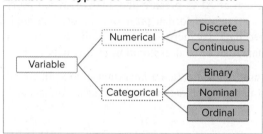

Numerical   Data are considered quantitative if numeric and arithmetic operations can be applied. For instance, sales data or visits to websites are numerical because they can be summed or averaged. Numerical data can be either *discrete* (**integer**) or *continuous* in nature. **Discrete data** is measured as whole numbers: 1, 2, 3, . . . The number of items purchased by a customer on a retailer's website is discrete. In contrast, **continuous data** can include values with decimals: 1, 1.4, 2, 2.5, 3.75, . . . The amount of time a customer spends on a retailer's website would be continuous.

Categorical   **Categorical data** exist when values are selected from a group of categories. A common example might be marital status. You may notice, categorical data can only be summarized by calculating the proportion and count of occurrences across and within categories.

Categorical variables can be one of three types: binary, nominal, or ordinal. **Binary** categorical data can have two values—for example, yes or no. This can be represented in different ways such as 1 or 0 or "True" and "False." Binary data is commonly used for classification in predictive modeling. Examples of binary variables include whether a person has purchased a product or not, or uses Twitter or not.

Nominal categorical data consist of characteristics that have no meaningful order. Marketers might inquire about the customer's country or marital status. There is no magnitude of value because a person cannot be half married and each category's characteristics are equally meaningful. The characteristics reflect the state of being: United States, China, Russia, Saudi Arabia, Mexico, United Kingdom, France, Germany, married, unmarried, divorced, widowed, and so on.

On the other hand, **ordinal** categorical data represent meaningful values. They have a natural order, but the intervals between scale points may be uneven (e.g., the rank order from the top product to the second may be large, but the interval from the second-ranked product to the third-ranked may be small). Customers might respond to a question such as do you prefer this brand more than or less than another brand. Another example might be when a company asks customers to rank products in order of preference.

Categorical variables require special consideration in preparation for modeling. How to prepare these variables will be discussed in a later chapter.

Metric Measurement Scales

Scales can also be metric. Metric scales can be measured as **intervals** or **ratios**. Both of these scales possess meaningful, constant units of measure, and the distance between each point on the scale are equal. However, there is a difference between these scales. Interval variables do not include an absolute zero. When thinking about weather, 0 degrees Fahrenheit means nothing, except that it is very cold. But ratio scales have an absolute zero point and can be discussed in terms of multiples when comparing one point to another. Product sales of $0 means nothing and sales of $100 is twice as much as $50. Similarly, zero indicates a lack of any weight, and 50 pounds is half of 100 pounds.

1.5 Predictors versus Target Variable

Types of Variables

Variables are characteristics or features that pertain to a person, place, or object. Marketing analysts explore relationships between variables to improve decision making. Consider a simple example. An analyst is investigating the relationship between two variables: weather conditions and ice cream sales. Does the weather impact customer ice cream purchases? Weather conditions would be considered the **independent variable** or what influences or drives the **dependent, target,** or **outcome variable** (ice cream sales). Warmer weather increases the likelihood that more ice cream will be purchased (see Exhibit 1-8). What other variables might impact ice cream sales? Although the example in Exhibit 1-8 only uses two variables, companies often use multiple variables at the same time as inputs to systems that process data and use it to predict dependent variables.

Exhibit 1-8 Example of Variable Types

In practical marketing analytics applications, variables are designated as independent (predictor) variables or dependent (target) variables.

1.6 Modeling Types: Supervised Learning versus Unsupervised Learning

Depending on the nature of the business problem being addressed, different types of algorithms can be used. In this book, we will focus on two types: *supervised learning* and *unsupervised learning*. **Supervised learning** suggests that the target variable of interest is known (e.g., ice cream sales; click or no click) and is available in a historical dataset.

The historical dataset can also be referred to as labeled data (because the target variable is available) and is divided into a training dataset, a validation dataset, and an optional testing dataset (also known as a holdout sample). The **training dataset** is the data used to build the algorithm and "learn" the relationship between the predictors and the target variable. The resulting algorithm is then applied to the **validation dataset** to assess how well it estimates the target variable, and to select the model that most accurately predicts the target value of interest. If many different algorithms are being compared, then it is recommended that a third data called **testing dataset** be used to evaluate the final selected algorithm and see how well it performs on a third dataset. The final selected algorithm is then applied to predict the target variable using new unlabeled data where the outcomes are not known, as shown in Exhibit 1-9.

Exhibit 1-9 Supervised Learning Steps

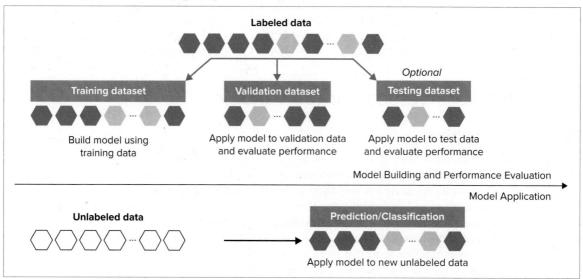

When the target variable is continuous, supervised learning is referred to as *prediction*. Let's say a retail company wants to understand customer buying behavior, specifically the purchase amount to create personalized offers. We will need to build a model to predict the purchase amount of customers against various products using labeled data (i.e., historical data that includes how much the customer spent on each product). The model can then be used to predict the purchase amount of new customers with similar characteristics.

When the target variable is categorical (typically binary—buy/no buy), supervised learning is called *classification*. Consider a large U.S. bank whose objective is to acquire new credit cardholders based on a special promotion. The historical data includes records of customers who have qualified (and not qualified) for past credit card offers after receiving the special promotion. An algorithm would be trained and validated on labeled data and then used to predict who should be targeted in the new promotional campaign. Exhibit 1-10 shows other examples of supervised learning applications using a variety of predictors.

Exhibit 1-10 Examples of Supervised Learning Applications

PREDICTOR (X)	TARGET (Y)	APPLICATION
Purchase histories	Future purchase behavior	Customer retention
Store transaction details	Is the transaction fraudulent?	Fraud detection
Faces	Names	Face recognition

Unsupervised learning has no previously defined target variable. The goal of unsupervised learning is to model the underlying structure and distribution in the data to discover and confirm patterns in the data. Examples of these techniques include association analysis and collaborative filtering Sephora runs for customers on its website using the "you may also like product X" based on an assortment of past purchases, or when Amazon indicates "others who bought this item also bought products X, Y and Z." Sephora and other companies also use cluster analysis to group customers into homogenous sets based on their loyalty (high, medium, and low) using their purchase history, the amount spent each year, and other key demographic and purchasing related variables.[18]

Supervised and unsupervised learning can be used together to gain more insights. For example, after conducting the unsupervised learning to determine customer loyalty segments, supervised learning can be used to predict purchase amounts for each of these segments. Whether the algorithm is supervised or unsupervised, the modeling process must be developed to represent how real-world problems begin, starting with a business problem and working toward a solution that makes a business impact. Modeling steps are discussed in greater detail in the following section.

1.7 The 7-Step Marketing Analytics Process

There are seven steps involved in the marketing analytics process (see Exhibit 1-11). Data modeling is only part of the journey, not the full marketing analytics journey. The 7-step marketing analytics process is iterative and continuously evolves to develop and manage improvements in the marketing analytics cycle. Each step plays an important role in achieving a successful outcome.

Exhibit 1-11 The 7-Step Marketing Analytics Process

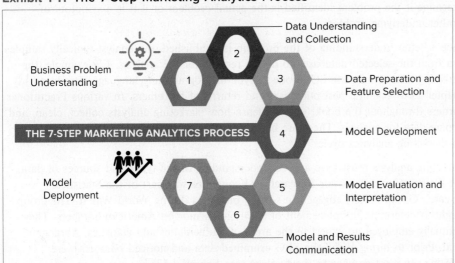

Step 1: Business Problem Understanding

Most marketing analytics models are developed when a business identifies a problem. The company may be experiencing low website traffic or conversion, high customer churn, or new product or market growth is slower than expected. The idea is to develop a model using analytics to understand the problem better and design a solution. One of the key elements in this step is to question whether the problem the business is presenting is, in fact, the correct problem, as was discussed in section 1.2. Due to today's dynamic business environment, companies frequently overlook or do not recognize problems. To avoid this situation, several questions should be asked:

- Exactly what are you trying to understand and solve?
- How will the stakeholder(s) use the results?
- Who will be affected by the results?
- Is this a single, short-term problem or an ongoing situation?

These initial questions are essential to make sure the right problem is being addressed.

MARKETING ANALYTICS EXTRAS

 Most experienced analysts recommend spending time thinking about defining the marketing analytics problem and determining its scope and feasibility before starting the next step. Given that most real-world problems are complex and often broad in scope, this recommendation is essential.

Step 2: Data Understanding and Collection

There are many different sources of data within an organization. The marketing analysts first job is to identify where the data is stored, its format, and how it can be combined to understand the question at hand. This step typically includes examining databases inside and outside the organization, and then talking with different key data owners and stakeholders (for example, the customer relationship manager, IT manager, or sales manager). It also includes observing and understanding organizational processes to determine if the problem identified is the actual problem or if it is a symptom of another underlying problem.

Once a better understanding of the problem is established, the analyst typically samples data from the selected databases to obtain records for the analysis. For example, the marketing analyst may use SQL code (a type of programming language introduced in Chapter 2) to examine past purchases and returns of customers. In various Practitioner Corners throughout the book, you will learn how marketing analysts collect, clean, and prepare data for analysis. These are basic tasks in the data understanding process of the marketing analytics cycle.

Marketing analysts must have a good understanding of the types and sources of data. The Cowles Commission for Research in Economics was part of the Statistical Research Group (SRG) engaged in solving problems during World War II. The group sought to determine the placement of additional armor on American bombers. They eventually employed an expert in the areas of mathematics and statistics, Abraham Wald. Prior to hiring Wald, the SRG examined data and noticed bombers were suffering the most damage to the fuselage (see Exhibit 1-12).[19]

Because the fuselage was also the location of the pilots, the group made the decision to include more protection in this area. Where would you have suggested more protection for the bomber? Did you ask the right questions before making a decision? Wald noticed the data was from a single source—only airplanes that had returned from combat. No data was available from destroyed airplanes. This meant the critical decision was based upon limited information from planes that successfully returned despite the amount of damage incurred. What would the information indicate about armor placement from the airplanes that sustained excessive damage and were not able to return? Fortunately, Wald recognized this would be important information, and he

Exhibit 1-12 Example of WWII American Bomber with Hypothetical Damage

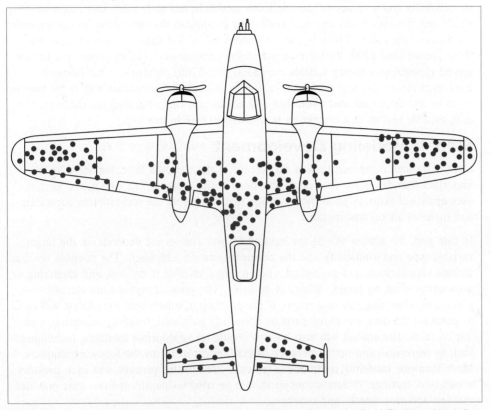

Source: Ethan Castro, "Hidden History: Abraham Wald and a Lesson in Survivorship Bias," *The News,* March 11, 2019, https://www.technewsiit.com/hidden-history-abraham-wald-and-survivorship-bias.

obtained information from pilots who survived by parachuting out of planes that failed to return. This emphasizes the importance of understanding the data prior to analysis. If Wald had not questioned or been made aware of the data's origin, the decision on armor placement could have been catastrophic or possibly ineffective.

Clearly, this is an important step today as well. What if Apple failed to test the strength of iPhone screens when they are dropped, or Tyson did not keep track of its chicken products so salmonella outbreaks could be tracked and resolved? Starting with all the information necessary in identifying, understanding, and solving a problem is clearly critical to finding the correct solution and optimizing the marketing analytics process.

Step 3: Data Preparation and Feature Selection

Data in different formats is combined in this step. To do so, the unit of analysis (e.g., customer, transaction, subscription plan) and the target and predictor variables are identified. The data columns (features) of the target and predictor variables are then visually and statistically examined. For example, scatterplots showing the relationship between the continuous target and each of the continuous predictors can be useful to identify patterns in this relationship. Data is cleaned by identifying and determining how to deal with missing values, data errors, or outliers. The data from different data sources describing the unit of analysis is also merged so data from both sources is measured consistently and can be used in developing the models.

Other features are further refined in this step. For example, dates might be adjusted to represent the day of the week, week, month, or year. In addition, predictors that have a strong relationship with the target variable and are not highly correlated with each other (predictors that are unique and not highly related) are included in the analysis to improve the reliability and accuracy of the predictive model. In this step, predictors might be eliminated, but they could also be transformed to improve the measurement. For example, the focus of the problem may be mobile phones priced less than or equal to $200 and those greater than $200. Rather than examining continuous monetary values, the feature can be changed to a binary variable ($=<$200$ or $>$200$). Similarly, if the research involves company size and performance, the focus could be companies with fewer than or equal to 500 employees and more than 500 employees. Understanding the meaning of each variable and its unit of analysis is an essential task in this step.

Step 4: Modeling Development

Steps 1 through 3 represent about 80 percent of the analyst's time, but serve as an important foundation for the rest of the steps in the process.[20] In step 4, the analyst uses analytical skills. A good model is one that represents the real-problem accurately and includes all key assumptions.

In this step, the analyst selects the method to use. The choice depends on the target variable type and availability and the business question addressed. The possible options include classification and prediction when a target variable is defined, and clustering or association when no target variable is available. The possible options are classification, prediction, clustering, or association. If the problem is supervised, the analyst will need to partition the data into three parts as previously indicated: training, validation, and test datasets. The analyst will also have to decide on appropriate modeling techniques such as regression and neural network, which are explained in the following chapters. More than one modeling technique is typically used in this process, and each includes a variety of features. Different models should be tried to identify the one that provides the best accuracy, speed, and quality.

A key idea to remember is that the model should be simple, practical, and useful. Netflix paid a million dollars for a model it never used due to its complexity.[21] Until recently, some of the most commonly encountered analytics problems were solved using simple techniques such as decision trees and regression analysis. The results were not necessarily as accurate, but the techniques were simple to understand and apply, and useful solutions could be developed.

Step 5: Model Evaluation and Interpretation

This step ensures the modeling is accurately performed and provides the best predictions for future applications. The model is evaluated to identify the algorithm providing the best solution. Initially, the algorithm is run on the validation dataset to determine how well it will predict the relevant target variable (dependent variable). If the validation results show high accuracy, then the model can be recommended to predict new cases and address the business problem. In some instances, the top model can be evaluated using an optional testing dataset to assess how well the final selected model might perform on new data.

Step 6: Model and Results Communication

The modeling step provides a set of recommendations. Understanding differences in the perspectives of problem-solving skills is critical because most people may not have a clear understanding of the modeling techniques used. It is key, therefore, for the analyst to present the model in a way that other people can understand, particularly management. Otherwise, the model may never be approved for implementation.

A good approach for this step is to collaborate with key stakeholders early in the process. If key stakeholders such as executives and managers have been involved in providing feedback from the beginning of the process (e.g., providing data and evaluating the progress), they are more likely to understand and support the recommended modeling approach.

A full understanding of the model is another important consideration. Whether the model is simple or complex, it should be explainable in straightforward terms with the appropriate visualization of results. For example, managers appreciate a regression model that includes a clear representation of the relationship between the target and predictors and that rapidly guides them in determining if their initial questions were answered.

Step 7: Model Deployment

The model completion and execution step is not finished until it has been implemented and is running on real-time records to offer decisions or actions. For example, a web recommender system is not considered complete until the system is used to make recommendations to customers during online purchases. Model implementation is typically approved by management for deployment, but only after full buy-in will the model add real value in making better decisions. Typically, this step involves other key stakeholders such as IT specialists, customer service representatives, or the sales team. These individuals should also train on implementing the system to ensure they understand how the model is executed and applied.

A key consideration throughout the 7-step marketing analytics modeling process is to evaluate the ethical dimensions of the analysis. Are the privacy and anonymity of the subjects being protected? Does a bias exist in the data that could impact the analytics results? Are the model results accurate? If not, some subjects may be misclassified and have a negative effect on the results. For example, applicants could be denied a bank loan, or purchase conversions may not increase as expected. At times, the model may be correct, but the objective is unfair to some subjects or unrealistic in its predictions. IBM, Microsoft, Facebook, Google, and other companies have created analytics review boards and ethical codes to evaluate the fairness of the analytics modeling. Another issue to keep in mind is that the data, features, data cleaning, and the model are determined by analysts. Thus, ethical training, ethical codes, and clear guidelines should be established and communicated to everyone working on developing the analytical model.

Continued from page 13

PRACTITIONER CORNER

Theresa Kushner | Advisory Board Member at data.world and Partner at Business Data Leadership

Q **What are the ethical considerations that marketing analytics students should pay attention to as they begin their career in analytics?**

A The one ethical consideration that marketing analytics students need to pay close attention to is bias. This takes various forms. There is bias in the data collected for analytics projects. There is bias in training data for AI/Machine Learning projects. There is bias in applying the learning from the analytics to the business problem. Not all bias is bad, but knowing that you have it and that it must be managed is something that most students in marketing analytics do not recognize. The way to avoid having bias enter the algorithms or the data

is to make sure you have checkpoints throughout the process that look for bias. Most data science processes do not consider this aspect. The other way to minimize bias is to create diverse teams that do the analytics. This doesn't necessarily mean diversity in race or gender, but it does mean diversity in thought. People who approach problems from different perspectives are a requirement in today's data science teams. Left-brained and right-brained people are needed. In fact, the most recent needed addition to a data scientist team is a data archeologist, someone who understands how data has been curated in the past—someone who uses both right- and left-brain thinking.

Continued to next page

1.8 Setting Yourself Apart

Marketing analytics experts work on solving complex and important problems. Regardless of which area in marketing, or even in the organization, you choose in your future career, knowledge of marketing analytics will be necessary. Marketing analytics is essential for students interested in distinguishing themselves in the job market. A study by PWC and the Business Higher Education Forum found that there were 2.35 million job postings in the U.S. for analytics-enabled jobs[22] and the number has continued to rise. More recently, an exploration of positions listed on Burning Glass suggested an average salary of $99,000 for analytics positions. The demand and salary for careers needing analytics training in all fields will continue to grow worldwide. Thus, job applicants with a knowledge of data science and analytics will be given preference over others without these skills.

Continued from previous page

PRACTITIONER CORNER

Theresa Kushner | Advisory Board Member at data.world and Partner at Business Data Leadership

Q **How does the knowledge of marketing analytics help students differentiate themselves from peers?**

A Marketing analytics is unique in that it aims the power of analytics at the customer and market—the place where companies make their money. Any student who understands how data analytics can be used to help increase revenues in a company has an edge over her peers.

Q **What is the potential career impact of understanding marketing analytics and the application to business problems?**

A My experience has taught me that understanding marketing analytics often grows into understanding market and business strategies. It's this understanding or experience that can catapult a career. Most companies are very interested in how they can apply analytics to their overall business as they move to transform to the digital age.

In the following chapters, marketing problems using a variety of powerful analytics software are discussed. The software platforms in Exhibit 1-13 are useful in many careers, particularly marketing, and are currently used by many organizations globally to solve complex business problems. Exhibit 1-14 displays the top software and the relative usage by companies based on a survey by KDnuggets, a leading provider of information on AI, analytics, big data, data mining, data science, and machine learning. Results were based on asking the question: What software did you use for analytics, data mining, data science, and machine learning projects in the past 12 months? In the remaining chapters of this book, you will learn how to solve specific marketing analytics problems through step-by-step instructions using a variety of software.

Results were based on asking the question: What software did you use for analytics, data mining, data science, and machine learning projects in the past 12 months?

This book provides the foundation and skills for successfully using analytical methods in marketing. Chapter cases cover a variety of tools and techniques to provide hands-on

Exhibit 1-13 Example of Software Platforms Introduced

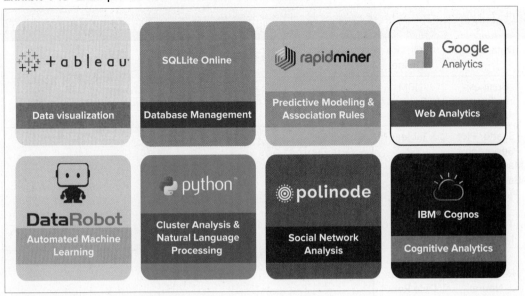

Exhibit 1-14 Top Analytics, Data Science, Machine Learning Software in KDnuggets Poll

SOFTWARE	2019 USAGE PERCENT
Python	65.8%
RapidMiner	51.2%
R Language	46.6%
Excel	34.8%
Anaconda	33.9%
SQL Language	32.8%
Tensorflow	31.7%
Keras	26.6%
scikit-learn	25.5%
Tableau	22.1%
Apache Spark	21.0%

Source: Gregory Piatetsky, "Python Leads the 11 Top Data Science, Machine Learning Platforms: Trends and Analysis," *KDnuggets,* May 2019, https://www.kdnuggets.com/2019/05/poll-top-data-science-machine-learning-platforms.html (accessed June 23, 2019).

experiences. The variety of methods and tools you will learn in this book will offer you a toolbox approach to solving different analytics problems. Exhibit 1-15 provides an overview of the chapters by topic, modeling type, software, and coverage of the four major areas of analytics: descriptive, predictive, prescriptive, and AI/cognitive. It is time now to start your journey to develop an understanding of the fundamental marketing analytics technologies, techniques, and business applications.

Exhibit 1-15 Topics and Software Coverage in This Textbook

TITLE	TYPE OF MODELING	SOFTWARE	CHAPTER	DESCRIPTIVE	PREDICTIVE	PRESCRIPTIVE	AI/COGNITIVE
Data Management	Data Query	SQL Lite Online	Chapter 2	 💡			
AI and Cognitive Analytics	Business Intelligence Analytics	IBM Cognos	Chapter 3	 💡	 💡		 💡
Visualization	Scatter Plot Geographic Map Heat Map Bar Chart Box Plot Network Graph Timeseries Line Graph	Tableau	Chapter 4	 💡			
Supervised Modeling	Linear Regression Neural Network Automated Machine Learning	Rapid Miner & Data Robot	Chapters 5, 6, and 7		 💡		
Unsupervised Modeling	Association Rules Cluster Analysis	Rapid Miner & Python	Chapters 8 and 9	 💡	 💡		
Natural Language Processing	Sentiment Analysis	Python	Chapter 10	 💡	 💡	 💡	
Social Network Analysis	Network Structure	Polinode	Chapter 11	 💡			
Web Analytics	Page View Click Through Engagement Time Conversion Optimization	Google Analytics	Chapter 12	 💡			

Summary of Learning Objectives and Key Terms

LEARNING OBJECTIVES

Objective 1.1   Define marketing analytics.

Objective 1.2   Discuss how to identify the right business problem.

Objective 1.3   Identify different data sources.

Objective 1.4   Describe different data types.

Objective 1.5   Explain the difference between predictors and target variables.

Objective 1.6   Differentiate between supervised and unsupervised modeling.

Objective 1.7   Discuss the 7-step marketing analytics process.

Objective 1.8   Explain the value of learning marketing analytics.

KEY TERMS

Artificial intelligence (AI)	Integer	Secondary data
Binary	Interval	SMART principles
Categorical data	Machine learning	Structured data
Cognitive analytics	Marketing analytics	Supervised learning
Continuous data	Nominal	Testing dataset
Dependent, target, or (outcome) variable	Ordinal	Training dataset
Descriptive analytics	Predictive analytics	Unstructured data
Discrete data	Prescriptive analytics	Unsupervised learning
Independent variable	Primary data	Validation dataset
	Ratio	Variables

Discussion and Review Questions

1. What is marketing analytics?

2. How are companies using marketing analytics to make strategic marketing decisions?

3. Name several external data sources that might be helpful to marketers.

4. How might a company use structured and unstructured data to better understand customers?

5. Define a target variable.

6. Discuss the difference between supervised and unsupervised learning.

7. What are the steps of the marketing analytics process?

Critical Thinking and Marketing Applications

1. Visit www.data.gov. Click on Consumer, then click on Data. How many datasets are currently located on this website for free? Select one dataset and develop a scenario where the data might be helpful for a marketing

manager. Discuss how exploring the data could guide the marketing manager in making more informed decisions.

2. Develop two questions that an airline company might be interested in answering. Describe types of unstructured and structured data that might be important to answering the questions. What data sources might be helpful?

References

1. Dana Mattioli, "On Orbitz, Mac Users Steered to Pricier Hotels," *The Wall Street Journal*, August 23, 2012, https://www.wsj.com/articles/SB10001424052702304458604577488822667325882 (accessed June 23, 2019).

2. Bernard Marr, "The Amazing Ways Spotify Uses Big Data, AI and Machine Learning to Drive Business Success," *Forbes*, October 30, 2017, https://www.forbes.com/sites/bernardmarr/2017/10/30/the-amazing-ways-spotify-uses-big-data-ai-and-machine-learning-to-drive-business-success (accessed June 23, 2019).

3. "Turning Fashion by the Numbers into A Billion-Dollar Business," *PYMNTS*, February 21, 2019, https://www.pymnts.com/news/retail/2019/stitch-fix-algorithm-data-innovation (accessed June 23, 2019).

4. Jared Council, "AI Helps Restaurant Chains Pick Sites for New Stores," *The Wall Street Journal*, May 13, 2019, https://www.wsj.com/articles/ai-helps-restaurant-chains-pick-sites-for-new-stores-11557739802?ns=prod/accounts-wsj (accessed June 23, 2019).

5. Kashmir Hill, "How Target Figured Out a Teen Girl Was Pregnant Before Her Father Did," *Forbes*, February 16, 2012, https://www.forbes.com/sites/kashmirhill/2012/02/16/how-target-figured-out-a-teen-girl-was-pregnant-before-her-father-did (accessed June 23, 2019).

6. Eric Knorr, "Hot Property: How Zillow Became the Real Estate Data Hub," *InfoWorld*, April 25, 2016, https://www.infoworld.com/article/3060773/hot-property-how-zillow-became-the-real-estate-data-hub.html (accessed June 23, 2019).

7. Neel Mehta, Parth Detroja, and Aditya Agashe, "Amazon Changes Prices on Its Products about Every 10 Minutes—Here's How and Why They Do It," *Business Insider*, August 10, 2018, https://www.businessinsider.com/amazon-price-changes-2018-8 (accessed June 23, 2019); and Jia Wertz, "6 Surefire Ways to Gain Sales Traction on Amazon FBA," *Forbes*, September 28, 2018, https://www.forbes.com/sites/jiawertz/2018/09/28/6-surefire-ways-to-gain-sales-traction-on-amazon-fba (accessed June 23, 2019).

8. "Kellogg Realigns Supply Chain to Help Achieve Cost-Savings Goals," *MHI*, http://s354933259.onlinehome.us/mhi-blog/kellogg-realigns-supply-chain-to-help-achieve-cost-savings-goals (accessed June 23, 2019); Clara Lu, "Kelloggs Supply Chain Process: From Factory to Supermarket Shelves," *TradeGecko*, July 22, 2014, https://www.tradegecko.com/blog/supply-chain-management/supply-chain-management-factory-supermarket-shelves-kelloggs (accessed June 23, 2019); and Gurjit Degun, "Kellogg's Looks to Supply Chain to Save £300 Million," *Supply Management*, November 6, 2013, https://www.cips.org/en/Supply-Management/News/2013/November/Kelloggs-looks-to-supply-chain-to-save-300-million (accessed June 23, 2019).

9. Matt Marshall, "How Olay Used AI to Double Its Conversion Rate," *Venture Beat*, July 19, 2018, https://venturebeat.com/2018/07/19/how-olay-used-ai-to-double-its-conversion-rate (accessed June 23, 2019); and Erica Sweeney, "Olay Doubles Conversion Rates with AI-Powered Skincare Advisor," *Marketing Dive*, July 20, 2018, https://www.marketingdive.com/news/venturebeat-olay-doubles-conversion-rates-with-ai-powered-skincare-advisor/528229 (accessed June 23, 2019).

10. J. Murawski, "Car Companies Curb AI Efforts" April 11, 2019, *The Wall Street Journal Online*, https://www.wsj.com/articles/car-companies-curb-ai-efforts-11554888601.

11. Bernard Marr, "The Amazing Ways Hitachi Uses Artificial Intelligence and Machine Learning," *Forbes*, June 14, 2019, https://www.forbes.com/sites/bernardmarr/2019/06/14/the-amazing-ways-hitachi-uses-artificial-intelligence-and-machine-learning (accessed June 23, 2019).

12. George T. Doran, "There's a S.M.A.R.T. Way to Write Management's Goals and Objectives," *Management Review* (AMA FORUM) 70(11): 35–36 (1981); and Graham Yemm, *Essential Guide*

to Leading Your Team: How to Set Goals, Measure Performance and Reward Talent (Pearson Education, 2013), pp. 37–39.

13. Yoni Heisler, "Walmart's Creepy Plan to Detect Unhappy Customers," *New York Post*, July 20, 2017, https://nypost.com/2017/07/20/walmarts-creepy-plan-to-detect-unhappy-customers (accessed June 23, 2019).

14. Kyle L. Wiggers, "Chick-fil-A's AI Can Spot Signs of Foodborne Illness from Social Media Posts with 78% Accuracy," *Venture Beat*, May 23, 2019, https://venturebeat.com/2019/05/23/chick-fil-as-ai-can-spot-signs-of-foodborne-illness-from-social-media-posts-with-78-accuracy (accessed June 23, 2019).

15. Lauren Johnson, "Taco Bell's Mobile Ads Are Highly Targeted to Make Users Crave Its Breakfast Menu," *AdWeek*, March 14, 2016, https://www.adweek.com/digital/taco-bells-mobile-ads-are-highly-targeted-make-users-crave-its-breakfast-menu-170155 (accessed June 23, 2019); Iris Dorbian, "Aki Technologies Takes in $3.75 Mln Seed," *PE Hub*, September 2016, https://www.pehub.com/2016/09/aki-technologies-takes-in-3-75-mln-seed/# (accessed June 23, 2019); Geoffrey Fowler, "It's the Middle of the Night. Do You Know Who Your iPhone Is Talking To?" *The Washington Post*, May 28, 2019, https://www.msn.com/en-us/news/technology/its-the-middle-of-the-night-do-you-know-who-your-iphone-is-talking-to/ar-AAC1Wvl (accessed June 23, 2019); and Lucy Sanovy, "Taco Bell Tracks Phone User Habits to Target Its Mobile Ads," *Mobile Commerce Press*, March 17, 2016, http://www.mobilecommercepress.com/taco-bell-tracks-phone-user-habits-target-mobile-ads/8521558 (accessed June 23, 2019).

16. "Walmart to Share Inventory Data with Suppliers in Battle with Amazon," *Reuters*, January 30, 2018, https://www.reuters.com/article/us-walmart-suppliers/walmart-to-share-inventory-data-with-suppliers-in-battle-with-amazon-idUSKBN1FJ1S0 (accessed June 23, 2019); Dan O'Shea, "Walmart Shares Inventory Data, Tightens Deadlines for Suppliers," *Retail Dive*, January 30, 2018, https://www.retaildive.com/news/walmart-shares-inventory-data-tightens-deadlines-for-suppliers/515962 (accessed June 23, 2019); and Kayla Webb, "Walmart Takes on Amazon by Sharing Inventory Data with Suppliers," *Deli Market News*, January 30, 2018, https://www.delimarketnews.com/retail/walmart-takes-amazon-sharing-inventory-data-suppliers/kayla-webb/tue-01302018-1130/5486 (accessed June 23, 2019).

17. Steven Melendez and Alex Pasternack, "Here Are the Data Brokers Quietly Buying and Selling Your Personal Information," *Fast Company*, March 2, 2019, https://www.fastcompany.com/90310803/here-are-the-data-brokers-quietly-buying-and-selling-your-personal-information (accessed June 23, 2019).

18. Cah, "Beauty in the Age of Individualism: Sephora's Data-Driven Approach," *Harvard Business School*, November 13, 2018, https://rctom.hbs.org/submission/beauty-in-the-age-of-individualism-sephoras-data-driven-approach (accessed June 23, 2019); and K.C. Cheung, "Sephora Uses AI to Transform the Way Its Customers Shop," *Algorithm-X Lab's Artificial Intelligence Newsletter*, January 26, 2019, https://algorithmxlab.com/blog/sephora-uses-ai-transform-way-customers-shop (accessed June 23, 2019).

19. Ethan Castro, "Hidden History: Abraham Wald and a Lesson in Survivorship Bias," *Tech News*, March 11, 2019, https://www.technewsiit.com/hidden-history-abraham-wald-and-survivorship-bias (accessed June 23, 2019); Kevin Drum, "The Counterintuitive World," *Mother Jones*, https://www.motherjones.com/kevin-drum/2010/09/counterintuitive-world (accessed June 23, 2019); and Walker Donohue, "7 Lessons on Survivorship Bias that Will Help You Make Better Decisions," *I Done This Blog*, July 24, 2018, http://blog.idonethis.com/7-lessons-survivorship-bias-will-help-make-better-decisions (accessed June 23, 2019).

20. Gil Press, "Cleaning Big Data: Most Time-Consuming, Least Enjoyable Data Science Task, Survey Says," *Forbes*, March 23, 2016, https://www.forbes.com/sites/gilpress/2016/03/23/data-preparation-most-time-consuming-least-enjoyable-data-science-task-survey-says (accessed June 23, 2019).

21. Casey Johnston, "Netflix Never Used its $1 Million Algorithm due to Engineering Costs," *Wired*, April 16, 2012, https://www.wired.com/2012/04/netflix-prize-costs (accessed June 23, 2019).

22. "Investing in America's Data Science and Analytics Talent," *PWC*, https://www.pwc.com/us/dsa-skills (accessed June 23, 2019).

2 | Data Management

LEARNING OBJECTIVES

2.1 Define big data and summarize the journey from big data to smart data.

2.2 Discuss database management systems, relational databases, and SQL query language.

2.3 Investigate the key elements of enterprise data architecture.

2.4 Define the dimensions of data quality and describe the importance of performing marketing analytics.

2.5 Explain the importance of understanding and preparing data prior to engaging in analytics.

Eugenio Marongiu/Image Source

2.1 The Era of Big Data Is Here

A marketing executive in a medium-sized U.S. retailer was surprised after reviewing the sales reports. One of the company's major competitors has been rapidly gaining market share. The executive was confused by the loss of market share because the firm had invested a large amount of money in improving their product design and online promotions. Upon reading a news article that examined decisions leading to the competitor's success, the executive was surprised by the challenge ahead. The competitor was investing heavily in collecting, integrating, and analyzing data from each of their stores and every sales unit. The competitor had integrated information technology (IT) infrastructure with the supplier databases, which enabled it to place orders automatically on high-demand items and shift product delivery from one store to another with ease. From e-commerce to in-store experiences, as well as across the supply chain, the competing company had become nimble and adaptive in the marketplace. What the competitor had witnessed was the game-changing impact of big data and analytics. Big data helps companies track demand and sales in real time, adapt quickly to market changes, and predict how customers will behave, thereby enabling them to personalize customer experiences.

In recent years, we have witnessed an explosion in the volume of data produced and stored. You have probably seen statements such as 90 percent of the world's data has been created in the last two years, or an estimated 2.5 quintillion bytes of data are generated every single day. However, that pace is only accelerating with data from web applications, social media, mobile apps, and sensors embedded in almost all everything we use. Large datasets are a core organizational asset that generates new opportunities and creates significant competitive advantages. Indeed, companies that adopt data-driven decision making typically achieve up to 6 percent higher productivity and output than their peers.

The Coca-Cola company is a good example of a business that has rebuilt itself on data to drive product development, customer retention, and engagement. With more than 500 drink brands sold in more than 200 countries, the Coca-Cola Company's customers consume more than 1.9 billion servings every day. Moreover, the company launched Cherry Sprite using data from self-service drink dispensers that allow customers to mix their own drinks. Finally, Coca-Cola identified the most popular flavor combinations and made them available to its customers.[1]

Another successful data-driven company is eBay, with an estimated 179 million active buyers and more than 1.2 billion live listings across 190 markets. eBay has invested in data management infrastructure that enables it to use two decades of data and customer behavior insights to train intelligent models to anticipate the needs of buyers, recommend items, and inspire every shopper based on interest and passions.[2] Mastercard too has built a data infrastructure that can process 75 billion transactions per year across 45 million global locations on the Mastercard network.[3] To do so, the company has moved from static data and fixed rules to fast-moving, real-time streams of transaction data, enhanced by external aggregated customer demographics and geographic information. In addition, using machine learning models, Mastercard has been able to prevent billions of dollars' worth of fraud.

Building a smart data infrastructure that enables real-time decision making requires a strong data strategy that is well aligned with overall business strategy. Many companies have adopted a data-driven strategy that encourages the use of data throughout the firm for decision making. With increased integration of both internal and external data, many companies are discovering that inter-department collaboration is a key success factor in optimizing data use. Analytics teams are increasingly interdisciplinary, and functional departments no longer operate in silos (see Exhibit 2-1). As a result, marketers are finding themselves collaborating with numerous departments throughout the company to create successful initiatives. In addition, new departments have emerged, such as data science, that focus on statistical computational algorithms and computer programming.

Exhibit 2-1 Collaborative Workgroups versus Traditional Silos

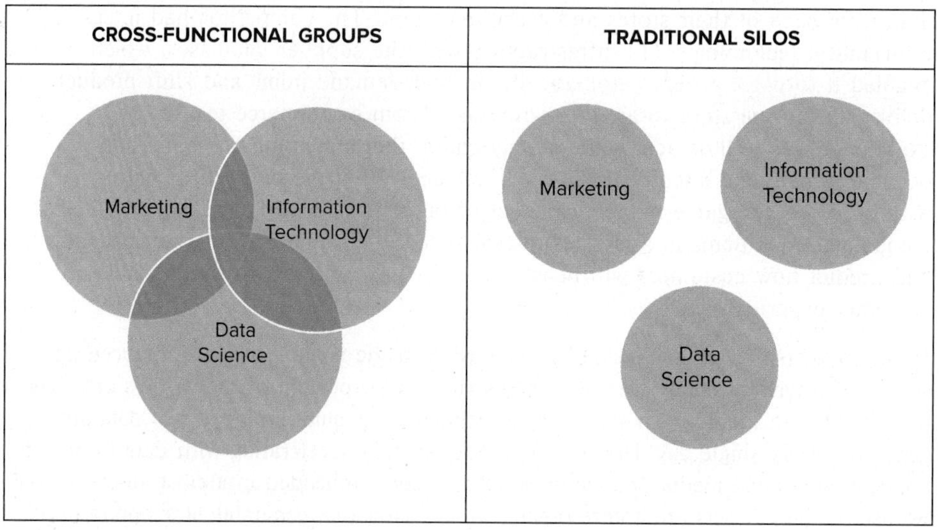

Companies such as General Electric and Zeta Global, a marketing services company, are developing cross-functional, collaborative structures between marketing, IT, and data science to ensure more accurate data collection and identification of useful insights.[4] Increasing applications of analytics and interdisciplinary collaboration mean marketers must have a basic understanding of data management fundamentals even if they do not have primary responsibility for managing these systems.

Integrated information technology infrastructure systems are collecting and maintaining massive amounts of data. In the airline industry, manufacturers utilize thousands of sensors and sophisticated real-time digital systems to collect more data. By 2026, over half of all wide-bodied aircraft are expected to produce 98 million terabytes of data. These advanced systems generate information surrounding engines, fuel consumption, crew deployment, and weather updates, to mention a few, with the goal of enhancing the customer experience.[5]

Multi-channel interactions are also producing large amounts of data. For example, data is generated from more than 100 million desktop and mobile visits to the Target website each month, 40 million users that downloaded the mobile app, as well as by customers shopping at over 1,800 brick and mortar stores.[6] Other types of external data are also collected, such as social media mentions, weather patterns, and economic developments. Another retailer, Walmart, processes over 2.5 petabytes (PB) of internal and external data every hour, seven days a week. But realistically, is it possible for us to understand how much data this truly is? To put this into perspective, a petabyte (PB) is a million gigabytes (GB), and a single petabyte can store about 225,000 movies. Imagine looking pixel by pixel at your favorite 225,000 movies, and that is only one petabyte. Consider the most recent thumb drive or cloud storage service you used. What was the storage capacity? While they range in size, many thumb-drive storage options for personal use hold 100 or more gigabytes (GB), and external laptop drives

Peter Drewes | Business Intelligence, Intellectual Property and Strategy at Lockheed Martin

Dr. Peter Drewes is a Business Intelligence and Intellectual property manager at Lockheed Martin focusing on the sustainment areas of the F35 program. His background is idea valuation and the business, strategic, and technical coordination necessary to bring those to life. Over his 30+ year career, he has developed and helped launch multi-billion dollar opportunities in unmanned systems, autonomous applications, and supercomputing. This has involved entering new markets for Underwater autonomous vehicles, transforming geospatial data into collective team knowledge, and advancing robotics through research into data analysis. His business focus has been that of combining business analytics and market analysis into cohesive strategic plans.

Peter Drewes

Q **Peter, from your perspective why is it critical for employees working in any function to understand or participate in the company's processes for data management, from collection to preparation, analysis, and ultimately strategy development?**

A The goal for every function is to understand the lifecycle of the data and processes that are being generated. What questions need to be answered? What requirements are placed on the data and the analysis? How long will the data and information be relevant, and how do you know data biases have been reduced so the information will be useful in answering questions?

The key is for those who ask questions to understand data lifecycle elements so they can ask and get answers to the right questions. For example, they must be able to bridge the silos between functional departments to provide detailed answers. Typically, in this situation, the marketing department is the question generator that wants to understand how customers are making decisions. As part of the journey, the marketing team will therefore have to bridge the gaps between silos to answer the fundamental questions. If marketers are uninvolved in the process or unable to collaborate, other departments such as data scientists must have the same understanding as the marketing department, but they seldom do. Functional departments can be adept in many areas, but the data science department does not make strategic marketing decisions. Similarly, the IT department does not specify how data scientists do their analysis. It is this bridging of the gaps between groups that facilitates appropriate technology investments, achieves desired returns on investment goals, while at the same time meeting their strategic goals. Utilizing each department's expertise is the only effective way to reach individual department and overall company goals.

Continued to page 37

hold a terabyte (TB) or more. For an understanding of computer technology measurement storage units, refer to Exhibit 2-2.

Big data is the term typically used to describe massive amounts of data. It is a relative term that requires special tools to manage and analyze. The amount of data collected by Target and Walmart would be considered big data by most standards. But Amazon, Google, and Facebook are other companies that have amassed large amounts of customer search history and purchase data. The existence of big data is a result of the digital transformation taking place in companies and among customers. Companies not only store historical and real-time data in a digital format, they also interact with suppliers and customers using a variety of digital methods that contributes to big data.

Exhibit 2-2 Computer Technology Storage Units of Measure

UNIT OF MEASURE	NUMBER OF BYTES	EXAMPLES[7]
Yottabyte (YB)	1000^8	as much information as there are atoms in 7,000 human bodies
Zettabyte (ZB)	1000^7	as much information as there are grains of sand on all the world's beaches
Exabyte (EB)	1000^6	about one-fifth of the words people have ever spoken
Petabyte (PB)	1000^5	half of the contents of all U.S. academic research libraries
Terabyte (TB)	1000^4	all the X-rays in a large hospital
Gigabyte (GB)	1000^3	Beethoven's 5th Symphony
Megabyte (MB)	1000^2	a small novel
Kilobyte (KB)	1000	a paragraph of a text document
Byte (B)	1	a single character of text

The word big, however, is somewhat subjective. In the case of big data, several characteristics illustrate the term (see Exhibit 2-3). Volume, variety, veracity, velocity, and value are several characteristics used to describe big data.

Exhibit 2-3 Characteristics of Big Data

Volume	Large Data at Rest	Companies must now store and analyze petabytes of data. Data is collected from a variety of sources and enables companies to examine the entire customer journey.
Variety	Diverse Data	Data can range from structured to unstructured. There are strengths and challenges to these different formats when creating an integrated database, but variety provides a more holistic understanding of customers and market situations.
Veracity	Messy Data	The data could have missing values, inconsistencies in the unit of measurement, erroneous information, and lack of reliability, which increases complexity and reduces confidence in the data.
Velocity	Fast Data in Motion	Troves of data are being produced by digital technology. This data is inundating companies at a rapid pace (taking milliseconds to seconds to send). This speed supports real-time response strategies.
Value	Useful Data	The extracted data must be converted into quality insights that add tangible and intangible benefits to the business. Achieving value requires an understanding of the goals and objectives of the business.

Volume refers to large amounts of data per time unit. The volume of data can be anticipated in the case of regular purchase behavior, but intense public attention on social media can bring inconsistent volumes of data, an amount a company might be unprepared to manage. Companies such as Walmart report more than 140 million customers visit a typical company-owned brick-and-mortar or ecommerce site each week.[8] These customers produce a vast quantity of data through purchase transactions, returns, browsing patterns, and search history. As you can imagine, the large quantity of data arrives with high **velocity** or speed. This high-volume, high-speed data moves constantly between the network of exchange relationships from suppliers to retailer stores to customers. Managing the volume and speed of incoming data can be challenging due to the potential **veracity** or **variety** of data. Recall from Chapter 1 that structured and unstructured types of data are constantly generated from various sources. Making a purchase online or in a store would yield structured data such as names, addresses, phone numbers, and purchase amounts. In contrast, data originating from social media through videos, text, and images would likely be unstructured. It is easy to understand how collecting similar data from several sources increases the potential for inconsistencies in the units of measure or missing data.

Big data is available to almost all companies throughout the world, but it is only an asset when it provides **value**. Value means the data is useful for making accurate decisions. Many professionals are moving away from the term "big data" and beginning to adopt the term "smart data." **Smart data** represents data that is valuable and can be effectively used. Big data should be well-organized and made smart prior to analysis by making sure it can be used to produce more accurate decisions.

2.2 Database Management Systems (DBMS)

Have you ever considered how big data is organized to create smart data that provides value? All data is stored and organized in a database. A **database** contains data collected from company operations. The data must be organized for efficient retrieval and analysis by different functional departments throughout the company. When employees search for customer information or customers search for products online, a database is working behind the scenes to provide the best results. Customer relationship management (CRM) and product search systems are commonly stored in relational databases.

A **relational database** is a type of database management system (DBMS). It is a collection of interrelated data items organized using software programs to manipulate and access data. The software programs involve a framework, often referred to as a schema, that captures the structure of how the database is constructed with tables, columns, data types, stored procedures, relationships, primary keys, foreign keys, validation rules, etc. A relational database stores data in structured columns and rows similar to an excel spreadsheet. Exhibit 2-4 shows sales for a specific plant variety: the Hass avocado. The relational table includes information about avocado sales and consists of a set of product or company attributes, including such items as region, average sales, total volume, and type. A set of tables is one component of a relational database, each of which has a unique name. As shown in Exhibit 2-4, a table typically includes a set of columns (also known as features, predictors or variables) and stores a large number of records. The row (also known as records) are often identified by a unique primary key and described by columns. A foreign key is a set of one or more columns in a table that refers to the primary key in another table. Primary keys and foreign keys are important in relational databases, because they help database users combine data from different tables, as shown in Exhibit 2-5.

Exhibit 2-4 Example of a Table Structure

OBSERVATION ID	REGION	AVERAGE PRICE	TOTAL VOLUME	TYPE
1	Albany	1.47	113514.4	Organic
2	Atlanta	0.95	649352.6	Conventional
3	Baltimore/ Washington	1.15	849487.6	Conventional
4	Boise	1.13	79646.97	Conventional
5	Boston	1.4	419696.6	Organic
6	Buffalo/Rochester	1.27	115508.3	Organic

Exhibit 2-5 Example of a Relational Database Structure

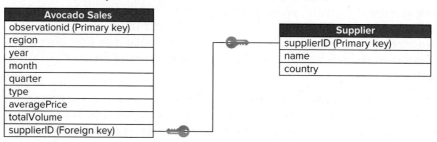

How can data in relational databases be accessed for greater meaning? Relational data is accessible by a database management language called **structured querying language (SQL)**. The language was developed by IBM and is used to access and update data stored in the database. A query can be used to join, select, manipulate, retrieve, and analyze data from relational databases. These databases are beneficial when data consistently maintain the same properties because they require predefined structures. If the company decides to begin collecting customer email addresses or locational information, the database tables would need to be altered to accept any new column.

On the other hand, non-relational databases (see Exhibit 2-6), also known as NoSQL databases, can store large volumes of structured or unstructured data. Non-relational databases show data vertically, combined together rather than in structured tables. For example, the first row in Exhibit 2-6 matches the first column of Exhibit 2-4 and refers to organic Hass avocados in Albany.

Exhibit 2-6 Non-Relational (NoSQL) Database Example

{"Name": "Average Sales Price: 1.47"},

{"Name": "Total Volume: 113514.4"},

{"Name": "Type: organic"},

  {"Name": "Region: Albany"}

NoSQL databases allow greater flexibility for storing ever-changing data and new data types, but drilling down to very specific types of data is more difficult. The flexibility of NoSQL databases is important for companies with dynamic sources of data, such as mobile devices or social media.

Most companies use both relational and non-relational type databases to store data. Data often resides in multiple sources with different data formats. As expected, managing data efficiently can be challenging. The difficulty of maintaining multiple databases is compounded by inappropriate data storage architecture.

2.3 Enterprise Data Architecture

Data storage architecture provides a framework for companies to systematically organize, understand, and use their data to make both small and large decisions. In recent years, companies have spent millions of dollars building enterprise-wide data architecture to help drive informed decision making in a fast-changing world. Many organizations view their data architecture as a competitive position to help them retain customers by learning more about their needs. Interestingly, new trends have evolved in data architecture with more companies investing in flexible cloud infrastructure and open-source architecture.

Exhibit 2-7 shows the basic architecture of a data storage environment for an organization. In principle, data analytics can be applied to analyze any kind of information repository. This includes Customer Relationship Management (CRM), Enterprise Resource Planning (ERP), and other Online Transaction Processing (OLTP) software that supports operational data transactions such as customer order entry, financial processing, material order, shipping process, and customer service. As an example, CRM solutions use an operational database to store customer data. Some of the most common CRM solutions are available through Microsoft, SAP, Salesforce, and Oracle. A CRM database might store recent customer transactions or responses to marketing promotions and allow marketers to monitor developments in real time. The data storage environment offers a place to combine different sources of data. Internal company data can be combined with data from other sources such as social media (e.g., Instagram, YouTube, Facebook) to capture customer opinions about products, reviews, and video comments, which also can be combined with web sales data. **Streaming data**, the continuous transfer of data from numerous sources in different formats, can also be included to capture customer data. This might include geographic mobile data, sensor data from physical stores, and logs from internal systems and web capturing of the type, content, and time of transactions made by the user interacting with the system.

Exhibit 2-7 Simple Architecture of a Data Repository

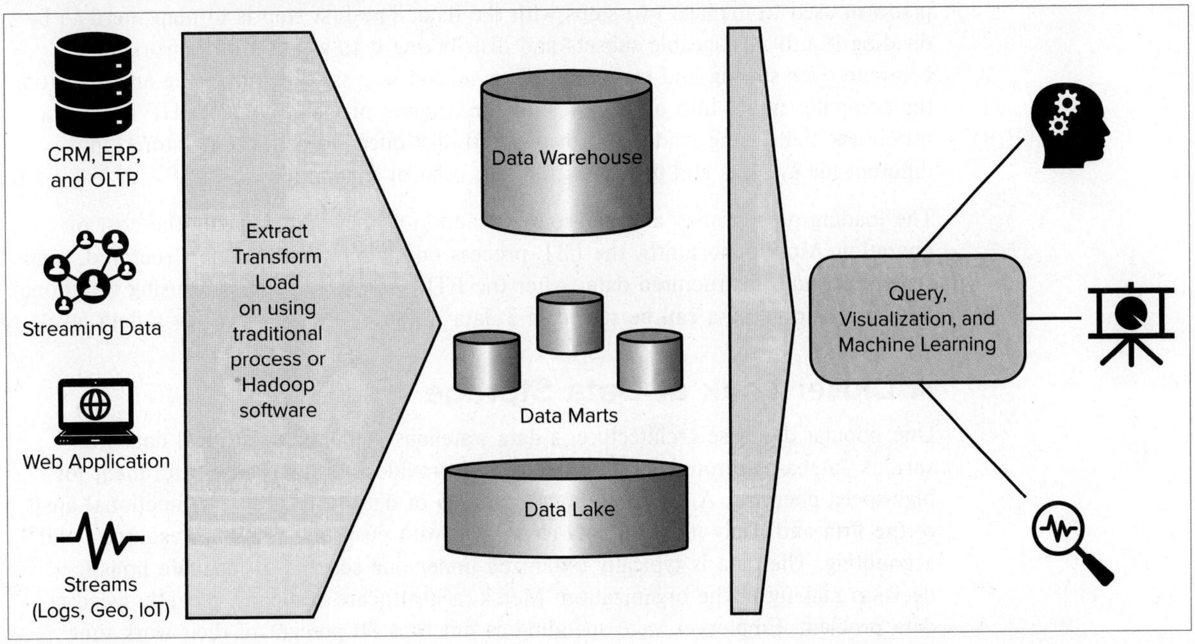

Traditional ETL

Extract, Transform, and Load (ETL) is an integration process designed to consolidate data from a variety of sources into a single location (see Exhibit 2-8). The functions begin with *extracting* key data from the source and converting it into the appropriate format. For example, the date is converted into data/time format. A rich transformation process then includes cleaning the data, applying transformation, and name conversion. *Transformation* requires conforming to the appropriate data storage format for where data will be stored. For example, a CRM database might require structured columns and rows such as first names, last names, and telephone numbers. But text from email communications, customer service interactions, or social media would be considered unstructured and must be specified differently. Because both structured and unstructured data are important, ETL solutions are being improved to efficiently integrate these various types of data. Most traditional ETL tools can process only relational datasets for semi-structured, unstructured data, and machinery sensor data, but newer systems are much more flexible. The third ETL step is *load*, in which the data is loaded into a storage system such as data warehouse, data marts, or a data lake.

Exhibit 2-8 Functions of Extract, Transform, Load (ETL)

FUNCTIONS
Data is **extracted** from the source.
Data is **transformed** into a useable form.
Data is integrated and **loaded** into a storage system.

ETL Using Hadoop

The massive volume of data led to the development of new technologies like Hadoop to capture, store, process, secure, and then analyze complex data (Exhibit 2-7). **Hadoop** is an open-source software that helps distributed computers solve problems of big data computation. Hadoop divides the big data processing over multiple computers, allowing it to handle massive amounts of data simultaneously at a reduced cost. Hadoop also facilitates analysis using MapReduce programming. MapReduce is a programming platform used to manage two steps with the data. The first step is to map the data by dividing it into manageable subsets and distributing it to a group of networked computers for storing and processing. The second step is to combine the answers from the computer nodes into one answer for the original problem handled. HIVE, a data warehouse built using Hadoop, provides SQL-like query to access data stored in different file systems and databases that are used by Hadoop.

The loading process uses an open-source Hadoop framework, reducing the cost of operation. Most importantly, the ETL process on Hadoop can handle structured, semi-structured, and unstructured data. After the ETL process is completed using traditional ETL or Hadoop, data can be stored in a data warehouse, data marts, or a data lake.

A Closer Look at Data Storage

One popular database architecture, a **data warehouse**, contains historical data from various databases throughout a company and provides a structured environment for high-speed querying. A data warehouse consists of data from different functional areas of the firm and likely includes data associated with customers, human resources, and accounting. The data is typically organized under one schema to facilitate holistic decision making in the organization. Merck, a healthcare company, recently faced a data problem. Employees were spending as much as 80 percent of their work time gathering data. The result was not enough time to complete other tasks.[9] Merck then developed a data warehousing system where data scientists can analyze both structured and unstructured data at the same time, and also develop reports using data visualization software for business analysts. Even though the databases might be located in different departments, the data warehouse system provides a central repository.

A **data mart** is a subset of the data warehouse that provides a specific value to a group of users. For example, a marketing data mart would be limited to data on customers, sales, products, and similar marketing metrics. There are two types of data marts: One is referred to as a dependent data mart, in which the data is directly obtained from an enterprise data warehouse. The second is referred to as independent data mart, in which the data is obtained from transactional systems, external providers, or specific geographic areas.

A **data lake** (often included in Hadoop systems) is a storage repository that holds a large amount of data in its native format. It is typically used to investigate data patterns and to archive data for future use. A variety of big data sources such as social media, weather data, logs, and sensor data, as well as online reviews, semi-structured (HTML) and unstructured data (e.g., videos, pictures), and machine-generated data (e.g., sensor data) can all be stored in a data lake. With data lakes, millions of customer records can be explored quickly without having to wait for data to be loaded into the data warehouse. At the same time, the contents of data lakes can be integrated with data warehouse. TD Bank Group is the sixth-largest bank in North America, employing around 85,000 people. TD Bank Group recently began to transform its digital infrastructure to a data lake architecture hosting customers' personal data such as demographics, preferences, opinions, and other external structured and unstructured data using a Hadoop private cloud.[10] Using tools like Hive, Apache Spark, and Tableau, the bank was able to explore massive amounts of data and build insightful reports and visualizations in a very cost-effective and quick manner. The data architecture enabled the company to move from "data-silos" to democratized access, providing information to employees across the organization. This data democratization enabled TD Bank to offer adaptive and customized products and services to its customers.

Consider the value of an enterprise-wide data repository for multi-channel retailers. Multi-channel retailers collect operational, transactional, and social media data from various sources. Customers make rapid decisions based upon information available to them at the right time. Companies rely on the real-time integration of multi-channel data to facilitate customer decision making through price modifications or streamlining inventory that help maintain customer satisfaction.

Continued from page 31

PRACTITIONER CORNER

Peter Drewes | Business Intelligence, Intellectual Property and Strategy at Lockheed Martin

Q **How are companies managing data from a variety of sources to create a full view of data and generate consistent value?**

A With modern computing power and inexpensive (temporary) data storage, large amounts of data can be stored and analyzed at will. The fundamental question is what to do with that data 2, 3, or 4 months after it has been stored? Is all of the data useful for market segments and analysis, or have they chosen to collect everything to prevent missing data that might be needed in the future? The key is the upfront setup of the inbound data

(Continued)

management and quality parameters. Each department within a company must be vocal and engaged in establishing a plan for data collection and management that provides answers to the questions relevant to them. It is very important to architect a solution up front to decide where the data is coming from and how often, how it will be stored, what analytics will be done on the data, and for how long. This will determine how to follow the data from field to useful information and how long you need to keep it handy.

Q How do marketers play an important role in data management?

A Marketers, business development teams, and process optimization teams work together to look at the problems and decide on the appropriate questions to answer. This will drive the requirements of data analytics that will ultimately deliver the insights to answer those questions.

The rate of internet-enabled devices/ processes continues to explode. More data is available from internal and external processes. It wasn't that many years ago that 1 MB of RAM was enough to solve many problems. Today's chasing of shiny objects might include "Let's use Artificial Intelligence / Machine Learning to make sense of our large datasets." But using a highly tuned algorithm to find relationships without a specific understanding could render unreliable results. Since the current trend is to accept what the computer has generated as a valid output, it is important the process of data management include functions across the enterprise.

Q How is the process of data management evolving to facilitate tangible results across the enterprise?

A It is an exciting time when internal questions can be asked, supporting data is identified and tied to external financial market analysis, and where predictive models answer the "what if" questions: "Should we go to market?" "Should we attempt to gain marketspace against company XYZ?" "Would this method be successful?" We are no longer limited by the quantity of data available, but by the ability to frame that data into successful business decisions. It is toward this point where the process of data management is evolving.

Business transformations based on governance and processes should be supported by massive amounts of "clean" data. Just because we have the resources to invest in a particular product does not mean we should. It might take too long to market to customers, be served by alternate means, be unrecoverable in terms of realizing an investment. No longer do we make the judgment "build it and they will come" or perform similar "guessing in the dark" exercises about a potential market analysis or a social media campaign. Using appropriate data management and numerical techniques, tangible results can be realized through insights that facilitate the analysis of markets or provide a value chain assessment with guidance for future endeavors. This type of power will influence businesses for the foreseeable future. Those that can take advantage of it and manage the incoming data will succeed; those that cannot will never realize their full potential.

Continued to page 40

For the data to be useful in addressing business problems, it must be properly managed. **Data management** as a process is the lifecycle management of data from acquisition to disposal. Prior to advancements in computing, data management consisted of paper copies placed in filing cabinets. If someone needed a file, they could review the paper copy and hopefully remember to replace it in the correct location. Today, data management provides a stable solution that facilitates efficient data access to appropriate people that reside both internally, such as the marketing team, and externally, such as suppliers, to the company. The management of data includes the strategy, structure, and processes to access and store data throughout the organization. Company data often consists of diverse data sources. The marketing, sales, and customer service departments collect different types of data from different sources. Marketing might collect information pertaining to customer responses to promotions, the sales department likely maintains data on current and churning customer accounts, and the customer service department acquires data through customer interactions from telephone calls, email, or chatbots. Although the data collected is usually required in making quick decisions for the particular department, it is not held in a vault only for their viewing. Most companies share access to data across functions or with external partners as necessary. Good data management provides a foundation for the delivery of high-quality data.

A major challenge of today's data management is that the inbound data continues to increase exponentially (Walmart, for example). These mountains of data are created each day and must be cleaned, verified, and validated so they can be used at some time in the future as high-quality data.

2.4 Data Quality

High-quality data is critical. Numerous success stories inspire current event articles recognizing the use of data by companies in decision making—to improve products, enhance customer relationships, adjust pricing strategies, and so forth. Unfortunately, not all companies experience the same level of success, because data too often contains errors that are not fixed. Coca-Cola used market research data of 200,000 people to create the New Coke product, one of the worst recorded product flops of all time. Based upon the research data, it was anticipated that consumers would adopt the new product. Unexpectedly, however, the new product development was a total failure that left customers upset, with 400,000 people expressing their dissatisfaction through phone calls and letters. The data was of poor quality and incomplete. It excluded important data, such as other predictors beyond taste—for instance, purchase behavior.

There is a common adage that people use when referring to deficient **data quality**: "garbage in, garbage out." The statement is reflected in the Coca-Cola example. If the database contains poor quality data, results or decisions emanating from that data will also be of poor quality. We can again follow the trail of bad data through a company to recognize the impact on multiple groups of people. Inaccuracies in a supplier's inventory management system will lead to confusion for corporate retail buyers whose job it is to maintain appropriate levels of products in stores. An absence in products on the shelves leads to frustrated store managers and disappointed customers who, in today's digitally connected environment, could effortlessly search for products elsewhere. Many companies have adopted site-to-store pickup options, but if their inventory is not current, then customers could place orders expecting to receive the item within a few hours, but receive a notice indicating the product is no longer in stock. The customer must then start from ground zero by either searching and purchasing the product from a competitor or online. Inaccurate data, missing fields, or data isolated in disparate sources can also be drivers of underperforming employees and dissatisfied customers.

If you consider the growth of data sources and vast amounts of data being generated, it is easy to comprehend how the quality of data might be negatively impacted. Customers or employees can easily input incorrect data by typing an incorrect ZIP code, using an invalid email address, misspelling a name, or inputting a decimal in the wrong location. These mistakes might seem harmless, but contemplate the effect of misspelled names. Jonh Smith, Jon Smith, and John Smith happen to be the same person but are currently registered as separate accounts in the company's CRM system, resulting in disconnected historical interactions by the same customer. This becomes an issue when the company decides to identify high-value customers based on purchase history. This customer would likely be eliminated because the transactions are divided into several customer names and subsequently smaller purchase amounts.

Let's examine another scenario. Consider purchasing your car at a dealership, then returning for regular service. If you purchase a service contract, for example, your car service is free for the first two years of purchase or 25,000 miles—whichever comes first. You schedule maintenance for your car to discover that the dealership's records indicate you already had your 25,000-mile service, even though you are positive the last maintenance visit was for 20,000 miles. They are using multiple software systems to store customer data and must investigate the claim prior to scheduling an appointment. As a result, the situation requires more of your time to search for vehicle maintenance records and to call back to verify they located the correct information. Data quality issues such as these—whether a result of incorrect data, missing data, or disconnected systems—are all too common and frequently lead to frustrated customers. Lack of quality data can also result in consequences to company employees because critical decisions are based upon data that is available to them in the system.

Continued from page 38

PRACTITIONER CORNER

Peter Drewes I Business Intelligence, Intellectual Property and Strategy at Lockheed Martin

Q **"Garbage in, garbage out." What are some major challenges companies encounter with data quality issues?**

A First and foremost is to determine how well a company follows their data governance policy. This will set the stage for everything following data collection. How is data collected, verified, and validated? How is it cleaned and parsed for later usage? These are all key elements in the reduction of the "garbage in" problem. Combining this with asking the right questions will reduce, but not eliminate, the garbage out.

A couple of common data quality issues are related to outliers or missing data. Are the outliers more distant from the curve true outliers or the data of interest? The dataset may have completely clean data that is relevant and useful, but still provides garbage output. In the case of outliers, they can be useful depending on the questions being asked, or they could produce erroneous results. Another area to consider is how missing data is addressed. One philosophy is to replace it with the mean to reduce deviations. However, there are always other questions to consider. Why is the data missing? Was there a valid reason that caused the data to be "missing"? Answers to these and similar relevant questions provide the basis to ensure usable information is provided throughout the process.

Q **What is the impact of bad data on decision making?**

A The major problem with bad, inconsistent, or biased data is that often times nothing jumps out to indicate the results are invalid. Technology will run analytics models for many hours through many terabytes of data to develop conclusions, but that does not mean the results are always correct. Analysts need to use training datasets to develop initial models that identify errors and revise as necessary. But in the real world, training datasets are not applied often enough because they reduce system efficiency and increase overhead costs to get to the answer. It is this recursive training using multiple datasets, however, that allows algorithms and data to be continuously analyzed and improved. If a test set of the highest 20 percent of data is used, does that change the results? What about using the lowest 20 percent? Which datasets will change the system conclusions? Examining questions such as these will yield more valuable information. Since we are relying on systems to provide a "faster" look at the data than we can do by hand, it becomes more challenging to watch the algorithms do their job given the volume of inbound data. This level of carelessness leads to business decisions we would never make if we had better data.

Another key area is the garbage in, hallelujah out concept. When biased or bad data isn't corrected, the results are skewed or potentially bad. However, since the algorithms and process have been approved and validated, we tend to trust the algorithms and the output data is believed to be true. Results are then often run up and down the management chain as good news (the hallelujah portion). But later when performance isn't met, or the biases are found, the decision-making process is questioned, reducing the chance management will accept the next analytical solution.

Continued to page 42

Unfortunately, when data are of poor quality, insights produced by marketing analytics will be unreliable. Data are important, but high-quality data is critical in developing an accurate understanding of trends and purchase patterns and in maintaining customer satisfaction. For data records to be valuable, they have to be timely, accurate, complete, and consistent. Many times, unsatisfied customers are a result of poor data quality.

Consider the restaurant chain example from Chapter 1. Restaurants are using a variety of data sources and machine learning to determine where to locate their next establishment. Included in the analysis might be internal information such as existing stores and competitor locations, store sales, area demographics, and traffic patterns, and could conceivably include lifestyle information such as healthy eating preferences of area customers from social media. What might be the financial repercussions of inaccurate data from a single one of the sources mentioned? Restaurants are relying upon the combination of this data as the foundation for AI driven analyses. Results will guide decisions to optimize placement and predict sales of new locations. Inaccuracies will taint the data and produce false information. Data has the potential to be a valuable resource for companies. But poor quality data can have a significant, negative impact.

Although data quality can be measured by numerous dimensions, the most common are timeliness, completeness, accuracy, consistency, and format:

- *Timeliness:* Have you ever found a product you wanted to quickly purchase at a brick-and-mortar store, but could not access a mobile phone or internet service to determine if it was available elsewhere at a lower price? You then left the store after purchasing the product only to realize a competitor was selling it for much less. The lack of timely information led to a decision that might have changed if the information was available when needed. Similar scenarios occur in other purchasing situations. Real-time data such as customer social media sentiment, responses to marketing campaigns, online and offline customer behavior patterns, customer service chatbots, or call centers are all critical in making current decisions. If customers communicate their dissatisfaction on social media or through call centers, companies prefer to know this sooner rather than later. They can then respond as quickly as possible in an effort to lessen damage to the brand. Having a complete set of data is also important to responding in a timely manner.

- *Completeness:* Imagine if a company wanted to send an email follow-up to their best customers and did not collect email addresses or wanted to personalize a communication using a first name, but it only had access to initials. Data completeness means maintaining the sufficient breadth, depth, and scope for the particular task. In this case, the company would need to forgo or delay the email campaign or personalized communications because the data was incomplete.

- *Accuracy:* Data accuracy is the extent to which the data is error-free. Is the data correct, reliable, and accurately measured? If it is, then decisions more often result in a favorable outcome.

- *Consistency:* Data inconsistencies can lead to embarrassing dilemmas and uncoordinated strategic decision making. Consider Nestlé USA as an example. The labeling of vanilla was different from one division and factory to another. When the data was being evaluated for integration, the inconsistent values created confusion and there was no efficient way to reconcile the differences. Because the data was inconsistent, the company was unaware the same supplier was charging different prices for each division and factory, when everyone should have realistically been paying the same price.

- *Format:* Format is the extent to which the information is adequately presented or delivered for efficient and effective understanding. When one person recently visited a Dallas, Texas, emergency room, the patient reported returning from a trip outside the country to the nurse, who documented the information. But the hospital later reported that although the records were accessible to the physician, his immediate computer screen did not contain the information and the patient was ultimately discharged. Unfortunately, it was later discovered the patient had Ebola, a highly contagious, often fatal disease and a panic ensued throughout the country. While this is a serious example, many functional departments make decisions from information dashboards. If the dashboard is difficult to read or clumsy to navigate, the impact could be detrimental.

2.5 Data Understanding, Preparation, and Transformation

For the curious mind, the idea of exploring data can be somewhat of a game. In a game, you use available information in hopes of making the best decisions, while also obtaining a high score or defeating your competitors. The data is used to satisfy an outcome—in this particular scenario, the outcome is winning. Data inspires curiosity for marketers because they are eager to use insights to strategize the next move. Marketers desire to explore data as quickly as possible because data is basically useless until analyzed. Consider rows and columns of data—there is no tangible benefit to data in raw form. But do not get distracted by the excitement of discovering fascinating new insights. There are important steps to consider in the process. Data is messy and must be tidied up before being used.

Data Understanding

Recall the 7-step marketing analytics process that was introduced in Chapter 1. First, marketers must grasp an understanding of the business. If there is a failure to understand the business situation, the marketer will have a difficult time defining the right business problem and asking the right questions.

Continued from page 40

PRACTITIONER CORNER

Peter Drewes | Business Intelligence, Intellectual Property and Strategy at Lockheed Martin

Q **Why is it so important that marketing analysts have a thorough understanding of the business and existing data?**

A Everything is related to asking the right question. If you ask the wrong question, you are heading toward a useless business answer. This is never done intentionally, but preventing this misstep requires a thorough understanding of the business processes, existing data, needed data, marketing and business outcomes. If only one person understands all of this, either their judgment must be completely trusted, or others should be brought up to speed to discuss different parts of the analysis. Without a collaborative, top-down view, everyone is operating in a silo environment. This may achieve local goals while creating system-wide inefficiencies. Thus, management and analysts must be able to see eye to eye and understand the same problem from the same perspective. System-wide efficiency can only be obtained through this understanding.

Continued to next page

Understanding available data is also critical to correctly addressing the desired business problems and reducing the potential for inaccurately reporting results. It might seem obvious to confirm you understand the data, but individual data fields are easily overlooked when dealing with large datasets. Pretend your company is struggling to understand sales over the last three years and your supervisor requests an analysis of sales data. Your job is to simply compare sales on an annual basis. You notice that the unit of measure for sales figures is reported monthly, and so you simply create an annual column for each year. In doing so, however, you do not realize the dataset only contained six months for the third year. Unfortunately, the mistake is not found until presenting the information, which erroneously reports third year sales have plummeted. Without a proper data understanding, you made an error in analyzing the data and the annual sales comparison is incorrectly reported.

Continued from previous page

PRACTITIONER CORNER

Peter Drewes | Business Intelligence, Intellectual Property and Strategy at Lockheed Martin

Q **"Chaos to Clarity." What are several key steps in the role of data cleaning and preparation (e.g., merging, aggregating) that are necessary for a marketing analyst to understand prior to data analysis?**

A Data analysis is the logistical execution of the data algorithms selected based on the questions to be answered. Following appropriate data management, the real work is done during the preparation and cleaning based on the question requirements. The design of the experimentation and the methods that will be used to test the data and algorithms should align with how the data is structured.

Therefore, merging sources or aggregating values might be necessary in answering certain questions.

The data governance process begins with studying what structured and unstructured data will arrive, how often it will arrive, what transport mechanism is involved (IoT, web socket, Excel sheet, or napkins). What does the timing mean compared to the decision I need to make? Having perfect data organized and correlated is a wonderful thing. But if the data is available six months after a corporate strategic decision is needed, it offers no value and can potentially hurt the company making decisions with only the data available at that moment.

Data Preparation

Extensive use of descriptive statistics and data visualization methods is necessary to gain an understanding of the data. First, the data must be properly prepared. During the process of preparing the data, tasks may include identifying and treating missing values, correcting errors and removing outliers in the data, deciding on the right unit of analysis, and determining how to represent the variables.

Feature Selection   In most data analytics projects, the analyst will have access to ample data to analyze a model. For this reason, it is important to pay close attention to the variables (also known as **features** or predictors) included in the model. In situations like these, the data is likely to have a large number of features. Some of these features (e.g., person's height and weight) might be highly correlated or measure the same thing. Other features could be completely unrelated to the variable of interest or the target variable. If features are correlated with each other or unrelated to the target variable, this can lead to poor reliability, accuracy, and what is referred to as overfitting of the model. But what is **overfitting**? Consider a dataset with 100 individuals, 40 percent of whom have purchased products at the same company before. Information about interest, income, number of children, neighborhood ZIP code, and past purchase behavior might do a good job predicting whether or not someone will purchase the product. But if we keep adding additional predictors such as height, number of pets, weight, and hair color, the accuracy of the model will likely improve.

This performance may be misleading, however, because it probably includes spurious effects that are specific to the 100 individuals, but not beyond the sample. Overfitting occurs from an overly complex model where the results are limited to the data being used and are not generalizable—which means future relationships cannot be inferred, and results will be inconsistent when using other data. Always keeping every variable available in the model is not necessary and often misleading. The analyst can determine which variables are sufficient to retain for the analysis. It is important, therefore, to know the features to include and which to eliminate to confirm that the model represents key variables of interest. Keeping too many variables can be unnecessary to achieve good model results and is costly to manage in terms of computer processing power. Typically, this step involves consulting stakeholders with domain specific knowledge (i.e., individuals with knowledge of the data and the business process) to ensure the features included are important from the end-user perspective.

Sample Size   As with feature selection, **sample size** is an important consideration. Political polls often report results of a certain sample size. Surveying every voter is impossible; therefore, these analyses focus on smaller, more reasonable proportions of the population. Sample size recommendations are based on statistical analysis concepts such as a power calculation. A **power calculation** helps determine that outcomes will be estimated from a sample with a sufficient level of precision. In a data mining project with a large dataset, the goal typically is not to estimate the *effect size* but to predict new records. When the goal is accurate prediction, a large sample of several thousand records is often required.

Unit of Analysis   A **unit of analysis** describes the what, when, and who of the analysis. To identify the appropriate unit of analysis, the first step is to identify the target (outcome) variable. Let's say we are trying to predict whether a customer is likely to churn (leave our business), then the customer is the unit of analysis. On the other hand, if the purpose is to predict brand satisfaction, then the brand is the unit of analysis. If a business is trying to determine the price of a mobile phone subscription plan for different customer levels, then the unit of analysis is the subscription rather than the person. At times, the unit of analysis may not be obvious. Therefore, it is a good practice to collaborate with other subject matter experts to collectively determine the correct unit of analysis.

Missing Values   It is common to have missing records for one or more of the variables in the dataset. Missing values result from various scenarios such as customers that, due to time constraints, overlook and leave fields blank. This creates a problem because analysts must make adjustments for missing data. There are several options to address missing data: (1) Imputing missing values with estimated new values (mean, median, regression value), (2) omitting the records with missing values, and (3) excluding the variables with the missing values.

If among 35 variables, the average sale is missing for only three records in that variable, we might substitute the mean sale for the missing records. This will enable us to proceed with the analysis and not lose information the record has for the other 34 complete variables. The imputation options are recommended when the missing values are missing at random and typically include the mean, median, and mode. For example, suppose the average sale for all customers is $45,000, marketing analysts could decide to use this value to replace the missing value for sales. Another option with missing values is to predict the missing value using regression or decision tree induction. For example, customer sales values might be missing. Relying on the other customer attributes in a dataset, we could use a decision tree to predict the missing values for sales. The missing values can then be replaced with predicted values using the results of the decision tree.

Removing incomplete observations when the number of missing values is small is also a reasonable option. It is important, however, to consider if the missing values are missing at random or if there is a pattern or reason for the missing values. For example, in a study of the relationship between product satisfaction and product performance, if participants with an above-average satisfaction skip the question "Rank the product performance," analyses may not identify the relationship between product performance and satisfaction. Information such as this is essential to understanding the relationships between variables.

When observations are missing for a large number of records, dropping the records will lead to a substantial loss in the dataset. It is good in cases like this to examine the importance of the variables with large missing values. If the variable is insignificant in the prediction of the model, it can easily be excluded. If the variable is a key indicator, however, then marketers must determine if it is worth the investment to collect data and obtain the missing records. When working with large datasets, removing many observations with missing values might have no effect on the overall analysis. This is particularly valid when the variable dropped has a high correlation with another variable in the dataset, and thus the loss of information may be minimal.

Outliers   Values that are at a considerable distance from any of the other data clusters are considered **outliers**. In large datasets, outliers are typically detected using a statistical test that assumes a distribution model of the data or distance measures. As a rule of thumb, an outlier is often determined as anything over three standard deviations from the mean. Although not grounds for immediate removal, outliers should be investigated further. For example, we know that an age observation of 140 indicates an error. However, it might be determined that an observation of 100 is within the possibility of accurate data and should be retained for the analysis. In cases when only a few outliers exist, removing them from the dataset is warranted. Most of the time, outliers need to be removed from the model as noise. In some applications such as fraud detection, however, these rare outlier events are what the model is trying to predict.

Consider several customer income levels in a dataset: $5,000, $45,000, $48,000, $50,000, $1,000,000. As a marketer, you are developing pricing strategies based upon customer demographics. In this simple case, two values stand out as obvious. The income levels of $5,000 and $1,000,000 do not conform with the general behavior of the data. You would need to decide whether the customers with an income of $5,000 or $1,000,000 would skew the results of purchase behavior based on the price of your product. To examine existing outliers in a data analytics project, we can review the maximum and minimum values for each variable. Are there values falling toward the minimum or maximum points of the value distribution? Here, the customer reporting an income of $1,000,000 would fall toward the maximum point of distribution. Another method of identifying outliers is to use **cluster analysis**, where groups are created based upon similarities to determine if any observations have a considerable distance to other clusters.

For a more detailed explanation of how to assess and deal with these data issues, refer to Hair, Babin, Anderson, and Black (2018).[11] Once data has been cleaned, the marketing analyst should determine whether the data warrants further transformation through aggregation, normalization, new variable construction, or dummy coding.

Data Transformation

- **Aggregation:** During this process, summary operations are applied to the data. For example, the weekly sales data may be aggregated to calculate the total sales by month, quarter, or year. This is a key process to help prepare data at the unit of analysis necessary for insights.

- **Normalization:** Variables (also known as features or predictors) may include different data ranges that vary greatly from each other. Some data might be measured weekly and other data annually. To normalize a variable, we scale it by subtracting the variable from the mean and then dividing it by the standard deviation. Normalization helps us bring all variables into the same scale. Normalization becomes critical in some data analytics techniques, such as cluster analysis, because large values will dominate the distance calculation.

- **New column (feature) construction:** A new feature (predictor or variable) can be calculated based on other existing values. If a dataset consists of a sales date, a marketer might want to know more about whether sales are more prevalent on certain days of the week, months, or seasonally. Using the sales date, new columns of data can be constructed by the day of the week, month, quarter, and year.

- **Dummy Coding:** This process can be useful when considering nominal **categorical variables**. A categorical variable is when the data represents one of a limited number of categories. Geographic location (e.g., Northeast, Southeast, Northwest, Southwest, Midwest) is an example of a categorical variable. In this case, geographic location is considered a nonmetric variable and need to be re-coded using a process called dummy coding. Dummy coding involves creating a dichotomous value from a categorical value. This type of coding makes categorical variables dichotomous using ones and zeroes. Dummy coding is covered in more detail in Chapter 5.

Case Study   Avocado Toast: A Recipe to Learn SQL

One of Americans' favorite "go to" breakfasts is avocado toast. In fact, it is reported that Americans spend almost $900,000 on avocado toast each month. How has this growth impacted avocado sales over the last few years? We can use SQL to query basic results that answer questions such as this and more. In this section, we will take a closer look at avocado sales data over four years across the United States. In exploring this data, you will learn how to manipulate thousands of rows using SQL language. This exercise will provide you with the knowledge to SELECT tables in SQL, JOIN data, CREATE and INSERT new tables, and modify data using UPDATE.

Getting Started

As mentioned earlier in this chapter, one of the most popular databases is a relational database. It is a framework made of tables (similar to a spreadsheet) where each row (also known as a record) represents a set of related data describing a customer or a product. On the other hand, each column (also known as a feature, predictor, or variable) represents data such as company name, region, street address, quantity sold, and so on. Exhibit 2-9 shows a subset of data in the avocado dataset. Columns include region, average price, and type. The rows contain the data for this table (for example, the first row shows Phoenix, 0.77, conventional).

Exhibit 2-9 A Subset of the Avocado Data (Year = 2018)

REGION	AVERAGE PRICE	TYPE
Phoenix	0.77	Conventional
Charlotte	1.23	Conventional
Denver	1.52	Organic
San Diego	1.15	Conventional

As previously mentioned, the way to manipulate data in a database is by using a query language. One of the most popular query languages is SQL. To demonstrate how SQL can be used to add and modify data, we will use SQLITE, a web version of SQL. SQLite is an introductory tool, but it will enable us to explore the basics of SQL programming. When you are ready to build a full application using an SQL server, this basic knowledge will help you get started.

Understanding the Dataset

This data can be downloaded from the student's resources page. Data for this exercise was downloaded from the Hass Avocado Board website but modified for this case study.[12] The data represents compiled weekly avocado sales for more than 3 years and comes from retailer's cash registers based on retail sales of Hass avocados. The Average Price (of avocados) in the table reflects a per unit (per avocado) cost, even when multiple units (avocados) are sold in bags. To get started, let's review the data elements in the table (Exhibit 2-10).

Exhibit 2-10 Data Elements Represented in the Hass Avocado Data

VARIABLE NAME (TYPE)	DESCRIPTION
observationid (typeless)	A unique identifier for each observation. This is a *primary key* that is located across multiple avocado datasets. A primary key can guide the integration of data from one table to the data of another table.
region (string)	The sales geographic location
year (date)	The year of the observation
month (date)	The month of the observation
quarter (date)	The quarter of the observation
type (string)	Conventional or organic
averageprice (numeric)	The average price of a single avocado
totalvolume (numeric)	Total number of avocados sold
supplierid (typeless)	An indentifier indicating the supplier of the avocado. Note that supplierid is a *foreign key* in the avocado table.

There are several tasks you will learn in SQL via the case study on how to prepare data for analysis and answer questions about it.

After reviewing the data, what questions can you ask to better understand avocado sales since 2016? Here are some ideas:

- What are the highest average prices customers are paying for a single avocado?
- What is the average price customers are paying per region?
- Where are avocados being sold over certain average prices?
- What is the average price that customers are paying in specific geographic regions?
- How can the data be aggregated to obtain the volume of conventional avocados per quarter versus per week?
- How are regions performing by volume sales?
- What is the company and country of origin for avocados supplied to each region?

You can use SQL for basic data analysis to answer these questions and more.

Applying the Concepts

There are several options for exploring SQL. For this short introductory exercise, you will use an online platform.

Step 1: Visit the website **https://sqliteonline.com**. Your screen should look like Exhibit 2-11.

Exhibit 2-11

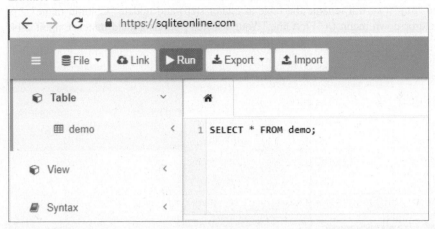

Source: SQLite

Step 2: To explore the data, it must be imported into the SQLite Online platform (Exhibit 2-12). Click on "Import" and then "Open."

Exhibit 2-12

Source: SQLite

Step 3: Click "Open" and browse for the csv file "AvocadoData" that you downloaded from the student's resources page (Exhibit 2-13).

Exhibit 2-13

Source: SQLite

Step 4: After selecting "Open," the data import specification will appear. Update "Table name" to "tmp" (we will rename the table at a later step) and update "Column name" from the drop-down menu to "First line." Your selected options should match Exhibit 2-14.

Exhibit 2-14

Source: SQLite

Step 5: After selecting "Ok," the data will upload and your screen should appear like that shown in Exhibit 2-15.

Exhibit 2-15

Source: SQLite

Step 6: You can now request certain information to begin exploring the data. In the open text area, enter your SQL code to view all the data. This is accomplished by using the asterisk * symbol. Perform this task by using the following query statement and then clicking "Run" in the menu bar (Exhibit 2-16):

SELECT * FROM tmp;

Exhibit 2-16

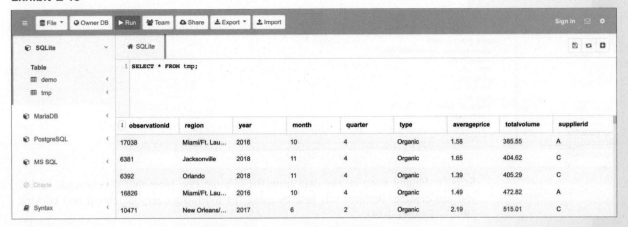

Source: SQLite

Step 7: Next, you must modify the avocado table so each column is given the appropriate data type. Because the Avocado table was created by importing the csv file, SQLite Online does not know the data type of each column. Instead, SQLite Online defaults each column to a string data type, which can be a problem for numerical values that need to be sorted. This can be fixed by creating the Avocado table with the appropriate column data types and then placing all the original data into the new table.

Step 7a: Perform this task by using the following DDL (data definition language) query statement to create the Avocado table with each column's appropriate data type (Exhibit 2-17):

```
CREATE TABLE avocado(
    observationid INT PRIMARY key,
    region TEXT,
    year INT,
    month INT,
    quarter INT,
    type TEXT,
    averageprice REAL,
    totalvolume REAL,
    supplierid TEXT
);
```

Exhibit 2-17

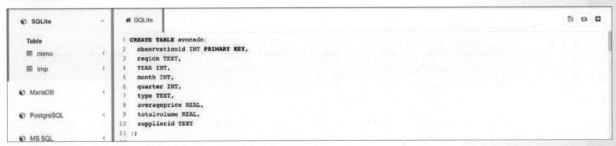

Source: SQLite

Step 7b: Click "Run" in the menu bar. You will see a new avocado entry created under "Table" (Exhibit 2-18).

Exhibit 2-18

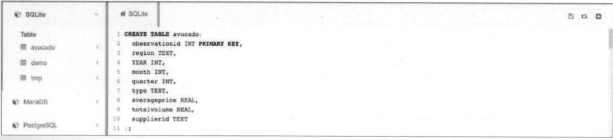

```
  1  CREATE TABLE avocado(
  2    observationid INT PRIMARY KEY,
  3    region TEXT,
  4    YEAR INT,
  5    month INT,
  6    quarter INT,
  7    type TEXT,
  8    averageprice REAL,
  9    totalvolume REAL,
 10    supplierid TEXT
 11  );
```

Source: SQLite

Step 7c: Finally, copy all the data from the original tmp table into the Avocado table you just created. Perform this task by using the following query statement and clicking "Run" (Exhibit 2-19):

INSERT INTO avocado(
observationid, region, year, month, quarter, type, averageprice, totalvolume, supplierid)
SELECT observationid, region, year, month, quarter, type, averageprice, totalvolume, supplierid
FROM tmp;

Exhibit 2-19

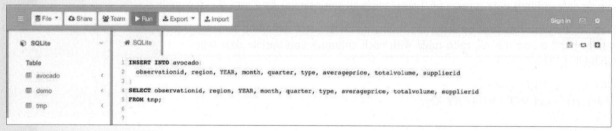

```
  1  INSERT INTO avocado(
  2    observationid, region, YEAR, month, quarter, type, averageprice, totalvolume, supplierid
  3  )
  4  SELECT observationid, region, YEAR, month, quarter, type, averageprice, totalvolume, supplierid
  5  FROM tmp;
  6
  7
```

Source: SQLite

Step 7d: Now, let's preview the data. Perform this task by using the following query statement and clicking "Run" (Exhibit 2-20):

SELECT * FROM avocado;

Exhibit 2-20

```
  1  SELECT * FROM avocado;
  2
  3
```

observationid	region	year	month	quarter	type	averageprice	totalvolume	supplierid
17038	Miami/Ft. Lau...	2016	10	4	Organic	1.58	385.55	A
6381	Jacksonville	2018	11	4	Organic	1.65	404.62	C
6392	Orlando	2018	11	4	Organic	1.39	405.29	C
16826	Miami/Ft. Lau...	2016	10	4	Organic	1.49	472.82	A
10471	New Orleans/...	2017	6	2	Organic	2.19	515.01	C
16985	Miami/Ft. Lau...	2016	10	4	Organic	1.58	542.85	A

Source: SQLite

Step 8: In this step, you will learn how to drop (or delete) a table from the database. Perform this task by using the following query statement and clicking "Run" (Exhibit 2-21):

Drop TABLE tmp;

Exhibit 2-21

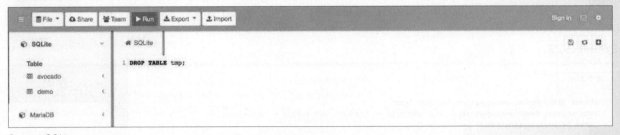

Source: SQLite

Step 9: You can view selected fields and sort your data. Suppose you are interested in just looking at the average price paid for an avocado by region but want to sort results by average price from high to low. Perform this task by using the following query statement and clicking "Run" (Exhibit 2-22):

SELECT averageprice, region, year FROM avocado ORDER BY averageprice DESC;

From sorting the data from high to low, we see that San Francisco has the highest average price from 2016.

Exhibit 2-22

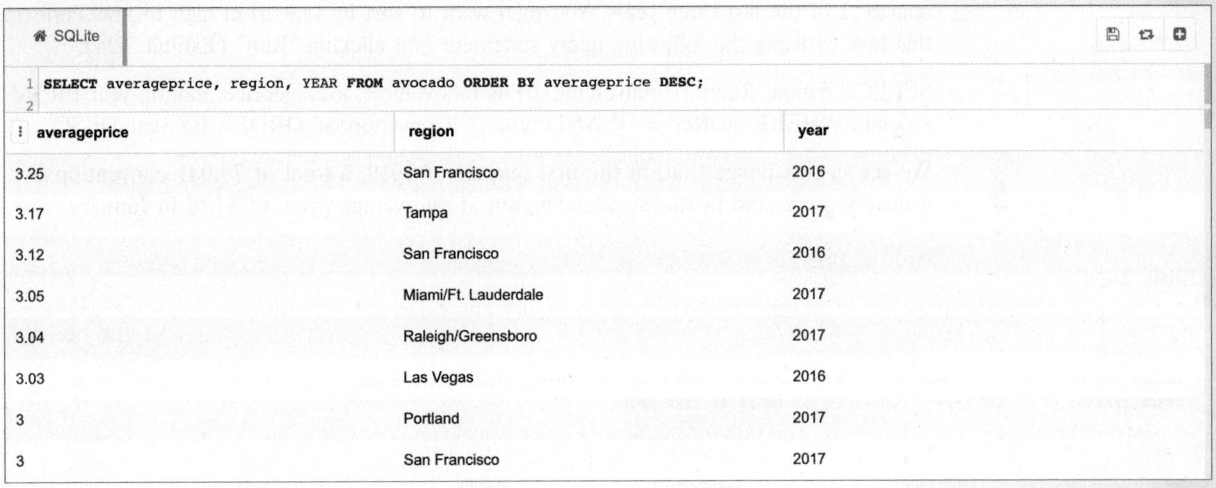

```
1 SELECT averageprice, region, YEAR FROM avocado ORDER BY averageprice DESC;
2
```

averageprice	region	year
3.25	San Francisco	2016
3.17	Tampa	2017
3.12	San Francisco	2016
3.05	Miami/Ft. Lauderdale	2017
3.04	Raleigh/Greensboro	2017
3.03	Las Vegas	2016
3	Portland	2017
3	San Francisco	2017

Source: SQLite

Step 10: What if you want to focus on reviewing a smaller subset of the data? To create smaller subsets, use a conditional statement (WHERE) to meet a condition. For example, you would like to examine sales where the average price is a certain value. You can include additional criteria (for example, region) to further narrow your query. To include this type of criterion (region), use what is referred to as a logical statement (AND, OR).

Maybe you would like to examine the average price of organic avocados in Charlotte, North Carolina, that are greater than $2.50. In this query, we will need to include some conditions that would limit the returned data specifically to the defined geographic area. Perform this task by using the following query statement and clicking "Run" (Exhibit 2-23):

SELECT year, month, averageprice, region, type
FROM avocado WHERE averageprice > '2.5' AND type = 'Organic' AND region = 'Charlotte'
ORDER BY averageprice DESC;

As you can see from the results, the highest average price of organic avocados sold in Charlotte, North Carolina, was $2.83 in August 2017.

Exhibit 2-23

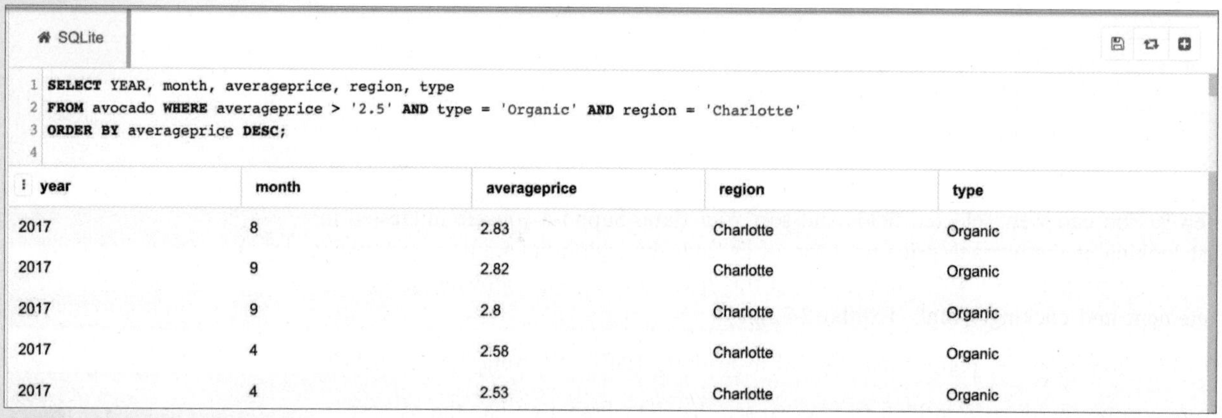

```
  SQLite                                                                                    🖫  ↻  ➕

1 SELECT YEAR, month, averageprice, region, type
2 FROM avocado WHERE averageprice > '2.5' AND type = 'Organic' AND region = 'Charlotte'
3 ORDER BY averageprice DESC;
4
```

year	month	averageprice	region	type
2017	8	2.83	Charlotte	Organic
2017	9	2.82	Charlotte	Organic
2017	9	2.8	Charlotte	Organic
2017	4	2.58	Charlotte	Organic
2017	4	2.53	Charlotte	Organic

Source: SQLite

Step 11: You need to better understand the total volume of conventional avocados in quarter 1 of the last three years. You then want to sort by year from high to low. Perform this task by using the following query statement and clicking "Run" (Exhibit 2-24):

SELECT region, Round((totalvolume),0) as totalvolume, averageprice, month, year FROM avocado WHERE quarter = '1' AND type = 'Conventional' ORDER BY year DESC;

We see in this image that, in the first quarter of 2019, a total of 79,041 conventional avocados were sold in the Syracuse region at an average price of $1.16 in January.

Exhibit 2-24

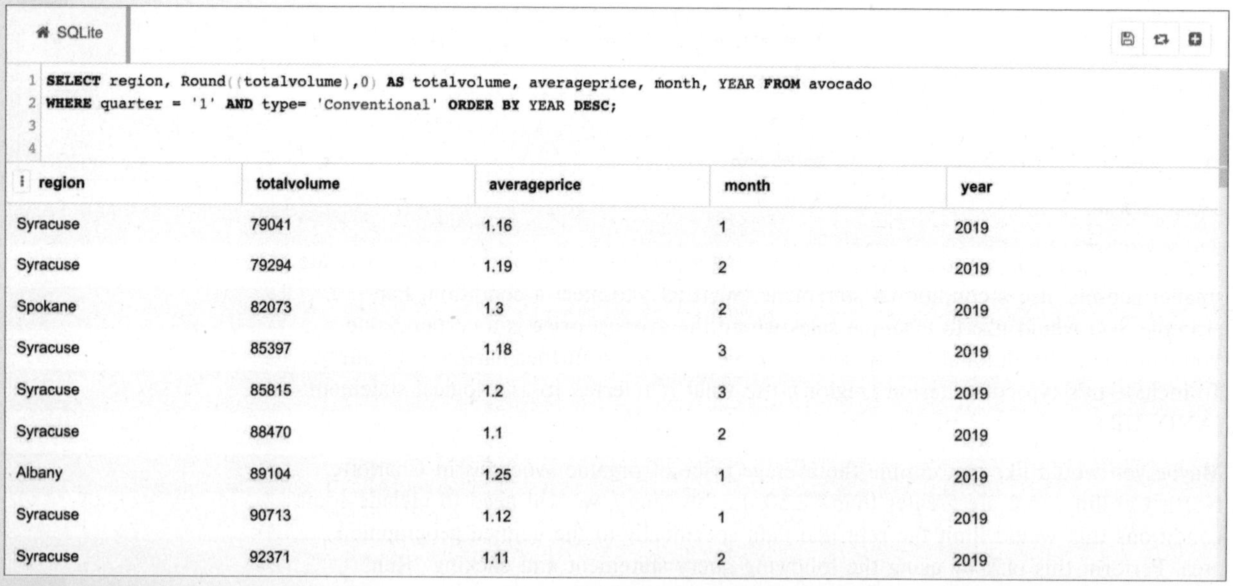

```
  SQLite                                                                                    🖫  ↻  ➕

1 SELECT region, Round((totalvolume),0) AS totalvolume, averageprice, month, YEAR FROM avocado
2 WHERE quarter = '1' AND type= 'Conventional' ORDER BY YEAR DESC;
3
4
```

region	totalvolume	averageprice	month	year
Syracuse	79041	1.16	1	2019
Syracuse	79294	1.19	2	2019
Spokane	82073	1.3	2	2019
Syracuse	85397	1.18	3	2019
Syracuse	85815	1.2	3	2019
Syracuse	88470	1.1	2	2019
Albany	89104	1.25	1	2019
Syracuse	90713	1.12	1	2019
Syracuse	92371	1.11	2	2019

Source: SQLite

Step 12: Another way to return a selected set of data that meets multiple criteria is using the statement IN. For example, if you want to understand only two cities from the results in step 9, consider returning all the fields to limit the focus on just those two cities—in this case, Boston and San Francisco. Perform this task by using the following query statement and clicking "Run" (Exhibit 2-25):

SELECT * FROM avocado WHERE region IN ("Boston", "San Francisco");

Now, you only see results from Boston and San Francisco.

Exhibit 2-25

observationid	region	year	month	quarter	type	averageprice	totalvolume	supplierid
16435	Boston	2016	8	3	Organic	1.23	7117.91	A
16329	Boston	2016	7	3	Organic	1.14	7313.26	A
14739	Boston	2016	1	1	Organic	1.26	7629.12	A
11188	Boston	2017	9	3	Organic	1.47	7698.45	C
14792	Boston	2016	1	1	Organic	1.32	7751.94	A
16965	Boston	2016	10	4	Organic	1.32	8153.98	A
14951	Boston	2016	1	1	Organic	1.52	8221.86	A
10696	San Francisco	2017	7	3	Organic	2.45	8311.12	C

The query shown: `SELECT * FROM avocado WHERE region IN ("Boston", "San Francisco");`

Source: SQLite

Aggregation

Most times when you get a dataset, you will need to roll it up to a higher level. For example, you can calculate the maximum average avocado price in our dataset, or the sum of total Volume by quarter or year. To do this, you will need to add a function to the variable you would like to roll up. For numeric type variables (e.g., averageprice, totalvolume), you can use the SQL aggregate functions for a set of values: sum, min, max, average, and so on (Exhibit 2-26). For categorical data (e.g., region and type), you can use functions such as count. When using aggregate functions, the result will be produced on a single row.

Exhibit 2-26 Aggregate Functions

FUNCTION	RETURNS
AVG ( )	The average value of the selected group.
COUNT ( )	The number of rows that correspond to a certain feature.
MAX ( )	The maximum value in a group.
MIN ( )	The minimum value in a group.
SUM ( )	The sum of values within a group.

Step 13: The averageprice column contains the average price of avocados by city and date. What if you want to search for the highest average price that customers have paid to date? Perform this task by using the following query statement and clicking "Run" (Exhibit 2-27):

SELECT MAX(averageprice) FROM avocado;

You will see that the highest average price that customers paid was $3.25. You can also use the MIN(averageprice) statement to find the lowest average price that customers paid to date.

Exhibit 2-27

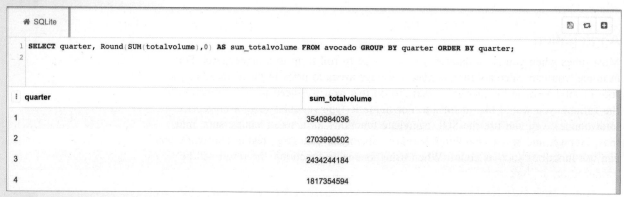

Source: SQLite

Step 14: Suppose your data contains the month/day/year in a single column, but you would like to examine data over each quarter instead. You can aggregate the total sales volume by summing the values by quarter. Perform this task by using the following query statement and clicking "Run" (Exhibit 2-28):

SELECT quarter, Round(SUM(totalvolume),0) as sum_totalvolume FROM avocado GROUP BY quarter ORDER BY quarter;

Using the Round function allows us to specifiy the number of decimal places for totalvolume. In this example, the number of decimals is set to zero. As you can see during quarter 1, customers from all regions purchased over 3.5 billion avocados. Now you can see the total avocado purchases by customers from all regions for each quarter.

Exhibit 2-28

```
SELECT quarter, Round(SUM(totalvolume),0) AS sum_totalvolume FROM avocado GROUP BY quarter ORDER BY quarter;
```

quarter	sum_totalvolume
1	3540984036
2	2703990502
3	2434244184
4	1817354594

Source: SQLite

Build Your Own Supplier Table

Step 15: The dataset also contains supplier information. If you are needing to know which supplier is providing avocados to certain cities, you might want to develop another table with the supplier information. Perform this task by using the following query statement and clicking "Run" (Exhibit 2-29):

CREATE TABLE supplier (supplierid TEXT PRIMARY KEY, name TEXT, country TEXT);

Exhibit 2-29

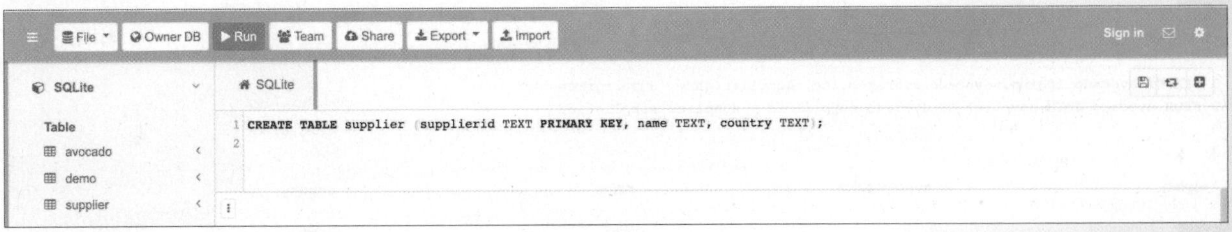

```
CREATE TABLE supplier (supplierid TEXT PRIMARY KEY, name TEXT, country TEXT);
```

Source: SQLite

Add Data to Your Table

Step 16: To add data to your data, you can insert supplier id, name, and country location. Perform this task by using the following query statement and clicking "Run" (Exhibit 2-30):

INSERT INTO supplier (supplierid, name, country) VALUES ("A", "Valex", "Spain");
INSERT INTO supplier (supplierid, name, country) VALUES ("B", "Cresco Produce", "Thailand");
INSERT INTO supplier (supplierid, name, country) VALUES ("C", "Shinesun Industry", "Viet Nam");

Exhibit 2-30

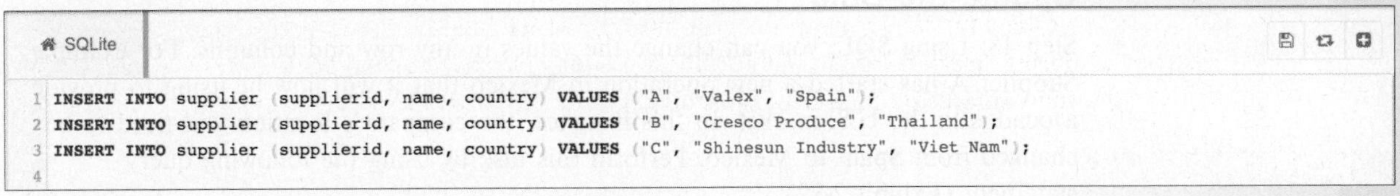

```
1  INSERT INTO supplier (supplierid, name, country) VALUES ("A", "Valex", "Spain");
2  INSERT INTO supplier (supplierid, name, country) VALUES ("B", "Cresco Produce", "Thailand");
3  INSERT INTO supplier (supplierid, name, country) VALUES ("C", "Shinesun Industry", "Viet Nam");
4
```

Source: SQLite

Join the Two Tables (MERGE)

Step 17: Currently, you have two tables. Table Avocado consists of observationid, region, year, month, quarter, type, averageprice, totalvolume, and supplierid, and table Supplier includes supplierid, name, and country. Note that supplierid is a common key between the Avocado table and the Supplier table. It is a primary key in the Supplier table, and it is a foreign key in the Avocado table. Thus, we can select attributes from both tables by joining the tables using the common key (supplierid). Perform this task by using the following query statement (Exhibit 2-31):

SELECT avocado.region, avocado.averageprice, supplier.name, supplier.country FROM avocado JOIN supplier ON avocado.supplierid = supplier.supplierid;

This table provides data in a cohesive form. We can now see that Valex from Spain supplied the product to the Miami/Ft. Lauderdale region where the average customer price was $1.58.

Exhibit 2-31

```
1  SELECT avocado.region, avocado.averageprice, supplier.name, supplier.country
2  FROM avocado JOIN supplier ON avocado.supplierid = supplier.supplierid;
3
4
```

⚆ SQLite

region	averageprice	name	country
Miami/Ft. Lauderdale	1.58	Valex	Spain
Jacksonville	1.65	Shinesun Industry	Viet Nam
Orlando	1.39	Shinesun Industry	Viet Nam
Miami/Ft. Lauderdale	1.49	Valex	Spain
New Orleans/Mobile	2.19	Shinesun Industry	Viet Nam
Miami/Ft. Lauderdale	1.58	Valex	Spain
Boise	1.67	Valex	Spain
Buffalo/Rochester	1.63	Valex	Spain
Boise	1.84	Valex	Spain

Source: SQLite

Update the Data

Step 18: Using SQL, you can change the values in any row and columns. For example, Supplier A has started a new operation in Mexico that it will now be using to provide avocados to the U.S. market. In this instance, the company's location will need to be changed from Spain to Mexico. Perform this task by using the following query statement (Exhibit 2-32):

UPDATE supplier SET country = "Mexico" WHERE name = "Valex";

Review your changes by using the following query statement:

Select* FROM supplier;

Exhibit 2-32

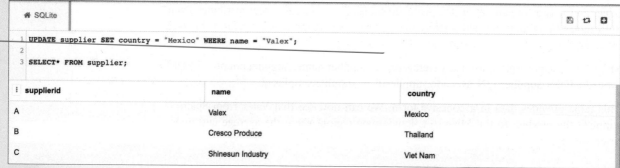

⚆ SQLite

```
1  UPDATE supplier SET country = "Mexico" WHERE name = "Valex";
2
3  SELECT* FROM supplier;
```

supplierid	name	country
A	Valex	Mexico
B	Cresco Produce	Thailand
C	Shinesun Industry	Viet Nam

Source: SQLite

Delete Values

Step 19: You might find that you no longer need to retain a row of data. Therefore, you must delete it to prevent it from being included in future analyses. To illustrate this, let's start with displaying observationid 5. Perform this task by using the following query statement (Exhibit 2-33):

Select * from avocado WHERE observationid = "5";

You now see observation 5 is visible on the screen.

Exhibit 2-33

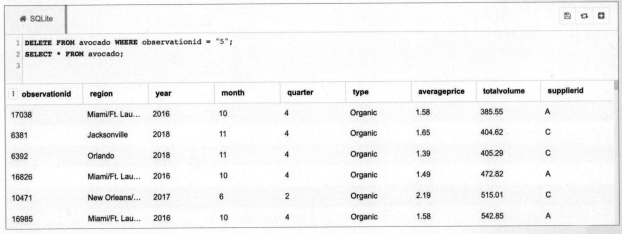

```
1  SELECT * FROM avocado WHERE observationid = "5";
```

observationid	region	year	month	quarter	type	averageprice	totalvolume	supplierid
5	Boston	2019	3	1	Conventional	1.32	835837.52	B

Source: SQLite

Step 20: We want to delete this observation from the data. Perform this task by using the following query statement (Exhibit 2-34):

Delete from avocado WHERE observationid = "5";

Select * from avocado;

As you see, observation 5 no longer exists in the table.

Exhibit 2-34

```
1  DELETE FROM avocado WHERE observationid = "5";
2  SELECT * FROM avocado;
3
```

observationid	region	year	month	quarter	type	averageprice	totalvolume	supplierid
17038	Miami/Ft. Lau...	2016	10	4	Organic	1.58	385.55	A
6381	Jacksonville	2018	11	4	Organic	1.65	404.62	C
6392	Orlando	2018	11	4	Organic	1.39	405.29	C
16826	Miami/Ft. Lau...	2016	10	4	Organic	1.49	472.82	A
10471	New Orleans/...	2017	6	2	Organic	2.19	515.01	C
16985	Miami/Ft. Lau...	2016	10	4	Organic	1.58	542.85	A

Source: SQLite

In this section, you have learned how to query data using SELECT in one table and across tables using JOIN, how to create a table using CREATE and INSERT, and how to modify data using UPDATE. Each query is helpful in identifying different pieces of information. By experiencing SQL, you have discovered how databases work. It is important to remember that the ideas you have learned here are just the beginning of your journey with SQL.

We encourage you to find more ways to work with SQL. Here are a few options for you to explore:

- *Google's BigQuery:* This Google database solution does not require a server and allows you to use SQL-like language to query and manipulate the data. BigQuery allows analysis in real time. It allows for 1 TB of data and 10 GB of data for free each month. To learn more, visit the Google BigQuery documentation at **https://cloud.google.com/bigquery**.

- *MYSQL on the server-side:* SQL can be used to manage data that is on the server side. You can set up a server-side database and access it using a client-based MySQL workbench used for data modeling, SQL development, and user administration. To learn more, review the MySQL documentation at **www.mysql.com/products/workbench**.

- *Amazon Aurora:* This relational database on Amazon Web Services is five times faster than MYSQL. Aurora is set up using Amazon Relational Database Service (RDS) on the virtual server. Data can be loaded into Aurora from MySQL and PostgreSQL. The data is backed up continuously on Amazon S3 servers to ensure reliability disaster recovery. To learn more, review the Aurora document at **https://aws.amazon.com/rds/aurora/getting-started**.

Summary of Learning Objectives and Key Terms

LEARNING OBJECTIVES

Objective 2.1 Define big data and summarize the journey from big data to smart data.

Objective 2.2 Discuss database management systems, relational databases, and SQL query language.

Objective 2.3 Investigate the key elements of enterprise data architecture.

Objective 2.4 Define the dimensions of data quality and describe the importance of performing marketing analytics.

Objective 2.5 Explain the importance of understanding and preparing data prior to engaging in analytics.

KEY TERMS

Aggregation	Database	Smart data
Big data	Feature	Streaming data
Categorical variables	Hadoop	Structured Query Language (SQL)
Cluster analysis	Normalization	Unit of analysis
Data lake	Outlier	Value
Data management	Overfitting	Variety
Data mart	Power calculation	Velocity
Data quality	Relational database	Veracity
Data warehouse	Sample size	Volume

Discussion and Review Questions

1. Define and describe the characteristics of big data.

2. Why is it important for marketers to have a basic understanding of the fundamentals surrounding data management?

3. What are some characteristics of data quality that need to be examined to avoid invalid analytics results?

4. How is the data prepared in ETL?

5. Explain several tasks that might be involved when preparing data for analysis.

6. What are some basic questions you can answer by querying data from a relational database using SQL?

Critical Thinking and Marketing Applications

1. Congratulations, you were just hired as a marketing analyst for a large company. The VP of Marketing has asked you to examine how the company might improve sales. What data might be helpful in your exploration? Where might you locate the data needed? What questions should you ask first?

2. Consider the avocado data within the Case Study. What additional data fields might be necessary to explore the following questions:

   a. What is the average income of customers in the cities that yield the largest sales?

   b. Do weather patterns impact the sale of avocados each week?

   c. Does social media chatter influence the purchase of weekly avocado sales?

References

1. Bernard Marr, "The Amazing Ways Coca-Cola Uses Artificial Intelligence and Big Data to Drive Success," *Forbes*, September 18, 2017, https://www.forbes.com/sites/bernardmarr/2017/09/18/the-amazing-ways-coca-cola-uses-artificial-intelligence-ai-and-big-data-to-drive-success (accessed June 15, 2019); and Bernard Marr, "How Coca-Cola Is Using AI to Stay at the Top of the Soft Drinks Market," *AI News*, May 7, 2019, https://www.artificialintelligence-news.com/2019/05/07/how-coca-cola-is-using-ai-to-stay-at-the-top-of-the-soft-drinks-market (accessed June 15, 2019).

2. Bernard Marr, "The Amazing Ways eBay Is Using Artificial Intelligence to Boost Business Success," *Forbes*, April 26, 2019, https://www.forbes.com/sites/bernardmarr/2019/04/26/the-amazing-ways-ebay-is-using-artificial-intelligence-to-boost-business-success (accessed June 15, 2019); and Sanjeev Katariya, "eBay's Platform Is Powered by AI and Fueled by Customer Input," eBay, March 13, 2019, https://www.ebayinc.com/stories/news/ebays-platform-is-powered-by-ai-and-fueled-by-customer-input (accessed June 15, 2019).

3. Bernard Marr, "The Amazing Ways How Mastercard Uses Artificial Intelligence to Stop Fraud and Reduce False Declines," *Forbes*, November 30, 2018, https://www.forbes.com/sites/bernardmarr/2018/11/30/the-amazing-ways-how-mastercard-uses-artificial-intelligence-to-stop-fraud-and-reduce-false-declines (accessed June 15, 2019); and Clinton Boulton, "3 Ways Mastercard Uses AI to Fight Fraud," *CIO*, December 3, 2018, https://www.cio.com/article/3322927/3-ways-mastercard-uses-ai-to-fight-fraud.html (accessed June 15, 2019).

4. Bob Violino, "The Secrets of Highly Successful Data Analytics Teams," *Insider Pro*, October 24, 2017, https://www.idginsiderpro.com/article/3234353/the-secrets-of-highly-successful-data-analytics-teams.html (accessed June 15, 2019); and Phil Weinzimer, "How CIO-CMO Partnerships Leverage Omni-Channel Marketing Strategy to Drive Business Value," *CIO*, February 21, 2017, https://www.cio.com/article/3171075/how-cio-cmo-partnerships-leverage-omni-channel-marketing-strategy-to-drive-business-value.html (accessed June 15, 2019).

5. Danny Bradbury, "How Big Data in Aviation Is Transforming the Industry," Cloudera, https://hortonworks.com/article/how-big-data-in-aviation-is-transforming-the-industry (accessed June 15, 2019); and Oliver Wyman, "The Data Science Revolution That's Transforming Aviation," *Forbes*, June 16, 2017, https://www.forbes.com/sites/oliverwyman/2017/06/16/the-data-science-revolution-transforming-aviation (accessed June 15, 2019).

6. J. Clement, "Combined Desktop and Mobile Visits to Target.com from May 2019 to February 2020," *Statista*, March 19, 2020, https://www.statista.com/statistics/714572/web-visits-to-targetcom (accessed June 15, 2019).

7. "Examples of Data Volumes," University of Delaware, https://www.eecis.udel.edu/~amer/Table-Kilo-Mega-Giga—YottaBytes.html (accessed June 15, 2019).

8. J.D. Byrum, "The Grocery List: Why 140 Million Americans Choose Walmart," Walmart, October 3, 2016, https://blog.walmart.com/business/20161003/the-grocery-list-why-140-million-americans-choose-walmart (accessed June 15, 2019); and Krishna Thakker, "Kroger and Walmart Outline Digital Transformations," *Grocery Dive*, January 14, 2019, https://www.grocerydive.com/news/kroger-and-walmart-outline-digital-transformations/545947 (accessed June 15, 2019).

9. Clint Boulton, "5 Data Analytics Success Stories: An Inside Look," *CIO*, February 25, 2020, https://www.cio.com/article/3221621/6-data-analytics-success-stories-an-inside-look.html (accessed June 15, 2019); Doug Henschen, "Merck Optimizes Manufacturing With Big Data Analytics," *InformationWeek*, April 2, 2014, https://www.informationweek.com/strategic-cio/executive-insights-and-innovation/merck-optimizes-manufacturing-with-big-data-analytics/d/d-id/1127901 (accessed

June 15, 2019); and Ken Murphy, "Merck Focuses on Data-Driven Platform Strategy," *SAPinsider*, https://sapinsider.wispubs.com/Assets/Case-Studies/2016/December/IP-Merck-Focuses-on-Data-Driven-Platform-Strategy (accessed June 15, 2019).

10. Penny Crossman, "TD Bank's Bold Bet on AI," *American Banker*, January 16, 2018, https://www.americanbanker.com/news/td-bank-investments-builds-on-ai-strategy (accessed June 15, 2019); Bernard Marr, "The Amazing Ways TD Bank, Canada's Second-Largest Bank, Uses Big Data, AI & Machine Learning," *Forbes*, December 18, 2018, https://www.forbes.com/sites/bernardmarr/2018/12/18/the-amazing-ways-td-bank-canadas-second-largest-bank-uses-big-data-ai-machine-learning (accessed June 15, 2019).

11. Joseph F. Hair, William C. Black, Barry J. Babin, and Rolph E. Anderson, *Multivariate Data Analysis*, 8th ed. (EMEA: Cengage Learning, 2019).

12. Hass Avocado Board, https://hassavocadoboard.com (accessed June 15, 2019).

PART
2

Ico Maker/Shutterstock

Exploring and Visualizing Data Patterns

3

Exploratory Data Analysis Using Cognitive Analytics

LEARNING OBJECTIVES

3.1 Assess the importance of exploratory data analysis.

3.2 Define cognitive analytics and knowledge discovery.

3.3 Investigate different use cases of cognitive analytics.

3.4 Examine the value of combining internal and external data sources for improved insight.

Image Source Trading Ltd/Shutterstock

3.1 The Importance of Exploratory Data Analysis

Data analysis through exploration is an essential process. Through this step, marketers become detectives exploring and identifying data patterns. **Exploratory data analysis** provides a summary of the main characteristics within the data. The purpose is to determine what is going on by exploring data trends, types, and values. The practice of understanding data is important before diving deep into the details of advanced analytics.

Many times, exploratory analysis results in graphical visualizations of data patterns. This format helps the analyst understand the existing data and patterns, and sheds light on potential issues. Exhibit 3-1 from the Bureau of Labor Statistics includes the percentage change in prices for household goods and services from March 2018–2019. Using visualization versus a data table enables us to quickly see the change in prices for the list of household goods. These visualizations in exploratory data analysis are helpful in obtaining an initial understanding of the data, but it is even more helpful when the data consists of hundreds or even thousands of variables.

Exhibit 3-1 Products that Represent the Largest Percentage Change in Prices for Household Goods and Services from March 2018–2019

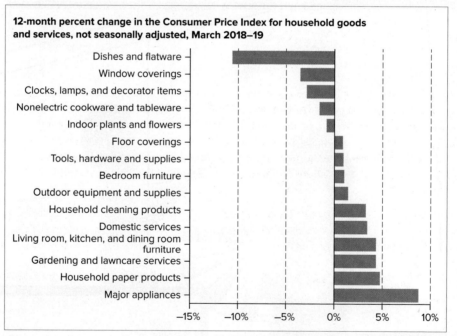

Source: "Consumer price changes for home furnishings and household goods and services," U.S. Bureau of Labor Statistics, April 15, 2019, https://www.bls.gov/opub/ted/2019/consumer-price-changes-for-home-furnishings-and-household-goods-and-services.htm.

Exploratory data analysis allows analysts to probe underlying relationships in data and investigate patterns. For example, you might visually examine customer purchasing patterns or trends. Exploratory data analysis in general, therefore, could also help determine if irregularities exist among other unique findings. You might discover that before a significant storm, or other weather event, customers are more likely to stock up on strawberry Pop-Tarts.[1] Also, are results like these a common or rare occurrence? Finally, if longitudinal data is available, you could determine if this is regular pre-storm behavior.

Exploratory data analysis can help detect:

- *Anomalies or outliers in the data.* Do undetected outliers exist?
- *Variables that are most important.* Are there certain variables that warrant more investigation than others?
- *Changes that occur within each variable.* What is the distribution of customer ages in the dataset?
- *Patterns or relationships between variables that warrant further exploration.* How does revenue per customer change over time?

Traditional exploration commonly relies upon predefined questions to uncover answers. What is the relationship between promotional emails and sales? Are there more customers shopping on Friday? In traditional exploration, the marketer would need to know what variables to explore by the questions they want to answer. However, this can be an overwhelming task. Consider a marketing analyst has data that includes 100 different variables, such as customer purchase history, demographic information, social media engagement data, and web search behavior. Where does the analyst begin? Is there a technology that could augment and amplify traditional exploration? Is it possible for technology to generate recommendations and answer questions from natural language? The answer is yes. Using advanced analytics, the analyst can uncover insights without designating predefined questions. Cognitive analytics and knowledge discovery applications can examine questions in natural language, generate recommendations, and pose new questions about the data.

3.2 Defining Cognitive Analytics and Knowledge Discovery

Cognitive analytics and **knowledge discovery applications** use advanced capabilities to draw conclusions and develop insights hidden in large volumes of data. These tools often involve advanced analytics approaches and capabilities. For example, cognitive analytics can recognize an image or understand the meaning of a text statement. **Machine learning, deep learning, natural language processing, computer vision,** or a combination of these applications facilitate the completion of advanced cognitive analytics tasks (see Exhibit 3-2).[2]

As cognitive applications interact more with data and humans, they continue learning and become smarter. This type of enhanced learning results in superior insights for the marketing analyst.

The Cognitive Analytics Technology that Won *Jeopardy*

At least one type of cognitive analytics technology has become famous. Does IBM Watson sound familiar?

IBM built a powerful computer. The computer could understand and process natural language. The technology combined high-speed data processing and machine learning to create a recommendation system. The process begins when questions are presented to Watson. This was demonstrated when IBM Watson competed on the quiz show, *Jeopardy*, with champions Ken Jennings and Brad Rutter. For example, the following clue was presented to the contestants: Nearly 10 million YouTubers saw Dave Carroll's clip call this "friendly skies" airline "breaks guitars." IBM Watson responded correctly with "What is United Airlines?" In three seconds, over 100 algorithms ran at the same time to analyze the question. The algorithms then ranked possible answers based on evidence that supports or rejects the answer. The final answer with the highest-ranking evidence was the one adopted by Watson. This was a turning point in the history of cognitive technologies.

Exhibit 3-2 Cognitive Technologies, Functionality, Adoption, and Examples

COGNITIVE ANALYTICS	FUNCTIONALITY	EXAMPLE OF USE
Machine learning	Describes the development of an algorithm that can improve its performance over time. Machine learning models improve by learning from the new data without being explicitly programmed. Most cognitive technologies are based on machine learning and its complex version, deep learning.	Provides personalized shopping experiences through automated product recommendations or website content based upon customer behaviors, interests, and purchases.
Deep learning	Involves many layers of abstract variables using neural network models. Neural networks have many levels of features or variables. Deep learning uses an algorithm to build models that classify or predict target variables. They are often used for speech recognition and image identification.	Simplifies the customer shopping experience by allowing customers to take photos of products and locate similar ones using a retailer's app or website.
Natural language processing	Facilitates extraction of text meaning in a readable, natural form. This technology supports virtual assistants, translators, and chatbots.	Expedites response times for customers needing basic assistance through website chatbots.
Computer vision	Extracts meaning from image pixels such as faces, scenes, and objects. Computer vision makes driverless cars possible. Many new mobile phones also allow users to unlock devices using the camera and facial recognition.	Enables retailers to reduce checkout times by facilitating automated checkout such as in the Amazon Go stores.

IBM Watson was successful on a game show, but are companies actually using cognitive analytics? In addition to IBM, numerous companies have further developed cognitive technology using AI. Many small and large companies across industries can now realize the value of using cognitive analytics and knowledge discovery tools. Deloitte conducted a survey of 1,100 business executives from U.S.-based companies.[3] Among early adopters, 63 percent reported AI initiatives are necessary to remain competitive or gain a lead over competitors. Business executives reported cognitive technologies are enhancing current products, optimizing current operations, and supporting better decision making.

Seth Wenig/AP Photo

3.3 Discovering Different Use Cases for Cognitive Analytics

Cognitive technology such as IBM Watson, IBM Cognos, Cogito, and Attivio are used by companies for two main reasons. First, cognitive analytics can be used to facilitate interactions between the customer and a company. Second, companies are using cognitive analytics to support internal operations and decision making.

Cognitive Analytics to Interface with the Customer

Cognitive analytics can be used in customer facing solutions that interact with the customer. Although there are many use cases, the companies introduced here use cognitive analytics to engage customers, convert shoppers to customers, provide customers with recommendations, and improve the overall customer experience:

- North Face uses cognitive analytics to help customers choose outerwear products that best fit their needs when shopping online or using the mobile app.[4] The customer initially answers a few questions in natural language such as "How do you plan to use the jacket?" and "What style do you like?" IBM Watson then displays filtered products to meet customer needs. During a pilot study, customers clicked on product recommendations 60 percent of the time. This unique shopping experience will likely lead to continued customer engagement and conversion. Moreover, as more customers use the platform, the system continues to learn and improve.

- Macy's uses cognitive analytics to improve in-store customer engagement. Their mobile tool named onCall was designed to answer shoppers' questions. A customer might have straightforward questions such as "Do you have Ralph Lauren shirts?" or "Where do I find the jewelry section?" While using the mobile application, the onCall AI system verbally responds to customer inquiries in the same manner as a sales associate.[5] If complex questions arise, the technology can elevate the customer inquiry to a real person. Using this technology, Macy's is able to meet customer needs more efficiently and understand customer priorities on a deeper level.

- At 1-800-Flowers.com, a computer automated gift concierge helps customers find a perfect gift. Using a natural language processing (NLP) application, customers can type "I am looking for a housewarming gift." The technology responds with questions for the customer to answer so the original inquiry can be clarified. What is the occasion? What is the relationship to the recipient? Gift recommendations are then selected from more than 7,000 products, including flowers, fruit, and chocolate.

- Cognitive analytics technology has also been used to drive player roster decisions for ESPN fantasy football.[6] IBM Watson and ESPN partnered to integrate player information from millions of news articles, blogs, videos, and podcasts each week. The trending media sentiments are used to make weekly score projections. More than 10 million fantasy football players then use the weekly score projections to make decisions about their teams. This added service improves ESPN fans' experiences and provides higher engagement.

Cognitive Analytics to Support Internal Operations and Decision Making

Cognitive analytics can be used to support internal business operations and enhance decision making, such as in these cases:

- Toyota Financial Services is a $100 billion organization that offers financing for Toyota car owners. Call center agents had limited access to customer information. This lack of information prevented agents from quickly answering customer inquiries.

In many instances, the customer was placed on hold while the agent reached out to other departments or a supervisor to acquire information. This created a disappointing customer experience. The addition of Watson cognitive analytics enabled call center representatives to obtain structured and unstructured data about customers (e.g., emails, social media content, reviews).[7] For example, using a dashboard, call agents were able to quickly access insights, answer customer inquiries, and provide exceptional customer experiences.

- Honda, one of the largest car manufacturers in the world, has $200 billion in annual revenue and over 20 million customers worldwide. Customer feedback is collected through a variety of channels such as dealers, suppliers, and global service centers. Data is collected in a variety of languages and formats. For example, Japan alone generates over 310,000 messages monthly. Cognitive analytics provides key insights to control quality and improve safety, including insights about preferred car enhancements and common car problems.[8] Using natural language processing, the time it takes to analyze customer's insights was reduced by 80 percent, enabling Honda to respond quickly to challenges faced by customers and to improve quality and productivity.

- Pebble Beach Resort in Monterey, California, operates 15 retail stores with almost 30,000 products. The resort struggled to maintain appropriate stock levels, resulting in low inventory and lost sales. Consumers were unable to purchase products they needed or wanted, and became dissatisfied with the retail experience. To solve this problem, the Resort now uses IBM Cognos to understand customer's purchasing patterns and optimize inventory levels.[9] Cognitive analytics not only helps reduce the cost of goods sold, it also can develop insights in minutes.

Companies also use cognitive analytics in exploratory data analysis. Exhibit 3-2 highlights cognitive technologies that companies have adopted.

PRACTITIONER CORNER
William Disch, Ph.D. | Educator, DataRobot

Used by permission of Dr. William Disch

Dr. William Disch is a DataRobot Educator and former Executive Director of Applied Analytics and Modeling, and Chief Statistician in marketing and business.

Working across multiple B2B and B2C verticals using machine learning and several multivariate regression and classification methodologies, he has driven client facing targeted marketing and proprietary analytics deliverables, as well as developed tools and products for high level and simple use of multi-source data (e.g., customer + consumer + third party). He has also consulted on the implementation of end-to-end ingest-to-deployment data and analytics workflow architecture, as well as analytics optimization and education, ran client analytics user optimization groups, and has authored several empirical articles, conference presentations, webinars, and blogs.

Bill's focus is on design, execution, and implementation of optimal analytics, with the goal of maximizing ROI and other outcomes. He is a proponent of both supervised and unsupervised learning, leveraging statistically independent segmentation to further optimize analytics. He earned his Ph.D. in experimental psychology and quantitative analytics from the University of Rhode Island, with a specialty in mixed-methods (quantitative, qualitative, mixed). Bill has been a college professor of research methods and statistics and has been working in the marketing and business space for the last 15+ years.

Q **What role do exploratory analytics play in advanced analytics?**

A Exploratory analytics are critical and should be a precursor and standard practice for all analytics. Exploratory analytics includes a full assessment of the datasets first, by a thorough assessment of population and audit reports (extended data dictionaries that include counts and percentages for every variable and cell), as well as full descriptive statistics. Once missing data and outliers are dealt with (outliers should be addressed before missing data). Descriptive statistics should include central tendency (mean, median, mode), variability/dispersion (standard deviation), and distribution (skewness, kurtosis). By neglecting full descriptive analytics, analysts and modelers can easily miss violation of assumptions that are required for many analyses. In addition, if unsupervised learning (e.g., Factor Analysis, Principle Component Analysis (PCA), two-step cluster, and other data reduction techniques) are used on non-optimized data, results will be less than optimal. Finally, multivariate inferential and predictive modeling and analytics should be performed on data that have been through a thorough exploratory/descriptive process.

PRACTITIONER CORNER

Jim Sterne | Co-founder and Board Chair Emeritus Digital Analytics Association, Creator Marketing Analytics Summit, author *Artificial Intelligence for Marketing: Practical Applications*

Jim Sterne

Jim Sterne focused his 40 years in sales and marketing on creating and strengthening customer relationships through digital communications. He sold business computers to companies that had never owned one in the 1980s, consulted and keynoted about online marketing in the 1990s, and founded a conference and a professional association around digital analytics in the 2000s. Following his humorous *Devil's Data Dictionary,* Sterne published his twelfth book, *Artificial Intelligence for Marketing: Practical Applications.* Sterne founded the Marketing Analytics Summit (formerly the eMetrics Summit) in 2002, which was the birthplace of the Digital Analytics Association. He served on the DAA Board of Directors for 15 years and is now Director Emeritus.

Q **What is an example of a cognitive knowledge discovery tool?**

A IBM Watson has a knowledge discovery capability that allows you to upload a large amount of data to discover patterns quickly and efficiently. It will tell you some interesting relationships between your Xs and your Y. This would be an exploratory type of application.

Q **Is there value in using an exploratory tool?**

A There is a value in exploring if there is a business purpose guiding this exploration.

For example, let's say I just want to research my customers. How much money and time do we want to spend on this? Well, maybe I just want to find some customer insights. What if the exploration yields that most customers' first names belong to the first half of the alphabet? Is that useful? No. Then we need to consider other questions and know when they are relevant to the business. This is where understanding your business and available data are critical.

Continued to next page

3.4 Combining Internal and External Data Sources for Improved Insights

Companies collect various types of data from diverse sources. Both internal and external data are used to drive unique insights. Recall from Chapter 1 that **internal sources of data** typically consist of customer sales and service data. In contrast, **external sources of data** are generally related to the economy, supply chain partners, competitors, weather, and customer-generated social media feedback. Many benefits are available from both internal and external data, but the value is greater when combined.

Continued from previous page

PRACTITIONER CORNER
William Disch, Ph.D. | Educator, DataRobot

Q **How important is it to add external and public data sources when addressing your business problems and questions?**

A The underutilization of available data is one of the easiest problems to address. House files alone (e.g., customers, patients, products) are generally incomplete, in that they lack real-world context. Consequently, even when modeling and analytics produce reliable and valid results, the generalizability is limited. Leveraging additional data sources allows for increases in generalizability because the information (signal) includes real-world context (e.g., behaviors, interests, demographic, economic, cultural, discretionary and disposable income) and the heterogeneous context of a prospect. There are three general levels of data in consumer (b2c) and business

(b2b) analytics: Internal (house file), External (third-party consumer and business appends such as Experian, Dun and Bradstreet, and others), and Public (e.g., U.S. Census, CDC, FDA, USGS). Segments, profiles, and personas are greatly enhanced when third-party data elements are included. Response rates, ROI, and model generalizability are nearly always optimized when using "multi-source" data elements. Finally, a powerful tool from multisource data elements is the creation of derived/composite variables. For example, instead of using ten separate "Outdoor Interest" variables in predicting propensity to buy outdoor products, creating a binary, continuous, or grouping variable from the ten variables is economical and parsimonious.

Continued to page 74

An advantage of cognitive analytics is it can be applied to explore structured and unstructured types of data. Exhibit 3-3 describes an example of a company's data. The data consists of sales information and aggregated values, showing when the company is mentioned on Facebook, Twitter, and Instagram. In this case, the data is matched by date. Basic sales data can be helpful for variety of reasons, such as managing inventory. But customers often provide substantial feedback on social media sites—indicating their honest sentiments about a product or brand. Thus, if a company limits itself to examining only annual sales data, they could miss critical details to help improve understanding of the bigger picture.

An exploratory data analysis graph combining internal and external data, as shown in Exhibit 3-4, can provide many marketing insights and lead to competitive advantages. These deep insights have the potential to empower better business decisions. Consider how the information in Exhibit 3-4 can be used to drive marketing insights and improve ROI on social media campaigns.

Exhibit 3-3 Hypothetical Daily Retail Sales Combined with Social Media Sentiment Data

DATE	SALES ($)	POSITIVE COMMENTS	NEGATIVE COMMENTS
1/1/20	50,000,000	50,000	40,000
1/2/20	63,000,000	60,000	50,000
1/3/20	70,000,000	65,000	55,000
1/4/20	60,000,000	50,000	60,000
1/5/20	45,000,000	60,000	80,000
1/6/20	43,000,000	70,000	90,000
1/7/20	40,000,000	60,000	88,000
1/8/20	50,000,000	50,000	40,000
1/9/20	55,000,000	100,000	50,000
1/10/20	80,000,000	80,000	40,000
1/11/20	80,000,000	75,000	40,000
1/12/20	40,000,000	60,000	40,000
1/13/20	40,000,000	40,000	56,000
1/14/20	35,000,000	50,000	80,000
1/15/20	35,000,000	60,000	75,000
1/16/20	60,000,000	65,000	40,000
1/17/20	70,000,000	40,000	60,000
1/18/20	50,000,000	70,000	40,000
1/19/20	43,000,000	30,000	60,000
1/20/20	40,000,000	40,000	65,000
1/21/20	50,000,000	65,000	40,000
1/22/20	55,000,000	70,000	34,000
1/23/20	70,000,000	80,000	40,000
1/24/20	83,000,000	70,000	30,000
1/25/20	54,000,000	50,000	40,000
1/26/20	50,000,000	40,000	70,000
1/27/20	40,000,000	45,000	60,000
1/28/20	35,000,000	43,000	55,000
1/29/20	40,000,000	50,000	40,000
1/30/20	50,000,000	48,000	50,000
1/31/20	40,000,000	40,000	35,000

Companies such as AMC Networks have discovered that combining internal and external data provides a more holistic view of customer behavior. Access to better data has been integral to maintaining pace with changing viewing habits in recent years. AMC integrates internal and external data from various sources (e.g., Nielson, iTunes, Amazon, Netflix, Hulu) in their search for new ways to market to viewers. Cognitive analytics predict viewing habits by exploring ratings, examining viewing numbers, and reviewing sales data.[10] AMC can then develop segmentation strategies to target viewers and promote each show. Results also help advertisers develop campaigns that reach the appropriate audience.

Exhibit 3-4 Hypothetical Daily Sales Combined with Social Media Sentiment Data Graph

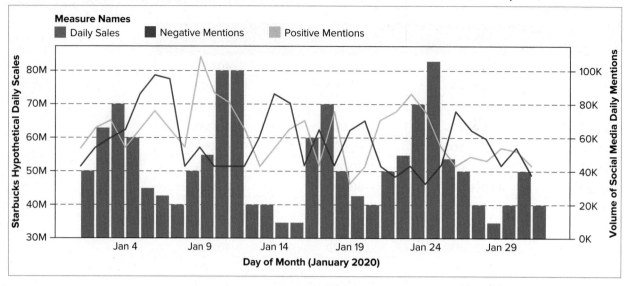

Continued from page 72

PRACTITIONER CORNER

Jim Sterne | Co-founder and Board Chair Emeritus Digital Analytics Association, Creator Marketing Analytics Summit, author *Artificial Intelligence for Marketing: Practical Applications*

Q **How can students prepare themselves for this era of AI and cognitive analytics?**

A The most important thing is for students to understand when to use a cognitive exploratory tool. I think about carpentry. If you have a hammer and a saw, that doesn't make you a carpenter. If you are a talented carpenter, then a hammer and a saw is all you need. At some point, however, I want to use another tool to smooth the wood. I want to use a certain sander because I have one problem. I just want to use a little bit of sandpaper on the side. I might need various tools for different sides of the wood so that the paint goes on well. Similarly, students or marketing analysts would need to be knowledgeable about their business problems so they understood when and how to use different tools for a different purpose. Some tools are more for exploratory analysis, some more for predictive and prescriptive analytics.

As evident through the examples, companies can integrate internal and external data to understand behaviors and attitudes on a deeper level. What other internal and external data might be helpful to combine for more insights?

A Closer Look at Online Customer Experience

Understanding the Business Problem

Red Ventures is a privately held Internet marketing company based in Charlotte, North Carolina. The company employs over 3,600 people and focuses on providing online experiences that bring together brands and customers. Red Ventures uses marketing technology and analytics to help clients in telecommunications and financial services industries attract new customers in the United States, Canada, and Puerto Rico.

On average, Americans have three to four credit cards each. Credit card debt in the United States has continued to increase over the last six years.[11] Although credit card debt is increasing, individuals are not seeking to increase the number of their credit cards. Consistent with this trend, Red Ventures has discovered that revenue from issuing credit cards has been declining. The general manager would like to better understand what is occurring. The manager is interested in revenue associated with each credit card and the conversions associated with each of the applications.

You have been asked to determine what drives conversion and revenue. Before starting, you need to understand your customer and their online behavior. This will enable the Sales, Customer Service, Marketing, and IT divisions to optimize website experiences and increase company revenues.

> Your marketing director sent an email asking you to analyze the online data from financial services:
>
> I am sending you 52,446 records from February to June 2018. The data consists of online activities for our financial services clients. The data represents credit cards that users have applied for and the conversion. It also includes the revenue associated with each application that is aggregated by customer.
>
> Please help me understand the origin of our customers. What is leading them to the site? What drives customer revenue? What drives conversion? Marketing, Sales, and IT need this information to personalize the online experience for each customer.
>
> Please review the attached data and provide suggestions on how we should build our marketing campaign.

Understanding the Dataset

The next step in the process is to understand what data is available for analysis. The Red Ventures data can be downloaded from the student resources page. The Red Ventures dataset was obtained from a client in the financial services industry and was collected from February to June 2018. The company owns and manages the complete digital marketing journey for this client. Red Ventures facilitates consumer needs throughout the buying cycle. This occurs by collecting and applying data from when the consumer becomes aware of the offer through the purchase stage of the process. How does this work? Suppose a potential customer is in the market for a new credit card. They submit a Google search for "credit card" to determine their options. A paid advertisement appears and the potential customer clicks it. They are directed to a website where they visit a few pages. Ultimately, they decide to apply for a credit card from the merchant provider. Red Ventures collects data at every touchpoint in this funnel. This data includes information from the performance of paid search advertisements to how the user interacts on the web page. Additionally, Red Ventures technology enables it to deliver unique website experiences to every visitor that comes to its web pages, including personalized options. For example, Red Ventures can suggest an offering based on a user's click stream pattern. This individual level of personalization helps meet the specific customer needs and facilitates the sale.

The data contains information such as how the customer came to the website, engagement with the website, and conversion information, and it can be used to optimize the end-user experience that drives revenue. To get started, review the data in Exhibit 3-5.

Applying the Concepts

In this case study, you will conduct exploratory data analysis with a cognitive analytics tool. IBM Cognos Analytics uses cognitive technology to execute data exploration and other analytics functions. During the analysis, patterns and key variables will be identified.

Exhibit 3-5 Information Available at the Time of Prediction

VARIABLE NAME (TYPE)	DESCRIPTION
date (date)	Date on which the online site browsing occurred.
first_page_topic (string)	First page topic visited.
last_page_topic (string)	Last page topic visited.
device_type (string)	Device type used to browse the online site.
browser_name (string)	Browser name used to the online site.
manufacturer (string)	Manufacturer of the device used to browse the online site.
country (string)	Country of user browsing the online site.
region (string)	State of user browsing the online site.
traffic_source (string)	The source of traffic leading the user to the online site (i.e., paid, organic, direct, or internal).
traffic_channel (string)	The channel the user came from (e.g., search, email, referral, etc.).
traffic_description (string)	The website the user came from (e.g., Google, Bing, Twitter, Facebook, etc.).
product_name (string)	Name of the product browsed (all names have been anonymized to products 1 to 85).
credit_needed_name (string)	Minimum credit level needed to apply for the credit card product on the online site (i.e., excellent credit, good credit, no credit check, or unknown).
merchant_name (string)	Merchant name of the products on the site (all names have been anonymized to Merchant 1 to Merchant 11).
sessions (numeric)	Number of sessions. A session is created when the user visits the site and expires when the user has no browsing activities for up to 30 minutes.
bounced_sessions (numeric)	User visited page on a site and left without interacting with it.
pages_viewed (numeric)	Number of pages viewed while browsing the site.
total_duration (numeric)	The entire time a user was on the site in milliseconds.
engagement_duration (numeric)	Amount of time the user was actively engaged on the site in milliseconds.
clicks (numeric)	Number of clicks on the site.
conversions (numeric)	Number of conversions that occurred. A conversion is defined as a web visitor completing a desired goal—for instance, making a purchase or filling out a credit card application.
revenue (numeric)	Amount of revenue generated based on the lead from the site.

It is critical to first review the dataset to understand its different fields. Open the Financial Services.csv file available with your book to examine the variable values. There are 52,446 records. Exhibit 3-6 shows a snapshot of the variables and records for 34 customer engagements.

Exhibit 3-6

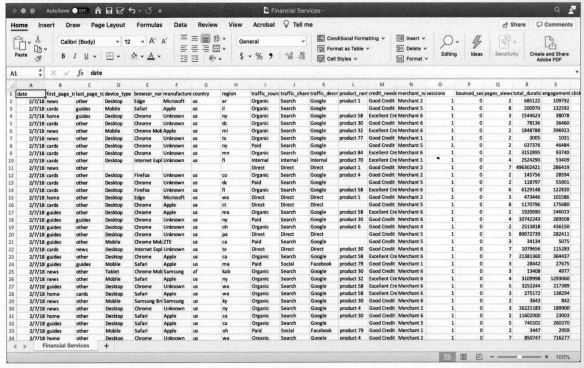

Microsoft Excel

To access IBM Cognos Analytics on the cloud, create an account in the Cognos Analytics system at https://myibm.ibm.com. You will receive an email informing you that your IBMid has been created. Once you log in, search for IBM Cognos Analytics and request a free trial. Once the setup is complete, you will see IBM Cognos Analytics as one of the software options available. Click "Launch" to open the Cognitive Analytics Cloud user interface, as shown in Exhibit 3-7.

Exhibit 3-7

IBM Cognos Analytics

Please note that IBM Cognos Analytics on the cloud is updated frequently, and there is a chance that, by the time you are using the system, some of the menu options will be slightly different. Despite any changes, however, you should still be able to follow along with the case study instructions.

Your screen will now appear similar to Exhibit 3-8. Start the process by uploading the data file into Cognos Analytics. You can either click "Browse" to locate the excel file "Financial Data.csv," or you can drag and drop the file into the drop zone indicated by the arrow in Exhibit 3-8.

Exhibit 3-8

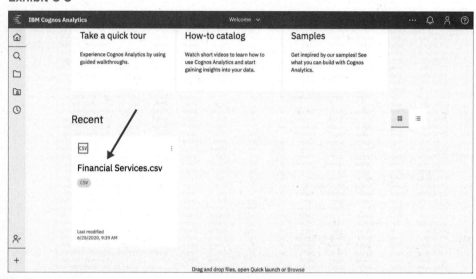

IBM Cognos Analytics

Cognos Analytics has now uploaded the Financial Services.csv file to your "Recent" folder (Exhibit 3-9). To expand the options, click on "⋮" next to the file name and click "Create exploration," as shown in Exhibit 3-9.

Exhibit 3-9

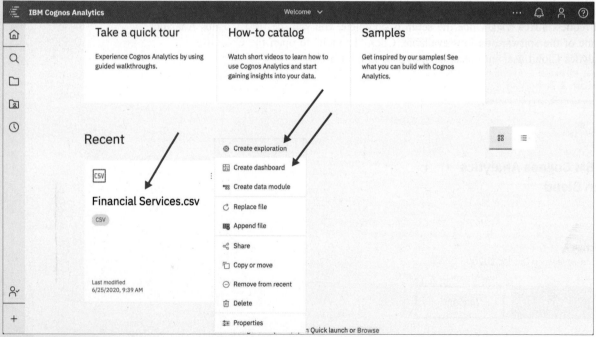

IBM Cognos Analytics

In the new exploration window, Cognos Analytics offers a variety of starting points based upon the data. Cognos Analytics will suggest entering column names from the dataset or even selecting one that is presented by Cognos. Using the [Skip - show me anything] option (Exhibit 3-10), Cognos will show interesting relationships in the data. These relationships are organized without guidance from the user. Click [Skip - show me anything] to see how this feature works.

Exhibit 3-10

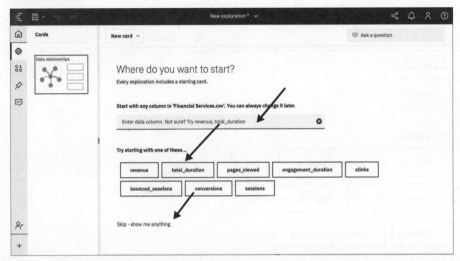

IBM Cognos Analytics

Once you click on [Skip - show me anything], the first diagram that opens is focused on key relationships in the data (Exhibit 3-11). This diagram shows "field of interest" in the center, and related fields based on a statistical evaluation. The concepts are represented as circles. The lines connect the field of interest (revenue) and the concepts (merchant name, product name, credit needed name, and so on) based on their statistical relationships, as shown in Exhibit 3-11. The thicker the line, the stronger the statistical relationship captured. For example, "product name," "merchant name," and "credit needed" have the strongest relationships with "revenue."

Exhibit 3-11

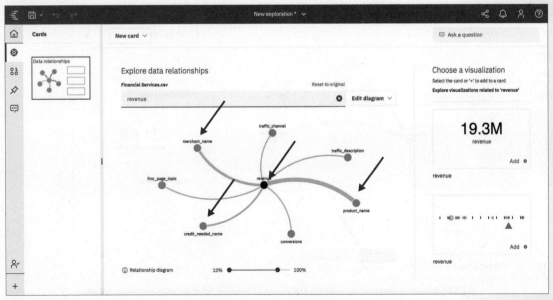

IBM Cognos Analytics

Click on the revenue search bar to examine other fields of interest such as "total_duration", "pages_viewed", and "engagement_duration", as shown (Exhibit 3-12). For this example, select engagement_duration .

Exhibit 3-12

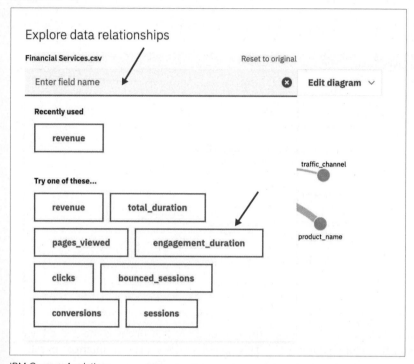

IBM Cognos Analytics

When another column is selected as a field of interest, the diagram is re-created (Exhibit 3-13). The strength of the relationship can also be selected. As in Exhibit 3-13, the slider can be used to see fields with only 35 percent or greater relationship strength with the variables of interest. Results indicate that the duration of engagement is mainly related to "total_duration" and "pages_viewed".

Exhibit 3-13

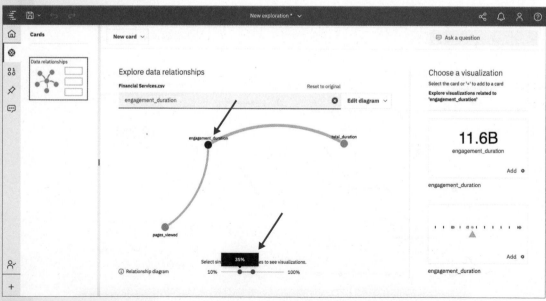

IBM Cognos Analytics

Reset the relationship diagram to show the field of interest revenue again. Now, press the control key (in Windows) or the command key (in MAC) to select revenue and first_page_topic, and credit_needed_name at the same time (Exhibit 3-14). As fields are selected, notice that to the right of the relationship diagram, new diagrams are created (Exhibit 3-14).

Click on the [Add ⊕] column visualization showing revenue by credit and first_page_topic on the right (Exhibit 3-14). This creates a new card with this visualization (Exhibit 3-15).

Exhibit 3-14

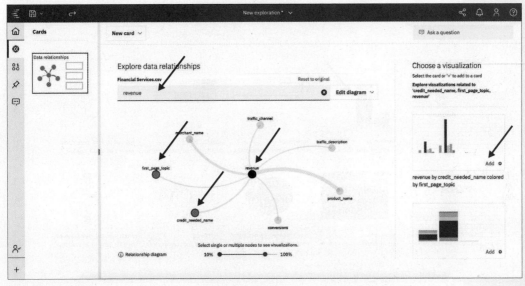

IBM Cognos Analytics

The visualization showing "revenue" by credit and "first_page_topic" in Exhibit 3-15 indicates that customers with good credit and who started browsing using the guides page generate the highest total revenue. The insights are also included in the Details panel to the right of the main diagram (Exhibit 3-15). This area contains information explaining data relationships in the chart. Notice in Exhibit 3-15 that there is also an unusually high value of revenue when customers have good credit as compared with other credit options.

Exhibit 3-15

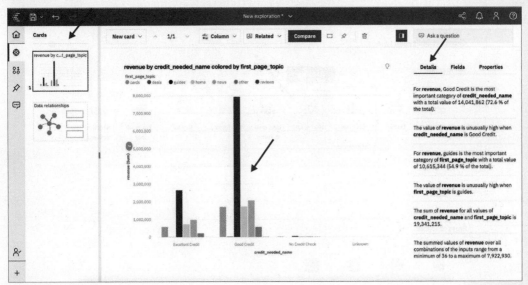

IBM Cognos Analytics

Additional relationships can now be visually explored. Using the Exploration toolbar on top of the visualization, click the down arrow next to [Column ˅] to access the visualization library.

The library will start with a recommended other visualization based on current relationships in the data (Exhibit 3-16).

Exhibit 3-16

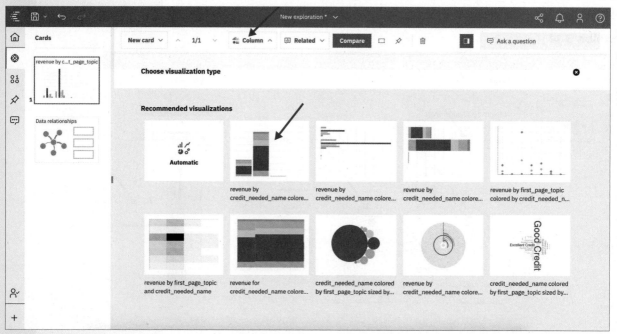

IBM Cognos Analytics

Scroll down through the recommended visualizations. In the Choose visualization type section under Comparison, locate and click on Heat map (Exhibit 3-17).

Exhibit 3-17

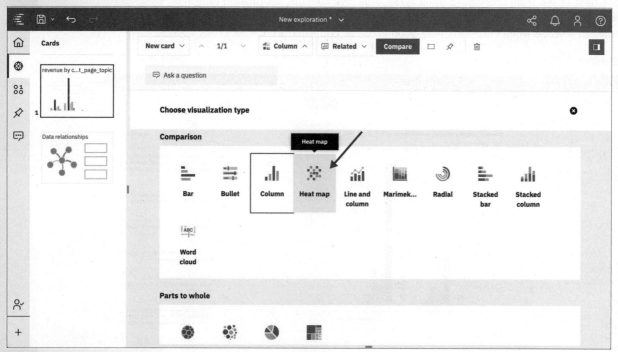

IBM Cognos Analytics

In Exhibit 3-18, the diagram shows that revenue is higher for customers with good credit and with excellent credit who start with the guide pages. Revenue is currently represented as total revenue, but the value can be changed to average. Click on "Fields."

Exhibit 3-18

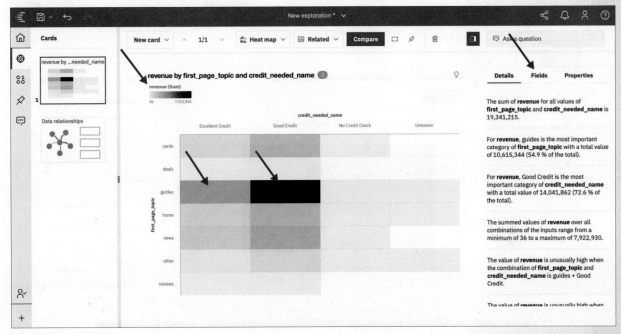

IBM Cognos Analytics

Under Fields, scroll down to locate Heat (Exhibit 3-19), click ". . ." next to revenue.

Exhibit 3-19

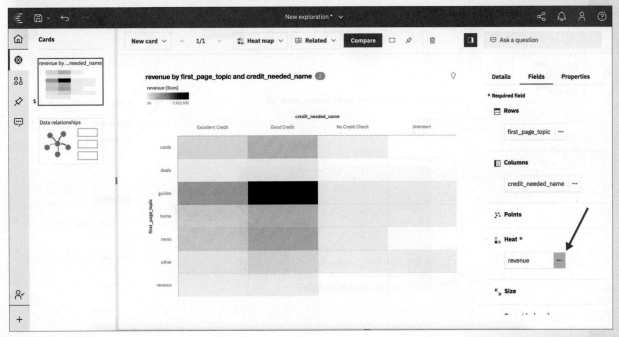

IBM Cognos Analytics

Select Summarize and click on Average. The Heat Map will update to show the average revenue value for different customer credit levels and start pages (Exhibit 3-20).

Exhibit 3-20

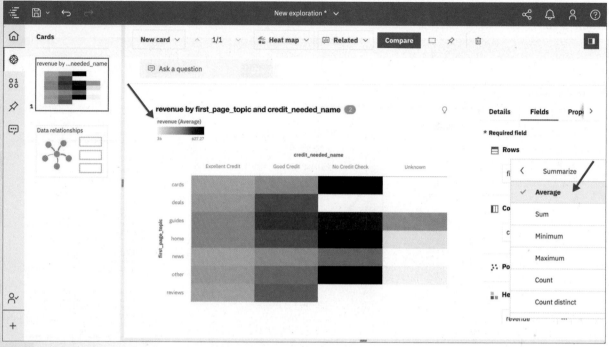

IBM Cognos Analytics

It appears that people with no credit check, and who also begin at the other pages, have the highest average revenue of $627.27 (Exhibit 3-21). How are the average values telling a different story than the sum of revenue?

Exhibit 3-21

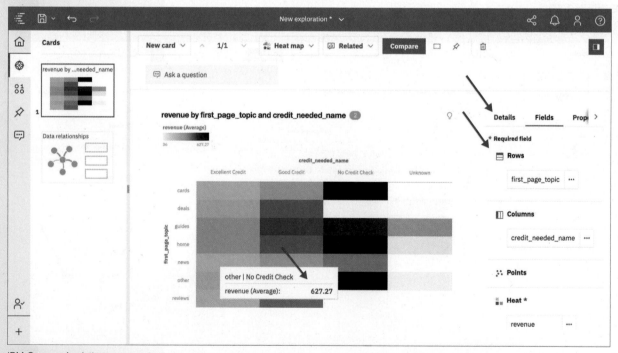

IBM Cognos Analytics

Looking at the Exploration toolbar, note that you can also search for related visualizations. Click on the down arrow to open the "Related" visualization (Exhibit 3-22).

Exhibit 3-22

IBM Cognos Analytics

The revenue by merchant_name card is displayed under the Related visualizations section. Click ⊕ to add to the Cards section (Exhibit 3-23). Don't forget to verify that your values are averaged. If you need to make changes to summarized values, you can repeat the steps similar to previous steps.

Exhibit 3-23

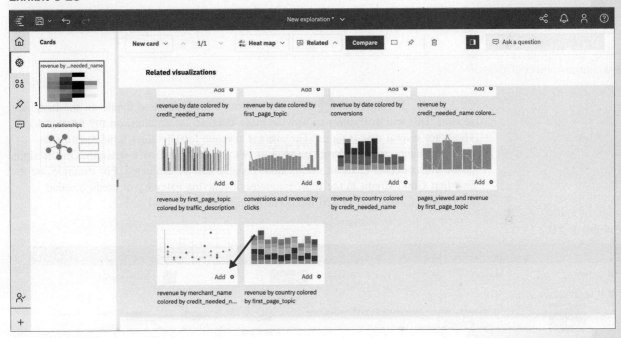

IBM Cognos Analytics

Under the Cards area, click on the revenue by merchant_name colored by credit_needed_name card to display it in the center screen (Exhibit 3-24). The highest average of 1,250 revenue is for Merchant 6 with no credit check.

Exhibit 3-24

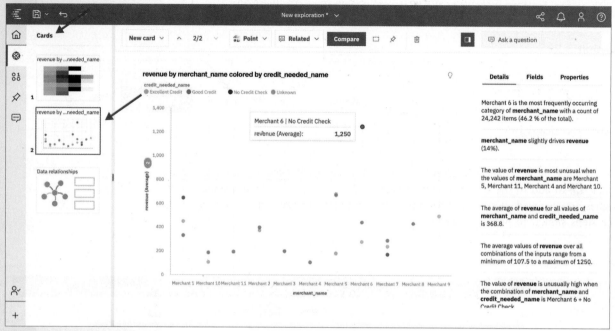

IBM Cognos Analytics

Click on the Insights icon [Q] at the top right of the figure and toggle on the Insights section. This will drill down to provide more detailed information on the relationships. There are several new insights. The average revenue for all values $368.8, and that merchant name, slightly drives revenue at (14 percent) predictive strength. On the right inside under details (Exhibit 3-25), more insights can be evaluated. For example, we find that Good Credit is the most frequently occurring category of credit_needed_name, with a count of 34,920 items (66.6 percent of the total).

Exhibit 3-25

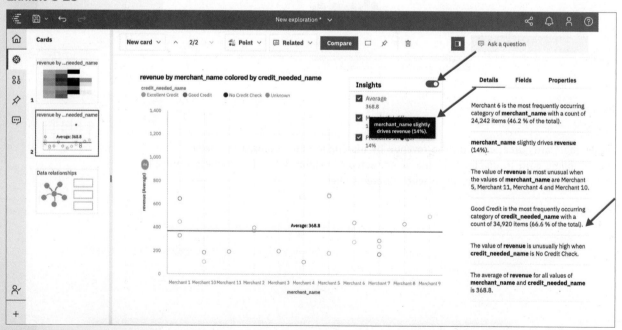

IBM Cognos Analytics

The next step is discovering additional patterns and relationships using natural language text. These results can be added to the original visualizations that were created. To start, click on the Assistant icon 😊 on the navigation panel (Exhibit 3-26). As shown in Exhibit 3-26, type "suggest questions" to show the questions suggested by IBM Cognos Analytics.

Hint: If you receive the following error message: "Sorry, I was not able to suggest questions for this data source. If it's an OLAP cube, this data source type isn't supported at this time. If it's a Framework Manager package, ensure that the package is enriched." click on the ⟳ icon next to Financial Services.csv in Exhibit 3-26. That should refresh the data source and let you review the suggested questions.

Now, click on "Which date has the top revenue?", as shown in Exhibit 3-26.

Exhibit 3-26

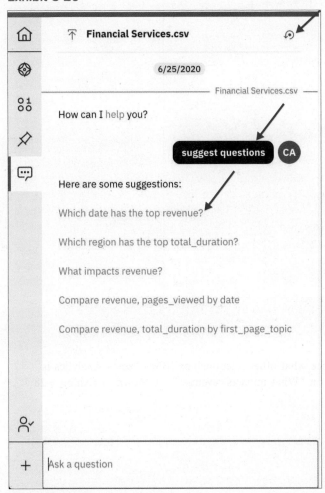

IBM Cognos Analytics

Exhibit 3-27 shows total revenue by date. Here, the user can ask many questions. What happened on 4/10/2018? Why is revenue much higher that day? What promotions were running on the website? What conversions are related to this revenue? You can view related visualizations by clicking on Show related visualizations . When selecting revenue by date, results appear to be incrementally decreasing (Exhibit 3-27). This was an insight that was originally pointed out by management.

Exhibit 3-27

IBM Cognos Analytics

Type "suggest questions" to see what other relationships IBM Cognos Analytics is proposing to examine. Click on "What impacts revenue?", as shown in Exhibit 3-28.

Exhibit 3-28

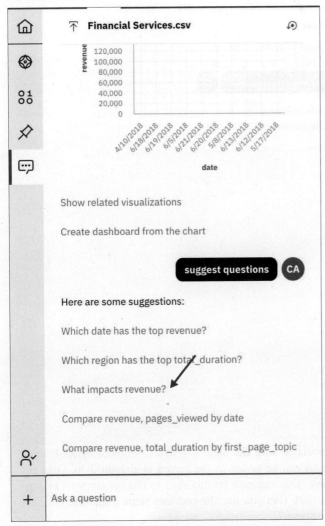

IBM Cognos Analytics

Cognos recognizes the meaning and display fields that have the greatest impact on this variable (Exhibit 3-29). Now, select device_type (Exhibit 3-29) to see how the device type is related to revenue.

Exhibit 3-29

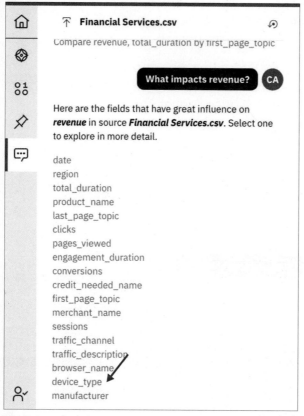

IBM Cognos Analytics

People using Desktops are associated with the highest revenue, followed by Mobile (Exhibit 3-30). This visualization can be added to the screen in Exhibit 3-30. Drag the visualization to the main screen. This can now be modified to change sums to average or change the type of visualization. Can you use the previous steps to determine the average revenue by customer browser?

Exhibit 3-30

IBM Cognos Analytics

Return to the Ask a question assistant and type "Create dashboard" (Exhibit 3-31).

Exhibit 3-31

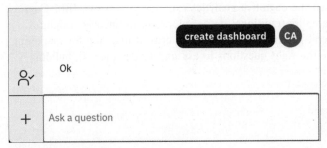

IBM Cognos Analytics

As in Exhibit 3-32, after a few seconds a dashboard will appear that shows interesting relationships in the dataset that have been organized into three topics: revenue, total duration, pages viewed. What can be determined by this dashboard? Could all of the manager's questions be answered? Summarize interesting insights and return to the data to determine other questions that can still be answered.

Exhibit 3-32

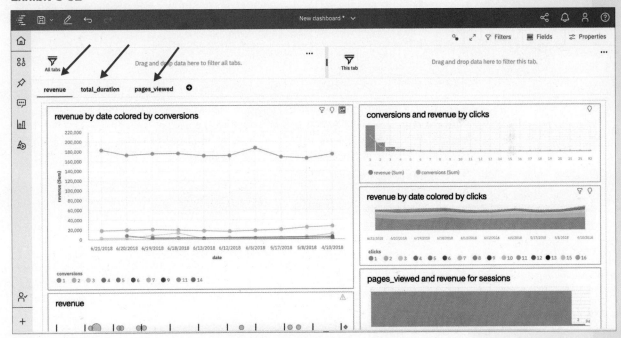

IBM Cognos Analytics

Insights Learned from Applying the Concepts

Exploratory analysis using cognitive analytics is a powerful tool to help a marketing analyst uncover and explore patterns in the data quickly.

The goal of the case was to explore online customer engagement in financial services. What drives customer revenue? What relates to engagement duration? We identified factors that are important to drive revenue, such as product name, merchant name, and credit needed. Results indicate that pages viewed are important to the duration of the session. Specific topics on the first page are associated with higher average revenue for customers across a variety of credit needs. Additional relationships can be explored in the dashboard created in Exhibit 3-32.

This case study has introduced the cognitive analytics exploratory process. IBM Cognos Analytics can augment and amplify traditional data exploration to uncover insightful patterns. Understanding general patterns in the data is a critical first step for marketing analysts. It helps them define the right questions to ask and guides them in building advanced analytics models.

Summary of Learning Objectives and Key Terms

LEARNING OBJECTIVES

Objective 3.1 Assess the importance of exploratory data analysis.

Objective 3.2 Define cognitive analytics and knowledge discovery.

Objective 3.3 Investigate different use cases of cognitive analytics.

Objective 3.4 Examine the value of combining internal and external data sources for improved insight.

KEY TERMS

Cognitive analytics

Computer vision

Deep learning

Exploratory data analysis

External sources of data

Internal sources data

Knowledge discovery applications

Machine learning

Natural language processing

Discussion and Review Questions

1. What is exploratory data analysis?

2. How does cognitive analytics augment traditional exploratory data analysis?

3. Why would a marketing analyst use cognitive analytics?

4. How might the integration of internal and external data provide value for a company?

Critical Thinking and Marketing Applications

1. Establish three different business scenarios where an exploratory data analysis using cognitive analytics might be helpful.

2. Using the different scenarios, determine internal and external data that might be useful in better understanding the relationship between the company and customers.

References

1. Meghan Overdeep, "You'll Never Guess What Surprising Product Walmart Stocks up on Before Big Storms," *Southern Living*, August 28, 2019, https://www.southernliving.com/news/walmart-strawberry-pop-tarts-hurricane.

2. Jeff Loucks, Tom Davenport, and David Schatsky, "State of AI in the Enterprise, 2nd Edition," Deloitte Insights, https://www2.deloitte.com/us/en/insights/focus/cognitive-technologies/state-of-ai-and-intelligent-automation-in-business-survey.html; "State of AI in the Enterprise, 2nd Edition," Deloitte Insights, https://www2.deloitte.com/content/dam/insights/us/articles/4780_State-of-AI-in-the-enterprise/DI_State-of-AI-in-the-enterprise-2nd-ed.pdf; and "The State of AI in the Enterprise," Irving Wladawsky-Berger blog, September 9, 2019, https://blog.irvingwb.com/blog/2019/09/the-state-of-ai-in-the-enterprise.html.

3. Loucks, Davenport, and Schatsky, "State of AI in the Enterprise, 2nd Edition."

4. Matt Marshall, "The North Face to Launch Insanely Smart Watson-Powered Mobile Shopping App Next Month," *Venture Beat*, March 4, 2016, https://venturebeat.com/2016/03/04/the-north-face-to-launch-insanely-smart-watson-powered-shopping-app-next-month; "The North Face, IBM,

and Fluid Launch New Interactive Shopping Experience Using Artificial Intelligence (AI)," IBM Press Release, December 14, 2015, https://www-03.ibm.com/press/us/en/pressrelease/48479.wss; and "The North Face & Watson: Bringing the In-Store Experience Online," *Olapic*, January 20, 2016, http://www.olapic.com/resources/the_north_face_ibm_artificial_intelligence.

5. "Increasing Customer Engagement," IBM, https://www.ibm.com/watson/advantage-reports/cognitive-business-lessons/customer-engagement.html.

6. Thor Olavsrud, "IBM Watson Brings Cognitive Computing to Fantasy Football," *CIO*, August 13, 2015, https://www.cio.com/article/2970347/ibm-watson-bring-cognitive-computing-to-fantasy-football.html.

7. "Case Studies: Toyota Financial Services," IBM, https://www.ibm.com/analytics/us/en/watson-explorer/whitepaper/case; and Michael Belfiore, "How Toyota Financial Services Uses Cognitive Solutions to Provide Personalized Service to Millions of Customers," IBM, September 15, 2016, https://www.ibm.com/blogs/watson/2016/09/toyota-financial-services-uses-cognitive-solutions-provide-personalized-service-millions-customers.

8. Amit Kumar, "How Honda Is Using Cognitive Search to Drive Real Changes in Quality Assurance," IBM Big Data & Analytics Hub, January 29, 2018, https://www.ibmbigdatahub.com/blog/how-honda-using-cognitive-search-drive-real-changes-quality-assurance.

9. Thor Olavsrud, "5 Ways IBM Cognos Analytics Is Transforming Business," *CIO*, May 1, 2019, https://www.cio.com/article/3391920/5-ways-ibm-cognos-analytics-is-transforming-business.html.

10. Samuel Greengard, "AMC Networks Scores Big with Advanced Analytics," *Baseline*, October 18, 2017, http://www.baselinemag.com/analytics-big-data/amc-networks-scores-with-advanced-data-analytics.html; and Olavsrud, "5 ways IBM Cognos Analytics is transforming business."

11. Matt Frankel and Kamran Rosen, "Credit Card Debt Statistics for 2019," The Ascent, February 5, 2020, https://www.fool.com/the-ascent/research/credit-card-debt-statistics; Jeff Herman, "Average credit card debt statistics," Creditcards.com, July 16, 2019, https://www.creditcards.com/credit-card-news/credit-card-debt-statistics-1276.php; Louis DeNicola, "How Many Credit Cards Does the Average American Have?" *Credit Karma*, August 7, 2019, https://www.creditkarma.com/credit-cards/i/how-many-credit-cards-does-the-average-american-have; and Jessica Dickler, "Consumer Debt Hits $4 Trillion," *CNBC*, February 21, 2019, https://www.cnbc.com/2019/02/21/consumer-debt-hits-4-trillion.html.

4 Data Visualization

LEARNING OBJECTIVES

4.1 Define data visualization and the objectives surrounding this technique.

4.2 Discuss the principles of design in data visualization.

4.3 Explain basic relationships in business data appropriate for visualization.

4.4 Assess key elements of data visualization that should be communicated.

NicoElNino/Shutterstock

4.1 What Is Data Visualization?

One of the key skills that distinguishes a good marketing analyst from a great one is the ability to communicate practical insights to a wide audience. In this chapter, you will learn what makes data visualization an effective way to quickly and clearly convey insights. For example, Exhibit 4-1 shows web traffic data for a large retailer. In your opinion, does the information in the table communicate clearly and directly the insights regarding the most common type of browser? Can you determine how the data is changing over time? Where are the inquiries coming from geographically?

In our opinion, the information is not clearly and directly communicated. To answer these questions, you need to visually examine each record and judge how it relates to the others. Furthermore, Exhibit 4-1 is only a small snapshot of over 20,000 existing rows of data that each consist of 21 columns of features (e.g., session start time, ZIP code, traffic source, and so on). As displayed in the exhibit, the data provides little value to understanding existing relationships among the data points.

Data is an asset only when it quickly and easily provides value. In the following pages, you will learn how to organize data visually using Tableau, one of the most popular visualization software tools in the business world today. The software helps you create a "data story" that adds value in a compelling way. Learning this tool will set you apart from your peers and facilitate your transition into becoming a highly sought-after marketing analyst.

Data visualization combines data analysis with computer graphics to efficiently identify trends, patterns, relationships, and outliers. Data visualization encodes quantitative values into graphical formats so data can be presented visually. This method of presentation improves the communication of information through comprehension, memory, and inference. Many companies use data visualizations throughout the company for better decision making. For instance, Coca-Cola sells soft drinks in Walmart. To gain insights, the companies work together to examine relevant prior data patterns to detect abnormal demand and to expose market trends. Let's say you visited Walmart to buy your favorite Coca-Cola drink. Upon arrival, you were disappointed when you found the shelf empty, and you left the store without buying your beverage. Due to empty shelves, the beverage industry loses billions of dollars in sales each year. To reduce this problem in Walmart stores, the company began sharing weekly product-level demand with Coca-Cola in Tableau format. The result: In a single 13-week period, the lost dollar sales of Coca-Cola products were reduced by $20 million by improving in-stock availability so customers could make purchases.

Exhibit 4-1 Does the Small Sample of Data Provide Clear Business Insights?

SESSION START TIME	BROWSER NAME	ZIP CODE	DEVICE TYPE	OPERATING SYSTEM NAME	TRAFFIC SOURCE
3/4/2018 15:37	Safari	36874	Mobile	iOS	Direct entry
2/22/2018 8:02	Firefox	36460	Desktop	Windows 10	Direct entry
2/27/2018 10:44	Chrome	36104	Desktop	Windows 7	Natural search
3/3/2018 16:49	Safari	36460	Mobile	iOS	Direct entry
2/27/2018 5:40	Chrome Mobile	36301	Tablet	Android	Direct entry
2/23/2018 16:10	Samsung Browser	35401	Mobile	Android	Direct entry
3/3/2018 15:37	Internet Explorer	35570	Desktop	Windows 7	Direct entry
2/21/2018 16:41	Chrome Mobile	35201	Mobile	Android	Paid search
2/18/2018 7:57	Samsung Browser	35201	Mobile	Android	Other
2/26/2018 12:38	Chrome Mobile	36535	Tablet	Android	Natural search

Exhibit 4-2 P&G Decision Cockpit and Meeting Space

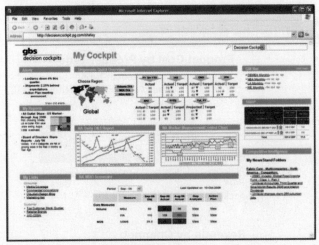 

Procter & Gamble

Many companies use data visualization as a strategic decision-making tool. P&G, for example, uses Decision Cockpits (see Exhibit 4-2), a data visualization tool that contains key indicators of worldwide market performance. The platform delivers information to over 50,000 employees' computers and in meeting spaces referred to as Business Spheres.[1] These digitally immersive data environments ensure the information is consistently distributed across the company. Using the Decision Cockpit displays has led to more efficient and accurate decision making, and it has also contributed to a data-driven cultural change. Employees now focus on how to address problems and seize challenges, rather than searching for and analyzing the data.

Although companies use different advanced analytics tools, data visualization enables different departments within companies to effectively share complex information. Data visualization through graphical depiction of quantitative values achieves two main objectives.

First, using charts and graphs to visualize data facilitates exploring and comparing results efficiently. Visualization software identifies and emphasizes the most important information. Let's say you are a marketing analyst for a snack food manufacturer. You want to develop a geographic display of retailer purchases over the last three years. Exhibit 4-3 shows how to emphasize points that could be used in a presentation to management. From a quick review, it is evident from the map, where darker colors represent higher sales, that customers in the United States produce the highest number of sales, gross profits were at their peak in 2017, chips and granola bars cost the most to produce, and the website produces the highest revenue.

Many visualization tools such as Tableau, Google Data Studio, Qlik, and Microsoft Power BI provide similar descriptive types of analysis, as well as more advanced functionality. Tableau, for example enables users to build in layers of additional information, and it includes filters so users can interact and make instant changes to the entire dashboard. These changes can be executed by simply clicking on, or hovering over, a particular area of interest to revise or update selected details. For example, if a user is interested only in examining the country purchasing the most chips, they could build in a filter for this display. The primary value of data

Exhibit 4-3 How to Efficiently Present Results

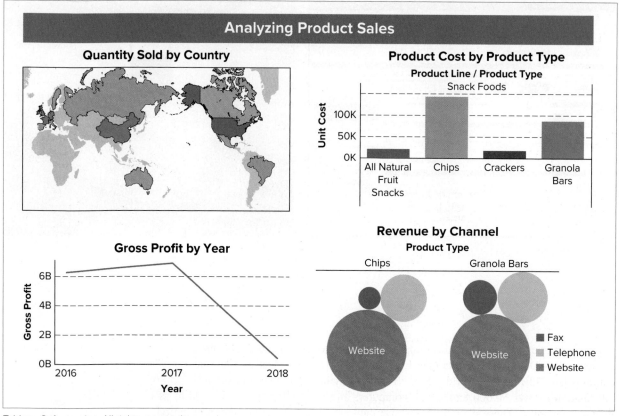

visualization is to efficiently obtain insights about what is occurring by highlighting opportunities and challenges. Are there any other apparent opportunities or challenges you notice when examining Exhibit 4-3?

Second, data visualization offers a simple and intuitive way to communicate complex topics to others. Data visualization engages the audience through simple and clear communication by highlighting trends and patterns. Through effective communication, data visualization gives meaning to ideas, articulates insights, and influences opinions. In addition, using data visualizations reduces audience fatigue by engaging them with vividly stimulating designs compared to numbers in tables. In sum, data visualization increases business understanding for the intended audience.

When designing data visualization outputs, it is important to apply some principles and consider basic elements of layout to ensure the reports are effective.

4.2 Principles and Elements of Design for Data Visualization

Psychology plays a powerful role in visual perception. Information presented visually affects the perception and cognition of the audience. Effective application of design principles can improve perception, attention, interpretation, comprehension, and memory of information. When designing visualizations for presentation, you must first answer questions about the structural components.

Principles of Design

How might audience brains respond to the information being shared? Understanding design principles guides the development of visualizations. If the principles are followed, it is more likely that the audience will be engaged and retain the information that is presented.

Principles of design are foundational rules to apply when creating visualizations. The six basic principles of design—balance, emphasis, proportion, rhythm, variety, and unity—are summarized next:

- **Balance:** Design elements should be balanced where the objects or shapes are distributed to correctly use the space. There are three different types of balance: symmetrical, asymmetrical, and radial (see Exhibit 4-4). *Symmetrical balance* occurs when each section of the visual is identical to the other sections. In *asymmetrical balance*, sections are different but maintain similar weights. *Radial balance* exists when an object is used as an anchor and other objects are equally distributed around the center point. Consider developing a visualization that contains several different charts. Each chart does not have to be an identical replica in terms of shape or size, but it is important that the output maintains the appearance of stability.

- **Emphasis:** This refers to placing emphasis on important insights to attract the viewer's attention. Our eyes focus quickly on elements such as pattern changes and dominant colors. As a result, insights can also be emphasized to attract attention by using different colors, shapes, sizes, and contrast.

- **Proportion:** This refers to the size of each object in the visualization. Proportion can be used to direct attention to certain insights, but it can also reflect the numerical value. It was found that large numbers on a visualization dashboard quickly attract viewer attention. Likewise, objects should be proportional to their level of importance or values. When using a pie chart, it is critical to verify that each part of the pie reflects the right proportion of the value. The visualization would not be accurate if the portion representing 30 percent of the whole appears larger than the area representing 50 percent.

- **Rhythm:** This is an important factor to ensure a perception of seamless, visually appealing transition between design elements. Complimentary, yet different shapes, colors, and proportions can be used to maintain an organized visual structure that facilitates eye movement.

- **Variety:** This is an important element in data visualization for two reasons. Variety in the type of visualizations used (e.g., bar graph, line chart, map, etc.) promotes engagement in the presentation, and it helps viewers process the information into long-term memory. Although designs should be complimentary, constant repetition should be avoided.

Exhibit 4-4 Three Types of Balance

Symmetrical Dashboard	Asymmetrical Dashboard	Radial Dashboard

  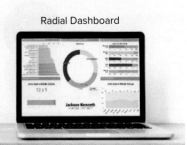

Source: Melissa Anderson, "What Are the 9 Principles of Design?" Dashboards, https://www.idashboards.com/blog/2017/07/26/data-visualization-and-the-9-fundamental-design-principles (accessed July 1, 2019).

- **Unity:** This is a result of the proper application of other design elements. Unity is achieved when there is a harmonious appearance and the design elements appear to belong together. It is a good idea to review your visualization dashboard design and ask yourself "does everything belong together?". If something doesn't contribute to the general story you have, consider removing it.

The Basic Elements of Design

What are some basic elements of design? **Design elements** are visual attributes describing various elements of a display. These building blocks of design can be represented by seven elements: color, form, line, shape, space, texture, and typography. Prior to determining which elements to use, thorough understanding of the data and the purpose of the visualization are imperative. Recall from Chapter 1 that there are different types of data. Some design elements represent only discrete data types, while others can be used for both continuous and discrete data types. The basic elements of design are:

- *Color* can impact human behavior and emotions. Applying color to visualizations is an important part of the process. Color can stimulate feelings or capture the attention of your audience. Product categories might be expressed using specific colors. A change in intensity of product sales could also benefit from the use of color. Do not forget, however, to remain consistent throughout the visualization dashboard.

    There are three main characteristics of color: hue, saturation, and value (see Exhibit 4-5). **Hue** is the name of the color, such as red, blue, or green. In contrast, **saturation** is a measure of the intensity or dullness of the color. Colors are highly saturated when they appear pure, whereas desaturated colors look dull. Finally, **value** is the lightness or darkness of the color as it transitions from white to black. Each of these characteristics can be used to emphasize certain products or differentiate between values.

Some situations involve consideration of specific colors. For example, red can be used to signal an action item or to identify a negative return on a marketing investment. But you would not use red to show positive sales growth. There are other instances,

Exhibit 4-5 Characteristics of Color

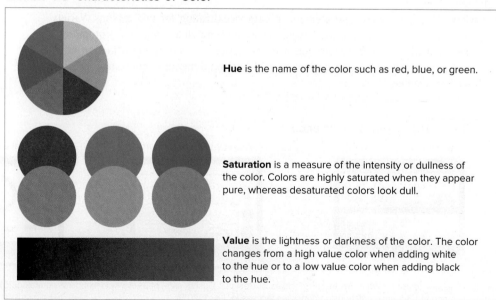

Hue is the name of the color such as red, blue, or green.

Saturation is a measure of the intensity or dullness of the color. Colors are highly saturated when they appear pure, whereas desaturated colors look dull.

Value is the lightness or darkness of the color. The color changes from a high value color when adding white to the hue or to a low value color when adding black to the hue.

Exhibit 4-6 Examples of Color Perceptions

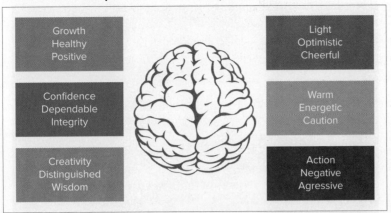

Growth Healthy Positive	Light Optimistic Cheerful
Confidence Dependable Integrity	Warm Energetic Caution
Creativity Distinguished Wisdom	Action Negative Agressive

however, when visualizations require many colors to define multiple values. Exhibit 4-6 shows the impact different colors can have on the perception of the viewer.

- *Form* can be created by adding lines, shadows, length, width, and depth.
- *Line* represents the path of a moving point in space. Lines can be different widths, but they must be longer than the width. Two elements of lines should be kept in mind: line type and line width (see Exhibit 4-7).
- *Shape* can be geometric, organic, or abstract. The most commonly used shapes in data visualization are generally geometric. The most frequently used shapes are squares, circles, and triangles, but other shapes may be used for unique appeals. Designers can use shapes to organize information, differentiate between ideas, or guide visual transitions from one element to another.
- *Space* is the area used within, around, or between design elements. There are two types of space: positive and negative. Positive space includes the area of the design, and negative space is the empty space between the design elements. The harmony between the positive and negative space is what creates a natural balance and enables your viewer to know where to focus (see Exhibit 4-8).

Exhibit 4-7 Line Type and Line Width

Line Type	Line Width

Exhibit 4-8 Positive and Negative Space Balance

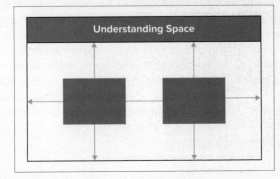

Understanding Space

Exhibit 4-9 Textured Map Using Satellite Image

- *Texture* is how the surface of the design suggests how a particular type of surface would feel to the viewer. Texture can be created by using the different characteristics of color (Exhibit 4-5) and shadows. Exhibit 4-9 shows how a satellite image can capture different topographies in Australia and New Zealand.
- *Typography* is characterized by the text itself, as well as the elements of the text. For example, font type, size, ligatures where letters are joined, and stylistic sets can be considered elements of typography (see Exhibit 4-10). Using different typographic styles can improve or hamper readability of the content.

Exhibit 4-10 Ligatures and Stylistic Sets

ff

Gross Profit vs. Gross Profit

PRACTITIONER CORNER
Nikola Cuculovski | Analytics Associate Director at 22squared

Nikola Cuculovski

Nikola Cuculovski is an Associate Analytics Director at 22squared, leading teams and clients to deliver on business goals. Nikola has a wealth of client experience ranging from Consumer Packaged Goods to Financial to Retail, across Brand and Direct Response marketing. He has worked with national brands like Publix, TIAA Bank, The Home Depot, and Cartoon Network, to name a few. As an agency analytics lead, he is at the forefront, interacting with clients and internal stakeholders to understand critical business challenges, identify strategic data-driven solutions, and implement and deploy data intelligence products at scale.

Continued

Q How do aesthetics and color play a role in data visualization?

A The field of semiotics explores how something is represented and how one reasons about it. While there is a set of foundational principles and widely used data visualizations allowing one to communicate their findings, the aesthetic component of the visual plays a vital role, because it can further intrigue or dismiss less-interested audiences based on the way the visual "feels." Aesthetics are often balanced by the clarity component of the data visual, because it is as important to communicate the right message to the audience as to fully engage with it.

As a result of the wide and easy understanding of its meaning, color plays as one of the most widely used and critical components in visual hierarchy of data visualizations. Through color, one is able to set the mood of the visual, emphasize certain points, and navigate the reader's eye throughout the narrative. Applying color in a visual is primarily dependent on the type of graph being used, and it can originate from a distinct color scheme where different types of categories can be easily identified, to a gradient approach where one color is applied based on the intensity of the data point. While applying color, considering culturally accepted intuitive colors, such as using the colors green and red for gain or loss in units, or providing visual encodings such as legends, will essentially improve the readability of the data visualization.

Q What is the result of poor data visualization designs?

A Communication is a two-way process where information is shared among at least two entities, hence introducing numerous opportunities and challenges for both the sender and receiver during the exchange to be deemed successful. From a sender's perspective, having almost limitless sources of information makes it very challenging to filter down and distill the most important and relevant information to be shared. Oftentimes, it is very easy and exciting to add just one more dimension or add just one more measure as a detail in the graph to tell the full story. However, this behavior will most likely lead to an overcomplicated piece that even the creator will have trouble explaining. Including a couple of additional dimensions or measures in the graph could lead to losing the context of the communication piece— which is usually why we started working on the visual in the first place. The simplest yet most overlooked rule of data visualization is to try to use a simple design over any fancy or complex-looking graph.

The more design elements there are, the more likely it will result in a poor data visualization that weakens the importance of the information being shared, thus making it easier to lose one's attention. Losing the opportunity to effectively receive the information can lead to inadequate decision making, hence making the data visual a critical piece during the information exchange.

Q What are the do's and don'ts of design?

A Although data visualizations are extremely powerful in simplifying complex messages to audiences, the wrong application of some of the data visualization components may often mislead and depict a misleading version of the truth. The Cleveland-McGill effectiveness scale is a visualization foundation that examines the graphical perception of how viewers decode information. The foundation provides a spectrum of visualization elements that are easier to understand, such as position, length, and slope, followed by attributes that require additional cognitive investment, such as color, depth, volume, and area representation. Although the Cleveland-McGill effectiveness scale recommends the type of visual elements to be used for certain data, every well-designed graph reflects additional considerations for implementation, such as balance, flow, readability, and proximity that are often directed by the medium (i.e., static or dynamic dashboard) of the data visual that is presented.

Because designing a data visual that opposes the mentioned principles would not be considered a best practice, data visuals that might be avoided could include pie charts, 3D charts, and to a lesser extent, charts that utilize two y-axes. This set of visuals are considered to be hard to read, and oftentimes there may be a simpler solution to improve the readability of the visual.

Continued to page 111

4.3 Fundamental Considerations When Developing Data Visualizations

Common Types of Charts and Graphs

When creating data visualizations to examine relationships, it is important to understand how the available data is measured and the various dimensions that are present. Remember, the data is considered quantitative if numeric and math calculations can be applied. Numerical values can be discrete or continuous. But categorical data represents values for groups and can only be summarized by calculating the proportion and count of occurrences across or within categories.

Businesses collect data representing both numerical and categorical types. Business types of data include measures and values that predominantly focus on customers, human resources, operations, supply chains, products, and services. There are several common types of relationships present in business data.[2] Zelany (2001) introduced five data relationships and Few (2012) later expanded these relationships to eight. For a more in-depth analysis on developing tables and graphs, please refer to these sources. The relationships describe different numerical connections or comparisons that exist within data and can be visually displayed in various ways.

Companies often use **time series** to understand how values evolve over time. Some examples of time series might be:

- The increase or decrease of annual social media engagement.
- The changing stock price trend throughout the week.
- The growth or decline of product sales over the past 5 years.

In these examples, line charts could be used to demonstrate the change or trend over time. Line charts represent comparisons of time series data. The line reflects variations of numerical data points over time. Exhibit 4-11 displays a line chart for changes to monthly average home prices from 2014 to 2015. The use of a specific time frame is guided by the available data and task at hand. The line chart shows there is a large variation in prices for homes with a water view (orange line) and homes with no water view (blue line).

Rankings are where the position is based upon importance, preference, or achievement. For example, Amazon uses algorithms to rank products in a category based upon sales and other values. The results reflect a product's popularity or ranking in the category. Examples of rankings could include:

- The company's product falls within the top 10 products of a market.
- The increasing price of products within a particular brand line.
- The location of retail stores by population.
- The position of salespeople based upon performance within the company.
- The number of automobiles by safety based on crash test results.

Although different methods might be appropriate, column charts (oriented vertically) could be used to show the ranked position and deviation in performance. A bar graph has two axes. One axis represents categories, while the other axis represents a numerical value. The bar length represents the value of a single statistic such as average, count, or percentage. Exhibit 4-12 shows a bar graph comparing exports by industry for the state of North Carolina. From the bar chart, we can see the state of North Carolina mainly exports chemicals followed by transportation equipment, machinery, and so forth.

Exhibit 4-11 Line Chart: Changes in Home Prices

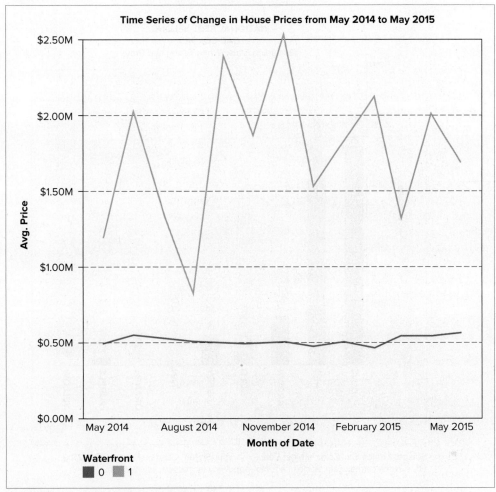

Time Series of Change in House Prices from May 2014 to May 2015

Exhibit 4-12 Bar Chart: Rankings

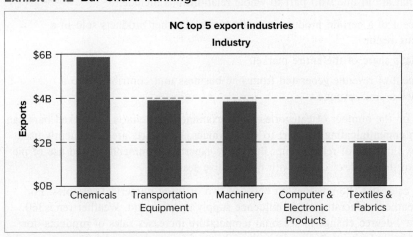

NC top 5 export industries

Part to whole relationships consist of categories measured as fractions or ratios. FedEx recently announced that Amazon made up less than 1.3 percent of the company's total revenue in 2018. Revenue from the business customer, Amazon, represents a proportion of the whole or total revenue during 2018. Carmax found that blue and red were the

Exhibit 4-13 Bar Chart: Part to Whole

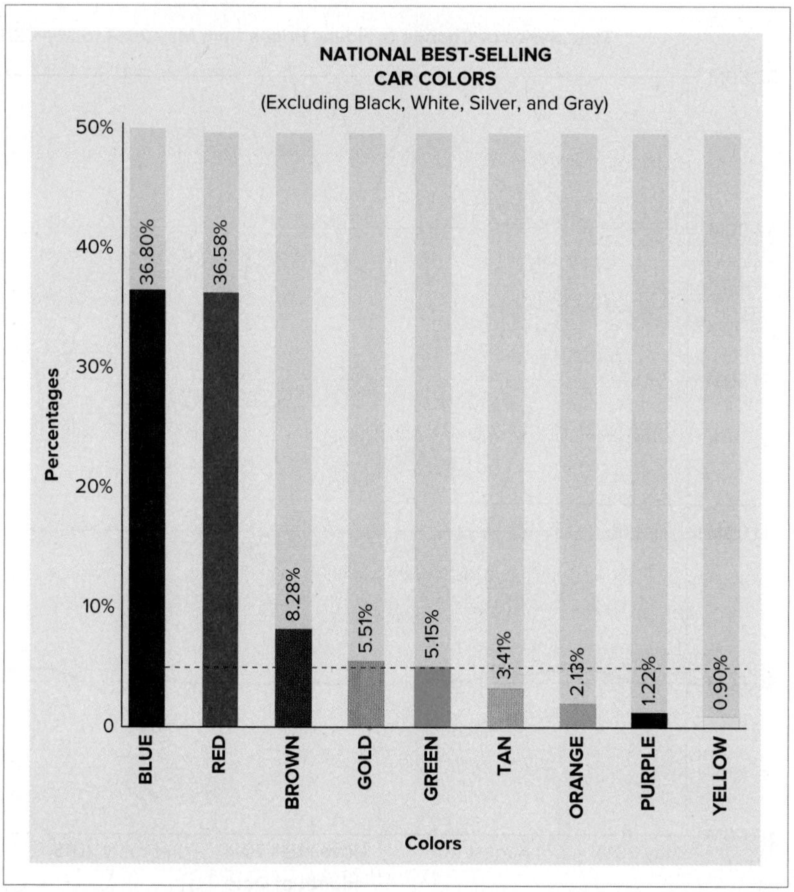

NATIONAL BEST-SELLING CAR COLORS
(Excluding Black, White, Silver, and Gray)

Source: "Which Car Color Is Most Popular in Your State?" Carmax, February 20, 2019, https://www.carmax.com/articles/car-color-popularity (accessed July 1, 2019).

top national best-selling car colors, as shown in Exhibit 4-13. Following the removal of black, white, silver, and gray, blue cars made up 36.80 percent of the other colors sold. Examples that are in line with part to whole relationships include:

- The percent of a certain product compared with all other products sold in a geographic region.
- A product's share of the entire market.
- The percent of revenue generated from one business unit contributing to a company's overall revenue.

Depending on the number of categories being examined, bar charts or stacked bars can be useful in communicating the part to whole values. Pie charts are a frequently used way to show this type of relationship. But many experts recommend limited use of pie charts due to their lack of clarity with quantitative scales.[3]

Correlation estimates the relationship between two or more numerical variables. For example, weather temperatures can influence supply and demand. Weathertrends360 found that a 1-degree change in seasonal temperature increases sales of products—for example, portable heater sales increased by 20 percent, strawberries by 8 percent, and jackets by 3 percent.[4] In this case, a scatter plot might be used to understand how temperature (x) impacts product sales (y). Other examples might include:

- The impact of consumer perceptions of brand quality on re-purchase intentions.
- How different sales prices would affect product purchases.

- The impact of population growth on the increase of the Gross Domestic Product (GDP) index.
- Whether consumer social media engagement on Facebook increases visits to the retailer's website.

Scatter plots display a collection of data points for two numerical variables. A single independent variable is plotted on the horizontal (X) axis and the dependent variable is plotted on the vertical (Y) axis. There are some cases, however, where two independent (or two dependent) variables exist and can also be displayed on a scatter plot. In this situation, the marketing analyst can decide how to plot variables along axes (X) and (Y). Sometimes, the scatterplot represents correlations between variables. There is a positive correlation when dots ascend from the lower left to the upper right area of the graph. A negative correlation is indicated by dots that descend from the upper left to the lower right area of the graph.

A scatter plot is an important visualization for advanced analytics tasks. It can enable a quick understanding of the relationship between two numerical variables in terms of information overlap and when considering clusters of observations. The scatter plot in Exhibit 4-14 shows a positive correlation between the average house price (in millions) and the square footage of living area in King County, Washington State.

Frequency distributions indicate how many observations fall within a certain interval, and the bars do not overlap or touch each other. The basic information in a frequency

Exhibit 4-14 Scatter Plot: Home Price by Square Feet

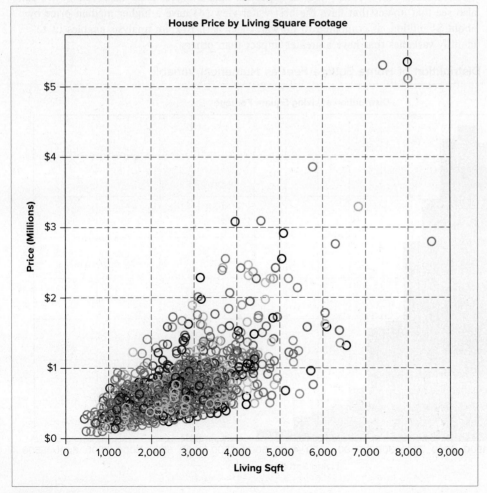

distribution enables us to easily understand how values are distributed among the objects we are examining. Examples of frequency distributions include:

- The distribution of product sales in different selling channels.
- The frequency of customers from various age or income groups.
- The variation of customer responses on a 5-point scale (strongly agree, somewhat agree, unsure, somewhat disagree, strongly disagree)—for example, how likely are customers to recommend a product to friends or family.

Histograms are a variation of frequency distributions that have bars that touch each other. The horizontal axis of a histogram displays quantitative data or data in specified ranges (e.g., 0 to 5, 5 to 10, 11 to 15) also known as bins and the vertical axis displays the corresponding frequency. The bars show the distribution of the quantitative (numerical) data related to a single variable. Because the data falls into a numerical sequence that does not overlap (i.e., from smaller numbers to larger numbers), the bars cannot be rearranged as in bar or column charts. In Exhibit 4-15, we see that most of the houses cluster between 1,800 and 2,000 square feet, and very few homes are over 6,000 square feet. The value 1,500 square feet represents the central or middle point for homes between 1,001 and 1,999 square feet.

Boxplots are another method to examine distributions and compare subgroups. Exhibit 4-16 shows boxplots that compare home prices by whether they have a better water view or do not have a water view (coded from 0 = no view to 4 = best water view). Homes with a better view, as expected, have a higher price distribution. We can also see that homes that have the best water view (4) have a higher median price by about $1 million, as compared to no water view (0). Boxplot analysis enables us to identify variables that have a greater impact than others.

Exhibit 4-15 Histogram: Distribution of Home Square Feet as Numerical Variable

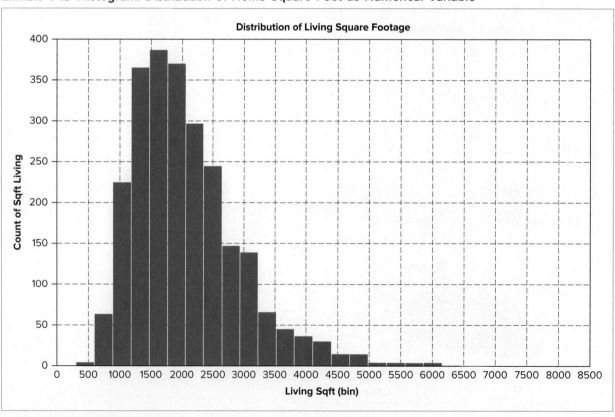

Exhibit 4-16 Boxplot: Home Prices Distribution by Water View

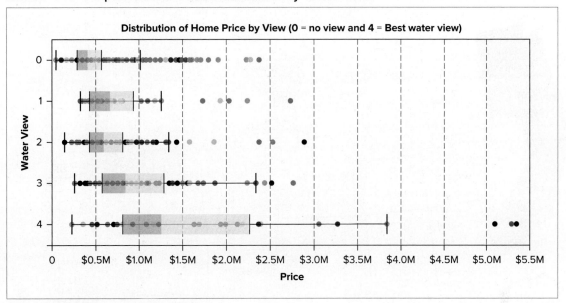

Geographic relationships can be compared by using maps. Geographic (geospatial) maps display "where"—the location on the map for types of information. When there is a food safety issue, for example, restaurants might use geographic relationships to determine if food-borne illnesses are located in many areas or only in specific areas, as shown in Exhibit 4-17. Other questions that could be answered using geographic representation:

- Where did customers make the most purchases last year by ZIP code?
- Where is the geographic location of our social media followers?
- Is positive or negative social media feedback centered around specific geographic locations?

Deviation analysis shows changes (departures) compared to another standard or value of reference. This type of analysis was recently applied to show the difference between Uber and Lyft. For example, the information in Exhibit 4-18 shows the extent to which net profit for Lyft and Uber differs from June 2016–June 2019. Deviation analysis can also answer questions such as:

- The variance between the actual product delivery date and the originally projected date.
- The extent to which retail sales differ in the 4th quarter of the calendar year from the prior year.
- The difference between forecasted sales and actual sales.

Nominal comparisons display different quantitative values of subcategories that are not in a specific order and do not share a particular relationship. For example, if the buyer for a large retailer wants to examine sales, they can use this type of information to determine whether certain categories are doing well or need to be reevaluated. Should the retailer carry more or less variety? What is the overall profit of one or more categories of products?

A bar chart could be used to display the sales of several different products. Exhibit 4-19 is a horizontal bar chart that shows a list of products in alphabetical order starting at the top bar and the sales of each product. Detergent has the highest sales volume, batteries the second highest, sunscreen the third highest, and so forth.

Exhibit 4-17 Geographic Map Chart: 2015 *E. coli* Breakout at Chipotle Mexican Grill

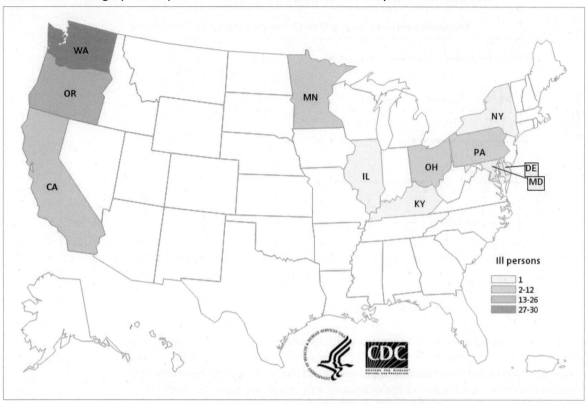

Ill persons

	1
	2-12
	13-26
	27-30

Exhibit 4-18 Deviation: Change in Net Income

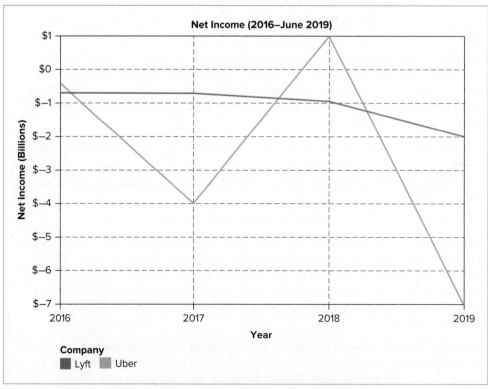

Net Income (2016–June 2019)

Company
■ Lyft ■ Uber

Exhibit 4-19 Nominal Comparison: Product Sales

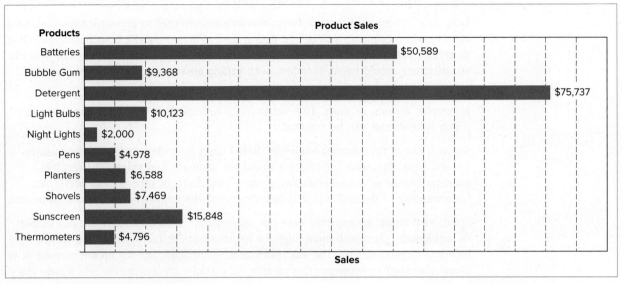

continued from page 103

PRACTITIONER CORNER

Nikola Cuculovski I Analytics Associate Director at 22squared

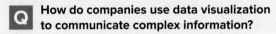

Q How do companies use data visualization to communicate complex information?

A Companies use data visualizations as the common language that enables one to simplify complex information for wider audiences with different types of backgrounds and experiences, and to cohesively communicate findings on a given question. With the continued growth in data and easier access to it, data visualizations have enabled professionals to become resident analysts within their companies, hence accelerating the process of uncovering and communicating interesting details, and using those findings for inspiration to solve the question at hand, as opposed to some historical quantitatively intensive approaches.

Oftentimes, data visualizations are seen as the final output and last step in the analytics journey that summarizes the findings for an audience. But data visualizations frequently can be the place where a new exploration journey begins based on the presented discoveries. While there are some veteran decision makers with longer industry experience who prefer a tabular view of the data and can notice trends through observing their Key Performance Indicators (KPIs), for the majority of decision makers, data visualizations are the outputs that communicate the findings leading them to their personal "eureka" moments. Following such moments, a good visualization may serve as a catalyst for a new set of questions that will require a further exploration of the data and the problem itself. Although many visualizations play a critical role in communicating the narrative, and provide context about the question at hand, most likely there are a couple of visualizations that summarize the majority of the analysis (i.e., explaining the relationship between sales and marketing, or how accurate the model predictions are) that will communicate the core message of the analysis.

Continued to next page

4.4 So, What's Your Story?

Data visualizations contribute to basic discovery and are used to present information, most often based on quantitative data. The data is used to create visualizations that are effective in telling a cohesive story to address the business question at hand. Development of these visualizations should begin, therefore, with getting answers to some critical questions.

First, what data is available? Data might be limited to certain products, services, geographic regions, or years. This would likely be important information in knowing which relationships can be explored.

Second, who is the intended audience? Based upon an understanding of the business and available data, what information would the audience find valuable? Does the audience consist of only the marketing team, executives, or other stakeholders? An understanding of the audience will help determine the information to be communicated.

Third, what results are expected from the visualization? What audience questions should be anticipated? The visualization might be informational, or the objective may be to influence decision making. The way information is displayed depends on the purpose. It is always important to remember that an effective narrative chronologically tells a clear story.

Fourth, what charts help to tell a clear story? Ultimately, it is always best to experiment with different visual displays. Many visualization tools, such as Tableau, offer suggestions while the data is being explored. While visualization tools are a great start, users need to be cautious in adopting auto-generated suggestions because they are not always the best choice. The visual principles, elements, and types described earlier should always be relied on in determining how to compose your story.

continued from page 111

PRACTITIONER CORNER

Nikola Cuculovski I Analytics Associate Director at 22squared

Q **How does a marketing analyst decide what information to include when preparing data visualizations for presentation?**

A As analysts, we often make a reasonable oversight and assume that our audiences' desires are to review the full depth of the analysis, including the exploratory as well as the explanatory analysis. However, while exploratory visualizations often help with educating the analyst about the dataset and discovering the underlying trends and findings, one needs to focus on the explanatory visualizations when building the final presentation. Given that decision makers have limited time and make many decisions throughout the day, the final output presented should mostly focus on the explanatory analysis and solving the question at hand. Nevertheless, this does not mean only showing the results slide and communicating the findings, since most of the time the audience will inquire how one arrived at the conclusions. This can be a challenging task for the analyst that will take multiple iterations to arrive at a final, well-balanced deliverable.

To narrow the scope of the presentation, the analyst will need to ask themselves several key questions that will define the final product, such as who is the target audience receiving this presentation, what is the key message that needs to be conveyed, what do we want our audience to do after listening to the presentation, and lastly choosing the right visual representation for the data presented. These questions will provide one with the context needed to successfully deliver the message and hopefully accomplish the desired outcomes.

Continued

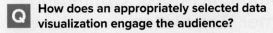

Q **How does an appropriately selected data visualization engage the audience?**

A Fueled by the recent exponential growth of data and increasing number of data visualization tools with low barriers to entry, one has the power to create and communicate their findings with only a few clicks. Partly due to this new wave of analytical empowerment, every day a number of new data visualizations and creative ways to visualize data are formed. While such creations push the boundaries of storytelling and the industry forward, most of the time a handful of properly used foundational data visualizations—such as simple text, bar and line graphs, scatterplots, heatmaps, and tables—and infrequent usage of area graphs continue to reach the full potential of audience engagement. Each one of those visual types has a specific application, and largely due to the simplicity of conveying the message—these types of visualizations have weathered the storms across the last couple of decades, while bearing the evolution of the data behind them.

By crafting the appropriate visual with a clearly defined purpose and message, such visuals will invite the audience to further examine and apply the presented learnings to their context and domain. Largely due to the explosion of data complexity, a new set of dynamic visualizations (i.e., animation, interaction and real time) have also started to be utilized. Since static visualizations oftentimes can limit the dimensionality of a message, dynamic visualization powered through a combination of functions allows one to interact with the data in a unique way that enables deeper learning.

Case Study Telecommunications: Optimizing Customer Acquisition

Red Ventures, a marketing company, has a strategic partnership with a telecommunications company that offers telephone, internet, and cable television subscriptions. One of the ways they partner is by optimizing customer acquisition through the telecommunication company's main website. On the site, customers can purchase internet, TV, and home phone services in two different ways. The first method of ordering is through an online cart. The second option is for customers to connect with the company through a call center sales agent. Red Ventures owns and operates both the online cart and the sales center for the telecommunications company. Red Ventures is responsible, therefore, for optimizing both ways to purchase services.

Preferences for both telecommunications products and digital engagement have been changing. While some website visitors prefer to purchase through an online cart, others prefer to transact with the help of a live sales agent. Therefore, the website optimization goal is to deliver the most appropriate purchase experience to each visitor based on what is known about them and their user behavior.

Since you are a marketing analyst for Red Ventures, how can you use visualization methods to find patterns in the data? Can you determine which segments of traffic should receive an online cart-focused versus a phone-focused website experience?

Understanding the Business Problem

Recently, the telecommunications industry has been negatively impacted by customers switching to alternative service providers for cable, home-telephone service, and internet connections. Because Red Ventures is responsible for improving telecommunications online sales, as well as those through call centers, the company is searching for ways to increase profits. Companies can acquire new customers by offering an exceptional experience. Thus, Red Ventures is focused on optimizing the customer experience when placing orders.

Understanding the Dataset

The next step in the process is to understand what data is available for analysis. The Red Ventures telecommunications data can be downloaded from the student's resources page. The Red Ventures dataset consists of data that has been collected over a two-week period. This data contains information such as visitor information, order information, and session time that were captured through the visitor interaction with the telecommunication company's website. To get started, let's review the data elements in Exhibit 4-20.

We will be using Tableau to further explore the data. There are several important things to know when using Tableau. When uploading data to Tableau, the software classifies data into different types (see Exhibit 4-21). **Dimensions** consist of qualitative or categorical information and usually identify variable names such as *browser name* and *metro name*. Dimensions can be summarized using counts. When data is quantitative or numerical—for example, *phone order monthly charge*—it is considered a **measure**. In setting up your analysis, your measures (quantitative or numerical data) can be aggregated. Aggregation occurs when summary operations are applied. For example, the monthly charges for all customers could be summarized as a sum, average, minimum, maximum, variance, or median. The type of data summary needed to address the business question can be decided in the visualization software.

Exhibit 4-20 Data Dictionary

VARIABLE NAME (TYPE)	DESCRIPTION
Session Id (typeless)	Unique ID representing one visitor session on the website
Session Start Time (date/time)	Timestamp of a visitor's session start time and date
Browser Name (string)	Browser from where a visitor entered
Sessions (numeric)	Active visitor session indicator (1 for active session)
Total Orders (numeric)	All orders (includes both cart and phone)
Cart Order (numeric)	Indicates a cart order
Phone Order (numeric)	Indicates a phone order
City (string)	City from where a visitor entered the website (based on IP address)
Connection Speed (string)	Local internet connection type (e.g., cable, mobile, broadband) of a visitor
Country (string)	Country from where a visitor entered the website (based on IP address)
Device Type (string)	Type of device that a visitor used to enter the website
Distinct Page Views (numeric)	The number of unique pages on the website that a visitor saw (refreshing the same page counts as one page view)
ISP Name (string)	Name of the internet service provider that a visitor used to access the website
Landing Page Raw (string)	Full URL of the page a visitor first landed on
Manufacturer (string)	Manufacturer of the device a visitor used to enter the website (generally only applies to mobile and tablet)
Metro Name (string)	Metro area that the visitor entered from (based on IP address)
OS Name (string)	Operating system on the device a visitor used when entering the website
Order Monthly Charge (numeric)	Monthly cost to the visitor for the purchased plan
State (string)	State from where the visitor entered the website (based on IP address)
Zip Code (numeric-categorical)	Zip code from where the visitor entered the website (based on IP address)
Traffic Source (string)	How a visitor accessed the site (Direct Entry = typing in the URL, Natural Search = unpaid search, Paid Search, Other)

Exhibit 4-21 Variables Types in Tableau

Dimension	Measure
These are categorical variables that can be summarized using count. However, these variables cannot be aggregated using sum, average, median, and so on. Examples: State, Date, Gender, Product Category.	These are numerical variables that can be aggregated using sum, average, median, standard deviation, variance, and so on. Examples: Sales, Price, Order Amount.

After reviewing the data, there are some other important questions to ask:

- *What does one row in the dataset represent?* Each row of the data represents one session. A session is a single visit to a website by a single visitor. It is possible there are multiple rows of data representing the same visitor, if they came to the website multiple times within this time period.
- *What do the distinct values of traffic source mean? Traffic Source* is captured by how the customer accessed the website. Direct entry refers to visitors that typed in the website URL. Natural search identifies visitors that searched the internet for information and clicked on the website. It does not include paid advertising.
- *What is the time zone of the Session Start Time field?* The time zone is reported in GMT.
- *What field represents the conversion?* The *Total Orders* column represents customer purchase or conversion.
- *How do we distinguish between cart and phone orders?* There is an order type column that has two types: *Phone* or *Cart Order*.

Data Preparation

A good practice before starting with any advanced analytics project is to review the dataset. Exhibit 4-22 can be used to understand the features available, data size, and categories under each column. Click on "Data," then "Filter" to further understand categories under each column.

Exhibit 4-22 Red Ventures Telecom Dataset Overview

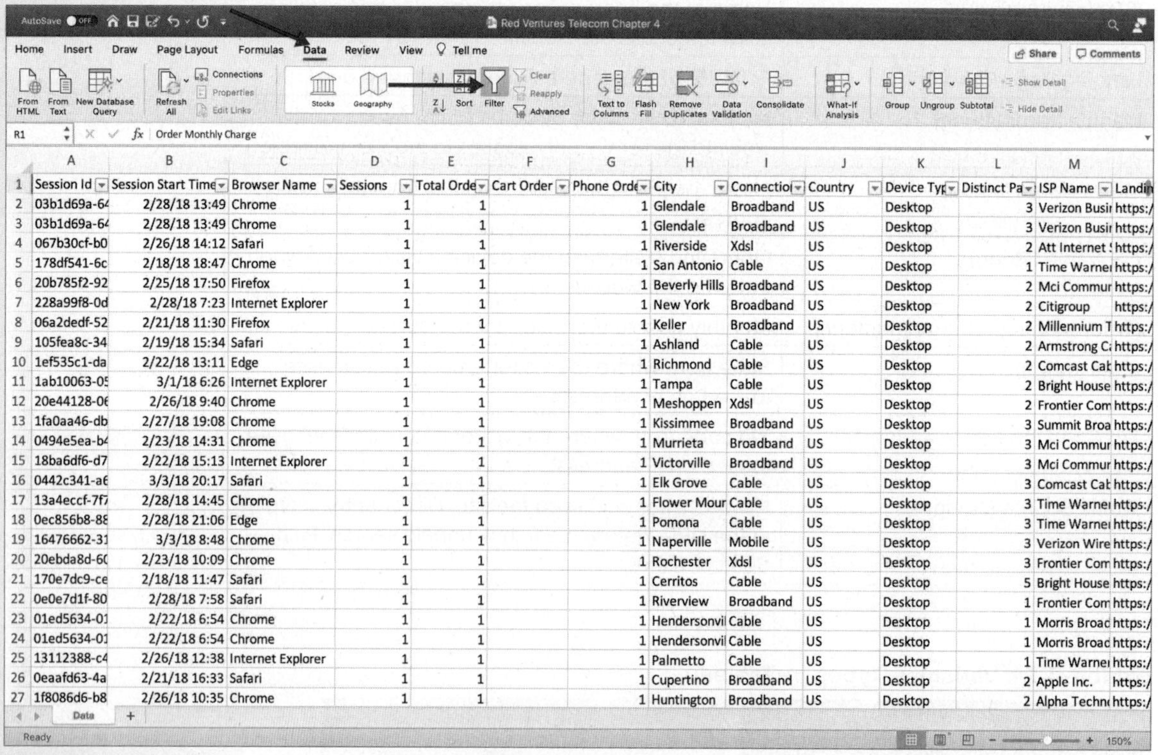

	A	B	C	D	E	F	G	H	I	J	K	L	M	
1	Session Id	Session Start Time	Browser Name	Sessions	Total Orde	Cart Order	Phone Orde	City	Connectio	Country	Device Typ	Distinct Pa	ISP Name	Landin
2	03b1d69a-64	2/28/18 13:49	Chrome	1	1		1	Glendale	Broadband	US	Desktop	3	Verizon Busir	https:/
3	03b1d69a-64	2/28/18 13:49	Chrome	1	1		1	Glendale	Broadband	US	Desktop	3	Verizon Busir	https:/
4	067b30cf-b0	2/26/18 14:12	Safari	1	1		1	Riverside	Xdsl	US	Desktop	2	Att Internet :	https:/
5	178df541-6c	2/18/18 18:47	Chrome	1	1		1	San Antonio	Cable	US	Desktop	1	Time Warnei	https:/
6	20b785f2-92	2/25/18 17:50	Firefox	1	1		1	Beverly Hills	Broadband	US	Desktop	2	Mci Commur	https:/
7	228a99f8-0d	2/28/18 7:23	Internet Explorer	1	1		1	New York	Broadband	US	Desktop	2	Citigroup	https:/
8	06a2dedf-52	2/21/18 11:30	Firefox	1	1		1	Keller	Broadband	US	Desktop	2	Millennium T	https:/
9	105fea8c-34	2/19/18 15:34	Safari	1	1		1	Ashland	Cable	US	Desktop	2	Armstrong C:	https:/
10	1ef535c1-da	2/22/18 13:11	Edge	1	1		1	Richmond	Cable	US	Desktop	2	Comcast Cat	https:/
11	1ab10063-05	3/1/18 6:26	Internet Explorer	1	1		1	Tampa	Cable	US	Desktop	2	Bright House	https:/
12	20e44128-06	2/26/18 9:40	Chrome	1	1		1	Meshoppen	Xdsl	US	Desktop	2	Frontier Com	https:/
13	1fa0aa46-db	2/27/18 19:08	Chrome	1	1		1	Kissimmee	Broadband	US	Desktop	3	Summit Broa	https:/
14	0494e5ea-b4	2/23/18 14:31	Chrome	1	1		1	Murrieta	Broadband	US	Desktop	3	Mci Commur	https:/
15	18ba6df6-d7	2/22/18 15:13	Internet Explorer	1	1		1	Victorville	Broadband	US	Desktop	3	Mci Commur	https:/
16	0442c341-a6	3/3/18 20:17	Safari	1	1		1	Elk Grove	Cable	US	Desktop	3	Comcast Cat	https:/
17	13a4eccf-7f7	2/28/18 14:45	Chrome	1	1		1	Flower Mour	Cable	US	Desktop	3	Time Warnei	https:/
18	0ec856b8-88	2/28/18 21:06	Edge	1	1		1	Pomona	Cable	US	Desktop	3	Time Warnei	https:/
19	16476662-31	3/3/18 8:48	Chrome	1	1		1	Naperville	Mobile	US	Desktop	3	Verizon Wire	https:/
20	20ebda8d-60	2/23/18 10:09	Chrome	1	1		1	Rochester	Xdsl	US	Desktop	3	Frontier Com	https:/
21	170e7dc9-ce	2/18/18 11:47	Safari	1	1		1	Cerritos	Cable	US	Desktop	5	Bright House	https:/
22	0e0e7d1f-80	2/28/18 7:58	Safari	1	1		1	Riverview	Broadband	US	Desktop	1	Frontier Com	https:/
23	01ed5634-01	2/22/18 6:54	Chrome	1	1		1	Hendersonvil	Cable	US	Desktop	1	Morris Broac	https:/
24	01ed5634-01	2/22/18 6:54	Chrome	1	1		1	Hendersonvil	Cable	US	Desktop	1	Morris Broac	https:/
25	13112388-c4	2/26/18 12:38	Internet Explorer	1	1		1	Palmetto	Cable	US	Desktop	1	Time Warnei	https:/
26	0eaafd63-4a	2/21/18 16:33	Safari	1	1		1	Cupertino	Broadband	US	Desktop	2	Apple Inc.	https:/
27	1f8086d6-b8	2/26/18 10:35	Chrome	1	1		1	Huntington	Broadband	US	Desktop	2	Alpha Techn	https:/

Microsoft Excel

A simple way to examine the data is the *Data Filter* option in Excel, as shown in Exhibit 4-23. Click on the arrow beside the field label. Look at each column to understand its content and levels. Make a note of features with unexpected data patterns.

Exhibit 4-23 Red Ventures Telecom Dataset Filter and Sort

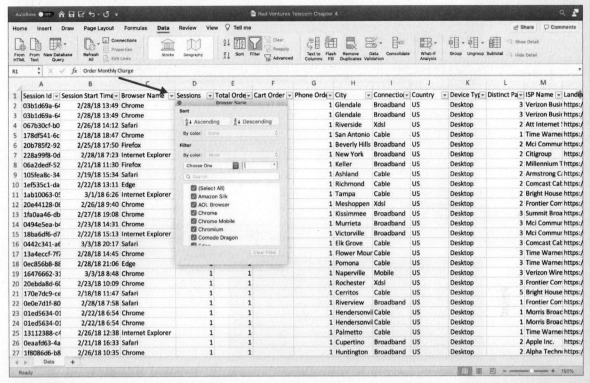

Microsoft Excel

Applying the Concepts

Are you ready for your adventure with Tableau? To download Tableau, go to www.tableau.com/academic/students and sign up for a student academic account. The good news is that Tableau works the same on Mac and Windows.

Step 1: Once the program has been downloaded on your computer, open Tableau to start creating a data visualization. Your screen should appear like Exhibit 4-24. Click on "Microsoft Excel" to locate the data file you will import into the program for analysis.

Step 2: On your computer, locate the data file you will be using for the analysis and click "Open" (Exhibit 4-25).

Exhibit 4-24

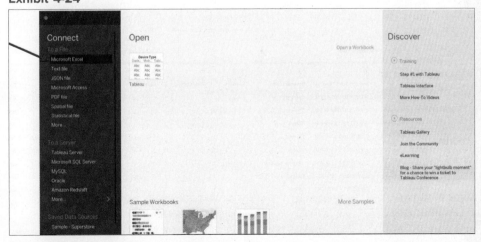

Tableau Software, Inc. All rights reserved.

Exhibit 4-25

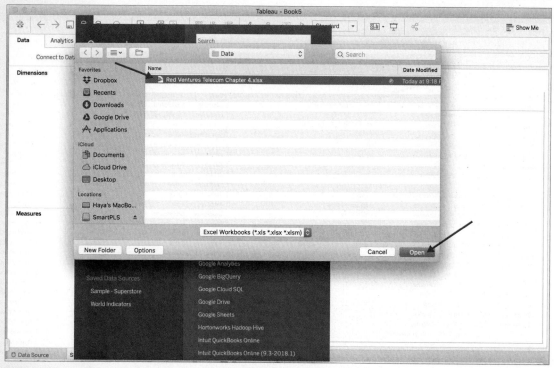

Step 3: Review the data that was imported into Tableau (Exhibit 4-26). In this step, make sure the data type appears accurately in Tableau. For example, *Session Start Time* has the type date and *City* has a geographic area. Click on "Sheet 1" to go to the Tableau worksheet. The worksheet screen is where you begin the data visualization.

Exhibit 4-26

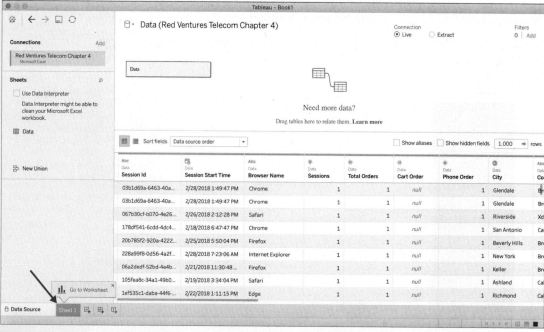

Step 4: Examine the dimensions (e.g., *Browser Name*, *City*, etc.) and measures (e.g., *Cart Orders*, *Distinct Page Views*, etc.) as shown in Exhibit 4-27. Remember that you can always review the data dictionary in Exhibit 4-20 for the meaning of the fields. You can also scroll down on the list of dimensions and measures to locate all of them.

Exhibit 4-27

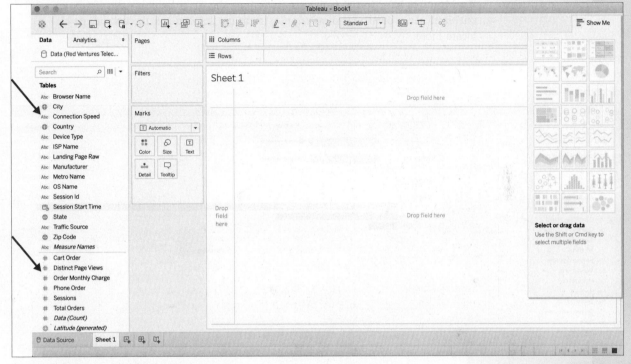

MARKETING ANALYTICS EXTRAS

Review Exhibit 4-27 to identify critical elements in Tableau, including:

- The *Columns* and *Rows* shelves allow us to represent dimensions as table headers or measures using quantitative axes.
- The *Filters* pane enables you to select a subset of the data; for example, view only Chrome Browsers data.
- The *Pages* pane will allow you to apply a filter to the entire page.
- The *Marks* card is one of the most important areas in Tableau. This is where you can control the types of data displayed, such as *details*, *colors*, *shapes*, *sizes*, and *text*.
- Finally, *Show Me* in the right corner is based on years of best practices and visualization principles. Tableau will suggest graphs depending upon the type of data in the rows and columns.

Now that the data has been imported, let's identify some characteristics of the visitors of the website by asking these questions:

- What devices are they using to access the website—mobile phone, tablet, laptop?
- What type of browser are they using—Safari, Chrome, Internet Explorer?
- Which operating system are they logging in with—macOS, Microsoft Windows?

Step 5: What devices are they using to access the website? To answer this question, drag *Device Type* under the Dimensions pane to the Rows section and *Sessions* under the Measures pane to the Columns section, as shown in Exhibit 4-28. If you are unable to see a particular dimension or measure, scroll down the on the list to locate more.

Exhibit 4-28

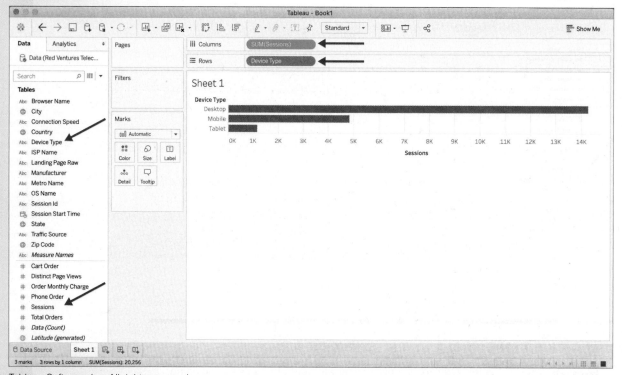

Step 5a: Recall that the Marks card gives you the ability to customize your view of the data or how it appears; the default color in Tableau is blue. Revisit our earlier discussion on how blue is a color of confidence, independence, and integrity.

You can include additional details on the chart. Now, drag *Sessions* under the Measures and drop it on the Marks card as shown in Exhibit 4-29.

Exhibit 4-29

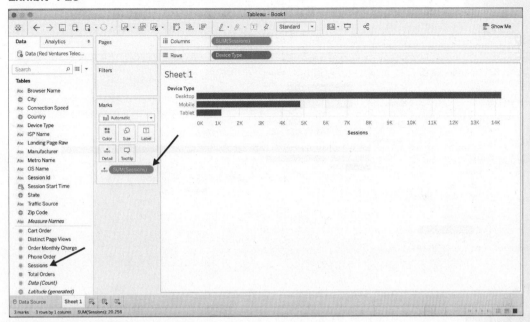

What changes appear on the chart? From the results, we can see that most visitors are visiting with a desktop computer.

Step 5b: After dragging the *Sessions* to the Marks card, you now see in Exhibit 4-30 that the total *Sessions* for each *Device Type* appears. The data view can easily be changed from total number to % of the total. To do that, right-click on *Sum(Sessions)* on the Marks card and select "Quick Table Calculation," as shown in Exhibit 4-30. Then, select "Percent of Total." On the Marks card, drag *Sum(Sessions)* onto the Label ⊤ box.

Exhibit 4-30

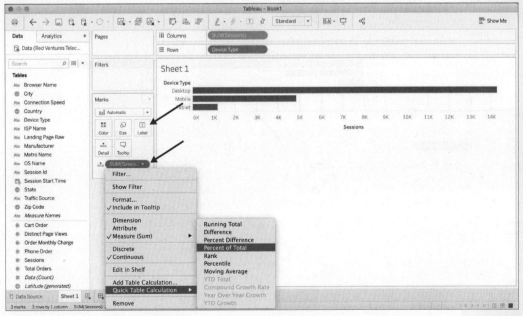

How is the *Device Type* value now reflected on the chart? The *Device Type* is now shown as a % of the total (Exhibit 4-31).

Exhibit 4-31

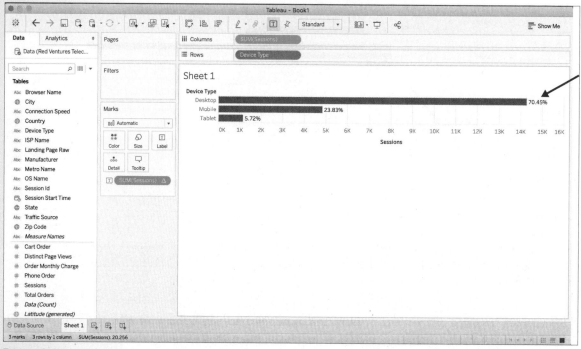

When you move your mouse over each of the *Device Type* bars, you will see the type of device you have and the total *Sessions* for each *Device Type* (Exhibit 4-32).

Exhibit 4-32

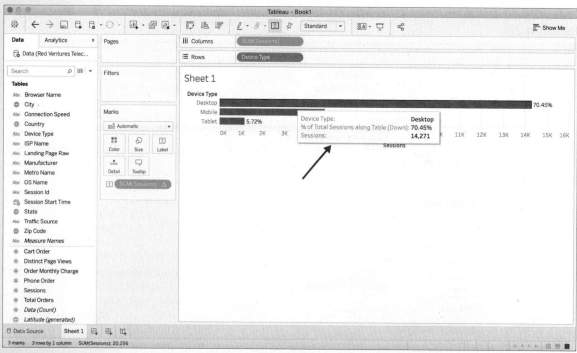

Step 5c: Let's relabel the *% of Total Number of Sessions* along Table (Down) to *% of Total Number of Sessions* and *Sessions* to *Number of Sessions* in the tooltip in the Marks card to *Number of Sessions*. To complete this step, right-click on ⌨ Tooltip box on the Marks card then edit the pop-up box as it appears in Exhibit 4-33.

Exhibit 4-33

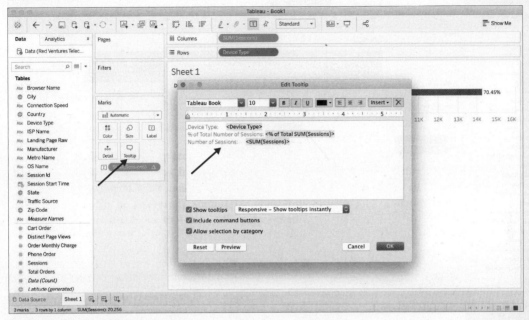

Step 5d: Let's drag *Device Type from Rows* and drop it on in the ⁚⁚ Color box on the Marks card. Exhibit 4-34 now shows the graph as a single, horizontal stacked bar chart and the *Device Type* is distinguished by color. Note that *Device Type* should no longer be present under Rows.

Exhibit 4-34

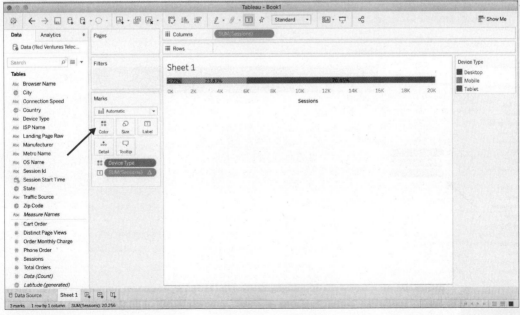

Step 5e: Now let's clean up the chart. To hide the header showing the *Sessions*, click on the X axis and uncheck "Show Header" (Exhibit 4-35).

Exhibit 4-35

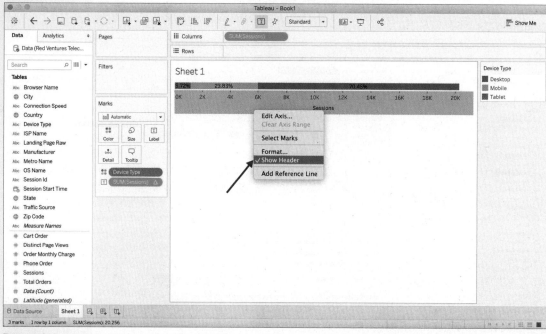

Let's increase the height of the single bar chart. Drag *Device Type* from left pane onto the Label ⊤ box on the Marks card. Now, hover over the edge of the horizontal stacked bar chart and expand the height by pulling the chart down using the double arrow symbol ↕ (Exhibit 4-36).

Exhibit 4-36

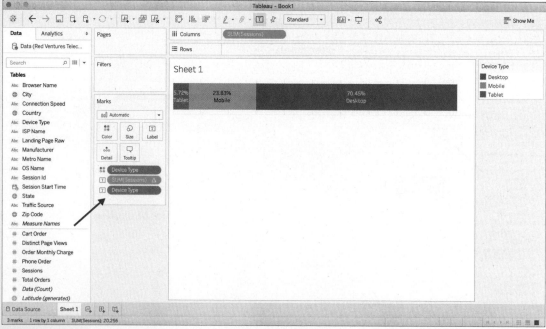

Currently, the Sheet name is labeled by default. To better understand the output at a quick glance, let's change the sheet name from "Sheet 1" to "Visitors by Device Type." Click on "Sheet 1" and relabel the sheet to name the page (Exhibit 4-37). When you change the sheet name, the title of the sheet changes as well to "Visitors by Device Type."

Exhibit 4-37

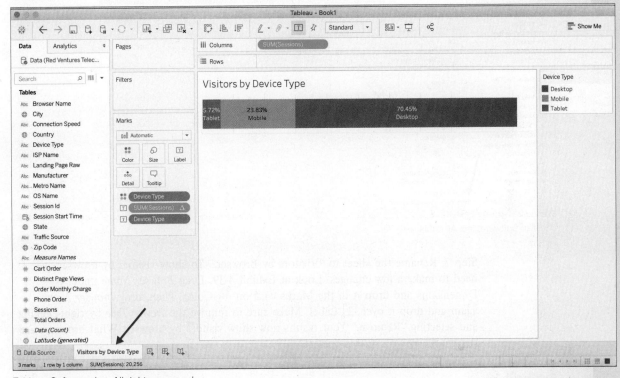

Step 6: To continue developing charts to answer our original questions, let's duplicate "Visitors by Device Type" to create two more sheets: "Visitors by Browser" and "Visitors by OS." Right-click on "Visitors by Device Type" as shown in Exhibit 4-38. Then, select "Duplicate."

Exhibit 4-38

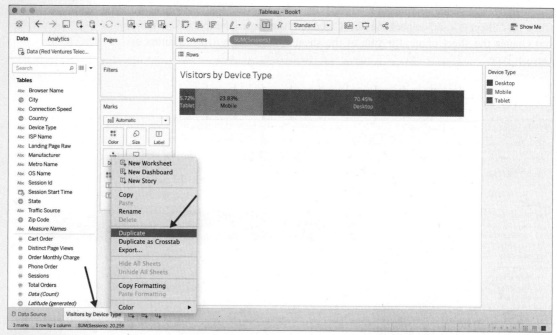

Step 7: Rename the sheet to "Visitors by Browser." To show visitors by browser, we need to make a few changes. Look at Exhibit 4-39. Drag *Browser Name* under Dimensions and drop it in the Marks card on ⠿ Color. Then, drag *Browser Name* again and drop it over T Label. Make sure to remove the *Device Type* by right-clicking and selecting "Remove." Your results now show visitors by browser. What browsers are the most common in this dataset?

Exhibit 4-39

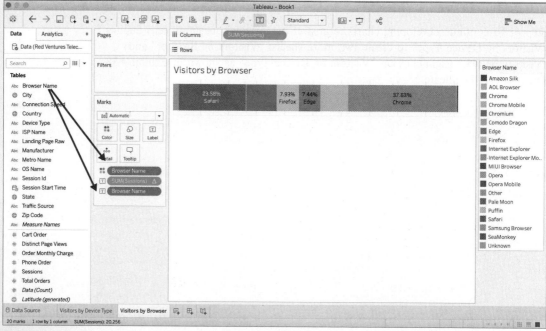

Step 8: Repeat the same steps for "Visitors by OS" and check your work against Exhibit 4-40. Results indicate that most of the visitors are using Windows 10.

Exhibit 4-40

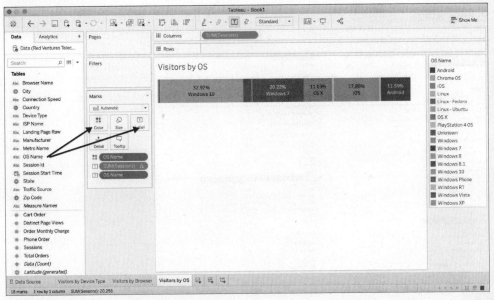

Do any of the captured patterns surprise you, and if so, why?

Step 9: Let's examine the data on a deeper level. Our next graph will focus on the *Conversion Rate* (%) by time (hour) of the day. Because this measure doesn't currently exist in the dataset, we will need to create it. Begin by clicking the ⊞ symbol and adding a new sheet to the workbook (Exhibit 4-41).

Exhibit 4-41

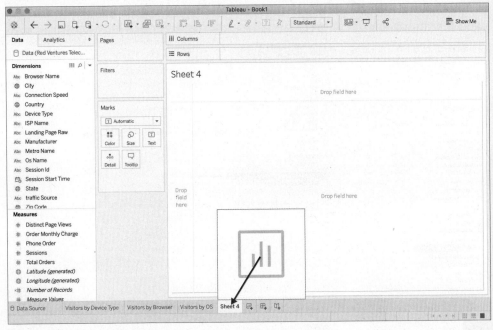

Step 9a: We will create a measure that reflects the conversion rate by time (hour) of the day. Drag and drop the *Session Start Time* to the Columns pane. It will appear by default as *Year(Session Start Time)*. Now, click the drop-down menu on *Year(Session Start Time)*, select "More," and click on "Hour," as shown in Exhibit 4-42.

Exhibit 4-42

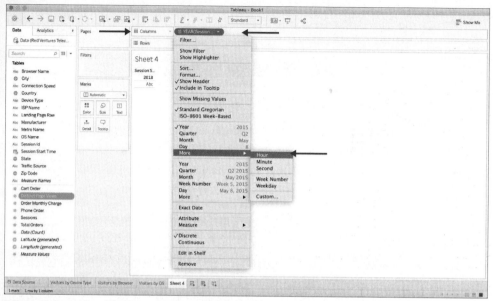

Step 9b: The measures we are interested in creating are *Cart Conversion Rate* and *Phone Conversion Rate*. First, click on "Analysis" in the menu bar and then click "Create Calculated Field" (Exhibit 4-43). The measures will tell us how many visitors became customers.

Exhibit 4-43

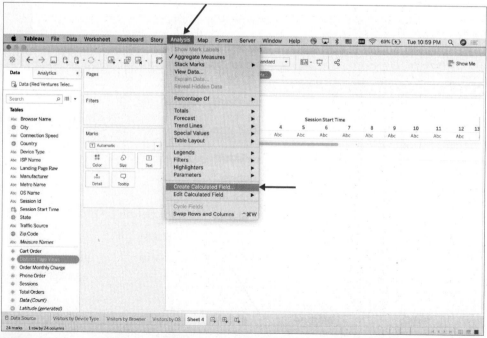

Step 9c: The *Phone Conversion Rate* is calculated as follows: total *Phone Order* measure divided by sum of *Sessions*. In the pop-up box, as shown in Exhibit 4-44, type the phone conversion rate formula, then click "OK."

Exhibit 4-44

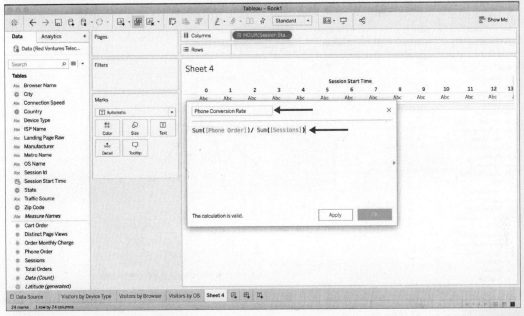

Step 9d: Repeat the earlier steps to create a calculated field for *Cart Conversion Rate*. The *Cart Conversion Rate* is calculated as follows: total *Cart Order* measure divided by sum of *Sessions*, then click "OK" (Exhibit 4-45).

Exhibit 4-45

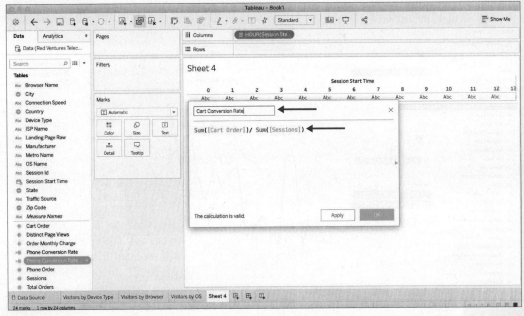

Step 10: Now that we've created the new measures, drag and drop *Phone Conversion Rate* into the Rows pane. The chart (see Exhibit 4-46) now shows the conversion rate by people contacting the company by telephone for the specific time of day.

Exhibit 4-46

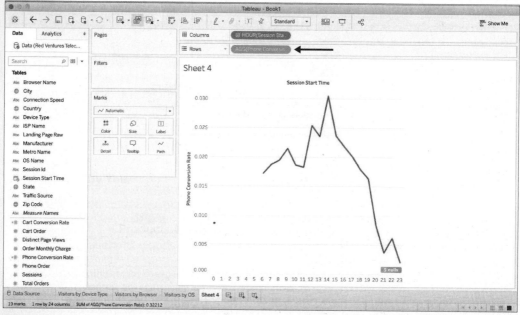

Step 11: To create a double-axis chart, drag *Cart Conversion Rate* and drop it over the Y axis *Phone Conversion Rate*. A double-axis chart is created showing the conversion rate for both cart and phone over time. The chart shows that the conversion rate for people ordering services by telephone peaks around hour 14 (Exhibit 4-47).

Exhibit 4-47

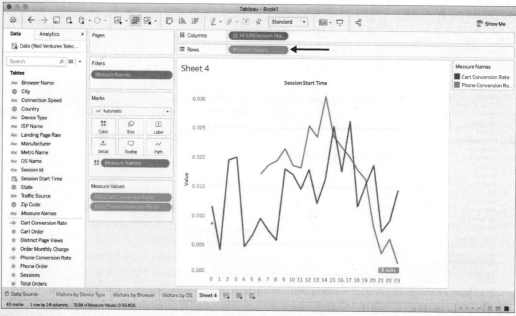

Step 11a: In Exhibit 4-48, you will notice five null values appearing. Null values means that no orders were placed at the time specified. Instead, you can allow Tableau to present those values as zero by clicking on "5 nulls" and then selecting "Show data at default position," as shown in Exhibit 4-48.

Exhibit 4-48

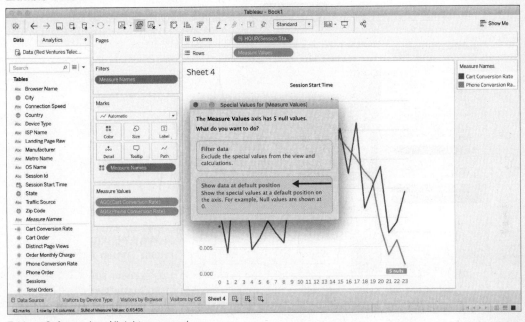

What has changed? The Phone Conversion Rate will appear at zero between the hours of 1 and 5 (Exhibit 4-49).

Exhibit 4-49

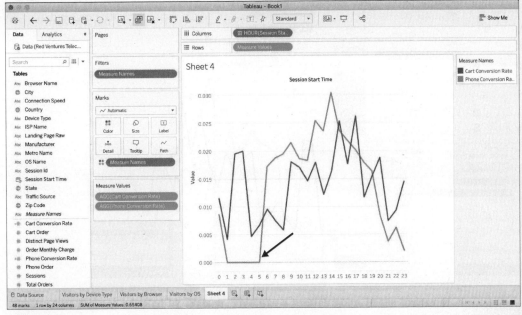

Step 11b: To change the scale from a decimal to %, right-click on the Y axis and click "Format" (Exhibit 4-50).

Exhibit 4-50

Select "Numbers," click "Percentage," and keep the decimal places at 2 (Exhibit 4-51).

Exhibit 4-51

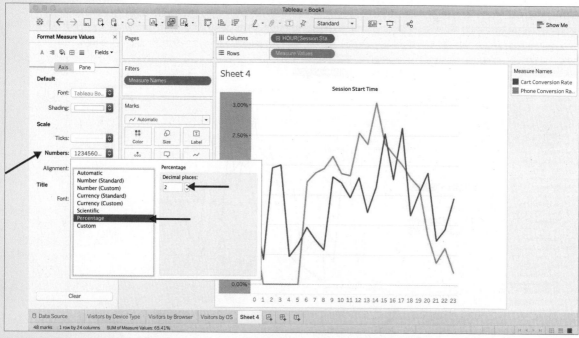

Step 11c: Now, right-click on the Y axis and click "Edit Axis." In the pop-up window (Exhibit 4-52), rename the Axis Title to "Conversion Rate".

Exhibit 4-52

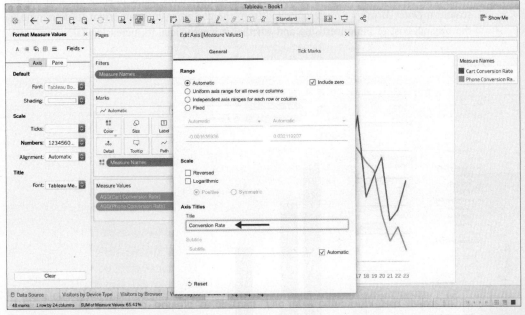

Step 11d: Rename Sheet 4 to "Conversion Rate by Hour of Day." Examine Exhibit 4-53. What patterns are you seeing in the data? What are the peak hours for cart orders? What about for phone orders? Are there any surprises?

Step 12: Now, let's test your skills. The marketing department needs to determine the performance of paid advertising. Follow the steps in prior examples to examine the

Exhibit 4-53

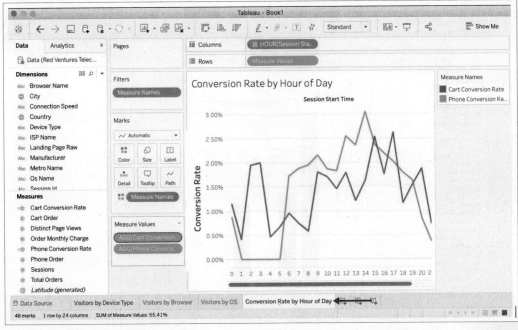

Traffic Source and *Order Monthly Change* to create a bar chart (Exhibit 4-54). Is paid advertising leading to purchases? If so, what is the impact?

It appears that customers entering the website by typing in the company name yields the highest *Order Monthly Charge*. Although paid advertising falls below direct entry and natural search in *Order Monthly Charge* collected from the customer, it is important to determine the original cost of the advertising and whether it is beneficial to increasing sales.

Exhibit 4-54

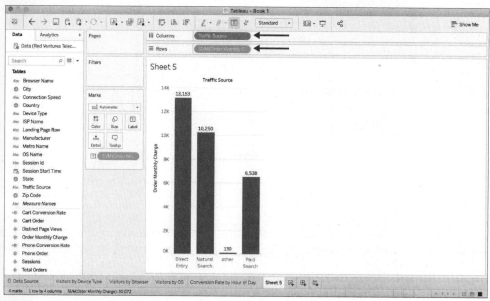

Step 12a: Currently, the bars are not in numerical order. To create a better flow in the chart, rank the bars from high to low using the Sort option. Click on the drop-down arrow on *Traffic Source* and click "Sort" (Exhibit 4-55).

Exhibit 4-55

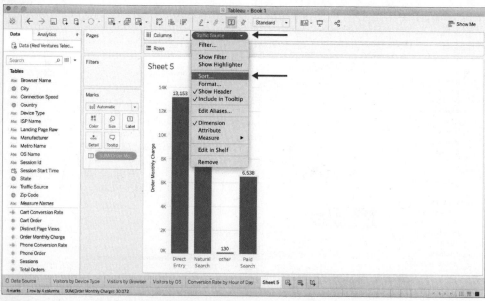

A pop-up window will appear (Exhibit 4-56). Sort by "Field."

Exhibit 4-56

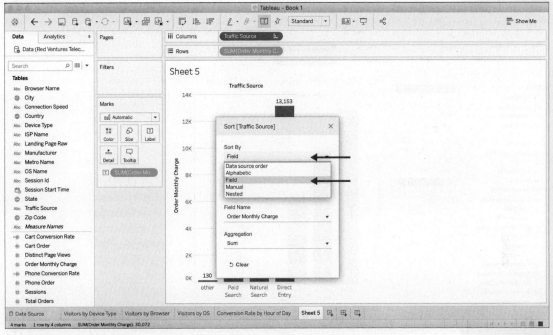

As in Exhibit 4-57, select *Order Monthly Charge* in descending order. Click the "X" to leave the window.

Exhibit 4-57

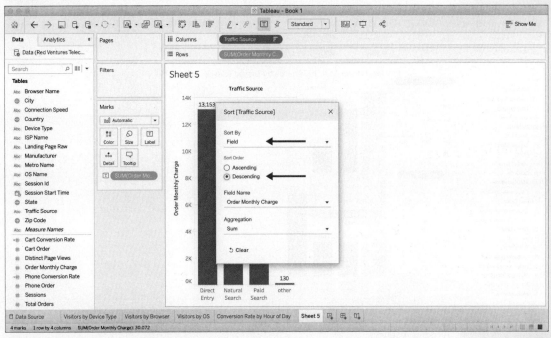

Step 12b: As described in a prior step, rename the sheet you created to "Total Order Monthly Charge by Traffic Source". Your new sheet should now appear like Exhibit 4-58.

Exhibit 4-58

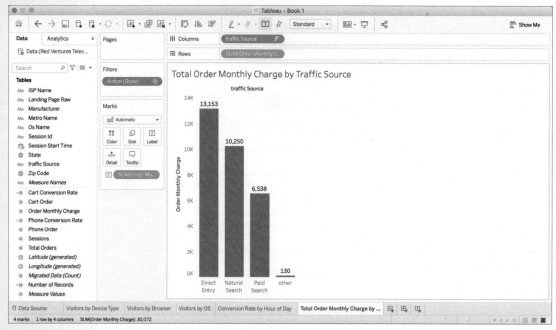

Because the numbers on the bars can be misleading, let's include a dollar sign. Right-click on the *Order Monthly Charge* label, and then select "Format" (Exhibit 4-59).

Exhibit 4-59

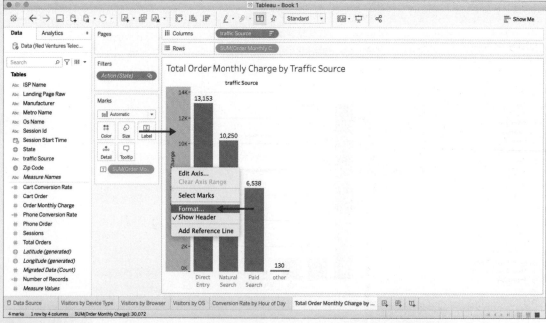

In the Default pane, under "Numbers," select "Currency (Custom)." Now, the values will include a $ and two decimal places, as in Exhibit 4-60.

Exhibit 4-60

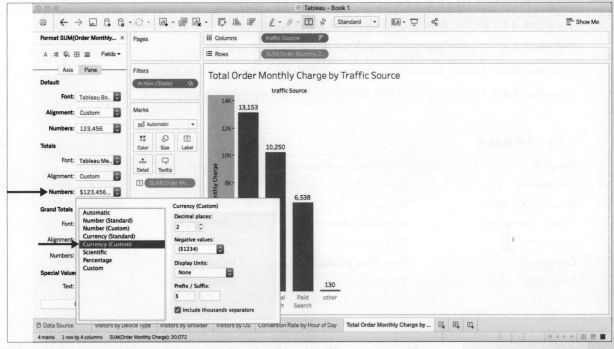

Insights Learned from Applying the Concepts

Data Visualization helps marketing analysts communicate practical insights to a wide audience. How is a data visualization an effective way to quickly and clearly convey insights? What insights were revealed in this case?

The goal of this case was to find patterns in the data that could help Red Ventures optimize customer acquisition. Consider the various segments of traffic. Which segment of traffic should receive an online cart-focused versus a phone-focused website experience? What other interesting patterns did you discover?

Tools such as Tableau allow users to create a visualization dashboard that combines all of the insights into a single screen. When examining the charts and graphs side-by-side, it is easy to see how principles of design play an important role in communicating different insights to the audience. This single source of potentially critical information represents relationships that describe different numerical connections or comparisons that exist within the data. Therefore, developing a visualization dashboard allows the marketing analyst to share several important insights at one time.

Summary of Learning Objectives and Key Terms

LEARNING OBJECTIVES

Objective 4.1 Define data visualization and the objectives surrounding this technique.

Objective 4.2 Discuss the principles of design in data visualization.

Objective 4.3 Explain basic relationships in business data appropriate for visualization.

Objective 4.4 Assess key elements that should be communicated.

KEY TERMS

Balance	Frequency distribution	Rankings
Correlation	Hue	Rhythm
Data visualization	Measure	Saturation
Design elements	Nominal comparison	Time series
Deviation	Part to whole	Unity
Dimension	Principles of design	Value
Emphasis	Proportion	Variety

Discussion and Review Questions

1. Define data visualization.

2. Why is it so important that marketers have a basic understanding of the fundamentals surrounding data visualization?

3. What are the two main objectives surrounding the graphical depiction of quantitative values?

4. What are the six basic principles of design?

5. Explain the basic elements of design.

6. Describe the eight common relationships that exist in business data.

Critical Thinking and Marketing Applications

1. Examine a public Tableau dashboard at https://public.tableau.com/en-us/gallery/?tab=viz-of-the-day&type=viz-of-the-day. How are the principles and elements of design used in the dashboard? How does the dashboard tell a story?

2. Suppose that you are presenting insights from the last two weeks to the management team at your company. You need to convey insights clearly and quickly. How would a dashboard facilitate your presentation?

References

1. Shilpi Choudhury, "How P&G Uses Data Visualization to Uncover New Opportunities for Growth," FushionCharts, April 9, 2014, https://www.fusioncharts.com/blog/how-pg-uses-data-visualization-to-uncover-new-opportunities-for-growth; and "Latest Innovations," P&G Business Sphere, https://www.pg.com/en_US/downloads/innovation/factsheet_BusinessSphere.pdf (accessed July 1, 2019); and Thomas Davenport, "How P&G Presents Data to Decision Makers," *Harvard Business Review*, April 4, 2013, https://hbr.org/2013/04/how-p-and-g-presents-data (accessed July 1, 2019).

2. Stephen Few, "Effectively Communicating Numbers Selecting the Best Means and Manner of Display," ProClarity, November 2005, https://www.perceptualedge.com/articles/Whitepapers/Communicating_Numbers.pdf (accessed July 1, 2019); Stephen Few, *Show Me the Numbers: Designing Tables and Graphs to Enlighten*, 2nd ed. (Analytics Press, 2012); and Gene Zelany, *Say it with Charts*, 4th ed. (McGraw-Hill, 2001).

3. Bernard Marr, "People, Please Stop Using Pie Charts," *Entrepreneur*, November 24, 2014, https://www.entrepreneur.com/article/239932 (accessed July 1, 2019); Stephen Few, "Save the Pies for Dessert," Perceptual Edge, August 2007, https://www.perceptualedge.com/articles/visual_business_intelligence/save_the_pies_for_dessert.pdf (accessed July 1, 2019); Tim Drexler, "Say NO to Pie (Charts)," TechBits, https://scls.typepad.com/techbits/2019/01/say-no-to-pie-charts.html (accessed July 1, 2019); Tom Brown, "Sorry Sir, We're All out of Pies," The Information Lab, February 8, 2011, https://www.theinformationlab.co.uk/2011/02/08/sorry-sir-were-all-out-of-pies (accessed July 1, 2019); and Tom Randle, "Think Before You Pie Chart (and More Effective Ways to Visualize Your Data)," Geckoboard, August 10, 2017, https://medium.com/geckoboard-under-the-hood/think-before-you-pie-chart-and-more-effective-ways-to-visualize-your-data-862ea3456b26 (accessed July 1, 2019).

4. Weathertrends360, https://www.weathertrends360.com (accessed July 1, 2019); Patrick Albin, "The Profit of 1 Degree," *Medium*, September 15, 2015, https://medium.com/@patrickalbin/the-profit-of-1-degree-c76d0988ee07 (accessed July 1, 2019); and "Weather, Consumer Behaviour and "The Profit of One Degree"," Project Ltd., June 14, 2017, http://www.pxltd.ca/2017/06/14/weather-consumer-behaviour-and-the-profit-of-one-degree/ (accessed July 1, 2019).

PART

3

ANALYTICAL METHODS FOR SUPERVISED LEARNING

5 Regression Analysis

LEARNING OBJECTIVES

5.1 Explain simple and multiple linear regression models.

5.2 Define a predictive regression model.

5.3 Differentiate between accuracy measures for predictive performance.

5.4 Assess predictive regression performance.

5.5 Discuss modeling of catagorical variables.

5.6 Discuss model independent variable selection.

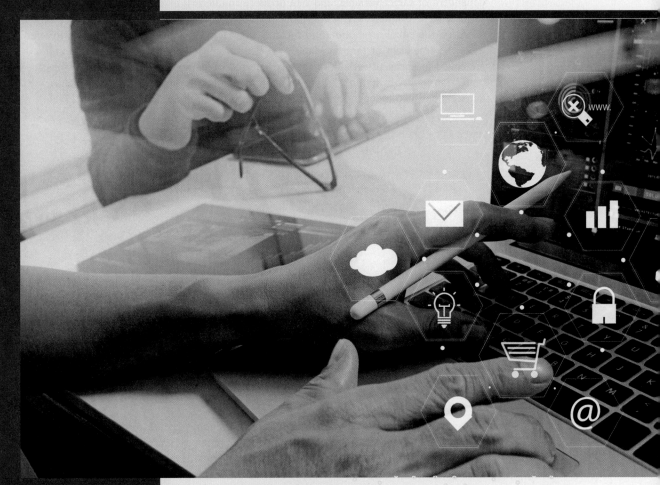

everything possible/Shutterstock

A large retail store would like to understand the impact of email promotions. To do this, the marketing analyst must predict sales amounts from customers that receive promotions by email. The store manager selected a sample of customers in the store's database and sent them promotional materials via email. Transaction data was then collected on the customers that made purchases. The transaction data included the amount spent by the customers responding to the promotional campaign, as well as other variables such as the last time they made a purchase from the store; their age, gender, and income level; and the day of the week. How can the store manager use this data to identify which variables are most likely to predict the purchase amount of a returning customer?

To answer this question, the store manager might use multiple regression. But what is multiple regression, and how do we determine which variables to examine? In the following pages, you will learn how to select variables and use regression models for predictions.

This chapter will only provide an overview of multiple regression. For a more detailed explanation of different types of regression, refer to Hair, Babin, Anderson, and Black (2019) or Hair, Page, and Brunsveld (2021).[1]

5.1   What Is Regression Modeling?

Regression modeling captures the strength of a relationship between a single numerical dependent or target variable, and one or more (numerical or categorical) predictor variables. For example, regression modeling could predict customer purchase spending based on the email promotion and income level. The variable being predicted is referred to as the **dependent** or **target variable (Y)**. The variables used to make the prediction are called **independent variables (X)** (also referred to as **predictors** or **features**). The regression model in Exhibit 5-1 has a single numerical dependent variable (purchase amount) and two independent variables (email promotion and income level).

Exhibit 5-1 Independent and Dependent Variables

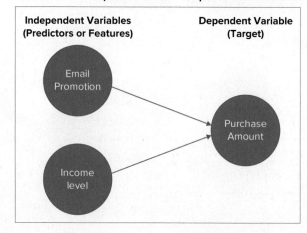

Using a regression model, we can identify which features (email promotion or income level) are more important in predicting customer purchase amount. Once the regression model has determined that one or more independent variables is a useful predictor, the next step is to identify which independent variable is the strongest predictor, then the second strongest, and so on, if there are more than two independent variables.

In **linear regression**, a relationship between the independent and dependent variables is represented by a straight line that best fits the data. The goal of the regression line is to minimize the distances between actual (observed) points (blue dots) and the regression line (red line), or what we refer to as error of prediction as shown in Exhibit 5-2.

Exhibit 5-2 Straight Line Linear Model

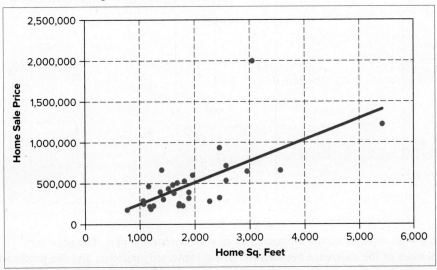

Simple Linear Regression

Simple linear regression is used when the focus is limited to a single, numeric dependent variable and a single independent variable. In Exhibit 5-1, simple linear regression was used to examine the relationship between the size of homes (independent variable/horizontal axis) and the sales price (dependent variable/vertical axis). For example, in analyzing the effect of home size in square feet (x) on home sale price (y), a marketing analyst would propose home sales price as the target (dependent) variable and home square feet as the predictor (independent) variable. Exhibit 5-3 displays the simple linear regression model equation and describes each value.

Exhibit 5-3 Simple Linear Regression Model

$$\hat{y} = b_0 + b_1 x + e$$

$\hat{y}$ = dependent variable

b_0 = The intercept is the value of $\hat{y}$ that we expect when x is zero

b_1 = slope of the line that explains the change in $\hat{y}$ when x changes by a single unit of measure.

x = independent variable

e = error in $\hat{y}$ for observations i. Accounts for the variability that is not explained by the linear relationship between x and $\hat{y}$.

In this equation, b_0 describes the estimated y-intercept and b_1 describes the slope of the regression line (red line in Exhibit 5-2). The estimated y-intercept is the point at which the linear regression line crosses the vertical axis (see Exhibit 5-4).

Exhibit 5-4 y-Intercept

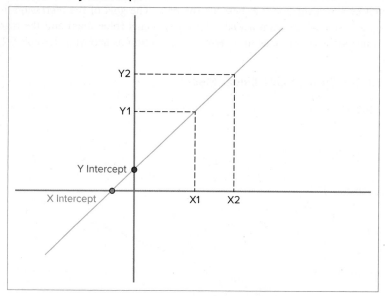

The $\hat{y}$ is an estimate of the average value of y for each value of x. The error term (e) is a measure of the difference between the actual (observed) outcome and the predicted value based on the model estimation. The error term (e) can also be thought of as the error in using regression to predict the dependent variable. A regression line always has an error term because independent variables are never perfect predictors of the dependent variables. Error terms tell us how certain we are in the estimate. Therefore, the larger the error the less certain we are about the estimation.

The information displayed in Exhibit 5-2 is based on 30 observations of home sales in King County, Washington. The relationship between the straight line and the dots shows the best fit of the line to the blue dots. The best fit of the straight line is measured by using the actual vertical distances of the blue dots from the red regression line. The vertical distance values of the blue dots from the red line are first squared. After the distances are squared, you sum the distance values to identify the position of the red line so the errors in calculating the squared distances are minimized. That is, the best fit of the straight line to the dots is obtained when the sum of the squared distance values compared to the actual distance values produces the smallest estimate of the errors. The regression equation for the best fit of the line for the 30 observations is:

$$\hat{y} = -11{,}696 + 262.13 \text{ Home Sq. Feet}$$

With this simple regression model, the analyst can use a new home square footage measure to estimate its price. For example, a home with square footage of 1,100 would be expected to have a price of $276,647. But many other variables may also affect the price of a house, such as the number of bedrooms, recent renovations, and so on. To determine if these additional independent variables can predict the dependent variable price, we must use multiple regression models. Multiple regression models also have a single numerical dependent variable, but in addition, they have several independent variables to improve your predictions.

What other variables might also affect the price of the home a purchaser is willing to pay? Examples of variables that might help you to predict include the quality of the workmanship in the home, customer's income level, number of past home shopping visits in the past 24 months, number of homes for sale in a particular area, and so forth.

How is the regression line estimated? The most common process is to estimate the regression line using the **Ordinary least squares (OLS)** method, which was summarized earlier. OLS minimizes the sum of squared errors. In this case, error represents the difference between the actual values and the predicted values of the distances between the straight line and the dots around the line.

The OLS method is a good way to determine the best fit for the set of data. The OLS process calculates the weights for the b_0 *and* b_1 and uses them to estimate the dependent variable. This procedure minimizes the errors and, ultimately, the differences between the observed and predicted values of the dependent variable. Whether the regression model includes one independent variable (simple regression) or several independent variables (multiple regression), the process estimates the value for only a single dependent variable. As noted earlier, the straight line is located in a position that minimizes the distances from the actual points to the estimated line. For example, Exhibit 5-5 shows the difference between a line of best fit (a) and a random line (b). The goal is to find the line that produces the minimum sum of squared errors in estimating the distances from the points to the straight line.

Exhibit 5-5 Line of Best Fit

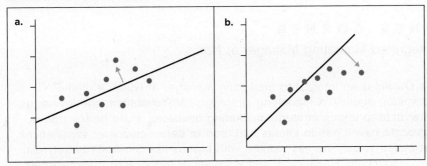

Multiple Linear Regression

Multiple regression is used to determine whether two or more independent variables are good predictors of the single dependent variable. For example, multiple regression could be used to determine whether several independent variables can improve the prediction of the single dependent variable sales. That is, what are some drivers (independent variables) that predict sales? In most instances, a marketing analyst could easily identify many possible independent variables that might predict the dependent variable sales such as promotion, price, season, weather, location and many more.

Evaluating the Ability of the Regression Model to Predict

A key metric to evaluate whether the regression model is a good predictor of the dependent variable is R^2. The **R^2** measures the amount of variance in the dependent variable that is predicted by the independent variable(s). The R^2 value ranges between 0 and 1, and the closer the value is to 1, the better the prediction by the regression model. When the value is near 0, the regression model is not a good predictor of the dependent variable.

A good fit of the straight line to the dots produces a tighter model (dots are consistently closer to the line) and a higher R^2, as shown in Exhibit 5-6. A poor fit of the straight line to the dots would produce a looser model than in Exhibit 5-6 (dots are consistently further away from the line) and the R^2 would be much lower. The R^2 goodness of fit measure is important for descriptive and explanatory regressions. When predicting new observations, however, there are other evaluation criteria that are important.

Exhibit 5-6 Regression Model Predicting R^2

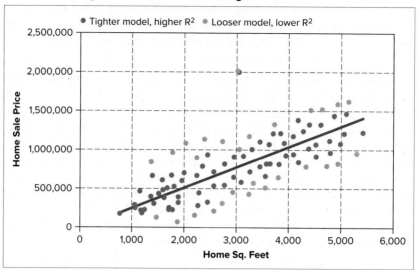

PRACTITIONER CORNER

Jessica Owens | Integrated Marketing Manager at Ntara

Jessica Owens is an integrated marketing manager at Ntara, a digital transformation agency. A marketing strategist and consultant, she leverages customer data to inform strategic marketing decisions, build better stories, and advocate new ideas to clients that lead to better customer experiences and increased sales. She has worked with brands like Simmons Beautyrest, Cardinal Innovations Healthcare, and a variety of global B2B manufacturers in chemical intermediates, flooring, transportation, and more. Jessica strives to help her clients understand, embrace, and connect data from all channels.

Jessica Owens

Q How do companies use predictive regression models to identify relationships that are important to their business?

A When our clients need to better understand what drives their customers to purchase more (or what doesn't!), we dig into their purchase and people data. By analyzing purchase data, demographic information, and qualitative data, we can determine factors that influence purchase behaviors and predict future opportunity.

Q When would using a predictive regression model be most appropriate?

A When million-dollar investment decisions are being considered, regression modeling helps turn assumptions and long-held beliefs about customer preferences into statistically

significant data that leadership can use to make informed decisions. If one of our clients believes launching into e-commerce is the answer, we use statistically significant historic data in order to predict sales opportunities.

Q How do we know when to explore relationships with predictive regression models?

A When a business seeks to understand how certain aspects of the marketing strategy will affect customer sales, for instance, you can analyze predictive regression modeling. If I invest $50,000 more into my advertising budget, what kind of return can I expect? If I offer free two-day shipping, will I increase sales volume? Answers like this can be found using predictive regression modeling.

Continued to page 148

5.2 The Predictive Regression Model

Determining the purpose of the analysis early on is critical when selecting regression as the analysis method to use. This journey starts with the business question at hand. For example, is your goal to identify the relationship between advertising and sales? Or are you interested in predicting sales amounts for new customers? For the former question, identifying the relationship between advertising and sales directs your attention to the coefficients, their significance, and goodness of fit using a descriptive or explanatory regression model. The regression model that emerges captures the relationship between independent variables and the dependent variable. This common approach to regression analysis could be one of two types: descriptive or explanatory regression modeling. Fitting a regression model to identify the relationship between the dependent and independent variables is considered descriptive modeling. In contrast, explanatory modeling focuses on identifying causal inferences based on theory-driven hypotheses.

Let's say the marketing manager wants to know future sales amounts for new or existing customers. The goal of this objective is to assess the predictive performance of the regression model. Predictive regression is most commonly used in advanced analytics modeling (e.g., machine learning). In explanatory, descriptive, and predictive modeling, a dataset is used to estimate the relationships between the target variable and predictors. To summarize, the goal in the explanatory model is to find the regression line that has the best fit to learn about the relationships in the dataset. On the other hand, predictive performance focuses on how well the model does when predicting new individual records that the model has never seen before. Recall from Chapter 1 that there are three datasets referred to as labeled data (because the target variable is known), a training dataset, a validation dataset, and an optional testing dataset (also known as a holdout sample). The training dataset is used to develop the initial sets of weights for the predictor variables (independent variables). The weights are the values for the Xs in the regression equation. The validation data is used to assess how well the regression model estimates the target variable when compared to the actual values. The third optional dataset is the test data, which can be used to evaluate how well the regression model performs on a third dataset. The final validated regression model is then applied to predict the target variable using new data where the outcomes are not known.

Exhibit 5-7 Differentiating Between Datasets

Training Data	A portion of the data is used to build a regression model.
Validation Data	The portion of the data that is used to assess the regression model which was developed from the training data.
Test Data (also known as holdout data)	Provides a final estimate of the regression model's performance after it has been trained and validated. The test data is not used to decide on which model to recommend or to improve an algorithm. It is instead used as a last check that the model is valid.

The key differences between descriptive/explanatory and predictive modeling are identified in Exhibit 5-8.

Exhibit 5-8 Key Differences Between Descriptive/Explanatory and Predictive Modeling

CATEGORY	DESCRIPTIVE/EXPLANATORY	PREDICTIVE
Main focus	*Retrospective:* Used to represent causation and association between dependent and independent variables.	*Prospective:* Used to predict a new observation.

CATEGORY	DESCRIPTIVE/EXPLANATORY	PREDICTIVE
Model use and reporting	The main focus is on interpreting the coefficients and the strength of the relationships between the dependent and independent variables.	The main focus is on predicting new data records. The interpretability of the x and y association is not required, but transparency is recommended.
Dataset	The entire dataset is used to build the model.	The dataset is divided into training and validation datasets (as explained earlier).
Performance measures	*In-Sample:* Uses coefficients, significance, goodness of fit, and overall model fit (R^2).	*Out-of-Sample:* Uses validation dataset metrics such as MAPE and RMSE (discussed in a later section), and compares these metrics against a set benchmark, as well as other predictive models.

Sources: Galit Shmueli, "To explain or to predict?" *Statistical Science,* 25, no. 3 (2010), pp. 289–310; and Galit Shmueli and Otto R. Koppius, "Predictive Analytics in Information Systems Research," *MIS Quarterly,* 2011, pp. 553–572.

Continued from page 146

PRACTITIONER CORNER

Jessica Owens | Integrated Marketing Manager at Ntara

Q **What is the value of using predictive regression versus other methods?**

A Simple linear regression helps us prove that significant *relationships* exist between variables, but *predictive* regression helps us estimate how much a new customer will spend when visiting our online store. We know that price and sales are related, but *what does it mean for the next customer*? Predictive regression modeling helps us understand how to target customers in a way that helps us improve business outcomes.

Q **What are some of the most popular tools used in businesses to explore relationships using predictive regression techniques (e.g., RapidMiner, R software)?**

A The right tool for the job really depends on the person doing the analysis, and the people they need to share the insights with. RapidMiner is great for this because of its strong visualization functionality and user-friendly interface. Many of our clients are pulling data in from multiple systems. No matter what tool you want to use, you must make sure you're avoiding duplications and errors in the way you store, import, and manipulate your data.

Continued to page 150

5.3 Predictive Regression Performance

In advanced analytics techniques, the goal is to build a model that has high predictive accuracy when applied to a new observation or data. To do so, we assess performance in predictive models with a numerical target. In this situation, relevant metrics are used to determine the quality of the predictive model.

As expanded upon in Exhibit 5-3, performance can be assessed with various metrics. To understand the amount of error that exists between different models in linear regression, we use metrics such as Mean Absolute Error (MAE), Mean Absolute Percentage Error (MAPE), and Root Mean Squared Error (RMSE) (described in

Exhibit 5-9). **Mean Absolute Error (MAE)** measures the absolute difference between the predicted and actual values of the model. **Mean Absolute Percentage Error (MAPE)** is the percentage absolute difference the prediction is, on average, from the actual target. **Root Mean Squared Error (RMSE)** indicates how different the residuals are from zero. **Residuals** represent the difference between the observed and predicted value of the dependent variable. As with each of these metrics, lower values indicate a better fit. These metrics assess the model's ability to predict new records. They are based on applying a model developed with the training dataset using the validation dataset. The main idea here is that if the future new records are similar to the validation dataset, the regression model that has good accuracy when using the validation dataset will produce good predictions.

Exhibit 5-9 Accuracy Measures for Predictive Modeling with Numerical Target

MEASURE NAME	EXPLANATION	EXAMPLE
Mean Absolute Error (MAE)	Measures the absolute difference between predicted and actual values of the model. This metric is the average prediction error. Lower MAE values indicate better fit.	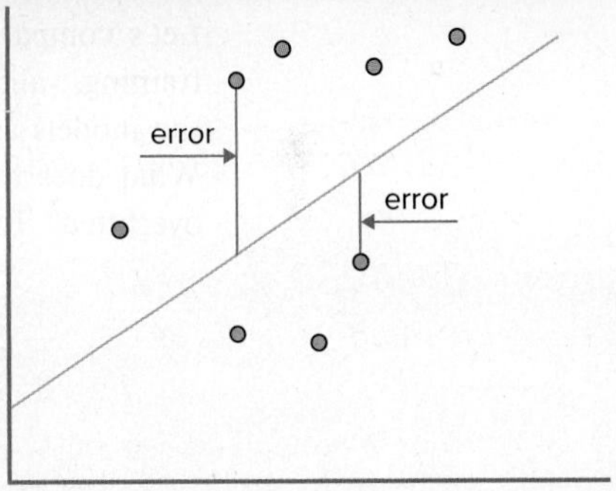 MAE = Average of all absolute errors
Mean Absolute Percentage Error (MAPE)	This metric is the percentage difference of the prediction, on average, from the actual target. Lower MAPE values indicate smaller percentages and therefore better fit.	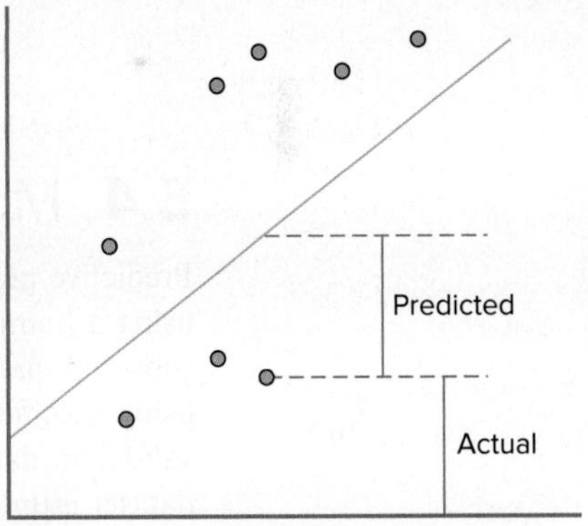 MAPE = Percentage difference of the prediction on average from the actual target
Root Mean Squared Error (RMSE)	This metric measures the standard deviation of the residuals. The plot of the residuals shows the distance of the data points from the regression line. The RMSE squares the residuals, averages the residuals and takes the square root. RMSE measures the difference of actual target from the predicted values. Lower RMSE values indicate shorter distances from the actual data point to the line and therefore better fit. RMSE uses the same units as the dependent (target) variable.	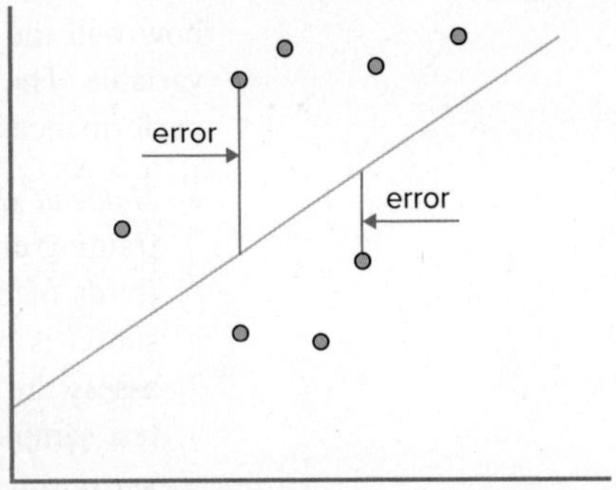 RMSE = Standard deviation of the residuals

Continued from page 148

PRACTITIONER CORNER

Jessica Owens | Integrated Marketing Manager at Ntara

Q **What are some of the most important elements of predictive regression that marketing analysts should know?**

A It's critical to work with quality data that accurately reflects your target population. When it comes time to analyze your model, pay attention to your errors—the lower the better. When we present findings to clients, we make sure we have a good validation outcome for our data, and that we have selected the model with the lowest RMSE error.

Continued to page 153

Let's compare the metrics (values) for the three measures of error. Examine the training, validation, and testing data in Exhibit 5-10. The values are similar in size, so the models are similar in terms of accuracy. But what if the values were very different. What does this mean and how might you reduce the error? Is it possible the model is overfitted? To answer these questions, we focus on understanding model validation.

Exhibit 5-10 Comparing MAE, MAPE, and RMSE Values

	MAE	MAPE	RMSE
Training Data	4.3	30%	6.5
Validation Data	4.5	35%	6.9
Testing Data	4.4	33%	6.7

5.4 Model Validation

Predictive performance is evaluated using a validation procedure. The model is built using a training subset of the data. Then, the model is validated on the remaining subset. A predictive model requires that the performance of the model be evaluated using specified metrics on a validation dataset. Recall from earlier in the chapter that a validation dataset is used to assess how well the resulting algorithm from the training dataset estimates the target variable, and to select the model that most accurately predicts the target value of interest.

Model evaluation is a critical step to estimate the error of the model. This step captures how well the model is expected to perform on unlabeled new data that has no target variable. The following evaluation methods are useful to ensure the model predictive performance can be extended to new data:

- *Hold-out validation:* Section 5.2 introduced the standard hold-out procedure for training and validation sets in supervised modeling. In this procedure, about two-thirds of the data is randomly selected to build the regression model. The remainder subset is referred to as the validation dataset. This validation sample is used to assess the predictive performance of the regression model. There is also an optional test sample that can be used to verify the model on a third dataset.

- *N-fold cross validation:* This procedure is commonly used in advanced analytics techniques. The dataset is divided into samples, as shown in Exhibit 5-11. The samples are mutually exclusive, and together they make up data subsets called folds (data subsets). It is typical to use ten folds. For each of the n-fold iterations, one dataset is selected as a validation dataset, and the remaining nine subsets are combined into a training dataset. The model is built using the training dataset and validated using the single selected validation set. The performance results of all n iterations are then averaged into a single score and evaluated. This method requires increased training time and more computer processing power. However, it is less sensitive to variation in the datasets than in hold-out validation.

Exhibit 5-11 N-Fold Cross Validation, where n = 10

Set 1	Set 2	Set 3	Set 4	Set 5	Set 6	Set 7	Set 8	Set 9	Set 10
Set 1	Set 2	Set 3	Set 4	Set 5	Set 6	Set 7	Set 8	Set 9	Set 10

...

Set 1	Set 2	Set 3	Set 4	Set 5	Set 6	Set 7	Set 8	Set 9	Set 10

5.5 Modeling Categorical Variables

Independent variables that are categorical in nature can be handled with many advanced analytics techniques. For example, nominal independent variables such as marital status (single, married, divorced, widowed), type of marketing promotion (flash sale, coupon giveaway, holiday promotion), sales territory (Northeast, Southeast, Northwest, Southwest, Midwest), employment status (unemployed, employed, student, retired), and so on. These variables need to be re-coded using a process called dummy coding. **Dummy coding** involves creating a dichotomous value from a categorical value. This type of coding makes categorical variables dichotomous using only ones and zeroes. Ordinal categorical variables representing rank order (e.g., order of preference of product or service, age group, etc.) can be coded numerically (1, 2, 3, etc.) and treated as if they were numerical variables. This approach should be avoided if the increments between each value are not equal.

Let's assume that a company wants to use a regression model to predict sales. The marketing analyst would like to include the type of customer promotions in the model which consist of three categories: flash sale, coupon giveaway, and holiday promotion. Because the type of promotion is a categorical variable with three different group types, we will need (k-1) dummy variables to show the relationship. K represents the number of categories. K-1 is then used to determine the number of dummy variables. In this scenario with three types of promotions, the three group promotion types are reduced to two or (k-1) variables. If you use all k-types (categories) in your regression model equation, it will cause the model to fail due to a perfect linear combination error. To rectify this, you can convert the data for the original categorical variable into the new dummy variable. As shown in Exhibit 5-12, the flash sale in this example is identified as the reference promotion, and the other two types of promotions Coupon Giveaway and Holiday Promotion are added in their own separate columns. For example, when the values for both Coupon Giveaway and Holiday Promotion are coded 0, that indicates the promotion type is flash sale. When the promotion type is coupon giveaway, the value in Coupon Giveaway will be coded 1, and the value in Holiday Promotion will be coded 0. When the promotion type is holiday promotion, the column Coupon Giveaway will be coded 0 and Holiday Promotion will be coded 1, as shown in Exhibit 5-12.

Exhibit 5-12 Binary Classification Problems

PROMOTION TYPE	COUPON GIVEAWAY	HOLIDAY PROMOTION
Flash sale	0	0
Coupon giveaway	1	0
Holiday promotion	0	1

The equation to estimate sales from promotion type looks like this:

$$Y = b_0 + b_1 \ Coupon \ giveaway + b_2 \ Holiday \ promotion$$

In this equation, b_0 is the estimated mean of sales for flash sale, b_1 is the estimated difference between the mean number of units sold using coupon giveaway and the mean number of units sold using flash sale, and b_2 is the estimated difference between the mean of the units sold in holiday promotion and the mean number of units sold in flash sale. The regression equation will include the two types of promotions as variables identified as coupon giveaway and holiday promotion. The point to remember here is that only k-1 is needed. Having more types of promotions will mean adding more variables.

5.6 Model Independent Variable Selection

Determining what and how many independent variables (also referred to as features or predictors) to use in the calculation depends upon the questions that need to be answered. It might be tempting to include all independent variables of a large set of data in a model. But remember, the best analytics model should be simple. Ultimately, the model needs to accurately represent the business problem at hand.

You might think that the more predictor variables, the better the regression model. But that is not always the result. Having too many independent variables in a model can have a negative effect. When too many independent variables are included, the model may be too complex for the data. As a result, irrelevant information can contribute to noise in the model calculations. Noise in the model results in an inaccurate representation of true relationships. Results might indicate a relationship between whether the customer took a nap prior to shopping and how much money they spent, when in reality, the relationship does not exist. This might result in a high level of accuracy for the training dataset. But the results will not be applicable to predicting models using new data. The name for this phenomenon is overfitting. **Overfitting** happens when sample characteristics are included in the regression model that cannot be generalized to new data. We identify overfitting when there is a significant difference between accuracy using the training data and accuracy using the validation data. To avoid the issue of overfitting, you should build a simple (or parsimonious) regression model. Best practice suggests that a model should be developed to accurately account for the dependent (target) variable and be easy to interpret and use.

When the model has too many independent variables, multicollinearity becomes a possible issue. **Multicollinearity** is a situation where the predictor variables are highly correlated with each other. If the predictors are not distinct concepts, the outcome is often misleading. High multicollinearity makes the independent variable coefficient estimates (weights) in a regression model unstable. It can also result in the size of the coefficients being incorrect, and the coefficient signs (positive or negative) may be reversed. In predictive modeling, issues involving multicollinearity can be mitigated to some extent. For example, using a large sample size improves the precision of the regression model and reduces the instability effects, as does combining two highly correlated independent variables using a procedure such as average sum scoring.

Detecting Multicollinearity

It turns out the type of predictor (i.e., numerical or categorical) plays an important role in detecting the type of multicollinearity you are examining.

When detecting multicollinearity for **numerical variables**, run a correlation matrix of the constructs. Examine correlations above 0.5 according to the rule of thumb (Hair, Black, Babin, and Anderson, 2019).

For Categorical Variables: Add a new dummy-coded categorical variable. Examine the estimated regression model with the dummy variables included in the regression model and with the dummy variables removed. If you see a major change in the estimated regression coefficients b_1, b_2, ..., b_n or in the p value for the independent variables included in the model, it can be assumed that multicollinearity exists.

There are several ways to reduce the impact of overfitting. We summarize one of the most popular approaches to solve this issue. It is referred to as feature selection.

Feature Selection

Identifying the optimal subset of features (independent variables) to explain a target variable can be challenging. **Feature selection** can be done quantitatively or qualitatively. Using a qualitative analysis, a marketer can depend on theory and domain knowledge as an initial guide. For example, marketers might suspect that recency of a customer's last visit and frequency of their purchase are important variables to include in a model. But customer service managers would consider other variables predicting customer churn as important, such as service failures, customer service dissatisfaction, or service recovery metrics. In large datasets, however, many features are often available to include in the regression model, and quantitative methods can be applied to eliminate irrelevant features.

The feature selection process is often repetitive when searching for the best combination of variables. First, all features in the dataset should be considered. Then, a subset of features should be selected. Next, additional selection criteria should be applied. Finally, the subset of features should be refined for improved performance. A general approach to feature selection (or elimination) is outlined in Exhibit 5-13.

Exhibit 5-13 General Approach to Feature Selection

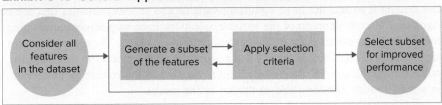

Continued from page 150

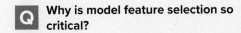

PRACTITIONER CORNER

Jessica Owens | Integrated Marketing Manager at Ntara

Q Why is model feature selection so critical?

A For the highest accuracy, it is best practice to remove less significant variables from your regression. Using irrelevant variables can greatly skew the model. When your goal is to accurately predict something, it's a no brainer to remove variables that will not help contribute to your model's performance.

Continued

Several quantitative approaches to identify the independent variable to include are summarized in the following bullet points.

- **Backward elimination** starts with the regression model that includes all predictors under consideration. For example, suppose the full model has 10 predictors $x_1, x_2, ..., x_{10}$. At each step in the model, predictors that contribute the least to model prediction are eliminated using a significance test. The least predictive feature is removed, and the model is rerun to reevaluate fit. The process continues until all variables remaining in the regression model are statistically significant. The criterion used to remove an insignificant variable is p-value > 0.05, but this value for the criterion can be adjusted up or down. The backward selection regression model stops when all predictors in the model are statistically significant.

- **Forward selection** begins by creating a separate regression model for each predictor. If there are ten predictors, then we will consider ten different models, each with one predictor. The predictor that has the best prediction score becomes the first predictor to be included in the forward selection model. The process is repeated for two variables by adding each of the remaining variables in combination with the variable chosen in the first step. The best two variables model next serves as the input for the next iteration to build the three variables set. The process continues until no additional variables improve the model prediction.

- **Stepwise selection** follows forward selection by adding a variable at each step, but also includes removing variables that no longer meet the threshold. Two criteria are typically applied with this approach. The first is when to add predictors to the model, and the second is when to remove variables from the model. An example of this criteria is to add the most significant variable and remove variables that are not significant at each iteration of the variable selection. Each step involves evaluating the remaining predictors not in the current regression model. Then, the next most significant predictors can be added if the significance still meets the threshold to remain in the model. The stepwise selection stops when the remaining predictors in a model satisfy the threshold to remain in the model.

Many software tools have the capability to perform regression analysis. For example, SPSS, RapidMiner, Python, R, and Excel software packages have the capabilities to execute regression. This chapter will introduce you to RapidMiner, which was identified by KDNuggets as one of the tools most often used for analytics.

Case Study: Need a Ride? Predicting Prices that Customers Are Willing to Pay for Ridesharing Services

Understanding the Business Problem

Since entering the market over 10 years ago, ride haling services have disrupted the consumer transportation industry. Companies such as Uber and Lyft offer customers a convenient and inexpensive transportation service in the palm of their hand—on a smartphone.

There are over 103 worldwide users of Uber each month, but in the U.S. alone over 35% of adults use ride-hailing services.[2] Even with their growing popularity, a recent study showed that Uber and Lyft contribute under 3% of the vehicle miles traveled (VMT) in major U.S. cities. The remaining 97% of travel is made up of personal and commercial vehicles.[3] Companies operating in this industry understand there is significant room for attracting new customers and enticing them to return.

While there are several reasons a customer might choose one ride service over another, one of the most common is related to the cost of the ride. Given this, how much are customers willing to pay?

Understanding the Dataset

The case data file has 19,160 records representing hypothetical rideshares from Lyft and Uber in the Boston area. The rideshare data has been matched with public weather data by location, day and time. The file rideshare.xlsx contains the data in Exhibit 5-14.

Exhibit 5-14 Data Dictionary

VARIABLE NAME	DESCRIPTION
Id (typeless)	A ride unique id for each observation
datetime (date)	Date and time of ride
hour (numerical)	Hour of day extracted from datetime
day (numerical)	Day of month extracted from datetime
month (numerical)	Month extracted from datetime
weekday (string)	Day of the week (Mon to Sun)
source (string)	Location of pickup
destination (string)	Location of drop-off
rideshare (string)	Name of ride sharing service (e.g., Lyft or Uber)
rideCategory (string)	Type of ride share service (e.g., shared, Uberpool)
price (numerical)	The total price of the ride
distance (numerical)	How good the condition is overall
surgeMultiplier (numerical)	Peak time price multiplier
weather (string)	The description of the weather (cloudy, rain, etc.)
temperature (numerical)	Temperature at the time and location of ride
precipProbability (numerical)	The likelihood of rain for a specific forecast period and location.
humidity (numerical)	Humidity at the time and location of ride

VARIABLE NAME	DESCRIPTION
windspeed (numerical)	Wind Speed at the time and location of ride
windGust (numerical)	Wind Gust measuring the increase in wind speed at the time and location of ride
ozone (numerical)	Ozone harmful level measuring air quality at the time and location of ride.

Data Preparation

Remember, an essential practice before starting with any analytics project is to first review and clean the dataset. Open the rideshare.xlsx file available with your book to examine the variable values in Excel. There are 19,160 records. Exhibit 5-15 shows a snapshot of the variables and records for 22 customer rides.

What does one row in the dataset represent? Each row of the data represents one customer. Two data sources have been combined using date and location: rider data including price, time of day, ride type, and public weather, including wind and temperature information.

You should also identify whether any variables seem unclear, or which variables (based on your understanding of the business problem) are likely to be the better predictors. Exhibit 5-15 will help in understanding variables and the records under each column.

A quick reminder: Click on Data, then Filter, as shown in Exhibit 5-15, to further understand variable categories under each column.

Exhibit 5-15

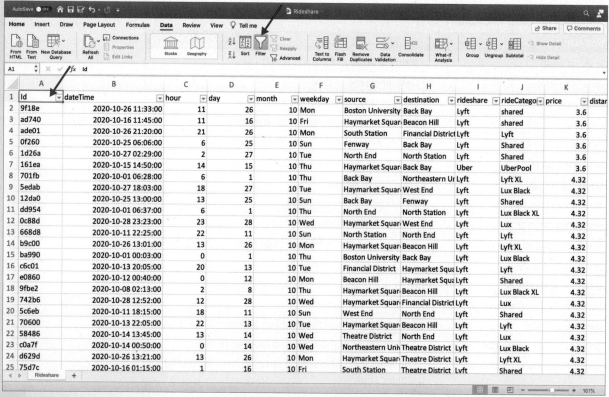

Microsoft Excel

After the initial review, are there any variables that need to be transformed? For example, variables such as date may be more useful if changed to represent hour, month, and day of the week, given the time-sensitive nature of the ride-sharing service.

The dataset rideshare.xlsx includes hour, day, month, and weekday (Exhibit 5-16). Click on cells C2, D2, E2, and F2 to review the equations used to calculate each of these fields. For example, in cell C2 we see the formula =Hour(B2), in cell D2 we see the formula =Day(B2), and so on. Each of these added fields are new variables (features) that will be used to build the predictive regression model.

Exhibit 5-16

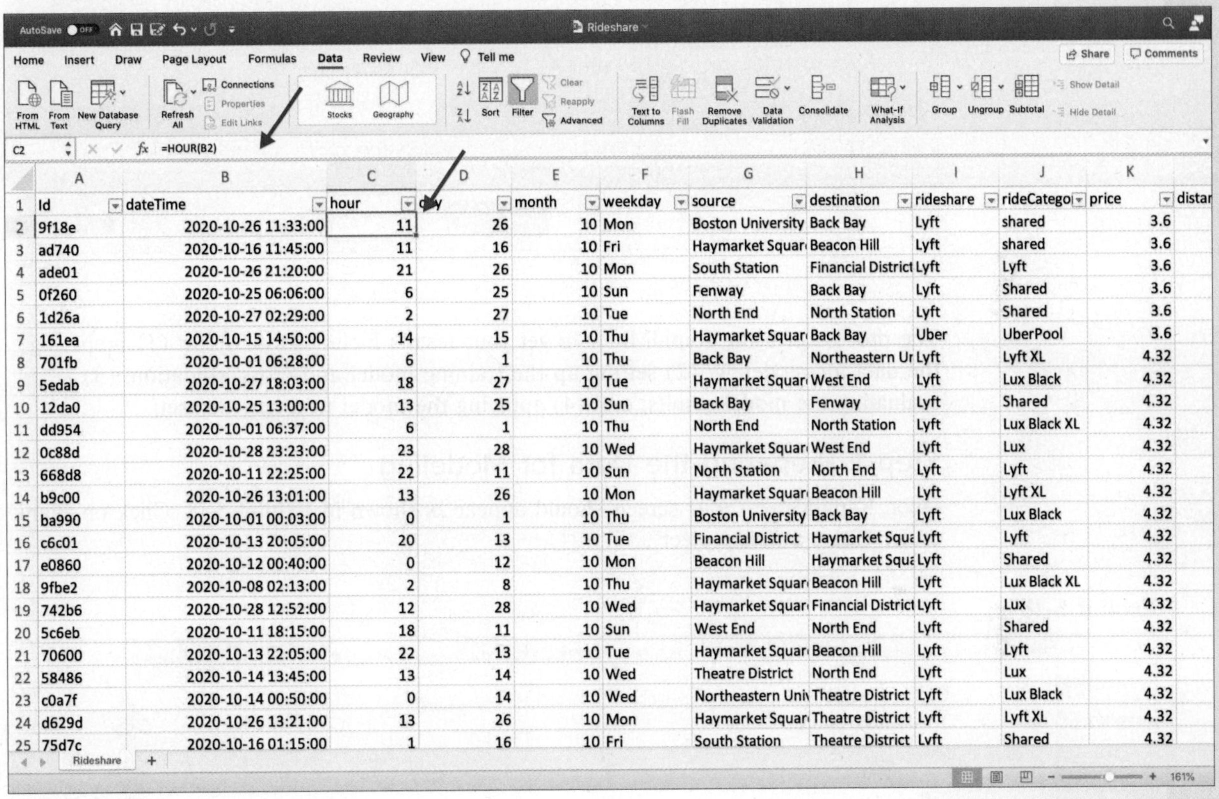

	Id	dateTime	hour	day	month	weekday	source	destination	rideshare	rideCategory	price	distar
2	9f18e	2020-10-26 11:33:00	11	26	10	Mon	Boston University	Back Bay	Lyft	shared	3.6	
3	ad740	2020-10-16 11:45:00	11	16	10	Fri	Haymarket Squar	Beacon Hill	Lyft	shared	3.6	
4	ade01	2020-10-26 21:20:00	21	26	10	Mon	South Station	Financial District	Lyft	Lyft	3.6	
5	0f260	2020-10-25 06:06:00	6	25	10	Sun	Fenway	Back Bay	Lyft	Shared	3.6	
6	1d26a	2020-10-27 02:29:00	2	27	10	Tue	North End	North Station	Lyft	Shared	3.6	
7	161ea	2020-10-15 14:50:00	14	15	10	Thu	Haymarket Squar	Back Bay	Uber	UberPool	3.6	
8	701fb	2020-10-01 06:28:00	6	1	10	Thu	Back Bay	Northeastern Ur	Lyft	Lyft XL	4.32	
9	5edab	2020-10-27 18:03:00	18	27	10	Tue	Haymarket Squar	West End	Lyft	Lux Black	4.32	
10	12da0	2020-10-25 13:00:00	13	25	10	Sun	Back Bay	Fenway	Lyft	Shared	4.32	
11	dd954	2020-10-01 06:37:00	6	1	10	Thu	North End	North Station	Lyft	Lux Black XL	4.32	
12	0c88d	2020-10-28 23:23:00	23	28	10	Wed	Haymarket Squar	West End	Lyft	Lux	4.32	
13	668d8	2020-10-11 22:25:00	22	11	10	Sun	North Station	North End	Lyft	Lyft	4.32	
14	b9c00	2020-10-26 13:01:00	13	26	10	Mon	Haymarket Squar	Beacon Hill	Lyft	Lyft XL	4.32	
15	ba990	2020-10-01 00:03:00	0	1	10	Thu	Boston University	Back Bay	Lyft	Lux Black	4.32	
16	c6c01	2020-10-13 20:05:00	20	13	10	Tue	Financial District	Haymarket Squa	Lyft	Lyft	4.32	
17	e0860	2020-10-12 00:40:00	0	12	10	Mon	Beacon Hill	Haymarket Squa	Lyft	Shared	4.32	
18	9fbe2	2020-10-08 02:13:00	2	8	10	Thu	Haymarket Squar	Beacon Hill	Lyft	Lux Black XL	4.32	
19	742b6	2020-10-28 12:52:00	12	28	10	Wed	Haymarket Squar	Financial District	Lyft	Lux	4.32	
20	5c6eb	2020-10-11 18:15:00	18	11	10	Sun	West End	North End	Lyft	Shared	4.32	
21	70600	2020-10-13 22:05:00	22	13	10	Tue	Haymarket Squar	Beacon Hill	Lyft	Lyft	4.32	
22	58486	2020-10-14 13:45:00	13	14	10	Wed	Theatre District	North End	Lyft	Lux	4.32	
23	c0a7f	2020-10-14 00:50:00	0	14	10	Wed	Northeastern Univ	Theatre District	Lyft	Lux Black	4.32	
24	d629d	2020-10-26 13:21:00	13	26	10	Mon	Haymarket Squar	Theatre District	Lyft	Lyft XL	4.32	
25	75d7c	2020-10-16 01:15:00	1	16	10	Fri	South Station	Theatre District	Lyft	Shared	4.32	

Microsoft Excel

Applying the Concepts

As you learned in Chapter 1, the RapidMiner software is one of the fastest-growing data analytics tools in the marketplace. In this example, you will learn how RapidMiner can be used to analyze the data displayed in the Excel spreadsheet using the linear regression model. To download RapidMiner, go to https://rapidminer.com/educational-program/ and register for a student academic account, as shown in Exhibit 5-17. The RapidMiner software works the same on Mac and Windows.

Once the program has been downloaded, open RapidMiner to start building the model.

Exhibit 5-17

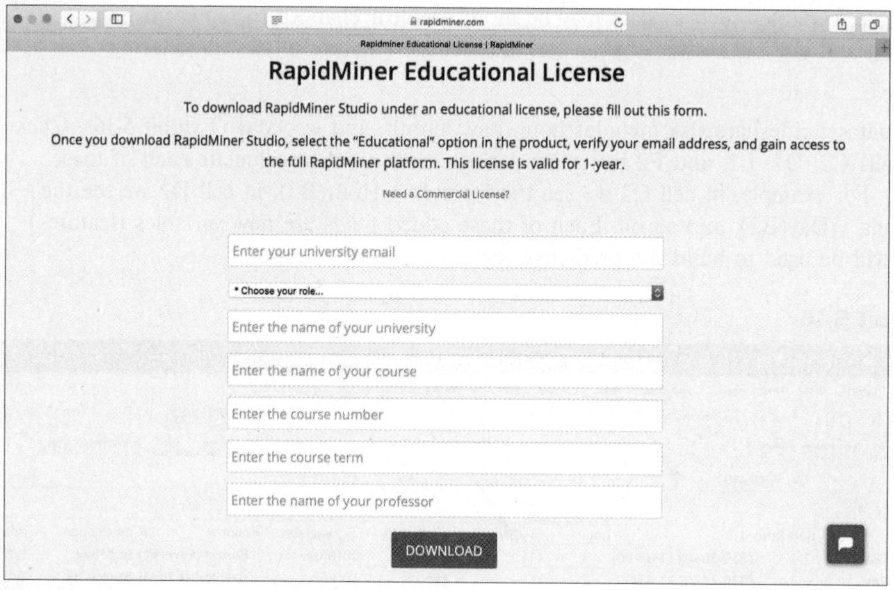

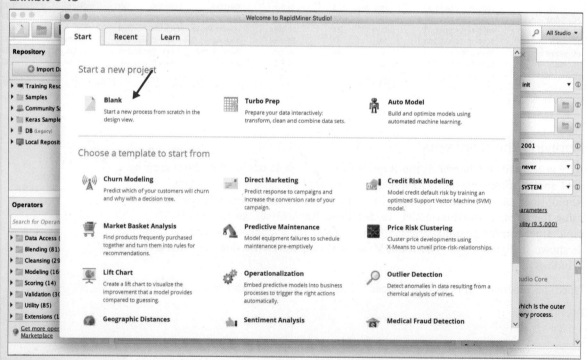

RapidMiner Educational License

To download RapidMiner Studio under an educational license, please fill out this form.

Once you download RapidMiner Studio, select the "Educational" option in the product, verify your email address, and gain access to the full RapidMiner platform. This license is valid for 1-year.

Need a Commercial License?

Enter your university email

* Choose your role...

Enter the name of your university

Enter the name of your course

Enter the course number

Enter the course term

Enter the name of your professor

DOWNLOAD

RapidMiner, Inc

The process of using RapidMiner to get your results includes four steps: (1) preparing the data for modeling; (2) setting up the training model and cross validation; (3) evaluating the model results; and (4) applying the model to a new dataset.

Step 1: Preparing the Data for Modeling

Open RapidMiner. Your screen should appear as shown in Exhibit 5-18. Click on Blank under "Start a new project".

Exhibit 5-18

RapidMiner, Inc

First, import the data into RapidMiner. Complete this step by clicking Import Data (Exhibit 5-19). To do so, click on My Computer and navigate to your folder where the data is saved.

Exhibit 5-19

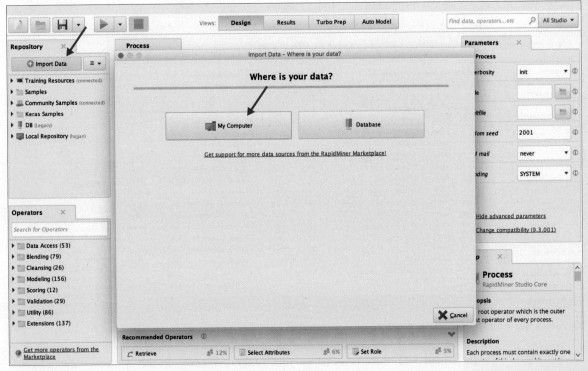

RapidMiner, Inc

Locate the Data for Chapter 5 and click on Rideshare.xlsx. Click on the file name, and then select →Next (Exhibit 5-20).

Exhibit 5-20

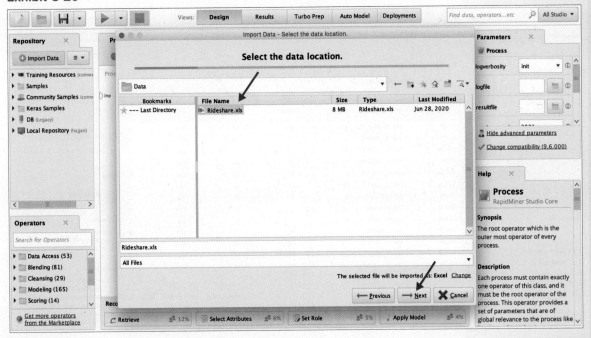

RapidMiner, Inc

Once the data is uploaded, your screen should look similar to Exhibit 5-21. Click →Next .

Exhibit 5-21

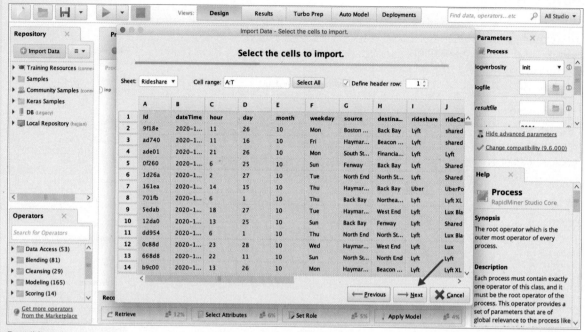

RapidMiner, Inc

In Exhibit 5-22, there is a Format your columns window. In this window, variables can be formatted. In addition, necessary changes can be made in the data type.

Notice the variable dateTime is interpreted as a data_time type. In contrast, the variables hour, day, and month are all interpreted as integers because they are whole numbers (e.g., 11,

Exhibit 5-22

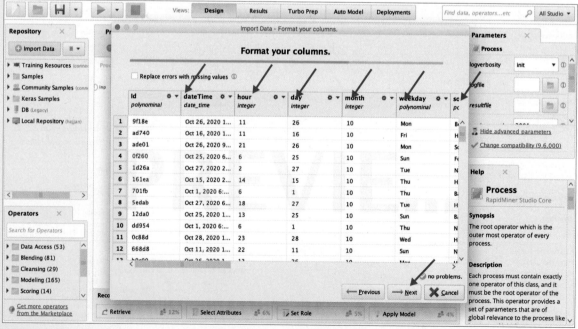

RapidMiner, Inc

26, 10). Both Id and weekday are read into RapidMiner as polynomial type (or string values). Review all the other variables and note the other data types in RapidMiner.

When you finish reviewing the data, click →Next , as shown at the bottom of Exhibit 5-22.

Determine in what folder on your computer the data will be stored. For this example, select Local Repository under data folder. Then, click ⚑ Finish , as shown in Exhibit 5-23.

Exhibit 5-23

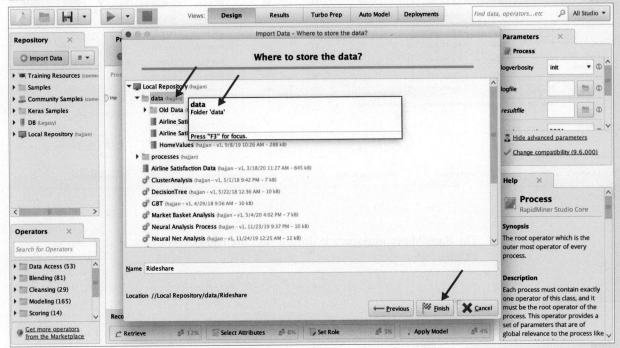

RapidMiner, Inc

The data is now read (or ingested) by RapidMiner and is available for review and analysis. Notice that the data in RapidMiner is referred to as ExampleSet with 19,160 examples and 20 variables (regular attributes) for the Rideshare dataset (see Exhibit 5-24).

In the top Views menu bar, click on Design (top of screen) to start building the model (Exhibit 5-24).

Exhibit 5-24

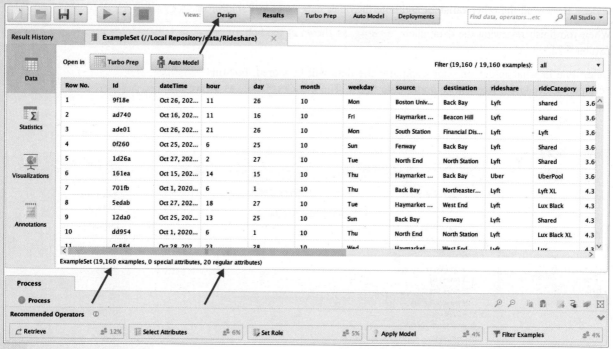

RapidMiner, Inc

The RapidMiner workspace is divided into five main default panels, as shown in Exhibit 5-25.

Exhibit 5-25

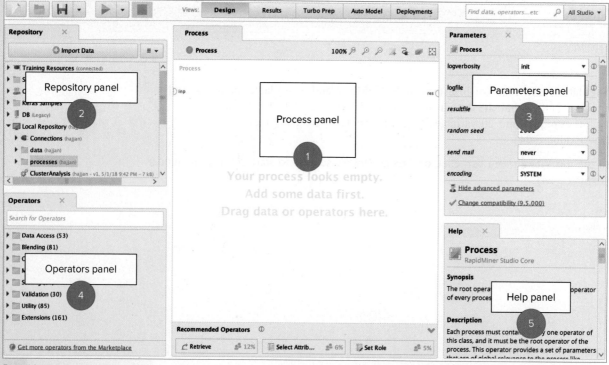

RapidMiner, Inc

If you close any of the panels during your setup, you can click on the View menu (top left; Exhibit 5-26) and select Restore Default View to reset the Design View to the default panel setup shown in Exhibit 5-26.

Exhibit 5-26

RapidMiner, Inc

To start building the model, import the data you just uploaded into the system to the process window. To do so, navigate to the Repository panel (the left side of the screen), and then in the Local Repository you will find the data folder, and below it the Rideshare dataset (see Exhibit 5-27).

Exhibit 5-27

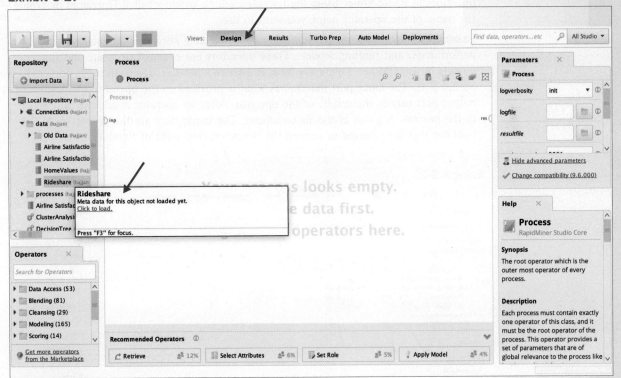

RapidMiner, Inc

Drag and drop the RideShare file to the Process panel, as shown in Exhibit 5-28.

Exhibit 5-28

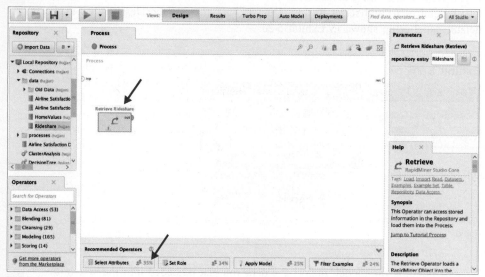

RapidMiner, Inc

At the bottom of the Process panel is a tab referred to as Recommended Operators. At any time, you can drag an operator from the Recommended Operators and drop it in the Process panel (Exhibit 5-29). Additionally, you can search for one of the 1,500 operators in Rapid-Miner using the lower-left search window called Operators by typing the name of the operator name you want to use.

Examples of operators include retrieving data, selecting attributes, evaluating analytical performance, and running models. These operators are essential to create and run models in RapidMiner. Operators have at least two ports. There is an input port and an output port. The input port determines what is provided to the operator, and the output port carries the results of the operator. After an operator is selected and added to the process, you can access its parameter. The parameters are the properties of the operator that are selected to control the operation (top right of Exhibit 5-29).

Exhibit 5-29

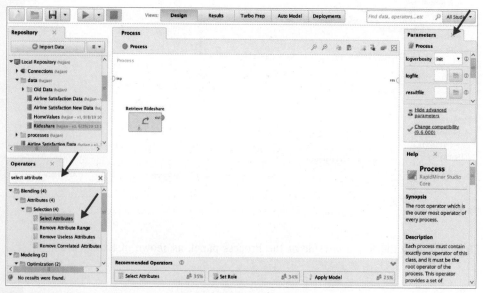

RapidMiner, Inc

Under the Operators panel, shown in the lower left corner of Exhibit 5-29, type "select attribute" in the Operators search window. You will see the Select Attributes operator appear under the Selection folder.

Under the Operators tab in the lower-left corner of the exhibit, locate the Select Attributes operator. Drag and drop it next to Retrieve Rideshare (Exhibit 5-30). Now, we are ready to connect the two operators. Hold your left mouse button down and drag the out port (out) from the Retrieve Rideshare over to the input port of Select Attributes (exa) (Exhibit 5-30). You will see a line is now connecting the two operators: the Retrieve Rideshare operator and the Select Attributes operator. At any time, you can remove this line by clicking on it and using the Delete key on your keyboard.

Next, click on the Select Attributes operator and review its Parameter panel on the top right side of the screen (Exhibit 5-30). Note, the first parameter under Select Attributes is called "attribute filter type." Click on the drop-down menu next to it and select subset. Using this subset parameter, you can select a subset of the attributes to include in the analysis.

Exhibit 5-30

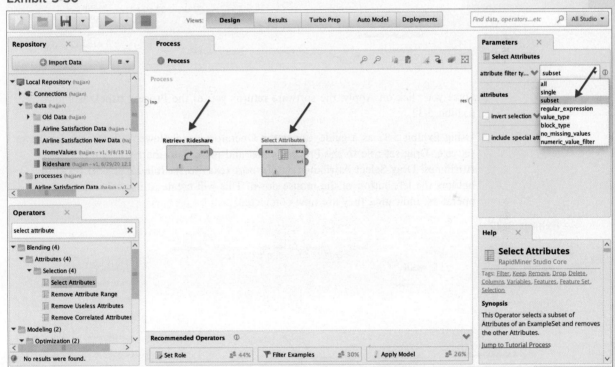

RapidMiner, Inc

Under parameters, a Select Attributes option appears (bottom right corner). Click on Select Attributes and you will see a Select Attributes window in the middle of your screen (see Exhibit 5-31). Now identify and start selecting the following attributes: day, distance, hour, humidity, month, ozone, precipProbability, price, surgeMultiplier, temperature, and weekday. These attributes are selected based on our knowledge of the variables and their likely importance in predicting the dependent variable (price).

Once you click on an attribute name, you can use the right arrow 🡢 to move specific attributes from the Attributes window on the left side to the Selected Attributes window on the right side. When you are finished selecting Attributes, click Apply (bottom of Exhibit 5-31). You can also use the Command key (for Mac) or Control key (for Windows) to select more than one attribute at the same time.

Exhibit 5-31

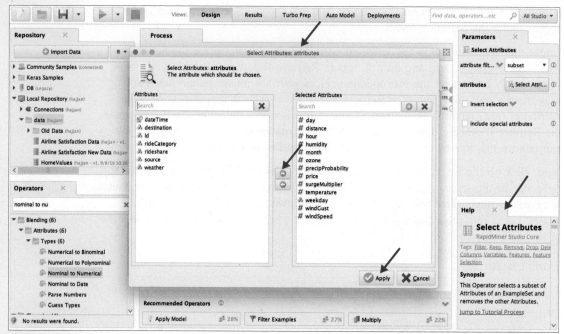

RapidMiner, Inc

Once you click on Apply, the software returns you to the Process panel, as shown in Exhibit 5-32.

Using Exhibit 5-32 as a guide, under the Operators panel (lower left corner) search for set role. Drag set role to the Process panel and place it to the right side of Select Attributes. Drag Select Attributes output port (exa) to set role input port (exa) by holding the left button of the mouse down. This will create a line between the two operators, indicating they are now connected.

Exhibit 5-32

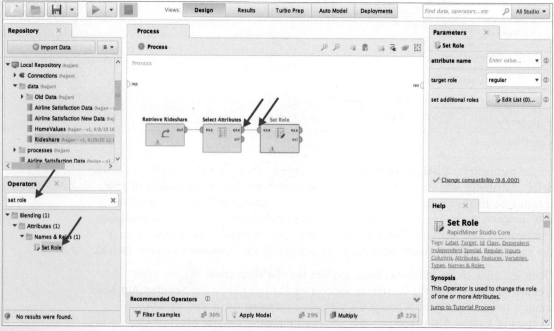

RapidMiner, Inc

Click set role processor and go to the Parameter panel (top right of screen). Under attribute name, click on the drop-down menu and select the dependent variable price (Exhibit 5-33).

Now click on target role (top right corner, below attribute name, Exhibit 5-33). Under this drop-down menu, there are several different possible roles for the variable selected. Now you must select the target role. In this case, select label using the drop-down menu target role to indicate that price is the target dependent variable.

Exhibit 5-33

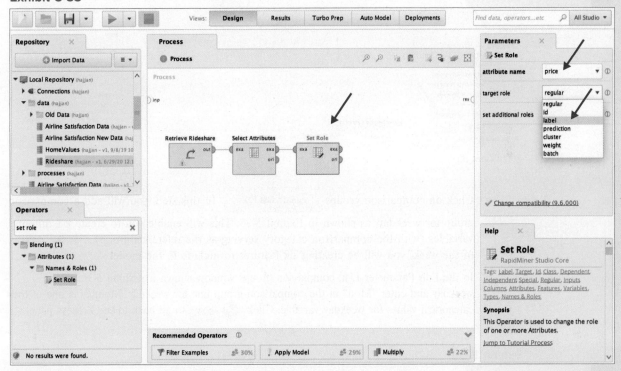

RapidMiner, Inc

In the next step, prepare variables to include in the predictive model. One of the variables (weekday) is measured as categorical. To use this variable in the model, you must convert it into numerical dummy-coded variables so you can run the linear regression model.

Under Operators (Exhibit 5-34; lower left corner), search for nominal to numerical. Drag nominal to numerical to the right side of set roles. Then, connect the output port (exa) from set roles to the input port (exa) on nominal to numerical. A line connecting the two operators will appear indicating the set roles operator is now able to pass on information to the nominal to numerical operator.

As mentioned earlier, the nominal to numerical operator is used to change any categorical variable into a dummy-coded variable.

Click on the nominal to numerical operator. The Parameters panel will appear at the top right corner of the screen (Exhibit 5-34). Under attribute, make sure attribute filter type has the default all selected, and under coding type, make sure dummy coding is selected. Now, check the box for use comparison groups.

Exhibit 5-34

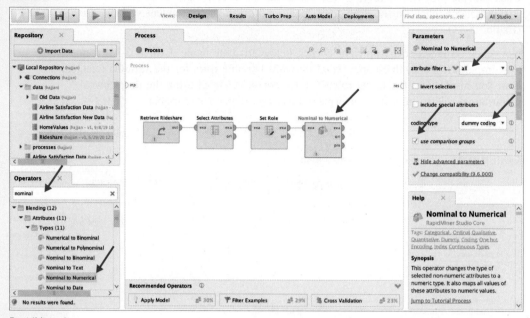

RapidMiner, Inc

Click on comparison groups ![Edit List (0)...] . In this step, you will add a comparison group for weekday, as shown in Exhibit 5-35. This will enable you to create k-1 dummy variables (with the comparison category serving as the reference group). For the days of the week, you will be creating six features to include in the model.

In the Edit Parameter List: comparison groups window shown in Exhibit 5-35, select weekday and enter "Mon" in the comparison group line for weekday. Monday is one of the categorical values for weekday variable. Click ![Apply] to go back to the Process panel.

Exhibit 5-35

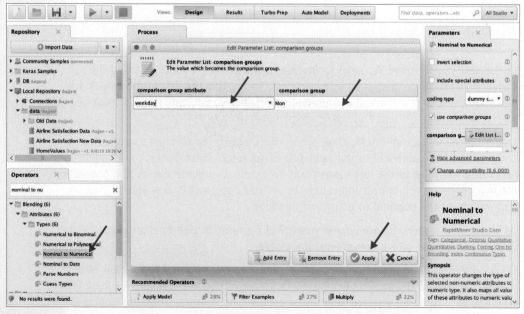

RapidMiner, Inc

Step 2: Setting Up the Training Model and Cross Validation

As you learned earlier in the chapter, different validation methods are available. To execute cross-validation for the model, the data will be randomly split into (k) subsets of the data. A single subset is then selected for validating the model (validation data)—the data subset that will be used to cross validate the model. For example, if the number of subsets is ten, then one subset is held out and becomes the validation test data, and the remaining nine subsets (k-1) are combined and used as the training data. This cross validation is repeated k times, with each of the k subsets used one time as the validation dataset. The (k) validation performance results from repeated procedures (in our example, the procedure is repeated ten times) are averaged to deliver a single estimate of the model's prediction performance.

To set up cross validation in this model, look in the Operators panel (Exhibit 5-36; lower left corner) and locate cross validation. Drag Cross Validation to the Process panel. Connect the nominal to numerical output port (exa) to Cross Validation's input port (exa). This will create a line between the two operators, indicating they are connected to share information.

Double-click on the Cross Validation processor to review its subprocesses.

Exhibit 5-36

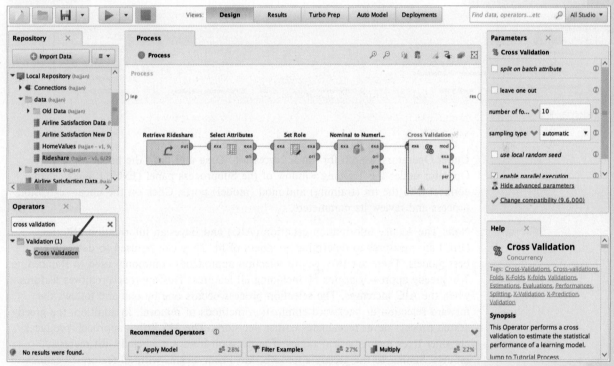

RapidMiner, Inc

When you double-click on the Cross Validation Operator, the content of Exhibit 5-37 becomes visible.

Note that the Cross Validation Operator is a nested operator. A nested operator means that several subprocesses are included within the operator (Exhibit 5-37). The Cross Validation Operator has two subprocesses: a training subprocess and a testing subprocess. The training subprocess is used for building a model (this subprocess learns which, if any, independent variables are good predictors). After the model is trained (good predictors are determined), it is then applied in the testing subprocess to see how well the model predicts the validation data subset.

Exhibit 5-37

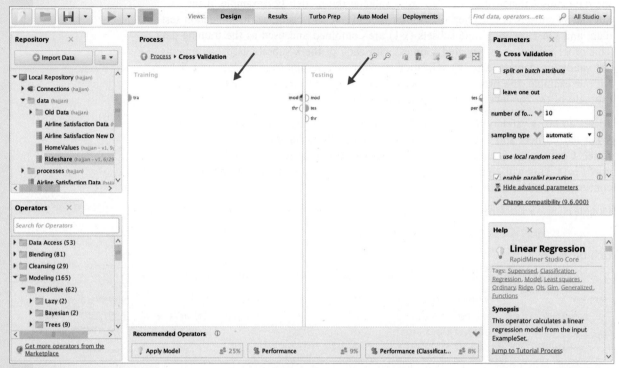

RapidMiner, Inc

Under Operators, search for linear regression. Drag and drop the linear regression Operator under the Training window of the Subprocess panel (Exhibit 5-38). Then, connect it to the tra (training) and mod (model) ports. Click on the linear regression process and review its parameters.

Note: The Akaike information criterion (AIC) and Bayesian information criterion (BIC) are measures to determine goodness of fit. They can be used to determine the best models. There are two feature selection approaches commonly used in RapidMiner. The greedy approach begins by including all features. This approach removes features when the AIC increases. The selection process occurs one by one and follows the forward selection or backward elimination methods of removal. In addition, the greedy search process never reevaluates earlier decisions. The M5 Prime approach produces classifier trees for numerical values. The decision trees are labeled with regression models. Similar to the greedy approach, M5 Prime begins with all features. Features consisting of the lowest standardized regression coefficients are considered for removal. The feature is eliminated if the step improves the AIC value. Both approaches continue until the AIC no longer improves.

M5 is a common method of feature selection and will be used in this example.

Exhibit 5-38

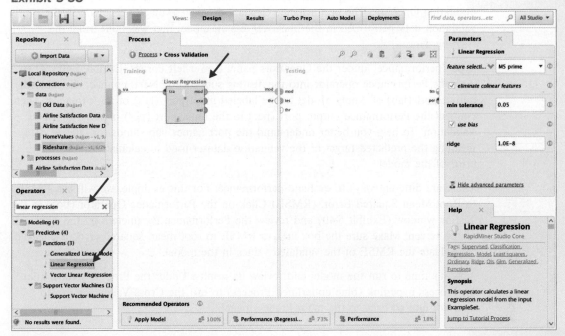

RapidMiner, Inc

When reviewing the Recommended Operators at the bottom of the screen, notice that
Apply Model is used 100% of the time after linear regression. Drag Apply Model
from the Recommended Operators option and drop it under Testing Subprocess
(Exhibit 5-39). Next, connect the output port (mod) from the Training area to the
input port (mod) on Apply Model. Then, connect the output port (tes) from the
Training area to the input port (unl) on Apply Model. Mod (Model) represents the
data in the validation dataset with a hidden dependent (target) variable. Now you are
ready to measure the predictive performance of the model.

Exhibit 5-39

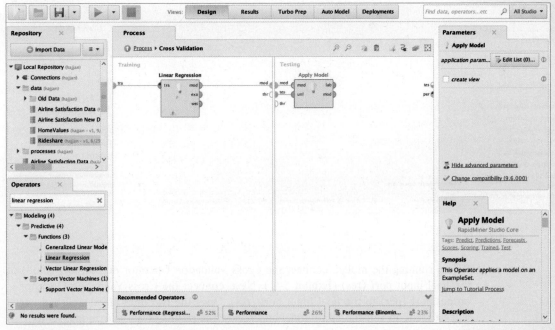

RapidMiner, Inc

To assess the performance of our regression model, we need to add the Performance evaluation Operator. The performance evaluation enables you to see how well the validation data performed in the linear regression model that was built using the training data.

Type "performance" under the Operators panel (lower left corner, Exhibit 5-40). Then, drag the Performance operator into the Testing subprocess. Next, connect the labeled output port (lab) of Apply Model to the labeled input port (lab) of Performance. Then, connect the Performance output port (per) to the input port (per) of the subprocess Validation. To help you better understand the port names, lab stands for labeled data, meaning the predicted target of the validation dataset used to calculate the RMSE to error of the model.

There are different ways to evaluate performance. For this example, we will use RMSE to Root Mean Squared Error. (RMSE) Click on the Performance Operator (box) in the Testing window (Exhibit 5-40) and review the Performance Parameters on the right side of the screen. Make sure the box next to RMSE to root mean squared error is checked to evaluate the RMSE of the validated values in the model.

Now it's time to run the model and review its results. Under the Process screen, click on Process hyperlink (blue underlined Process) to exit the Cross Validation nested operator and go back to the main Process panel.

Exhibit 5-40

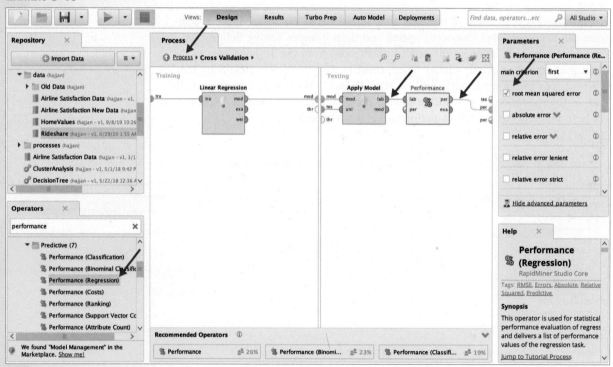

RapidMiner, Inc

Before running the model, connect the Cross Validation Operator output port (mod) to the final input port (res) (Exhibit 5-41). Next, connect the Cross Validation Operator output port (per) to the final input port (res). Once the two lines are established, you will be ready to run the final model and review the results of all your model setup work.

Exhibit 5-41

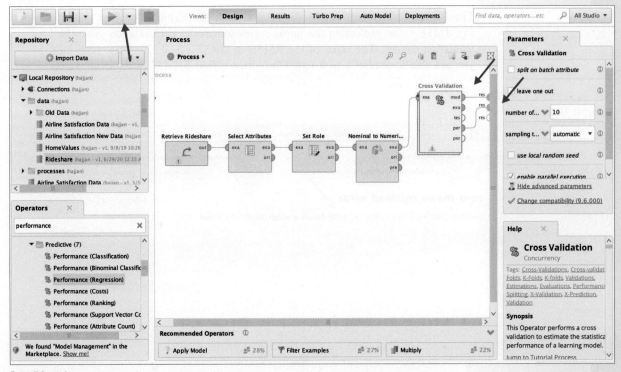

RapidMiner, Inc

To run the model, click ▶ in the View menu bar. The results will take a few minutes to run, depending on your computer processor speed. Exhibit 5-42 shows the Cross Validation process at this point is 30% completed.

Exhibit 5-42

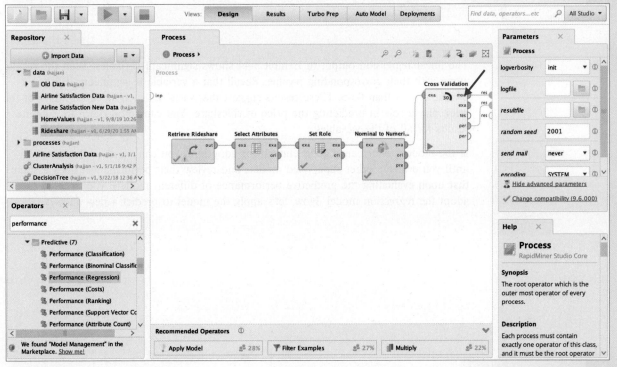

RapidMiner, Inc

Step 3: Evaluating the Model Results

The Performance Vector output should now look like Exhibit 5-43. The output shows the RMSE value, indicating the linear regression model performance using the validation dataset. The value of the RMSE is 11.437 +/− 0.130. This result means you are able to predict a new Lyft/Uber price within $11.437 of its actual value.

Exhibit 5-43

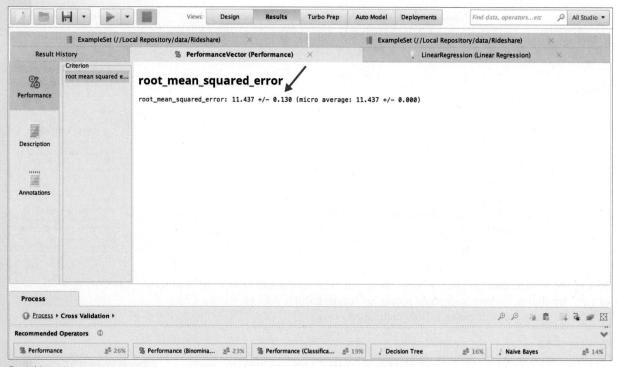

RapidMiner, Inc

The linear regression output in Exhibit 5-44 shows significant variables. Scan the results along with their corresponding p-value. Recall that a variable is significant if it has a p-value of less than 0.05. These results suggest that variables such as certain days of the week play a role in predicting the price of rideshare. You can scroll down to examine results for all of the variables.

Is the model performance good enough for adoption? You can't answer this question until you evaluate other supervised models and review their performance. Let's assume that upon evaluating the predictive performance of different models, you decided to adopt the regression model. Now, let's apply the model to predict a new dataset.

Exhibit 5-44

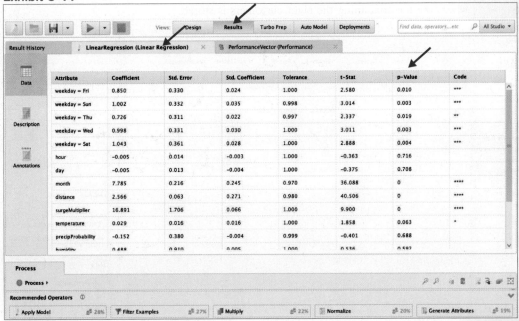

Attribute	Coefficient	Std. Error	Std. Coefficient	Tolerance	t-Stat	p-Value	Code
weekday = Fri	0.850	0.330	0.024	1.000	2.580	0.010	***
weekday = Sun	1.002	0.332	0.035	0.998	3.014	0.003	***
weekday = Thu	0.726	0.311	0.022	0.997	2.337	0.019	**
weekday = Wed	0.998	0.331	0.030	1.000	3.011	0.003	***
weekday = Sat	1.043	0.361	0.028	1.000	2.888	0.004	***
hour	−0.005	0.014	−0.003	1.000	−0.363	0.716	
day	−0.005	0.013	−0.004	1.000	−0.375	0.708	
month	7.785	0.216	0.245	0.970	36.088	0	****
distance	2.566	0.063	0.271	0.980	40.506	0	****
surgeMultiplier	16.891	1.706	0.066	1.000	9.900	0	****
temperature	0.029	0.016	0.016	1.000	1.858	0.063	*
precipProbability	−0.152	0.380	−0.004	0.999	−0.401	0.688	
humidity	0.488	0.910	0.005	1.000	0.536	0.592	

RapidMiner, Inc

Step 4: Applying the Model to New Dataset

The model has been created and validated using historical data with a known target variable. Now it's time to apply the linear regression model to a new dataset with no known target. As an example, assume there are eight new rides. The objective is to use the parameters developed in training the model to predict how much the customer will pay.

The first step is to import the new data that has no price (no target variable) information. In RapidMiner, this data is referred to as unlabeled data. To import the new data, click on Import Data (Exhibit 5-45).

Exhibit 5-45

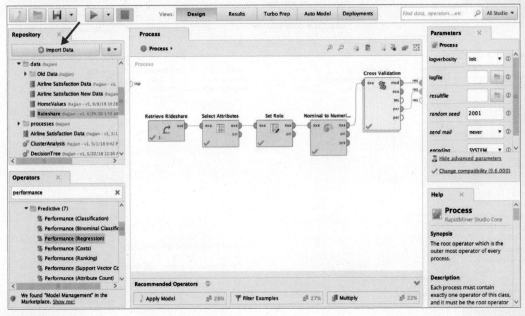

RapidMiner, Inc

After clicking on Import Data, click on My Computer (Exhibit 5-46) and navigate to where the file containing the eight customers is stored.

Exhibit 5-46

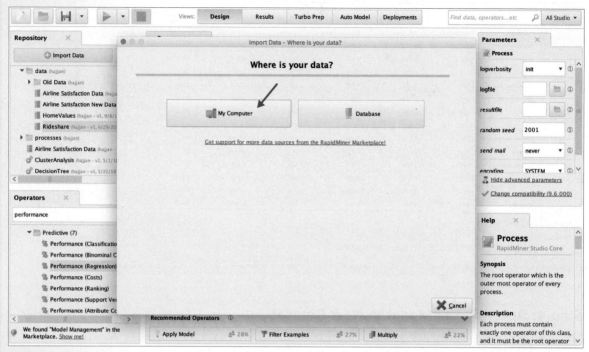

RapidMiner, Inc

Add the file Rideshare New Data.xlsx available with your textbook (Exhibit 5-47). The data contains new customers with the same variables as in the original model.

Exhibit 5-47

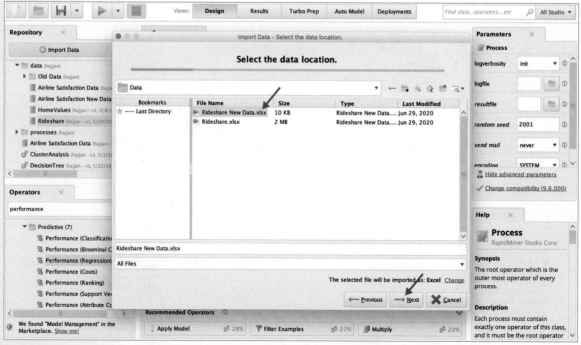

RapidMiner, Inc

Using a process similar to what we followed earlier to upload the training data file, the new data can be previewed as seen in Exhibit 5-48. After reviewing and verifying the data, click ⟶ Next.

Exhibit 5-48

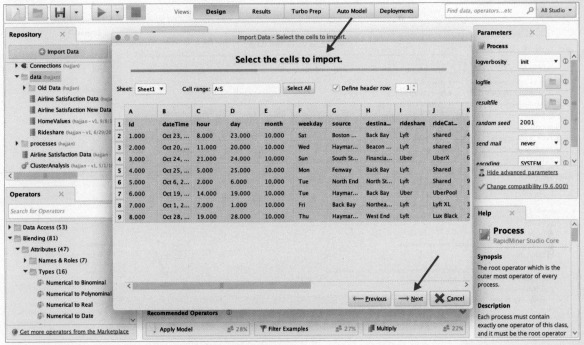

RapidMiner, Inc

Review the type of variables, as shown in Exhibit 5-49.

Exhibit 5-49

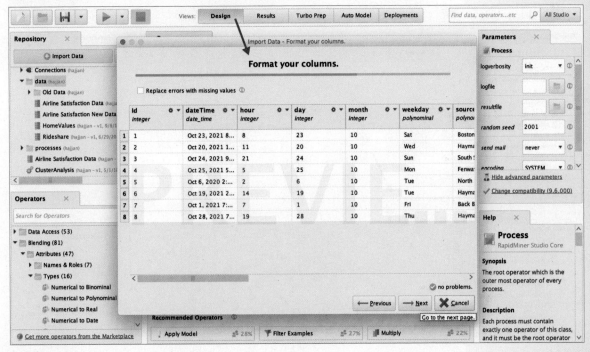

RapidMiner, Inc

Specify where the data will be stored in the data repository. For this example, select the data folder under Local Repository. Then, click ⚑ Finish, as shown in Exhibit 5-50.

Exhibit 5-50

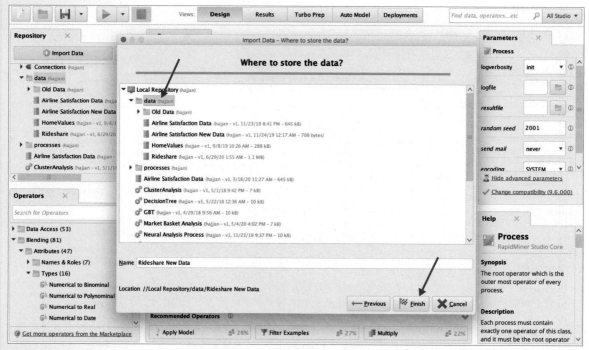

RapidMiner, Inc

Next, drag the Rideshare New Data from the Local Repository to the Process window, as shown in Exhibit 5-51.

Exhibit 5-51

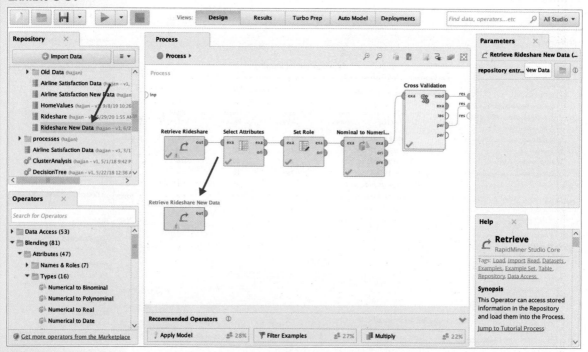

RapidMiner, Inc

Under Operators (lower left corner), drag and drop the nominal to numerical to the process screen (Exhibit 5-52). Similar to the first data set, the categorical variables will need to be converted into dummy codes because the linear regression does not accept text values. Next, connect the output port (out) on the Retrieve Rideshare New Data to the input port (exa) on the nominal to numerical.

Exhibit 5-52

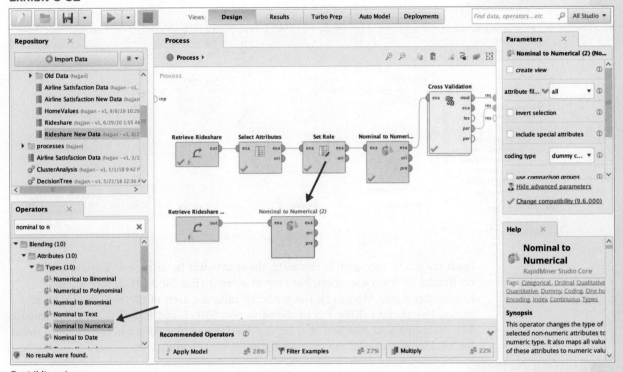

RapidMiner, Inc

Now, look under the Operators panel again (Exhibit 5-53). From the Recommended Operator (lower bottom of screen), add the Apply Model.

Next, connect the output port (exa) from nominal to numerical to the input port on the Apply Model (unl). Recall that port (exa) stands for example dataset being passed on, and port (unl) means data that dependent (target) variable or label is not present in the new dataset (Exhibit 5-53). Connect the Cross Validation Operator output port (mod) to the input port (mod) on the Apply Model. This will ensure the regression model equation will be used to calculate a prediction score for the eight new rides. Now, the final step is to connect the Apply Model output port (lab) to the input port (res) line to obtain the final results.

To execute the model, click Run ▶ in the View menu bar at the top left. The results will take only a few seconds to run.

Exhibit 5-53

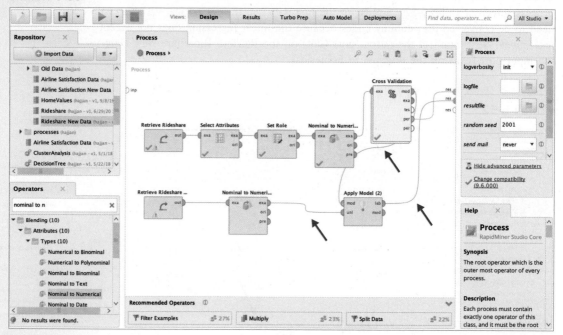

RapidMiner, Inc

Once the model execution is complete, the results will be displayed. You can click on Results on the Views menu bar (top of screen) (Exhibit 5-54). Under the tab ExampleSet Apply Model (2), the predicted value for each of the eight new rides is shown. For example, Ride 1 is predicted to cost $20.17, and Ride 7 is predicted to cost $92. Note that your numbers may be slightly different from those in the exhibits, given the random selection of the training and validation datasets.

Exhibit 5-54

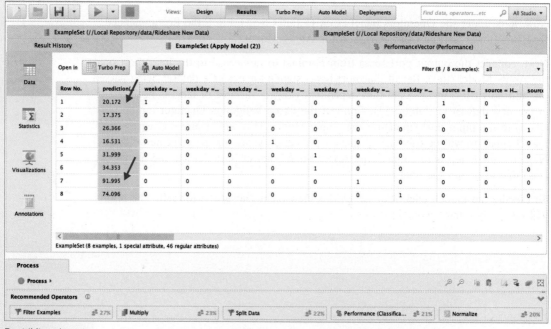

RapidMiner, Inc

Now, click to save your model (Exhibit 5-55). Name it "LinearRegression Model" and click ✓ OK .

Exhibit 5-55

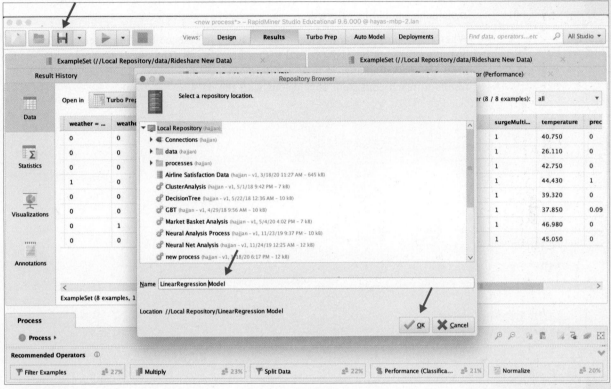

RapidMiner, Inc

Insights Learned from Applying the Concepts

Many useful marketing problems can be solved with linear regression analysis. In fact, linear regression is a commonly used model, given its ease of use and explainability. In this case, what insights were revealed?

The goal of this case was to predict price per ride. Results from this model would tell you the cost a customer might pay. There are different decisions that could be made to help meet customer needs and wants. First, predicting price per ride could help the company maintain the right prices at the right time. If the cost is too expensive, customers might search for alternative options, so it is important that price reflects what a customer is willing to pay. Predicting price per ride also allows ridesharing services to support their drivers. This information can help drivers plan the best times to work and maximize their income. Ridesharing services could also use the information to confirm that there are plenty of drivers available during peak or higher cost times.

Other things to consider include how rideshare information and weather data were combined to create a predictive model. How could revenue be increased for each of the customers? Would more data and additional variables provide better model performance? It is important to remember that the performance of the model needs to be evaluated by comparing the linear regression results to the performance of other modeling techniques, such as neural network and gradient boosted tree model. When comparing several models, the one that has the lowest RMSE and is the most explainable should be selected.

When developing a RapidMiner model, you are in essence building a template of operators that can be easily reused with a new dataset. Therefore, developing the model saves the marketing analyst time in future analyses and improves the reproducibility of results to reach consistent conclusions with the data.

Summary of Learning Objectives and Key Terms

LEARNING OBJECTIVES

Objective 5.1   Explain simple and multiple linear regression models.

Objective 5.2   Define a predictive regression model.

Objective 5.3   Differentiate between accuracy measures for predictive performance.

Objective 5.4   Assess predictive regression performance.

Objective 5.5   Discuss modeling of catagorical variables.

Objective 5.6   Discuss model independent variable selection.

KEY TERMS

Backward elimination

Dependent (target) variable (Y)

Dummy coding

Feature selection

Forward selection

Independent (predictor or feature) variable (X)

Linear regression

Mean Absolute Error (MAE)

Mean Absolute Percentage Error (MAPE)

Multicollinearity

Multiple regression

Numerical variable

Ordinary least squares (OLS)

Overfitting

R^2

Regression modeling

Residuals

Root Mean Squared Error (RMSE)

Simple linear regression

Stepwise selection

Test data

Training data

Validation data

Discussion and Review Questions

1. What is a simple linear regression?
2. How is multiple regression different from simple linear regression?
3. Explain how predictive regression performance is assessed.
4. Name some techniques used for selecting features to use in a model.

Critical Thinking and Marketing Applications

1. Locate an article on a struggling business. Identify a business problem from the article. List 15 features that could be helpful in predicting a target variable.
2. Use the features identified in question 1. Draw two different models that include features and a target variable. The first model should be developed using all of the 15 features that could predict the target variable. The second model should be limited to the top five features that could predict the target variable following a qualitative analysis.

References

1. Joseph F. Hair, Barry J. Babin, Rolph E. Anderson, and William C. Black, *Multivariate Data Analysis*, 8th edition (Cengage Learning, UK, 2019); and Joseph F. Hair, Michael Page, and Niek Brunsveld, *Essentials of Business Research Methods*, 4th edition (Routledge, 2021); **2.** https://investor.uber.com/news-events/news/press-release-details/2019/Uber-Announces-Results-for-Third-Quarter-2019/default.aspx https://www.wired.com/story/uber-lyft-ride-hail-stats-pew-research/ https://www.pewresearch.org/fact-tank/2019/01/04/more-americans-are-using-ride-hailing-apps/; **3.** https://www.prnewswire.com/news-releases/new-study-finds-over-97-of-vehicle-miles-traveled-in-major-us-cities-are-completed-by-personal-and-commercial-vehicles-300896095.html https://drive.google.com/file/d/1FIUskVkj9lsAnWJQ6kLhAhNoVLjfFdx3/view

6 Neural Networks

LEARNING OBJECTIVES

6.1 Define neural networks.

6.2 Identify and compare various uses for neural networks.

6.3 Explain the elements of a neural network.

6.4 Investigate how neural networks function.

6.5 Review important considerations when using neural networks.

ra2studio/Shutterstock

6.1 Introduction to Neural Networks

Which customers are likely to purchase a product or service following exposure to a digital marketing campaign? How much will a customer spend? These types of prediction or forecasting questions can be examined using a number of methods for analyzing data. For example, answers to some of these questions might be obtained by using predictive linear regression. Recall from Chapter 5 that regression is the appropriate method when the predictive relationships are linear. Linear regression could identify the relationship between the number of times a customer visits a website and whether they are likely to make a purchase. But other relationships might be non-linear in nature, such as examining seasonal visits to a website and the likelihood of a purchase. In this situation, a non-linear method such as neural networks can provide more accurate answers to these questions. **Neural networks** are algorithms that are trained to recognize patterns in data that are non-linear.

The logic of neural networks is based on patterns identified by observing biological activities in the human brain. Brains have networks of neurons (connections) that transfer information. The neurons learn from past experiences and use this knowledge to solve problems. For example, a brain recognizes a chair is in fact something to sit on based upon the learned knowledge of selected experiences. A similar process occurs within a neural network. That is, relationships (networks) between data, and the learned patterns are applied to solve complex problems.

PRACTITIONER CORNER

Stephen Brobst | Chief Technology Officer at Teradata

Stephen Brobst

Stephen Brobst is the Chief Technology Officer for Teradata Corporation. His expertise is in the identification and development of opportunities for the strategic use of technology in competitive business environments. Over the past 30 years, Stephen has been involved in numerous engagements in which his combined expertise in business strategy and high-end parallel systems has been used to develop frameworks for analytics and machine learning to leverage information for strategic advantage. Clients with whom he has worked include leaders such as eBay, Staples, Fidelity Investments, General Motors Corporation, Kroger Company, Wells Fargo Bank, Walmart, AT&T, Verizon, T-Mobile, CVS Health, Metropolitan Life Insurance, VISA International, Vodafone, Blue Cross Blue Shield, Nationwide Insurance, American Airlines, Mayo Clinic, and many more.

Stephen has particular expertise in the deployment of solutions for maximizing the value of customer relationships through use of advanced customer relationship management techniques with omni-channel deployment. Stephen is a TDWI Fellow and has been on the faculty of The Data Warehousing Institute since 1996. During Barack Obama's first term, he was also appointed to the Presidential Council of Advisors on Science and Technology (PCAST) in the working group on Networking and Information Technology Research and Development (NITRD), where he worked on development of the Big Data strategy for the U.S. government. In 2014, he was ranked by ExecRank as the #4 CTO in the United States (behind the CTOs from Amazon.com, Tesla Motors, and Intel) out of a pool of 10,000+ CTOs.

Continued

Q With technology and analytics advancing at such a rapid pace, many companies have established interdepartmental teams. These teams eliminate silos throughout the organization and reduce communication inefficiencies by bringing together a variety of experts. As a result, interdepartmental collaboration is critical to successfully achieving business goals. In this case, however, collaboration is more than the concept of working with other people. These interdepartmental teams possess different types of knowledge from a variety of fields. While this knowledge creates a powerful team, understanding discipline-specific terminology (e.g., information technology, marketing, data science) and communicating effectively can be challenging.

What elements are most important for marketers to understand when engaging in conversations or collaborating with experts in the fields of information technology or data science about advanced analytics such as with neural networks?

A The important thing to understand for a marketing person is that there are many different algorithms that can be used to predict customer behaviors. Moreover, no one algorithm will be the right choice for all types of behaviors. It is also important to understand that there is an ability to make tradeoffs in the accuracy of the models as they are deployed. There are different kinds of "wrong" when deploying predictive models, and marketers need to understand the difference between false positives and false negatives, as well as the expected value outcomes related to different scenarios, to make the right tradeoffs during deployment. Defining models that create

outcomes that are actionable is essential. Marketers must think about how the output of a model will be used to influence business processes and actions taken within the company.

Q Neural networks can be a complex method for modeling data. Because the use of neural networks continues to increase, the area remains important for marketers to grasp a basic understanding of it. What advice do you have for marketers when first learning about neural networks?

A Do not be seduced by the hype. Although neural networks represent a very important tool for increasing accuracy for certain scenarios, they are not a panacea. Understand where neural networks add value and where other techniques will be more appropriate. For example, linear mathematical models are much cheaper to execute for most predictions and can be nearly as accurate with more transparency than neural networks in many cases. Think about using deep learning and traditional machine (shallow) learning as complements to yield cost-effective predictive capabilities.

Q Why might neural networks be adopted over other advanced analytics methods such as regression and decision trees?

A They would be used when data is highly dimensional and/or dirty/incomplete. In addition, neural networks should only be considered when very large training sets are available (orders of magnitude larger than what is required for linear regression, for example).

Continued to page 188

6.2 How Are Neural Networks Used in Practice?

Marketers use neural network technology to identify patterns and make accurate predictions. Neural networks can aid marketers in predicting customer behavior, understanding buyer segmentation, developing brand strategies, optimizing inventory, forecasting sales, improving marketing automation, developing digital content, and much more.

Their flexibility in application and the prediction effectiveness of neural networks have enabled them to be successfully deployed in a variety of marketing contexts. The following are just a few of their uses, along with examples of how companies employed them.

- **Classify new customers by their potential profitability when planning direct marketing strategies.** Microsoft used BrainMaker, a neural network software, to determine which customers are most likely to open their direct mail based on past purchase behavior.[1] Using data from 20 direct mail campaigns, the neural network trained itself to examine the impact of 25 features and develop recommended solutions. The results almost doubled customers' response rates to 8.2 percent, which in turn, reduced direct marketing costs by 35 percent. Estimating the number of customers likely to purchase a product from exposure to a marketing campaign offers many practical insights. Companies can use the information to improve conversion rates for specific marketing campaigns, to adjust communications to target segments more closely, and to reallocate marketing budgets toward more profitable opportunities, to mention a few.

- **Generate customized digital content.** Under Armour has a health-tracking mobile application called Record.[2] The app collects health-related data from a variety of sources, such as wearable devices, manually entered user data, and other third-party applications. The data includes sleeping patterns, workouts, nutrition, and related information that is used in a neural network to develop customized digital content for its app users.

- **Predict lead scoring.** DialogTech provides neural network–driven marketing analytics solutions to manage customer inbound call centers.[3] The collected data includes incoming caller objectives, interactions with the salesperson, and conversation outcomes. The solution predicts a lead score of incoming customer service calls to improve the quality of customer phone calls and develop solutions for future sales opportunities.

- **Personalize customer experiences.** The Proctor & Gamble brand Olay has a mobile application that enables customers to obtain skincare assessments.[4] The app examines the customer's image to determine potential skin issues and then recommends specific products to address areas of concern. Customers are treated to a personalized experience, and specialized recommendations are tailored to their needs. The digital interaction mimics an in-store transaction, while allowing customers to remain in the comfort of their home.

- **Entice customers to visit a brick-and-mortar store.** Cricket Wireless works with Cognitiv[5] to increase in-store visits during the holiday season. Cognitiv uses mobile phone location data from current Cricket stores' customers to train the neural network. The solutions predict the likelihood of non-Cricket customers visiting the store and are used to develop digital advertising campaigns. Using the Cognitiv recommendations, the cost per customer visit was reduced and in-store visits were increased.

- **Determine customer lifetime value and defined customer segments.** ASOS, an online retailer in the UK, is a leader in AI adoption.[6] ASOS uses neural networks to analyze customer behavior that occurs on the website to predict the value of a customer. The prediction method provides a score indicating whether online users will be purchasers or non-purchasers. The ASOS neural network method can target users with specific promotions that increase the likelihood of future purchases.

- **Increase new customers that request online product quotes.** An automotive insurance company hired Cognitiv[7] to apply their deep learning platform, Neuralmind, to drive new customers to log on to their website and complete an online insurance quote. The results were used to examine digital marketing patterns and website impressions with strategies to predict purchases.

Create products or make product and service recommendations. Netflix uses neural networks to recommend movies to subscribers.[8] In addition, neural networks develop insights to improve production decisions and procurement of relevant movies.

Analyze audience sentiment to alter film stories. Disney collects data using cameras to execute sentiment analysis to better understand audience reactions to films.[9] The information enables Disney to understand how the audience is processing and reacting to films. These camera-executed sentiment insights are used to make changes to films and will soon be applied to other aspects of the business, such as theme parks and restaurants.

Acquiring and retaining satisfied, loyal customers is critical to maintaining financial stability. Using neural networks in marketing contexts offers new insights to achieve this objective.

Continued from page 186

PRACTITIONER CORNER

Stephen Brobst | Chief Technology Officer at Teradata

Q Several examples of companies using neural networks have been introduced in this chapter. In which marketing scenarios might neural networks be most beneficial? For example, are there certain marketing use cases that might benefit from the use of neural networks?

A When data is highly dimensional, the use of multi-layer neural networks will be more effective than traditional machine learning in a majority of cases. The hidden layers in the multi-layer neural networks provide a transformation capability against complex datasets that is more effective than purely linear mathematical models. In addition, if data is dirty and/or incomplete, then the use of deep learning with multi-layer learning networks will generally be more robust in dealing with "noisy" data than traditional machine learning. Predicting product demand and predicting fraud are the two most commonly deployed uses where multi-layer neural networks have delivered proven business value.

Continued to page 195

6.3 What Are the Basic Elements of a Neural Network?

Neural networks are layered structures. The neural network shown in Exhibit 6-1 consists of an **input layer**, a **hidden layer**, and **output layer**. Each pattern in one layer connects to a pattern in another layer. The data is entered into the neural network analysis in the **input layer**. The hidden layer sits in between the input and output layers. Calculations are performed in the **hidden layer** to produce weights from the input layer. Information from the hidden layer is then transferred to the next hidden layer or output layer. In the **output layer**, the model arrives at a prediction. Algorithms within each layer modify the data patterns to produce the outcomes requested by the analyst.

The input layer in Exhibit 6-1 represents some general customer demographics, including age and location and whether they were exposed to a digital marketing campaign. This layer consists of customer information that potentially influences whether customers will make a purchase or not, which is identified in the output layer.

Exhibit 6-1 Basic Terminology of Neural Networks

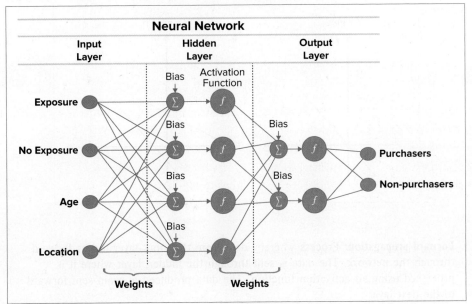

The overall neural network represents a classification problem. A marketing manager wants to predict customers that are most likely to make a purchase. The purpose is to classify the customers into two groups: purchasers and non-purchasers. In this case, the neural network has two output layers. However, some software will produce only one outcome node (e.g., purchasers). Input layers send values to the hidden layer, which in turn processes the data and sends the predicted results to the output layer (purchasers or non-purchasers).

There are some important terms to be familiar with to understand how neural networks function. These relevant terms are explained next.

- **Neurons or nodes:** A set of inputs (features) that are multiplied by their weights. To do so, the values are summed and applied to what is referred to as an activation function. The result is to convert the inputs into a single output.
- **Inputs:** Values representing features (variables) from the dataset that pass information to the next layer via connections.
- **Connections:** Transmit information from one neuron to another. Each network consists of connected neurons and each connection is weighted.
- **Weights:** Determines how important each neuron is. Connections between the neuron layers are assigned a weight. Features that are important in predicting the output have larger weights. In contrast, less important features have smaller weights. Weights are produced in the hidden layers.
- **Learning weight:** Determines the amount of adjustment made to the weights in the network.
- **Learning rate:** Determines the speed at which the model can arrive at the most accurate solution. The learning rate consists of positive values that generally range between 0 and 1.
- **Hidden layer:** Calculations are performed in the hidden layer to produce weights from the input layer. The weights are then transferred to the next hidden layer or output layer.
- **Outputs:** Where the model arrives at a prediction. The output is calculated as:

$$\text{Output} = \text{sum (weights} \times \text{inputs)} + \text{bias}$$

Exhibit 6-2 Basic Relationships with and without Bias

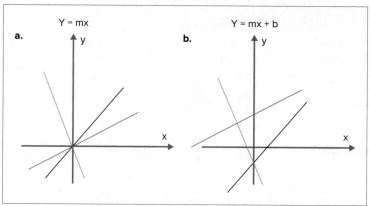

- **Forward propagation:** Process whereby data from the input layer moves forward through the network. The data is sent through the hidden layer where it is processed using an activation function. The data produced is again sent forward to the next layer.

- **Backpropagation:** Transmits the total loss back into the neural network to understand the amount of loss from each neuron. Using this information, weights are then adjusted to reflect the loss. Nodes with higher error rates are given lower weights, and those with lower error rates are given higher weights.

- **Biases:** The constant value given to the weighted input of each node. This constant value changes the weighted sum of the inputs, which in turn, adjusts the output. If bias is absent, then the neuron might not be activated. As a result, the neuron's information would not be passed to the next layer.

Bias is learned by the model and helps to create the best model fit for the data. Exhibit 6-2 shows a simple illustration of how bias works in a neural network. Consider Exhibit 6-2a ($Y = mx$). The model will try to fit the data, but the lines are always forced to pass through the origin (0,0) as a result of the equation $Y = mx$. Bias creates flexibility in the model, so adjustments can be made to improve the model. It can be thought of as the intercept b in a line equation shown in Exhibit 6-2b ($Y = mx + b$). It makes it possible to move the model freely (up or down, left or right) along the x and y axes. Thus, the model has the flexibility to provide the best fit for the data and is not constrained to only move through the origin (0,0).

- **Activation functions:** Consist of mathematical calculations that are performed within the hidden and output layers of the neural network. Data within each layer is adjusted before being transferred to the next layer. The activation functions enable the model to detect non-linear relationships. For example, recall from Chapter 5 that the output of a linear regression is bound by a straight line (see Exhibit 6-3a). The cost of customer acquisition for a digital marketing campaign might exhibit a linear relationship. But some relationships might be non-linear, such as the increase in customers over time (see Exhibit 6-3b). The activation function is controlled by weights and bias. Weights increase the speed in switching on the activation function, whereas bias works to delay the activation function.

There are different types of activation functions. The ones most often applied are sigmoid, hyperbolic tangent (Tanh), rectified linear unit (ReLU), and leaky ReLU. These activation functions have different equations, and each, therefore, serves different objectives.

Exhibit 6-3 Linear versus Non-linear Relationships

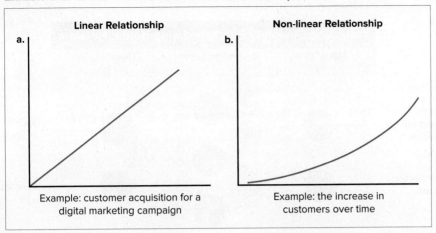

Linear Relationship

a.

Example: customer acquisition for a
digital marketing campaign

Non-linear Relationship

b.

Example: the increase in
customers over time

6.4 How Does a Neural Network Learn?

The best way to understand how neural networks learn is to illustrate the process using an example. To do so, you will not need to build a neural network model by hand. The software itself will execute the neural network analysis and provide the results. Here, we will provide a brief overview of what happens when a neural network is created. This will help demonstrate the basic elements of what happens when you use the software.

Using the small sample of customers in Exhibit 6-4, we will explain how neural networks function. Remember in real-life applications neural networks require a large sample size to produce accurate results. The purpose of the example below is to illustrate the operations behind neural networks.

There are five customers in the sample. The data represents purchase behavior of customers, such as past purchase amounts and the customer's satisfaction, which will be used to predict whether new customers will make a purchase. The network for the data is shown in Exhibit 6-5, and each node is numbered. The input layers are numbered i_1, i_2; the hidden layers are numbered h_3, h_4, h_5; and the output layers are numbered o_6 and o_7. Weights are shown on the arrows connecting the nodes. The additional nodes (grey circles) are referred to as the bias (e.g., b_3, b_4, b_5). Recall that the purpose of the bias factor is to control the contribution level of the node.

Exhibit 6-4 Small Sample Size of Data

CUSTOMER	PAST PURCHASE AMOUNT	CUSTOMER SATISFACTION SCORE	WILL THE CUSTOMER PURCHASE?
Raghu	20	90	Yes
Ann	10	61	No
Steven	40	40	No
Bita	57	63	No
Dennis	50	75	Yes

Exhibit 6-5 Predicting Customer Purchase Using a Neural Network

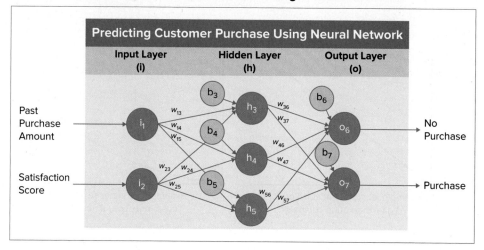

The values passed from the input layer to the hidden layer consist of two values: i_1 and i_2. The hidden layer (node) takes this input and computes a weighted sum of the inputs. Then, the activation algorithm discussed in Section 6.3 is applied to determine the output (O_6 and O_7).

What Does This Process Look Like in Action?

Step 1: Calculate the weighted sum of the inputs adjusted for bias in the hidden layer (node h) using the formula that follows. Initially, weights are randomly set. As the network "learns" from the data, weights are adjusted to minimize the error.

$$\text{Weighted sum of previous layer} = b_k + \sum_{j=1}^{p} w_{jk}\, x_j$$

b = bias value randomly initialized at a small value

p = input predictors in the model

w = weight randomly initialized at a small value

x = input value from the previous layer

Where $j = 1, 2, 3, 4,$ and 5

and $k = 3, 4, 5, 6,$ and 7

Step 2: Apply an *activation function* to the weighted sum for the hidden layer. One popular example of the form of the function is sigmoid:

$$\text{Node output} = \frac{1}{1 + e^{-(\text{weighted sum of previous layer})}}$$

Determining the initial weights in the network: The values of b and w are initially set randomly and are small values. The initial values indicate no knowledge of the network, but, as the network learns from the training, new weights are assigned to minimize the error in the network.

Let's start by calculating the output of hidden node 3. To do this, we begin with the following values:

$$b_3 = -0.05, \qquad w_{13} = 0.03, \qquad and \qquad w_{23} = 0.02$$

In Exhibit 6-4, input values for the first node (i_1 and i_2) are past purchase amount = 20 and customer satisfaction score = 90. The output values of node i_1 and i_2 remain unchanged $x_1 = 20$ and $x_2 = 90$.

Using the formulas introduced earlier, you can now calculate the output of the first hidden node:

$$\textit{weighted sum of hidden node } h_3 = -0.05 + (0.03)(20) + (0.02)(90) = 2.35$$

$$h_3 \textit{ output} = \frac{1}{1+e^{-(2.35)}} = 0.913$$

$$b_4 = -0.04, \qquad w_{14} = 0.02, \qquad \textit{and} \qquad w_{24} = 0.03$$

$$\textit{weighted sum of hidden node } h_4 = -0.04 + (0.02)(20) + (0.03)(90) = 3.06$$

$$h_4 \textit{ output} = \frac{1}{1+e^{-(3.06)}} = 0.955$$

$$b_5 = -0.05, \qquad w_{15} = 0.01, \qquad \textit{and} \qquad w_{25} = 0.04$$

$$\textit{weighted sum of hidden node } h_5 = -0.05 + (0.01)(20) + (0.04)(90) = 3.75$$

$$h_5 \textit{ output} = \frac{1}{1+e^{-(3.75)}} = 0.977$$

Apply a similar approach as steps 1 and 2 to calculate the output layer values, while also accounting for the initial bias and weights:

$$b_6 = 0.02, \qquad w_{36} = 0.01, \qquad w_{46} = 0.04, \qquad \textit{and} \qquad w_{56} = 0.06$$

$$\begin{aligned}\textit{weighted sum of output node } o_6 &= 0.02 + (0.01)(0.913) + (0.04)(0.955) \\ &\quad + (0.06)(0.977) \\ &= 0.126\end{aligned}$$

$$o_6 \textit{ output} = \frac{1}{1+e^{-(0.126)}} = 0.531$$

$$b_7 = 0.06, \qquad w_{37} = 0.03, \qquad w_{47} = 0.02, \qquad \textit{and} \qquad w_{57} = 0.04$$

$$\begin{aligned}\textit{weighted sum of output node } o_7 &= 0.06 + (0.03)(0.913) + (0.02)(0.955) \\ &\quad + (0.04)(0.977) \\ &= 0.146\end{aligned}$$

$$o_7 \textit{ output} = \frac{1}{1+e^{-(0.146)}} = 0.536$$

To determine if the first customer (Raghu) will be predicted as a purchaser or not a purchaser, you have to normalize the output nodes results to make sure they add up to 1. To do that, apply the following process:

$$\textit{Normalized } (P(Y = \textit{Not Purchase})) = \frac{o_6 \textit{ output}}{(o_6 \textit{ output} + o_7 \textit{ output})}$$

$$\textit{Normalized } (P(Y = \textit{Not Purchase})) = \frac{0.531}{(0.531 + 0.536)} = 0.498$$

$$\textit{Normalized } (P(Y = \textit{Purchase})) = 1 - \textit{Normalized}((Y = \textit{Not Purchase}))$$

$$= 1 - 0.498 = 0.502$$

Because the output is normalized to one (binary), the cutoff value is 0.50, with a higher value representing purchase, and a value lower than 0.50 representing not a purchaser. The resulting normalized value at 0.502 would therefore be classified as a purchaser.

How Does the Network Learn?

To train the model, you must estimate the bias and weights that lead to the best predictive results. The process described earlier is repeated for all records in the dataset. After each run, we compare prediction to actual and calculate the error. Earlier you learned about backpropagation. In this example, the error is propagated back and used to update the weights of the hidden nodes. With large errors leading to large weight changes and small errors leading to unchanged weights.

Recall that the learning rate ranges from 0 to 1 and controls the amount of change in the weight from one iteration to the next. To compute the error, we subtract the estimated from the actual and multiply the result by a correction factor using the following equation:

$$\text{error for output node} = \hat{Y}(1 - \hat{Y})(Y - \hat{Y})$$

The weights and bias are then updated at each iteration using this equation:

$$w_{jk_{new}} = w_{jk_{old}} + l + \text{Error for output node}$$

$w_{jk_{old}}$ = the initialized weight in the network

l = learning rate that controls the rate of change in the weights from one learning iteration to the next

Error from previous node = the error associated with the previous node error

Y for first record is equal to 1 given that purchase = yes

Let's start by calculating the error associated with o_6. The calculations for o_6 and o_7 error are shown next.

$$o_6 \ error = 0.531(1 - 0.531)(1 - 0.531) = 0.117$$
$$o_7 \ error = 0.536(1 - 0.536)(1 - 0.536) = 0.115$$

The new weights and new bias are calculated using the earlier equation:

$$w_{36_{new}} = w_{36_{old}} + l \ o_6 \ error$$

The network can be updated after running the first customer record as follows:

$$\text{Assume that } l = 0.2$$

Use the values from our initial calculations:

$$w_{36} = 0.01, \quad w_{46} = 0.02, \quad w_{56} = 0.05, \quad and \quad b_6 = 0.02$$

From the results previously stated, we find that $o_6 \ error = 0.117$.

$$w_{36_{new}} = 0.01 + (0.2)0.117 = 0.033$$
$$w_{46_{new}} = 0.02 + (0.2)0.117 = 0.043$$
$$w_{56_{new}} = 0.05 + (0.2)0.117 = 0.073$$
$$b_6 = 0.02 + (0.2)0.117 = 0.0434$$

The new weights and new bias are calculated using the earlier equation:

$$w_{37_{new}} = w_{37_{old}} + l \ o_7 \ error$$

Use the values from our initial calculations:

$$w_{37} = 0.03, \quad w_{47} = 0.02, \quad w_{57} = 0.04, \quad and \quad b_7 = 0.06$$

From the preceding results, we find that $o_7 \ error = 0.115$.

$$w_{37_{new}} = 0.03 + (0.2)0.115 = 0.530$$
$$w_{47_{new}} = 0.02 + (0.2)0.115 = 0.043$$
$$w_{57_{new}} = 0.04 + (0.2)0.115 = 0.063$$
$$b_7 = 0.06 + (0.2)0.115 = 0.083$$

The new weights are used to calculate the first customer record repeating steps 1 and 2 and are then updated after the second and third customer records, until all of the five customer records are used. After each iteration is completed, the process is repeated starting again with the first customer record.

When Does the Network Stop Learning?

The network is constantly learning until the final optimized solution is obtained. If the network is not well-trained, then the result will be underfitting of the model and it will not predict well. But, if a model is trained too much, the result will be overfitting and it will yield poor performance on new data. It is important, therefore, to understand when to halt training of neural networks to avoid both underfitting and overfitting.

The first step is to monitor the model's performance when training. Then, select a metric from which to monitor this performance. For example, model loss, prediction error, or accuracy could be used as performance metrics. Users can trigger early stopping when the metric reaches a particular threshold or when the system reaches its maximum run limits. The final optimal solution is reached when model prediction is no longer improving.

Continued from page 188

PRACTITIONER CORNER

Stephen Brobst | Chief Technology Officer at Teradata

Q **What is the necessary level of algorithmic comprehension when exploring the use of neural networks and collaborating with interdepartmental teams?**

A It is an unreasonable expectation for most people in marketing to acquire a deep understanding of the underlying mathematics associated with multi-layer neural networks. However, "explainability" when deploying neural networks is essential. To make better business decisions, as well as to be in compliance with regulations such as CCPA (California Consumer Privacy Act) and GDPR (General Data Protection Regulation), it is critical to understand which features are having a positive or negative impact on predictions/classifications being put forth by the neural network. When these decisions impact the customer experience, it is not acceptable to treat deep learning as a "black box" with no understanding of how decisions are made.

Continued to next page

6.5 Key Reminders When Using Neural Networks

The following are some important questions to consider when using neural networks.

- **Can a neural network be applied to out-of-range data?** Neural networks are known for their good predictive performance and can be generalized to new values. However, the network is often not able to extrapolate outside the range of values that were used to build the model. For example, the network could offer little value if the original range of values in the training data was 1 to 1,000, but the values we want to estimate ranged from 20,000 to 50,000.

- **How many features (variables) should be used?** Only key predictors are required to be included in the model. Feature reduction methods (eliminating predictors) discussed in Chapter 5 can be used to identify which features should be included in the model.

- **What determines the size of a neural network?** Neural networks vary in size. The complexity of the question for analysis and the number of features used in the analysis impacts the actual size of the network. In general, the simplest network that achieves an acceptable level of prediction is the best model.

- **Are neural networks a black box?** Neural network architectures can be complex. Thus, the structure inside the nodes is often recognized as a black box. Sometimes it is difficult to explain why and how the neural network arrived at a solution—and that may lead to a lack of trust in the model. But if the network exhibits an acceptable prediction rate, the analyst should analyze the prediction logic to develop a reasonable explanation and justification.

- **What are data and computer requirements of neural networks?** Neural networks require a large dataset to perform well. At the same time, large datasets are expensive to obtain and manage and require extensive computational power.

- **What programs can be used to develop neural networks?** Quite a few commercial options are available to consider when developing neural networks such as RapidMiner, SPSS Modeler, and SAS. In many instances, however, open-source programs such as R programming or Python can be used to develop and apply neural networks.

Continued from previous page 195

PRACTITIONER CORNER

Stephen Brobst | Chief Technology Officer at Teradata

Q What questions should be asked when the neural network arrives at an output? How might a team detect an abnormality that should be examined further?

A Outputs should always be evaluated for bias. This is important for all predictive models, but even more so for neural networks because of the "black box" nature of the mathematics. The output of the predictive model should be tested to understand if there are built-in biases against specific demographic cohorts. More than 180 types of human bias have been identified by sociologists—and many of these will be translated into AI algorithms. Social biases related to race, gender, sexual preference, ethnicity, political affiliation, and so on should be identified and avoided.

Q Many individuals refer to neural networks and deep learning as a black box. What ethical concerns should be the focus of analysts using this model?

A Emerging regulations such as GDPR and CCPA require transparency for any use of data that impacts a consumer. Black box algorithms violate consumer rights associated with these regulations. Cathy O'Neil in her book, Weapons of Math Destruction, points out that by ". . . insulating algorithms and their creators from public scrutiny, rather than responding to civic concerns about bias and discrimination, the existing system propagates the myth that those algorithms are objective and fair . . ."

Understanding the Business Problem

Historically, passenger airlines have experienced an increase in customers each year. In fact, the rise in passengers from January through November 2019 was up 3.9 percent over the prior year.[10] Exhibit 6-6 shows the increase in airline passengers from January through November since 2003.

Despite the positive increase in the number of passengers, the American Customer Satisfaction Index of overall customer satisfaction is 74/100.[11] This value means the airline industry falls below hotel, video streaming services, banking, and apparel industries. Customer satisfaction is important in building loyalty and increasing lifetime value. For that reason, many airlines are making efforts to better understand the needs and wants of their customers.

Understanding the Dataset

For this case study, a hypothetical 2019 dataset will be used.[12] The dataset consists of customer survey and airline data that reflects customer relationships with the airline. A neural network will be developed to predict satisfaction of a customer based on customer demographics (e.g., age, gender), flight-related information (e.g., time, cancelation, flight departure, arrival delays), and behavioral data (e.g., shopping habits in the airport, type of travel—business or personal). The goal is to predict

Exhibit 6-6 Number of Airline Passengers, 2003 to 2019

Passengers in millions, unadjusted (000,000)

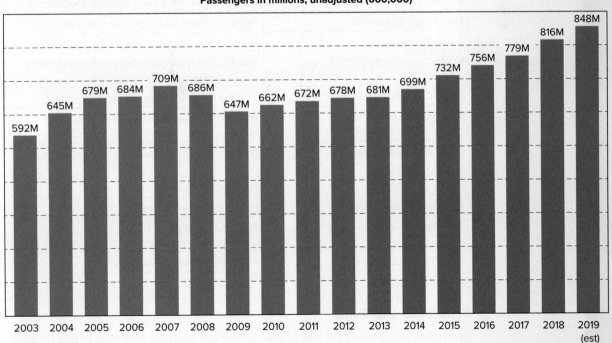

Source: Bureau of Transportation Statistics, "Estimated November 2019 U.S. Airline Traffic Data," United States Department of Transportation, December 12, 2019, https://www.bts.gov/newsroom/estimated-november-2019-us-airline-traffic-data.

customer satisfaction. If the customer is dissatisfied, the airline can evaluate when and how to improve customer service through interventions such as communication or compensation.

To get started, review the data elements in Exhibit 6-7.

RapidMiner will be used to predict customer satisfaction using a neural network. First, the data variables will be reviewed in Excel and then loaded into RapidMiner for analysis.

Exhibit 6-7 Data Dictionary

VARIABLE NAME (TYPE)	DESCRIPTION
Customer Id (typeless)	Unique ID representing a customer
Satisfied? (string: target)	A binary measure indicating if a customer is "satisfied" or "not satisfied"
Airline Status (string)	Customer's airline status (Blue, Silver, Gold, Platinum)
Age (numeric)	Customer's age ranging from 15 to 85
Gender (string)	Customer's gender (Male or Female)
Type of Travel (string)	Business, Mileage, or Personal travelers
Shopping Amount at Airport (numeric)	$ amount for customer spending on shopping while at airport
Eating and Drinking Amounts at Airport (numeric)	$ amount for customer eating and drinking expenditures while at airport
Class (string)	Travel class (Business, Eco, Eco Plus)
Flight Date (numeric)	Date of flight
Day of Flight Date (date)	Day of month for travel (1 to 31)
Month of Flight Date (string)	Month of year for travel (January–December)
No of Flights (numeric)	Number of previous flights by customer
Airline Name (string)	Name of the flight's airline (Primera Air, Wow Air)
Flight Time (numeric)	Number of minutes the flight takes from origin city to destination city
Flight Cancelled (string)	The flight was canceled or not (Yes or No)
Arrival Delay (numeric)	Number of minutes the flight is delayed for arrival
Departure Delay (numeric)	Number of minutes the flight is delayed for departure
Origin State (string)	Flight origin state
Destination State (string)	Flight destination state
Scheduled Departure Hour (numeric)	The hour the flight is scheduled for departure (24-hour military time)
Flight Distance (numeric)	Flight distance in miles

Preparing the Data

Remember, an essential practice before starting any analytics project is to first review and clean the dataset. Open the Airline Satisfaction Data.xlsx file available on the

Exhibit 6-8 Airline Satisfaction Data

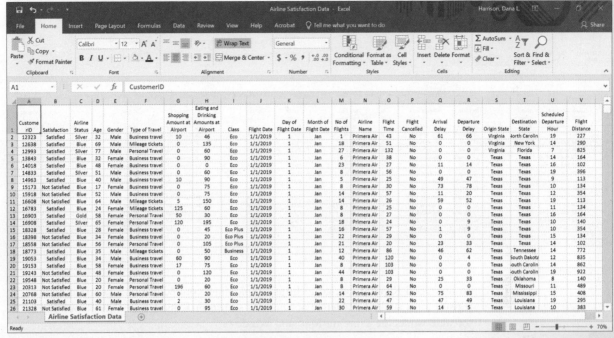

Microsoft Excel

Student Resources page to examine the variable values in Excel. There are 10,600 records. Exhibit 6-8 shows a snapshot of the variables and records for 25 customers.

What does one row in the dataset represent? Each row of the data represents one customer. Two data sources have been combined: survey data and airline secondary data.

What do the distinct values for *satisfaction* mean? Customer satisfaction was captured via survey using a binary variable: satisfied or not satisfied.

After the initial review, are there any variables that need to be transformed? For example, variables such as date may be more useful if changed to represent day of the week, given how travel patterns vary by day of the week.

You should also identify whether any variables seem unclear or which variables based on your understanding of the business problem are likely to be the better predictors. Understanding which variables may be more or less important in predicting customer satisfaction will enable you to more easily interpret the results. Exhibit 6-8 can be used to improve your understanding of variables and values in the dataset under each column.

Quick reminder: Click on *Data*, then *Filter* as shown in Exhibit 6-9 to further understand variable categories (e.g., Business Travel, Personal Travel, Mileage Tickets) under each column.

Applying the Concepts

The RapidMiner software is one of the fastest-growing data analytics tools in the marketplace. In this example, you will learn how RapidMiner can be used to analyze the data displayed in the Excel spreadsheet using a neural network.

Exhibit 6-9 Airline Dataset Overview

	A	B	C	D	E	F	G	H	I	J	K	L	M	N	O	P	Q	R	S
1	Customer	Satisfaction	Airline St	Age	Gender	Type of Tr	Shopping	Eating an	Class	Flight Dat	Day of Fli	Month of	No of Flig	Airline Na	Flight Tin	Flight Car	Arrival De	Departure	Origin Sta
2	12323	Satisfied	Silver	32	Male	Business tra	10	46	Eco	1/1/19	1	Jan	1	Primera Air	43	No	61	66	Virginia
3	12638	Satisfied	Blue	69	Male	Mileage tick	0	135	Eco	1/1/19	1	Jan	18	Primera Air	51	No	0	0	Virginia
4	12993	Satisfied	Silver	77	Male	Personal Tra	0	60	Eco	1/1/19	1	Jan	27	Primera Air	132	No	0	0	Virginia
5	13843	Satisfied	Blue	32	Female	Business tra	0	90	Eco	1/1/19	1	Jan	6	Primera Air	38	No	0	0	Texas
6	14018	Satisfied	Blue	48	Female	Business tra	0	0	Eco	1/1/19	1	Jan	23	Primera Air	27	No	11	14	Texas
7	14833	Satisfied	Silver	51	Male	Business tra	0	60	Eco	1/1/19	1	Jan	8	Primera Air	56	No	0	0	Texas
8	14963	Satisfied	Blue	40	Male	Business tra	10	90	Eco	1/1/19	1	Jan	5	Primera Air	25	No	49	47	Texas
9	15173	Not Satisfied	Blue	17	Female	Business tra	0	75	Eco	1/1/19	1	Jan	8	Primera Air	30	No	73	78	Texas
10	15918	Not Satisfied	Blue	52	Male	Business tra	0	75	Eco	1/1/19	1	Jan	14	Primera Air	57	No	11	20	Texas
11	16608	Not Satisfied	Blue	64	Male	Mileage tick	5	150	Eco	1/1/19	1	Jan	14	Primera Air	26	No	59	52	Texas
12	16783	Satisfied	Blue	24	Female	Mileage tick	125	60	Eco	1/1/19	1	Jan	8	Primera Air	25	No	0	0	Texas
13	16903	Satisfied	Gold	58	Female	Personal Tra	50	30	Eco	1/1/19	1	Jan	8	Primera Air	27	No	0	0	Texas
14	16908	Satisfied	Silver	65	Female	Personal Tra	120	195	Eco	1/1/19	1	Jan	18	Primera Air	24	No	0	9	Texas
15	18328	Satisfied	Blue	28	Female	Business tra	0	45	Eco Plus	1/1/19	1	Jan	16	Primera Air	57	No	1	9	Texas
16	18398	Not Satisfied	Blue	34	Female	Business tra	0	20	Eco Plus	1/1/19	1	Jan	22	Primera Air	29	No	0	0	Texas
17	18558	Not Satisfied	Blue	56	Female	Personal Tra	0	105	Eco Plus	1/1/19	1	Jan	21	Primera Air	20	No	23	33	Texas
18	18773	Satisfied	Blue	35	Male	Mileage tick	0	50	Business	1/1/19	1	Jan	12	Primera Air	86	No	46	62	Texas

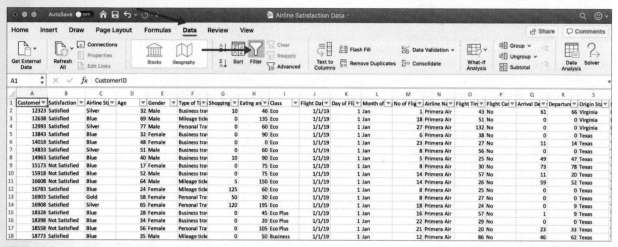

Microsoft Excel

To download RapidMiner, go to https://rapidminer.com/educational-program and register for a student academic account, as shown in Exhibit 6-10. The RapidMiner software works the same on Mac and Windows.

Exhibit 6-10

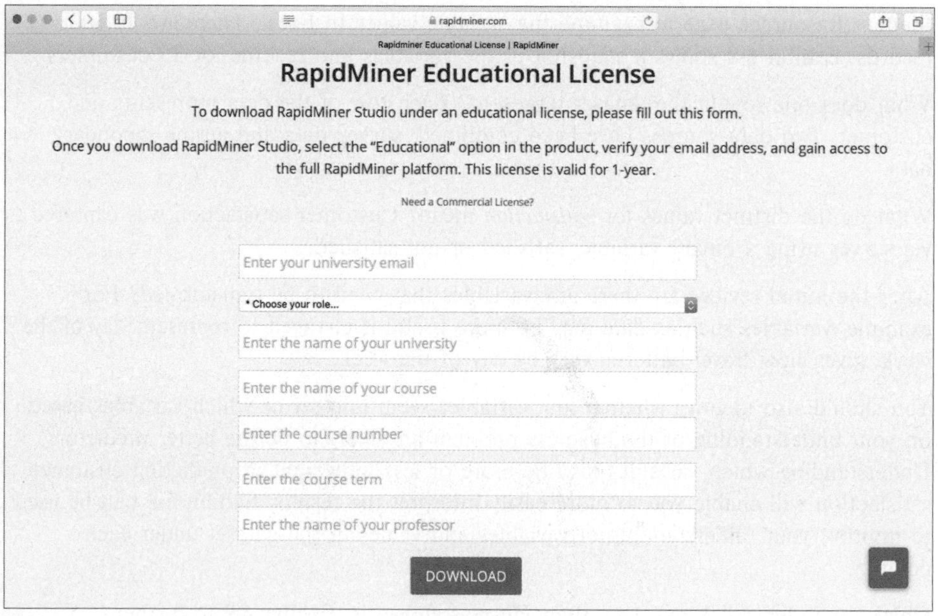

RapidMiner, Inc.

Once the program has been downloaded, open RapidMiner to start building the model.

The process of using RapidMiner to get your results includes four stages: (1) preparing the data for modeling; (2) setting up the training model and cross validation; (3) evaluating the model results; and (4) applying the model to a new dataset.

Stage 1: Preparing the Data for Modeling

Your screen should appear like Exhibit 6-11. Under "Start a new project," click *Blank*.

Exhibit 6-11

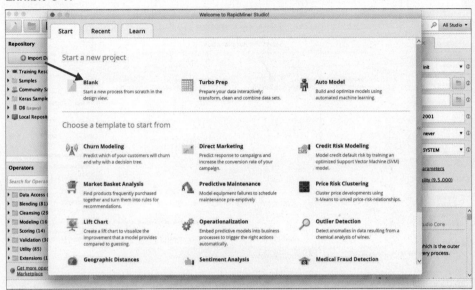

RapidMiner, Inc.

First, import the data into RapidMiner. Complete this step by clicking *Import Data* (Exhibit 6-12). Then, click on "My Computer" and navigate to the folder where the data is saved.

Exhibit 6-12

RapidMiner, Inc.

Locate "Data" for Chapter 6 and click on the Airline Satisfaction Data.xlsx file. Then, select "Next" (Exhibit 6-13).

Exhibit 6-13

RapidMiner, Inc.

Your screen should look like Exhibit 6-14. Click "Next."

Exhibit 6-14

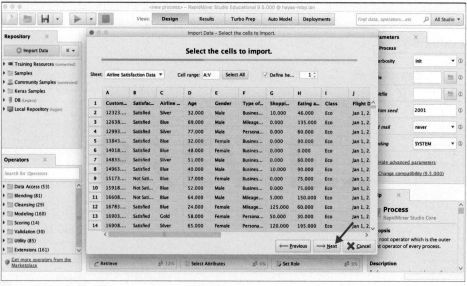

RapidMiner, Inc.

You will now see a "Format your columns" window, as shown in Exhibit 6-15. You can format your variables in this window or make any necessary changes for data type.

Exhibit 6-15

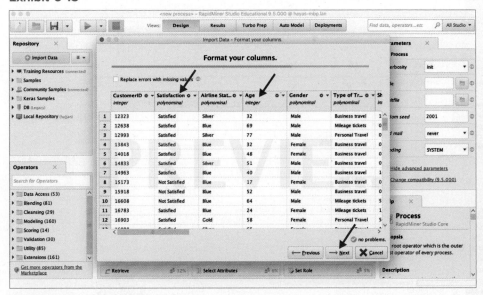

RapidMiner, Inc.

Notice that the variable "Satisfaction" is processed as a polynomial type in RapidMiner. This is because the variable has string values stored: Satisfied and Not Satisfied. The variable "Airline Status" is processed as a polynomial type as well because it also has string values stored: Blue, Silver, Gold, and Platinum. In contrast, the variable "Age" is classified as integer because it is a whole number (e.g., 32, 69, 77).

In Exhibit 6-16, you will see data types in RapidMiner that can be assigned to variables. Note that any variable with two string values such as "Satisfaction" or "Gender" can be changed to binomial type because it has exactly two unique string values. However, given that it does not impact the upcoming analysis, we will continue to process it as polynomial.

Exhibit 6-16

TYPE NAME: DESCRIPTION	EXAMPLE
Polynomial: string values	Blue, Silver, Gold, Platinum
Binomial: exactly two unique string values	True or False Yes or No Male or Female
Real: fraction number	11.250
Integer: Whole number	1, 2, 3, 4
Date_time: Date with time	01.12.2021 15:40
Date: Date without time	01.12.2021
Time: time of day	15:40

When you finish reviewing your data, click "Next," as shown at the bottom of Exhibit 6-15.

Determine where you will store the data. For this example, select *Local Repository*, then the "data" folder. Click "Finish," as shown in Exhibit 6-17.

Exhibit 6-17

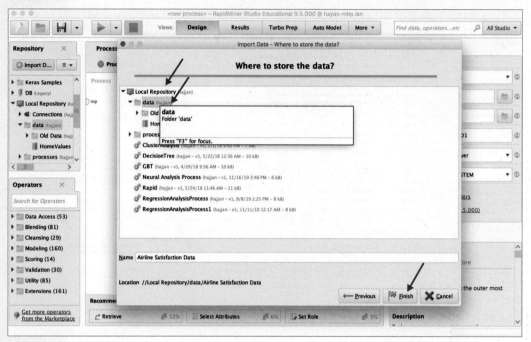

RapidMiner, Inc.

The data is now read by RapidMiner and is available for review and analysis. Notice that the data in RapidMiner is referred to as ExampleSet with 10,600 examples and 22 variables (regular attributes) (see Exhibit 6-18).

In the top *Views* menu bar, click on "Design" to start building the model (Exhibit 6-18).

Exhibit 6-18

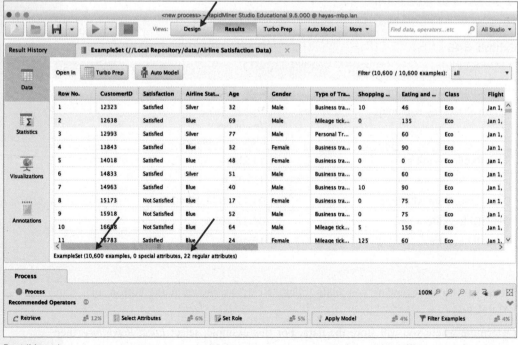

RapidMiner, Inc.

The RapidMiner workspace is divided into five main default panels, as shown in Exhibit 6-19.

Exhibit 6-19

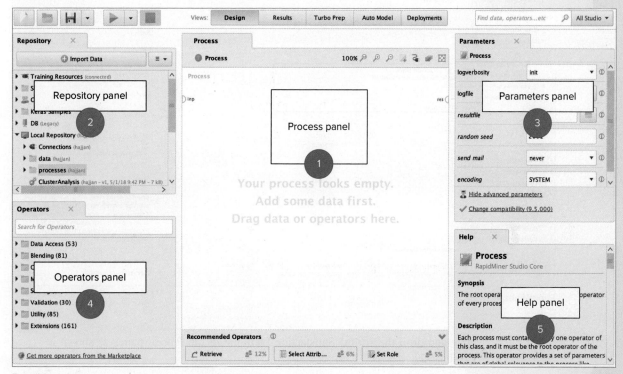

RapidMiner, Inc.

If you close any of the panels during your setup, you can click on the top *Views* menu bar (Exhibit 6-20) and select "Restore Default View" to reset the Design View to the default panel setup shown in Exhibit 6-19.

Exhibit 6-20

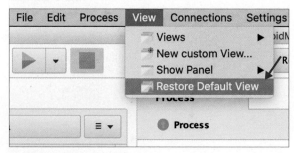

RapidMiner, Inc.

To start building the model, import the data you just uploaded into the system to the Process panel. To do so, navigate to the *Repository* panel (left side of screen) and then in *Local Repository*, you will find the "data" folder, which contains the Airline Satisfaction Data dataset (see Exhibit 6-21).

Exhibit 6-21

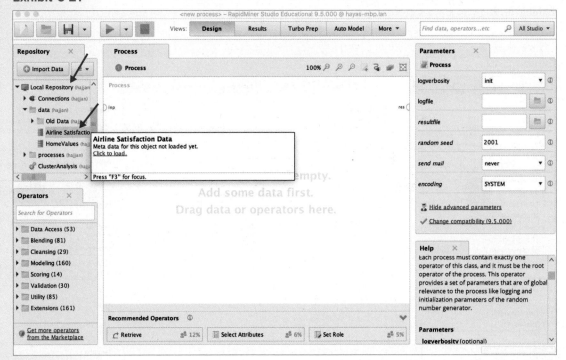

RapidMiner, Inc.

Drag and drop the Airline Satisfaction Data file to the *Process* panel, as shown in Exhibit 6-22.

Exhibit 6-22

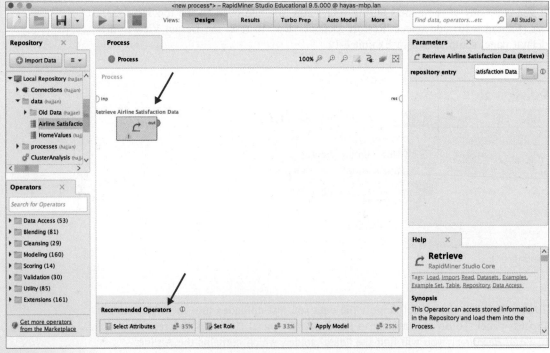

RapidMiner, Inc.

At the bottom of the Process panel is a tab called *Recommended Operators*. At any time, you can drag an operator from the Recommended Operators and drop it in the Process panel (Exhibit 6-22). Additionally, you can search for other operators using the lower left search window in the *Operators* panel by typing the name of the operator you want to use. There are over 1,500 operators available in RapidMiner.

You may be wondering "What is an operator?" An operator is used to create and execute the RapidMiner analytical process. Examples of operators include retrieving data, selecting attribute, evaluating analytical performance, and running models. Operators have at least two ports. There is an input port and an output port. The input port determines what is provided to the operator, and the output port carries the results of the operator. After an operator is selected and added to the process, you can access its parameter. The parameters are the properties of the operator that are selected to control the operation (top of Exhibit 6-22).

Under the Operators panel, type "select attributes" in the search window (Exhibit 6-23). You will see the *Select Attributes* operator appear under the "Selection" folder.

Exhibit 6-23

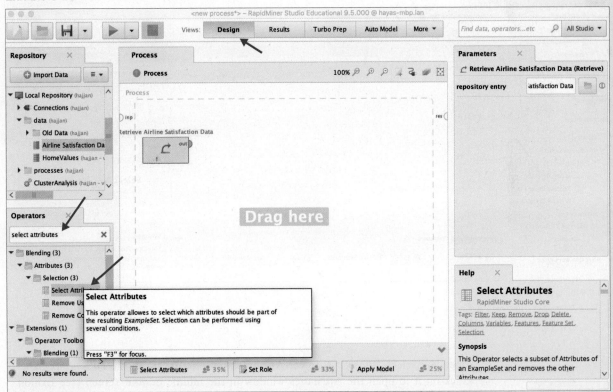

RapidMiner, Inc.

Drag and drop the *Select Attributes* operator to the Process panel and place it on the right side of the *Retrieve Airline Satisfaction Data*, as shown in Exhibit 6-24. Now we are ready to connect the two operators. Hold your mouse left button down and drag the output port (out) from the *Retrieve Airline Satisfaction Data* operator over to the input port (exa) for the Select Attributes (Exhibit 6-24). You will see a line is now connecting the two operators—the Retrieve Airline Satisfaction operator and the Select Attributes operator. You can remove this line at any time by clicking on it and using the Delete key on your keyboard.

Next, click on the *Select Attributes* operator and review its *Parameter* panel on the top right side of the screen (Exhibit 6-24). Note, the first parameter under *Select Attributes* is called "attribute filter type." Click on the drop-down menu next to it and select "subset." Using this subset parameter allows you to select a subset of the attributes you want to include in the analysis.

Exhibit 6-24

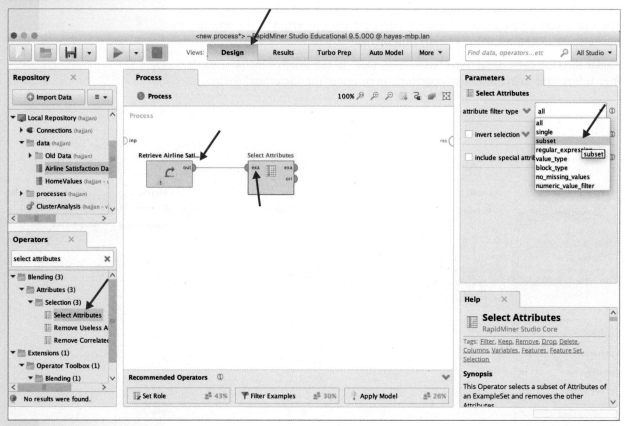

RapidMiner, Inc.

Once you select "subset," a Select Attributes option appears in the *Parameters* panel. Click on it to open the Attributes window in the middle of your screen (see Exhibit 6-25). Here, you can select the specific attributes you want to use. Click on them and then use the arrow to move the attributes from the left to the right side.

Select the following attributes: Age, Arrival Delay, Day of Flight Date, Departure Delay, Flight Time, No of Flights, Satisfaction, and Type of Travel. These attributes are selected based on our knowledge of the variables and their likely importance in predicting the dependent variable (Satisfaction). When you are finished selecting attributes, click "Apply" (Exhibit 6-25). Note: You can use Command key (for Mac) or Control key (for windows) to select more than one attribute at the same time.

Exhibit 6-25

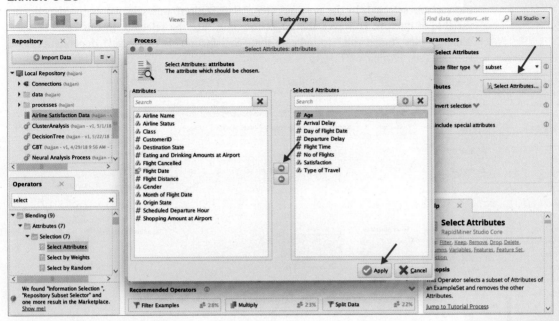

RapidMiner, Inc.

The software returns you to the Process panel. Under the Operators panel, search for "set role" (Exhibit 6-26). Drag the *Set Role* operator to the Process panel and place it to the right side of *Select Attributes*. Drag *Select Attributes* output port (exa) to *Set Role* input port (exa) by holding down the left button of the mouse. This creates a line between the two operators, indicating they are now connected.

Click *Set Role* to go to the Parameter panel (Exhibit 6-26). Under "attribute name," click on the drop-down menu and select "Satisfaction" as the dependent variable.

Exhibit 6-26

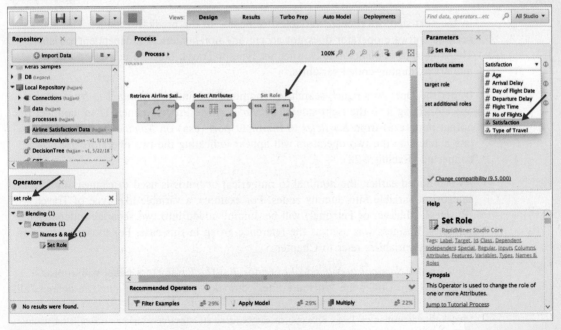

RapidMiner, Inc.

Still under the Parameters pane, the "target role" lists several different roles possible for the variable selected. In the previous step, "Satisfaction" was selected as the dependent variable of interest. However, the target role must also be selected. In this case, select "label" under "target role" to indicate that "Satisfaction" is the target* dependent variable (see Exhibit 6-27).

Exhibit 6-27

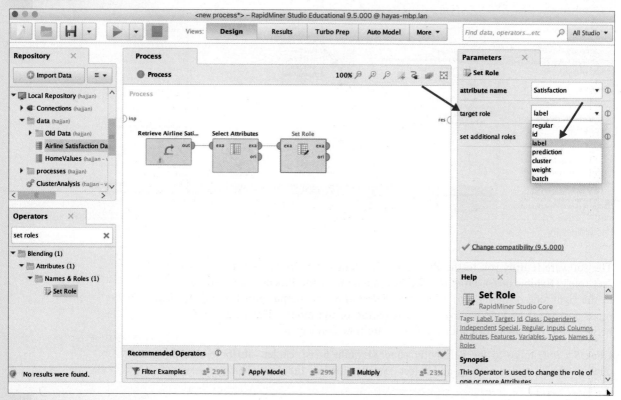

RapidMiner, Inc.

In the next step, we prepare variables to include in the predictive model. The neural network software operator does not accept any non-numerical independent variables. Therefore, polynomial variables, such as Type of Travel, must be converted into numerical, dummy-coded variables.

Under the Operators panel, search for "nominal" to find the *Nominal to Numerical* operator. Drag it to the right side of *Set Roles* in the Process panel. Then, connect the output port (exa) from *Set Roles* to the input port (exa) on *Nominal to Numerical*. A line connecting the two operators will appear indicating the two operators are now connected (Exhibit 6-28).

As mentioned earlier, the nominal to numerical operator is used to change any categorical variable into dummy codes. For example, a variable like Type of Travel (Business, Mileage, or Personal) will be dummy coded into two separate independent variables. Business was used as the reference group in this case. For more information on dummy variables, refer to Chapter 5.

Click on the *Nominal to Numerical* operator and the Parameters panel will appear (Exhibit 6-28). Under the "attribute filter" drop-down menu, make sure the default "all"

*Additional information on Target Role options can be found at: https://docs.rapidminer.com/latest/studio/operators/blending/attributes/names_and_roles/set_role.html

is selected. Under the "coding type" drop-down menu, make sure "dummy coding" is selected.

Now, check the box for comparison groups by selecting "Edit List."

Exhibit 6-28

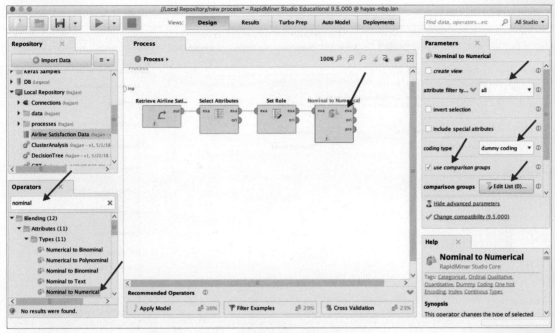

RapidMiner, Inc.

An *Edit Parameter List: comparison groups* window will pop up. Under the "comparison group attribute" drop-down menu, select "Type of Travel" (Exhibit 6-29).

Exhibit 6-29

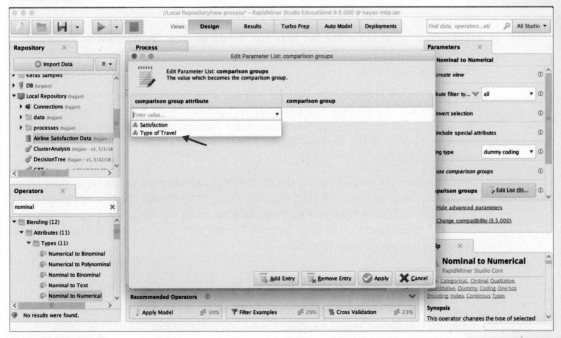

RapidMiner, Inc.

In the *Edit Parameter List: comparison groups* window, enter text "Business travel" in the "comparison group" field (Exhibit 6-30). Business travel is one of the three categorical values under Type of Travel variable. Click "Apply" to go back to the Process panel.

Exhibit 6-30

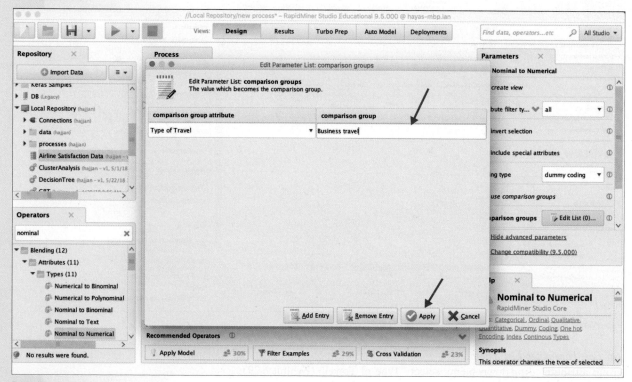

RapidMiner, Inc.

To continue setting up the model, you need to move the Nominal to Numerical part of the model below the Set Role box. To do so, drag the *Nominal to Numerical* operator down under *Set Role* to have more space in the Process window (Exhibit 6-31).

The next step in preparing the data for analysis is to handle missing values. To manage missing values in your data, you must add an operator called Replace Missing Values. To do so, go to the Operators panel, search for "replace missing values" and select the operator. Now, drag the *Replace Missing Values* operator to the right side of *Nominal to Numerical* (Exhibit 6-31).

Next, connect the output port (exa) of *Nominal to Numerical* to the input port (exa) of *Replace Missing Values*. A line will now appear to connect the two operators. Click on the *Replace Missing Values* operator to go to the Parameters panel. The "default" replacement method is "average," make sure it is selected before moving to set up the training model (Exhibit 6-31).

Stage 2: Setting Up the Training Model and Cross Validation

The next step in setting up your model is cross validation. As you learned in Chapter 5, different model validation methods are available. To execute cross

Exhibit 6-31

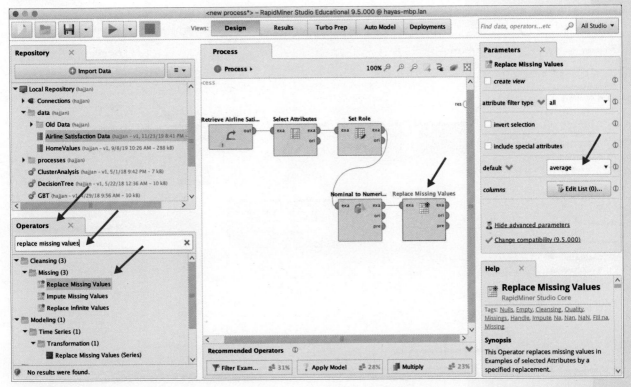

RapidMiner, Inc.

validation for our model, the data will be randomly split into k subsets of the data. A single subset is then selected for validation data—the data subset that will be used to cross validate the model. For example, if the number of subsets is five, then one subset k is held out and becomes the validation data and the remaining four subsets (k-1) are combined and used as the training data. This cross validation is repeated k times, with each of the k subsets used one time as the validation dataset. The k validation results from repeated procedures (in our example, the procedure is repeated five times) are averaged to deliver a single estimate of the model's prediction performance.

To set up cross validation in your model, search for "cross validation" in the Operators panel (Exhibit 6-32). Drag the *Cross Validation* operator to the Process panel. Connect *Replace Missing Value* output port (exa) to *Cross Validation*'s input port (exa). This will create a line between the two operators, indicating they are connected.

Note that the *Cross Validation* operator is a nested operator (Exhibit 6-32). A nested operator means that several subprocesses are included within the operator. The *Cross Validation* operator has two subprocesses: a training subprocess and a testing subprocess. The training subprocess is used for building a model (this subprocess learns which, if any, independent variables are good predictors). After the model is trained (a prediction equation is determined), it is then applied in the testing subprocess to validate how well the model predicts the validation data subset.

Exhibit 6-32

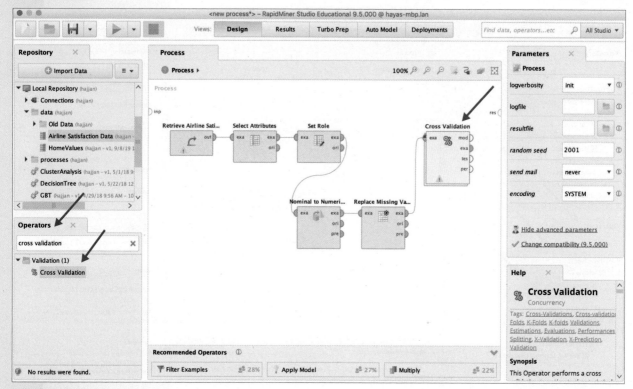

RapidMiner, Inc.

When you double-click on the *Cross Validation* operator shown in Exhibit 6-32, you will get the screen in Exhibit 6-33. Two sub processors are displayed: a training subprocess and a testing subprocess. As mentioned earlier in the training subprocess, we first build the neural net model, and then the results are passed to the test subprocess to apply the model on the validation dataset. The predictive performance of the model is measured in the test subprocess by applying the trained model on the k cross-validation datasets and then evaluating the results to see how well the model predicts.

The purpose of this RapidMiner case exercise is to develop a neural net model to use for prediction of an outcome—in this example, the dependent (outcome) variable is "Satisfaction." The next step is to search for "neural net" under the Operators panel. Then, drag the *Neural Net* operator into the Training subprocess window (Exhibit 6-33).

Now connect the output port (tra) line of the *Cross Validation* operator to the input port (tra) of the *Neural Net* operator in the Process window. Then, connect the output port (mod) of *Neural Net* to the input port (mod) on the line separating the training and testing windows. To help you better understand those connections, tra stands for training dataset and mod stands for model. In our case example, this is the neural network algorithm that is produced using the training dataset.

Click on the *Neural Net* operator in the Training window of the Process panel. You can now review the Parameters panel, which enables users to manage the architecture of the network. As you build your experience with neural nets, you can

Exhibit 6-33

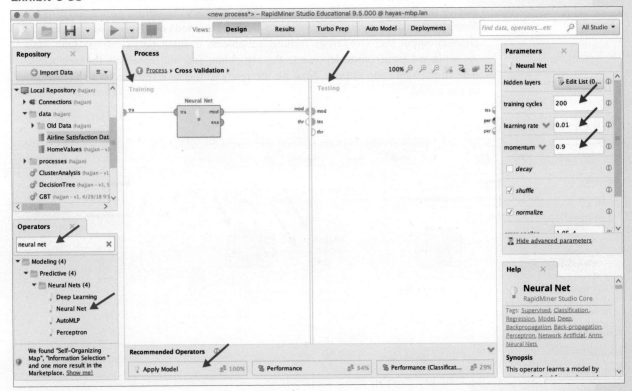

RapidMiner, Inc.

customize the options under the Parameters panel*, as shown in Exhibit 6-33. The default "hidden layer" is set to one hidden layer, and its number of nodes is equal to ((number of input variables + number of classes)/2) + 1. For our case, we have ((8 input variables including 2 dummy variables and threshold node explained earlier + 2 output classes (satisfied and not satisfied))/2) + 1 = 6 hidden nodes + 1 threshold node.

The other parameter you can set up is "training cycles." The default value is 200, and it indicates the number of times the predicted values are compared with the actual values to compute an error function. Using backpropagation, the error function is then entered into the neural net model to adjust the weights of each connection in order to reduce the error. The training cycle of 200 indicates the number of times the error function is calculated and entered into the neural network model before the network stops learning. Other parameters that can be controlled are "learning rate" and "momentum." The learning rate default value is 0.01. Note that a smaller learning rate results in a more stable solution but increases the processing time of the model. The momentum default value is set to 0.9. This parameter represents the acceleration in the model. That is, how fast the model changes the weights in order to optimize the solution.

Note under Recommended Operators (bottom of the Process panel) that *Apply Model* is used 100 percent of the time after *Neural Net*.

*Additional information about neural net parameters can be found at: https://docs.rapidminer.com/latest/studio/operators/modeling/predictive/neural_nets/neural_net.html

Drag and drop *Apply Model* from Recommended Operators to the Testing subprocess side of the Process panel (Exhibit 6-34). Next, connect the output port (mod) from *Neural Net* in the Training subprocess to input port (mod) on *Apply Model*. Then, connect output port (tes) from Training subprocess to input port (unl) on *Apply Model*. As explained earlier, mod represents the algorithm, and unl represents the unlabeled data in the validation dataset. Now we are ready to measure the predictive performance of the model.

Exhibit 6-34

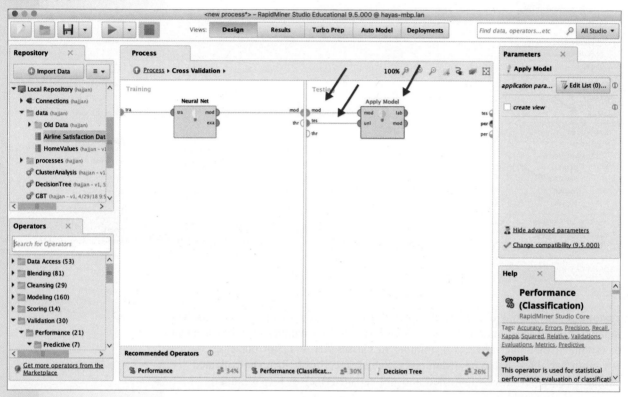

RapidMiner, Inc.

To measure performance, we need to add a performance evaluation operator. The performance evaluation enables us to see how well the validation data performed in the neural net model that was built using the training data.

Search for "performance class" under the Operators panel (Exhibit 6-35). Then, drag the *Performance (Classification)* operator into the Testing subprocess. Next, connect the output port (lab) of *Apply Model* to the input port (lab) of *Performance*. Then, connect the *Performance* output port (per) to the input port (perf) of the subprocess *Cross Validation*. To help you better understand the context, lab stands for labeled data, meaning the predicted target of the validation dataset used to calculate the accuracy of the model.

There are different ways to evaluate performance. For this example, we will use prediction accuracy. Click on the *Performance* operator in the Testing subprocess to review the Parameters panel. Check the box next to "accuracy" to evaluate the percentage of accuracy of the actual versus predicted values in the model (Exhibit 6-35).

Now it is time to review the model results. Under the Process panel, click on the Process hyperlink to exit the Cross Validation nested operator and go back to the main Process panel (Exhibit 6-35).

Exhibit 6-35

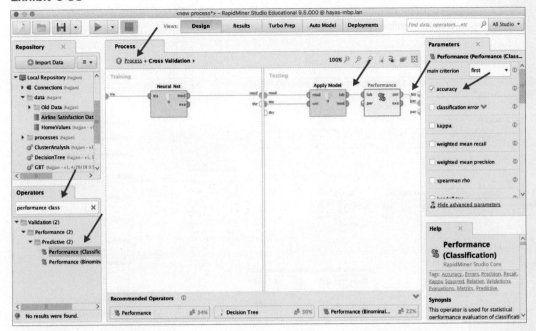

RapidMiner, Inc.

First, as shown in Exhibit 6-36, connect the *Cross Validation* operator output port (mod) to final input port (res). Mod represents the neural network model and res represents the results that will be displayed under the Results tab. Second, connect the *Cross Validation* operator output port (per) to final input port (res). Per represents the performance outcome of the model connected to res to display the results under the Results tab. Once your two lines are established, you will be ready to run the final model and review the results of all your model setup work.

Exhibit 6-36

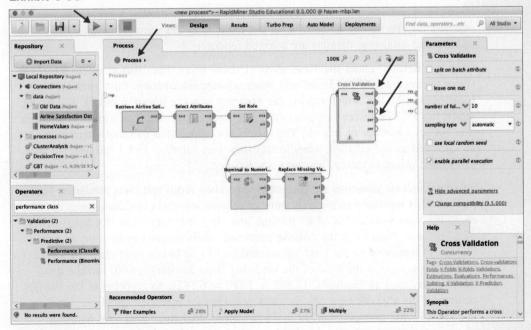

RapidMiner, Inc.

To execute the model, click Run, which is the blue "play" button at the top. The results will take a few minutes to run. Exhibit 6-37 shows the *Cross Validation* process at this point is 55 percent completed.

Exhibit 6-37

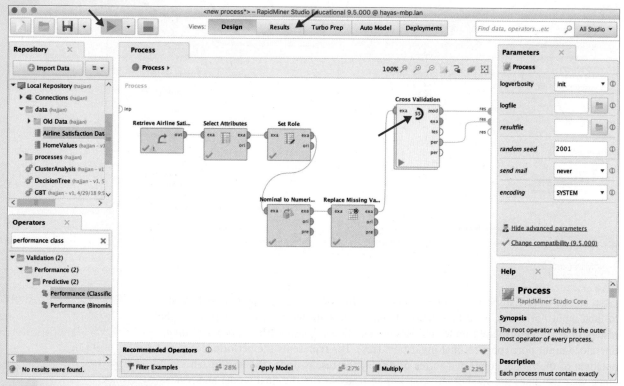

RapidMiner, Inc.

Stage 3: Evaluating the Model Results

Once the model execution is complete, the results will be displayed. Note that your numbers may be slightly different from the Exhibits in this example because the training and validation datasets are selected randomly.

Click on "Results" under the *Views* menu (Exhibit 6-38). The "PerformanceVector" tab shows the accuracy of the model and other relevant information. First, evaluate the Classification Matrix, which reports the accuracy of a classification model. The example model has a 77.28 percent accuracy rate. Accuracy is calculated as correct predictions over the total number of records. The matrix also shows that 628 customers were misclassified as not satisfied, when in fact they were satisfied, and 1,780 were classified as satisfied, when in reality they were not satisfied.

Two key outcome measures are presented here: class recall and class precision. The *class recall* is measured as the total number of class members classified correctly. Class recall for "true Satisfied" is 88.43 percent, and class recall for "true Not Satisfied" is 65.57 percent. *Precision* is the positive predicted values (correct prediction) in a class (category) compared to the total values predicted to be in the same class. In this example, precision is the ratio of the predicted "true Satisfied" (4,802) to the total number predicted as "Satisfied" (4,802 + 1,780 = 6,582). As reported in the far-right column of the Classification Matrix, class precision for predicted "pred. Satisfied" is 72.96% (4,802 divided by 6,582 = 72.96%). For predicted "pred. Not Satisfied," *class precision* is 84.37%. To obtain this number, first calculate the row sum of the "pred. Not Satisfied" (628 + 3,390 = 4,018). Then, divide 3,390 (correct predictions) by 4,018 and the result is 84.37%, as shown in Exhibit 6-38.*

Exhibit 6-38

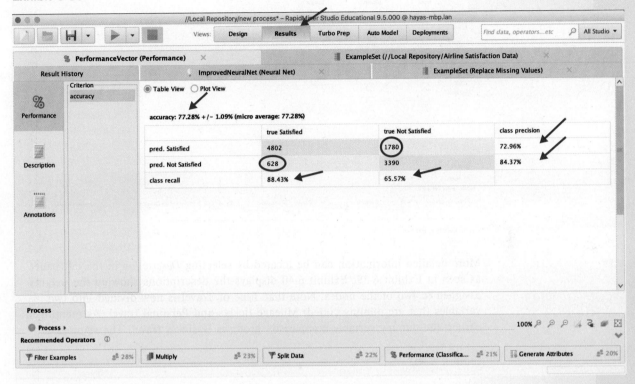

RapidMiner, Inc.

Recall that a neural net has hidden layers that assume the weights of each input. RapidMiner shows the weights of the neural network and the hidden nodes when you click on the "ImprovedNeuralNet" tab. The input layer corresponds to the selected independent variables in the model (e.g., Age). The Input layer shows eight input variables. The categorical variable (Type of Travel) has been converted to two dummy variables (business travel is the reference group). The Input layer variables include these variables and a threshold node that was explained earlier. The hidden layer shows the nodes in the model. The number of hidden nodes is calculated using this equation: (8 input variables + 2 output classes (satisfied or not satisfied)) / 2) + 1 = 6 hidden nodes + 1 threshold node. The Output layer corresponds to the number of outputs (dependent variables) we are examining. In this example, we have two outputs: customers who are satisfied or not satisfied. The width (thickness) of the lines connecting the input node to the output varies, with more important relationships represented by thicker lines (Exhibit 6-39).

Using this as a guide, you can see that the customer's Age line is thicker, which means that age is a relatively more important predictor variable in the model. Review the other lines and see what other input variables are important. Place your cursor over a circle to see what it is.

*Additional information about how recall and precision are calculated is available at: https://docs.rapidminer. com/latest/studio/operators/validation/performance/predictive/performance_classification.html

Exhibit 6-39

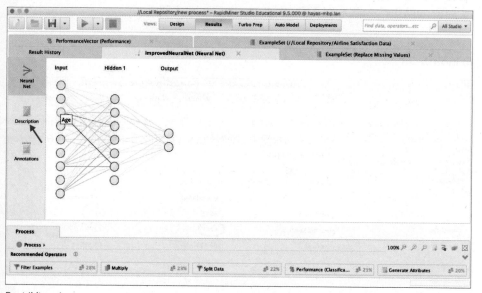

RapidMiner, Inc.

More detailed information can be located by selecting *Description* in the left panel as seen in Exhibit 6-39. Exhibit 6-40 displays the descriptions showing the weights assigned to two of the nodes. Note that Type of Travel is now divided into two variables that are dummy coded: Mileage tickets and Personal travel. As mentioned earlier, the dummy variable comparison group is Business travel. The sigmoid

Exhibit 6-40

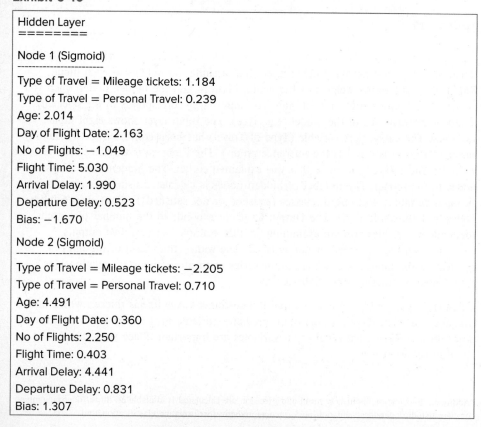

```
Hidden Layer
========

Node 1 (Sigmoid)
-----------------------
Type of Travel = Mileage tickets: 1.184
Type of Travel = Personal Travel: 0.239
Age: 2.014
Day of Flight Date: 2.163
No of Flights: −1.049
Flight Time: 5.030
Arrival Delay: 1.990
Departure Delay: 0.523
Bias: −1.670

Node 2 (Sigmoid)
-----------------------
Type of Travel = Mileage tickets: −2.205
Type of Travel = Personal Travel: 0.710
Age: 4.491
Day of Flight Date: 0.360
No of Flights: 2.250
Flight Time: 0.403
Arrival Delay: 4.441
Departure Delay: 0.831
Bias: 1.307
```

activation function is used to calculate the function output. The value of the bias for each node and the weights associated with each of the input to nodes 1 and 2 are also shown here. These weights are estimated and updated as the model is run by using the error reduction iterative process explained earlier in the chapter.

We are ready to save our work before we apply our model. Click the "Save" icon, name the file "Neural Net Analysis," and click "OK" (Exhibit 6-41).

Is the model performance good? We do not know until we compare it to the prediction performance of other supervised models. Let's assume that upon comparison we decided to adopt this model, now what? Now it is time to apply the model to a new dataset. Remember, the key to creating any predictive model is to apply it to new observations.

Exhibit 6-41

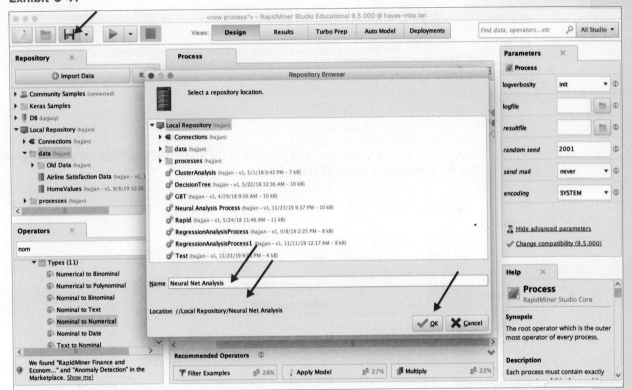

RapidMiner, Inc.

Stage 4: Applying the Model to a New Dataset

As an example, assume we have ten new customers. The objective is to use the parameters developed in training the model to predict the likelihood of the customers being satisfied or not satisfied.

The first step is to import the new data that has no target (dependent) variable (satisfied or not satisfied) information. In RapidMiner, this data is referred to as unlabeled data. To import the data, click on *Import Data* (Exhibit 6-42).

Exhibit 6-42

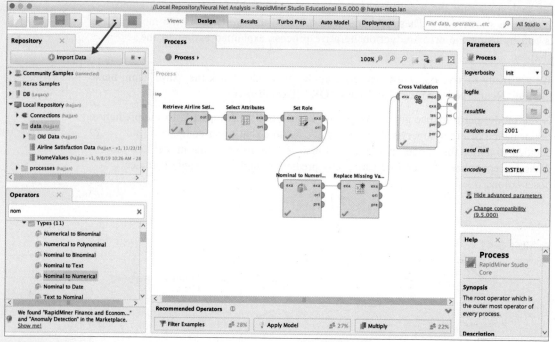

RapidMiner, Inc.

Next, click on "My Computer" and navigate to the folder for where the file containing the ten customers is stored (Exhibit 6-43).

Exhibit 6-43

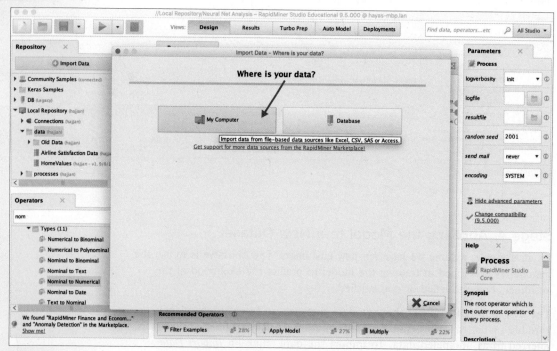

RapidMiner, Inc.

Add the "Airline Satisfaction New Data.xlsx" file (Exhibit 6-44). The data contains 10 new customers with the same features as in the original model.

Exhibit 6-44

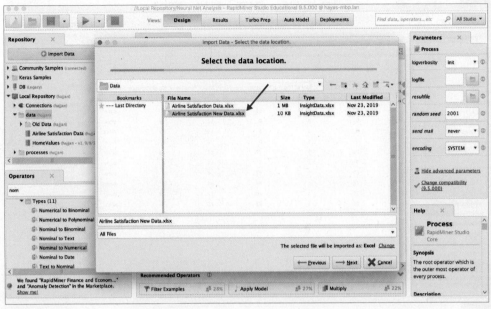

RapidMiner, Inc.

Using a process similar to what we followed earlier to upload the training data file, the new data can be previewed as seen in Exhibit 6-45. After reviewing and verifying the data, click "Next."

Exhibit 6-45

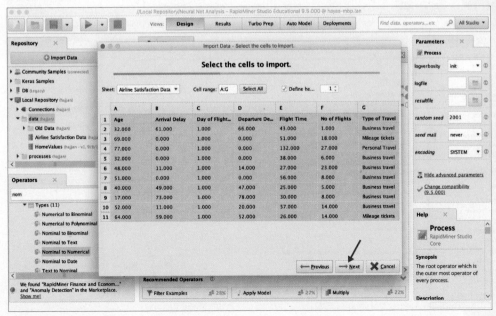

RapidMiner, Inc.

Don't forget that the types of the variables should be examined for accuracy (integer or polynomial) and corrected if needed (Exhibit 6-46).

Exhibit 6-46

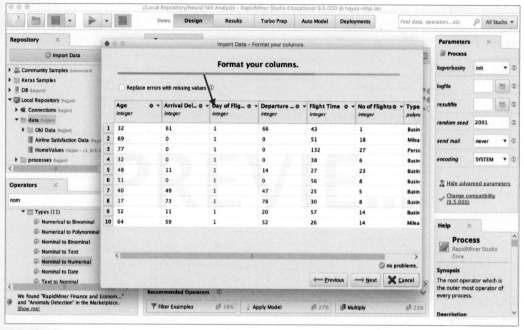

RapidMiner, Inc.

You now need to specify where the data will be stored. The new data storage location can be selected under the "Where to store the data?" window in the *Repository* panel. For this example, select "Local Repository" under the "data" folder. Then, click "Finish" (Exhibit 6-47).

Exhibit 6-47

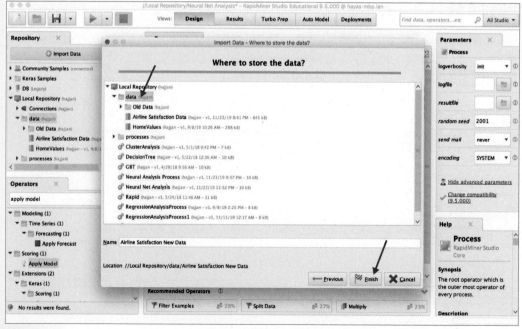

RapidMiner, Inc.

Next, drag the new *Airline Satisfaction New Data* from the Local Repository to the Process panel, as shown in Exhibit 6-48.

Exhibit 6-48

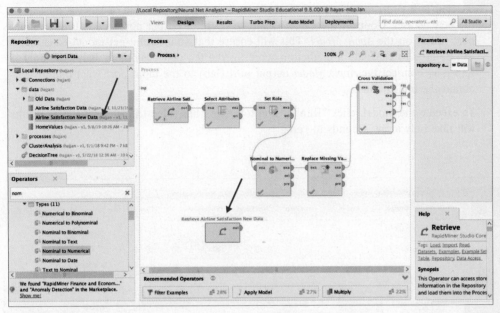

RapidMiner, Inc.

Under the Operators panel, find the *Nominal to Numerical* operator and drag it to the Process panel (Exhibit 6-49). Similar to the first dataset, the categorical variables will need to be converted into dummy codes because the neural network does not accept any categorical predictors. Next, connect the output port (out) on the *Retrieve Airline Satisfaction New Data* to the input port (exa) on the *Nominal to Numerical*.

Exhibit 6-49

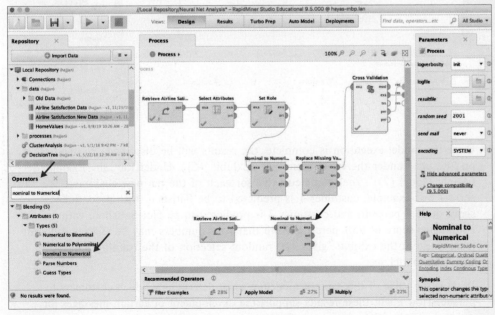

RapidMiner, Inc.

Under the Operators panel again, search for the *Apply Model* operator and drag it into the Process panel next to *Nominal to Numerical* (Exhibit 6-50).

Next, connect the output port (exa) from *Nominal to Numerical* to the input port on the *Apply Model* (unl). Recall that port (exa) stands for example dataset being passed on, and port (unl) means data that no dependent (target) variable or label is present in the new dataset. Connect the *Cross Validation* operator output port (mod) to the input port (mod) on the *Apply Model*. This will ensure that your neural net model equation will be used to calculate a prediction score for the ten new customers. Now, the final step is to connect the *Apply Model* output port (lab) to the input port (res) line to obtain the final results.

To execute the model, click "Run" in the top menu bar (blue triangle icon). The results will take only a few seconds to run.

Exhibit 6-50

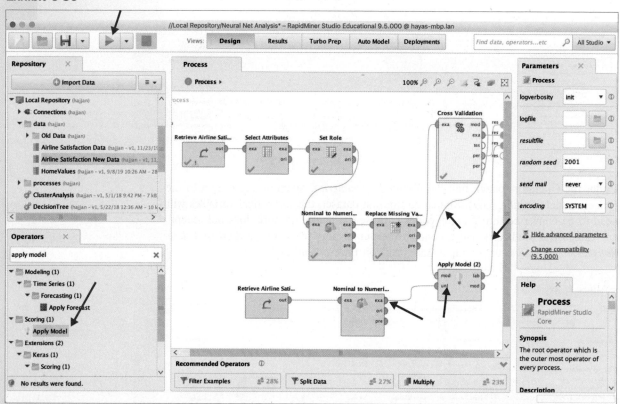

RapidMiner, Inc.

Once the model execution is complete, the results will be displayed. You can click on "Results" under the *Views* menu bar (Exhibit 6-51). Under the tab "ExampleSet (Apply Model (2))", the predicted value for each of the ten new customers is shown. For example, customer 1 is predicted to be Satisfied, with a confidence score of 75.7 percent, and customer 3 is predicted to be Not Satisfied, with a confidence score of 95.1 percent. Note that your numbers may be slightly different from those in the exhibits, given the random selection of the training dataset to build the model.

What is the value of this type of modeling when determining which customers to pursue? How might these results support the development of certain messages for satisfied and dissatisfied customers?

Customers 3, 8, and 10 are most likely to be unsatisfied (as shown in Exhibit 6-51). Consider the reasons for this dissatisfaction. What type of personalized messaging and action could be used to improve their experience as a customer?

Exhibit 6-51

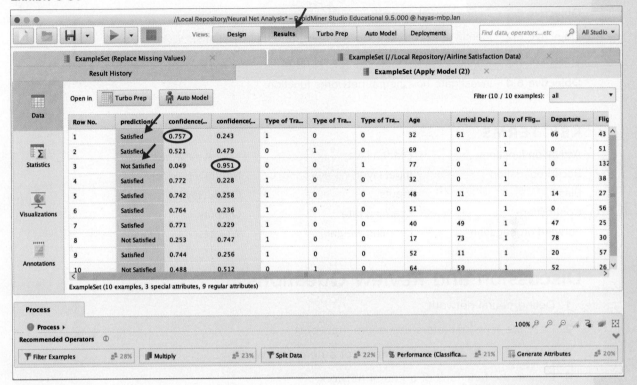

RapidMiner, Inc.

Insights Learned from Applying the Concepts

Many useful marketing problems can be solved with neural network analysis. In this case, what insights were revealed?

The goal of this case was to predict customer satisfaction. The analysis revealed three customers out of ten (30 percent) are likely to be dissatisfied with airline services. The airline can use this knowledge to identify options on how to improve their customer satisfaction, particularly through personalized communications and compensation. Consider how many customers will be retained with this understanding. Furthermore, consider the potential revenue that could be generated from customer retention.

This case provides an understanding of how a complex neural network model can be developed and results obtained using a relatively simple software. Models developed using RapidMiner are seldom a one-time effort. Once developed, the models can be used over and over again, until market circumstances change. Now that you have created a process template, you can change the dataset and use the same process to apply a neural network model to other datasets.

Summary of Learning Objectives and Key Terms

LEARNING OBJECTIVES

Objective 6.1   Define neural network.

Objective 6.2   Identify and compare various uses of neural networks.

Objective 6.3   Explain the elements of a neural network.

Objective 6.4   Investigate how neural networks function.

KEY TERMS

Activation functions	Hidden layer	Neural networks
Backpropagation	Input layer	Neurons (nodes)
Bias	Inputs	Output layer
Connections	Learning rate	Outputs
Forward propagation	Learning weight	Weights

Discussion and Review Questions

1. Define neural network.

2. Describe how marketers use neural networks.

3. What are basic structural elements of a neural network?

4. Explain the functions of a neural network.

5. What types of neural networks exist?

6. How does a neural network learn?

Critical Thinking and Marketing Applications

1. Review the data fields in Exhibit 6-7. What are some additional variables not contained in the dataset that could be used to predict whether customers might be satisfied?

2. What outcomes other than customer satisfaction would be helpful for marketing managers to predict?

References

1. Michael Brenner, "Artificial Neural Networks: What Every Marketer Should Know," Marketing Insider Group, January 23, 2018, https://marketinginsidergroup.com/content-marketing/artificial-neural-networks-every-marketer-know; Sooraj Divakaran, "The Future of Marketing & Neural Networks," Digital Uncovered, http://digitaluncovered.com/future-marketing-neural-networks; and Magnus Unemyr, "Use AI for Social Media Analytics and Consumer Insights," personal blog, May 4, 2018, https://www.unemyr.com/social-media-analytics-crimson-hexagon.

2. Brenner, "Artificial Neural Networks."

3. DialogTech, https://www.dialogtech.com.

4. Jennifer Faull, "How P&G Harnessed AI to Create 'First of Its Kind' Olay Skin Advisor," *The Drum*, February 28, 2017, https://www.thedrum.com/news/2017/02/28/how-pg-harnessed-ai-create-first-its-kind-olay-skin-advisor; and Barrett Brunsman, "P&G Goes Global with Selfie Skin Analysis," *Cincinnati Business Courier*, February 27, 2017, https://www.bizjournals.com/cincinnati/news/2017/02/27/p-g-goes-global-with-selfie-skin-analysis.html.

5. Case Studies from Cognitiv, https://cognitiv.ai/case-studies.

6. Karen Nyawera, "Fashion Forward—Using Deep Learning at ASOS to Predict Customer Lifetime Value in Online Fashion Retail," HBS Digital Initiative, January 12, 2019, https://digital.hbs.edu/platform-rctom/submission/fashion-forward-using-deep-learning-at-asos-to-predict-customer-lifetime-value-in-online-fashion-retail; Ka Lai Brightley-Hodges, "How Do ASOS Use Deep Learning to Optimise Performance?" ReWork blog, January 10, 2018, http://blog.re-work.co/how-do-asos-use-deep-learning-to-optimise-performance; and Ed Targett, "ASOS Bloodbath: AI Retail Opportunity?" *Computer Business Review*, December 17, 2018, https://www.cbronline.com/news/ai-retail-asos.

7. Case Studies from Cognitiv.

8. Allen Yu, "How Netflix Uses AI, Data Science, and Machine Learning—From a Product Perspective," *Medium*, February 27, 2019, https://becominghuman.ai/how-netflix-uses-ai-and-machine-learning-a087614630fe; and Trey Williams, "Netflix Uses Frame-by-Frame Machine Learning to Decide What You Really Want to Watch," *Market Watch*, September 28, 2017, https://www.marketwatch.com/story/netflix-uses-frame-by-frame-machine-learning-to-decide-what-you-really-want-to-watch-2017-09-27.

9. Bernard Marr, "Disney Uses Big Data, IoT and Machine Learning to Boost Customer Experience," *Forbes*, August 24, 2017, https://www.forbes.com/sites/bernardmarr/2017/08/24/disney-uses-big-data-iot-and-machine-learning-to-boost-customer-experience.

10. Bureau of Transportation Statistics, "Airlines and Airports," U.S. Department of Transportation, https://www.bts.gov/topics/airlines-and-airports-0.

11. "Benchmarks by Industry," ACSI, https://www.theacsi.org/acsi-benchmarks/benchmarks-by-industry.

12. Parul Pandey, "Data Science with Watson Analytics," *Medium*, August 26, 2018, https://medium.com/analytics-vidhya/data-science-with-watson-analytics-7dddcc34d3a9; and Parul Pandey, "Airline Satisfaction Survey.csv," GitHub, August 25, 2018, https://github.com/parulnith/Data-Science-with-Watson-Analytics/blob/master/Airline%20Satisfaction%20Survey.csv.

7 Automated Machine Learning

LEARNING OBJECTIVES

7.1 Define Automated Machine Learning.

7.2 Identify and compare various uses of automated modeling.

7.3 Investigate the Automated Machine Learning process.

7.4 Summarize the value of ensemble models.

7.5 Construct and assess an Automated Machine Learning model.

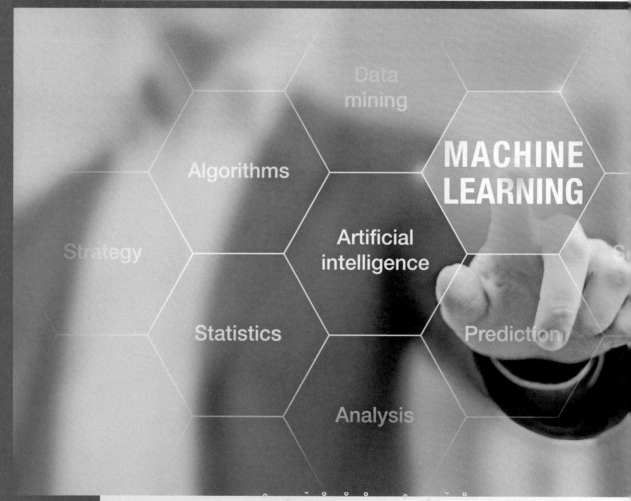

NicoElNino/Shutterstock

7.1 What Is Automated Machine Learning (AutoML)?

Who will win? Every year, people make predictions of who will be the winners of sporting events, entertainment awards, elections, and more. These predictions are often based upon personal intuitions, anecdotal evidence, or current polls. But what if you could accurately predict, for example, Grammy winners? That is exactly what DataRobot, an enterprise artificial intelligence (AI) platform, did for song and record winners of the 62nd Grammy awards. Using publicly available information, a data analyst from DataRobot applied Automated Machine Learning to make accurate predictions.

Delivering accurate predictions can have significant implications for companies as well. How many Apple iPhones will people buy next year? What motivates people to post on Instagram or communicate on Twitter? Why is customer loyalty so high for Amazon? How much will salespeople generate next quarter? Although these types of questions do not capture who will come out on top, they enable companies to anticipate results and determine how they can "win" in their decision making.

Previous chapters introduced commonly used supervised models for prediction and classification. These supervised models, such as neural networks, can help marketers answer important business questions. Recall that there are two main types of analytics methods: A **supervised model** is one that consists of a defined target variable, whereas an **unsupervised model** has no target variable. Running each supervised technique individually and comparing the results for best accuracy can be time consuming. As a more efficient alternative, marketers can rely on **Automated Machine Learning (AutoML)**, a mainly supervised approach that explores and selects models using different algorithms and compares their predictive performance.

AutoML is a process that automates the task of developing analytical models with machine learning. When applied, AutoML has helped to overcome the shortage in advanced data analytics skills—enabling more businesses to benefit without the traditional, manual approach of standard machine learning. In addition, AutoML has led to democratizing machine learning efforts so machine learning capabilities can now be extended to populations beyond traditional data scientists, particularly in medium- and smaller-sized businesses. Several of the new technology platforms automate the analysis process, support comparing predictive performances, and enable businesses of all sizes to develop accurate predictive models.

Even though the process has some automated features, users still must understand the underlying elements involved in developing the model. Imagine you are an analyst presenting results predicting that selected customers of a mobile phone provider, like Verizon, would be switching to AT&T. Specifically, your predictive model shows that increasing customer retention rates by 5 percent will likely increase profits by 25 percent or more. With predictions like this, the marketing team would likely want to intervene as soon as possible in an effort to prevent customers from leaving the company and switching to competitor brands. When presenting the model's decision or recommendation, the audience will want to know how it arrived at the conclusion. Typical questions would be what data was used to build the model, how the model was developed, what assumptions were made, and the specifics about the accuracy of prediction outcomes, because inaccurate results could lead to ineffective decision making.

What Questions Might Arise?

When looking at and reporting the model's decision or recommendation, some questions may need to be asked, including:

- How was the data collected and prepared for analysis?
- How did the model arrive at a particular conclusion? What is the blueprint of the model?
- Why did the model arrive at a particular conclusion?
- What variables had the greatest impact on the predicted outcome? What patterns exist in the data?
- What are the reasons behind why the recommended model produced the most accurate decision? For example, are there data issues that could be impacting the validity of the model? Is the model consistent in its predictions? Why is the model a good predictor? How accurate is the model?

Fortunately, software companies such as dotdata Enterprise, H2O.ai, RapidMiner, DMway, Google AutoML, and DataRobot offer several alternative AutoML solutions that can be evaluated. Expediting the process of modeling formulation and model selection afforded by AutoML is a good way for marketing analysts to focus on the best model to predict future customer behaviors. Thus, marketing analysts can recommend models that are more effective in offsetting consequences of customers leaving, reducing negative comments posted on websites, or generating new streams of revenue and profits through opportunities.

Marketers need to remember that implementing AutoML does not replace human expertise. The AutoML platform is only capable of the analytical discovery of relationships that actually are present in the dataset. Understanding the context of the data and ensuring that it meets quality standards will result in the most effective models. Predictive models, for example, such as those based on relationships between customer social media feedback and call center interactions, or between website postings and purchase likelihood, are examples that produce meaningful results.

PRACTITIONER CORNER

Elpida Ormanidou | Advanced Analytics and Insights at Starbucks

Elpida Ormanidou

Before joining Starbucks, Elpida Ormanidou worked as the Vice President for Advanced Analytics and Testing at Chico's FAS. She started her career at Sam's Club as a member trends analyst, and with a team of internal and external scientists, she developed a new analytical framework for the Membership organization, resulting in the company's member-centric strategy. She then worked as a senior pricing manager before moving to Walmart U.S. in 2008. She spearheaded an effort at Walmart to standardize the HR data analysis processes, making it faster and more accurate, while ensuring confidentiality and data integrity. Her most important priorities are enabling an organization to leverage actionable data science and achieve business objectives and to establish and expand their advanced analytics capability as a competitive advantage.

Continued

Q There has been increasing discussion about AutoML democratizing AI. AutoML solutions such as H2O.ai, RapidMiner, DMway, Google AutoML, and DataRobot allow marketing analysts to efficiently and effectively leverage the power of machine learning and AI to solve business problems. What are the advantages of using these tools?

A One of the biggest challenges we are faced with is that the rate of change today is faster than any other time in history. Business and our society need the ability to move at speed and agility. That involves processing vast amounts of data and turning them into simple, actionable, and consumable insights. While still viewed with skepticism, ML and AL applications are already transforming the world, and marketing is no exception. In fact, marketing competes for ML and AI capabilities against every other industry. Continued innovation in this space can significantly improve the experience for customers, employees, and their communities.

Earlier this year, Blake Morgan, a customer experience futurist and author, expertly underscored the need for personalization in the marketing world in a recent *Forbes* article.[1] The spike in demand and the shortage of talent created a prime space for the plethora of "out of the box" ML software and data science platforms that allow business users to harvest insights with the power of ML, without having deep expertise in deploying and fine-tuning ML learning models.

One advantage, of course, is that marketing can be much more responsive to customers' demanding 1:1 personalized experience. With some basic training, Marketing analysts can deliver individualized recommendations. In turn, by marketing analysts absorbing the need to apply and execute on ML recommendation, they free up more specialized and trained data scientists to continue to elevate capabilities, generate new, more sophisticated algorithms and respond to customer demands in new innovative ways in a perpetual productive loop.

One benefit that is not as obvious and does not often get the spotlight is the moderating or catalyzing function these marketing analysts play. For example, they often "humanize" the ML recommendations, which can appear crude, insensitive, or biased. Or they balance the ethicality of an application—because we can do something, does not mean we should. Additionally, they help define functional problems in ways that data scientists can easily understand and then develop algorithms to recommend solutions. On the other hand, they help individuals in marketing to increase their analytic literacy and also their ability to integrate more progressive solutions into their daily work.

Q What are the challenges marketers might face?

A The biggest and most fundamental challenge for marketers is buy-in. Most marketers take the classic approach to adopting AI and ML by basically asking how this new capability will fit into our existing operations. The better question to ask is how marketing should be organized around an AI-first strategy. This is important because we are not talking about a common change as, for example, implementing a new CRM solution. We are talking about a transformation—a radical reorganization and bifurcation of marketing activities, based on value-added solutions that can be led by both humans and machines. Marketers have to move past the fear, fight their protectionist instincts, and lead this transformation.

After marketers resolve these more existential challenges, they have to tackle another major challenge with privacy and the regulatory gaps: the classic can-versus-should dilemma, given diverse customer needs and slow regulatory evolution. While this problem is not driven necessarily by AI, it is definitely intensified and magnified by broader adoption of AI and ML solutions.

Other challenges are more mainstream. For example, marketers have to consider and invest in the technology/data infrastructure necessary to enable ML/AI, which can compete with other marketing-specific investment. Short-term versus long-term ROI in the right balance will be a consideration. A lot of those solutions come with a hefty price tag that is often "pay first get return later" and this does not fit well with the current profit-centric model, especially that of publicly traded companies.

Finally, there are challenges around recruiting and developing technical talent. The right talent that can facilitate and enable this marketing evolution is motivated differently than what some of the traditional existing programs can afford us.

Continued to page 236

7.2 AutoML in Marketing

AutoML has become more commonly used in marketing analytics. AutoML facilitates accurate decision making for users with limited coding and modeling experience. In a recent survey conducted by Accenture, 40 percent of companies reported already using machine learning to improve sales and marketing performance, and the adoption rate for AutoML is expected to increase substantially over the next few years.[2]

Companies representing many different industries have adopted AutoML to improve marketing efforts. Exhibit 7-1 shows examples of potential AutoML marketing applications.

Which Companies Are Actively Using AutoML?

It might not be surprising that some of the most successful companies are using AutoML. Typical examples include Facebook, Google, Microsoft, Amazon, Apple, and so on, as well as many other not-so-well-known companies.

Every time a user logs into Facebook, they are interacting with an algorithm developed by the company's AutoML platform. Facebook was previously able to roll out new advanced analytics models only every 60 days. But with AutoML, Facebook now trains and tests over 300,000 models every month and releases a new model every week.[3] These predictive models are used to further understand Facebook user patterns in an effort improve business performance, such as increasing ad revenues and user engagement.

Airbnb has also been using advanced analytics for years. The company experimented with several AutoML tools such as Auto-Sklearn, TPOT, and DataRobot. Airbnb is currently using AutoML to predict customer lifetime value for hosts and guests. Models predict the spending of each guest over time by taking into consideration variables such as demographics, location, and mobile and web activity. What Airbnb and other users learn from their models is then used to develop personalized messages based on the host or guest's lifetime value. Through automation of this process, Airbnb has had a positive impact on employee productivity and been able to reduce prediction errors by over 5 percent.[4]

Sumitomo Mitsui Card Company (SMCC) is the largest credit card company in Japan. The company applies AutoML for risk modeling and marketing applications, such as enhancing customer product upsell and cross-sell opportunities, managing customer attrition, and identifying the likelihood of default.[5] Insights from AutoML models are also used to support customer relationship management, marketing, and sales.

Exhibit 7-1 Examples of AutoML Applications in Marketing

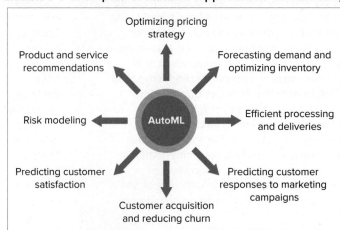

Kroger, the second-largest supermarket company in the world, is using AutoML, to help it resolve industry challenges from customers who want new service capabilities, such as home delivery. AutoML helps Kroger leverage data and better understand their 60 million household customers.[6] Using AutoML, Kroger is able to develop marketing campaigns uniquely personalized for customers.

Sports teams are also adopting AutoML. The Philadelphia 76ers of the National Basketball Association (NBA) was interested in better understanding both individual and season ticket sales.[7] How could they increase individual ticket sales and season ticket packages? What was the likelihood a ticket holder would renew their package? The team used AutoML to optimize its renewal process and thereby increase season ticket sales by four times. The team is now number one in the NBA for season ticket sales.

AutoML has been implemented by many companies in the healthcare industry to manage large volumes of data. For example, Blue Health Intelligence (BHI) uses AutoML to improve the quality of care for 180 million members.[8] Using public data sources, claims, and enrollment data, BHI identifies socioeconomic and behavioral factors associated with health risk outcomes. BHI is then able to develop methods of intervention to help manage healthcare costs.

The airline industry is highly competitive and customer satisfaction is extremely important. Customers want convenient reservations and check-in processes but often report concerns about in-flight service. In an effort to develop deeper customer relationships, United Airlines has adopted AutoML. Advanced analytics helps the company manage customer expectations and satisfaction. United Airlines can respond to customers in areas such as recommended flights and destinations, anticipate the number of bags a flight will hold—thus avoiding customers needing to check bags after boarding—and alerting customers in advance when WiFi might be unreliable.[9] With few exceptions, the company has been able to improve overall customer experiences.

URBN is a portfolio of apparel brands that includes Urban Outfitters, Anthropologie, Free People, and BHLDN. URBN previously struggled with the tedious and time-consuming task of manually coding product attributes such as color, patterns, neckline style, fabric, and so on. Yet, having these items coded is critical in delivering online personalized recommendations, as well as accurate and quick search results. Customers value and expect positive experiences. And meeting e-commerce expectations leads to an increase in customer satisfaction and loyalty. Until recently, many e-commerce sites were struggling with their search accuracy. For example, when customers use product-related synonyms, websites typically produce relevant search results only 30 percent of the time.[10] Furthermore, customers who search using just a product number or accidentally misspell a word by a single character experience poor search results 34 percent of the time. The company's data analytics teams turned to AutoML to manage similar deficiencies. When URBN began using AutoML, they substantially enhanced the overall customer shopping experience.[11]

Disney adopted AutoML to develop vision models that can recognize images and add details of products and their characteristics. These characteristics are then integrated with their e-commerce search engine. Results from this initiative included quick product recommendations and discoveries based on words searched by customers and improved overall customer experience.[12]

Pelephone is one of the oldest and largest mobile phone providers in Israel with more than 2.5 million customers. In an effort to increase revenues, Pelephone used AutoML to develop a predictive model and then trained a team of customer representatives to upsell devices and accessories. They prepared their data to include customer variables such as purchasing habits, past mobile phone usage, operating systems, and demographics. Using AutoML, the company was able to predict which customers were most likely to purchase a device. Before using the AutoML model, customers previously purchased from the representatives approximately 1.5 percent of the time. But after adoption of the AutoML model, purchase rates increased to almost 5 percent.[13]

Some companies use standalone AutoML technology. Other companies, however, such as Carfax, Comcast/Xfinity, and Farmers Insurance, use AutoML tools embedded in their technology platforms.[14] Salesforce Einstein, for example, uses an AutoML tool integrated into their existing Customer Relationship Management (CRM) tools. Companies using Salesforce CRM tools can then discover hidden insights and predict customer relationship outcomes so customers can be better managed in real time. Salespeople using the AutoML system can quickly develop lead scores for prospects, calculate the likelihood of sales for a customer, determine overall brand engagement, and assess the likelihood of closing a deal.

continued from page 233

PRACTITIONER CORNER
Elpida Ormanidou | Advanced Analytics and Insights at Starbucks

Q **Numerous companies are now adopting AutoML into their practices. It is predicted that companies will spend $77.6 billion on artificial intelligence systems such as those with machine learning capabilities by 2022 and that this technology could "create an additional $2.6 trillion in value for marketing and sales." How do you see AutoML learning playing a role in marketing and sales decision making?**

A In the early spring of 2020 during a pandemic that some argue will permanently impact our way of life and customer behaviors, we have a prime example of why using data democratization with AI tools can make a tangible difference in our day-to-day operations and even in society. During this time, the challenges marketers face got magnified enough to make them easier to identity and describe.

The United States adopted a very decentralized approach to deal with this pandemic. Local, municipal, and state governments made independent decisions. That meant that customers in different communities had different access, expectations, and availability of products and services. Marketing was faced with the need to, overnight, modify their strategy and be responsive to those heavily localized customer needs. Where marketing effectively supported a touchless digital-first approach, companies gained competitive advantage and were able to differentiate themselves in terms of customers. We are currently building models and using AI and ML to understand what products our customers really need and how to serve them, while keeping the highest levels of safety for our employees and our customers.

Almost every company was negatively impacted at some degree initially. However, many companies, powered by effective use of AutoML, are adopting and recovering faster. Walmart is a great example of a successful player, as the biggest publicly traded company with both physical and digital presence. AutoML serves as the canary in the coal mine, and very early on, before humans realize it, it can register and incorporate trends and data signals into recommendations. Adopting these algorithms drives value for the company in terms of speed of identification or message differentiation. Deploying them in parallel or with human supervision protects value by currently prioritizing and strategically implementing the ones that are relevant and make sense.

While organizations are asked to do more with less, AutoML can drive additional value when implemented correctly. Once companies

Continued

are able to achieve high levels of data accuracy and put the right infrastructure in place, AutoML reduces onboarding time for new employees, drives incremental output by taking over repetitive tasks (i.e., operational reporting). While executives and business leaders often struggle to frame a question, and technical talent gets sidetracked by answering wrong or ill-defined questions, AutoML helps users, especially newly placed ones, "learn" what questions to ask and focus on the right problem with more discipline.

Q What use cases are most benefited by AutoML?

A Use cases should be driven by business strategy and should be selected to ensure they deliver a competitive advantage. A very interesting and common application is around recommendation engines. Time and time again, we see that AutoML beats human-curated recommendations. Therefore, we can comfortably conclude that such an application will be very beneficial.

Continued to next page

7.3 What Are Key Steps in the Automated Machine Learning Process?

There are four key steps in the AutoML process: (1) preparing the data, (2) building models, (3) creating ensemble models, and (4) recommending models (see Exhibit 7-2).

Data Preparation

Successful use of AutoML begins with data preparation. Data preparation involves several considerations. These can include handling missing data, outliers, variable selection, data transformation, and data standardization to maintain a common format. In considering these issues, do not forget about the common adage that people use when referring to invalid and unreliable data: "garbage in, garbage out." Appropriate data preparation to ensure the quality of data is a fundamental first step in producing accurate model predictions.

Model Building

During model building, tens of models are usually built automatically after the analyst specifies the dependent (e.g., continuous or categorical) variable of interest. Models are complex, statistically based forms of analysis. The purpose of a model is to extract insights from data. Using features of a dataset, models are able to provide an understanding into relationships and patterns. AutoML uses preestablished modeling techniques that create access for anyone from novices to data science experts at the click of a button.

Exhibit 7-2 Key Steps in the AutoML Process

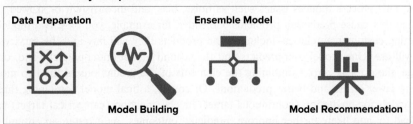

continued from previous page 237

PRACTITIONER CORNER

Elpida Ormanidou | Advanced Analytics and Insights at Starbucks

Q **There are essentially four high-level steps to AutoML: preparing the data, building models, creating ensemble models, and recommending models. What is your advice to approaching each of these steps?**

A From over two decades of experience in this space, here is my advice. I seriously doubt you will ever find yourself solving a real-life problem with perfectly clean or complete data. I also seriously doubt you need it in order to build effective models. Don't let data perfection be a distraction. Accept "good enough," derive the value you can from it, and call out its limitations. Iterate, don't overinvest.

Another point about data is to not hoard it. So many analysts and even data scientists have the mentality that data is power. It is not. Knowledge is power. Share data in the pursuit of knowledge.

In terms of models, at the risk of being cynical, I would argue that the best model is the one that will get used. My advice again for practitioners is to keep an eye on where the value gets created. Don't chase the perfect model; start with one that brings incremental value fast and that continues to evolve and innovate. As a data science professional, you deserve and reserve the right to get smarter.

Analytics capability is like an organizational muscle that companies need to build. This is because a successful analytics infrastructure touches every element and process of the business from data to deployment. Huge value gets unlocked from the optimized and coordinated application of analytics. Success is contingent to adoption and absorption, which explains one statistic that claims that over 70 percent of organizations that attempt to build analytics teams fail, even though analytics is considered a critical function in the organization.

Q **Workflow and explainability seem to be a key concern with AutoML. How do different AutoML tools simplify the workflow and provide transparency for the modeler?**

A Today's tools are more intuitive than previous generations. Some allow the user to build models with drag/drop interfaces, and most help reduce the lead time for cleaning data, building the workflow, and incorporating common drilldowns.

Simplicity is a major consideration. On the other hand, the problems that ML is tackling are multidimensional and very complex. Often, there is no silver bullet or simple explanation. Therefore, one should be balancing the tradeoffs between simple and simplistic.

Continued to page 240

Creating Ensemble Models

When making big decisions such as purchasing a laptop or an automobile, you are likely to consult various sources of information to obtain the most accurate information to make your decision. Developing an accurate model follows the same premise. Sometimes the best approach is to combine different algorithms, blending information from more than one model into a single "super model." This type of model is referred to as an **ensemble model**. It combines the most favorable elements from all models into a single model. This process reduces issues such as noise, bias, and inconsistent or skewed variance that cause prediction problems. Consider, for example, you have two models predicting customer purchases—including the products they will buy and the services they will use. One model over-predicts and the second model under-predicts, and, on average, the error is zero. Combining the elements of the predictions of the two models leads to fewer errors and better predictions. Of course, a final model combining three or four models for prediction (continuous target) or classification (categorical target) can also lead to, and likely further improve, predicted outcomes. As a result, an ensemble model usually generates the best overall predictive performance. Although an ensemble model offers several advantages, it is important to keep in mind that understanding how different variables have contributed to an outcome can be difficult.

Simple Approaches to Ensemble Modeling Several options are available when considering ensemble modeling. For continuous target variables, one method is to take the average of predictions from multiple models. This method can be useful for predicting regression problems or analyzing probabilities in classification problems. For instance, you could average a regression tree and linear regression. You first run each model separately to create two prediction scores and calculate the average of the two models to create a new ensemble score.

Another more advanced technique involves using a weighted average. Weights can be assigned based on the importance of each model in prediction. For example, one model might consist of higher quality data or could have higher levels of accuracy. The higher quality data would be assigned greater importance and thus weighted higher in the model.

For categorical target variables, the most common category of "majority" rule can be used. For example, let's say three separate models were run using logistic regression, neural network, and classification tree. The final estimates for the target (dependent) variables for the three respective models might be the following: (purchase), (purchase), and (no purchase). The models predict purchase more often. According to the majority rule, we decide the new case is purchase.

Advanced Ensemble Methods

Bagging **Bagging** is short for "Bootstrap Aggregating." There are two main steps in bagging, as displayed in Exhibit 7-3. Step 1 generates multiple random smaller samples from the larger sample. Each sample has a set of observations. But because the

Exhibit 7-3 Bagging (Bootstrap Aggregating)

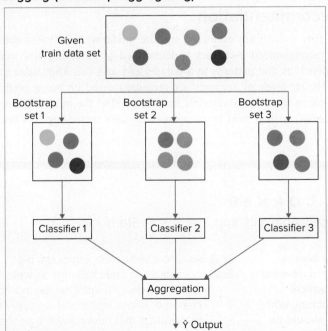

Source: Amey Naik, "Bagging: Machine Learning Through Visuals. #1: What Is 'Bagging' Ensemble Learning?" *Medium*, June 24, 2018, https://medium.com/machine-learning-through-visuals/machine-learning-through-visuals-part-1-what-is-bagging-ensemble-learning-432059568cc8.

observation is not actually removed from the original sample, only copied, it can be copied again and placed in a second or even a third sample. Note in Exhibit 7-3 that the green observation was copied twice in bootstrap set 1, and only once in bootstrap samples 2 and 3. This process is referred to as "bootstrap sampling."

The second step in bagging is to execute a model on each sample and then combine the results. The combined results are developed based on taking the average of all samples for continuous outcomes or the majority of case results for categorical outcome variables.

Boosting   The objective of **boosting** is reducing error in the model. Boosting achieves this by observing the error records in a model and then oversampling misclassified records in the next model created.

During the first step, the model is applied to a sample of the data. A new sample is then drawn that is more likely to select records that are misclassified in the first model. Next, the second model is applied to the new sample. The steps are repeated multiple times by fitting a model over and over (see Exhibit 7-4). The purpose of boosting is to improve performance and reduce misclassification. The final model will have a better prediction performance than any of the other models.

Exhibit 7-4 Boosting

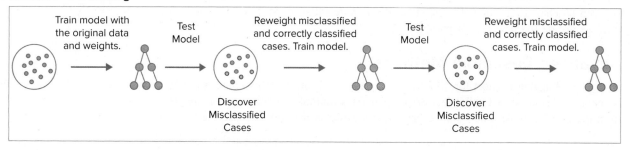

Model Recommendation

Multiple predictive models are examined and the model with the most accurate predictions is recommended. Accuracy is determined by observing how well a model identifies relationships and patterns in a dataset and uses this knowledge to predict the outcome. Higher levels of accuracy are measured based on better predictions of observations, not in the original datasets used to develop the model. The most accurate prediction model(s) is then used by companies to make better business decisions.

continued from page 238

PRACTITIONER CORNER
Elpida Ormanidou | Advanced Analytics and Insights at Starbucks

 Since AI systems are taught our biases, marketers have a responsibility to develop principles and systems for the ethical management of AI to benefit society. What are some ethics questions that should be addressed when adopting AutoML?

A As discussed earlier, Ethics is a big consideration and challenge as well. If we clearly understand what the individual customer is looking for and we apply AutoML to deliver to that desire, we are generally OK. For example, people have no problem

Continued

providing their own DNA, just to find out what part of the world they come from. The moment trust breaks down and the data is used for other reasons, an ethical question will arise.

Going back to the point of personalization, we need to keep a balance between which data is a must-have versus nice-to-have, and how the output will be perceived by the end user. Key, and very close, partnerships between Privacy, Legal, and HR teams are critical to ensure that we follow GDPR (General Data Protection Regulation) and other new guidelines by country, state, and local authorities. Each (not just in aggregate) customer must feel that we use their data to improve their experience above all else. If data is used to maximize profit or add complexity to their life, that becomes problematic. This has led to customers' disengaging from email communications that spam their email because they aim at driving sales versus serving each specific customer.

This challenge is already demonstrated now in certain social media that almost discriminately spam customers.

The main questions that I always ask myself as I approach data analytics problems are:

- What is the value to the customer (each individual not segments)?
- What additional value will this particular data provide?
- Did our customers opt in for us to be able to use this data in this way?
- How will this application be perceived given the cultural and demographic differences of our global customer base?
- How long do we need to keep data in our systems to inform the business?
- Do we have a secure and reliable process to host and share the data?
- Do I have the right technology and policies in place to monitor that data is safe at all times and to safeguard its integrity from internal and external threats?

Loan Data: Understanding When and How to Support Fiscal Responsibility in Customers

Understanding the Business Problem

The peer-to-peer (P2P) lending industry, where borrowers are extended loans by personal investors, is a $2.0 billion industry and is expected to continue growing. Lending Club is an online peer-to-peer lending platform that indirectly connects investors and borrowers. The company is a leader in the industry and has almost 40 percent in market share.[15] Customers who use the online platform are typically looking to refinance their credit card, consolidate their debt, cover medical expenses, or finance a business. The platform offers a quick process where customers can be approved in only a few minutes. Lending Club has facilitated over 4 million loans, totaling almost $50.4 billion.

Due to the company's peer-to-peer style of lending, it also offers opportunities to individuals and institutional investors, as well as bank partnerships. Individuals invest in "notes" that represent their proportion of the loans. When customers make monthly principal and interest loan payments, individual investor accounts are credited for the amount that corresponds to their particular "note". The loans are appealing to individual investors because they typically make a 4 to 7 percent return on their investment. There are risks, however, because approximately 10 percent of the loans default. The creditor assumes the debt will remain unpaid, and the remaining balance is written off as bad debt.

The Chief Operating Officer at Lending Club has charged the marketing team with reducing the default rate from 10 to 8 percent within 12 months. The expected savings from this 2 percent reduction equates to almost $10 million annually. Equally important, however, is that reducing the default rate will improve the reputation and brand equity of Lending Club as a low-risk investment with good returns.

The marketing team at Lending Club started their journey by conducting comprehensive stakeholder interviews. These interviews included three groups of people. One was a diverse group of borrowers who have defaulted. This group was interviewed to understand what interventions could have been helpful in avoiding default. The second group were internal financial analysts, who were interviewed to better understand the financial impact and support programs the company could offer for high-risk borrowers. The last group were investors, who were interviewed to obtain ideas on how to best engage the borrowers. The marketing team also collected historical data, such as demographics and various outcomes, from 2007 to 2014.

After evaluating their options, the marketing team decided the best approach was to build a supervised model. The objective of the model was to identify borrowers that have a high chance of default. Borrowers likely to default would be targeted each month with personalized digital messages, reminding them to pay their bills and to save money by avoiding penalties. In addition, they would be offered free access to a financial advisor to help manage their budget. Now, let's develop a model to identify individuals at high risk of default.

Understanding the Dataset

The first step in the model development process is to understand what data is available for analysis. You can download the Lending Club sample dataset from the student

Exhibit 7-5 Lending Club Information Available at the Time of Prediction

VARIABLE NAME (TYPE)	DESCRIPTION
default_status (binary string: target)	Current status of loan (yes for default, or no for no default)
loan_amnt (numeric)	Listed amount of the loan applied for by the borrower
term (string)	Number of payments on the loan; values are in months, and length can be either 36 months or 60 months
int_rate (numeric)	Interest rate on the loan (%)
grade (string)	Loan grade assigned by Lending Club (A best to G worst); corresponds to the loan applicant's credit rating and risk values, such as debt-to-income ratios or loan amount
emp_title (string)	Job title supplied by the borrower when applying for the loan
emp_length (numeric)	Employment length in years supplied by the borrower; values include (<1, 1 to 10, and n/a)
home_owners (string)	Home ownership status provided by the borrower during registration or obtained from the credit report; values are RENT, OWN, MORTGAGE, and OTHER
annual_inc (numeric)	Self-reported annual income provided by the borrower during registration
verification (string)	Employment verification status
purpose (string)	A category provided by the borrower for the loan request
addr_state (string)	Address by state of the borrower
dti (numeric)	A ratio calculated using the borrower's total monthly debt, payments on the total debt obligations, excluding mortgage and the requested Lending Club loan, divided by the borrower's self-reported monthly income
revol_bal (numeric)	Total credit revolving balance
total_acc (numeric)	Total number of credit lines currently in the borrower's credit file

resources page. The Lending Club dataset was a random sample of 30,000 customers from 2004 to 2014. The company website has the complete digital application journey for all borrowers. The sample data includes the dependent variable default status (default or not default) and key independent variables, including loan amount, borrower's employment information, home ownership status, self-reported annual income, loan purpose, debt-to-income ratio, number of credit lines, and similar data. To get started, review the variables in Exhibit 7-5.

Uploading the Data

In this case study, you will conduct exploratory data analysis with DataRobot software. DataRobot is an AutoML tool that automates feature selection, exploratory analysis, and modeling. During the analysis, patterns and key variables will be identified and the best model will be selected. You should first look at the 30,000 records in the Excel file LendingClub_2007_2014.xlsx (Exhibit 7-6) and examine each field and its range of values.

Exhibit 7-6

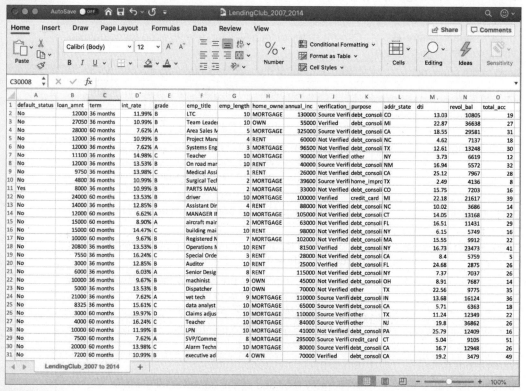

Microsoft Excel

To access DataRobot, you will have to obtain login information from your professor. DataRobot is free for educational use. Your professor will provide you with your username and password. Please note that DataRobot is updated constantly, and there is a chance that by the time you are using the system, some of the menu options will be slightly different. You should still be able to follow along with the instructions in the next sections.

Go to app.datarobot.com and type in your username and password (Exhibit 7-7).

Exhibit 7-7

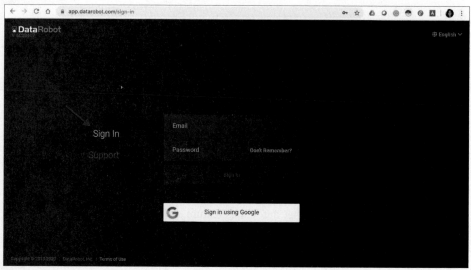

DataRobot, Inc.

When you first log into DataRobot, you will see a window to upload your dataset (Exhibit 7-8). Note that you cannot clean a dataset in DataRobot. Data cleaning (e.g., removing missing data, correcting data entry errors, etc.) should be completed prior to uploading the data into DataRobot. The data file LendingClub_2007_2014.xlsx for this case study has already been cleaned and is ready to be uploaded into DataRobot.

The default background in DataRobot consists of a dark theme. If you prefer a light themed background, please click on ![icon], then click on Settings. Scroll to find Theme and change it to the Light Theme. The display will then change to a light background.

Select "Local File" to navigate to the directory where the data for this case study is stored (Exhibit 7-8).

Exhibit 7-8

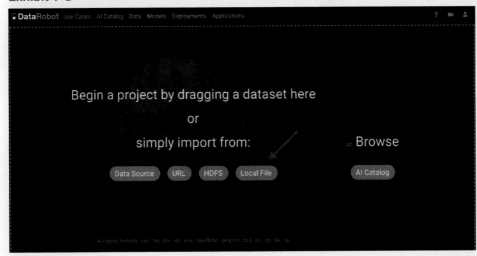

DataRobot, Inc.

Next, as shown in Exhibit 7-9, select the LendingClub_2007_2014.xlsx file and click "Choose."

Exhibit 7-9

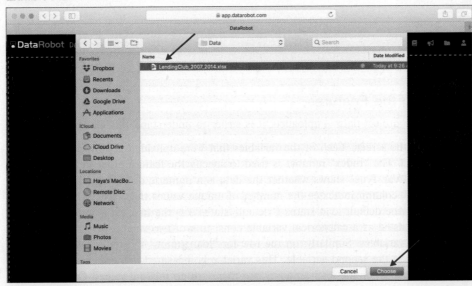

DataRobot, Inc.

As shown on the right side of Exhibit 7-10, there are three green checkmarks when this process is completed: Uploading Data, Reading raw data (Quick) into the cloud platform, and Exploratory Data Analysis. After completion, DataRobot will instruct the user to identify a target or dependent variable that will be predicted (Select target). You may be tempted to jump ahead at this point and select a target variable. However, it is a good idea to first examine the features (variables) that have been uploaded before selecting the target variable.

Exhibit 7-10

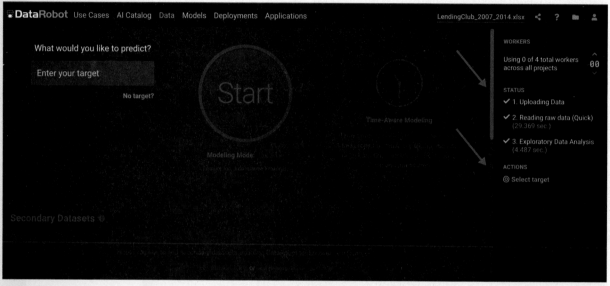

DataRobot, Inc.

In the upper right corner, the project name can be changed by clicking on the dataset name and typing in a new name (Exhibit 7-11). For now, we will keep the same project name.

Exhibit 7-11

DataRobot, Inc.

Examining the Features

Now that the project data is uploaded, it is easier to understand the features.

Scroll down the screen. Each of the variables that were uploaded is now visible (Exhibit 7-12). The "Index" number is used to specify the feature order in the dataset. The column "Var Type" shows whether the data is a numeric or categorical variable. The "Unique" column indicates the number of unique values that exist for the variable. For example, the default loan status ("default_status") is the first variable in the dataset. It is listed as a categorical variable consisting of two values—yes or no—and has zero missing variables. Similarly, on the row for "loan_amnt," the Index number of two indicates this is the second variable. This variable is measured numerically, there are 887 unique values for the loan amount, and there are no missing values. Other values shown here include, for example, the mean and standard deviation for numeric

Exhibit 7-12

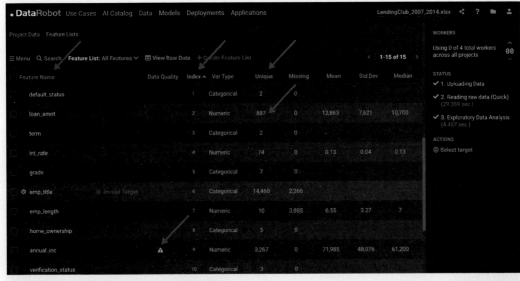

DataRobot, Inc.

variables. The variable annual-inc (annual income) has a warning sign ⚠. This means that the variable has outliers and should be treated with caution when running a linear model. Other variables impacted by the same warning are revol_bal (Total credit revolving balance) and total_acc (Total number of credit lines). These are important variables for the analysis. As of now, we will retain the variables and carefully assess interpretations if the recommended model is linear.

Clicking on the variable name will return more details about the specific variable (Exhibit 7-13). For example, click on "default_status." The feature list expands to show more details. This detailed view shows how many loans out of the 30,000 total in the dataset are in each of the two categories: not in default ("No") or in default ("Yes"). The distribution indicates that 18 percent of customers are in default on their loan (N = 5,540).

Exhibit 7-13

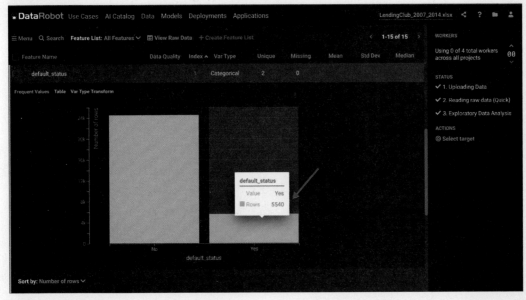

DataRobot, Inc.

The distribution and descriptive statistics of each variable can also be examined. Note, for example, the numerical variable interest rate ("int_rate") in Exhibit 7-14. Only a few loans in the dataset have 6 percent (Min) or 26 percent (Max) interest rate, and the mean value for interest rate is 13 percent.

Exhibit 7-14

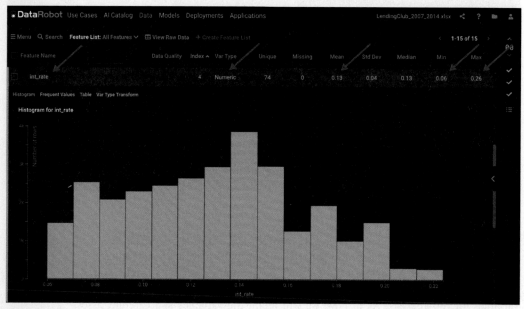

DataRobot, Inc.

In further examining the categorical variable "Grade" in Exhibit 7-15, there are seven unique variable category grades: A to G. Recall that grade corresponds to the loan applicant's credit rating and risk values, such as debt-to-income ratios or loan amount. The top three grades that have been assigned are B, C, and A (bottom of bar chart).

Exhibit 7-15

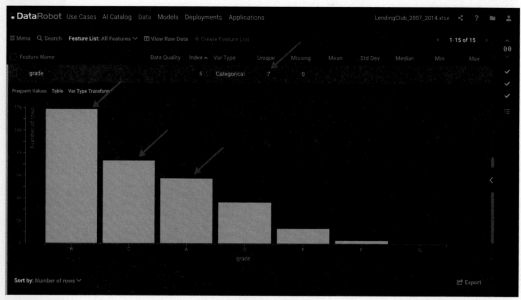

DataRobot, Inc.

Other variable transformations typically take place at this stage. For example, if a date feature was included in the dataset, the date will automatically be changed to Day of the week, Month, and Year. This is helpful to gain a better understanding if a particular day or days of the week lead to different outcomes.

Defining the Target Variable

It is now time to define the target variable and review the advanced parameters for the model. In the section *What would you like to predict?*, begin typing "default_status" (Exhibit 7-16). The field will auto populate based on text input. Select "default_status" to set it as a target.

Exhibit 7-16

DataRobot, Inc.

After the target variable is selected, the distribution of the variable is shown for default_status (Exhibit 7-17). The distribution is displayed with the bar chart in the top left corner. Note the bar for "No" (loan not in default) is much taller than for "Yes," indicating loans in default are much smaller than the number of loans not in default.

Note how the top window now has default_status in it and the Start button is highlighted. The Feature List selected is *Informative Features* (duplicates and variables with too few values are excluded) and the optimization metric selected by default is *LogLoss* (see the highlighted Start button). LogLoss means the model is evaluated based on the probability of positive classification generated by the model and how far it is from the correct answer. Therefore, a LogLoss of zero would reflect a perfect model. When the model assigns a probability of 0.95 to the case being "Yes," the model is considered to have done better than if the probability it assigned was 0.75 (75 percent) to the same case. But if the model assigned a probability of 0.20 to a case that is actually a "Yes," LogLoss will penalize the model a lot for being close to zero and wrong. See the DataRobot documentation section—the ❓ question mark icon in the top right corner—for more information about LogLoss and other modeling techniques.

Now click on *Show Advanced Options* at the bottom of the screen.

Exhibit 7-17

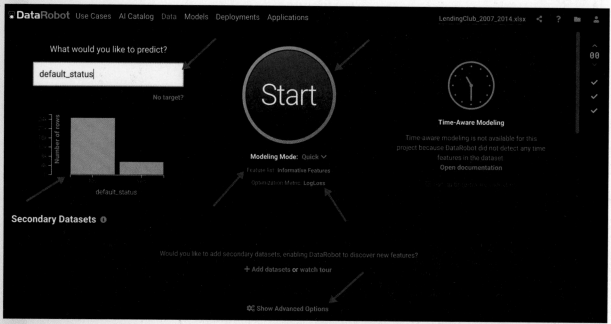

DataRobot, Inc.

Click on Show Advanced Options (bottom of Exhibit 7-17). Several options appear under Partitioning (Exhibit 7-18). DataRobot supports several partitioning methods: Random, Partition Feature, Group, Date/Time, and Stratified. To be prepared for the next steps, review each of the different types of partitioning in the DataRobot resources community. Each of these options can be reviewed in the DataRobot documentation section by clicking on the question mark icon **?** in the top right corner.

The Random partitioning option enables you to divide the total sample into two separate groups—a training sample and a hold-out sample. Under *Select partitioning method:*, first select Random. Next, select the percentage to be used for the hold-out sample. You can pull the slider to change the size of the hold-out sample as needed. For the current sample size, a good hold-out sample size is 20 percent (indicated by the red portion of the line in Exhibit 7-18), leaving 80 percent of the sample for training the model. For larger samples, it might be acceptable to increase the size of the hold-out sample.

The hold-out sample data is kept in a "lock-box" for use later. This is equivalent to the optional testing dataset you learned about in Chapter 1. The hold-out sample must be unlocked before the model starts predicting new cases. However, it is critical to finalize model decisions before unlocking the hold-out sample, because it cannot be relocked.

Although not selected here, Stratified partitioning is also a useful method in supervised learning. The Stratified partitioning method works the same way as Random except that it maintains a similar proportion of positive and negative target examples in each subgroup. As a result, the original ratio of default to non-default cases is maintained in both the training and the hold-out samples.

In Exhibit 7-18 under *Run models using:*, there are two options: Cross Validation and Train-Validation Holdout. For this exercise, select "Cross Validation." Cross validation was introduced in Chapter 5. Recall that predictive performance is evaluated using a cross validation procedure. The model is built using a training subset of the data. Then, the model is validated on the remaining subset for each n-fold iteration.

Exhibit 7-18

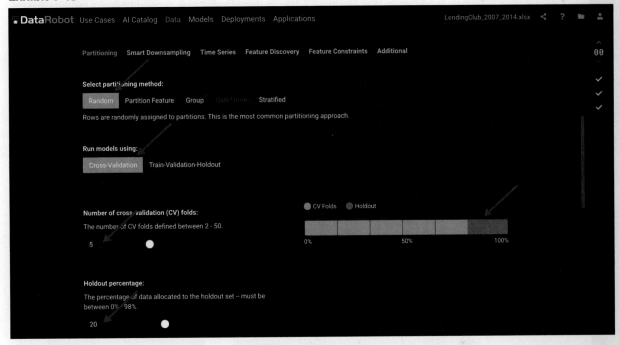

DataRobot, Inc.

Let's revisit how cross validation works. After determining the hold-out sample size of 20 percent, this sample is put in a lock box and the remainder of the data is randomly divided into n-folds (n separate groups). The most often used number of folds is either five or ten. The choice of the appropriate number of folds is based on the total sample size, with larger samples making it possible to increase the number of folds. For our sample, recall the hold-out sample size based on 20 percent of the total sample, so 6,000 observations. Thus, we have 24,000 cases (30,000 − 6,000 = 24,000) left for the training sample. If we use five folds, that means each of the five folds has 4,800 cases used for the cross validation process (24,000 / 5 = 4,800). That is, four of the folds combined would total 19,200 cases (4 × 4,800 = 19,200) to run the training model, and the fifth fold of 4,800 cases would be used to cross validate the model for each fold. Exhibit 7-19 shows the five-fold concept visually.

Exhibit 7-19

Training	Training	Training	Training	Validation	Hold-out
Training	Training	Training	Validation	Training	Hold-out
Training	Training	Validation	Training	Training	Hold-out
Training	Validation	Training	Training	Training	Hold-out
Validation	Training	Training	Training	Training	Hold-out

For cross validation, the average of all predicted validation scores are used to obtain the final validation score for the model. Then, before applying the model to new cases, the hold-out sample score should be calculated. This ensures the model performs well before adopting it in a real-life setting.

Running the Model

Click Modeling Mode: "Quick". Select the "Autopilot" option as the *Modeling Mode*, click the Start button (Exhibit 7-20). If your DataRobot account doesn't include the "Autopilot" option, proceed with the "Quick" option. "Quick" is "Autopilot" applied to a smaller subset of models.

Exhibit 7-20

DataRobot, Inc.

Exhibit 7-21

DataRobot, Inc.

The Start option triggers a seven-step set of processes (Exhibit 7-21):

1. Setting the target feature (default_status) in the analytics process.
2. Creating cross validation and hold-out samples.
3. Characterizing the target variable by saving the distribution of the target variable to the analysis process to choose which models to run.
4. Loading the dataset and preparing it for analysis. This option is relevant when the dataset is larger than 500 MB.
5. Saving target and partition information. This step is where actual validation folds and hold-out samples are stored.
6. Analyzing features where each feature (variable) is sorted by importance in predicting the target variable.
7. Generating a blueprint that determines models based on the target variable distribution and the previous steps.

Earlier, we examined the distribution of the different features (independent variables) in our dataset (see Exhibit 7-14). Reviewing this data again shows each of the features relative to the target (dependent) variable. Each feature can be compared to the target using one of two methods: regular linear regression or logistic regression. In our example, the method is logistic regression because the target variable is categorical (yes = default on loan; no = did not default). Recall that with regular linear regression the target variable is continuous.

The green bars displayed in the "Importance" column of the *Data* page are a measure of how much a variable, by itself, is related to (predicts) the target variable (Exhibit 7-22).

Exhibit 7-22

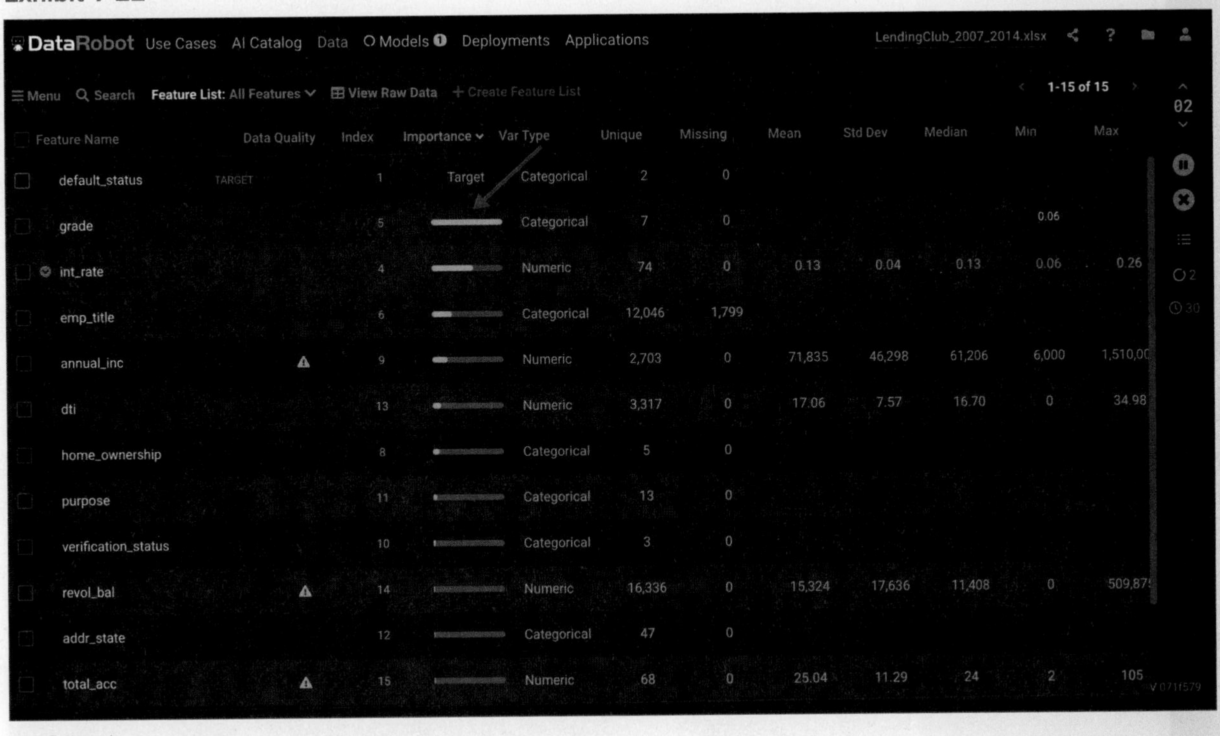

Feature Name	Data Quality	Index	Importance ⌄	Var Type	Unique	Missing	Mean	Std Dev	Median	Min	Max
default_status	TARGET	1	Target	Categorical	2	0					
grade		5		Categorical	7	0				0.06	
int_rate	⊘	4		Numeric	74	0	0.13	0.04	0.13	0.06	0.26
emp_title		6		Categorical	12,046	1,799					
annual_inc	⚠	9		Numeric	2,703	0	71,835	46,298	61,206	6,000	1,510,00
dti		13		Numeric	3,317	0	17.06	7.57	16.70	0	34.98
home_ownership		8		Categorical	5	0					
purpose		11		Categorical	13	0					
verification_status		10		Categorical	3	0					
revol_bal	⚠	14		Numeric	16,336	0	15,324	17,636	11,408	0	509,87
addr_state		12		Categorical	47	0					
total_acc	⚠	15		Numeric	68	0	25.04	11.29	24	2	105

DataRobot, Inc.

Hover the cursor over the importance score for "grade" (green line), as shown in Exhibit 7-23. The importance score provides two values: Value and Normalized Value. The first, Value, is a univariate value showing univariate model results using the validation dataset. The number for Value shows the approximate validation score you would get if you build a model with that one variable—in this model, Value is 0.44435. Below Value is the Normalized Value. This number ranges from 0 to 1, where a higher value indicates a stronger relationship. These scores indicate the predictive power of a model using only this one variable to predict the selected target variable.

The green line length corresponds to the normalized value and shows the feature's predictive value relative to the other features included in the model. The longer green line shows that "grade" has a relatively stronger predictive relationship with the default target variable as compared to other predictor variables. Note that the stronger predictor variables are shown at the top of the list, and as you move down, the predictive ability of the variables decreases, with several of the variables showing no predictive ability of the target variable.

Notice in Exhibit 7-23 the Value is 0.44435. A Value of 1 would indicate the feature fully predicts the target variable, while a 0.5 would indicate the feature predicts 50 percent of the change in the target, and a 0 indicates no relationship between the feature and the target variable (in this example, default status of a loan). Thus, this value is interpreted in a manner similar to R^2.

Exhibit 7-23

DataRobot, Inc.

Earlier, the descriptive statistics and distribution of the predictor variable interest rate were reviewed. Now that the target variable has been processed (classified with the model), the output provides the distribution of the predictor variable relative to the target dependent variable (Exhibit 7-24). The line shows the percentage of loan defaults increases as the interest rate increases. The pattern of higher interest rates associated with higher rates of loan defaults is logical, given that a higher interest rate typically indicates a higher risk loan.

Exhibit 7-24

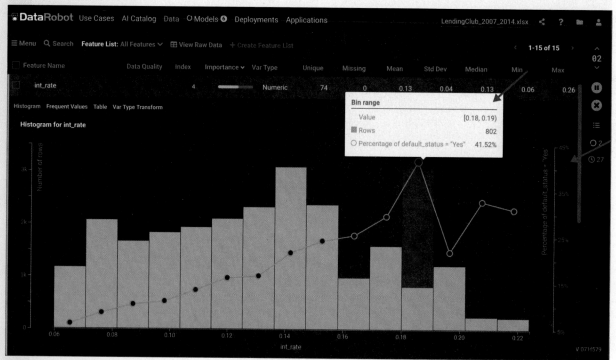

DataRobot, Inc.

Recall the categorical variable grade had seven unique variables and the top three grades are B, C, and A (Exhibit 7-15). The number of customers assigned each credit value is represented by the height of the blue bars (Exhibit 7-25). The data in Exhibit 7-25 shows that Grade A has the lowest likelihood of default compared to all the other categories (the percentage of defaults is identified by the orange circle for a particular bar). This is expected because Grades are based upon various factors such as the borrower's credit score and a risk assessment. In addition, we would expect that borrowers from the Grade A loans category would be less likely to default, given their more positive financial position. In contrast, we would expect Grade E to have the highest default rate, and it does at 46.46 percent. Click on the circle on top of each of the bars to see the specific percentage of default-status results.

Exhibit 7-25

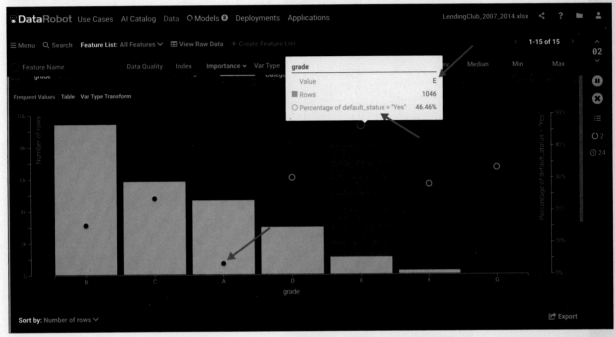

DataRobot, Inc.

Now, let's examine each of the variables and identify any surprising trends. For example, scroll down on the feature list and select "emp_title." This will generate a chart similar to Exhibit 7-25, but it will provide information related to which line of employment seems to be associated with the highest default rates.

Consider exploring other features in the list to answer the following question: What is the default rate associated with Nevada?

Note that running the models on the cloud will take between 10 and 12 minutes. The good news is there is plenty to explore in the system while the final models are running.

The model processing runs on Amazon Web Services workers (or servers). The default workers variable is set to two, but you may have an option to increase the number of workers to four (Exhibit 7-26). Increasing the number of workers improves the speed of the process.

Exhibit 7-26

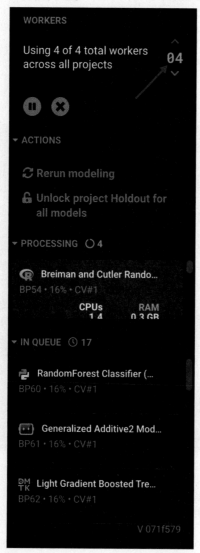

WORKERS

Using 4 of 4 total workers
across all projects   04

ACTIONS

↻ Rerun modeling

🔓 Unlock project Holdout for
   all models

PROCESSING ○ 4

Ⓡ Breiman and Cutler Rando...
BP54 · 16% · CV#1
              CPUs   RAM
              1.4   0.3 GB

IN QUEUE 🕐 17

⛁ RandomForest Classifier (...
BP60 · 16% · CV#1

⊡ Generalized Additive2 Mod...
BP61 · 16% · CV#1

DM
TK Light Gradient Boosted Tre...
BP62 · 16% · CV#1

                           V 071f579

DataRobot, Inc.

Evaluating the Model Results

Finally, when the models are finished running, the Leaderboard (top left of Exhibit 7-27) will appear and show the ranking of the models. Next, a cross validation is run for the top models. The models are then sorted by cross validation scores and two types of ensemble models are created: AVG Blender and ENET Blender (lower left in Exhibit 7-27). The AVG Blender model averages the probability score of the top models based on the probability produced for each case. For example, if the probabilities for the top three models return probabilities of 0.90, 0.87, 0.90 for case 1, the average of the results is 0.89.

Exhibit 7-27

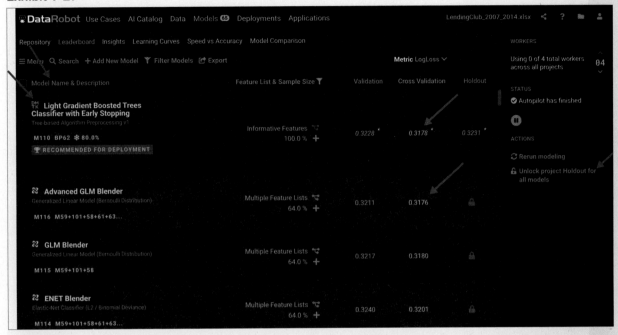

DataRobot, Inc.

The ENET Blender model runs two options—one option blends the top three models and the other the top eight models. In this example, the ENET blender blended the top eight models. (Note: To determine which models were used, click on "ENET Blender," then "Describe," and then "Blueprint.") Each probability in the ENET Blender model is treated as a feature and is used with the target variable to predict the output value. The Leaderboard shows the *Light Gradient Boosted Trees Classifier with Early Stopping* as the recommended model for deployment.* This model is recommended based upon accuracy and understandability. The Advanced GLM blender has the lowest error (0.3178), as shown in the "Cross Validation" column (Exhibit 7-27), but the sample size is less than the recommended model. Focusing only on cross validation results, this blender model is the most accurate.

Recall that after the models are trained, the predictions are applied to the hold-out sample. Remember that you will need to unlock the hold-out sample to evaluate the quality of your models once they are trained. To unlock the sample and obtain the model's hold-out score, click on "Unlock project Holdout for all models" on the right side of the screen (Exhibit 7-27). Hold-out values will not be generated in the "Holdout" column.

Confirm that the *Light Gradient Boosted Trees Classifier with Early Stopping* is sorted by cross validation (Exhibit 7-28). Select "Understand," then "Feature Impact," and click "Compute Feature Effects".

This will start a process to assess the importance of each feature in the model using a permutation importance technique. This technique calculates how much worse a model would perform if DataRobot made predictions after randomly shuffling the values in the variable. This calculation is usually run after normalizing all values, so the value of the most important column is 1. In other words, the feature impact measures how the accuracy of the model would change if the feature is removed from the model.

---

*For more information on Gradient Boosting Decision Trees, go to: https://papers.nips.cc/paper/6907-lightgbm-a-highly-efficient-gradient-boosting-decision-tree.pdf

Exhibit 7-28

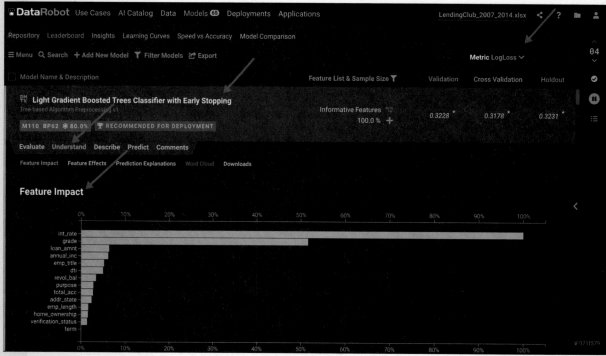

DataRobot, Inc.

The *Light Gradient Boosted Trees Classifier with Early Stopping* is sorted by cross validation. To understand this ranking, select "Understand" and then click "Prediction Explanation" (Exhibit 7-29).

The results show a granular understanding of the customers. Individual customer's feature values are examined to determine the reasons a customer has defaulted or not defaulted. You can set the thresholds for examining the individual feature contributions to the target variable. Exhibit 7-29 shows the top and bottom 10 percent of cases. For

Exhibit 7-29

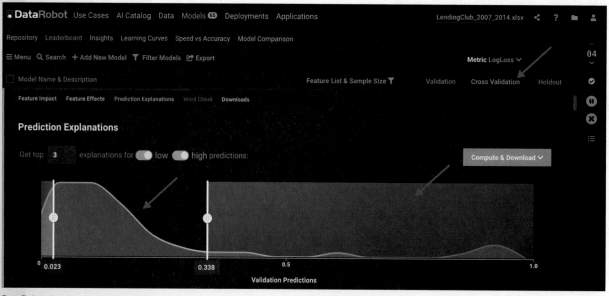

DataRobot, Inc.

example, blue thresholds show all customers with probabilities of default ranging between 0 and 0.023. Red thresholds, on the other hand, show customers between 0.338 and 1 who are likely to default.

Continue scrolling down the chart from Exhibit 7-29. The next portion of your screen should appear similar to Exhibit 7-30. The left column shows the customer ID number assigned by DataRobot, and the probability of default is shown in the second column under "Prediction." The top three probabilities of default are shown at the top of the "ID" column. The three cases with the lowest probability of default are shown at the bottom of the "ID" column. In addition, the plus or minus signs in the "Explanations" columns show the prediction importance of the features: very important is $+++$, not important at all is $---$, medium important is $++$, medium unimportant is $--$, and weak important/unimportant is $+/-$.

Exhibit 7-30

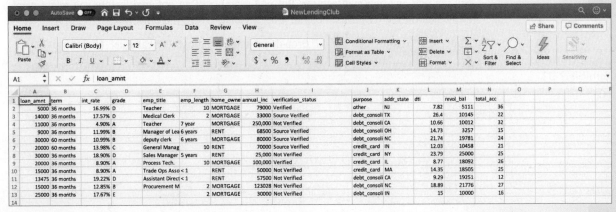

Preview of explanations for predictions from validation data within highlighted area(s):

ID	PREDICTION	EXPLANATIONS		
29930	0.975	+++ int_rate = 0.1433	++ annual_inc = 27000	++ emp_title
27864	0.972	+++ grade = "E"	++ int_rate = 0.079	++ annual_inc = 18500
29989	0.970	+++ int_rate = 0.1875	++ annual_inc = 35000	++ emp_title = "winco foods"
4692	0.004	--- int_rate = 0.079	--- grade = "A"	-- emp_title = "Chief Operating Offi...
22805	0.004	--- int_rate = 0.0762	--- grade = "A"	-- emp_title = "Systems Engineer"
14835	0.003	--- int_rate = 0.0662	--- grade = "A"	-- emp_title = "Department Manag...

DataRobot, Inc.

Results for the first loan customer indicate that the estimated likelihood of default at 97.5 percent, an interest rate of 14.33 percent, annual income of $27,000, and no employment title provided. This output provides granular detail and insights to explain the results as they relate to actual customers.

Applying the Model to Predict New Cases

Lending Club has 12 new borrowers and they would like to examine their likelihood to default (Exhibit 7-31). These potential borrowers were not included in training or validating the model, and the Lending Club wants to use the model to determine

Exhibit 7-31

	loan_amnt	term	int_rate	grade	emp_title	emp_length	home_owne	annual_inc	verification_status	purpose	addr_state	dti	revol_bal	total_acc				
1	loan_amnt	term	int_rate	grade	emp_title	emp_length	home_owne	annual_inc	verification_status	purpose	addr_state	dti	revol_bal	total_acc				
2	5000	36 months	16.99%	D	Teacher		10 MORTGAGE	79000	Verified	other	NJ	7.82	5111	36				
3	14000	36 months	17.57%	D	Medical Clerk		2 MORTGAGE	33000	Source Verified	debt_consoli	TX	26.4	10145	22				
4	11000	36 months	4.90%	A	Teacher	7 year	MORTGAGE	250,000	Not Verified	debt_consoli	CA	10.66	10012	32				
5	9000	36 months	11.99%	B	Manager of Lea	6 years	RENT	68500	Source Verified	debt_consoli	OH	14.73	3257	15				
6	30000	60 months	10.99%	B	deputy clerk	6 years	MORTGAGE	80000	Source Verified	debt_consoli	NC	21.74	19781	24				
7	20000	60 months	13.98%	C	General Manag		10 RENT	70000	Source Verified	credit_card	IN	12.03	10458	21				
8	30000	36 months	18.90%	D	Sales Manager	5 years	RENT	25,000	Not Verified	credit_card	NY	23.79	25000	25				
9	20000	36 months	8.90%	A	Process Tech.		10 MORTGAGE	100,000	Verified	credit_card	IL	8.77	18092	26				
10	15000	36 months	8.90%	A	Trade Ops Asso	< 1	RENT	50000	Not Verified	credit_card	MA	14.35	18505	25				
11	13475	36 months	19.22%	D	Assistant Direct	< 1	RENT	57500	Not Verified	debt_consoli	CA	9.29	19251	12				
12	15000	36 months	12.85%	B	Procurement M		2 MORTGAGE	123028	Not Verified	debt_consoli	NC	18.89	21776	27				
13	25000	36 months	17.67%	E			2 MORTGAGE	30000	Not Verified	debt_consoli	IN	15	10000	16				
14																		

Microsoft Excel

whether to lend them money. High-risk borrowers will be closely examined by the marketing department and targeted with personalized messaging. They also will be offered support through complimentary access to a financial advisor. The dataset of the new borrowers does not include the target (dependent) variable of likelihood of defaulting on a loan–that is, what the model will predict. Let's apply the model to identify individuals in this new dataset who are at a high risk for defaulting on their loan.

The next step is to use the model to develop a prediction. Under the model identified as *Light Gradient Boosted Trees Classifier with Early Stopping*, click "Predict" and then "Make Predictions" (Exhibit 7-32).

You can import new data to make predictions using the drop-down menu or simply drag and drop the data into the specified area of the screen (Exhibit 7-32).

Exhibit 7-32

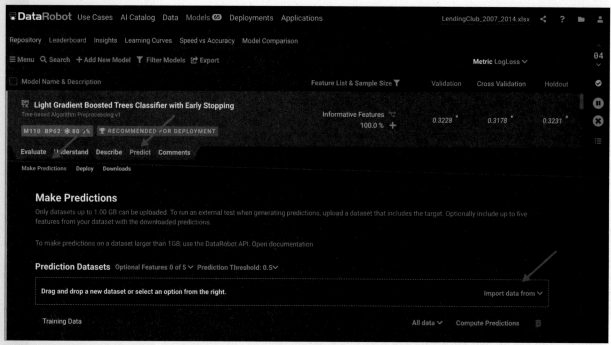

DataRobot, Inc.

In addition, if you click "Optional Features 0 of 5," as shown in Exhibit 7-33, it will add to the features DataRobot will display when the data is downloaded. For this example, we will not add any optional features. But one example of an optional feature you might want to include on the output is the emp_title associated with the borrower.

Under the "Import data from" drop-down menu, choose "Local File" (Exhibit 7-33).

Exhibit 7-33

DataRobot, Inc.

Navigate to where your file is stored, and click "Open" to upload it (Exhibit 7-34).

Exhibit 7-34

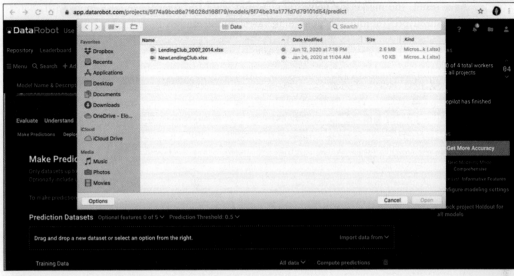

DataRobot, Inc.

Once your file is uploaded, click on "Compute Predictions" (Exhibit 7-35). This will start the process to apply the predictive model algorithm to the new dataset to calculate a target score for each record (potential borrower). The process will take only a few minutes.

Exhibit 7-35

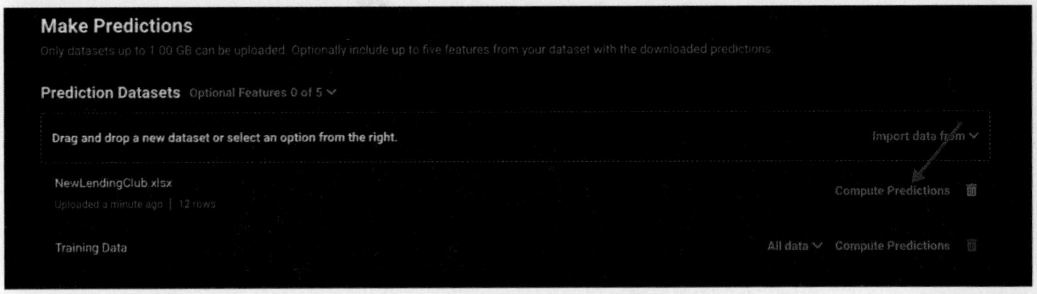

Make Predictions

Only datasets up to 1.00 GB can be uploaded. Optionally include up to five features from your dataset with the downloaded predictions.

Prediction Datasets Optional Features 0 of 5 ∨

Drag and drop a new dataset or select an option from the right.   Import data from ∨

NewLendingClub.xlsx   Compute Predictions 🗑
Uploaded a minute ago | 12 rows

Training Data   All data ∨ Compute Predictions 🗑

DataRobot, Inc.

Once the prediction calculation is completed, you can click "Download predictions" to get a comma-separated values file (.csv). The file will include all of the customer cases, with the predictions of the likelihood of defaulting on their loan (Exhibit 7-36).

Exhibit 7-36

DataRobot, Inc.

After the file is downloaded, open it in Excel to review the results. In Excel, it is helpful to sort the data by prediction probability. In Exhibit 7-37, notice the prediction values in column B. Customers 11 and 6 have the highest probability of defaulting on their loan. As a result, the marketing department would want to target these customers with specialized programming or may make a recommendation to not issue a loan for them.

Exhibit 7-37

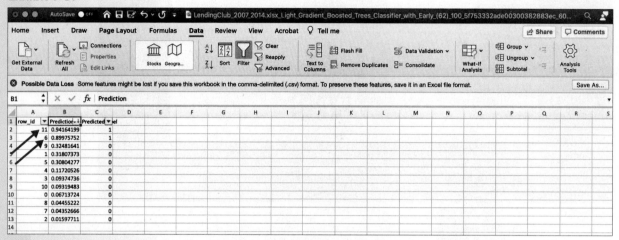

Microsoft Excel

Insights Learned from Applying the Concepts

Many useful marketing problems can be solved with AutoML. In this case, what insights were revealed?

The goal of this case study was to identify borrowers who have a high chance of default. The results of the AutoML revealed that 2 customers out of 12 (17 percent) were more likely to default on their loan. As a result of this analysis, Lending Club can send personalized digital messages to these customers. Messages might consist of inquiries determining if there is a financial hardship or simple reminders to pay bills and how to save money by avoiding penalties. In addition, the company can offer these borrowers access to a free financial advisor to help manage their budget.

This case study introduced the AutoML process. You have learned how the AutoML process works, the modeling and evaluation criteria, and how to score new cases to help Lending Club implement its new customer-based campaign to reduce the default rate.

AutoML models can be deployed in a production environment that provides instant predictions as new customer data becomes available. Remember that the deployed model analyzing data in real time should be actively monitored to know when to retrain and update the model.

Summary of Learning Objectives and Key Terms

LEARNING OBJECTIVES

Objective 7.1 Define Automated Machine Learning.

Objective 7.2 Identify and compare various uses of automated modeling.

Objective 7.3 Investigate the Automated Machine Learning process.

Objective 7.4 Summarize the value of ensemble models.

Objective 7.5 Construct and assess an Automated Machine Learning model.

KEY TERMS

Automated Machine
Learning (AutoML)

Bagging

Boosting

Ensemble model

Supervised model

Unsupervised model

Discussion and Review Questions

1. Explain Automated Machine Learning (AutoML).

2. What questions might arise when presenting AutoML learning results?

3. How can AutoML learning be used in marketing?

4. Describe an ensemble model.

5. What are the key steps in the AutoML process?

Critical Thinking and Marketing Applications

1. Identify other business problems you might face as a marketer in the P2P lending industry. Considering your new business problem, what other free data sources can be blended with Lending Club data to evaluate loan applications in real time.

2. Examine Exhibit 7-37. Are there other customers that should be monitored for default? Should the marketing team consider developing communications for customers that are not at risk for defaulting?

3. Identify the variables necessary when using AutoML to predict customer churn (customers that stop purchasing from the brand) for your favorite clothing brand.

References

1. Blake Morgan, "50 Stats Showing the Power of Personalization," *Forbes*, February 18, 2020, https://www.forbes.com/sites/blakemorgan/2020/02/18/50-stats-showing-the-power-of-personalization/#2872199c2a94.

2. Louis Columbus, "Machine Learning Is Redefining the Enterprise in 2016," *Forbes*, June 4, 2018, https://www.forbes.com/sites/louiscolumbus/2016/06/04/machine-learning-is-redefining-the-enterprise-in-2016/#3dd49eee1871; and H. James Wilson, Narendra Mulani, and Allan Alter, "Sales Gets a Machine-Learning Makeover," *MIT Sloan*, May 17, 2016, https://sloanreview.mit.edu/article/sales-gets-a-machine-learning-makeover.

3. Cade Metz, "Building AI Is Hard—So Facebook Is Building AI That Builds AI," *Wired*, May 6, 2016, https://www.wired.com/2016/05/facebook-trying-create-ai-can-create-ai.

4. Hamel Husain, "Automated Machine Learning—A Paradigm Shift That Accelerates Data Scientist Productivity @ Airbnb," *Medium*, May 10, 2017, https://medium.com/airbnb-engineering/automated-machine-learning-a-paradigm-shift-that-accelerates-data-scientist-productivity-airbnb-f1f8a10d61f8.

5. Tom Davenport and Dave Kuder, "Automated Machine Learning and the Democratization of Insights," Deloitte, March 25, 2019, https://www2.deloitte.com/us/en/insights/topics/analytics/automated-machine-learning-predictive-insights.html; and Ryohei Fujimaki, "Accelerating SMBC's Data-Driven Culture with AutoML 2.0," *Forbes*, September 17, 2019, https://www.forbes.com/sites/cognitiveworld/2019/09/17/accelerating-smbcs-data-driven-culture-with-automl-2-0/#21e75ebd5b78.

6. Noah Bricker, "A Machine Learning Pioneer in Grocery: You Guessed It Kroger," HBS Digital Initiative, November 12, 2019, https://digital.hbs.edu/platform-rctom/submission/a-machine-learning-pioneer-in-grocery-you-guessed-it-kroger; and Bernard Marr, "How U.S. Retail Giant Kroger Is Using AI and Robots to Prepare For the 4th Industrial Revolution," *Forbes*, July 20, 2018, https://www.forbes.com/sites/bernardmarr/2018/07/20/how-us-retail-giant-kroger-is-using-ai-and-robots-to-prepare-for-the-4th-industrial-revolution/#13b8249b17d6.

7. Braden Moore, "How the Philadelphia 76ers Win Off the Court Using Machine Learning from DataRobot," DataRobot, 2019, https://www.datarobot.com/wp-content/uploads/2019/11/DataRobot_How_the_Philadelphia_76ers_Win_Off_the_Court_Using_Machine_Learning_Case_study_v3.0.pdf.

8. Gareth Goh, "Blue Health Intelligence Selects DataRobot to Build and Deploy Powerful Machine Learning Models," DataRobot, November 27, 2018, https://www.datarobot.com/news/blue-health-intelligence-selects-datarobot-build-deploy-powerful-machine-learning-models; and BHI, "Predicting and Prescribing Meaningful Interventions to Manage Rising Member Costs," September 20, 2019, https://bluehealthintelligence.com/predicting-and-prescribing-meaningful-interventions-to-manage-rising-member-costs.

9. Press Release, "As Airline Satisfaction Climbs to Record Highs, Line Blurs Between Low-Cost and Traditional Carriers, J.D. Power Finds," J.D. Power, May 29, 2019, https://www.jdpower.com/business/press-releases/2019-north-america-airline-satisfaction-study; and Gareth Goh, "AI Experience Chicago: Highlights from TD Ameritrade, United Airlines, and Symphony Post Acute Network," DataRobot, May 22, 2018, https://blog.datarobot.com/ai-experience-chicago-highlights-from-td-ameritrade-united-airlines-and-symphony-post-acute-network.

10. Zohar Gilad, "72% of Sites Fail Ecommerce Site Search Expectations: 3 Steps + a Checklist to Ensure Yours Isn't One of Them," Big Commerce, https://www.bigcommerce.com/blog/ecommerce-site-search/#3-ways-to-optimize-mobile-search-for-increased-sales.

11. "Why Google's Cloud Auto ML Is Its Most Important ML Launch Yet," Maven Ware, August 5, 2018, https://www.mavenwave.com/white-papers/why-googles-cloud-auto-ml-is-most-important-launch-yet.

12. Ibid.

13. Maayan, "DMway Helps Israel's Oldest, Largest Cellular Phone Provider Increase Sales for Success," DMway, March 1, 2019, http://dmway.com/dmway-helps-israels-oldest-largest-cellular-phone-provider-increase-sales-for-success.

14. "Companies Currently Using Salesforce Einstein Analytics," HG Insights, https://discovery.hgdata.com/product/salesforce-einstein-analytics.

15. https://my-ibisworld-com.iris.etsu.edu:3443/us/en/industry-specialized/od4736/industry-performance

Ico Maker/Shutterstock

PART 4

Analytical Methods for Unsupervised Learning

8 Cluster Analysis

LEARNING OBJECTIVES

8.1 Define cluster analysis.

8.2 Identify and compare various uses for cluster analysis.

8.3 Investigate how cluster analysis functions.

8.4 Explain and assess the common types of cluster analysis.

Dan Dalton/Caiaimage/Getty Images

8.1 What Is Cluster Analysis?

To be successful, marketers must understand the market(s) they serve. That is, what people in a particular market buy and why they buy one product or service instead of another. A market is a group of people who gather together to buy and sell products and/or services. But within each market, there are subgroups of people with different needs and/or preferences. Marketers need to know who the subgroups are and how their needs and preferences differ. For example, Nissan needs to know how to design its car models to target customers who want to buy its cars instead of a Toyota. Lowe's needs to develop messages that will appeal to its customers versus customers who shop at Ace Hardware. Companies also need to answer questions about how to target those customers. For example, how should Procter & Gamble optimize supply chain networks to meet the needs of various markets? What is the ideal pricing strategy for Walmart in different geographic regions? These questions and more can be answered using cluster analysis to identify different market segments.

Market segmentation—the process of separating markets into segments (subgroups)—enables companies to divide consumer and business markets into smaller groups that have shared characteristics. These characteristics are based on demographic and lifestyle information related to customers, geographic location, attitudes and behavioral traits, psychological orientation, and other similar types of information.

Claritas, a leader in developing segmentation strategies for companies, uses market characteristics developed through market segmentation to identify clusters of similar groups. Claritas has created four unique segmentation approaches that provide insights for companies such as Nordstrom, Sprint, PepsiCo, and Mastercard. The segmentation approaches are generated from characteristics related to customer behaviors, shopping patterns, technology habits, demographics, lifestyle preferences, and more. Segmenting a market using shared characteristics is referred to as **cluster analysis**. Exhibit 8-1 shows three clusters with different characteristics.

Cluster analysis uses algorithms to explore different types of relationships, and then develops smaller groups from larger populations based upon similar characteristics. Marketers can use these insights to improve marketing strategies and better allocate resources when creating messages that resonate with a particular group, gauging new product development, or even selecting test markets that might be most receptive. SPSS Modeler, SAS Enterprise Miner, R Programming, and Python are reliable market segmentation tools to conduct a cluster analysis.

Exhibit 8-1 Market Segmentation Through Cluster Analysis

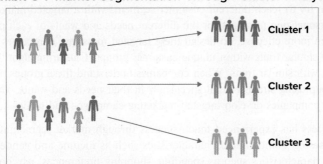

8.2 How Is Cluster Analysis Used in Practice?

Marketers often try to reach different customer segments with a targeted marketing message or product. Personalizing messages for the different needs and wants of each customer segment is often more effective. To design these targeted messages, companies need to be able to identify similar traits within unique customer groups. Clustering algorithms can identify groups with similar traits. When companies understand these groups, they can then target each group using strategies that specifically fit their needs and wants. The results of clustering help companies develop targeted marketing campaigns and tactics.

American Express has experienced much success through market segmentation. The company focuses on demographic characteristics such as income and gender, as well as behavioral characteristics such as spending, shopping preferences, psychographic behaviors, and lifestyles. Using a combination of these characteristics, American Express can identify different clusters of loyal customers. Understanding the different needs and wants of these customers enables them to develop new products and targeted marketing. The result has been a sizable increase in market share for the consumer card market, a decline in customer turnover, deeper customer loyalty, and increased card spending.[1]

Auto companies often use segmentation strategies. Nissan Motor Group manufactures and sells cars and trucks under the Nissan and Infiniti brand names, among others. Each vehicle produced by the brands is targeted at a specific customer segment. Consider the variety of sedans, sports cars, electric cars, crossovers, SUVs, and trucks offered by the company. It is logical that Nissan customers have substantially different characteristics because vehicles range from starting prices of $15,000 to over $113,000. Another automotive manufacturer, Daimler AG, manufactures and sells cars and trucks under the Mercedes-Benz and Daimler brand names. Daimler Mercedes-Benz developed the CLA model car that started at under $30,000 to appeal to a younger audience of potential customers, including Generations X and Y. The company also created an online community known as Generation Benz to engage likeminded customers and capture insights from social interactions. All automobile manufacturers use segmentation strategies to maximize marketing capabilities, such as new product development, pricing strategy, and advertising.

Take, for example, Buzz (young, tech enthusiasts), Jill (suburban soccer moms), and Barry (wealthy, professional men).[2] These groups are three of five consumer segments Best Buy, a technology retailer, identified and assigned a category name. These segments of loyal customers were developed from similarities in demographic, lifestyle, and marketplace data. Based on this segmentation, Best Buy spent $50 million remodeling some stores and provided training to serve each of the segments. The company also used these insights to enhance in-store customer experiences and improve sales. Stores that underwent changes and focused on these customer segments reported almost 10 percent in sales growth.

Clustering enables marketers to identify hidden patterns and structures in the data. For example, Best Buy didn't hypothesize or predefine the groups of different customers. Instead, the clustering process generated clusters, and the company provided meaning to the clusters. After clusters are identified, companies typically assign names and definitions to each customer cluster. Distinguishing clusters from the larger population is necessary for understanding and responding to different engagement or buying behaviors.

But how does a cluster analysis work?

8.3 How Does a Cluster Analysis Function?

Cluster analysis organizes data into two or more, similar groups. A measure of similarity between observations and within groups is computed. Groups exhibit within cluster (intra-cluster) homogeneity or similarities, and dissimilar characteristics (heterogeneity) between groups (inter-cluster). Similarities between groups are calculated using various measures of the distance between groups. The measures of distance between groups are applied to individual members in the groups, and individuals are assigned to the group with which they have the most in common. Smaller distances between individual observations represent greater similarity. Moreover, no previous established dependent variable is specified with cluster analysis, so the technique is considered an unsupervised learning. The goal of cluster analysis, therefore, is to model the underlying structure and distribution of characteristics in the data to separate a dataset into homogenous subgroups.

Using cluster analysis, a retailer might be interested in segmenting customers based upon data such as income, distance to the store, and the number of purchases at a particular location. Exhibit 8-2a reflects all customers in the retailer's database—there is no application of cluster analysis and therefore no subgroups.

Exhibit 8-2a All Customers Within a Database

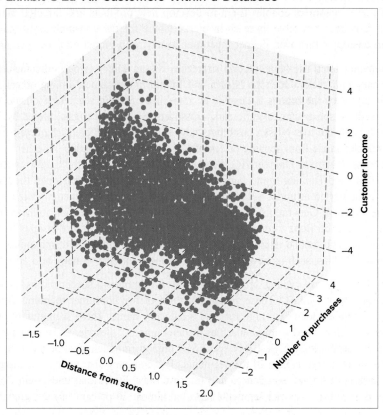

Exhibit 8-2b Cluster Analysis Applied to Customer Database

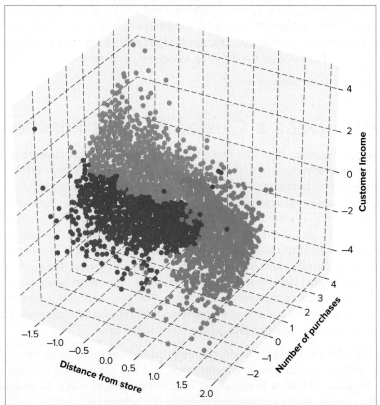

Using the data for the three specified variables (income, distance, and number of purchases), a cluster analysis can be used to develop separate subgroups. When cluster analysis is applied, Exhibit 8-2b shows the results of a typical market segmentation outcome. What homogenous clusters of customers emerge when considering customer income, their distance to the store, and their number of purchases? In this situation, three clusters emerge from the cluster analysis—shown as red, purple, and green.

Cluster analysis is an efficient and effective method of executing market segmentation to identify subgroups of customers to use in improving business and marketing decisions and therefore performance.

To apply cluster analysis, you must know how the technique works. First, there are several different types of cluster analysis. The two most common cluster analysis techniques are k-means clustering and hierarchical clustering.

8.4 What Are the Types of Cluster Analysis?

K-Means Clustering

K-means clustering uses the mean value for each cluster and minimizes the distance to individual observations. In this type of analysis, the number of clusters (k) is initially specified by the analyst. Different values of k can be examined, for example, ranging from 2 clusters to 12 clusters. The results for the different clusters are then examined with the best number of different homogenous groups chosen, based on what helps the business develop the most effective strategy.

Exhibit 8-3 captures a visual representation of the k-means clustering algorithm. The process begins with the analyst deciding on k initial subgroups to experiment with the number of clusters. A good number k to start with is 2 (for two groups). After determining the initial k (2) clusters, the algorithm randomly assigns each observation to one of the k (2) clusters. A cluster seed is randomly selected and designated as the initial cluster centroid. Then, cluster centroids (means) are calculated. Using cluster centroid values, the k-means algorithm continues to reassign observations based upon the proximity of each observation to the cluster centroid. An observation may start out in one cluster it is close to, but when a new cluster is started, the observation may be reassigned to the new cluster if the observation is closer to the centroid of the new cluster. The k-means cluster algorithm reduces the dispersion within a cluster based on the distance or proximity to the centroid (overall group mean) of an observation within a particular cluster. In short, an overall group mean is calculated, and observations are assigned to the group they are closest to in terms of their characteristics. The clustering

Exhibit 8-3 K-Means Clustering

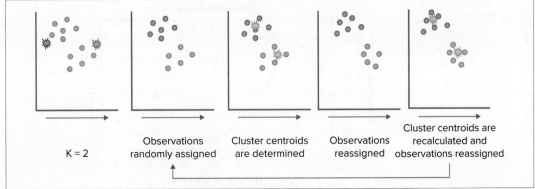

<table>
<tr><td>K = 2</td><td>Observations
randomly assigned</td><td>Cluster centroids
are determined</td><td>Observations
reassigned</td><td>Cluster centroids are
recalculated and
observations reassigned</td></tr>
</table>

Exhibit 8-4 Elbow Chart

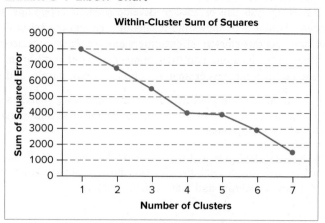

process continues to evolve until moving observations between clusters can no longer minimize the within-cluster distance. This method is efficient in obtaining solutions and is most often used with large sample sizes because of its simplicity.

How is the quality of clusters objectively evaluated? The marketing analyst typically uses a line chart (also referred to as an "elbow chart") to evaluate the reduction in cluster error (reduction in heterogeneity) as a larger number of clusters is developed. Note in Exhibit 8-4, we see that moving from one to two clusters provides a significant reduction of within-cluster distance (sum of squared error), and so does the move from three to four clusters, but not from four to five. The results in Exhibit 8-4 indicate the optimal number of k (clusters) is four, because the five-group cluster solution does not show a further reduction in the amount of error.

Another approach to determining the number of clusters is calculating a silhouette score. The **silhouette score** is another way to identify the optimal number of clusters for the data. The silhouette score is calculated after the cluster algorithm has assigned each observation to a cluster. To obtain the silhouette score, you determine the average distance between each observation in the cluster and the cluster centroid. Note that the cluster centroid is the average of all observations included in a cluster. The average distance of an individual observation to the centroid of its assigned cluster is then compared to the average distance of that observation to the centroid of the next nearest cluster. Typically, a silhouette score is between $+1$ and -1. To interpret the value of the silhouette score, a $+1$ means the observation is part of the correct cluster, and a value of -1 indicates a poor fit showing the observation is in the wrong cluster. You can use the "elbow" and silhouette score charts to select the optimal number of clusters. For example, Exhibit 8-5 shows that the

Exhibit 8-5 Silhouette Score

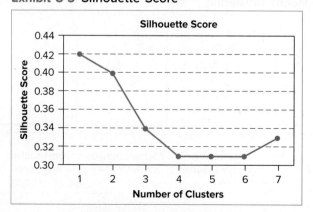

optimal number of clusters is four. In addition to examining four clusters, the analyst may decide to also examine solutions for three and even five clusters, and compare them to the four cluster solution. To do so, you would carefully evaluate how meaningful each of the alternative cluster solutions would be in developing a marketing segmentation strategy. The correct number of clusters would be the solution that enables the business to develop the most effective marketing strategy for its customers.

K-Means Issues to Remember

When running k-means clustering, it is best to begin with data that has been standardized using z-scores or min-max. Standardization is necessary to obtain the most accurate cluster results—when the clustering variables are measured on very different scales. Recall that in our previous cluster example, we were using the variables income, distance, and number of purchases within a specified time period. Each of the variables is measured differently—income measured in dollars, distance in miles, and the number of purchases measured using a scale of zero to ten purchases. Standardizing converts all three variables to be comparable measures.

Another consideration is that the k-means clustering method can only be applied to numerical data. Why is numerical data a requirement? Recall that k-means uses the average datapoint in the cluster as a starting point. Therefore, the mean value is applicable only when the mean is relevant for all of the data used in the clustering process, which requires all data is numerical. If the data is categorical (e.g., Yes or No), the mean would not be meaningful because you cannot average two categories. Thus, if possible, categorical data must be numerically coded before using the k-means algorithm or k-modes algorithm can be used.

Hierarchical Clustering

A second widely used method for identifying subgroups to use in market segmentation is **hierarchical clustering**. This method of clustering produces solutions in which the data is grouped into a hierarchy of clusters. Individual observations are combined into subgroups using a measure of distance between observations. There are two commonly used approaches to hierarchical clustering: agglomerative clustering and divisive clustering.

With **agglomerative clustering** (a bottom-up approach), each observation is initially considered to be a separate cluster. That is, if you have 100 observations, you start with 100 separate clusters—one for each observation. Then, in a step-by-step process, each observation is assigned to a cluster that has common characteristics. A linkage method is used to merge smaller clusters into larger clusters. This process of merging observations continues until all observations are included in a single cluster that includes all 100 observations.

With **divisive clustering** (a top-down approach), all records are initially assigned to a single cluster. That is, if you have 100 observations, all 100 observations are specified as being in a single cluster. Then, a step-by-step process follows in which the most dissimilar observations (records) are sequentially separated from the initial 100-observation cluster. Thus, the process starts with a single cluster of 100 and ends up with 100 different clusters.

How is the similarity between observations measured with hierarchical clustering? (See Exhibit 8-6 for a description of the different methods.) For numerical variables, similarity is most often measured using approaches such as the Euclidean distance or Manhattan distance (see Exhibit 8-7). But if categorical variables are used to cluster, similarity is generally measured using Matching or Jaccard's coefficient.

Exhibit 8-6 Ways to Measure Similarity

FUNCTION	DEFINITION
Euclidean	The distance is measured as the true straight line distance between two points.
Manhattan	The distance between two points is not straight—it is a path with right turns as if you are walking a grid in a city. It is also referred to as the "City Block" distance measure.
Matching	Measures the similarity between two observations with values that represent the minimum differences between two points.
Jaccard's	Measures the similarity between two observations based on how dissimilar two observations are from each other.

Exhibit 8-7 Euclidean versus Manhattan

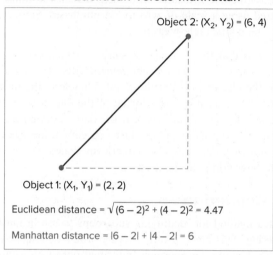

Object 2: $(X_2, Y_2) = (6, 4)$

Object 1: $(X_1, Y_1) = (2, 2)$

Euclidean distance $= \sqrt{(6-2)^2 + (4-2)^2} = 4.47$

Manhattan distance $= |6-2| + |4-2| = 6$

To measure similarity (dissimilarity), a linkage criterion can be used to capture the distance between the resulting clusters. Linkage can be computed using one of the following methods, which are based on linking individual observations both within and between clusters:

- **Complete linkage:** Similarity is defined by the maximum distance between observations in two different clusters.
- **Single linkage:** Similarity is defined by the shortest distance from an object in a cluster to an object from another cluster.
- **Average linkage:** Similarity is defined by the group average of observations from one cluster to all observations from another cluster.

A visual example of the three similarity measures based on linking observations is shown in Exhibit 8-8.

Exhibit 8-8 Similarity Measures

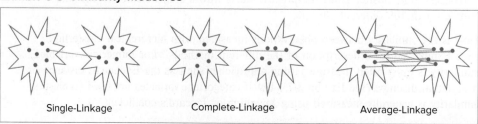

Single-Linkage   Complete-Linkage   Average-Linkage

Exhibit 8-9 Hierarchical Clustering Dendrogram

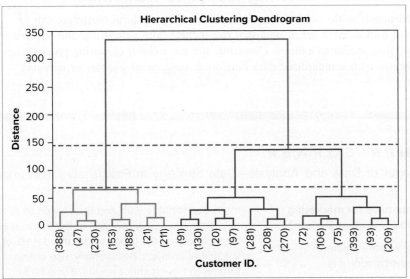

A fourth method of measuring distances with hierarchical clustering is Ward's method. **Ward's method** applies a measure of the sum of squares within the clusters summed over all variables. The Ward's method process selects two clusters to combine based on which combination of clusters minimizes the within cluster sum of squares for all clusters across all of the separate clusters.

All four measurement approaches for determining clusters when applying hierarchical clustering can be illustrated with a dendrogram. Exhibit 8-9 shows a dendrogram that illustrates the process for hierarchical clustering. The treelike graph provides an illustration of the hierarchy of clusters in the dataset.

We can see in the dendrogram example in Exhibit 8-9 that there are two main branches. Each of these branches represents a possible cluster. The height of each branch indicates the distance, measuring dissimilarity. In other words, the longer the vertical line is, the more separated the cluster is from the other clusters. Thus, when you look at the graph, you may be able to visually decide how many clusters are needed to represent the correct number of clusters for the data. As an example, if you impose a horizontal line on the dendrogram and count the number of vertical lines it crosses, it will suggest the number of clusters. The two gray dotted lines suggest the possibility of either two clusters (higher line) or three clusters (lower line).

Identifying the correct number of clusters using a dendrogram is a subjective process. The analyst takes into account their knowledge of the markets served by the business to assess the practical meaning of the clusters emerging from the dendrogram. To develop an understanding of the markets served, it is helpful to review the descriptive statistics for each cluster to define the characteristics of the clusters and assign them an appropriate name. For example, a grocery delivery service may find there are two clusters. The characteristics of the one cluster include higher income, weekend shoppers, between the ages of 40 and 50, and less price sensitive. The second cluster is made up of weekday shoppers, with medium incomes, between the ages of 25 and 35, and shopping mainly for discounted items. This understanding will enable the marketing analyst to identify the first cluster as a market segment that represents "Higher Income, Weekenders" and the second cluster as representing "Weekday, Price Sensitive" customers. Additionally, the number of clusters is two, so it should be relatively easy to develop a cost-effective strategy to serve both clusters. If you are developing a marketing strategy, segmenting customers into a smaller number of clusters will be easier to manage than a larger number.

Hierarchical Clustering Issues to Remember

While k-means works only with numerical values, hierarchical clustering can be executed with a mixed set of data that can include both categorical and numerical values. Also, similar to k-means clustering, the hierarchical clustering process should be executed with standardized data developed using either z-scores or min-max.

continued from page 268

PRACTITIONER CORNER

Kaitlin Marvin | Manager of Data and Analysis—Data Strategy at Progressive Insurance

Q **What suggestions do you have for marketing analysts learning new tools, such as Python?**

A It can be easy to get overwhelmed when trying to learn a new analytical tool. It is important to remember that you don't have to be an expert to begin using the tool. Just try! There are many online tutorials to help you get set up and learn some basics. Jupyter Notebook is a great way to get going. I find taking an analysis I have done in a tool I am more comfortable with and then trying to re-create it in a new tool can help me focus on the nuances of the tool and not the details of the actual analysis. Additionally, use online forums to troubleshoot issues. If you have availability in your class schedule, sign up for a programming class. When you begin applying for jobs, this can be a great question to ask your interviewers about what support they offer around training or tuition reimbursement.

Online Perfume and Cosmetic Sales: Understanding Customer Segmentation through Cluster Analysis

Understanding the Business Problem

The online perfume and cosmetic industry includes companies that sell products such as cosmetics, fragrances, and skin care. Many of these retailers also sell these products in brick-and-mortar stores. In recent years, purchasing patterns have shifted, however; and many customers regularly purchase these products using an online channel, such as Amazon. Revenue in this industry exceeds $16.2 billion annually and is expected to grow substantially over the next several years.[3]

The tremendous growth in this industry has also been met with heightened competition. Bloggers and social media influencers are using their platform to engage large numbers of followers and introduce them to products. They often include personal reviews and direct links to products for customers that make purchasing easy by only requiring a couple of clicks. Online consumers can explore products, compare prices, and make purchases from the comfort of their own home within minutes.

The Chief Marketing Officer at one of the leading beauty care companies wants to better understand customer behavior. The goal is to segment the market to more effectively engage their customers in marketing campaigns. The marketing department understands that developing relationships and strong brand loyalty will translate into greater value for both the customers and the company. In the past, marketing has targeted customers who are periodic "big spenders," but this thinking is potentially flawed. Focusing on single large purchases rather than on other behavioral variables overlooks the frequency of visits, the recency of purchases, and the overall customer lifetime monetary value. The company has collected basic behavioral characteristics from online purchases of cosmetics, fragrances, and skin care. This behavioral purchasing data will be used to develop more successful market segmentation strategies.

Understanding the Dataset

The first step in the model development process is to understand what data is available for analysis. You can download the hypothetical online perfume and cosmetic sales sample dataset from the student resources page. This dataset consists of 250,000 records (observations) and includes key variables such as customer id, the number of products purchased in each transaction, the price per unit for purchased products, total revenue per customer transaction, and a description of the purchased products. To get started, let's review the data elements in Exhibit 8-10.

Exhibit 8-10 Data Dictionary

VARIABLE NAME (TYPE)	DESCRIPTION
TransactionNo (typeless)	Unique transaction number for each online sale
CustomerID (typeless)	Number assigned to the customer who purchased the product(s)
Quantity (numeric)	Number of products purchased in the transaction
UnitPrice (numeric)	Price per unit for the product purchased
Revenue (numeric)	A calculated field (Quantity × UnitPrice) representing the total revenue per transaction
TransactionDate (date)	Date the online sale occurred
Product Description (string)	Description of product purchased online

Applying the Concepts

In this case study, you will conduct cluster analysis using k-means clustering analysis with Python. Python is a software programming language that enables marketing analysts to execute many different types of data analysis, including cluster analysis. There are several steps to follow before using Python. The first step is to review the 250,000 records in the Excel file "OnlineSales.xlsx" and examine each field's values.

The data for this case study is at the transaction level. That is, for each customer, there are multiple transactions they completed online, including the quantity, unit price, a revenue variable derived by multiplying quantity by unit price, and beauty and health product descriptions. A portion of the data is shown in Exhibit 8-11.

Exhibit 8-11 Segmentation Data for Clustering

	TransactionNo	CustomerID	Quantity	UnitPrice	Revenue	TransactionD	Product Description
2	1082862	24692	74213	3.34	247871.42	2/20/20	Neutrogena Body Oil, Light Sesame Formula, 8.5 Ounce
3	1075252	24694	10	4.4	44	1/9/20	Olay Total Effects 7-In-1 Anti-Aging Daily Moisturizer 1.7 Fl. Oz.
4	1075252	24694	2	6.55	13.1	1/9/20	Aveeno Positively Radiant Skin Brightening Daily Scrub, 5 Ounce
5	1075252	24694	10	5.55	55.5	1/9/20	Blue Lizard Australian Sunscreen, Regular, SPF 30+, 8.75-Ounce Bottle
6	1075252	24694	34	2.95	100.3	1/9/20	Aveeno Active Naturals Skin Relief Hand Cream, 3.5 Ounce
7	1075252	24694	10	3.55	35.5	1/9/20	Eucerin Daily Protection Moisturizing Face Lotion, Broad Spectrum SPF 30
8	1075252	24694	10	3.55	35.5	1/9/20	Thayers - Rose Petal Witch Hazel with Aloe Vera Alcohol-Free Toner - 12 oz.
9	1075252	24694	10	3.55	35.5	1/9/20	Miracle of Aloe Miracle Hand Repair Cream 8 Oz Relieve Dry, Cracked, Flacking Hands Immediately! Therapeutic Formula Contains 60% Ultra Aloe - The Purest Most Potent Fo
10	1075252	24694	10	3.55	35.5	1/9/20	Suave Naturals Conditioner, Tropical Coconut - 22.5oz.
11	1075252	24694	10	3.55	35.5	1/9/20	Vidal Sassoon VS14434 No Headache Headbands (2 Headbands)
12	1075252	24694	10	3.55	35.5	1/9/20	Essie Nail Lacquer, Sugar Daddy, 0.5 Fluid Ounce
13	1075252	24694	2	6.05	12.1	1/9/20	CND: Treatments/Prep Stickey Base Coat, 2.3 oz
14	1075252	24694	2	6.05	12.1	1/9/20	Bella B Tummy Honey Cream - 4 oz
15	1075252	24694	2	6.05	12.1	1/9/20	Conair BC171NCS Ceramic Ionic Hot Air Brush, Black, 1.25 Inch
16	1075252	24694	2	6.05	12.1	1/9/20	Floxite Fl-10h 10x Hand Held 2-sided Mirror with Stand, Clear
17	1075252	24694	2	6.05	12.1	1/9/20	Max Green Alchemy Scalp Rescue Shampoo 8.8 oz
18	1075252	24694	4	4.4	17.6	1/9/20	Fruit Of The Earth 100% Aloe Vera 24oz Gel Pump
19	1075252	24694	28	3.55	99.4	1/9/20	Silver Metallic Perfume Atomizer Spray 10 ML for purse or travel Refillable
20	1075252	24694	10	3.75	37.5	1/9/20	Shea Moisture Shea Butter Leave in Conditioner 8oz
21	1075252	24694	10	3.95	39.5	1/9/20	NOW Foods - Red Clay Powder Moroccan, 6 OZ.
22	1075252	24694	4	6.55	26.2	1/9/20	Coty Airspun Loose Powder, Naturelle, 2.3 Ounce
23	1075252	24694	4	6.05	24.2	1/9/20	WR Medical Therabath Paraffin Wax Refill With Heat Retaining Capacity Lavender Harmony
24	1075252	24694	4	6.05	24.2	1/9/20	Olay Regenerist Eye Lifting Serum, 0.5 Fluid Ounce
25	1075252	24694	4	6.05	24.2	1/9/20	Method Foaming Hand Wash, Green Tea & Aloe, 10 Ounce (Pack of 6)
26	1075252	24694	10	3.55	35.5	1/9/20	Blue Lizard Australian Sunscreen, Sensitive SPF 30+, 5-Ounce
27	1075252	24694	2	6.55	13.1	1/9/20	Infiniti Professional Nano Tourmaline Ceramic Curling Iron, 1 1/2-Inch
28	1075252	24694	1	7.25	7.25	1/9/20	Olay Regenerist Microdermabrasion & Peel System 1 Kit
29	1075252	24694	4	8.25	33	1/9/20	Queen Helene Mint Julep Masque, 2 Ounce Travel Size Tube
30	1075252	24694	10	3.95	39.5	1/9/20	Nexxus Humectress Ultimate Moisturizing Conditioner, 33.8 fl oz (1l)
31	1075252	24694	22	5.25	115.5	1/9/20	Nexxus Emergencee Restorative Strength Conditioning Treatment 3.3 Ounce
32	1075252	24694	10	6.95	69.5	1/9/20	Almay intense i-color Play Up Liquid Liner, Raisin Quartz 024, 0.8-Ounce Package
33	1075252	24694	4	7.79	31.16	1/9/20	Revlon Super Lustrous Creme Lipstick, Pink in the Afternoon 415, 0.15 Ounce
34	1084474	24694	22	3.15	69.3	2/28/20	Deva Curl Angell Hyper-Allergic Conditioning Gel 32oz

Microsoft Excel

After reviewing the data, what questions can you ask to better understand customer sales? Here are some suggestions:

- How can the data be grouped using the behavioral characteristics of a customer's recency, frequency, and monetary value?
- How can the data be prepared for cluster analysis?
- What is the correct number of clusters based on the silhouette score?
- What are the characteristics of clusters from the analysis?

Python can be used to cluster the data, answer these questions, and more. Before getting started with the instructions that follow, you will need to download Anaconda (**https://www.anaconda.com**), an open-source distribution platform for Python that simplifies the Python download process. Anaconda is available for both Windows and Mac. You can find detailed download instructions in this textbook's student resources.

Opening Python Using Anaconda

Step 1: Before beginning your work with Python, create a folder in which to save your work. Create a new folder on your Desktop or under Documents, and name it "Cluster Analysis" (Exhibit 8-12). Save the data file "OnlineSales.xlsx" from the student resources website in the Cluster Analysis folder you just created.

Exhibit 8-12

Microsoft

Step 2: There are several options to run Python on your computer. For this case study, you will use a Jupyter notebook.

Exhibit 8-13 Opening Jupyter Notebook on Windows

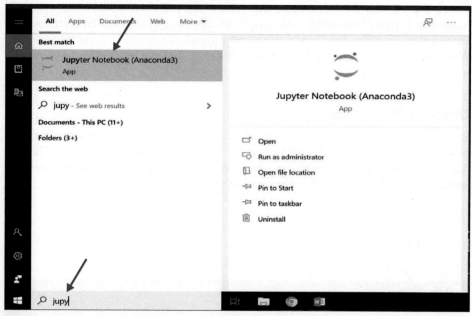

Jupyter

On a Windows computer, search for "jupyter" and click on "Jupyter Notebook (Anaconda3)" Exhibit 8-13.

On a Mac computer, navigate to Applications and locate "Anaconda-Navigator" (Exhibit 8-14).

Exhibit 8-14 Opening Jupyter Notebook on Mac Using Anaconda-Navigator

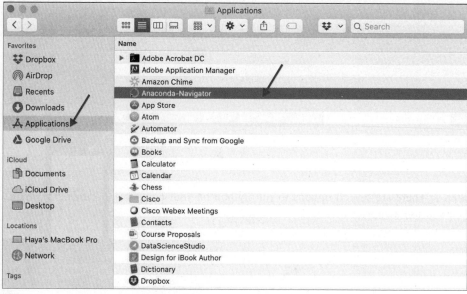

Jupyter

Exhibit 8-15 Launching Jupyter notebook: on Mac

Jupyter

Open it and click on "Launch" under Jupyter Notebook (Exhibit 8-15). Note that Jupyter notebook is updated constantly and the version number you see on your screen might differ from the one in Exhibit 8-15.

Step 3: Your default web browser will automatically open a Jupyter notebook page. Using the menu, navigate to the Cluster Analysis folder you created in Step 1 (Exhibit 8-16).

Exhibit 8-16

Jupyter

Then, click on "New" and use the drop-down menu to select "Python 3" (Exhibit 8-17).

Step 4: A new screen should open after completing step 3 (Exhibit 8-18).

Step 5: Click on the "Untitled" label next to the Jupyter logo. A Rename Notebook window will open. Replace "Untitled" with "Cluster Analysis" and click "Rename" (Exhibit 8-19).

Step 6: You will see the new window (Exhibit 8-20). You are now ready to begin preparing the Python environment for your analysis.

Exhibit 8-17

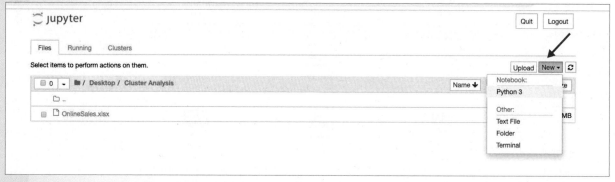

Jupyter

Exhibit 8-18

Jupyter

Exhibit 8-19

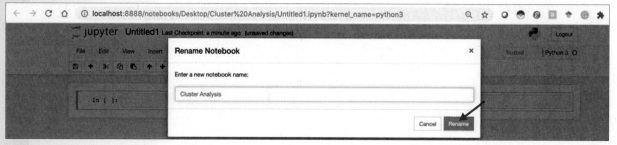

Jupyter

Exhibit 8-20

Jupyter

Preparing the Python Environment

Step 7: Python needs packages in the Jupyter notebook environment to run the analysis. For that reason, we will download packages that will execute important functions such as import data, run cluster analysis, and visualize different aspects of our data. In this case study, we will follow the clustering python code described by Lim, 2019.[4] To add a comment in Python, use the symbol # and then type a comment. It is a good idea to leave notes to review later when programming in Python or other languages. This will help you remember the tasks that were executed in each step when you return to your work.

To download the necessary packages, enter the following text on your screen (Exhibit 8-21):

```
import pandas as pd
import numpy as np
from scipy import stats
import datetime as dt
# Clustering
from sklearn.cluster import KMeans
from sklearn.preprocessing import StandardScaler
from sklearn.metrics import silhouette_score
# Visualization
import seaborn as sbn
import matplotlib.pyplot as plt
from mpl_toolkits.mplot3d import Axes3D
```

Now, click "Run" as shown in Exhibit 8-21.

Exhibit 8-21

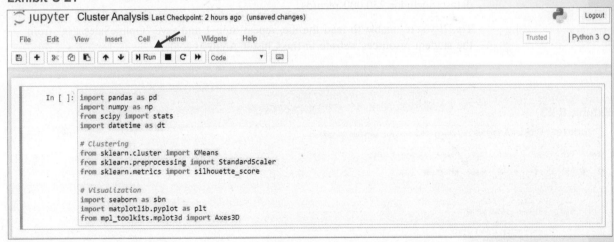

Jupyter

Step 8: To add a new segment of code into Jupyter Notebook, you can type the code in the new box that appears after you ran the code in Step 7 (Exhibit 8-22). This will enable you to run each segment of the Python code separately. This also makes it easier to debug any errors that have been made during the coding process. In case the new box doesn't auto populate, click the plus button in the menu bar (Exhibit 8-22). This will open a new box to enter your next segment of code.

Tip: To delete any code segment box, click the scissors button next to the plus (+).

Exhibit 8-22

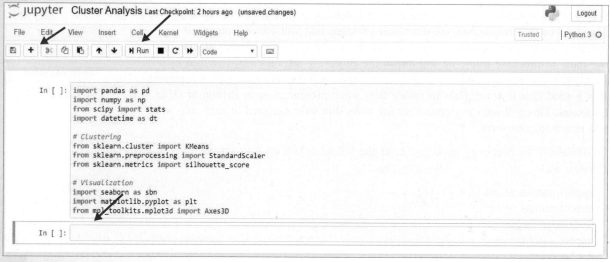

Jupyter

Step 9: To read the data in the Python environment, you will need to input the correct code. To do this, use a new code box and type the following code on your screen (Exhibit 8-23):

```
#Import data into a dataframe and read it in our environment.
sales = pd.DataFrame(pd.read_excel('OnlineSales.xlsx'))
```

Now, click "Run." Note this process may take a few seconds to complete, because the dataset includes 250,000 records.

Tip: If you're unable to read the file, repeat Step 1 and save "OnlineSales.xlsx" from the student resources website in the Cluster Analysis folder.

Exhibit 8-23

Jupyter

Exhibit 8-24

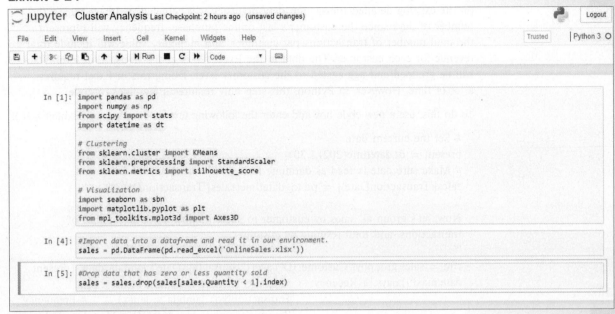

Jupyter

Step 10: The Online Sales data needs to be cleaned to include only positive quantity units sold. Negative quantity sold values signal returns. Therefore, zero or negative quantity sold values should be removed. To do this, use a new code box and type the following code (Exhibit 8-24):

```
#Drop data that has zero or less quantity sold
sales = sales.drop(sales[sales.Quantity < 1].index)
```

Now, click "Run."

Step 11: In this step, you will view the first few records in the data. To do this, use a new code box and enter the following text on your screen (Exhibit 8-25):

```
sales.head() # Read the first 5 rows in our data
```

Now, click "Run."

Exhibit 8-25

Jupyter

Step 12: Now, we will create the recency, frequency, and monetary value data based on the existing detailed transaction data. Recency will be calculated based upon the number of days since the customer's last online purchase, frequency will represent the total number of transactions per customer, and monetary value will include total revenue for each customer. The data in the Excel file is at the transaction level. Data will be grouped and aggregated to the customer level. Doing this in Excel requires a lot of time. However, in Python, this step only requires a few lines of code.

To do this, use a new code box and enter the following text on your screen (Exhibit 8-26):

```
# Set the current date
present = dt.datetime(2021,1,30)
# Make sure date is read as datatime format
sales['TransactionDate'] = pd.to_datetime(sales['TransactionDate'])
'''
```

Now, let's group all sales by customer to show number of days, number of transactions, and total revenue by customer.
```
'''

rfm = sales.groupby('CustomerID').agg({'TransactionDate': lambda date: (present - date.max()).days, # Recency
                                        'TransactionNo': lambda x: len(x),      # Frequency
                                        'Revenue': lambda x: x.sum()}) # Monetary Value
# Let's rename columns from TransactionDate, TransactionNo, and Revenue to Recency, Frequency, and MonetaryValue.
rfm.rename(columns={'TransactionDate': 'Recency',
                    'TransactionNo': 'Frequency',
                    'Revenue': 'MonetaryValue'}, inplace=True)
```

Now, click "Run." Note that for this example, we are assuming that the current date is January 30, 2021 and recency will be calcuated as the number of days since the last visit. The smaller the value, the more recent the visit, and conversely, the higher the number, the older the visit. For instance, a recency of 10 means that the last time the customer purchased a product was 10 days ago, and a recency of 25 means that the last time the customer purchased a product was 25 days ago.

Exhibit 8-26

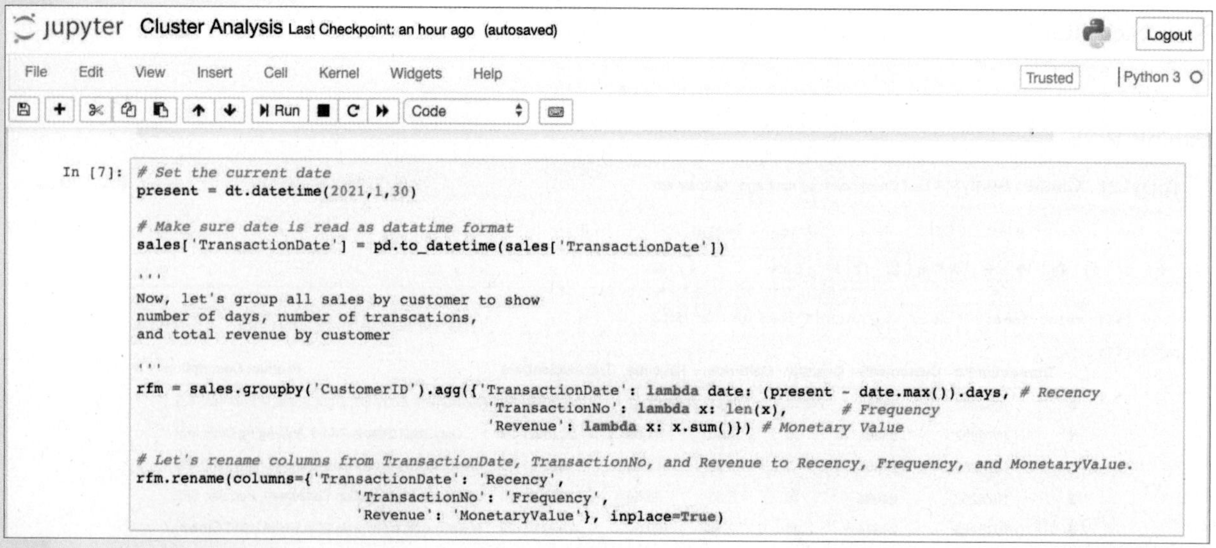

Jupyter

Step 13: You can define the variable types to ensure the type matches your need. To illustrate this process, make sure that the Monetary Value is an integer number with no decimal places. To do this, use a new code box and enter the following text on your screen (Exhibit 8-27):

```
# Let's make sure MonetaryValue values are defined as an integer with no decimal places
rfm['MonetaryValue'] = rfm['MonetaryValue'].astype(int)
```

Now, click "Run."

Exhibit 8-27

Jupyter

Step 14: You are probably eager to see the data containing your new variables. To do this, use a new code box and enter the following text on your screen (Exhibit 8-28):

```
rfm.head()
```

Now, click "Run."

Exhibit 8-28

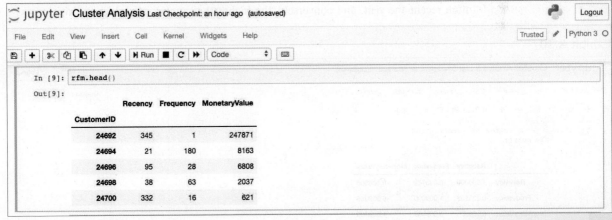

Jupyter

Step 15: To review general statistics (e.g., count, mean, standard deviation) of the data, complete the following procedure. Use a new code box and enter the following text on your screen (Exhibit 8-29):

```
# Review descriptive statistics for our rfm data
rfm.describe().round(2)
```

Now, click "Run."

Exhibit 8-29

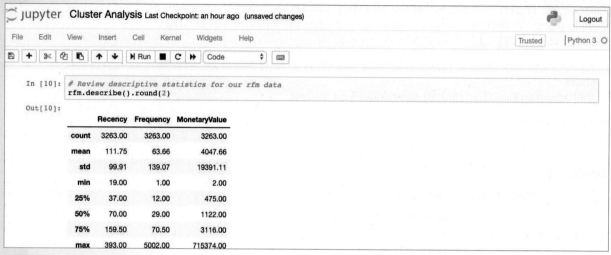

Jupyter

Let's review the correlations among the three variables: recency, frequency, and monetary value. To do this, use a new code box and enter the following text on your screen (Exhibit 8-30):

```
# Let's review the correlation
rfm.corr()
```

Now, click "Run."

Note the correlation between monetary value and frequency is 0.56. Recency and frequency have a correlation of −0.23. Finally, monetary value and recency has a correlation of −0.11. The negative correlations can be explained by how recency is calculated—as the number of days since the last visit. The smaller the value, the more recent the visit, and conversely, the higher the number, the older the visit.

Exhibit 8-30

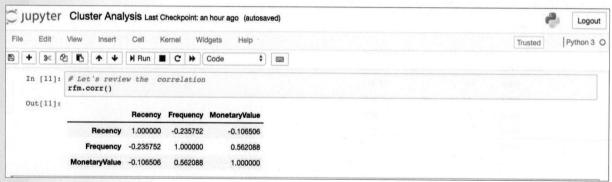

Jupyter

Step 17: It is always nice to add a visual representation to the correlation matrix using a heat map. To do this, use a new code box and enter the following text on your screen (Exhibit 8-31):

```
sbn.heatmap(rfm.corr(), annot=True);
plt.title('Correlation for rfm data');
```

Now, click "Run."

Exhibit 8-31

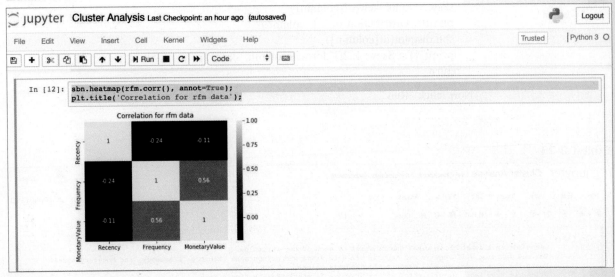

Jupyter

Step 18 (optional): You may want to create a csv file with the dataframe that was created. To do this, use a new code box and enter the following text on your screen (Exhibit 8-32):

```
# You have an option here to save the rfm table to csv on your computer
rfm.to_csv('rfm.csv')
```

Now, click "Run."

You can now navigate to the Cluster Analysis folder to see the newly created file (rfm.csv).

Exhibit 8-32

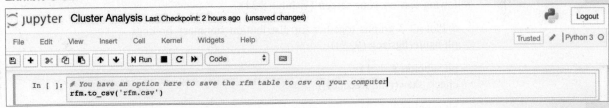

Jupyter

Step 19: Cluster analysis is sensitive to data distribution. Therefore, you will need to examine the skewness of the data. That is, review the data to see whether it appears to be distributed more so to the left (negative) or to the right (positive). To do this, use a new code box and enter the following text on your screen (Exhibit 8-33):

```
'''
Let's set up a function to check the skewness of each of our variables.
The new function will require two inputs: rfm data frame and column name
(Recency, Frequency, and MonetaryValue)
Using the skew values we will capture the skewness values for each column
Using the skew test, we will check if the skewness is statistically significant
Using the plt.title, we will control the title of each of distribution plots
Using the sbn.distplot we will plot the data
Using the print function we will post in a table skew values and skewness test results
'''
```

```
def check_skew(df, column):
  skew = stats.skew(df[column])
  plt.title('Distribution of ' + column)
  sbn.distplot(df[column])
  print("{}'s: Skew: [:.2f]".format(column, skew))
return
```

Now, click "Run."

Exhibit 8-33

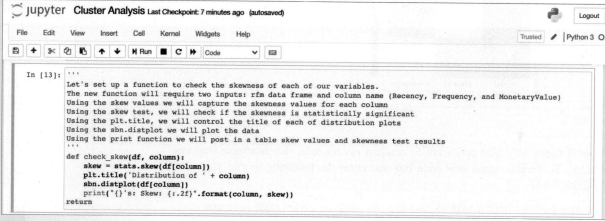

Jupyter

Step 20: In this step, you will visualize the data and examine its skewness using the function created earlier: check_skew. To do this, use a new code box and enter the following text on your screen (Exhibit 8-34):

```
# Plot all 3 graphs together for distribution summary findings
plt.figure(figsize=(9, 9))

plt.subplot(3, 1, 1)
check_skew(rfm,'Recency')

plt.subplot(3, 1, 2)
check_skew(rfm,'Frequency')

plt.subplot(3, 1, 3)
check_skew(rfm,'MonetaryValue')

plt.tight_layout()
return
```

Now, click "Run."

Exhibit 8-34

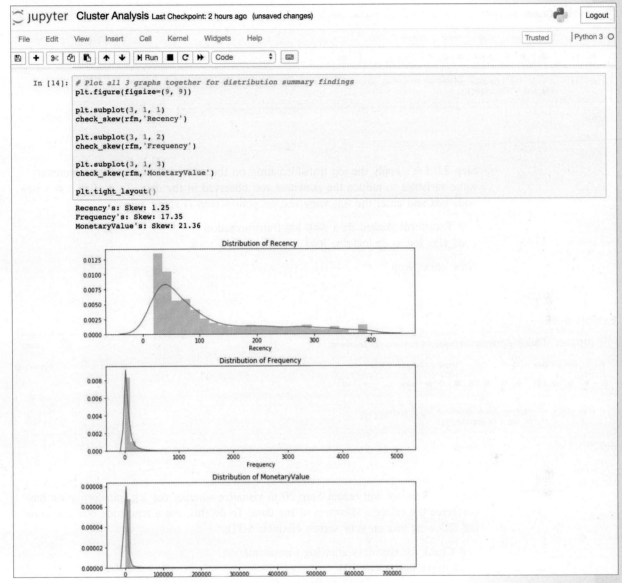

```
In [14]:  # Plot all 3 graphs together for distribution summary findings
          plt.figure(figsize=(9, 9))

          plt.subplot(3, 1, 1)
          check_skew(rfm,'Recency')

          plt.subplot(3, 1, 2)
          check_skew(rfm,'Frequency')

          plt.subplot(3, 1, 3)
          check_skew(rfm,'MonetaryValue')

          plt.tight_layout()
```

```
Recency's: Skew: 1.25
Frequency's: Skew: 17.35
MonetaryValue's: Skew: 21.36
```

Jupyter

Step 21: Examining the data shows you that skewness is a concern for Frequency and Monetary Value, as we can visually see in Step 20. To correct this, we will take the log of the variables. This will help reduce skewness in the data. First, make a copy of the rfm data so the original file remains unchanged. Then, use a new code box and enter the following text on your screen (Exhibit 8-35):

Copy the rfm data to new df so we can perform data log data transformation, rfm_log = rfm.copy()

Now, click "Run."

Exhibit 8-35

Jupyter

Step 22: Let's apply the log transformation on the recency, frequency, and monetary value variables to reduce the skewness you observed in the data. To do this, use a new code box and enter the following text on your screen (Exhibit 8-36):

```
# Transform skewed data with log transformation
df_rfm_log = np.log(rfm_log)
```

Now, click "Run."

Exhibit 8-36

Jupyter

Step 23: Now, we will repeat Step 20 to visualize whether the log transformation has corrected the extreme skewness in the data. To do this, use a new code box and enter the following text on your screen (Exhibit 8-37):

```
# Check for skewness after log transformation
plt.figure(figsize=(9, 9))

plt.subplot(3, 1, 1)
check_skew(df_rfm_log,'Recency')

plt.subplot(3, 1, 2)
check_skew(df_rfm_log,'Frequency')

plt.subplot(3, 1, 3)
check_skew(df_rfm_log,'MonetaryValue')

plt.tight_layout()
```

Now, click "Run."

Upon reviewing Exhibit 8-37, the distribution of each of the variables appear more normal.

Exhibit 8-37

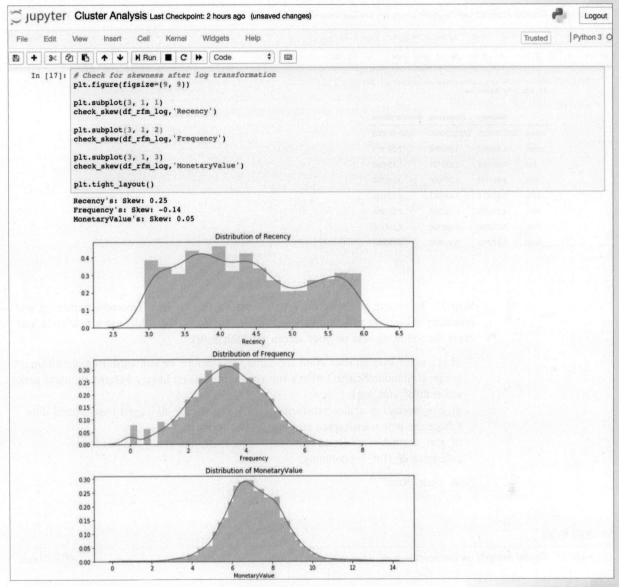

Jupyter

Step 24: You may recall earlier in the chapter we discussed that unit of analysis influences the results of cluster analysis. Let's review the current scale of the variables. To do this, use a new code box and enter the following text on your screen (Exhibit 8-38):

```
#note that the values are on different scales
df_rfm_log.describe()
```

Now, click "Run."

Exhibit 8-38

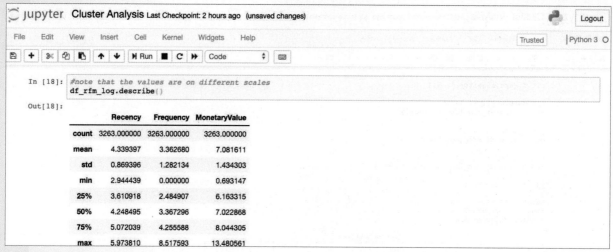

Jupyter

Step 25: To correct the scale discrepancy among the variables (recency, frequency, and monetary value), we will run standard scaler function. To do this, use a new code and enter the following text on your screen (Exhibit 8-39):

#Let's make sure all data is on the same scale before we run clustering algorithm
scaler = StandardScaler() #Let's run the preprocessing library Sklearn standard scaler
scaler.fit(df_rfm_log)
df_rfm_normal = scaler.transform(df_rfm_log) #Scale all logged transformed data
#Store the new transformed rfm into a data frame
df_rfm_normal = pd.DataFrame(df_rfm_normal, index=df_rfm_log.index, columns=df_rfm_log.columns)

Now, click "Run."

Exhibit 8-39

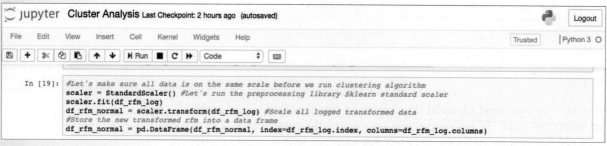

Jupyter

Step 26: Let's review if Step 25 yielded a one scale for all variables with a standard deviation of 1 and a mean of 0. To do this, use a new code box and enter the following text on your screen (Exhibit 8-40):

# Check result after running the Standard Scaler
df_rfm_normal.describe().round(3)

Now, click "Run."

Exhibit 8-40

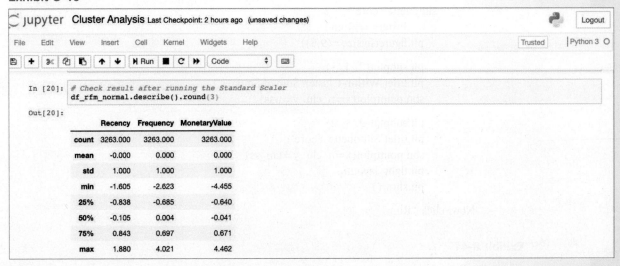

Jupyter

Step 27: Recall in our earlier discussion that finding the right number of clusters can be challenging. For this reason, in this step, we will develop a function that calculates both the silhouette and within-cluster sum of squares for different cluster numbers starting with 2 until 11 clusters. In this step, you will use the elbow and silhouette score charts to identify the optimal number of clusters. To do this, use a new code box and enter the following text on your screen (Exhibit 8-41):

```
#Let's use a function that calculates the optimal number of clusters for K-Means
def optimal_kmeans(df, start=2, end=11): #using a dataset, we will start with 2
clusters and try up to 11 clusters
    # Create empty lists to save values needed to plot graphs
    n_clu = []
    km_ss = []
    wss = []

    # Create a for loop to find optimal n_clusters
    for n_clusters in range(start, end):

    # Create cluster labels
        kmeans = KMeans(n_clusters=n_clusters)
        labels = kmeans.fit_predict(df)

    # Review model performance using silhouette_avg and inertia_score
        silhouette_avg = round(silhouette_score(df, labels, random_state=1), 3)
        wss_score = round(kmeans.inertia_, 2)

    # Add score to lists created earlier
        km_ss.append(silhouette_avg)
        n_clu.append(n_clusters)
        wss.append(wss_score)

    # Print n_clusters, silhouette_avg, and inertia_score
        print("No. Clusters: {}, Silhouette Score(SS): {}, Within-Cluster Sum-of-Squares:
        {}".format(
            n_clusters,
            silhouette_avg,
            wss_score))
```

```
# Plot two graphs at the end of loop: Within cluster sum of squares and
silhouette score
if n_clusters == end - 1:
    plt.figure(figsize=(9,6))

    plt.subplot(2, 1, 1)
    plt.title('Within-Cluster Sum-of-Squares')
    sbn.pointplot(x=n_clu, y=wss)

    plt.subplot(2, 1, 2)
    plt.title('Silhouette Score')
    sbn.pointplot(x=n_clu, y=km_ss)
    plt.tight_layout()
    plt.show()
```

Now, click "Run."

Exhibit 8-41

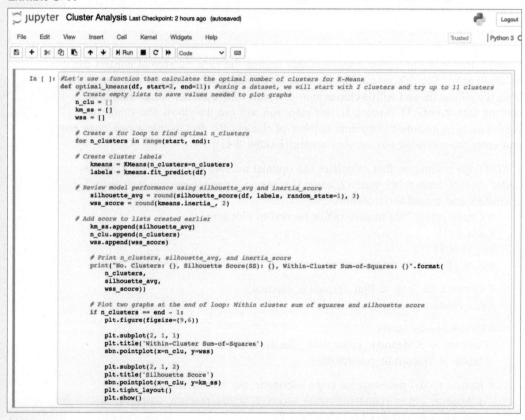

Jupyter

Step 28: This step will execute the function built and ran in Step 27. To do this, use a new code box and enter the following text on your screen (Exhibit 8-42):

```
optimal_kmeans(df_rfm_normal)
```

Now, click "Run."

The elbow and silhouette score charts in Exhibit 8-42 help evaluate the reduction in cluster error since a larger number of clusters is developed (explained earlier in section 8.4). The results indicate the optimal number of k clusters is three or four.

Exhibit 8-42

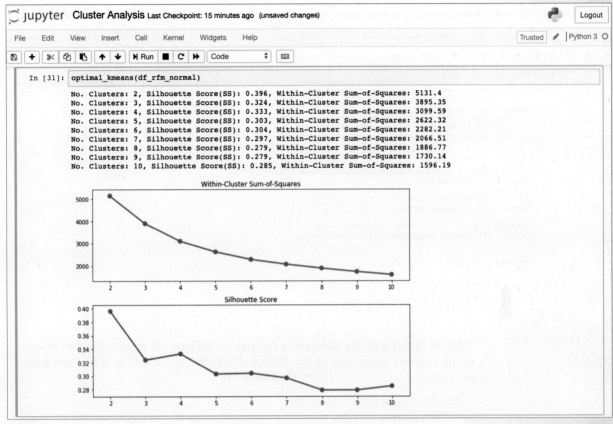

Jupyter

Step 29: In this step, you will build a function to apply the k-means algorithm to three and four clusters. To do this, use a new code box and enter the following text on your screen (Exhibit 8-43):

```
# Now, we apply the k-means cluster with two cluster sizes: 3 and 4 to see which
provides us with customer segments
def kmeans(normalized_df, clusters_number, original_df):
'''
```

Implement k-means clustering on dataset
   normalised_df_rfm : dataframe. Normalised rfm dataset for k-means to fit.
   clusters_number : int. Number of clusters to form.
   original_df_rfm : dataframe. Original rfm dataset to assign the labels to.
'''

```
kmeans = KMeans(n_clusters = clusters_number, random_state = 1)
kmeans.fit(normalized_df)
```

```
# Extract cluster labels
cluster_labels = kmeans.labels_
```

```
# Create a cluster label column in original dataset
df_new = original_df.assign(Cluster = cluster_labels)
```

```
return df_new
```

Now, click "Run."

Exhibit 8-43

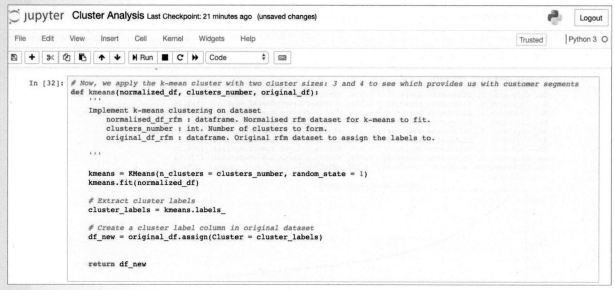

Jupyter

```
In [32]:  # Now, we apply the k-mean cluster with two cluster sizes: 3 and 4 to see which provides us with customer segments
          def kmeans(normalized_df, clusters_number, original_df):
              '''
              Implement k-means clustering on dataset
                  normalised_df_rfm : dataframe. Normalised rfm dataset for k-means to fit.
                  clusters_number : int. Number of clusters to form.
                  original_df_rfm : dataframe. Original rfm dataset to assign the labels to.

              '''

              kmeans = KMeans(n_clusters = clusters_number, random_state = 1)
              kmeans.fit(normalized_df)

              # Extract cluster labels
              cluster_labels = kmeans.labels_

              # Create a cluster label column in original dataset
              df_new = original_df.assign(Cluster = cluster_labels)


              return df_new
```

Step 30: In this step, we will build a function to evaluate the mean and count of each of the variables under each of the clusters. To do this, use a new code box and enter the following text on your screen (Exhibit 8-44):

```
def rfm_values(df):
    '''x
    Calculate average rfm values and size for each cluster

    '''
    df_new = df.groupby(['Cluster']).agg({
        'Recency': 'mean',
        'Frequency': 'mean',
        'MonetaryValue': ['mean', 'count']
    }).round(0)
    return df_new
```

Now, click "Run."

Exhibit 8-44

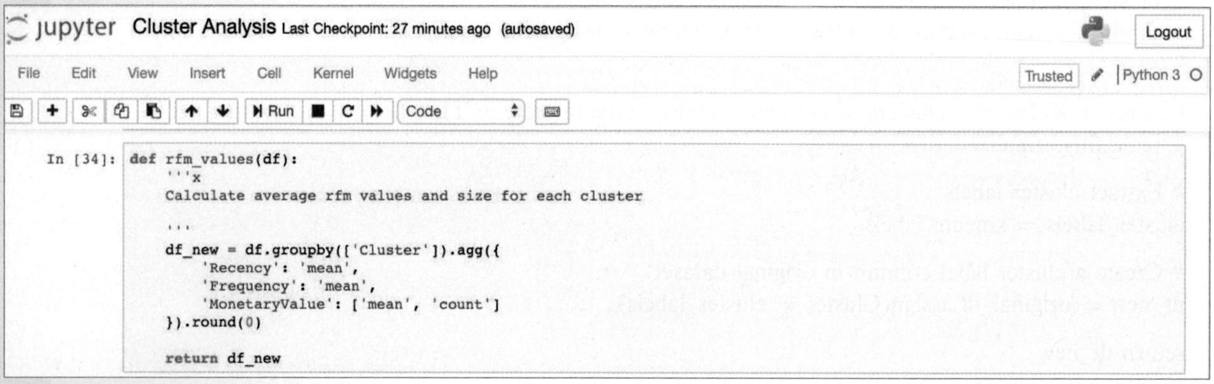

Jupyter · Cluster Analysis · Last Checkpoint: 27 minutes ago · (autosaved) · Logout

File · Edit · View · Insert · Cell · Kernel · Widgets · Help · Trusted · Python 3 ○

```
In [34]:  def rfm_values(df):
              '''x
              Calculate average rfm values and size for each cluster

              '''
              df_new = df.groupby(['Cluster']).agg({
                  'Recency': 'mean',
                  'Frequency': 'mean',
                  'MonetaryValue': ['mean', 'count']
              }).round(0)

              return df_new
```

Jupyter

Step 31: Let's apply both functions we built in Steps 29 and 30 to the normalized data. To accomplish this task, complete the following procedure for three clusters. Use a new code box and enter the following text on your screen (Exhibit 8-45):

```
df_rfm_k3 = kmeans(df_rfm_normal, 3, rfm)
rfm_values(df_rfm_k3)
```

Now, click "Run."

The results in Exhibit 8-45 show the means for recency, frequency, and monetary value and observation counts of three clusters. Note, how customers in cluster 1 have a higher monetary value (amount of money customers spent), higher frequency (generally visit the online store often) with more recent visits (a lower value refers to more recent visits) over the time span (i.e., 18 months) of the data compared to clusters 0 and 2.

Exhibit 8-45

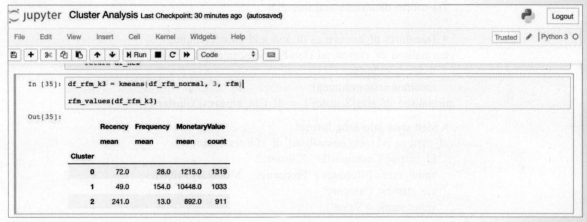

Jupyter

Step 32: We repeat Step 31 for four clusters. To accomplish this task, complete the following procedure to build your clusters. Use a new code box and enter the following text on your screen (Exhibit 8-46):

```
df_rfm_k4 = kmeans(df_rfm_normal, 4, rfm)
rfm_values(df_rfm_k4)
```

Now, click "Run."

Exhibit 8-46

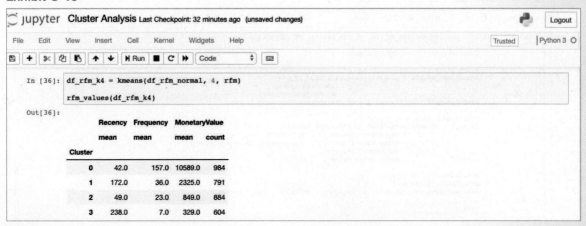

Jupyter

Take a moment to understand each of the four clusters and their behavior (Exhibit 8-46). For instance, note that cluster 0 has high recency (a lower value is a customer who visited the online store recently), a higher frequency (they generally visit the online store very often), and have spent a modest amount of money (monetary value) over the time span (i.e., 18 months) of the data.

Step 33: You have learned before that visual representation can help to better understand cluster characteristics. For that reason, it is necessary to write a function that builds a line plot visualization of the clusters. Take a moment to evaluate the clusters and determine if they will be useful in segmenting the market.

To accomplish this task, complete the following procedure to build the clusters. Use a new code box and enter the following text on your screen (Exhibit 8-47):

```
def line_plot(normalised_df_rfm, df_rfm_kmeans, df_rfm_original):
    '''
    Transform dataframe and line plot
    '''
    # Transform df_normal as df and add cluster column
    normalised_df_rfm = pd.DataFrame(normalised_df_rfm,
        index=rfm.index,
        columns=rfm.columns)
    normalised_df_rfm['Cluster'] = df_rfm_kmeans['Cluster']

    # Melt data into long format
    df_melt = pd.melt(normalised_df_rfm.reset_index(),
        id_vars=['CustomerID', 'Cluster'],
        value_vars=['Recency', 'Frequency', 'MonetaryValue'],
        var_name='Category',
        value_name='Value')

    plt.xlabel('Category')
    plt.ylabel('Value')
    sbn.pointplot(data=df_melt, x='Category', y='Value', hue='Cluster')

    return
```

Now, click "Run."

Exhibit 8-47

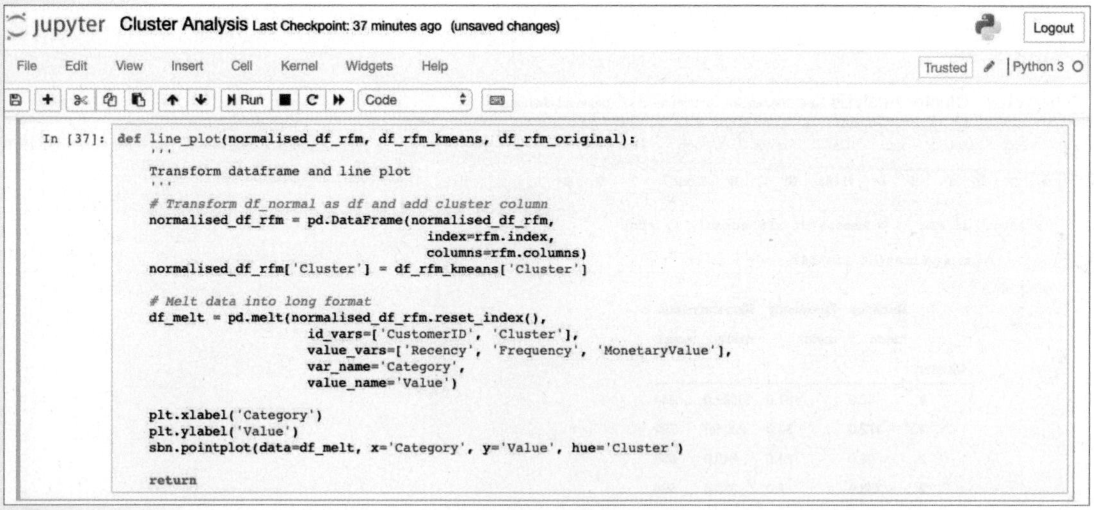

Jupyter

Step 34: In this step, we will visualize our graphs for three and four clusters by applying the function we built in Step 33. To accomplish this task, complete the following procedure for three and four clusters. Use a new code box and enter the following text on your screen (Exhibit 8-48):

```
plt.figure(figsize=(9, 9))

plt.subplot(3, 1, 1)
plt.title('Line Plot of K-Means = 3')
line_plot(df_rfm_normal, df_rfm_k3, rfm)

plt.subplot(3, 1, 2)
plt.title('Line Plot of K-Means = 4')
line_plot(df_rfm_normal, df_rfm_k4, rfm)
plt.tight_layout()
```

Now, click "Run."

Recall that you will need to explore two cluster sizes (three and four). Upon evaluating the line plot (Exhibit 8-48), which do you feel provides a better business meaning of the customer segmentation?

Upon evaluation, it was determined that the four segments could assist in developing a more targeted marketing strategy.

Exhibit 8-48

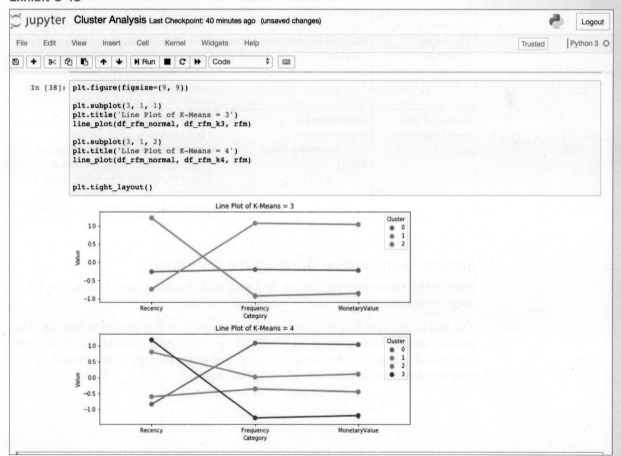

Let's revisit the meaning of the variables. Higher recency values mean that the customer has not visited the store recently, and lower recently values mean that the customer has visited recently. Higher frequency means the customer generally visits the online store very often. High monetary values mean the customer spent a relatively high amount in the online store. Review the four clusters identified in Exhibit 8-49. Using the definition of the different clusters, what type of marketing strategy might be beneficial?

Exhibit 8-49 Customer Segments

SEGMENT NAME	CUSTOMER CHARACTERISTICS	DEFINITION
Silver: weakest customers.	High Recency Low Frequency Low Monetary Value (Red)	Low value customer because they produce less monetary value, have not visited the online store in a while, and do not have a history of frequent purchases. This segment can potentially benefit from new product announcements.
Gold: valuable customers when they decide to shop.	Medium Recency Medium Frequency Medium-Low Monetary Value (Green)	Medium value customer because they produce a modest monetary value and fall in the middle when it comes to the frequency of purchase history and most recent visit to the online store. This segment might benefit from cross-selling offers.
Platinum: valuable customers with significant potential.	High Recency Medium Frequency Medium-High Monetary Value (Orange)	Valuable customer because they produce a modest monetary value, fall in the middle when it comes to the frequency of purchase history, and have a history of recent purchases. This segment could use a reminder to return for special offers.
Ambassadors: best customers.	Low Recency High Frequency High Monetary Value (Blue)	Extremely valuable customer because they produce high monetary value, have a history of frequent purchases, and have recently visited the online store. This segment could be targeted with exclusive offers for best customers.

Insights Learned from Applying the Concepts

Many useful marketing problems can be solved with cluster analysis. In this case, what insights were revealed?

The goal of this case was to show how market segmentation is applied in practice. The analysis revealed four customer segments that can be targeted differently (Exhibit 8-49). The retailer can use this knowledge to engage customers through targeted outreach programs and grow revenue through customer retention.

Summary of Learning Objectives and Key Terms

LEARNING OBJECTIVES

Objective 8.1   Define cluster analysis.

Objective 8.2   Identify and compare various uses for cluster analysis.

Objective 8.3   Investigate how cluster analysis functions.

Objective 8.4   Explain and assess the common types of cluster analysis.

KEY TERMS

Agglomerative clustering	Euclidean	Matching
Average linkage	Hierarchical clustering	Silhouette score
Cluster analysis	Jaccard's	Single linkage
Complete linkage	K-means clustering	Ward's method
Divisive clustering	Manhattan	

Discussion and Review Questions

1. Define cluster analysis.

2. How is cluster analysis useful in marketing segmentation?

3. How can marketers use cluster analysis?

4. How does a cluster analysis function?

5. Differentiate between hierarchical and k-means cluster analysis techniques.

Critical Thinking and Marketing Applications

1. Review Exhibit 8-48. What are the differences seen in the groups when examining the three cluster results versus four cluster results?

2. Review Exhibit 8-49. What are some marketing strategies that might meet the needs and wants of customers within the four different clusters?

References

1. Rob Markey, Gerard du Toit, and James Allen, "Find Your Sweet Spot," *Harvard Business Review*, February 27, 2008, https://hbr.org/2008/02/find-your-sweet-spot-1.html.

2. Mike Mancini, "Building Loyalty—One High Profit Customer Segment at a Time," Nielsen, August 5, 2009, https://www.nielsen.com/us/en/insights/article/2009/building-loyalty-one-high-profit-customer-segment-at-a-time; Rick Moss, "Best Buy Builds a Store for Jill...and Buzz, Barry and Ray," *Retail Wire*, August 18, 2005, https://retailwire.com/discussion/best-buy-builds-a-store-for-jill-and-buzz-barry-and-ray; and Best Buy Press Release, "Best Buy Rolls Out Customer-Segmented Stores in California," *Business Wire*, October 13, 2004, https://www.businesswire.com/news/home/20041013005822/en/Buy-Rolls-Customer-Segmented-Stores-California.

3. https://my-ibisworld-com.iris.etsu.edu:3443/us/en/industry-specialized/od5090/about

4. Tern Poh Lim, "The Most Important Data Science Tool for Market and Customer Segmentation," Towards Data Science, January 7, 2019, https://towardsdatascience.com/the-most-important-data-science-tool-for-market-and-customer-segmentation-c9709ca0b64a

9 Market Basket Analysis

LEARNING OBJECTIVES

9.1 Define market basket analysis.

9.2 Identify and evaluate various uses for market basket analysis.

9.3 Investigate and explain association rule using the apriori algorithm.

9.4 Evaluate and interpret results from the apriori algorithm.

9.5 Explain how collaborative filtering functions.

Uber Images/Shutterstock.com

9.1 What Is Market Basket Analysis?

Suppose you are a marketing manager for a retailer. You realize there are some important challenges and opportunities to consider:

- Customers who are unable to locate products will try to locate them at another retailer.
- Thirty-five percent of a close competitor's revenue comes from recommendations.[1]
- Over 60 percent of people say they make purchases due to an email message.[2]
- Empty shelves cost retailers nearly $1 trillion a year.[3]

Based on information like this, there are several questions you would want to answer. How should product placement be optimized in a store to minimize lost sales? What products should be recommended to customers searching the website? How can email promotions be personalized to attract more customers? To answer these questions, you need to learn more about the buying habits of your customers.

Market basket analysis, sometimes referred to by marketers as association discovery, uses purchase transaction data to identify associations between products or combinations of products and services that occur together frequently. A market basket analysis can be applied on past customer transactions at the store or on the website to understand customer buying habits.

Exhibit 9-1 gives an example of a market basket analysis and what it can tell us about customer purchases in a supermarket. Let's say a customer places two items (soda and milk) in their grocery cart. How likely is it that other certain specific items will also be included? In short, market basket analysis tells us that if a customer purchases *milk* and *soda* in a supermarket, they will also probably purchase *bread, beer,* and *salty snacks*.

These five products represent the topmost commonly purchased products in grocery baskets and will likely be purchased at the same time. Other complimentary items, such as chips and salsa, are also likely to be purchased together. The combinations of items purchased are then used to serve customers better by anticipating and understanding customer purchase behavior.

Exhibit 9-1 The Basics of Market Basket Analysis

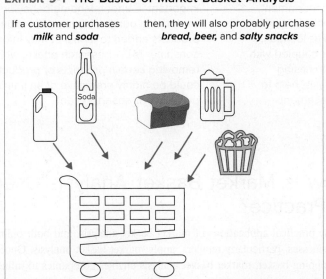

If a customer purchases **milk** and **soda** then, they will also probably purchase **bread, beer,** and **salty snacks**

PRACTITIONER CORNER

Rob Taylor | Principal Business Solutions Manager at SAS

Rob is part of the SAS Global Customer Intelligence Practice and has actively been involved in Digital Intelligence and Marketing for over 20 years. Having held positions within Decision Management at Citigroup and Moneysupermarket.com as the Customer Insight and Web Analytics Manager, he is focused on leveraging granular online behavioral data with traditional predictive analytics and machine learning techniques to understand customer behaviors and actioning them through real-time personalization and customer journeys.

Rob Taylor

Q **Companies in different industries, such as supermarkets and retailers, spend considerable time determining where products should be placed. Some stores use heat maps to determine which aisles are walked more frequently. For example, milk, bread, and eggs are often located in the back corner of stores even though they're commonly purchased. How does the knowledge of what customers might place in their baskets help with general product placement?**

A There are many factors that contribute to how products are presented to a customer. Combining consumer intelligence with business factors provides all the necessary data points needed to deliver against any desired strategic ambition for a store or website. That strategic ambition could be anything from increased sales, reduced cart abandonment, or increased share of wallet. From a brick-and-mortar perspective, factors such as location, store size, and local competition, coupled with consumer demographics and purchasing behaviors, including basket analysis, help to drive both product range and placement.

Q **How do companies in both brick-and-mortar and online channels anticipate and respond to purchase habits differently?**

A In digital channels, behavioral data is even more accessible and granular. The ability to not just use basket analysis against purchased products, but against every single product viewed makes it even more powerful to any data scientist. Digital channels also provide the ability to change product content in real time, which lends itself further to basket analysis techniques, such as recommendation engines and matrix factorization.

Digital channels, however, come with slightly different challenges than bricks and mortar. There is a greater opportunity of cart abandonment, while purchases can be made across multiple sessions. It is these factors that make basket analysis even more important in understanding behaviors, as well as defining purchase cycles. An initial flurry of products added to a basket may inform us the consumer is in a research phase, while removing certain products or product lines could be highly predictive of an imminent purchase or abandonment.

Continued to page 312

9.2 How Is Market Basket Analysis Used in Practice?

There are many practical applications of market basket analysis, and both online and brick-and-mortar businesses, particularly retailers, apply market basket analysis. Once a product is placed in a shopping basket, market basket analysis enables companies to influence a customer's selection of other products. Some of these products might be on a customer's shopping list. Other customer product selections could be influenced by marketers using different strategies to remind or introduce customers to additional products or services they are likely to purchase. While market basket analysis is useful for in-store recommendations, it is even more valuable for online purchasing because the information on product selection is in real time—once you place an item in the online shopping cart for purchase, the retailer can provide immediate suggestions of other items customers are likely to purchase.

Online retailers such as Amazon have mastered the analysis of shopping baskets showing items frequently bought together. These insights are used in developing recommendations for advertising other products and services likely of interest to a customer. For instance, searching for the *Blue Ocean Strategy* book listed on numerous MBA program reading lists produces results for products frequently bought together (see Exhibit 9-2). Amazon informs potential customers of other products that might be of interest to them. In addition to market basket analysis, Amazon uses collaborative filtering in most of its customized recommendations such as with what other customers purchase after viewing a particular item. **Collaborative filtering** uses the idea of identifying relevant items for a specific user from a large set of items by taking into consideration the preferences of many similar users. Collaborative filtering is based on data such as what a user has bought in the past, which items a user liked, and what the other similar customers have viewed and bought. A discussion on collaborative filtering is revisited in Section 9.4.

Target has also been very successful using transaction data to engage customers. The urban dictionary even defines this success as the "Target Effect"—or entering a store website with a short shopping list but departing with a cart full of products. Target is focused on developing customer-centered strategies in store and online to show customers what they need and want—often before they know. Using market basket analysis, Target can understand customer sales patterns and then use this information to influence and assist with product selections. This can be accomplished by optimizing product placement through product adjacencies (i.e., locating certain products near each other), maintaining appropriate merchandise assortment, and improving the use of space.[4] The company realizes that the more they capture the attention of customers, the more they can continue to engage them through personalized connections and create satisfying experiences that could also result in extended customer loyalty.

Traditional supermarkets carry about 15,000 products in smaller stores to as many as 50,000 products in larger stores.[5] Consider the top five products on most shopping lists mentioned earlier. Where are these items located in a store? Are milk and bread usually

Exhibit 9-2 Examples of Products Frequently Purchased Together

Amazon

located directly beside each other, or even on the same side of the store? No, locating these items further apart requires customers to cover more ground in the store. This in-store location strategy is based on the knowledge that about two-thirds of supermarket product purchases are based on impulse decisions while in the store. Moreover, end-aisle displays can increase product sales a minimum of 100 percent during the time products are placed there. Thus, requiring customers to walk past other aisles or intriguing displays can trigger additions to the shopping basket or impulse purchases. In contrast, sometimes placing complimentary products together such as beer and snack items, or chips or nuts, could be a successful cross-selling strategy that encourages customers to purchase more products.

Market basket analysis enables marketers to identify what products are being purchased together. Uncovering relationships between product and service bundle purchases is important for understanding customer purchase patterns and maximizing sales.

But, how does a market basket analysis work?

9.3 Association Rules: How Does a Market Basket Analysis Identify Product Relationships?

Market basket analysis is an unsupervised learning algorithm that explores patterns between two or more items using association rules (or affinity analysis). An **association rule** helps define relationships in a transaction dataset using if-then statements. By analyzing transaction data, we discover dependencies between items purchased in the form of IF [item A] THEN [item b] statements. For example, if soda (antecedent) is purchased, then milk (consequent) will also likely be purchased. Thus, the antecedent corresponds to the IF item, and the consequent corresponds to the THEN item in the association rule. Association analysis identifies that the antecedent and consequent of the rule share a co-occurrent relationship. These rules are commonly generated using the Apriori algorithm.

The **Apriori algorithm** identifies combinations of items in datasets that are associated with each other. Associations are identified based on the frequency in which the products occur together in the basket.

Exhibit 9-3 provides an example of ten customer transactions. The products are consistent with the most commonly purchased items at the grocery store. Using this

Exhibit 9-3 Transaction Data of a Grocery Store

TRANSACTION NUMBER	ITEMS PURCHASED
1	Soda, Milk, Bread
2	Soda, Milk
3	Beer, Salty Snacks, Milk, Soda
4	Soda, Milk, Bread
5	Salty Snacks, Milk, Soda
6	Beer, Salty Snacks
7	Soda, Salty Snacks
8	Beer, Soda
9	Beer, Bread
10	Beer, Soda, Milk, Bread, Salty Snacks

small dataset, you can determine, for example, the likelihood that soda and milk will be purchased together.

Another way to represent this dataset is to create a binary matrix of the transactions and use 1 if the item is present and 0 if the product is not present (see Exhibit 9-4).

From the coded data in Exhibit 9-4, we can create a frequency data table showing the number of times each item and itemset have appeared in the total transactions (see Exhibit 9-5).

Exhibit 9-4 Binary Matrix of Transaction Data of Grocery Store

TRANSACTION NUMBER	SODA	MILK	BREAD	SALTY SNACKS	BEER
1	1	1	1	0	0
2	1	1	0	0	0
3	1	1	0	1	1
4	1	1	1	0	0
5	1	1	0	1	0
6	0	0	0	1	1
7	1	0	0	1	0
8	1	0	0	0	1
9	0	0	1	0	1
10	1	1	1	1	1

Exhibit 9-5 Frequency Data for Grocery Store

(showing items with a two or more itemset)

ITEMS	FREQUENCY
Soda	8
Milk	6
Bread	4
Salty Snacks	5
Beer	5
Soda, Milk	6
Soda, Bread	3
Soda, Salty Snacks	4
Soda, Beer	3
Milk, Bread	3
Milk, Salty Snacks	3
Milk, Beer	2
Bread, Beer	2
Salty Snacks, Beer	3
Soda, Milk, Bread	3
Soda, Milk, Salty Snacks	3
Soda, Milk, Beer	2

When you use market basket analysis, there are three measures that indicate the reliability of the associations. The three measures are (1) support, (2) confidence, and (3) lift. In the case study later in this chapter, you will be able to apply these measures.

Support measures the frequency of the specific association rule. Support shows the number of transactions that include the items of interest divided by the total number of transactions:

$$Support = \frac{\text{Number of transactions that includes both antecedent and consequent}}{\text{Total number of transactions}}$$

Consider, for example, the itemset {Soda; Milk} in which soda and milk are both included in the same transaction a total of six out of ten times, as shown in Exhibit 9-5. Using the association rule IF [soda] THEN [milk], support would be calculated as:

$$Support = \frac{\text{Frequency\{Soda, Milk\}}}{\text{Total number of transactions}} = \frac{6}{10} = 0.60$$

In this case, 60 percent of baskets (transactions) contain both soda and milk.

Confidence measures the conditional probability of the consequent actually occurring given that the antecedent occurs. It is calculated as the count of purchases consisting of both items in the association rule divided by the total number of times the antecedent item is purchased. This measure indicates the percentage of times the association rule is correct. The formula is:

$$Confidence = \frac{\text{Support of transactions that includes both antecedent and consequent}}{\text{Support of transactions that includes antecedent only}}$$

Using the association rule IF [soda] THEN [milk], confidence would be calculated as:

$$Confidence = \frac{\text{Support\{Soda, Milk\}}}{\text{Support\{Soda\}}} = \frac{.6}{.8} = 0.75$$

The itemset {soda, milk} is included together in six transactions. Whereas, {soda} is included in eight transactions. The example shows that when grocery baskets contain soda, 75 percent of them also contain milk.

Lift enables us to evaluate the strength of the association. In a lift ratio, we divide the confidence with a benchmark score that is called *expected confidence*. Expected confidence is calculated as the number of total transactions that includes the consequent item divided by the total number of transactions:

$$Expected\ Confidence = \frac{\text{Number of transactions that includes consequent}}{\text{Total number of transactions}}$$

Using the association rule IF [soda] THEN [milk], the expected confidence would be calculated as:

$$Expected\ Confidence = \frac{\text{Frequency\{Milk\}}}{\text{Total number of transactions}} = \frac{6}{10} = 0.60$$

Lift ratio is calculated as the ratio of the confidence divided by the expected confidence. For the association rule IF [soda] THEN [milk], the lift would be calculated as:

$$Lift = \frac{\text{Confidence}}{\text{Expected Confidence}} = \frac{0.75}{0.60} = 1.25$$

Lift validates that a transaction containing both products is not random. A lift value of 1 indicates no relationship within the itemset. A lift value higher than 1 indicates a relationship between the products or services that is higher than would be expected if they were independent. A lift value below 1 indicates a negative relationship that the products or services in the itemset are unlikely to be purchased together.

If soda is purchased, then with a confidence of 75 percent milk will also be purchased. The lift of 1.25 suggests that the purchase of milk is 1.25 times more likely when soda is purchased compared to shoppers just purchasing milk.

How do we ensure that rules generated are not due to random chance effect and are meaningful? It is critical to remember when using market basket analysis that the higher number of transactions will ensure that we have more robust conclusions.

9.4 Special Topics in Market Basket Analysis

What if an analyst is interested in understanding customer patterns across demographics, seasons, store locations, and so on? **Differential market basket analysis** is the use of market basket analysis techniques across stores, locations, seasons, days of the week, and so forth. Using this approach, a marketing analyst would run a market basket analysis in one location, then compare it to other locations to see if the results in one location are consistent with the other locations. If the results are different, the analyst can focus on what makes the locations different. Is it the placement of the products? Is it the type of promotions run? Or is it the customers served? This in-depth analysis technique can help the business potentially improve its sales.

In association rules, the goal is to find items that are frequently purchased together and to make a customer recommendation every time one of those items is added to the basket. This application is useful when there are products or services that are frequently purchased together time after time (e.g., personal garments: blouse and scarf; grocery shopping: chips and soft drinks). What if a company wants to offer personalized recommendations for the user when items are not purchased as frequently? Consider music downloads, audiobook purchases, or movie streaming. In cases like this, an analytics solution referred to as collaborative filtering can be used.

Collaborative filtering examines users' preferences for a set of items. The preferences can be captured explicitly—for example, when a user rates a product or service or likes a song—or implicitly—for instance, when a user clicks on a webpage. Collaborative filtering is commonly used by companies like Netflix, Amazon, YouTube, and Spotify.

Collaborative filtering enables us to analyze data on user preferences, and then recommend what customers would potentially like based on their similarity to other customers. The main idea is that customers who have rated a movie similarly or liked the same song will also likely express similar agreement in their future behavior. The goal of collaborative filtering is to recommend new products and services to a customer who has not purchased them before.

There are two main types of collaborative filtering:

- *Item to item filtering* considers items that were previously co-purchased or co-rated with the item of interest, and then recommends the most highly correlated items among similar items. An example of this is when a retailer promotes products using the promotional language "Customers who liked this item also liked..."
- *User to item filtering* will find customers who are similar in their preferences and consider items they have purchased, then recommend the ones that are highly rated by the customer's neighbors. An example of this is when a retailer promotes products using the promotional language "Customers who are similar to you also liked..."

Exhibit 9-6 Customer Rating Matrix of Songs on 1- to 5-Star Scale

	SONG NAME				
Customer	*Memories* by Maroon 5	*Love of My Life* by Queens	*Come Out and Play* by Billie Eilish	*Death & Taxes* by Daniel Caesar	*Streetcar* by Daniel Caesar
Faith	2	5	4	4	5
Mason	4	2	5	3	2
Julian	3	5	4	4	
Alexander			2	3	1
Prachi	5	5	4		2

To measure similarities in collaborative filtering, a distance measure needs to be selected. There are several popular measures of distance in collaborative filtering, including calculating the average Pearson Correlation between ratings and Cosine Similarity. Both measures produce values that range from –1 to 1. Values that are closer to –1 indicate non-similar relationships, whereas values that are closer to 1 indicate similarity.

A simplified example of the collaborative filtering concept that companies like Spotify can use to make recommendations for their customers is shown in Exhibit 9-6. This chart shows customers and the songs they have rated on a 1- to 5-star scale. Organizing data in this matrix helps us visualize similarities in the ratings across customers and songs. For example, we see that Faith and Julian have similar song ratings. Based on this information, we can recommend *Streetcar* by Daniel Caesar to Julian as a next song to listen to.

While collaborative filtering is very useful, it does have some limitations, including:

- *Cold start:* A new item cannot be recommended until enough users have rated it.
- *Popularity bias:* Items with a lot of recommendations will be assigned a higher weight. Thus, popular items are recommended more often than items that do not have a lot of recommendations.

continued from page 306

PRACTITIONER CORNER

Rob Taylor | Principal Business Solutions Manager at SAS

Q Recent reports show that companies like Mastercard might collaborate and share real-time transaction information with retailers to help them optimize promotional strategies. How do you collect and use data to offer the products and personalized service customers want and need without compromising their trust and adhering to privacy laws?

A If you look at your own experiences as a consumer, the way we expect organizations to engage with us has evolved substantially over time. We expect the organization to "know" us—our needs, our expectations, and our attitudes to price, quality, and service. We also expect organizations to engage with us in a channel that we choose or prefer, at convenient times with relevance.

Continued

This new standard of "expected customer experience" brings a great deal of responsibility to the marketing analyst to get the balance right between privacy and personalization. There is no right answer to this balance, and this can only be found through customer journey analysis and personalization testing against KPI's such as increased brand loyalty, customer lifetime value (CLV), and customer satisfaction scores (e.g., Net Promoter Score).

In Europe, GDPR (General Data Protection Regulation) has helped marketers to draw broad guidelines to follow. However, interpretation of the regulations varies substantially between businesses, in-house data protection officers, and privacy experts. The safest way is to focus on the consumer. Use any data collected to enhance their individual experiences and customer journey, while being transparent with them about what you are collecting and why. If you are delighting your consumers with great customer experiences, they will be more than happy to provide personal data for a seamless customer journey.

Case Study Online Department Store: Understanding Customer Purchase Patterns

Understanding the Business Problem

Department stores represent a $136 billion industry. Traditional department stores such as Macy's and Nordstrom are key players in terms of market share. However, for the last several years, brick-and-mortar department stores have been struggling. In January 2020, clothing store sales fell 3.1 percent, the largest decline since 2009. The industry is losing customers to changing habits and preferences. Shoppers are gravitating toward efficient, online transactions with more product options and often the promise of fast, free shipping to their doorstep. While this is a challenge to traditional brick-and-mortar department stores, it also represents an opportunity.

Companies want to understand customer purchase patterns and then encourage or influence customers' purchases. In marketing, this can be done by broadening a customer's awareness of other options and improving online conversions. This is also referred to as a "nudge" or potential to alter someone's behavior. Nudging theory considers both psychology and behavioral economics to understand how people think, how they make decisions, and what can impact those choices.[6] Department stores can nudge customers in the form of certain anchors. These anchors, such as product placements and recommendations, on ecommerce sites can then influence different behaviors. In this case study, the objective is to explain how to use the data to optimize product placement and develop recommendations.

Understanding the Dataset

In this example, a hypothetical online retailer dataset will be used. The dataset consists of customers' online transactions for activewear. A market basket analysis will be used to capture the patterns of which products customers frequently buy together in a basket. If two products are often bought together, this could be used to alert customers about other products they may be interested in—before they check out.

To get started, let's review the data elements in Exhibit 9-7.

RapidMiner will be used to execute the market basket analysis. First, the data variables will be reviewed in Excel and then loaded into RapidMiner for analysis.

Exhibit 9-7 Data Dictionary

VARIABLE NAME (TYPE)	DESCRIPTION
TransactionID (typeless)	Unique ID representing a transaction (also known as a basket online)
CustomerID (typeless)	Unique ID representing a customer
Order_Date (date)	Date of the transaction
Brand (string)	Retailer brand (e.g., Adidas, New Balance, Under Armour)
Product (string)	Product type (e.g., Jacket, Visor, V-Neck)
Color (string)	Color of the product (e.g., Red, Maroon, Navy, White)
Size (string)	Product size (e.g., S, M, L, XL)
Sales_Amount (numeric)	Dollar amount of customer spending on the product

Data Preparation

An essential practice to remember before starting any analytics project is to first review and clean the dataset. Download and open the Online Retailer Dataset.xlsx file (available on the student resources site) to examine the variable values in Excel. There are 198,433 records and eight variables. Exhibit 9-8 shows a snapshot of the variables and records for the first 35 transactions.

What does one row in the data set represent? Each row of the data represents one product transaction. For example, the first row is a Neon V-Neck shirt. The second row is Bright Pink Shorts.

After the initial review, you should see that there is a large number of transaction-level data of what customers have purchased from 2017 through 2020. When you have an understanding of what these customers often buy together, you can develop more effective sales and promotion strategies.

Quick reminder: Click on *Data*, then *Filter* to further understand variable categories under each column.

Exhibit 9-8 Online Retailer Dataset Overview

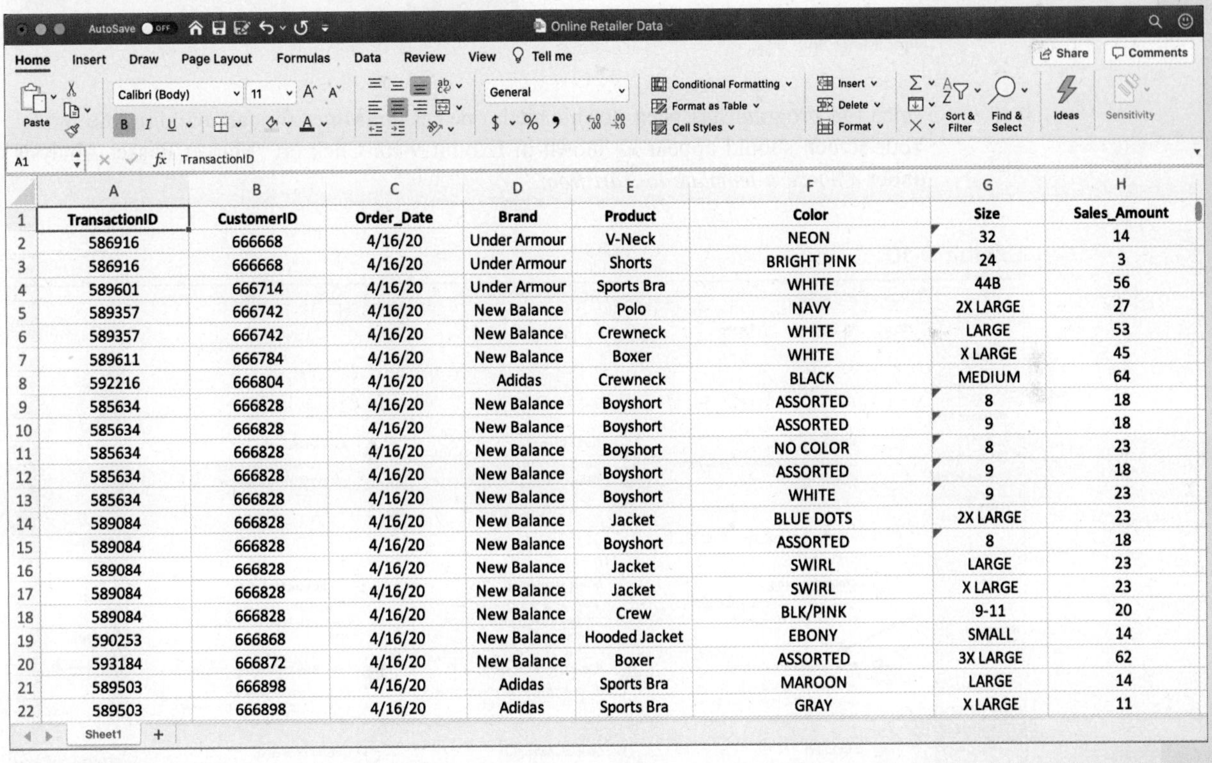

	TransactionID	CustomerID	Order_Date	Brand	Product	Color	Size	Sales_Amount
1	TransactionID	CustomerID	Order_Date	Brand	Product	Color	Size	Sales_Amount
2	586916	666668	4/16/20	Under Armour	V-Neck	NEON	32	14
3	586916	666668	4/16/20	Under Armour	Shorts	BRIGHT PINK	24	3
4	589601	666714	4/16/20	Under Armour	Sports Bra	WHITE	44B	56
5	589357	666742	4/16/20	New Balance	Polo	NAVY	2X LARGE	27
6	589357	666742	4/16/20	New Balance	Crewneck	WHITE	LARGE	53
7	589611	666784	4/16/20	New Balance	Boxer	WHITE	X LARGE	45
8	592216	666804	4/16/20	Adidas	Crewneck	BLACK	MEDIUM	64
9	585634	666828	4/16/20	New Balance	Boyshort	ASSORTED	8	18
10	585634	666828	4/16/20	New Balance	Boyshort	ASSORTED	9	18
11	585634	666828	4/16/20	New Balance	Boyshort	NO COLOR	8	23
12	585634	666828	4/16/20	New Balance	Boyshort	ASSORTED	9	18
13	585634	666828	4/16/20	New Balance	Boyshort	WHITE	9	23
14	589084	666828	4/16/20	New Balance	Jacket	BLUE DOTS	2X LARGE	23
15	589084	666828	4/16/20	New Balance	Boyshort	ASSORTED	8	18
16	589084	666828	4/16/20	New Balance	Jacket	SWIRL	LARGE	23
17	589084	666828	4/16/20	New Balance	Jacket	SWIRL	X LARGE	23
18	589084	666828	4/16/20	New Balance	Crew	BLK/PINK	9-11	20
19	590253	666868	4/16/20	New Balance	Hooded Jacket	EBONY	SMALL	14
20	593184	666872	4/16/20	New Balance	Boxer	ASSORTED	3X LARGE	62
21	589503	666898	4/16/20	Adidas	Sports Bra	MAROON	LARGE	14
22	589503	666898	4/16/20	Adidas	Sports Bra	GRAY	X LARGE	11

Microsoft Excel

Applying the Concepts

We worked with RapidMiner in Chapters 5 and 6. As you learned, the RapidMiner software is one of the most widely used data analytics tools available. In this example, you will learn how RapidMiner can be used to analyze the data displayed in the Excel spreadsheet using market basket analysis.

If you have not yet downloaded RapidMiner, go to https://rapidminer.com/educational-program and register for a student academic account, as shown in Exhibit 9-9. The RapidMiner software works the same on Mac and Windows.

Exhibit 9-9

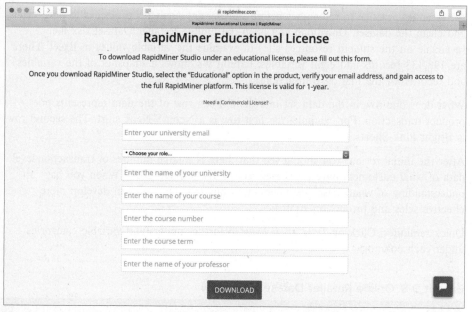

RapidMiner, Inc.

Once the program has been downloaded, open RapidMiner to start building the model. Your screen should appear as shown in Exhibit 9-10. Click on "Market Basket Analysis" under *Choose a template to start from*.

Exhibit 9-10

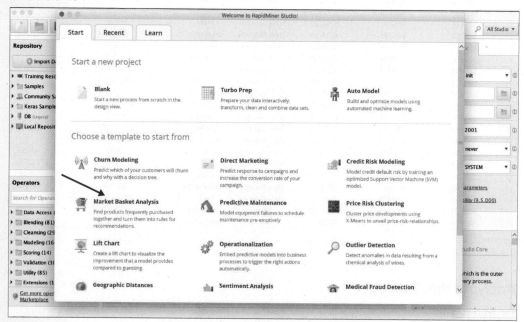

RapidMiner, Inc.

The Market Basket Analysis template shown in Exhibit 9-11 is now open with all operators preloaded and ready for you to load the data and analyze it. The template has four main steps: (1) loading the data operator; (2) preparing the data for analysis using aggregate, rename, and set role operators; (3) running the FP-growth model using the FP-Growth operator; and (4) running association rules analysis using the Create Association Rules operator. The properties of these operators will eventually be changed. But before proceeding with these changes, you need to import the data into the RapidMiner software. To do so, click on "Import Data," shown in Exhibit 9-11 under Repository.

Exhibit 9-11

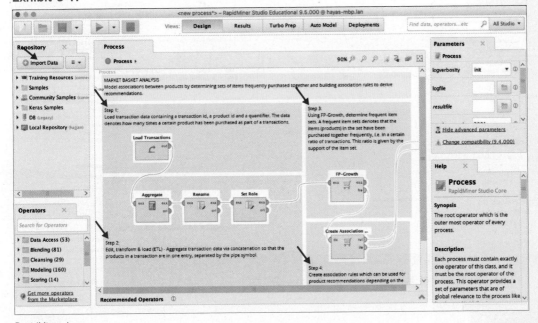

RapidMiner, Inc.

To import the data, click on My Computer and navigate to the folder where you saved the Online Retailer Data.xlsx file (Exhibit 9-12).

Exhibit 9-12

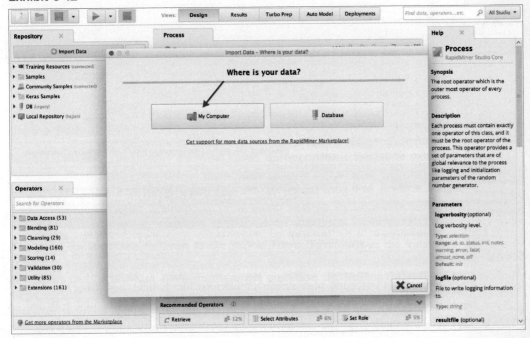

RapidMiner, Inc.

Click the Online Retailer Data.xlsx file name and then select "Next" at the bottom of the screen (Exhibit 9-13).

Exhibit 9-13

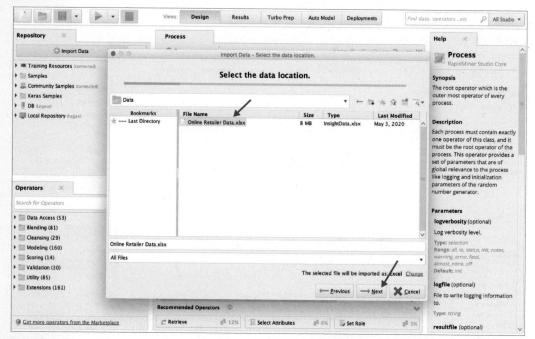

RapidMiner, Inc.

Exhibit 9-14

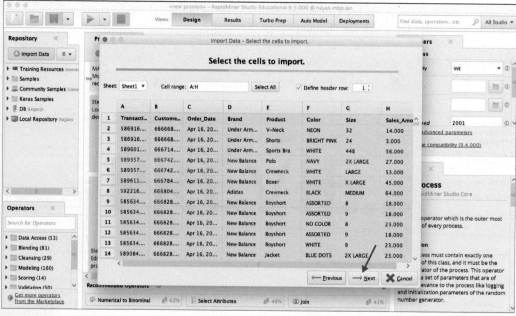

RapidMiner, Inc.

Once your data is uploaded, your screen should look like Exhibit 9-14. Click the "Next" button to move to the "Format your columns" window, as shown in Exhibit 9-15.

Next, review Exhibit 9-15. You can format your variables in this window or make any necessary changes for data type. Notice that the variables TransactionID and CustomerID are processed as integers because they are numerical values with no decimal places. The variable Order Date is processed as a date. In addition, Product is processed as a polynomial type in RapidMiner. This is because the variable has string values stored: V-Neck, shorts, jacket, and so on. Note that Brand and Color are also processed as polynomial types because they are also string data.

When finished reviewing your data, click "Next," as shown at the bottom of Exhibit 9-15.

Exhibit 9-15

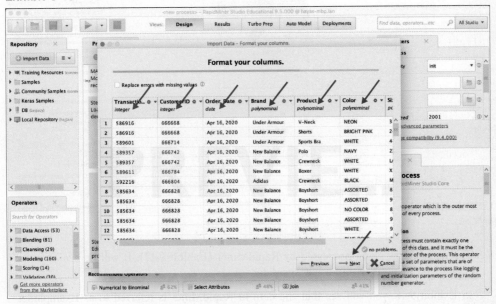

RapidMiner, Inc.

Determine in what folder inside the RapidMiner repository the data will be stored. For this example, select "Local Repository" and then "data" folder. Then, click "Finish," as shown in Exhibit 9-16.

Exhibit 9-16

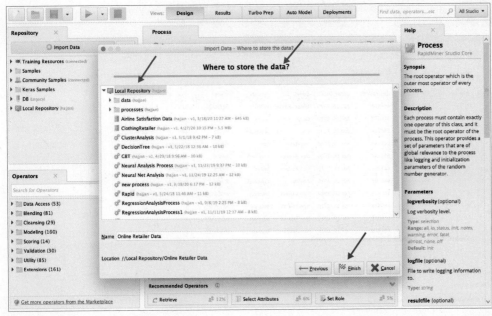

RapidMiner, Inc.

Exhibit 9-17

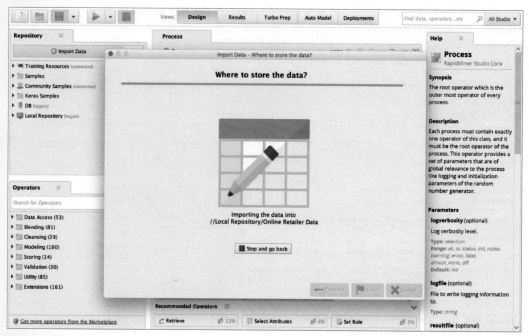

RapidMiner, Inc.

The data is now being processed by RapidMiner (Exhibit 9-17). It will be available for review and analysis within a few seconds.

In Exhibit 9-18, you will see that the data in RapidMiner is referred to as ExampleSet with 198,433 examples and 8 variables (regular attributes). In the top Views menu bar, click on "Design" (top of screen) to return to your Market Basket Analysis model (Exhibit 9-18).

Exhibit 9-18

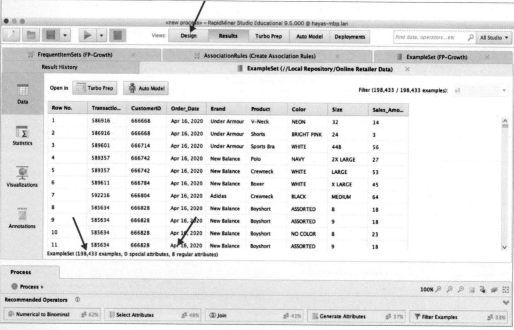

RapidMiner, Inc.

Exhibit 9-19

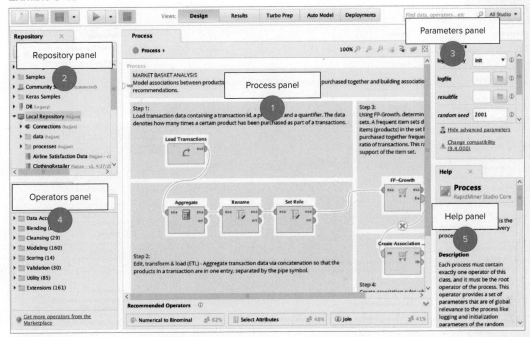

RapidMiner, Inc.

You may recall from Chapter 6 that the RapidMiner workspace is divided into five main default panels, as shown in Exhibit 9-19.

If you close any of the panels during your setup, you can click on the Views menu (top screen of Exhibit 9-20) and select "Restore Default View" to reset the Design View to the default panel setup.

Exhibit 9-20

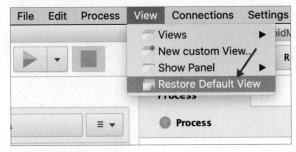

RapidMiner, Inc.

Loading Data

To start with the Market Basket Analysis, we begin with Step 1 in the template to update the Load Transactions operator. To do so, click on the *Load Transaction* operator, as shown in Exhibit 9-21. Then, click on the file folder icon under the Parameters panel at the top right of the screen to update the repository entry.

As we learned in Chapter 6, an operator is used in RapidMiner to create and execute analytical processes. Examples of operators include retrieving data, selecting attributes, aggregating data, renaming it, and running models. Operators have at least two ports—an input port and an output port. The input port determines what is provided to the operator, and the output port carries the results of the operator.

Exhibit 9-21

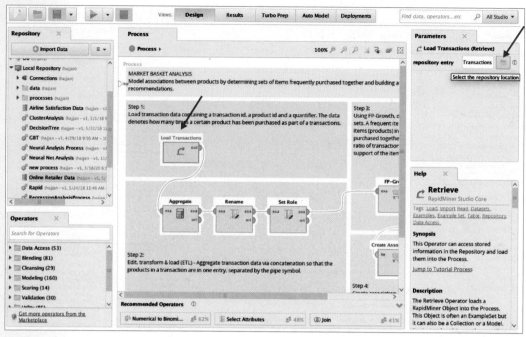

RapidMiner, Inc.

After an operator is selected and added to the process, you can access its parameters in the *Parameters* panel. The parameters are the properties of the operator that are selected to control the operation (top right of Exhibit 9-21).

To import the Online Retailer Data we uploaded earlier, navigate to the Local Repository folder and click on the Online Retailer Data dataset (see Exhibit 9-22). Now, click "OK."

Exhibit 9-22

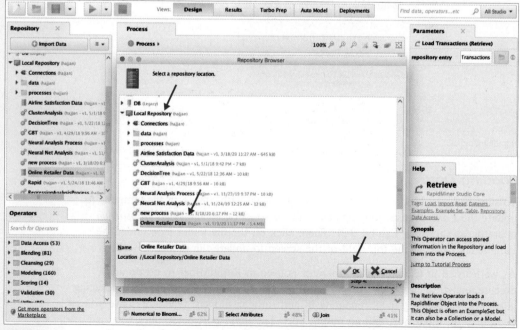

RapidMiner, Inc.

Preparing the Data

Exhibit 9-23 shows that Step 2 in the template is made up of three sub-steps: Aggregate, Rename, and Set Role. Each of these operators will help prepare the data to apply the market basket analysis.

Now, click the *Aggregate* operator (as shown in Exhibit 9-23) to update the template values with the Online Retailer Data variables. The Aggregate operator enables you to prepare the transaction data by product. Under the Parameters panel, click on "Edit List" under the "aggregation attributes" selection to choose the Product variable (top right of Exhibit 9-23).

Exhibit 9-23

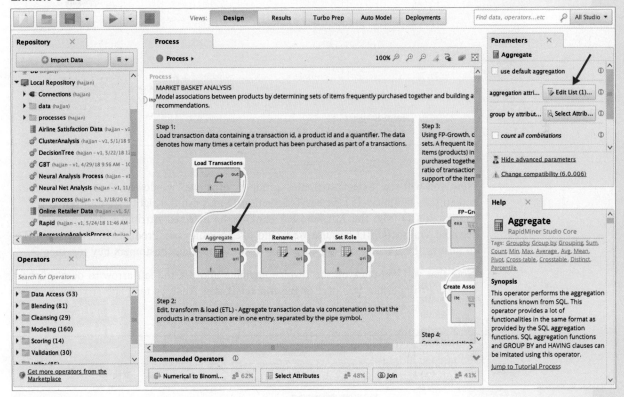

RapidMiner, Inc.

Using the drop-down menu, select "Product" and click "Apply" (Exhibit 9-24). The Product variable is selected because you are interested in examining what products customers often buy together. The aggregation function "concatenation" will enable us to combine all products in a transaction occurring in multiple rows into one row.

For example, assume we have the following transactions:

- Transaction 1: {V-Neck}
- Transaction 1: {Jacket}
- Transaction 2: {Visor}

The results of the aggregate function will be Transaction 1 {V-Neck; Jacket}, Transaction 2 {Visor}, and so on.

Still under the Parameters panel, click on "Select Attribute" in the "group by attribute" section (Exhibit 9-24).

Exhibit 9-24

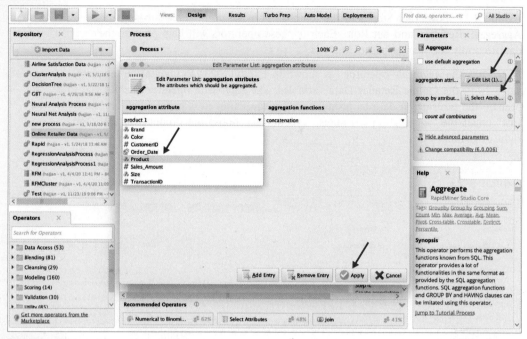

RapidMiner, Inc.

Now, you will see "Select Attributes: group by attribute" window in the middle of your screen (see Exhibit 9-25). Select TransactionID and use the right arrow to send TransactionID from the Attribute left pane to the Selected Attributes right pane. We selected TransactionID because we would like to group our Products by TransactionID to answer the question we posed earlier on what products customers buy together.

Note that you can click on the Invoice attribute and use the left arrow to deselect the Invoice attribute that was part of the Market Basket Analysis template (Exhibit 9-25).

Exhibit 9-25

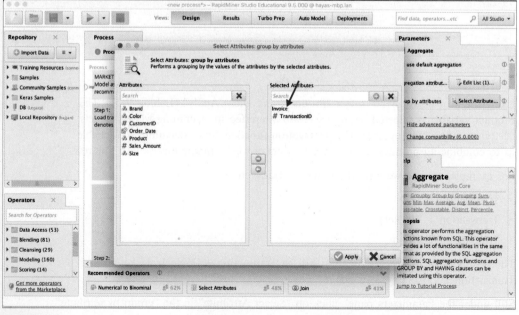

RapidMiner, Inc.

Exhibit 9-26

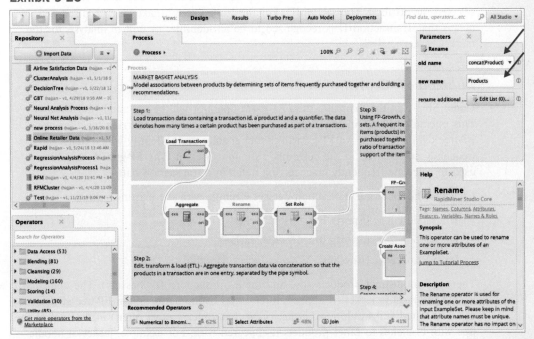

RapidMiner, Inc.

Next, click on the *Rename* operator, as shown in top right of Exhibit 9-26. This operator enables you to change the name of any of the attributes. For example, you can change the name of the concat(Product) to Products. To do so, under "old name" in the Parameters panel, select "Concat(Product)" from the drop-down menu and type the name "Products" under the "new name" section.

Next, click on the *Set Role* operator (Exhibit 9-27). Under the Parameters panel, click on the "attribute name" drop-down menu and select TransactionID. If you don't see

Exhibit 9-27

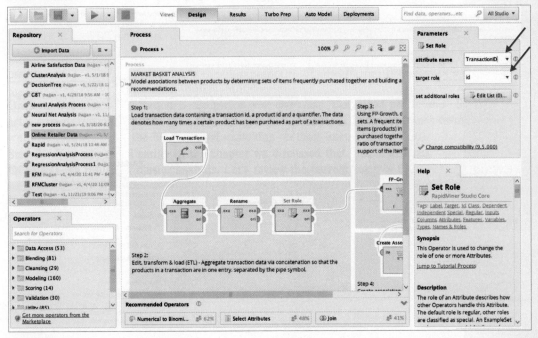

RapidMiner, Inc.

TransactionID, go back to the *Aggregate* operator instructions and make sure you selected the attribute TransactionID. For the "target role," make sure id is selected. id means that TransactionID is recognized to be an identifier or unit of analysis for the market basket analysis.

Running FP-Growth

Under Step 3 in the template, the *FP-Growth* operator will be executed (Exhibit 9-28). This operator will calculate the products that are frequently occurring together using an FP-tree data structure. An FP-growth model enables us to identify which items most frequently co-occurred in the customer's shopping basket. The **FP-growth algorithm** is used to calculate frequently co-occurring items in a transaction dataset.

Consider the following transaction dataset example with the existing values:

- Transaction 1 = {Sports Bra, Visor, Jacket}
- Transaction 2 = {Sports Bra, Hoodie, Jacket}
- Transaction 3 = {Boyshort, V-Neck, Jacket, Hoodie}

There are six distinct products sold and three transactions (or baskets). The item that is sold the most is jacket (it appears three times in the dataset). An FP-tree structure will be created and would have jacket (item that appears most often) in the root of the tree with branches to other products it appeared with. For example, jacket to hoodie and jacket to sports bra, and so on.

This is an important step before building an association rule to show what customers often purchase together. The default parameter values in RapidMiner will be used for this operator.

Exhibit 9-28

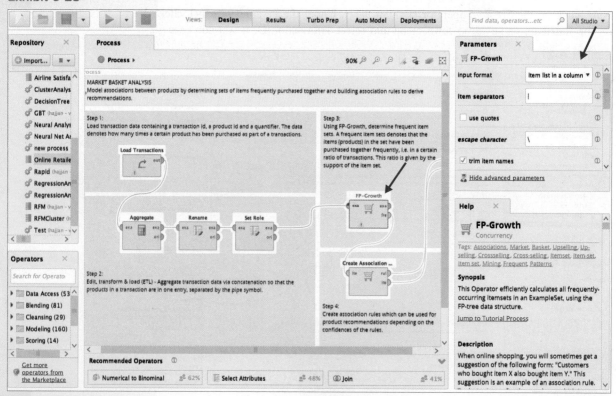

RapidMiner, Inc.

Creating Association Rules

Step 4 consists of creating association rules. Now, examine the default parameter values (Exhibit 9-29). Note that here you can set up the confidence min value, gain theta, and Laplace k. These terms are defined on page 330 so you can decide how different options may affect your results.

Confidence min value ranges from 0 to 1, and it is used to estimate the probability of observing product Y given product X. Confidence is useful in determining the business viability of a rule. A higher confidence will make it worthy to invest in a marketing campaign.

The attributes *lift* and *gain* can also be changed to ensure the minimum values we require in the basket before displaying the products.

We will not change the default values suggested in the template in our case study. But we recommend you try changing them later to see how the changes impact your results.

To execute the model, click "Run" (the blue play button) in the Views menu bar (Exhibit 9-29). The results will take a few minutes to run depending on your computer processor speed.

Exhibit 9-29

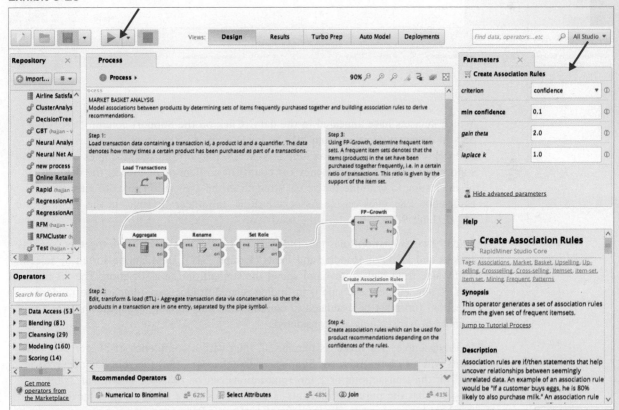

RapidMiner, Inc.

Once the model execution is complete, the results will be displayed as in Exhibit 9-30. The results show the frequent items purchased based on the FP-growth model. It appears that Crewneck and Underwire are products purchased often. In reviewing the support number, it appears that 24.3 percent of the baskets had Crewneck, 15.6 percent had Underwire, and 10.8 percent had Pants.

Exhibit 9-30

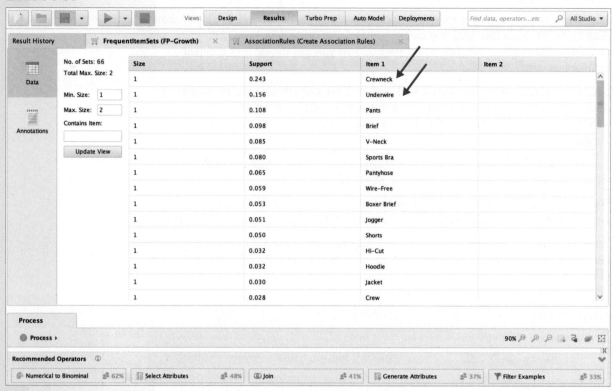

RapidMiner, Inc.

Which itemsets have appeared in the data? Click on the Support column to sort the data in descending order (from high to low) (Exhibit 9-31). Note that Crewneck is often purchased with Pants, as well as V-Necks. Recall from our examples earlier that support only shows the frequency (or count) of an item or itemset in the data. It will be interesting to examine the actual strength in the association rule. To view the association rule, click on the AssociationRules tab under "Results" in the Views menu bar (Exhibit 9-31).

Under the AssociationRules tab, there are two items that often come together, such as Jackets and Pants or Hoodies and Pants (Exhibit 9-32). Data can be sorted by selecting a lift value from high to low and shows the strength in the association. The lift ratio tells us how efficient the rule is in finding related products as compared to random selection. Lift must be evaluated in combination with support to ensure that enough number of transactions are considered.

In the example, if a Jacket is purchased, then with a confidence of 30 percent Pants will also be purchased. Support of 0.009 means that the rule has occurred in 0.9% of the transactions or 1,786 transactions out of 198,433. The lift of 2.769 suggests that the purchase of Pants is 2.769 times more likely when a Jacket is purchased, compared to shoppers just purchasing Pants.

Similarly, if a Hoodie is purchased, then with a confidence of 24.9 percent Pants will also be purchased. The lift of 2.293 suggests the purchase of Pants is 2.293 times more likely when a Hoodie is purchased compared to shoppers who only purchased Pants.

In this case study, association rules are evaluated with the most commonly applied criteria: support, confidence, and lift. Note that adding more customer transactions will most likely allow us to derive rules that have higher support, confidence, and lift values.

Exhibit 9-31

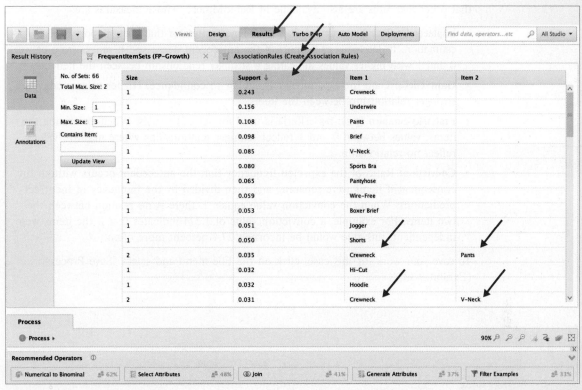

RapidMiner, Inc.

Exhibit 9-32

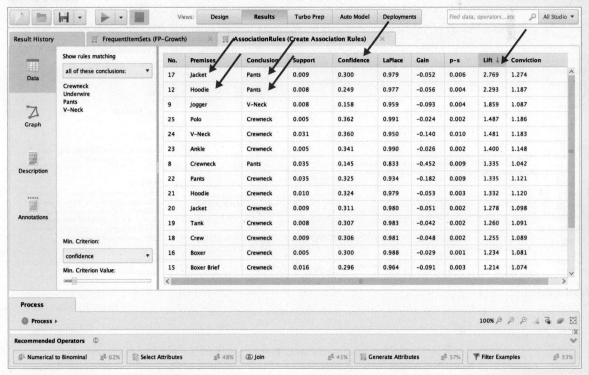

RapidMiner, Inc.

These measures were explained earlier in the chapter. However, it is important to note that other measures are also available in RapidMiner*. Those measures are:

- **Laplace:** Laplace K parameter is a confidence estimator that uses support in its estimation. It decreases as support of the antecedent decreases. It ranges from between 0 and 1 with higher values indicating a stronger relationship between the items.

- **Gain Theta:** Gain theta parameter is similar to confidence. Higher values indicate a stronger relationship between the items.

- **Piatetsky-Shapiro (p-s):** p-s criteria is used for selecting rules. When examining the items, values between 0 and 1 reflect stronger relationships where negative values reflect no relationship.

- **Conviction:** Ratio of the expected frequency that the antecedent occurs without the consequent if items were separate, and then divided by the frequency of incorrect predictions. When the conviction value equals 1, there is no relation between the two items. For example, a conviction value of 1.274 indicates that if the items were independent, this rule would be incorrect 27.4 percent more often.

To save your work for this case, click on the File menu and select "Save Process as..." (Exhibit 9-33).

Exhibit 9-33

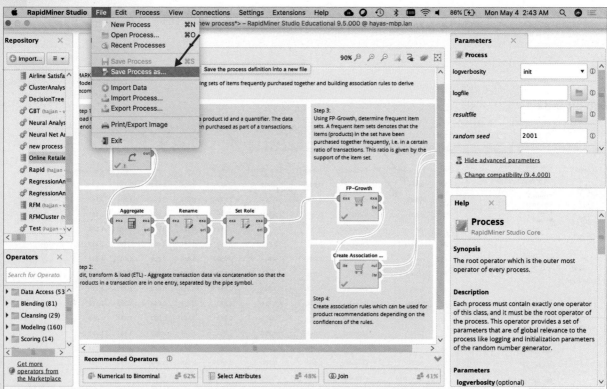

RapidMiner, Inc.

*If you are interested in learning more about Laplace, gain theta, p-s, and conviction, review the RapidMiner documentation at: https://docs.rapidminer.com/latest/studio/operators/modeling/associations/create_association_rules.html.

Exhibit 9-34

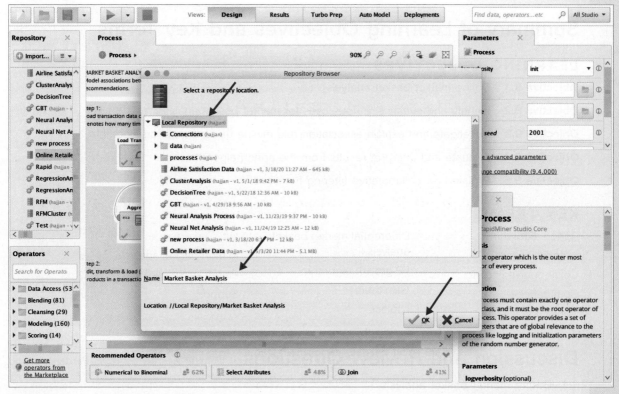

RapidMiner, Inc.

Save the file as "Market Basket Analysis" under your Local Repository and click "OK" (Exhibit 9-34). Now you can exit RapidMiner.

Insights Learned from Applying the Concepts

Marketers can use these and other market basket analysis insights to develop different, more targeted marketing strategies for different market segments, such as ordering accurate product quantities, knowing where to place products in a store or on a website, offering post-purchase coupons, developing promotional campaigns, and understanding how customers might respond to cross-selling tactics. It is easy to see the benefits of market basket analysis for making many different marketing decisions.

In this case, what insights were revealed? One insight is that when a customer adds a Jacket to the basket, it is likely they also will add Pants. What does that mean for marketing? Understanding that customers are likely to add pants if they add a jacket will assist in making product placement decisions. Perhaps this means that pants and jackets are placed near each other. Or, when developing promotional materials or sending coupons, it would be best to consider both items.

Summary of Learning Objectives and Key Terms

LEARNING OBJECTIVES

Objective 9.1   Define market basket analysis.

Objective 9.2   Identify and evaluate various uses for market basket analysis.

Objective 9.3   Investigate and explain association rule mining using the apriori algorithm.

Objective 9.4   Evaluate and interpret results from the apriori algorithm.

Objective 9.5   Explain how collaborative filtering functions.

KEY TERMS

Apriori algorithm

Association rule

Collaborative filtering

Confidence

Conviction

Differential market basket analysis

FP-growth algorithm

Gain theta

Laplace

Lift

Market basket analysis

Piatetsky-Shapiro (p-s)

Support

Discussion and Review Questions

1. Define market basket analysis.

2. How can marketers use market basket analysis insights in decision making?

3. What are association rules?

4. What does an apriori algorithm identify?

5. Explain the difference between support, confidence, and lift.

6. What is the difference between collaborative filtering and association rule?

Critical Thinking and Marketing Applications

1. Upon evaluation of Exhibit 9-32, what is Support, Confidence, and Lift indicating for results of the association rule IF [Hoodie] THEN [Pants]?

2. How could marketing managers use the results from Exhibit 9-32 when making email marketing and general promotion decisions?

References

1. Daniel Faggella, "The ROI of Recommendation Engines for Marketing," MarTech Today, October 30, 2017, https://martechtoday.com/roi-recommendation-engines-marketing-205787; and Ian MacKenzie, Chris Meyer, and Steve Noble, "How Retailers Can Keep Up with Consumers," McKinsey & Company, October 1, 2013, https://www.mckinsey.com/industries/retail/our-insights/how-retailers-can-keep-up-with-consumers.

2. Jacinda Santora, "Email Marketing vs. Social Media: Is There a Clear Winner?" Optinmonster, December 19, 2019, https://optinmonster.com/email-marketing-vs-social-media-performance-2016-2019-statistics; Lisa Gennaro, "50+ Wild Email Marketing Statistics You Need to See," WP Forms, June 16, 2020, https://wpforms.com/email-marketing-statistics; and "Email Marketing Statistics," 99 Firms, https://99firms.com/blog/email-marketing-statistics/#gref.

3. Daphne Howland, "Out-of-Stocks Could Be Costing Retailers $1T," *Retail Dive*, June 22, 2018, https://www.retaildive.com/news/out-of-stocks-could-be-costing-retailers-1t/526327; and "Out of Stocks Affecting Retail On and Offline," On Time Logistics blog, September 5, 2018, https://www.otlusa.biz/out-of-stocks-affecting-retail-on-and-offline.

4. Debbie Haus, "Target Uses Guest Intelligence to Drive Marketing Strategies," Retail Touch Points, January 21, 2020, https://retailtouchpoints.com/topics/store-operations/target-uses-guest-intelligence-to-drive-marketing-strategies; and "Target Selects DemandTec for Assortment Optimization," Retail Customer Experience, March 23, 2010, https://www.retailcustomerexperience.com/news/target-selects-demandtec-for-assortment-optimization.

5. Alessandra Maltio, "Grocery Stores Carry 40,000 More Items Than They Did in the 1990s," MarketWatch, June 17, 2017, https://www.marketwatch.com/story/grocery-stores-carry-40000-more-items-than-they-did-in-the-1990s-2017-06-07; "Understanding the Grocery Industry," The Reinvestment Fund, September 30, 2011, https://www.reinvestment.com/wp-content/uploads/2015/12/Understanding_the_Grocery_Industry-Brief_2011.pdf; and "How Many Grocery Stores Are There in the United States?" FoodIndustry.com, April 2019, https://www.foodindustry.com/articles/how-many-grocery-stores-are-there-in-the-united-states.

6. H. Conick, "Read This Story to Learn How Behavioral Economics Can Improve Marketing," AMA, January 12, 2018, https://www.ama.org/marketing-news/read-this-story-to-learn-how-behavioral-economics-can-improve-marketing/; H. S. Sætra, "When Nudge Comes to Shove: Liberty and Nudging in the Era of Big Data," *Technology in Society*, 59, 101130, 2019; and R. H. Thaler and C. R. Sunstein, *Nudge: Improving Decisions About Health, Wealth, and Happiness* (Penguin, 2009).

Ico Maker/Shutterstock

PART 5

Emerging Analytical Approaches

10 Natural Language Processing

LEARNING OBJECTIVES

10.1 Define natural language processing.

10.2 Identify and evaluate various uses for natural language processing.

10.3 Investigate and explain the steps of text analytics.

10.4 Evaluate and interpret results from the text analytics.

Rawpixel.com/Shutterstock

10.1 What Is Natural Language Processing?

With the rise of the internet and social media, a large amount of data is increasingly available for marketing decision making. About 25 percent of the data is structured and therefore directly usable by most statistical analysis methods. Recall from Chapter 1 that *structured data* is made up of records that are organized in rows and columns. This type of data can be stored in a database or spreadsheet format so it is easy to analyze. The format of structured data is numbers, dates, and text strings that are stored in a clearly defined rows and columns. In contrast, *unstructured data*, which represents more than 75 percent of the emerging data, does not have a predefined structure and does not fit well into a table format (within rows and columns). Moreover, unstructured data requires further processing before it can be analyzed using statistical methods and when possible must be converted into structured data prior to analysis. This type of data includes, for example, text (words and phrases), images, videos, and sensor data. Customers, employees, and competitors produce a large amount of unstructured data that can be very useful in marketing decision making. Unstructured data is, therefore, increasingly being used to develop more effective marketing strategies.

The focus of this chapter is on using natural language processing to identify patterns in text data. Social media posts, product reviews, emails, customer service call records, sales calls, and chatbots are just some common sources of text data. The sources shown in Exhibit 10-1 produce a huge volume of text data useful for solving marketing problems.

How can insights be obtained from text data? **Natural language processing (NLP)** is a branch of artificial intelligence (AI) used to identify patterns by reading and understanding meaning from human language. Through NLP, companies can analyze and organize internal data sources, such as customer service calls, as well as external data sources, like social media content. Analyzing and interpreting text data provides answers to a variety of questions and produces insights about the company, customers, products, services, and market. NLP can be used by marketers to extract information that can be applied in both proactive and reactive ways, including responding to customer comments and complaints and building on product preferences. Ultimately, NLP can help companies reduce potential conflicts and prioritize the level of urgency when responding to concerns and opportunities.

Exhibit 10-1 Example of Text Data Sources

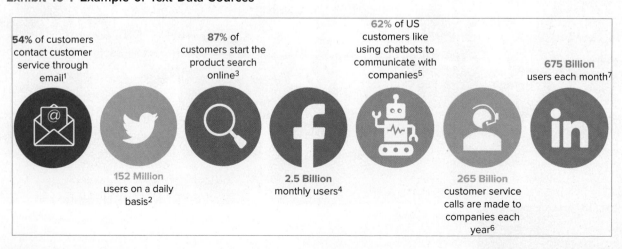

54% of customers contact customer service through email[1]

87% of customers start the product search online[3]

62% of US customers like using chatbots to communicate with companies[5]

675 Billion users each month[7]

152 Million users on a daily basis[2]

2.5 Billion monthly users[4]

265 Billion customer service calls are made to companies each year[6]

Consider these examples:

- *Brand reputation:* What is customer sentiment or emotion toward the brand? How much of the conversation is focused on the brand versus other issues?
- *Customer satisfaction:* How do customers feel about their in-store or online experience?
- *Market intelligence:* What are competitors doing and how are customers responding? Are certain topics or keywords trending?
- *Product or service quality:* Do customers prefer certain product features or are there quality issues?

PRACTITIONER CORNER

Jasmine Jones | Database Administrator at MetLife

Jasmine Jones

Jasmine Jones graduated from Elon University in 2019 with a bachelor's degree in computer science. While there, she nourished her love for data by minoring in data science and most importantly, working at the university's Center for Analytics. During that time, she was able to advance her data analytics skills by working with companies, both large and small, doing tasks such as coding, text mining, and web scraping in order to advise their decisions with the use of data. She is now fortunate to continue working with data in her first career after college as a database administrator at MetLife, further nurturing her love for all things data.

Q Many companies are implementing NLP-driven interactions with customers. From chatbots to conversational analytics platforms used to derive sentiment analysis and monitor social media chatter, companies are using NLP to understand customers, create efficiencies, and personalize service. How can natural language processing be applied to help companies engage and interact with customers?

A Natural language processing enables companies to engage and interact with the customer in a pointed manner. The best way to engage a customer can be determined by understanding the interests of the customer with tools such as topic modeling and sentiment analysis. Once engaged, companies are able to have more meaningful interactions with their customers with the help of chatbots that have the customers' best interest in mind and continue to learn and adapt with each customer they interact with.

Q How do marketers use NLP to create a successful customer journey quickly, and with minimal friction?

A Marketers utilize natural language processing to better understand their customers. Marketers can analyze a large number of product or service reviews without much effort. They can do this by utilizing tools such as sentiment analysis, which will allow them to quickly understand whether a product was perceived positively or negatively, or tools such as topic modeling to suggest other products related to their interests.

Q What is the potential for natural language processing in marketing?

A Natural language processing can help marketers extract insights quickly from social media posts, online forums, chatbot conversations, call center transcripts, emails, and so on. These insights can reveal what customers like or dislike about the company.

Continued

Such understanding can be used for advertising, marketing campaigns and to personalize the customer's experience.

Q Is there a unique use case that you could share?

A Marketers can generate new advertisements using information from natural language processing tools such as topic extraction and summarization of customer conversations. They can use what the customer cares about to create new advertisements. The customer reaction to the new advertisements can be captured and analyzed in real-time, which makes it possible to test the efficacy of new advertisements quickly and effectively.

Continued to page 348

10.2 How Is Natural Language Processing Used in Practice?

Marketers use NLP to understand the "what," "how," "when," and "why" of customer and market behavior. For example, marketers can use NLP to extract underlying intentions, beliefs, and attitudes behind the behavior. Whether companies are using chatbots or monitoring social media, companies can analyze text data records to learn more about what their customers want and need. NLP has been applied in a variety of contexts, as described in the following text.

Optimize Inventory and Engage Customers in Marketing Campaigns

Do you ever mention your cold or flu on social media? Clorox uses social listening to monitor discussions occurring on social media that might impact its brands.[8] Applying NLP, Clorox analyzes social media conversations around symptoms that could accompany these viruses, including most recently with the COVID-19 pandemic. By combining this information with data from the Centers for Disease Control and Prevention, the company assists retailers in understanding appropriate inventory levels and targeting certain customers with marketing campaigns for products such as Clorox disinfectant wipes.

Produce New Products to Meet Customer Needs

The hashtag #sriRancha began trending on Twitter, which captured the popularity of mixing ranch dressing and hot sauce. Social media chatter indicated customers were creating their own flavors of Hidden Valley's ranch dressing (see Exhibit 10-2). The

Exhibit 10-2 #sriRancha on Twitter

If you don't put your cheese fries in #sriRancha then you're living a lie #foodie #realtalk @srirachasauce

♡   ↻ 3   ♡ 2   ↑

Source: Kate @ChemistK8, Twitter, April 22, 2015, https://twitter.com/ChemistK8/status/590786488826273793/photo/1.

company listened to the conversation and seized on the opportunity to develop new products such as siracha-flavored ranch dressing.[9]

Simplify Guest Travel to Improve Hospitality

Chatbots, driven by NLP, have become common for the hospitality industry. Companies like Marriott are using chatbot virtual assistants to enhance connections with customers and answer questions any time of the day. These chatbots can understand and respond in different languages. They also recognize certain behaviors and understand preferences to then make recommendations. The goal of chatbots is to engage customers when and where they want and to personalize service.

Create a Better Experience for Customers

The success of Uber is highly dependent upon the reliability and ease of use of the technology that powers their mobile phone application. Uber gauges driver and user experiences using Brand 24, a social media monitoring technology. Following the rollout of a new app, Uber observed a spike in people talking about the company on social media. Social media mentions went from around 9,000 instances to almost 22,000 within the first few weeks after the app release.[10] But the insights for Uber were not limited to the increase in number of mentions. They also obtained both positive and negative sentiments, enabling them to improve the app and be more responsive to customer needs. Thus, Uber was able to determine whether the app created a better customer experience or whether they needed to make additional improvements.

Add Unique Features to Products

Companies often monitor social media to see what customers are saying about their products. How do customers rate a product compared to competitive products? What features do they like or want, or what do they dislike? Ford uses NLP to make discoveries in social media conversations.[11] When Ford decides to add new features to products, they often monitor conversations about a similar option on another vehicle. For example, adding features such as power lift gates or seat heaters can be costly if customers are not receptive to the change. Understanding what customers really want helps Ford determine if the change is worth pursuing.

Improve Customer Service

Companies such as Avis and Dish Network use chatbots to enhance customer service. The use of chatbots powered by NLP enables companies to respond to customers quickly, manage a large volume of simple inquiries, and reduce operating costs. If a customer has questions outside of business hours, the chatbot is available. In addition, chatbots enable customer service representatives to prioritize responses and stay focused on addressing more complex customer issues. For example, Dish Network's chatbot manages about 30 percent of the incoming volume, whereas Avis chatbots can manage almost 70 percent of customers' questions.[12] When a higher percentage of inquiries are addressed by chatbots, companies can reduce costs and satisfy more customers.

Facilitate Customer Ordering

"Alexa, can you order a pizza?" "Alexa, can you turn off the lights?" Companies such as Amazon and Domino's Pizza use voice recognition software so customers can order and track products. Domino's uses technology powered by natural language processing to facilitate customer orders for pizza using voice commands.[13] Customers can easily customize, select pickup locations, and pay using their natural language app. Domino's

Exhibit 10-3 Ordering Domino's Pizza through Amazon Alexa

Order Domino's with

AMAZON ALEXA

Amazon Alexa can hear your voice from across the room. That means you don't even have to get up to order Domino's. With the Domino's Skill for Amazon Alexa you can build a new order, reorder your most recent order, place your Easy Order, or track an order using Domino's Tracker®. The future is now.

LEARN MORE

Source: "Domino's Anywhere," Domino's Pizza, https://anyware.dominos.com.

and other companies have now extended their ordering capability to virtual assistants such as Amazon Alexa (see Exhibit 10-3) and Google Home. This method has been so successful, the company started testing similar voice-guided technology for incoming phone orders. Of course, when deciding to implement NLP, companies must consider whether a particular customer segment is receptive to that approach of responding, because some segments prefer traditional person-to-person communications.

Strengthen Customer Relationships

The Royal Bank of Scotland uses text data from various structured and unstructured data sources when applying NLP.[14] Customer emails, surveys, and call center interactions can be examined to discover reasons behind customer dissatisfaction. By effectively uncovering the drivers of customer dissatisfaction using NLP, the company is able to understand service failures, resolve issues faster and with greater success, and improve profitability.

10.3 How Is Text Analytics Applied?

Text analytics is an NLP technique that includes text acquisition and aggregation; text data preprocessing through cleaning, categorizing, and coding; text exploration; and text modeling (see Exhibit 10-4).

Step 1: Text Acquisition and Aggregation

The first step in text analytics is to determine the marketing analyst's business question. Understanding the question to be answered will dictate the text data that needs to be acquired. For example, let's say the marketing analyst is interested in knowing how customers feel about the quality of their products. Once the question is defined, the analyst can collect text data using multiple sources, such as online reviews downloaded from the company's e-commerce site or scraped from a third-party website, and from call center transcripts, surveys, or social media posts. Typically, posts from social media, such as Twitter and Facebook, are downloaded using application programming interfaces (APIs). An API is a programming code that enables the user to connect one

Exhibit 10-4 Text Analytics Steps

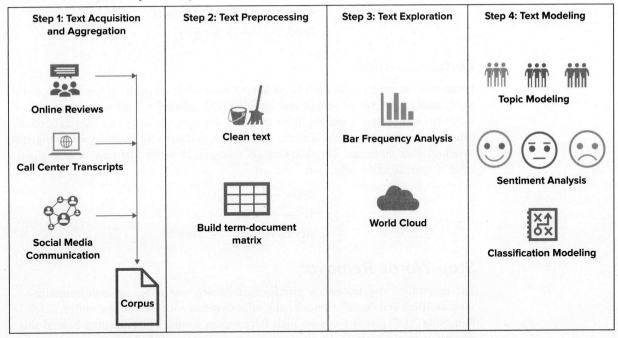

Step 1: Text Acquisition and Aggregation	Step 2: Text Preprocessing	Step 3: Text Exploration	Step 4: Text Modeling

Step 1: Online Reviews, Call Center Transcripts, Social Media Communication → Corpus

Step 2: Clean text; Build term-document matrix

Step 3: Bar Frequency Analysis; World Cloud

Step 4: Topic Modeling; Sentiment Analysis; Classification Modeling

application program to another to access and download data seamlessly. Once the text data is collected, it needs to be combined and uploaded into the text analytics software program. Most software such as Python and R enable the user to define all text data into a **corpus** ("body" in Latin). A corpus refers to a collection of a large body of text that is ready to be preprocessed.

Step 2: Text Preprocessing

The second step includes processing and cleaning the data. The data often contains punctuation, variations in capital and lowercase letters, or special characters such as % or @. As a result, the data must be preprocessed. This step reduces noise in the data, creating consistency and removing special characters. Preprocessing prepares data for the text exploration and modeling. Critical concepts under text preprocessing include the following:

Tokenization

Tokenization is the process of taking the entire text data corpus and separating it into smaller, more manageable sections. These smaller sections are also known as **tokens**. A token is known as the basic unit of analysis in the text analytics process. Text analytics computer programs have their own predefined delimiters such as spaces, tab, and semicolons to divide the text into tokens. For example, the sentence "I love bread" would need to be separated into three tokens: "I," "love," and "bread." After the data are tokenized, the tokens can be reduced even further by applying stemming and lemmatization.

Stemming

Stemming is the process of removing prefixes or suffixes of words, thus reducing words to a simple or root form. Different algorithms can be used for stemming, such as the common Porter stemmer. The following are examples of words that have been changed using the Porter stemmer algorithm:

$$\text{Happiness} \longrightarrow \text{Happi}$$
$$\text{Connection} \longrightarrow \text{Connect}$$
$$\text{Service} \longrightarrow \text{Servic}$$

Lemmatization

Lemmatization reduces the word to its lemma form while considering the context of the word, such as the part of speech and meaning. This process will allow for groupings of words to be processed together, those that may not have the same root. Several online databases, such as WordNet, function similar to a thesaurus by grouping words together based on their meanings. The following are examples of words that have been changed using a lemmatization algorithm:

$$\text{Better} \longrightarrow \text{Good}$$
$$\text{Is} \longrightarrow \text{Be}$$
$$\text{Reviewing} \longrightarrow \text{Review}$$

Stop Words Removal

The removal of **stop words** is a process that deletes words that are uninformative, such as "the" and "and." Consider the following sentence "I love the coffee." Removing "the" places focus on high information words. The reasoning behind this process is to concentrate on words that are of greater value. Analysts can also specify their own stop words depending on context. For example, if analyzing online reviews from Amazon, it is reasonable to add Amazon as a stop word since it will likely appear many times in the reviews and not add much value to understanding the text.

N-Grams

N-grams is a simple technique that captures the set of co-occurring or continuous sequences of n-items from a large set of text. N-grams identifies words for different values of n. For example, consider the following sentences:

- The customer service representative was exceptional.
- The responsiveness of the customer service representative was terrific.
- I consider myself a loyal customer.

A unigram will show the most frequent single words (customer), a bigram will show the most frequent two co-occurring words (customer-service), and a trigram will show the most frequent three co-occurring words (customer-service-representative). The higher the considered n value in n-grams, the more the context will be understood from the results. This technique is commonly used in search engines to recommend the next character or word in real time as the user is typing the search inquiry.

Bag of Words

The **bag of words** technique counts the occurrence of words in a document while ignoring the order or the grammar of words. A term-document matrix can be created for this purpose.

Term-Document Matrix

The **term-document matrix (TDM)** uses rows and columns to separate the text, as shown in Exhibit 10-5. The rows correspond to terms (or words), while columns show document names, and a count of occurrence in binary form fills the cells of the matrix.

Exhibit 10-5 Term-Document Matrix Example

Documents	Stop Words	Term Document Matrix			

Terms	Document 1	Document 2	Document 3
Love	1	0	0
Product	1	1	1
Useful	0	1	0
Need	0	0	1
Return	0	0	1

Documents column:
- Document 1: I love this product
- Document 2: The product is useful
- Document 3: I need to return the product

Stop Words Removed: I, this, is, to, the

For example, the term "Love" is found in Documents 1 (coded 1 or present), but not in Documents 2 and 3 (coded 0 or not present).

How does a term-document matrix work? Consider the following three online reviews:

- Document 1: I love this product.
- Document 2: The product is useful.
- Document 3: I need to return the product.

Each of the three sentences is referred to as a document, and each word is recognized as a term. Using these three sentences, a term-document matrix can be created (see Exhibit 10-5). Each row consists of a word (order is not important), and in each column, there is a number that matches the document number. The entire collection of data—or in this case, all three sentences—is the corpus. Exhibit 10-5 shows how text mining makes it possible to convert unstructured data into structured data in a matrix format. A 1 in the matrix indicates the word is present in the document, and a 0 means the word is not present in the document. For example, the word "Product" is present in all three documents.

Converting text data into a structured matrix makes it possible to conduct meaningful analyses of the data. The preprocessed text is now represented in a structured form and ready for exploration.

How can we measure the importance of a term in a document? To do that, we calculate term frequency–inverse document frequency or TF-IDF. The **term frequency (TF)** measures the number of times a term (or word) occurs in a document. The **inverse document frequency (IDF)** measures the frequency of a term (or word) over all the documents. In this case, a term occurring less frequently is considered to provide more information versus terms that are common.

The main concept behind TF–IDF is to find documents that have frequent occurrences of rare terms that could be interesting for our understanding of the text. The algorithm balances the frequency of the words (TF), which might not represent relevance by penalizing these terms (IDF). A document with a high TF-IDF score means it has a relatively high frequency for terms that are relatively rare overall, while a small value indicates that the terms are missing in the document or that they exist in most documents.

Step 3: Text Exploration

Text exploration consists of reviewing common words, type of content, and relationships using basic statistics.

Consider all of the written text in sections 10.1 and 10.2 of this chapter. The text has been prepared and cleaned according to steps 1 (text acquisition and aggregation) and 2 (text preprocessing). This was completed by changing all text to lowercase, removing punctuation, removing stop words, stemming all words, and preparing a term-document matrix. Results can be explored visually using a frequency bar chart or word cloud.

Frequency Bar Chart

A frequency bar chart consists of the x-axis representing terms (words) and the y-axis representing the frequency of a particular term occurring. Exhibit 10-6 shows a plot of the text in sections 10.1 and 10.2 of this chapter and the results when stemming is used to clean the data. Using the Porter Stemmer, words like customers and companies have been stemmed to "custom" and "company." Additionally, words like "chatbots" and "chatbot" have been combined into a single category identified as "chatbot."

What happens when lemmatization is used instead of stemming? The results will be different, as shown in Exhibit 10-7. Note how "customers" and "customer" are now combined into the single category of "customer," while "data" is converted into "datum". Also, "chatbot" and "chatbots" are now combined into one category ("chatbot"), as was done with stemming.

Exhibit 10-6 Term Frequency Chart Using Porter Stemming Algorithm

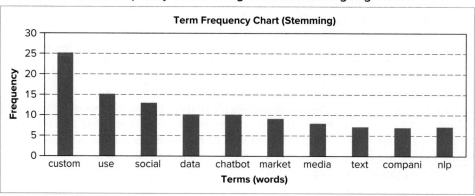

Exhibit 10-7 Term Frequency Chart Using Lemmatization Algorithm

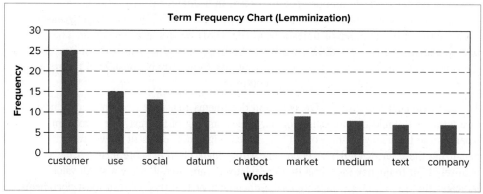

Word Clouds

A **word cloud** provides a high-level understanding of frequently used terms. The word cloud shows the occurrences of terms, with the size of the word in the cloud representing the frequency of the term. Word clouds display similar information to frequency charts, but use a visual representation of the frequency. Exhibit 10-8 shows frequent words that have been stemmed during cleaning. Note how the word *custom* (i.e., customer) appears larger than the word *text* or *nlp*. This means the word *customer* appears more frequently than words that are smaller.

Exhibit 10-8 Word Cloud Using Porter Stemming Algorithm

Applying lemmatization instead of stemming when cleaning the data will result in the word cloud in Exhibit 10-9. The word *customer* dominates the word cloud figure, followed by *use* and *social*.

Exhibit 10-9 Word Cloud Using Lemmatization Algorithm

Step 4: Text Modeling

In text modeling, the preprocessed data is used to build models. A few popular algorithms are commonly used by marketers for text modeling.

Topic modeling enables the analyst to discover hidden thematic structures in the text. Topics can be identified to better describe a set of documents. One popular algorithm for topic modeling is **Latent Dirichlet Allocation (LDA)**. The goal of the LDA method is to maximize the separation between the estimated topics and minimize the variance within each projected topic. LDA identifies important words in the text and groups them into topics.

There are three steps to building an LDA structure:

1. Start with k topic clusters. The analyst typically randomly selects the number of topics to begin the process. LDA then temporarily assigns the terms in each document to one of the k topics.

2. Words will be reassigned to a new topic based on two criteria:

   a. The proportion of words to a topic.

   b. The extent to which a topic is widespread across all documents.

3. Repeat step 2 until coherent topics emerge.

Exhibit 10-10 Topic Modeling Example

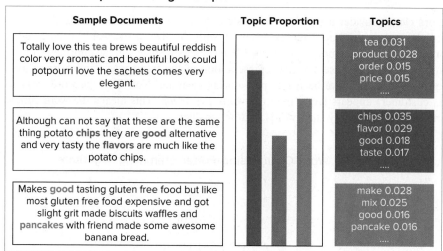

Sample Documents	Topic Proportion	Topics
Totally love this **tea** brews beautiful reddish color very aromatic and beautiful look could potpourri love the sachets comes very elegant.		tea 0.031 product 0.028 order 0.015 price 0.015 ....
Although can not say that these are the same thing potato **chips** they are **good** alternative and very tasty the **flavors** are much like the potato chips.		chips 0.035 flavor 0.029 good 0.018 taste 0.017 ....
Makes **good** tasting gluten free food but like most gluten free food expensive and got slight grit made biscuits waffles and **pancakes** with friend made some awesome banana bread.		make 0.028 mix 0.025 good 0.016 pancake 0.016 ....

Exhibit 10-10 provides an example of topic modeling. Words have been assigned to different topics based upon the LDA method. Notice that the colors in the documents, bar chart, and topic boxes are represented by three colors. For example, the words "chips," "good," and "flavor" correspond to the blue bar chart and topic box. Three topics have emerged from this process: tea, chips, and making pancakes.

Sentiment analysis is a measure of emotions, attitudes, and beliefs. The purpose of sentiment analysis is to identify the customer's thoughts as they relate to products, features, services, quality, and so on. Although there are numerous options, these insights can be found by using sources such as social media posts, online reviews, and emails to the company. People are often willing to share how they feel about a product, service, or brand. Is the customer's opinion neutral, positive, or negative? Understanding customer sentiments is critical because attitudes and beliefs can impact customer decision making and behavior. Customers that are satisfied will likely recommend the company to others or become a loyal customer. In contrast, customers that feel negatively toward a brand or product might share their poor experience with others or select an alternative competitor's product. Sentiment analysis offers a wide range of applications for marketers.

Several popular libraries can be used for sentiment analysis, such as Vader (Valence Aware Dictionary and sEntiment Reasoner) Library and Blob Text. Out-of-the-box sentiment analysis solutions, such as TextBlob and Vader, may not always yield perfect results. Nevertheless, they still offer insights in understanding large text in context. Both are available for free using the Python programming language. Note that these libraries can also process symbols such as popular emojis. Using sentiment analysis of online reviews, the Vader library analyzed the text in Exhibit 10-11. The output of the Vader text analysis captures negative, positive, and neutral sentiment scores ranging from 0 (low) to 1 (high). These three scores are then combined into one sentiment measure called a "compound score" ranging from -1 (most extreme negative) to $+1$ (most extreme positive).

Exhibit 10-11 Sentiment Analysis Example Using Vader Library

DOCUMENT	NEGATIVE	NEUTRAL	POSITIVE	COMPOUND SCORE
The product quality was great.	0	0.494	0.506	0.624
I feel 😊 today.	0	0.476	0.524	0.670
The service I received today made me sad.	0.341	0.659	0	−0.476

Exhibit 10-12 Online Review Form for a Clothing Retailer

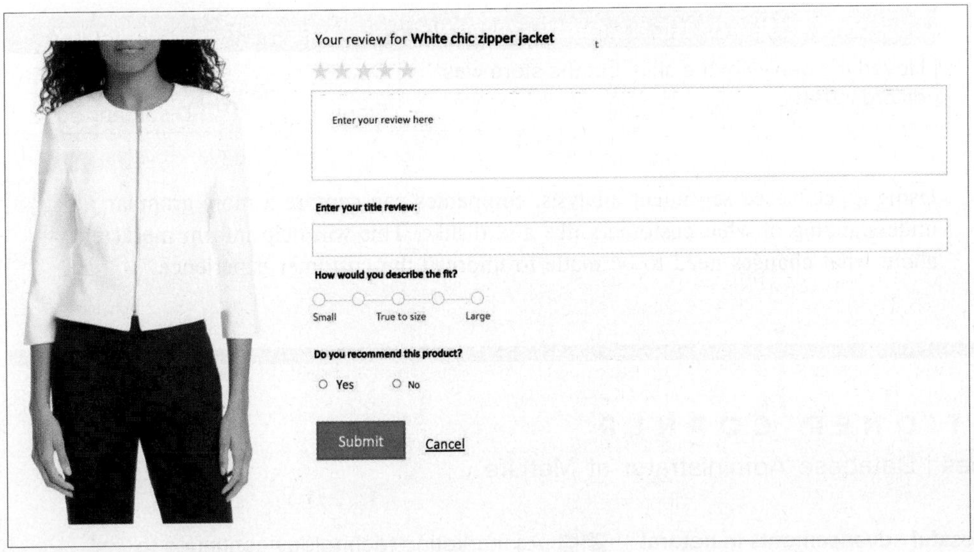

Source: Nordstrom.

Text classification creates categories or groups that are associated with the content. Numerically represented text data can be used in a classification model. For instance, consider the example of an online form in Exhibit 10-12.

By completing the form, the customer can rate a product they own, add a review, describe the fit, and even recommend it to other shoppers. A marketing analyst can build a classification model to see what words are associated with recommending a product. Using a tokenized term-document matrix and modeling method, such as logistic regression or random forest, words such as "unfortunate," "tight," "rough," and "return" might be associated with the product not being recommended. At the same time, words like "love," "fit," and "comfortable" are likely associated with the product being recommended. This type of analysis is useful to classify new customers using their online reviews and whether they would recommend the product.

10.4 Special Topics in Text Analytics

The internet has made it easy for customers to quickly share their opinions. Not only do customers enjoy communicating their experiences, they also often provide complex thoughts and suggestions. Many times, this type of detailed feedback contains contradictory or different opinions, known as **sentiment polarity**. Customers might share different sentiments for different features that represent their experiences. Features, such as product quality, customer service, or the store, are known as aspects. Aspects capture the "what" or main topic for which the opinion is expressed. For example, a customer might write the following review: "I loved the quality of the shirt, but the store was disorganized." In this single review, there is more than one sentiment ("loved" is positive, whereas "disorganized" is negative) and more than one aspect (quality, store).

Typical sentiment analysis would assign one score for the review. But a single score would be inaccurate given that the review contains mixed feelings. In cases like this example, it is best to use aspect-based sentiment analysis. Aspect-based sentiment analysis derives different aspects (or features) from the text statement and then assigns a sentiment score (see Exhibit 10-13).

Exhibit 10-13 Aspect-Based Sentiment Analysis

CUSTOMER REVIEW OF THE PURCHASE EXPERIENCE	ASPECT	POLARITY
I loved the quality of the shirt, but the store was disorganized.	Quality	Love
	Store	Disorganized

Using aspect-based sentiment analysis, companies can capture a more granular understanding of what customers like and dislike. This will help inform marketers about what changes need to be made to improve the customer experience.

Continued from page 338

PRACTITIONER CORNER

Jasmine Jones | Database Administrator at MetLife

Q Driven by successful advancements in natural language processing and AI, the chatbot industry is poised to reach $2.1 billion by 2024. Studies show 62 percent of customers actually enjoy using chatbots to interact with companies. Experts are even suggesting marketers will be developing specialized bots in the near future. At 1-800-Flowers.com, for instance, a computer automated gift concierge helps customers find a perfect gift. Using a natural language processing (NLP) application, customers can type "I am looking for a housewarming gift." The NLP technology responds with questions for the customer to answer so the original inquiry can be clarified. What is the occasion? What is the relationship to the recipient? Gift recommendations are then selected from more than 7,000 products, including flowers, fruits, and chocolate.

How is the adoption of this and other advanced marketing technologies fueling the necessity for marketers to minimize the data skills gap?

A As marketing technology continues to advance, it will be expected by the customers when they interact with the company. If companies do not minimize the data skills gap and adopt these advances in technology, they will quickly fall behind their competitors.

Q What is a good starting point for marketers to learn the basics of NLP? What knowledge and skills will be helpful?

A To begin to understand natural language processing, marketers should first build an understanding of data and the many forms it may come in so they can understand the need for NLP tools. Other helpful skills would be text data cleaning and pre-processing, as well as modeling and coding. Software like Python has commonly been used for NLP. Furthermore, strong communication skills can help marketers properly validate the output of NLP tools and communicate effective insights.

Case Study Specialty Food Online Review: Understanding Customer Sentiments

Understanding the Business Problem

Over the last few years, customer food preferences have been changing. Demand for specialty foods, such as those produced in small quantities, as well as non-GMO, gluten-free, natural, or imported foods, has increased substantially and is strong across age groups. In fact, grocery stores have seen specialty food sales grow 10.3 percent, whereas conventional products have only grown 3.1 percent.[15] While this presents an opportunity for stores to offer new food items, companies in the industry are struggling to understand customer perceptions of different options and quickly changing food preferences.

How might a company better understand these perceptions? Let's say you are a marketing analyst at one of the largest grocery store providers of specialty foods: HealthyFoods, Inc. The Chief Marketing Officer sends you an email asking for information about customer product reviews of specialty food items. Insights from your analysis will be used in helping the company determine whether products are meeting customer expectations, which products have potential, whether new products should be acquired, and which should be discontinued. In addition, the specialty foods company will share the information with the product manufacturers so they can make improvements to their products.

Understanding how customers are responding to the products and their overall sentiment in the reviews will be key in your shared results.

Understanding the Dataset

You have acquired a dataset of 5,000 product reviews from the grocery store website. In this example, a hypothetical online review dataset will be used. The dataset consists of online reviews expressing what customers liked or disliked about the product. The data includes the number of other shoppers that indicated the review was helpful, a star rating on a scale of 1 to 5 indicating the satisfaction with the product, the title of the review the customer has assigned, and the customer's full text review.

To get started, review the data elements in Exhibit 10-14.

An NLP text analytics methodology will be applied to extract meaning from the data. Python will be used to assess the topic and sentiment of the online reviews. Data variables will be reviewed in Excel and then loaded into Python for analysis.

Exhibit 10-14 Data Dictionary

VARIABLE NAME (TYPE)	DESCRIPTION
ProductID (typeless)	Product ID representing a product
Helpfulness_Score (numeric)	Number of people indicating that the review was helpful
Rating (numeric)	Score from 1 (low rating) to 5 (high rating) indicating the customer's opinion of the product
Review_Title (string)	Title assigned by the customer to describe the review
Text (string)	Customer's online review describing the experience with the product

Data Preparation

It is critical to first review the dataset to understand its different fields. Download and open the FoodReviews.xlsx file available on the student resource page to examine the variable values in Excel. There are 5,000 records. Exhibit 10-15 shows a snapshot of the variables and records for 15 customer reviews.

What does one row in the dataset represent? Each row of the data represents one customer review.

After the initial review, you may notice the reviews vary in length. Sometimes it is useful to engineer or add new features to your dataset, such as the number of words in a review. Past research has shown that the number of words may be related to a customer's rating and helpfulness of the review, because it is likely more thorough.

Exhibit 10-15 Food Reviews Dataset

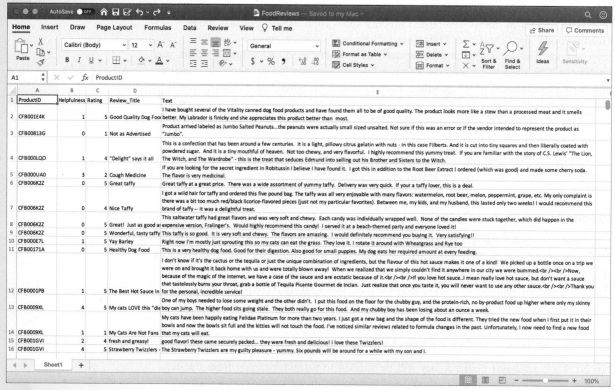

Microsoft Excel

Applying the Concepts

Several steps remain in the analysis. After reviewing the data, what questions can you ask to better understand customers' opinions? Here are some suggestions:

- What are the most frequently used words in customer reviews?
- How can the data be prepared for text analysis?
- You can conduct topic modeling. Thus, what are the key topics emerging from in customer reviews?
- You want to apply sentiment analysis. What are the customers' overall sentiments toward the products?

Python can be used to prepare and analyze text data, answer these questions, and more. Before getting started with the instructions that follow, you need to download Anaconda (https://www.anaconda.com), an open-source distribution platform for Python that simplifies the Python download process. Anaconda is available for both Windows and Mac. You can find detailed download instructions in this textbook's student resources.

Opening Python Using Anaconda

Step 1: Before beginning your work with Python, create a folder in which to save your work. Create a new folder on your Desktop or under Documents, and name it "Text Analytics" (Exhibit 10-16). Save the data file "Food Reviews.xlsx" from the student resources website in the Text Analytics folder you just created.

Step 2: There are several options to run Python on your computer. For this case study, you will use a Jupyter notebook.

Exhibit 10-16

Microsoft Corporation

Exhibit 10-17 Opening Jupyter on Windows

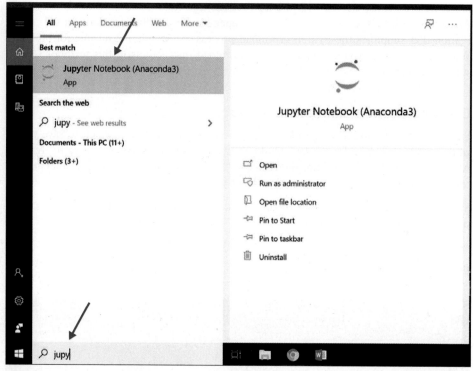

Jupyter

On a Windows computer, search for "jupyter" and click on "Jupyter Notebook (Anaconda3)," as shown in Exhibit 10-17.

On a Mac computer, navigate to Applications and locate "Anaconda-Navigator" (Exhibit 10-18).

Exhibit 10-18 Opening Jupyter on Mac

Jupyter

Exhibit 10-19 Launching Jupyter on Mac

Jupyter

Open it and click on "Launch" under Jupyter Notebook (Exhibit 10-19). Note that Jupyter notebook is updated constantly and the version number on your screen might differ from Exhibit 8-15.

Step 3: Your default web browser will automatically open a Jupyter notebook page. Using the menu, navigate to the Text Analytics folder that was created in Step 1 (Exhibit 10-20).

Exhibit 10-20

Jupyter

Then, click on "New" and use the drop-down menu to select "Python 3" (Exhibit 10-21).

Step 4: A new screen should open after completing Step 3 (Exhibit 10-22).

Step 5: Click on the "Untitled" label next to the Jupyter logo. A Rename Notebook window will open. Replace "Untitled" with "TextAnalytics" and click Rename (Exhibit 10-23).

Step 6: You will see the new window (Exhibit 10-24). You are now ready to begin preparing the Python environment for your analysis.

Exhibit 10-21

Jupyter

Exhibit 10-22

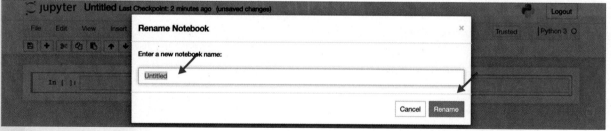

Jupyter

Exhibit 10-23

Jupyter

Exhibit 10-24

Jupyter

Preparing the Python Environment

Step 7: As you learned in Chapter 8, Python needs packages in the Jupyter notebook environment to run the analysis. For that reason, you will download packages that will execute modules, such as importing data, performing data cleaning, visualizing different aspects of the data, and running sentiment analysis.

To add a comment in Python, use the symbol # and then type a comment. It is a good idea to leave notes to review later when programming in Python or other languages. This will help you remember the tasks that were executed in each step when you return to your work.

To download the necessary packages, enter the following text on your screen (Exhibit 10-25):

```
# library for loading data
import pandas as pd

# libraries for text preprocessing
import nltk
from nltk import FreqDist
nltk.download('stopwords') # run this one time
import spacy
!python3 -m spacy download en # one time run

#library for Topic Modeling
import gensim
from gensim import corpora

#library for sentiment analysis

from textblob import TextBlob
from nltk.sentiment.vader import SentimentIntensityAnalyzer

# libraries for visualization
import matplotlib.pyplot as plt
import seaborn as sns
%matplotlib inline
```

Now, click "Run."

Exhibit 10-25

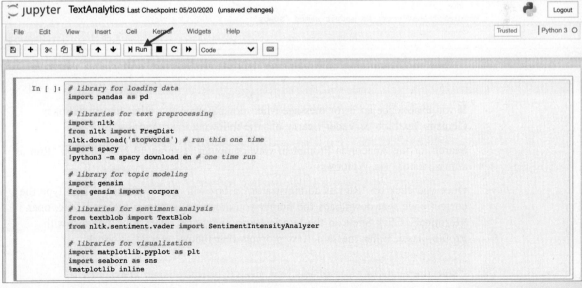

Jupyter

Tip: If you experience an error message when downloading NLTK (Natural Language Toolkit), you can try to correct it by entering and running the following code:

```
import nltk
import ssl
try:
    _create_unverified_https_context = ssl._create_unverified_context
except AttributeError:
    pass
else:
    ssl._create_default_https_context = _create_unverified_https_context
nltk.download()
```

Now, click "Run." A new NLTK Downloader window will open. Select all and click download. This process will take a few minutes to download packages needed for text analysis.

Tip: Did you receive an error message identical or similar to Exhibit 10-26?

Exhibit 10-26

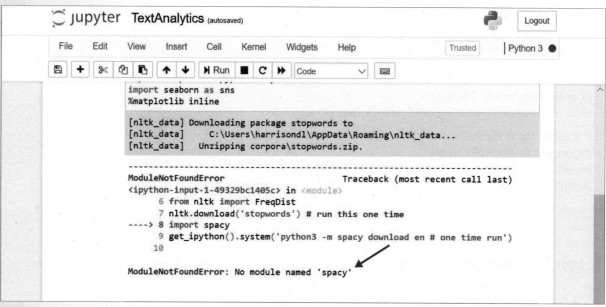

Jupyter

If you experience an error message when downloading the other libraries (Spacy, Genism, Textblob or Vader), carry out the following instructions.

Search for the Anaconda Prompt in your computer (Exhibit 10-27). Click on "Run as administrator" (in Windows).

Once you click on "Run as administrator," a box will appear where you can type the correct code that downloads the library you are missing. If you are on a Mac, open "Terminal". Click Shell on the terminal app menu and select New Window with Profile—Basic. Enter the same text prompts that follow.

Exhibit 10-27

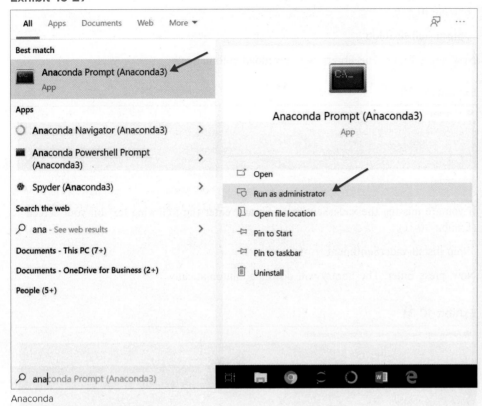

Anaconda

If you are missing the spacy library, enter the following text on your screen (Exhibit 10-28):

> pip install -U spacy

Now, press Enter. The library will download automatically.

Exhibit 10-28

Anaconda

If you are missing the gensim library, enter the following text on your screen (Exhibit 10-29):

> pip install --upgrade gensim

Now, press Enter. The library will download automatically.

Exhibit 10-29

Anaconda

If you are missing the textblob library, enter the following text on your screen (Exhibit 10-30):

pip install textblob

Now, press Enter. The library will download automatically.

Exhibit 10-30

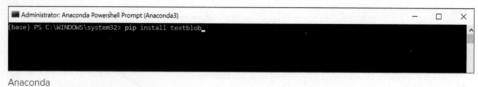

Anaconda

If you are missing the vaderSentiment library, enter the following text on your screen (Exhibit 10-31):

pip install vaderSentiment

Now, press Enter. The library will download automatically.

Exhibit 10-31

Anaconda

Once all of the libraries are downloaded, repeat Step 7 and proceed with the case.

Step 8: Once you run the libraries, you may receive a notice of package downloads (Exhibit 10-32). These messages are useful to confirm that the libraries downloaded successfully in your Jupyter work environment.

Exhibit 10-32

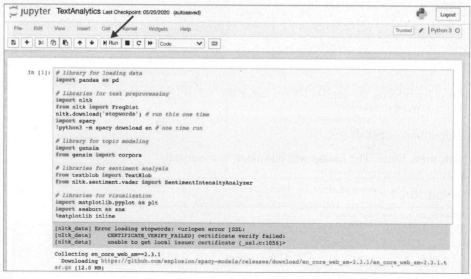

Jupyter

As you start moving into the analysis, recall from Chapter 8 that to add a new segment of code into Jupyter notebook, click the plus button in the menu bar. This will open a new box to enter code and enable you to run each segment of the Python code separately. This also makes it easier to debug any errors made during the process. (**Tip:** To delete any code segment, click the scissors button next to the plus.)

Step 9: To read the data into your Python environment, you will need to input the correct code. To do this, use a new code box and type the following code (Exhibit 10-33):

#Import data into a dataframe and read it in our environment.

reviews = pd.DataFrame(pd.read_excel('FoodReviews.xlsx'))

Now, click "Run." Note this process may take a few seconds to complete because the dataset includes 5,000 records.

Exhibit 10-33

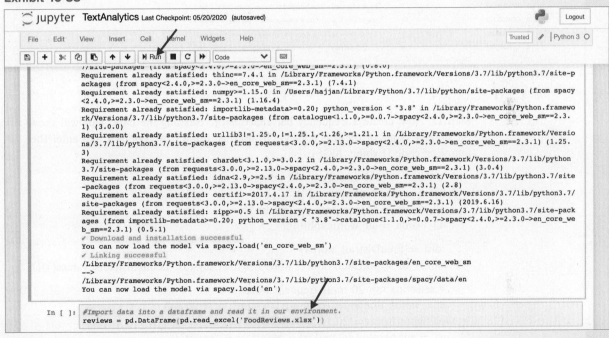

Jupyter

Step 10: In this step, view the first few records in the data. To do this, use a new code box below the previous code and enter the following code (Exhibit 10-34):

reviews.head() # Read the first 5 rows in our data

Now, click "Run."

Exhibit 10-34

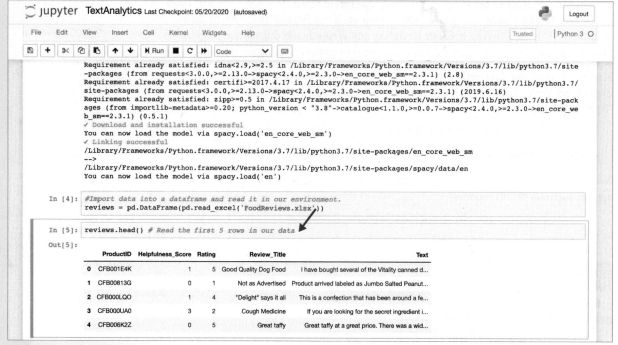

Jupyter

Step 11: Now, create a frequency bar chart before cleaning the data. This will show the "messy" state of the text reviews. To do this, use a new code box and enter the following code (Exhibit 10-35):

```
# function to plot most frequent terms
def freq_words(x, terms = 20):
    all_words = ' '.join([text for text in x])
    all_words = all_words.split()

    fdist = FreqDist(all_words)
    words_df = pd.DataFrame(['word':list(fdist.keys()), 'count':list(fdist.values())])

    # selecting top 20 most frequent words
    d = words_df.nlargest(columns="count", n = terms)
    plt.figure(figsize=(20,5))
    ax = sns.barplot(data=d, x= "word", y = "count")
    ax.set(ylabel = 'Count')
    plt.show()

# let's apply the function to Text field in reviews data

freq_words(reviews['Text'])
```

Now, click "Run." In Exhibit 10-35, note that words like "the" and "I" appearing most frequently are not useful in understanding customers' opinions and should be removed.

Exhibit 10-35

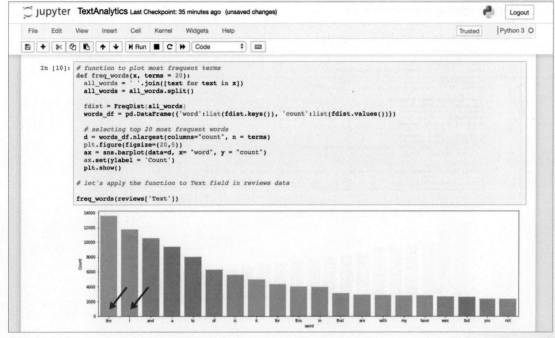

Jupyter

Text Preprocessing

Step 12: Let's start preprocessing the text data by changing all review text to lowercase, removing all punctuation and special characters, removing stop words, removing words with less than two words, and displaying a frequency bar chart to review the outcome. To do this, use a new code box and enter the following code (Exhibit 10-36):

```
# Data Preparation
# make entire text lowercase
reviews['Text'] = [r.lower() for r in reviews['Text']]
# remove unwanted characters, numbers and symbols
reviews['Text'] = reviews['Text'].str.replace("[^a-zA-Z#]", " ")
from nltk.corpus import stopwords
stop_words = stopwords.words('english')
# add our own stopwords based on context
MyStopWords = ['healthyfoods', 'really', 'also']
stop_words.extend(MyStopWords)

# function to remove stopwords
def remove_stopwords(rev):
    rev_new = " ".join([i for i in rev if i not in stop_words])
    return rev_new

# remove short words (length < 2)
reviews['Text'] = reviews['Text'].apply(lambda x: ' '.join([w for w in x.split() if len(w)>2]))

# remove stopwords from the text
Text = [remove_stopwords(r.split()) for r in reviews['Text']]

freq_words(Text, 20)
```

Now, click "Run."

Exhibit 10-36

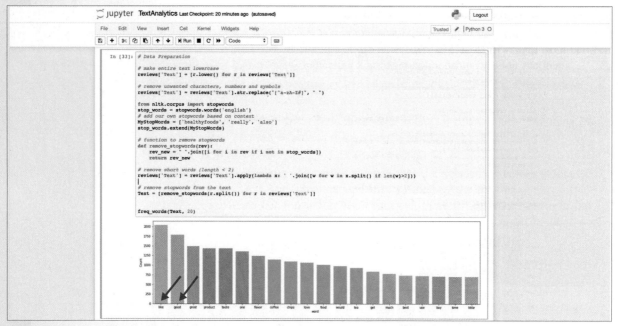

Jupyter

In Exhibit 10-36, note the words that appear most frequently now are more useful in understanding that the customers are using the words "like," "good," "great," "product," "taste," and so on frequently to describe products.

Step 13: What happens when you tokenize the reviews? Tokenization will break up each review into single words. To do this, use a new code box and enter the following code (Exhibit 10-37):

```
# tokenizing reviews
tokenized_Text = pd.Series(Text).apply(lambda x: x.split())
# printing tokenized reviews
print(tokenized_Text[1])
```

Now, click "Run."

Exhibit 10-37

Jupyter

Step 14: We discussed the value of stemming and lemmatization earlier in the chapter. Let's apply lemmatization to our tokenized words to see how each word from the sample shown in Exhibit 10-38 will change. To do this, use a new code box and enter the following code (Exhibit 10-38):

```
nlp = spacy.load('en', disable=['parser', 'ner']) # disable loading of dependency labels and named entities assignment.
# lemmatization of reviews
def lemmatization(texts, tags=['NOUN', 'ADJ', 'VERB']): # filter noun and adjective and verbs
    output = []
    for sent in texts:
        doc = nlp(" ".join(sent))
        output.append([token.lemma_ for token in doc if token.pos_ in tags])
    return output
Text_lem = lemmatization(tokenized_Text)
print(Text_lem[1]) # print lemmatized review
```

Now, click "Run."

Note that if you experience the following error message "can't find model en", then follow the instructions in Exhibit 10-27 to download the library spacy using Anaconda Prompt. Enter the following text on your screen: python -m spacy download en.

Now, press Enter. The library will automatically download.

Exhibit 10-38

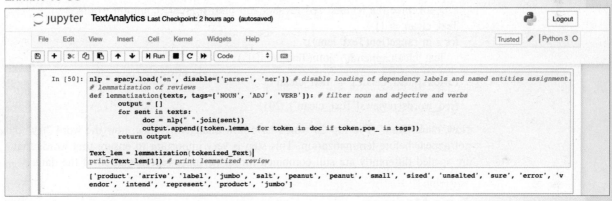

Jupyter

Exhibit 10-39

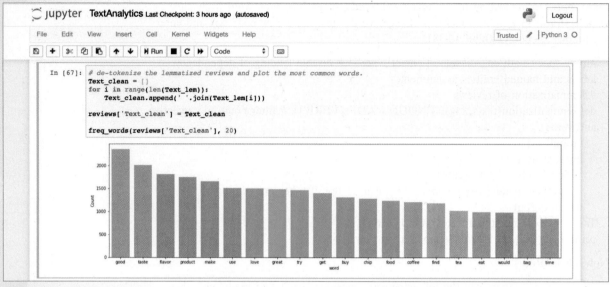

Jupyter

Step 15: In this step, combine the lemmatized word into one document. Remember that lemmatization will allow a grouping of words to be processed together that may not have the same root. To do this, use a new code box and enter the following code (Exhibit 10-39):

```
# de-tokenize the lemmatized reviews and plot the most common words.
Text_clean = []
for i in range(len(Text_lem)):
    Text_clean.append(' '.join(Text_lem[i]))

reviews['Text_clean'] = Text_clean

freq_words(reviews['Text_clean'], 20)
```

Now, click "Run." The top 20 words have now changed. Notice, how the word "try" did not appear before lemmatization. This step is very important to ensure that words that are spelled differently are still combined for an accurate representation of the data.

Topic Modeling

Step 16: Topic modeling is a process to identify topics that are present in the text and to uncover potential hidden connections in the data. Using the tokenized and lemmatized text, you will create a term-document matrix and apply the LDA algorithm, as discussed in section 10.3. Note that your results may be different than the results in Exhibit 10-40 because LDA is not deterministic and it depends on sampling. To do this, use a new code box and enter the following code (Exhibit 10-40):

```
#Topic Modeling using LDA

dictionary = corpora.Dictionary(Text_lem)# This creates a collection of words to its
bag-of-words representation.

# Convert list of tokenized reviews into a Document Term Matrix using the
dictionary prepared above.

doc_term_matrix = [dictionary.doc2bow(rev) for rev in Text_lem]
# Note that doc2bow only takes tokenized data to be processed.
```

Exhibit 10-40

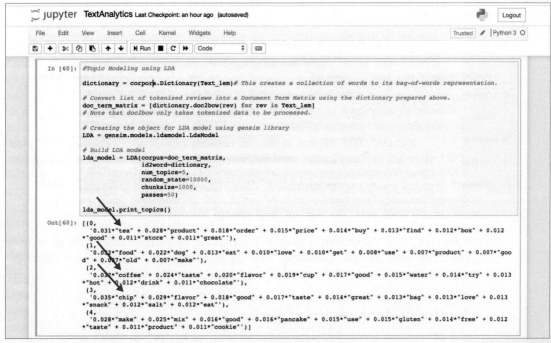

Jupyter

```python
# Creating the object for LDA model using gensim library
LDA = gensim.models.ldamodel.LdaModel
```

```python
# Build LDA model
lda_model = LDA(corpus=doc_term_matrix,
   id2word=dictionary,
   num_topics=5,
   random_state=10000,
   chunksize=1000,
   passes=50)
```

```python
lda_model.print_topics()
```

Now, click "Run." Notice the topics that have emerged are describing products such as "tea," "coffee," and "chips" (Exhibit 10-40). This process may take a few minutes depending on your computer processor speed. Topics emerging in your output may be slightly different from Exhibit 10-40.

Sentiment Analysis Using TextBlob

Step 17: Understanding customer sentiment is critical when developing a report for the project. To understand sentiment, apply TextBlob, an MIT library. In TextBlob, polarity indicates sentiment. These values range between −1 and 1. Note, that polarity measures are not perfect and sometimes will miss the context of the statement. Sentiment analyzers, however, continue to improve. It is a good idea to experiment between using the full text versus clean text. This step will analyze sentiment using the full text. To do this, use a new code box and enter the following code (Exhibit 10-41):

```python
# Apply iterates the function accross the data rows
reviews['polarity'] = reviews.apply(lambda x: TextBlob(x['Text']).sentiment.polarity,
axis=1)
```

```python
reviews.head() # view the first 6 rows in your data.
```

Exhibit 10-41

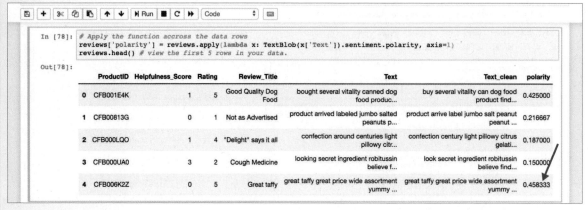

Jupyter

Now, click "Run." A sentiment analysis score should be assigned quickly for all reviews. The review with the title "Great taffy" has the highest polarity score (Exhibit 10-41), which indicates a higher level of satisfaction based upon the review.

Sentiment Analysis Using Vader

Step 18: Vader is another popular sentiment analyzer by MIT. In Vader, sentiment is measured using three values: negative, positive, and neutral. The values range from 0 to 1. These three values are combined into one sentiment measure called a "compound score" ranging from −1 (most extreme negative) to +1 (most extreme positive). The output is similar to the polarity measure from TextBlob. To do this, use a new code box and enter the following code (Exhibit 10-42):

```
sid = SentimentIntensityAnalyzer()
reviews["sentiments"] = reviews["Text"].apply(lambda x: sid.polarity_scores(x))
reviews = pd.concat([reviews.drop(['sentiments'], axis=1),
reviews['sentiments'].apply(pd.Series)], axis=1)
reviews.head() # view the first 5 rows in your data
```

Exhibit 10-42

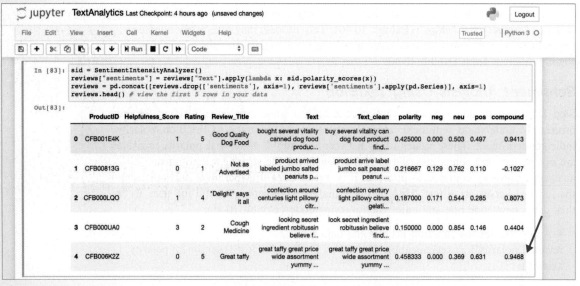

Jupyter

Now, click "Run." Notice again that that review with the title "Great taffy" continues to have the highest positive sentiment when examining the same five reviews.

Tip: If you experience an NLTK error message when running Vader, you can try to correct it by entering and running the following code:

```
import nltk
nltk.downloader.download('vader_lexicon')
```

Step 19: You may want to examine all of the reviews in a spreadsheet. You can create a csv file with the sentiment. To do this, use a new code box and enter the following code (Exhibit 10-43):

```
# You have an option here to save the reviews table to csv on your computer
reviews.to_csv('reviews_updated.csv')
```

Now, click "Run." Note, if you navigate to the Text Analytics folder you created in Step 1, you will find a *reviews_updated.csv* file created.

Exhibit 10-43

Jupyter

Step 20: In this step, open the *reviews_updated.csv* file (Exhibit 10-44). Filter the data to look at values with a TextBlob polarity of −1 and then evaluate the reviews. How can these results be interpreted? Values that are −1 indicate negative reviews. Examine if the Vader compound scores align with the TextBlob scores. Is one algorithm more accurate than the other?

Exhibit 10-44

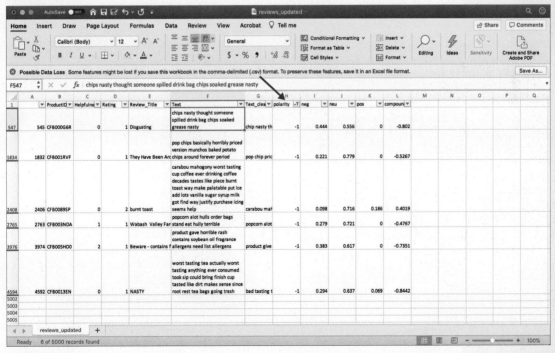

Microsoft Excel

Insights Learned from Applying the Concepts

In this case, what insights were revealed? One goal was to identify topics that were present in the text. In Exhibit 10-40, it was discovered that topics such as tea, coffee, and chips emerged from the text. What does that mean for marketing? This information can be used to understand potential hidden connections in the data. It provides an idea of what customers are discussing in their reviews.

Second, the reviews in Exhibit 10-44 contain negative sentiments. Marketers can use these reviews to determine why customers are unhappy. While it is important to know different reasons customers are unhappy, it is also critical to know if it is a pervasive issue. Do many customers express that the chips are "nasty" or "horribly priced"? If these are common reasons, there are some responses to consider. For example, the company can reevaluate pricing or which products to stock and provide this feedback to the manufacturer to make improvements as well. Values that are 1, indicate positive reviews. The same evaluation can be conducted on positive reviews. Why are customers satisfied? If customers are satisfied with the price of this product, the company could use these results to determine incentives or pricing strategies moving forward.

Text analytics will continue to be an important topic in the future. Building your skills in this area is definitely valuable for career advancement.

Summary of Learning Objectives and Key Terms

LEARNING OBJECTIVES

Objective 10.1 Define natural language processing.

Objective 10.2 Identify and evaluate various uses for natural language processing.

Objective 10.3 Investigate and explain the steps of text analytics.

Objective 10.4 Evaluate and interpret results from the text analytics.

KEY TERMS

Bag of words

Corpus

Inverse document frequency (IDF)

Latent Dirichlet Allocation (LDA)

Lemmatization

Natural language processing (NLP)

N-grams

Sentiment analysis

Sentiment polarity

Stemming

Stop words

Term-document matrix (TDM)

Term frequency (TF)

Text classification

Tokenization

Tokens

Topic modeling

Word cloud

Discussion and Review Questions

1. Define natural language processing.

2. How can marketers use natural language processing?

3. What are the basic steps of text analytics?

4. What is the difference between stemming and lemmatization?

5. How does removing stop words improve the analysis?

6. How does a term-document matrix work?

Critical Thinking and Marketing Applications

1. Collect five reviews from your favorite retail website for one product. Using the reviews, develop a term-document matrix similar to Exhibit 10-5. What terms appear most frequently?

2. Create a scenario in which this text data might be helpful to a company. Then, consider which data sources (e.g., customer service transcripts, customer-generated social media posts, etc.) would be useful, and the insights that would be needed to address the issue. For example: An innovative company introduced several new products. They are in the process of developing a new marketing communications strategy. In the meantime, they are interested in knowing how customers feel about existing and new products.

References

1. Lindsay Willott, "Customer Service Stats for 2020," Customer Thermometer, November 25, 2019, https://www.customerthermometer.com/customer-service/customer-service-and-satisfaction-statistics-for-2020; Swetha Amaresan, "40 Customer Service Stats to Know in 2020," *HubSpot*, December 26, 2019, https://blog.hubspot.com/service/customer-service-stats; and Kate Leggett, "2018 Customer Service Trends: How Operations Become Faster, Cheaper—And Yet, More Human," *Forrester*, January 24, 2018, https://www.forrester.com/report/2018+Customer+Service+Trends+How+Operations+Become+Faster+Cheaper+And+Yet+More+Human/-/E-RES142291.

2. Todd Spangler, "Twitter Hits $1 Billion in Q4 Revenue on Solid User Growth, Misses Profit Target," *Variety*, February 6, 2020, https://variety.com/2020/digital/news/twitter-q4-2019-earnings-1203494873; Paul Sawers, "Twitter Hits $1 Billion in Quarterly Revenue, 'Monetizable Daily Users' Jump 21% to 152 Million," *VentureBeat*, February 6, 2020, https://venturebeat.com/2020/02/06/twitter-hits-1-billion-in-quarterly-revenue-monetizable-daily-users-jump-21-to-152-million; and Ingrid Lunden, "Twitter Reports $1.01B in Q4 Revenue with 152M Monetizable Daily Active Users," *TechCrunch*, February 6, 2020, https://techcrunch.com/2020/02/06/twitter-q4-earnings.

3. Dan Alaimo, "87% of Shoppers Now Begin Product Searches Online," *Retail Dive*, August 15, 2018, https://www.retaildive.com/news/87-of-shoppers-now-begin-product-searches-online/530139; and Heike Young, "Nine Stats About the Retail Customer Journey in 2019," Salesforce blog, April 9, 2019, https://www.salesforce.com/blog/2019/04/customer-retail-statistics.html.

4. Josh Constine, "Facebook Hits 2.5B Users in Q4 But Shares Sink from Slow Profits," *TechCrunch*, January 29, 2020, https://techcrunch.com/2020/01/29/facebook-earnings-q4-2019; J. Clement, "Number of Monthly Active Facebook Users Worldwide as of 1st Quarter 2020," Statista, April 30, 2020, https://www.statista.com/statistics/264810/number-of-monthly-active-facebook-users-worldwide; and Andrew Hutchinson, "Facebook Climbs to 2.5 Billion Monthly Active Users, But Rising Costs Impede Income Growth," Social Media Today, January 30, 2020, https://www.socialmediatoday.com/news/facebook-climbs-to-25-billion-monthly-active-users-but-rising-costs-imped/571358.

5. Devon McGinnis, "40 Customer Service Statistics to Move Your Business Forward," Salesforce blog, May 1, 2019, https://www.salesforce.com/blog/2013/08/customer-service-stats.html; and Amaresan, "40 Customer Service Stats to Know in 2020."

6. Trips Reddy, "How Chatbots Can Help Reduce Customer Service Costs by 30%," IBM blog, October 17, 2017, https://www.ibm.com/blogs/watson/2017/10/how-chatbots-reduce-customer-service-costs-by-30-percent; "How Enterprise Is Putting Conversational AI to Work," *VentureBeat*, February 10, 2020, https://venturebeat.com/2020/02/10/how-enterprise-is-putting-conversational-ai-to-work; and Abinash Tripathy, "The Contact Center Is Having Its Model T Moment," *Forbes*, December 7, 2017, https://www.forbes.com/sites/forbestechcouncil/2017/12/07/the-contact-center-is-having-its-model-t-moment/#18f4265330ec.

7. Paige Cooper, "20 LinkedIn Statistics That Matter to Marketers in 2020," *Hootsuite*, March 9, 2020, https://blog.hootsuite.com/linkedin-statistics-business; Andrew Hutchinson, "LinkedIn Reaches 675 Million Members, Continues to See 'Record Levels of Engagement,'" *Social Media Today*, January 31, 2020, https://www.socialmediatoday.com/news/linkedin-reaches-675-million-members-continues-to-see-record-levels-of-en/571435; and "About LinkedIn," LinkedIn, https://about.linkedin.com.

8. Christine Birkner, "How Clorox Used Social Media to Curb Flu Season," AMA, February 12, 2016, https://www.ama.org/marketing-news/how-clorox-used-social-media-to-curb-flu-season; and The Clorox Company, "Clorox Launches Cold & Flu Pulse: A Socially Predictive Cold & Flu Tracker," press release, October 27, 2015, https://www.thecloroxcompany.com/release/clorox-launches-cold–flu-pulse-a-socially-predictive-cold–flu-tracker/67b4208f-ca0e-4a1f-9353-3f8512f753de.

9. Sharon Terlep, "Focus Groups Fall Out of Favor," *The Wall Street Journal*, September 18, 2016, https://www.wsj.com/articles/focus-groups-fall-out-of-favor-1474250702?ns=prod/accounts-wsj; and Nicole Jarvey, "Focus Groups: Marketing's Oldest Technique Adapts to the Digital Age," Digital Current, July 14, 2014, https://www.digitalcurrent.com/digital-marketing/focus-groups-in-digital-age.

10. "Case Study," Uber, https://brand24.com/case-study/uber; and "15 Social Media Monitoring Tools for 2020 [Tools to Monitor Brand Mentions]," Influencer Marketing Hub, https://influencermarketinghub.com/social-media-monitoring-tools.

11. Eileen McNulty, "How Ford Uses Data Science: Past, Present and Future," Dataconomy, November 18, 2014, https://dataconomy.com/2014/11/how-ford-uses-data-science-past-present-and-future; and Jason Hiner, "Ford's Big Data Chief Sees Massive Possibilities, But the Tools Need Work," ZDNet, July 5, 2012, https://www.zdnet.com/article/fords-big-data-chief-sees-massive-possibilities-but-the-tools-need-work.

12. Daniel Newman, "Does Your Company Need That Chatbot?" *Forbes*, July 245, 2019, https://www.forbes.com/sites/danielnewman/2019/07/24/does-your-company-need-that-chatbot/#6ce1c9a130f1; and P.V. Kannan and Josh Bernoff, "Does Your Company Really Need a Chatbot?" *Harvard Business Review*, May 21, 2019, https://hbr.org/2019/05/does-your-company-really-need-a-chatbot.

13. Alex Woodie, "How AI Is Revolutionizing Fast Food," Datanami, July 30, 2019, https://www.datanami.com/2019/07/30/how-ai-is-revolutionizing-fast-food; Allie Coyne, "Domino's Debuts Virtual Assistant for Ordering," *IT News*, March 1, 2017, https://www.itnews.com.au/news/dominos-debuts-virtual-assistant-for-ordering-453024; and "Domino's Anywhere," Domino's Pizza, https://anyware.dominos.com.

14. Tom Groenfeldt, "RBS Uses Analytics to Make Customer Service More Than Just a Slogan," *Forbes*, May 3, 2018, https://www.forbes.com/sites/tomgroenfeldt/2018/05/03/rbs-uses-analytics-to-make-customer-service-more-than-just-a-slogan/#5f893e2108e3; "SAS Helps Royal Bank of Scotland to Become the Number One Bank for Customer Service, Trust and Advocacy by 2020," SAS, https://www.sas.com/en_gb/customers/rbs.html; and "Natural Language Processing (NLP)," SAS, https://www.sas.com/en_us/insights/analytics/what-is-natural-language-processing-nlp.html.

15. Russell Redman, "Specialty Food Market Stays on Growth Path," *Supermarket News*, June 5, 2019, https://www.supermarketnews.com/deli/specialty-food-market-stays-growth-path; "The State of the Specialty Food Industry, 2019-2020 Edition," Specialty Food Association, May 31, 2019, https://www.specialtyfood.com/news/article/state-specialty-food-industry-2019-2020-edition; Monica Watrous, "Fueling the $148.7 Billion Specialty Food Industry," *Food Business News*, January 22, 2020, https://www.foodbusinessnews.net/articles/15254-fueling-the-1487-billion-specialty-food-industry; "Specialty Food Sales Near $150 Billion: 2019 State of the Specialty Food Industry Report Released," Specialty Food Association, June 11, 2019, https://www.specialtyfood.com/news/article/specialty-food-sales-near-150-billion-2019-state-specialty-food-industry-report-released; "Specialty Food Sales Near $150 Billion," *Gourmet News*, July 8, 2019, https://www.gourmetnews.com/specialty-food-sales-near-150-billion; and "Specialty Food Sales Near $150 Billion: 2019 State of the Specialty Food Industry Report Released," *Cision PR Newswire*, June 4, 2019, https://www.prnewswire.com/news-releases/specialty-food-sales-near-150-billion-2019-state-of-the-specialty-food-industry-report-released-300861728.html.

11 Social Network Analysis

LEARNING OBJECTIVES

11.1 Define social network analysis.

11.2 Understand the importance of social network analysis.

11.3 Investigate and explain different use cases of social network analysis.

11.4 Evaluate and interpret results from the social network analysis.

REDPIXEL.PL/Shutterstock

11.1 What Is Social Network Analysis?

Have you heard of six degrees of separation? This theory developed from the idea that everyone is linked to within about six people from each other. Several years ago, Microsoft found support for this theory when their research discovered that everyone is linked to Madonna, the Dalai Lama, and the Queen within seven or fewer people.[1] Exhibit 11-1 is a hypothetical example showing seven connections (e.g., 1, 2, 3, ...). All connections (blue circles) also have their own vast network of other connections.

How are you linked to these people? You are connected with others through networks of family, friends, and acquaintances. The development and widely adopted use of digital platforms have facilitated these connections—to some people to which we might never have connected. LinkedIn, Facebook, WhatsApp, Twitter, and Pinterest are just some of the most popular social network platforms that connect us on a global level. It is estimated that by 2023, there will be 3.43 billion social network users worldwide. To put this into perspective, as recently as 2010, worldwide social network users had not yet reached 1 billion.

So, how do people connect? Followers of a Home Depot Facebook account share different connections than an individual's personal account. What discussions and terms are guiding the structure of each network? Consider Subaru's Twitter followers. Some people in their network might be more interested in discussing gas mileage, whereas others might be more focused on discussing safety. Who are the influencers and who are the followers in the network? **Influencers** are individuals who initiate or actively engage others in conversation and are often well-connected to others in the network. These questions and more can be answered by exploring social networks.

Social network analysis identifies relationships, influencers, information dissemination patterns, and behaviors among connections in a network. Social network analysis results in visual maps that trace connections in the population and ultimately represent the size and structure of the networks.

Exhibit 11-1 Social Network Example

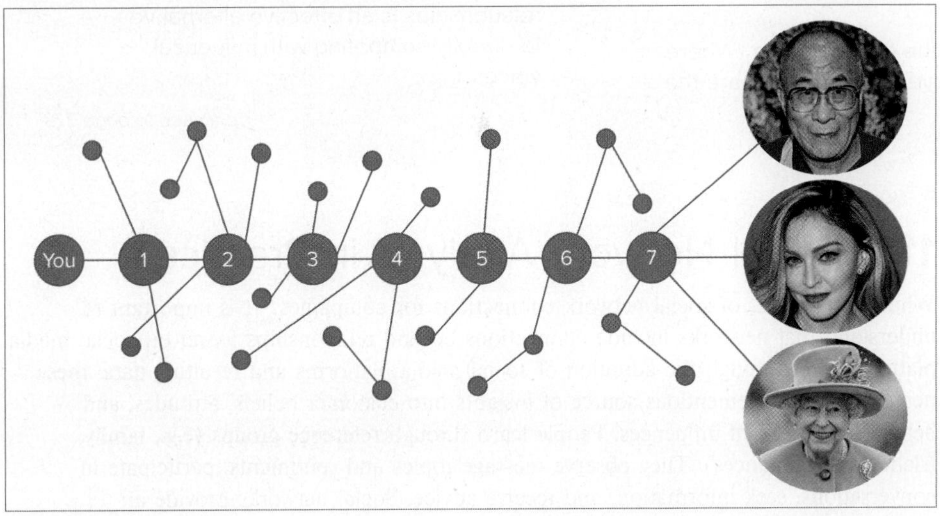

(Top): Steve Azzara/Getty Images; (Middle): Steve Granitz/Getty Images; (Bottom): Samir Hussein/Getty Images

PRACTITIONER CORNER

Marc Smith | Director at the Social Media Research Foundation

Marc Smith

Dr. Marc A. Smith is a sociologist specializing in the social organization of online communities and computer-mediated interaction. Smith leads the Connected Action consulting group and co-founded the Social Media Research Foundation (http://www.smrfoundation.org), a non-profit devoted to open tools, data, and scholarship related to social media research. He contributes to the open and free NodeXL project (http://nodexl.codeplex.com) that adds social network analysis features to the familiar Excel spreadsheet. NodeXL enables social network analysis of email, Twitter, Flickr, WWW, Facebook, and other network datasets. Along with Derek Hansen and Ben Shneiderman, he is the co-author and editor of *Analyzing Social Media Networks with NodeXL: Insights from a Connected World*, which is a guide to mapping connections created through computer-mediated interactions. Smith has published research on social media extensively, providing a map to the landscape of connected communities on the Internet.

Q There is a theory of six degrees of separation, suggesting that everyone is only six connections away from everyone else. This idea of the "small world phenomenon" can be witnessed by examining social networks. Social networks encompass connections to other people and businesses. People acquire knowledge, share information, and influence others. What can the exploration of social networks uncover for marketers?

A Like Google Maps for social relationships, networks are a way to represent visually and analytically the web of connections that link people to one another.

Like Google Maps, the result is a way to answer the three basic questions: "Where am I?", "Where do I want to be?", and "How do I get there?"

For marketers, the questions are "Where is the relevant conversation?", "Who are the leading voices?", and "How do I engage with them?"

Q Given that we are highly connected through a digital world, and social networks make connections easier, how can marketing analysts use this information in decision making?

A With network analytics, it becomes a simple task of identifying the major divisions, subgroups, or communities within the larger population. Market segmentation can be discovered through the shape of the data. Once major segments are defined, network analysis can also identify the key leaders who drive the conversation.

Engaging with influencers via organic relationships is an effective alternative to directly competing with influential voices.

Continued to page 378

11.2 Social Network Analysis in Practice

What is the power of social network connections for companies? It is important to understand that networks include connections beyond relationships found on social media platforms. But through the adoption of social media platforms and resulting data, these networks offer a tremendous source of insights into customer beliefs, attitudes, and behavior from social influences. People learn through reference groups (e.g., family, friends, acquaintances). They observe message topics and sentiments, participate in conversations, seek information, and receive advice. Social networks provide an opportunity for companies to communicate with, and start conversations with, customers. But they also enable individuals to share and exchange information with each other.

What are these communities saying about the product? Customers might be more concerned with hedonic or enjoyment features versus utilitarian or functional product attributes. How are subcommunities created from the conversations occurring between people in the network? Subcommunities could be developing from why customers are purchasing certain products or their sentiment about particular products. Could these conversations provide knowledge to develop innovative products or services? Social network analysis ultimately provides a picture of the network. Companies can use this picture to better understand communities, influencers and conversations that emerge.

Companies approach social media networks differently. They can rely on social networks to communicate with followers and personally extend their reach. But companies also want followers to engage with them on social media platforms and to further spread the message to their own networks. Consider the company Blendtec. Several years ago, Blendtec set up a brand page and started using YouTube to promote their blenders. Instead of blending common food items, the company took a unique approach to blending items that you would never place inside a blender, such as marbles, glow sticks, and electronics like Apple products and the Amazon Echo (see Exhibit 11-2). They titled the videos "Will It Blend?" The videos became a viral sensation.

Social media interactions among participants in the network develop organically from the company's original posts. Customers then regularly engage with the company and share

Exhibit 11-2 Blendtec's "Will It Blend?"

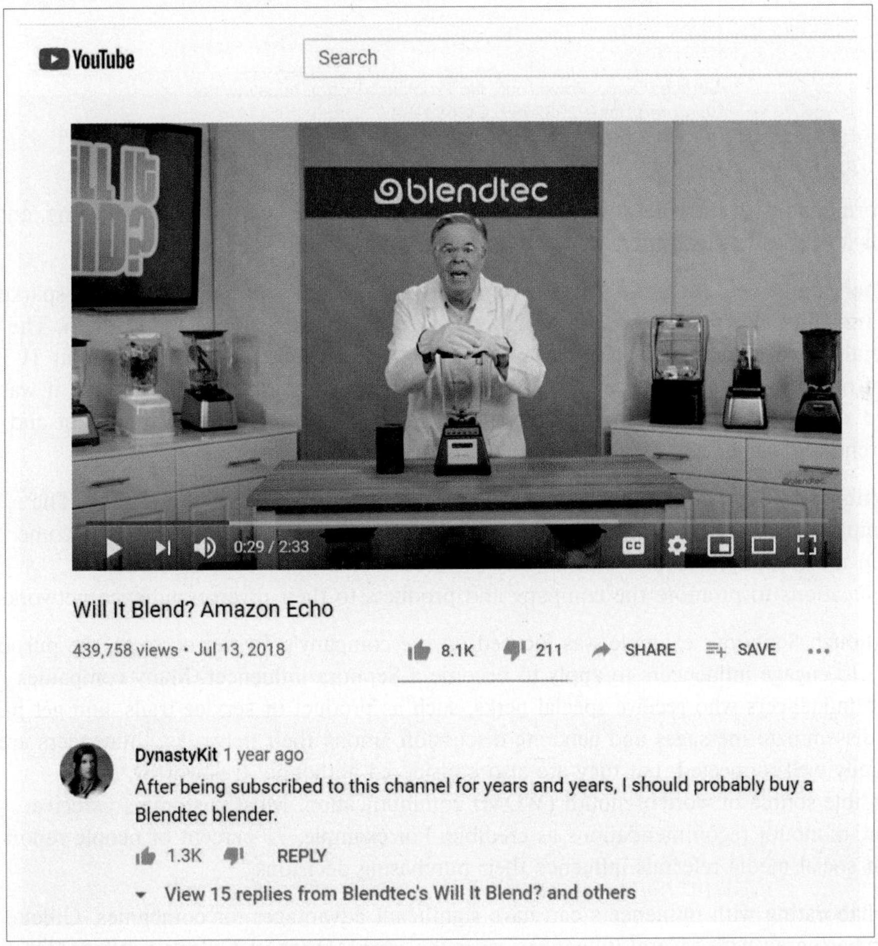

Source: Blendtec, "Will It Blend – Amazon Echo," YouTube, https://www.youtube.com/watch?v=NpP3rrNoEqo.

Exhibit 11-3 Oreo's Super Bowl Tweet

Source: Oreo, "Power out? No Problem," Twitter, https://twitter.com/oreo/status/298246571718483968.

information with their networks. These follower interactions are naturally occurring, and individual participants interact, develop conversations, and disseminate messages.

Other companies, such as Oreo and Sephora, also maintain brand pages. Oreo sparked conversation during Super Bowl XLVII when the lights went out in the stadium. The social media team leaped into action by quickly sending out a tweet (see Exhibit 11-3). Not only did the clever tweet successfully garner the attention of followers, but it was also shared far and wide among other networks of people, creating awareness of and purchase consideration for their products by potential customers.

Exhibit 11-4 shows Sephora inviting followers to apply for the Sephora Squad. The company used their Twitter platform to encourage followers of the brand to become even more engaged. Sephora ultimately selected over 20 people from 15,000 applications to promote the company and products to their diverse audience networks.[2]

Although Sephora's example was focused on the company's Twitter account, the purpose was to engage influencers to apply to become a Sephora influencer. Many companies hire influencers who receive special perks, such as product or service trials, and get paid to disseminate messages and generate discussion among their networks. Influencers are usually well-connected, but they are also considered authentic, trustworthy, and a credible source of word-of-mouth (WOM) communication. Most customers perceive word-of-mouth recommendations as credible. For example, 71 percent of people report that social media referrals influence their purchasing decisions.[3]

Collaborating with influencers can have significant advantages for companies. Gillette has partnered with several influencers over the years. Three of Gillette's influencers, identified in Exhibit 11-5, have a combined network of almost 2.3 million followers.

Exhibit 11-4 The #SephoraSquad of Beauty Influencers

Source: Sephora, "Sephora Squad," Twitter, https://twitter.com/sephora/status/1106656520190586880.

Exhibit 11-5 Gillette's Influencers on Instagram

Source: "Case Study: Gillette Gets Personal With Influencers," Mediakix, https://mediakix.com/blog/gillette-influencer-marketing-case-study-instagram. (Top): Shaquem Griffin screenshot; (Bottom Left): Summer Shores screenshot; (Bottom Right): Nyle Dimarco screenshot.

Exhibit 11-6 Disney Partners with the Bucket List Family on Instagram

(Left): thebuckelistfamily on Instagram, https://www.instagram.com/p/B8yw8tYDtKC/; (Right): thebuckelistfamily on Instagram, https://www.instagram.com/p/BY_pH83Aab4/?utm_source=ig_embed

These Instagram posts alone generated more than 213,000 likes and almost 2,000 comments.

Walt Disney World partnered with The Bucket List Family to stay in each of their resorts for 30 days. During this time, the family recorded videos and developed posts about their experiences for Instagram (see Exhibit 11-6). The Bucket List Family has over 2.4 million followers on Instagram and over 1 million on YouTube.

Regardless of the strategy a company chooses, interacting with existing and potential customers through networks can introduce products or services, increase brand awareness, and improve sales. Using social network analysis, companies can monitor conversations about brands and relationships occurring from those interactions. Using these insights, companies can better understand consumption behavior and brand preferences.

Continued from page 374

PRACTITIONER CORNER

Marc Smith | Director at the Social Media Research Foundation

 Q What a customer wants and how they act often varies. Research indicates, however, that customers can be influenced by their peers and what they perceive to be social norms. Should marketers engage in social networks to give their company a voice and communicate their message to existing or potential customers?

A Marketers must go to where the people are. Today, that means getting eyeballs on the screens their users are spending time with.

The challenge is to reduce the volume and "mass" marketing focus—to a voice that is one among many in a conversation based on context and local concerns. A shift emphasize to personalization is required.

Continued

Q Social networks are often led by influencers. Influencers are highly connected with a large following of people that listen, respond to, and share their posts. Sometimes these influencers receive perks from companies to experience their products and subsequently develop content to share with their large networks. Connections in the network generally view the posts as authentic and from a trusted source, versus a company's advertisements. This form of word-of-mouth communications has the potential for big impacts. On the positive side, these efforts can generate outcomes such as excitement for a new product or service. But consumers might unfollow an influencer if they perceive a relationship with a company is not being disclosed.

How can companies work with influencers to communicate their message to large audiences while protecting customers and maintaining trusted relationships?

A Organic influencers are more valuable than paid influencers.

Influencer relationship management is not a marketing relationship. It is more like an advisory board.

The most valuable influencers are not told to repeat marketing messages.

Identifying and engaging influencers is a productive way to remain part of their awareness and to potentially gain editorial endorsement.

11.3 How Does a Social Network Analysis Function?

Companies use social network analysis to measure entities (e.g., customers, products, services) and the relationships among them. Several key elements involved in a social network analysis are:

- **Nodes:** An entity (e.g., people or product) that is also known as a vertex. Exhibit 11-7 shows seven nodes represented as blue circles.

- **Edges:** The links and relationships between nodes. Edges can explain friendship or family ties. Exhibit 11-7 shows five edges represented by the orange lines that connect the nodes.

- **Edge weight:** The strength of the relationship between two nodes. The thicker the line, the higher the exchange between the two nodes. For instance, the relationship between A and B has a higher edge weight than between B and C in Exhibit 11-7.

- **Graph:** A visualization that enables viewers to understand the relationship between nodes and the importance of nodes. For example, the network in Exhibit 11-7 indicates that A and B are connected. Based on the width of the orange line, it also shows there is a higher intensity (weight) of conversations or other similar relationships back and forth between A and B, when compared to relationships between other nodes.

Exhibit 11-7 Social Network Graph: Defining Nodes and Edges

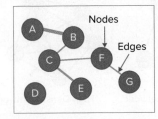

- **Singleton:** A node that is unconnected to all others in the network. Consider, for example, a network user that created a LinkedIn account but never added anyone to their network. In Exhibit 11-7, node D is a singleton.
- **Egocentric network:** An individual network. A personal social media network on Facebook or LinkedIn, for example, is considered an egocentric network. The person is considered the ego and the nodes to which they are connected are referred to as *alters*. The alters are people such as close family, friends, and professional networks. Marketers can use information about the ego to target alters by making generalizations as to their shared attitudes and beliefs.
- **Directed** vs. **undirected network:** Network connections can be directional, showing how one node in the network is connected to the other. For instance, B might follow A on Twitter, and A might not follow B (see Exhibit 11-8). A directed network relationship is typically depicted using a line with a directional arrow from one node to another, such as the arrow from B to A. Network edges can also be undirected. When no arrow is directed toward a node, there is either a two-way direction or the relationship is referred to as undirected. For example, as shown in the Facebook example in Exhibit 11-8, if node F is connected to node G, then G is also connected to F (bi-directional). This is the type of connection that exists on social media networks like Facebook. It is typically depicted using a line with no arrows pointing at a node.

Exhibit 11-8 Social Network Graph: Directed and Undirected Networks

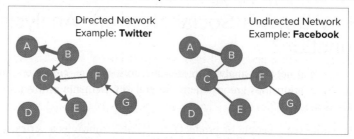

Network Measures

In addition to describing the elements of networks, you also need to understand the measures used to evaluate networks. We first describe two general measures and then several additional measures of centrality.

Density measures the extent to which the edges are connected in the network and indicates how fast the information is transmitted. The measure is determined by calculating the ratio of the actual number of edges to the maximum number of potential edges. A value of 0 indicates no density, lower values (closer to 0) indicate a sparse network, higher values (closer to 1) represent a denser network, and a value of 1 indicates a dense network. The higher the density, the faster information is transmitted in a network. In Exhibit 11-9, the high-density network has many more edge connections than the low-density network.

Exhibit 11-9 Types of Network Density

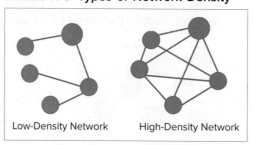

Exhibit 11-10 Distribution of Node Degrees Based on Exhibit 11-7

NODE DEGREES	FREQUENCY	NODE
Degree 0	1	D
Degree 1	3	A, G, E
Degree 2	2	B, F
Degree 3	1	C

The **distribution of node degrees** measures the degree of relationship (or connectedness) among the nodes. For example, node C of the social network graph in Exhibit 11-7 is connected to three people (B, E, and F), as indicated by the Degree 3 label in Exhibit 11-10.

Measures of Centrality

Measures of centrality indicate the influence a node has in the network and also a node's strategic network position. As an example, we will use NodeXL and the alphabet network dataset provided by the Social Media Research Foundation to explore a couple measures of centrality.[4] To help you understand these measures, we will use the information in Exhibit 11-11. The Vertex column identifies each node (individual), from A to Z (not all vertices are visible in Exhibit 11-11). The other columns display all of the centrality metrics.

Degree centrality measures centrality based on the number of edges that are connected to a node. If the network is directed, there are two measures of degree: indegree and outdegree. Indegree is the number of connections that point in toward a node. In contrast, outdegree is the number of arrows that begin with the node and point toward other nodes. This is an important measure to show how connected a node (or someone) is in the network. Nodes with a higher degree of centrality have more links and are more central. Exhibit 11-11 shows Z with the highest degree of centrality (6) in the network (see Degree column).

Exhibit 11-11 Example of Betweenness Centrality

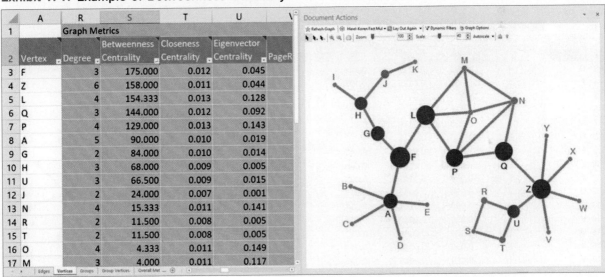

Used by permission of Marc Smith

Betweenness centrality measures centrality based on the number of times a node is on the shortest path between other nodes. Betweenness assesses positional centrality and it shows which nodes serve as bridges between nodes in the network. This measure helps identify individuals who influence the flow of information in a social network. Looking at the graph network on the right in Exhibit 11-11, let's assume Z has to travel and does not have access to social media for a week. As a result, individuals (nodes) U, V, W, X, and Y will lose their information broker and will not be exposed to information in the network that week. Notice that nodes V, W, X, or Y are not positioned on the shortest path between other nodes. Thus, their betweenness centrality is zero.

Closeness centrality measures the proximity of a node to all other nodes in the network. The measure is calculated for each node based on its sum of shortest paths. The higher the closeness score, the shorter the distance to other nodes in the network. This measure identifies individuals who can spread information quickly in their network. In Exhibit 11-12, individual L has the highest closeness centrality at 0.0127, and the next highest individual is P with a closeness centrality of 0.0125. These two individuals can spread information within the network very quickly.

Eigenvector centrality measures the number of links from a node and the number of connections those nodes have. Eigenvector centrality, also referred to as relational centrality, shows whether a node is well-connected to other nodes, who in turn are also well-connected. This is a useful measure to identify individuals with influence over the network, not just the individuals directly connected to them. The higher the eigenvector centrality value assigned to the node (letter) in Exhibit 11-12, the more the node has influence over the entire network. Eigenvector values can range from 0 (no centrality) to 1 (highest centrality). The overall range in a network depends on its structure. In Exhibit 11-12, L, M, N, O, and P (see the Vertex column) are well-connected to others that have numerous connections and also have the highest eigenvector centrality values (the range is from lowest at 0.117 to highest at 0.149). In contrast, Z is the only connection for V, W, X, and Y and has a much lower eigenvector centrality value (0.044), which means this individual has much less influence over the network.

Exhibit 11-12 Example of Eigenvector Centrality

	A	R	S	T	U
1		Graph Metrics			
2	Vertex	Degree	Betweenness Centrality	Closeness Centrality	Eigenvector Centrality
3	O	4	4.333	0.0112	0.149
4	P	4	129.000	0.0125	0.143
5	N	4	15.333	0.0110	0.141
6	L	4	154.333	0.0127	0.128
7	M	3	4.000	0.0111	0.117
8	Q	3	144.000	0.0119	0.092
9	F	3	175.000	0.0120	0.045
10	Z	6	158.000	0.0109	0.044
11	A	5	90.000	0.0101	0.019
12	U	3	66.500	0.0091	0.015
13	G	2	84.000	0.0101	0.014
14	V	1	0.000	0.0086	0.012
15	W	1	0.000	0.0086	0.012
16	X	1	0.000	0.0086	0.012
17	Y	1	0.000	0.0086	0.012

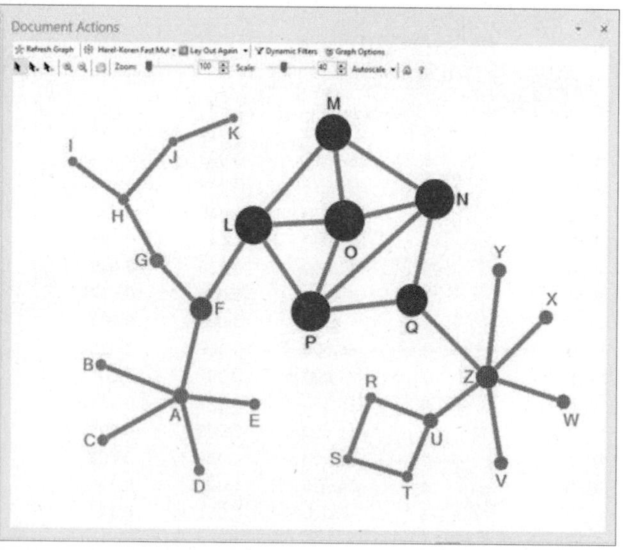

Used by permission of Marc Smith

Exhibit 11-13 Example of Louvain Communities

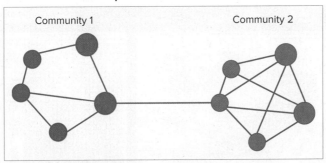

Community 1   Community 2

In addition to centrality measures, there are benefits to identifying communities within a network. Communities can share similar characteristics and display a common behavior. Using this information, marketers can customize how they target the communities within the network.

Louvain communities measure non-overlapping communities, or groups of closely connected nodes, in the network. The Louvain algorithm measures the density of edges inside the communities versus edges outside the communities. The objective of the algorithm is to produce the best possible clustering of the nodes in a network where connections between nodes within the community are dense, but where connections with other external communities are sparse. For example, in Exhibit 11-13 there are two network communities. Each community cluster connects nodes that are closely connected in the network.

Network Structures

The previous section introduced network measures that can be used to assess relationships within the networks. You also need to understand network structures, which enable you to visually examine which types of interactions are occurring and how the network is evolving. We define and describe these concepts next.

Different structures emerge in network maps depending upon the network measures. Consider the six structures of networks identified in Exhibit 11-14. These network structures were developed based on Twitter topics.[5] While the network structures are not comprehensive, they are examples that are the result of interactions occurring in the network. The six structures are:

- The *polarized crowd* structure is split into two groups. These groups are clearly separated and represent different conversations where there is little connection between them. For example, political conversations on Twitter.

- The *tight crowds* structure indicates the Twitter topics are all highly interconnected by similar conversations. For example, the conversations of digital marketing managers on Twitter.

- *Brand clusters* structures often have many independent participants that might share information about a popular topic or brand but are not interacting much with each other. For example, the Apple brand page on Twitter.

- The *community cluster* structure represents groups that are large and connected, but also have quite a few independent participants. For example, initial news stories from The World Health Organization (WHO) regarding COVID-19 likely engaged different news outlets that also had their own group of followers.

Exhibit 11-14 Example of Six Network Structures

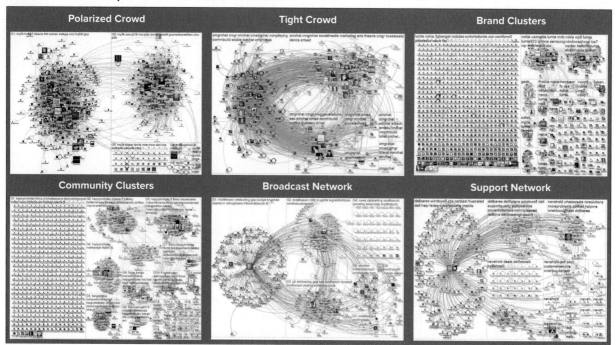

- The *broadcast networks* structure represents participants that disseminate and appear like a hub-and-spoke structure that has a central anchor (larger circle). From this central anchor, many participants disseminate the anchor's information and create inward spokes. For example, the *Wall Street Journal* might release a message on Twitter where spokes of people repeat the message.

- The *support network* structure represents unconnected participants that are connected by the anchor, and the result is outward spokes. For example, the Dell Support Twitter page.

Tools like NodeXL, Polinode, and Gephi, as well as general-purpose analytics tools such as Python and R, have developed powerful packages to analyze social networks and identify network influencers and participants and how they relate to others in the network.

11.4 Link Prediction Using Social Network Analysis

Can social network analysis predict the next most likely link to be established in the network? Social media networks like LinkedIn and Facebook often suggest "People You May Know," Tinder proposes "New Matches," and Amazon recommends "Items to Purchase." These recommendations result from predictions using social network analysis.

How can these prediction problems be solved? The answer is through **link prediction** where the objective is to predict new links between unconnected nodes. Link prediction uses a variety of methods such as similarity and machine learning algorithms. A similarity (or proximity measure) algorithm is one of the most widely used algorithms in link prediction.

The similarity measure algorithm assumes that two nodes sharing similar graph features, such as common connections, are most likely to also be connected to each other. For example, two people with a common friend may be introduced to each other by that friend. Consider how similarity can also be measured on platforms like YouTube. Similarity features may include customers who subscribe to the same brand account or who share favorite brand videos. Another similarity feature could be different YouTube channels that share the same subscribers.

Exhibit 11-15 Link Prediction

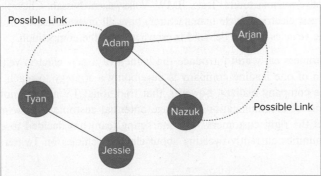

In Exhibit 11-15, the common connection for Tyan and Adam is Jessie. If a relationship exists between Tyan and Jessie, and also between Adam and Jessie, then it is possible to predict whether a relationship might form between Tyan and Adam, who are currently displayed as unconnected nodes.

Machine learning methods are becoming more popular tools in social network analysis. In these models, social network data is typically split into training and validation sets. A prediction algorithm such as a gradient boosting classifier or a random forest is run and then evaluated for prediction accuracy. The goal of the machine learning algorithm is to predict whether a pair of nodes will or will not establish a link between them. When splitting the social network data into training and validation datasets, the potential for data leakage should be considered. This might occur when pairs of nodes in the training dataset are also connected to those in the validation dataset. To deal with this challenge, data can be split based on time (if the data is available). For example, the data can be sorted from older to newer connections, and about 70 percent of older data is used for training, while about 30 percent of data from the newer time period is used for validation.

When nodes are closer together, the more likely there will be a relationship between them. Using link prediction, future associations that are likely to occur can be more accurately predicted.

Auto Industry: Understanding
Network Influencers

Understanding the Business Problem

Customer demand, increasing emissions standards, and global government initiatives designed to promote manufacturing of vehicles with improved fuel economy are driving changes in the automotive industry. The electric vehicle market is estimated to increase from just over 3 million units in 2019 to over 26 million units by 2030.[6] The industry consists of several leading automotive manufacturers. Tesla, BMW, Volkswagen, Nissan, Chevrolet, and BYD (the world's largest electric vehicle manufacturer) have all invested heavily in innovations to produce electric vehicles. But as demand is growing, so is the competition.

To engage customers early and introduce the launch of a new electric vehicle, the marketing team of one leading company is developing a strategy to reach potential customers. The company realizes, however, that traditional TV ads are not the most effective channel of communication to engage potential customers. How might a company target the right customers? The marketing team has decided to explore network communities currently tweeting about electric vehicles on Twitter.

Understanding the Dataset

The social network connections of current customers on Twitter will be used to identify customers with influence. In this example, hypothetical data of network relationships will be used. The data consists of a sample of users tweeting about electric cars during the previous quarter. The dataset includes customer names (nodes) and all retweets (edges). The data has been prepared in Excel using a template downloaded from the social network analysis tool Polinode. The template has two different sheets—one showing edges and one showing nodes.

To get started, review the data elements in Exhibit 11-16.

Exhibit 11-16 Data Dictionary

VARIABLE NAME (TYPE)	DESCRIPTION
Nodes Sheet	
Name (string)	Name of Twitter user
Gender (string)	Gender (e.g., Male, Female)
Number of Followers (numerical)	Number of followers on Twitter
Edges Sheet	
Source (string)	Twitter user originating the tweet
Target (string)	Twitter user retweeting the tweet

A Social Network Analysis methodology will be applied to extract meaning from the data. Polinode will be used to assess the relationships among customers. The objective is to identify influencers in the network so they can be targeted to help spread information about the new electric vehicle. Data variables can be reviewed in the Excel file and then loaded into Polinode for analysis.

Data Preparation

It is important to first review the dataset to understand the data and fields. Download the SocialNetwork.xlsx file available on the student resources page. Next, open the Excel file to examine the variable values. There are two sheets in the Excel file. Exhibit 11-17a has three columns of data: Name, Gender, and Number of Followers. Exhibit 11-17b has two columns (Name of Source and Target) that show the variables and records.

What does one row in the dataset represent? In the Nodes sheet (Exhibit 11-17a), each row of the data represents one Twitter user in the network. For example, Lucy Matthews is a Twitter user who is female and has 50,043 followers.

Exhibit 11-17a Social Network Dataset: Sheet Nodes

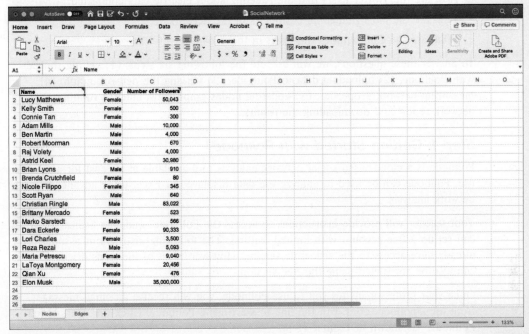

Microsoft Excel

Exhibit 11-17b Social Network Dataset: Sheet Edges

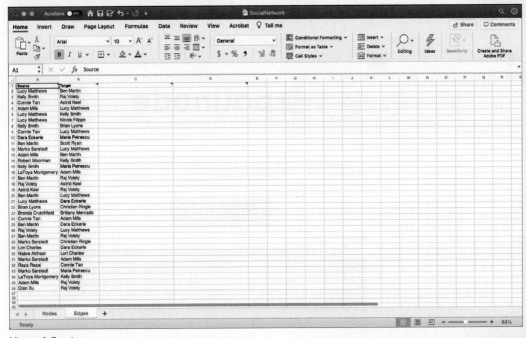

Microsoft Excel

In the Edges sheet (Exhibit 11-17b), each row represents one relationship or retweet. For example, in this sheet Lucy Mathews is the source of the tweet (or retweet) and the target is Ben Martin (i.e., Ben Martin has retweeted the tweet by Lucy Matthews).

Applying the Concepts

After reviewing the data, what questions can you ask to better understand customers' relationships? Here are some suggestions:

- How are the Twitter users that are tweeting about electric cars connected?
- Who are the most influential customers in the network?
- What are the communities that exist in the network?

To answer these questions, we will execute the following six steps: (1) getting started with Polinode, (2) uploading data to Polinode, (3) viewing the network graph, (4) measuring network properties, (5) updating nodes graph view, and (6) running a network report and downloading the results.

Step 1: Getting Started with Polinode

Polinode is a cloud-based social network analysis tool available at no cost for academic use. Polinode can be used to analyze the data displayed in Excel using advanced social network analysis.

Your teacher will provide instructions to access the Polinode academic license, or you can set up a free account with limited features. The following instructions assume you already have access to the academic version. However, most of the steps discussed next can also be completed using the free version.

Once your professor invites you to use Polinode, you will receive an email message from info@polinode.com with the link to start using Polinode. Click on "Start Using Polinode," as shown in Exhibit 11-18.

Exhibit 11-18 The Polinode Start Page

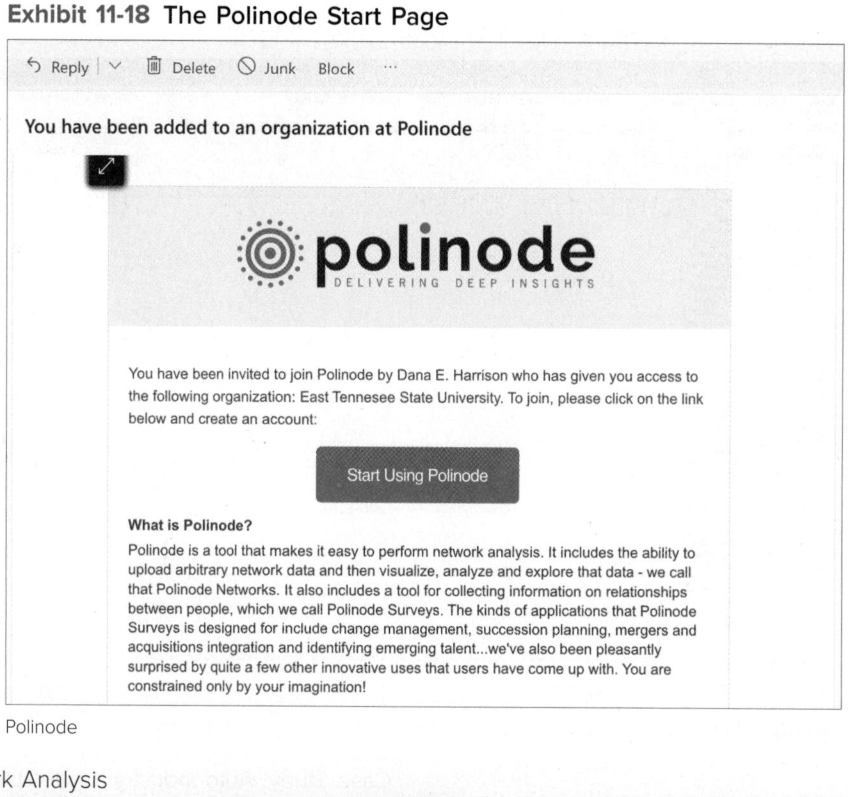

Polinode

Exhibit 11-19 The Polinode Account Creation Page

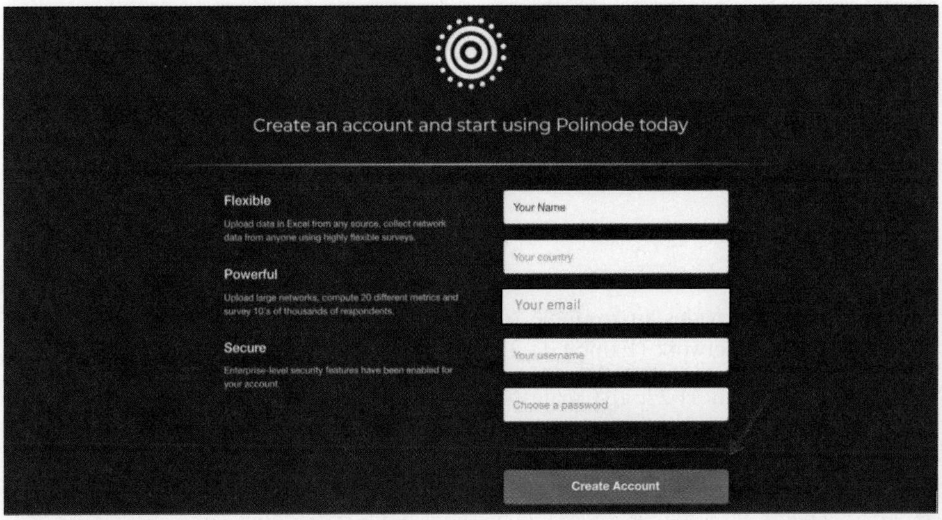

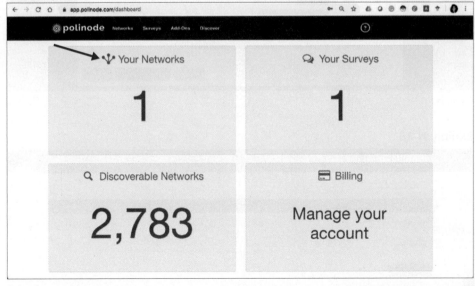

Polinode

A new webpage with your name and email address prepopulated will open (Exhibit 11-19). Enter your country, username, and a (strong) password of your choice. Now, click "Create Account."

Step 2: Uploading Data to Polinode

Your Polinode account is now set up and you are ready to build a social network graph.

Once you click "Create Account" from the previous step, your web browser will automatically open the Polinode dashboard, as shown in Exhibit 11-20. Click on "Your Networks" to access the network list available through Polinode.

Exhibit 11-20

Polinode

Exhibit 11-21

Polinode

Polinode initially provides an Example Network. Click on "+ New Network" to start building your own network (Exhibit 11-21).

As you see in Exhibit 11-22, a "Create New Network" window will open. To complete the form, enter the Network Name as "Twitter Network" and the File Type as "Excel." For the File, click "Choose File" and navigate on your computer to where you downloaded the "SocialNetwork.xlsx" dataset. Select the Excel file and click "Open." The Excel data has already been matched to the Polinode template that requires Nodes and Edges be set up on separate Excel sheets.

Next, you can choose who can see and access this network. Where it asks to select Access, choose "Private." The academic account does not allow the creation of a Public network.

Review Exhibit 11-22 to confirm you have selected the correct fields, and then click "+ Create."

Your network will take only a few seconds to be created and will be added to the network list (Exhibit 11-23). In the "Twitter Network" row, click on the Explore icon to visualize the newly created Twitter Network, as shown in Exhibit 11-23.

Exhibit 11-22

Polinode

Exhibit 11-23

Polinode

Step 3: Viewing the Network Graph

The network is built automatically so you can see all the nodes (the blue circles in Exhibit 11-24). On the right side of the screen, attribute features can be accessed. When you move your cursor over any of the nodes, you will be able to see the data attributes that were loaded for each node, such as gender and the number of followers. For instance, if you move the cursor over the node "Dara Eckerle," you will see her specific attributes, including gender (female) and number of Twitter followers (90,333) (Exhibit 11-24).

Exhibit 11-24

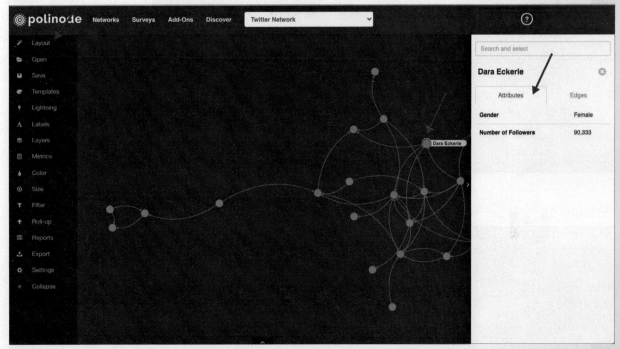

Polinode

On the left side of the screen, you can access the Polinode options to update the network graph. Examples of the options include Layout, Templates, Labels, and so on. We will dive deeper into several of these options in the next steps.

When the graph first loads in Polinode, it shows the details of Attributes and Edges as previously described (Exhibit 11-25). Click on the right arrow on the right side of the screen to hide the Attributes and Edges detailed window view. This will allow for more space on the screen to see the full graph.

On the left side navigation panel, click on "Layout" (Exhibit 11-26). The algorithm that determines the layout visual structure of the graph can be selected. The default option is Force Directed. Forced Directed uses an algorithm to reduce the crossing edges and set the edges in a visually pleasing way. For this case study, keep the default layout. Later on, you can select other layouts for your network to see which one you like best.

Your network might become difficult to visualize as you proceed with the case. If this happens, you can return to Layout, click on "Advanced" and select "Yes" under "Prevent Overlap" (Exhibit 11-26). Then, click "Start" to update the layout.

Exhibit 11-25

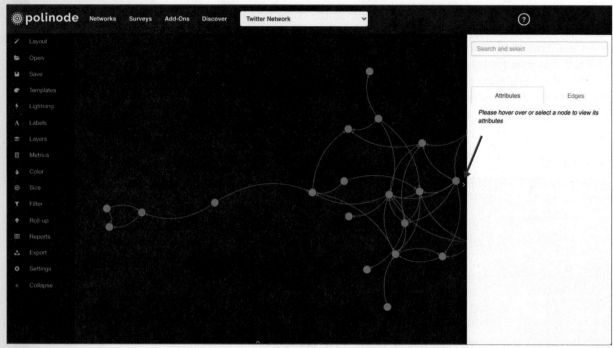

Polinode

Exhibit 11-26

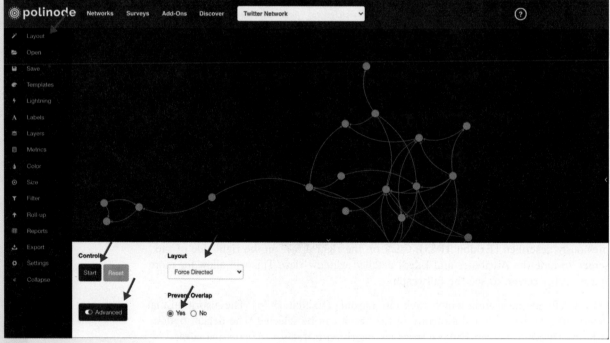

Polinode

Next, click on "Labels" (Exhibit 11-27). Under "Show Labels," you can view the name of the person associated with the node. Using the drop-down menu, change "Show Labels" to "Always." This option is only advised when the network is smaller in size, otherwise the labels on the screen will overlap, and it will be difficult to see the information on the layout.

Exhibit 11-27

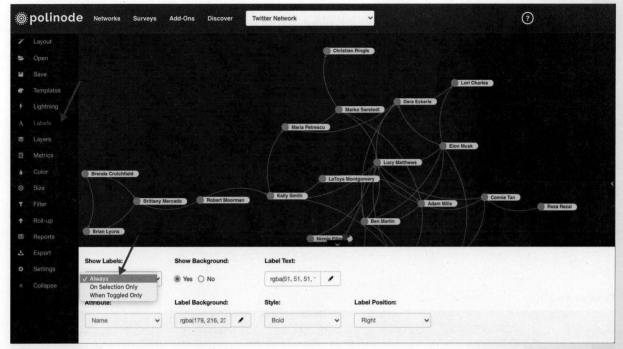

Polinode

Exhibit 11-28

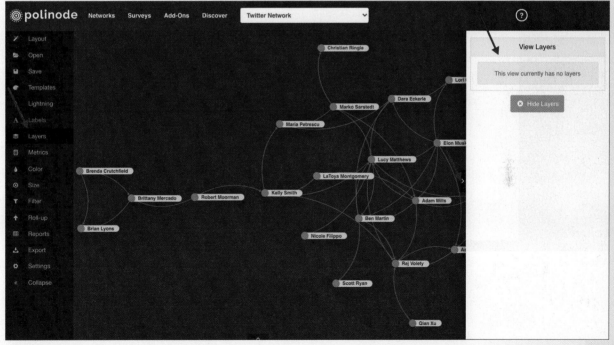

Polinode

Next, hide the bottom window by clicking on the down arrow in the lower middle of the screen (Exhibit 11-27).

Now, click on "Layers" (Exhibit 11-28). A "View Layers" window will open on the right side of the screen, indicating there are no layers available. Polinode metrics and filters are stored as Layers in this platform. As a result, the underlying network data is not affected. Each time a view is opened, the metric is recalculated. Once calculations and filters are added, you should revisit Layers to update the view of the graph. For now, hide the "View Layers" window by clicking on the right arrow (Exhibit 11-28).

Step 4: Measuring Network Properties

Now, click on "Metrics" (Exhibit 11-29). There are 21 Polinode algorithms to identify communities and calculate centrality measures (closeness, degree, betweenness, and eigenvector) of influencers in the network.

Start with identifying communities in the network. In the "Manage Metrics" window, select "Communities" and then click "Calculate and Add as Layer" to finalize this step (Exhibit 11-29). A new layer for communities will be created and added to the Layers section that was reviewed earlier.

Exhibit 11-29

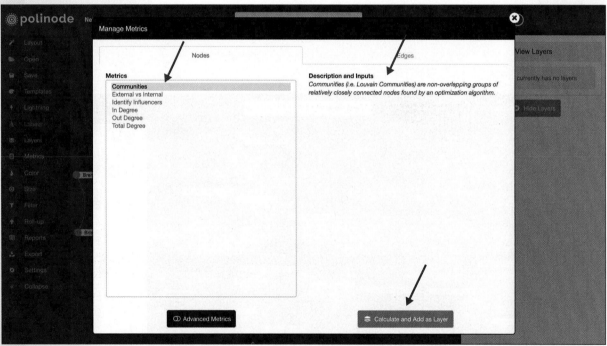

Polinode

In the "Manage Metrics" window, select "Total Degree" and then click "Calculate and Add as Layer" (Exhibit 11-30). A new layer for total degree will be created and added to the Layers section that was reviewed earlier.

Next, in the "Manage Metrics" window, click on "Advanced Metrics" and select "Betweenness Centrality" (Exhibit 11-31). Then, click "Calculate and Add as Layer." A new layer for betweenness centrality will be created and added to the Layers section that was reviewed earlier.

Exhibit 11-30

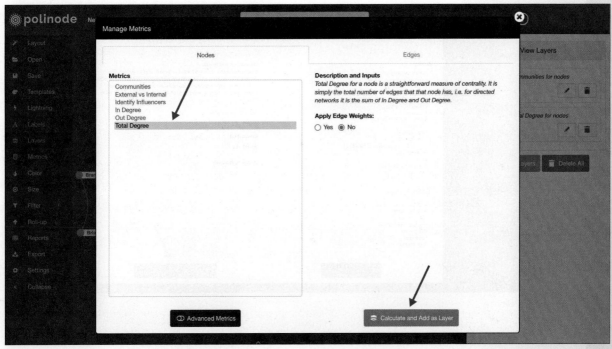

Polinode

Exhibit 11-31

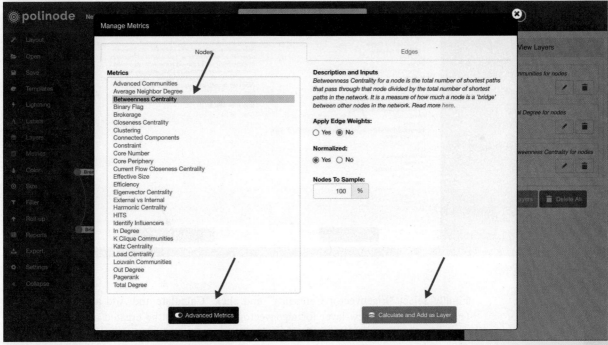

Polinode

Under "Advanced Metrics," select "Closeness Centrality," and click "Calculate and Add as Layer" (Exhibit 11-32). A new layer for closeness centrality will be created and added to the Layers section that was reviewed earlier.

Exhibit 11-32

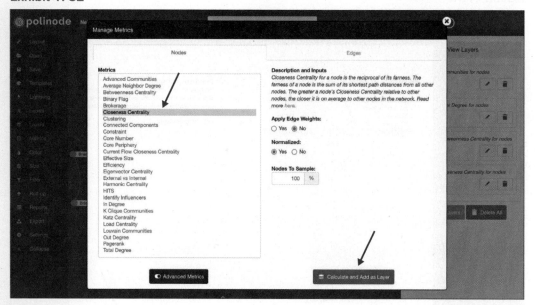

Polinode

Exhibit 11-33

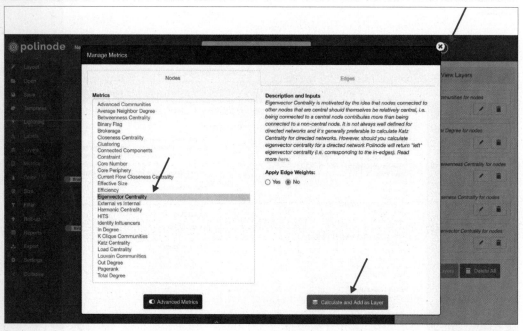

Polinode

Finally, select "Eigenvector Centrality" and click "Calculate and Add as Layer" (Exhibit 11-33). A new layer for eigenvector centrality will be created and added to the Layers section that was reviewed earlier.

Click the "X" button at the top right to close the metrics window and review the layers added (Exhibit 11-33).

Review the five layers that were added in the "View Layers" window (Exhibit 11-34). These layers will be used to update graph colors, size, and filter options. Hide the right pane window by clicking on the right arrow (Exhibit 11-34).

Exhibit 11-34

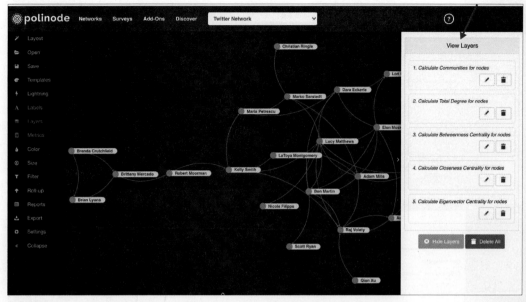

Polinode

Step 5: Updating Nodes Graph View

On the left side navigation panel, click on "Color" (Exhibit 11-35). The bottom window will bring up color options. Under Color Nodes By: select "Communities." It appears there are six communities detected in the network (Exhibit 11-35). This will change the colors of your nodes by the community where they have been assigned. It is easy to see from Exhibit 11-35, that nodes like Robert Moorman, Brittany Mercado, Brenda Crutchfield, and Brian Lyons belong to the same community.

Exhibit 11-35

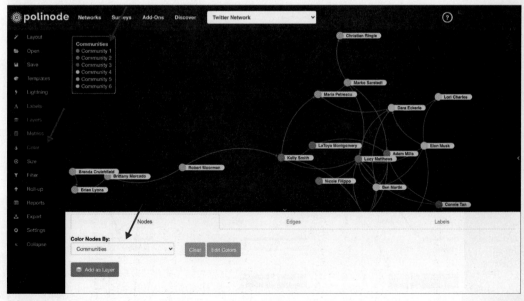

Polinode

Exhibit 11-36

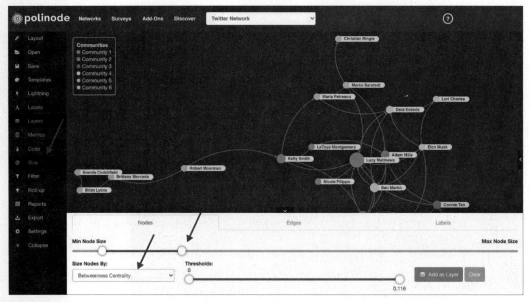

Polinode

Next, click on "Size" and then select "Betweenness Centrality" (Exhibit 11-36). Adjust the Min and Max Node Sizes by using the slider so the more important nodes appear bigger relative to the smaller nodes (Exhibit 11-36).

Next, click on "Filter" (Exhibit 11-37). Under "Filter Nodes By," select "Gender." Under "Selected Attribute Values," click on "Female" or "Male" to see only female or male Twitter users in the graph (Exhibit 11-37). You can also filter by number of followers and all the centrality measures that were calculated earlier.

Now, hit "Clear" to review the graph. Hide the bottom window by clicking on the down arrow (Exhibit 11-37).

Exhibit 11-37

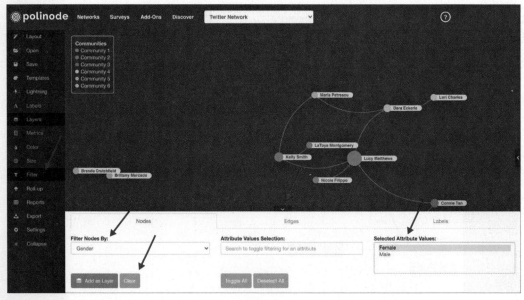

Polinode

Exhibit 11-38

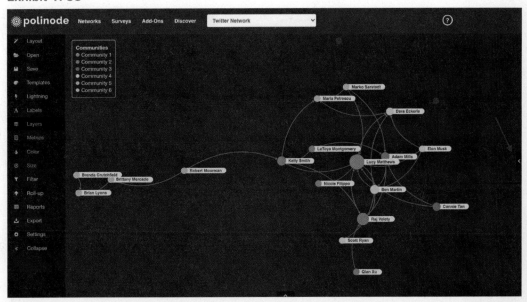

Polinode

When reviewing the size of the nodes, we see that certain nodes (larger ones) appear to have higher betweenness than others (Exhibit 11-38). Consider, for example, Lucy Matthews and Raj Volety. They seem to have higher centrality in the network. To examine the calculated metrics further, review the properties of each node. Click the left arrow to expand the properties section on the right side of the screen (Exhibit 11-38).

Now, move your cursor over the largest node associated with Twitter user Lucy Matthews (Exhibit 11-39). Note that Lucy belongs to Community 1 and her Total Degree value is 10. She has the highest betweenness centrality in the network, a high closeness centrality, and a high eigenvector centrality.

Exhibit 11-39

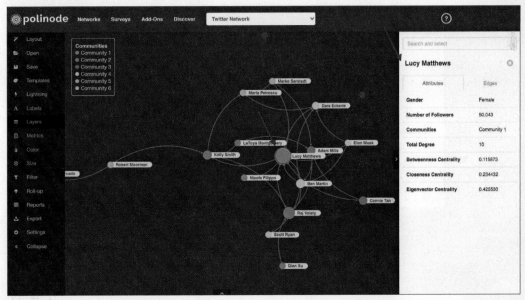

Polinode

Exhibit 11-40

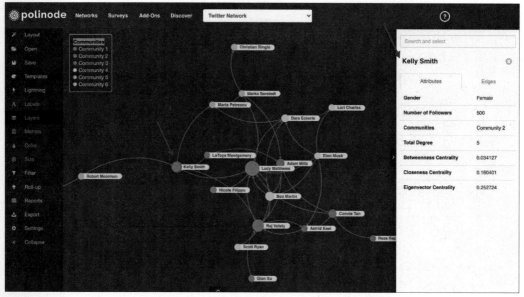

Polinode

You can compare the node for Lucy Matthews with another one, such as Kelly Smith (Exhibit 11-40). Move your cursor over the node for Kelly Smith to get the panel on the right side of the screen to show her Attributes. She is part of Community 2 and has Total Degrees of 5 (number of edges in and out of her nodes). She also has lower betweenness centrality, closeness centrality, and eigenvector centrality than Lucy. Kelly still holds a good position in the network because she connects different communities that otherwise would not be connected.

Step 6: Running a Network Report and Downloading Results

To evaluate all the nodes systematically, run a report to show the overall network measures. To do so, click "Reports" on the left side navigation panel, as shown in Exhibit 11-41.

Exhibit 11-41

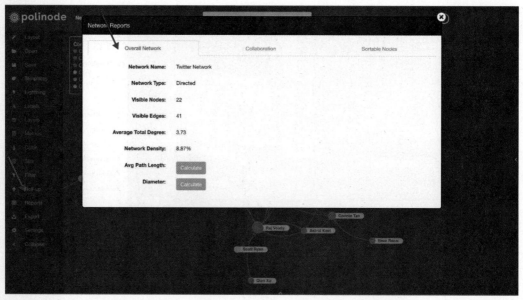

Polinode

Exhibit 11-42

Polinode

This will open a "Network Reports" window showing the network measures, which include type of network (directed or undirected), number of nodes, number of edges, average number of degrees in the network, and density of the network (Exhibit 11-41).

In the "Network Reports" window, click on the "Sortable Nodes" tab (Exhibit 11-42). Select "Export Nodes." This will download an Excel output that has all the nodes and their calculated centrality measures.

The export function will download a "Twitter Network Nodes.xlsx" file that will help you examine the different community and centrality measures in Excel (Exhibit 11-43).

Exhibit 11-43

	A	B	C	D	E	F	G	H	I	J
1	Name	Gender	Number of Followers	Label	Size	Communities	Total Degree	Betweenness Centrality	Closeness Centrality	Eigenvector Centrality
2	Adam Mills	Male	10000	Adam Mills	1	Community 2	7	0.029365079	0.241071429	0
3	Astrid Keel	Female	30980	Astrid Keel	1	Community 3	4	0.003174603	0.132505176	0.275435577
4	Ben Martin	Male	4000	Ben Martin	1	Community 4	8	0.034920635	0.253968254	0.25272408
5	Brenda Crutchfield	Female	80	Brenda Crutchfield	1	Community 5	2	0	0.095238095	0
6	Brian Lyons	Male	910	Brian Lyons	1	Community 5	2	0	0	0
7	Brittany Mercado	Female	523	Brittany Mercado	1	Community 5	3	0.002380952	0.047619048	0
8	Christian Ringle	Male	83022	Christian Ringle	1	Community 6	1	0	0	0
9	Connie Tan	Female	300	Connie Tan	1	Community 3	4	0.023809524	0.250626566	0
10	Dara Eckerle	Female	90333	Dara Eckerle	1	Community 4	5	0.015873016	0.047619048	0.402818122
11	Elon Musk	Male	35000000	Elon Musk	1	Community 4	6	0	0.360119048	0
12	Kelly Smith	Female	500	Kelly Smith	1	Community 2	5	0.034126984	0.160401003	0.25272408
13	LaToya Montgomery	Female	20456	LaToya Montgomery	1	Community 2	2	0	0.216450216	0
14	Lori Charles	Female	3500	Lori Charles	1	Community 4	2	0	0.063492063	0
15	Lucy Matthews	Female	50043	Lucy Matthews	1	Community 1	10	0.115873016	0.234432234	0.425529619
16	Maria Petrescu	Female	9040	Maria Petrescu	1	Community 6	3	0	0	0.389329655
17	Marko Sarstedt	Male	566	Marko Sarstedt	1	Community 6	4	0	0.288095238	0
18	Nicole Filippo	Female	345	Nicole Filippo	1	Community 1	1	0	0	0.25272408
19	Qian Xu	Female	476	Qian Xu	1	Community 1	1	0	0.154285714	0
20	Raj Volety	Male	4000	Raj Volety	1	Community 2	8	0.076190476	0.19047619	0.463770593
21	Reza Rezai	Male	5093	Reza Rezai	1	Community 3	1	0	0.192063492	0
22	Robert Moorman	Male	670	Robert Moorman	1	Community 5	2	0	0.185867896	0
23	Scott Ryan	Male	640	Scott Ryan	1	Community 4	1	0	0	0.150094042

Microsoft Excel

Exhibit 11-44

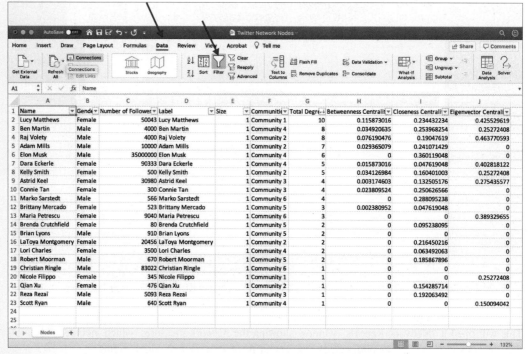

Microsoft Excel

The data now can be sorted by clicking "Data" and then "Filter" in Excel (Exhibit 11-44). The data can be sorted from high to low by each of the centrality measures to better understand the different influencers in the network.

Return to your web browser with the Polinode application and close the Report window using the "X" button at the top right (Exhibit 11-45).

Exhibit 11-45

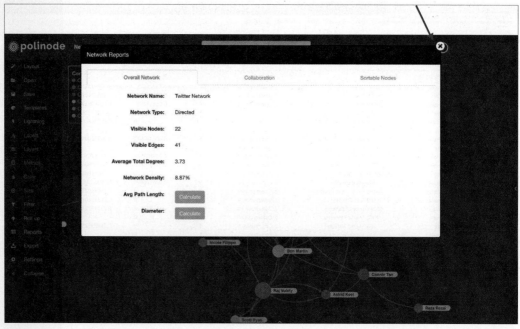

Polinode

Exhibit 11-46

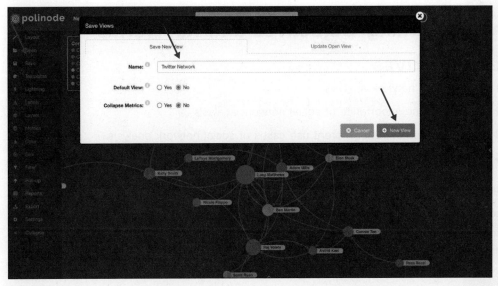

Polinode

On the left side navigation panel, click "Save" (Exhibit 11-46). This will bring up a "Save Views" window, allowing you to save the network information. In the name field, type "Twitter Network," and then click "+ New View" (Exhibit 11-46). This will save the network settings and calculations for future access. Click the "X" button at the top right to close the Save Views window.

Insights Learned from Applying the Concepts

We can solve many useful marketing problems with social network analysis. In this case, what insights were revealed?

Recall the initial questions in the case:

- How are the Twitter users tweeting about electric cars connected?
- Who are the most influential customers in the network?
- What are the communities that exist in the network?

The structure of the network was discovered through the graph, and the influential Twitter users in our sample were identified. Influencers in the network can be engaged by the company to promote the new electric car being developed. In this case, Lucy Matthews was identified as having the highest number of connections measured by total degrees. She also has the highest betweenness in the network. Thus, she has the highest influence in the network, connecting people who otherwise will not be connected. Raj Volety has the highest eigenvector centrality. This means that Raj has power in connecting two well-connected parts of the network. Without him, the other parts of the network would not be connected. Note that Elon Musk had the highest closeness centrality, which means he can transmit messages in the social network through the shortest paths fairly quickly. Finally, recall that six communities were identified. These six communities (groups) of people are closely connected in the network.

As the proliferation of social networks into our daily lives continues, the importance of social network analysis will continue to grow. This case is an example of how to identify important customers and segments in a network. Social network analysis can help optimize a viral marketing campaign and promote new ideas, information, products, and services in the right networks.

Summary of Learning Objectives and Key Terms

LEARNING OBJECTIVES

Objective 11-1 Define social network analysis.

Objective 11-2 Understand the importance of social network analysis.

Objective 11-3 Investigate and explain different use cases of social network analysis.

Objective 11-4 Evaluate and interpret results from the social network analysis.

KEY TERMS

Betweenness centrality	Edge weight	Link prediction
Closeness centrality	Edges	Louvain communities
Degree centrality	Egocentric network	Nodes
Density	Eigenvector centrality	Singleton
Directed network	Graph	Social network analysis
Distribution of node degrees	Influencer	Undirected network

Discussion and Review Questions

1. Define social network analysis.

2. How can marketers use social network analysis?

3. Differentiate between a node and an edge.

4. What information does a graph provide?

5. Explain the difference between degree centrality, betweenness centrality, and eigenvector centrality.

6. How can link prediction be used?

Critical Thinking and Marketing Applications

1. How does knowledge of what Twitter users are tweeting about regarding electric cars help refine and develop innovative products? What are some other sources of information that might also be helpful?

2. A company wants to identify three influencers in the network to discuss and review the new electric car model. Using Exhibit 11-43, which three people could serve as influencers? Why did you select them?

References

1. David Smith, "Proof! Just Six Degrees of Separation Between Us," *The Guardian*, August 2, 2008, https://www.theguardian.com/technology/2008/aug/03/internet.email; Joe Fay, "Microsoft 'Proves' Six Degrees of Separation Theory," *The Register*, August 4, 2008, https://www.theregister.co.uk/2008/08/04/six_degrees_microsoft; and Dan Farber, "Proof of six degrees of separation," *CNET*, March 15, 2008, https://www.cnet.com/news/proof-of-six-degrees-of-separation.

2. Elizabeth Segran, "Sephora Picks 24 Influencers for its Coveted #SephoraSquad Program," *Fast Company*, March 29, 2019, https://www.fastcompany.com/90326765/sephora-brings-25-influencers-into-its-coveted-sephorasquad-program; and Diana Pearl, "Sephora Turned Applications for Its Influencer Program Into a Social Media Event," *Adweek*, May 21, 2019, https://www.adweek.com/brand-marketing/sephora-turned-applications-for-its-influencer-program-into-a-social-media-event.

3. Mike Ewing, "71% More Likely to Purchase Based on Social Media Referrals," HubSpot, January 9, 2019, https://blog.hubspot.com/blog/tabid/6307/bid/30239/71-More-Likely-to-Purchase-Based-on-Social-Media-Referrals-Infographic.aspx; Andrew Arnold, "4 Ways Social Media Influences Millennials' Purchasing Decisions," *Forbes*, December 22, 2017, https://www.forbes.com/sites/andrewarnold/20317/12/22/4-ways-social-media-influences-millennials-purchasing-decisions/#2e586233539f.

4. "NodeXL," Social Media Research Foundation, https://www.smrfoundation.org/nodexl.

5. Marc Smith, Lee Raine, Ben Shneiderman, and Itai Himelboim, "Mapping Twitter Topic Networks: From Polarized Crowds to Community Clusters," Pew Research Center, February 20, 2014, https://www.pewresearch.org/internet/2014/02/20/mapping-twitter-topic-networks-from-polarized-crowds-to-community-clusters.

6. Research and Markets, "Global Electric Vehicle (EV) Market Forecasts to 2030," Intrado Globenewswire, August 6, 2019, https://www.globenewswire.com/news-release/2019/08/06/1897431/0/en/Global-Electric-Vehicle-EV-Market-Forecasts-to-2030-Market-Volume-Projected-to-Grow-from-3-269-671-Units-in-2019-to-26-951-318-Units-by-2030.html.

12

Fundamentals of Digital Marketing Analytics

LEARNING OBJECTIVES

12.1 Define digital marketing.

12.2 Understand the importance of digital marketing.

12.3 Investigate different use cases of digital marketing.

12.4 Evaluate and interpret results from digital marketing analytics.

GaudiLab/Shutterstock

12.1 What Are the Basics of Digital Marketing?

Have you ever visited a company website, clicked on an advertisement, or posted an online review about a product or service? Customers interact with firms through numerous electronic marketing touchpoints. **Digital marketing** is the use of marketing touchpoints that are executed electronically through a digital channel to communicate and interact with current and potential customers and partners. Examples of digital channels are social media, email, search engines, and websites that facilitate connections with current and potential customers. There are several critical elements of a successful digital marketing strategy. The major elements include advertising (e.g., social media, display), search engine optimization, website design, branded social media, and email marketing. These digital marketing touchpoints can be categorized as different types of media, including owned, paid, and earned digital media (see Exhibit 12-1).

What Is Owned Digital Media?

Owned digital media is managed by the company and includes touchpoints such as email marketing, social media pages, and company websites. For example, the corporate website of Dunkin' would be an example of owned digital media. Website visitors expect accurate and current information and determine whether to remain on a site within the first 10 to 15 seconds.[1] Customers unable to locate information or an item of interest rather quickly will likely leave the site. Company-owned digital media is developed as a source of information that is about a company's products and services.

What Is Paid Digital Media?

Exposure that the company pays others to provide is referred to as **paid digital media**. Examples of paid digital media include sponsored posts (e.g., influencers), display advertisements, and social media advertisements. Companies can target specific groups of people to be the recipient of an advertisement using demographics or online searches. These advertisements often appear at the top of the page of an internet search, when scrolling through a social media platform, or even on another web page.

What Is Earned Digital Media?

Communication or exposure not initiated or posted by the company is called **earned digital media**. Earned digital media is likely an outcome of owned and paid efforts. When owned and paid efforts increase, awareness surrounding the company is also likely to increase. Reviews, social media shares, and media coverage are some touchpoints considered earned digital media.

Exhibit 12-1 Owned, Paid, and Earned Digital Media

TYPE OF MEDIA	DESCRIPTION	EXAMPLES
Owned digital media	The media is managed by the company	Websites, blogs, and social media accounts
Paid digital media	The company pays for exposure	Display advertising, influencer promotions, and social media advertisements
Earned digital media	Communication or exposure that is not initiated by the company	Customer reviews, social media shares, media coverage, and organic search placement

How Is Digital Marketing Used?

These digital marketing media touchpoints create challenges and opportunities. Companies are challenged by the large number of possible touchpoints. The more touchpoints there are, the more difficult it is to understand, monitor, and control the customer experience. On the other hand, numerous digital touchpoints provide an opportunity for the company to better understand behavior and interact with a current or potential customer.

Over 85 percent of people indicate their search for a product or service begins in a digital touchpoint.[2] However, the path to discovering, researching, and potentially purchasing products or services varies. While some people discover products on social media advertisements, others research products through social networks and so on. Exhibit 12-2 shows the different influences of touchpoints (e.g., owned, paid, and earned) based on research from GlobalWebIndex. These influences are based on almost 285,000 individuals between the ages of 16 and 64 that used the internet.[3] The larger circles indicate more frequent usage of a particular social path, depending upon age.

How does a company better understand patterns and trends in the three digital marketing media categories? **Digital marketing analytics** enables marketers to monitor, understand, and evaluate the performance of digital marketing initiatives.

Exhibit 12-2 GlobalWebIndex Social Path to Purchase

THE SOCIAL PATH TO PURCHASE
% who say they do the following applies to them

● Global ● 16-24 ● 25-34 ● 35-44 ● 45-54 ● 55-64

	Global	16-24	25-34	35-44	45-54	55-64
Discover brands/products via ads on social for discovery	27%	31%	29%	27%	23%	19%
Discover brands/products via recommendations on social	24%	26%	26%	24%	21%	15%
Research products online via social networks	43%	50%	46%	41%	33%	25%
Lots of likes/good comments would increase chance of purchase	23%	27%	26%	23%	19%	13%
A 'buy' button would increase chance of purchase	13%	14%	16%	14%	10%	6%

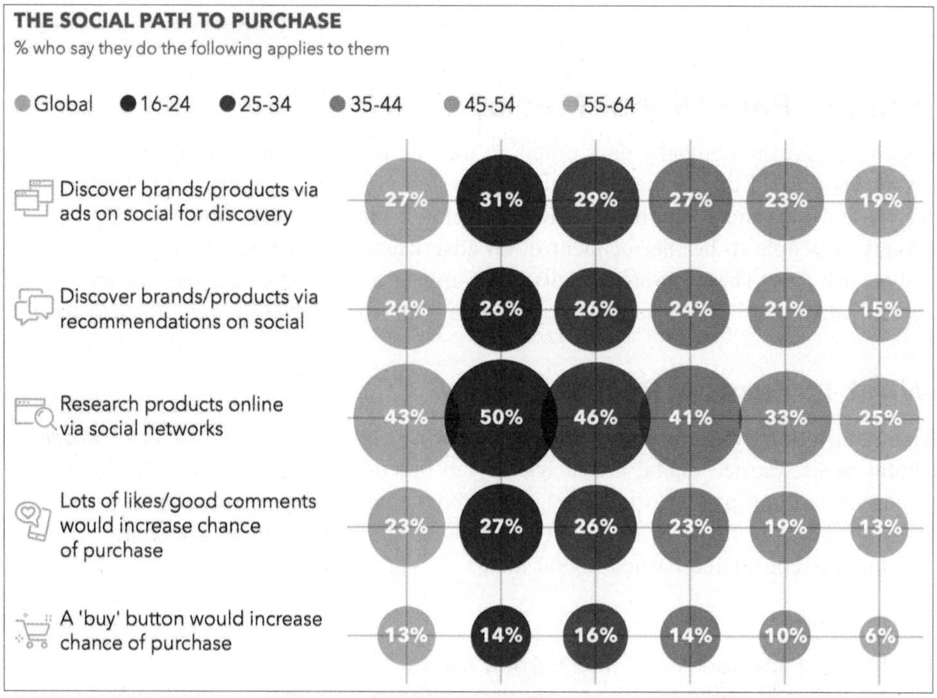

Source: "Social GlobalWebIndex's Flagship Report on the Latest Trends in Social Media," GlobalWebIndex, Flagship Report 2020.

12.2 Digital Marketing Analytics in Practice

Insights from digital marketing analytics can be used to better understand and enhance the customer purchase journey. The goal for marketers is to increase the likelihood that customers will complete the journey and actually purchase a product or service, and also that they return in the future to make additional purchases.

PRACTITIONER CORNER

Aran Moultrop | Analytics Advisor at Alteryx

Aran Moultrop is an Analytics Advisor to enterprises across a variety of industries. He has helped numerous companies apply best of breed Analytic solutions to organizations in roles at SAP, SAS, Sisense, and Alteryx.

Aran has built workflows to help companies identify customers for personalized retention and marketing efforts powered by prediction algorithms. He enjoys communicating technical topics with diverse audiences.

Aran Moultrop

Q **Companies have been making efforts to track the customer journey for many years. Whether online or at a brick-and-mortar location, companies understand the value of mapping the customer's journey from search to purchase to post-purchase reviews to follow-up customer service. Over 85 percent of shoppers now begin product searches using digital touchpoints. How can companies use web analytics to understand their customer journey?**

A Companies today have a wide variety of tools at their disposal to create a "golden record" of the customer's journey. In the retail space, in particular, tools related to data management, data quality, and a variety of web analytics tools are deployed to capture transactions made in brick-and-mortar locations, while also capturing online purchases. Some of the most common uses of web analytics tools for online activity tracking include AdWords from search engines and advertising platforms, referral/channel source, A/B landing page testing, tracking mouse movement across web pages, drop-off points, and market basket conversion. Working in conjunction with those uses are email optimization platforms that nudge or offer up incentives for customers to come back and complete their purchase.

A useful chart that shows common web page flows by your customers is a Sankey Diagram.

After a customer makes a purchase, Marketing departments can now use that data to cross-sell and up-sell similar or complementary products. Over the course of the relationship with a customer, Analytics can drive and recommend more specific products based on the interests of the individual consumer. These targeted campaigns should yield better results than a typical "spray and pray" methodology.

Q **A recent study indicated that people using smartphones are more willing to share personal information than desktop users. How does this type of information help marketers when examining the incoming visitor's device type?**

A Understanding customer preferences and being able to serve those preferences up at the right time is what will make or break the best brands in the future. Knowing that customers utilizing shopping platforms on mobile devices are more likely to share information should motivate marketers to develop a deep understanding of when and where the customers want to be served. This will help them market more effectively when building predictive models for campaigns. Effectively capturing and storing data about customers should be a continuous process across all channels.

Continued

How does this information help marketers make decisions about website design?

 Marketers need to have a consistent brand feel across all platforms, but the preceding study about sharing personal information shows that the best marketers will understand where they can ask more questions to gain deeper insights about their customers. Being able to adapt across different channels, while presenting the same brand experience, is a challenge and an opportunity for marketers to drive further customer insights.

Continued to page 414

The purchase journey is a process that has several stages, including (1) previous experiences the customer might possess, (2) the pre-purchase stage when the customer becomes aware of or searches for the product or service, (3) the purchase stage when the customer selects a product or service, and (4) the post-purchase stage where the customer uses the product or service and shares information with the company and others. During the purchase journey, customers seek information and interact with companies through multiple digital touchpoints. Properly managing interactions throughout the customer purchase journey can lead to brand awareness, brand engagement, word-of-mouth marketing, and conversion to purchase. Interactions during the customer purchase journey take place across owned, paid, and earned digital marketing media.

Owned Digital Marketing Media

How can the information footprint that website visitors leave behind on company websites, by opening an email or visiting a social media page, help to personalize customer experiences? Using this information and more, companies can develop personalized content for email campaigns or create optimized website content for certain customer profiles. Sprint, the PGA Tour, and Nissan Motor Company have used Adobe products to measure their owned digital marketing media, understand the customer journey and improve the customer experience (see Exhibit 12-3). As a result, Sprint, for example, improved equipment protection program sales by 29 percent.[4] Nissan customized emails to generate 200 percent higher open and click rates.[5] The PGA Tour increased global digital visits by 26 percent.[6] Measuring results from owned digital marketing media offers substantial advantages to companies that have the capabilities to integrate insights into strategic decision making.

What do Toys "R" Us, Sears, and J.Crew have in common? These retailers have been impacted by the "Amazon effect." The **Amazon effect** refers to the often-disruptive influence e-commerce and digital marketplaces have had on traditional brick-and-mortar retailers. Amazon was established in July 1995. The main goal was to create a virtual store that achieved a lower fixed cost while maintaining a higher inventory level than brick-and-mortar stores. Today, Amazon has become the largest retailer in the world. But how did the company become so successful? Many argue that Amazon's secret to success can be attributed to harnessing its digital capabilities. All interactions with Amazon are digital and produce a vast amount of data. Using this data, the company develops a deep knowledge of customers, an optimized logistics network, and an exceptional technology infrastructure. Strong digital strategies facilitate a deep understanding of customers and give predominantly online companies an edge over brick-and-mortar stores. Companies operating mainly

Exhibit 12-3 Examples of Owned Digital Marketing Media

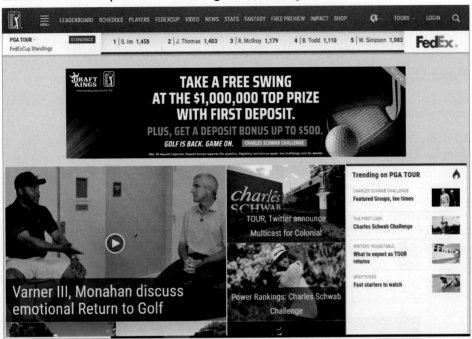

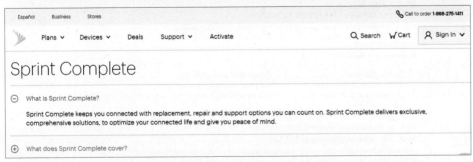

Sources: PGA Tour, https://www.pgatour.com; Nissan, https://www.nissanusa.com; and Sprint Complete, https://www.sprintcomplete.com.

as brick and mortar stores such as Toys "R" Us, Sears, and J.Crew were unable to maintain pace with those managing a successful digital strategy and have filed for bankruptcy.

Paid Digital Marketing Media

Digital advertising budgets continue to increase. Exhibit 12-4 provides examples of paid advertisements in Facebook and on a search engine.

Likewise, targeting online users with advertising has become more sophisticated and complex. For example, GumGum uses artificial intelligence computer vision technology

Exhibit 12-4 Examples of Paid Digital Marketing Media

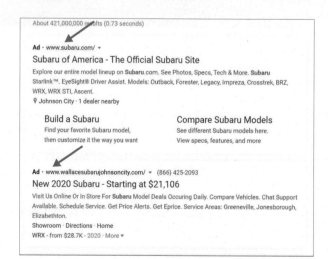

Sources: "Life is Good" sponsored ad on Facebook; and "Subaru" sponsored ads on Google.

Exhibit 12-5 Example of GumGum Advertisement Placement

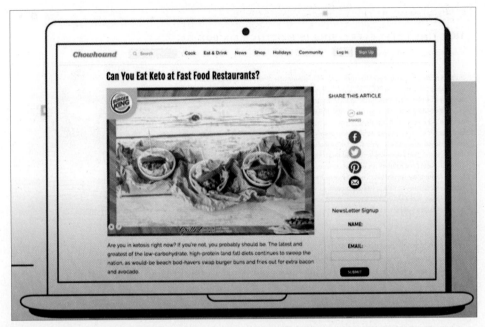

Source: GumGum, https://gumgum.com.

to examine images and videos a website user is viewing. The company can then place advertisements in content areas that will catch the potential customer's attention (see Exhibit 12-5). This technology is an advantage to businesses in their efforts to improve return on investment of marketing budgets. Targeting the right customer at the right time and at the right place enables them to capture the audience's interest and drive increased advertising success.

Earned Digital Marketing Media

A company does not produce earned digital marketing media—it only takes actions to increase the likelihood of earned media emerging. Because the company is not the source of earned digital media, the positive or negative sentiment associated with earned media is uncontrollable. For example, if companies engage in unethical behavior, then the public sentiment displayed online will likely be negative. This negative sentiment can create substantial challenges for companies. Information spreads quickly and continues to live online for a long time—which helps keep the story alive. For example, run a quick search on the company Enron. The company ceased operations in 2007 after engaging in unethical accounting practices, but online articles over the last 14 years still appear online and more continue to be published.

Many companies, however, benefit from earned media. Earned media or user-generated content is highly trusted by potential customers as authentic and accurate. Exhibit 12-6 is a post from Erin Schrader's Living in Yellow blog in which she gives her personal opinion of Stitch Fix, an online personalized styling service. The post specifically mentions that it is not sponsored by the company. Stitch Fix, though, can use technology tools such as Brand24 and Mention to scan websites and collect information when a company or keyword is discussed, such as in this example.

Exhibit 12-6 Example of Earned Digital Marketing Media

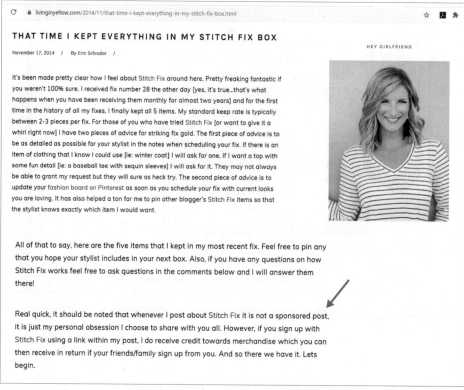

Source: Erin Schrader, "That Time I Kept Everything in My Stitch Fix Box," Living in Yellow blog, November 17, 2014, https://livinginyellow.com/2014/11/that-time-i-kept-everything-in-my-stitch-fix-box.html. Used by permission.

Companies use different tools to collect data, track results, and analyze digital marketing media performance. Google Analytics, Brandwatch, Mention, Brand24, Adobe products (e.g., analytics, audience manager, campaign, experience manager, and target), Keyhole, Kissmetrics, Optimizely, Hootsuite Analytics, Talkwalker, Owler, crunchbase, SpyFu, Moat, and HubSpot are just some of the many tools used to examine and assess digital marketing media performance. These tools can conduct simple or more complex analyses of customer interactions. Determining which measures are important can be overwhelming. Ultimately, companies should select key measures that align with their business strategy.

Continued from page 410

PRACTITIONER CORNER

Aran Moultrop | Analytics Advisor at Alteryx

Q Web analytics is focused on visitors' behaviors regarding websites, such as traffic due to an advertising campaign or internet searches, as well as how visitors act once they enter a website. Given this, what can web analytics *not* tell us about a customer?

A Web analytics can track many user behaviors and patterns across platforms, but it can be difficult to discern the true buying intentions of customers. Most buyers are now more informed than ever. They will do months of research for large or strategic purchases.

Continued

Understanding timelines of purchases can be very difficult, unless a timing question is introduced into the buying process.

Q What is complementary data that can enhance web analytics insights?

A There is a wealth of data that can be used to augment analyses. Credit scores, census, demographic, drive time, and household income are all examples of external data sources that can be found or purchased to enhance marketing campaign effectiveness.

Q Companies have increased their social media activity and engagement over the last several years. eMarketer.com predicts increased use particularly in Instagram, Pinterest, and Snapchat. How are marketers using different platforms?

A Marketers are using social media to track and target their customers. Social media marketing is a cost-efficient and effective way to reach customers. Marketers can do everything from targeting their customers on social media based on location or based on behaviors. If a consumer looks at a product on a website, with the use of analytics, marketers can then target them on say Facebook and serve them up an ad with the product they were just looking at. They can even provide a direct link to buy the product.

Marketers can also utilize social media to complete "social listening" exercises, where marketers essentially listen in on social media and see what consumers are talking about. This can be utilized to see if consumers are talking about their brands or their competitors, so they can adjust their marketing strategy based on their consumers.

A perfect example of the large increase in social media engagement since 2016, has been pharmaceutical companies. When social media started to become more popular, it was difficult for pharmaceutical companies to have product-specific branded ads versus disease (e.g., diabetes) awareness campaigns, because the FDA hadn't released any regulations about social media. Now, the FDA has put regulations in place and pharmaceutical companies can also have ads on social media platforms.

Q What changes do you anticipate in the next several years?

A One large change we will see is that LinkedIn currently doesn't allow branded (product-based) ads on its platform. However, it is now piloting and testing branded ads, so in the near future, marketers will be able to utilize LinkedIn for reaching more customers. This is a signficiant shift in the LinkedIn business model to further monetize on the connections.

At some point, social media could become so inundated with ads that they are not as effective anymore because there is so much clutter, and so some new platform may come along to take their place.

12.3 Digital Marketing Analytics Measures

The digital environment makes it possible for companies to test and refine practices quickly. Companies should adopt a comprehensive approach to examining the real-time performance and success of digital marketing. Website or social media analytics independent of the entire digital marketing environment provides only a snapshot of how customers are interacting with the company. Digital marketing analytics connects and examines all digital business activity.

Companies should determine a comprehensive but manageable set of measurements that align with the overall business strategy. Some digital marketing metrics help answer questions about what is happening, but do not clarify more advanced questions such as why. These basic metrics are as important as more complex metrics when considering digital marketing performance in a holistic manner. A good digital marketing report will consider owned, earned, and paid digital media.

Digital marketing reports should include an analysis of the digital audience as they interact with the company. For example:

- How digital company platforms are acquiring visitors or customers.
- The behavior of visitors as they interact or share information about the company.
- Whether people interacting with the company online are becoming customers through conversion analysis.
- The digital path visitors take to interact with the company and become customers.
- Which digital content (e.g., text, images, colors) is most attractive to potential customers and therefore most effective in turning them into actual customers.
- Which digital strategies lead to customer retention.

Although not a comprehensive list, the following are a few measures to consider when determining important customer journey aspects to measure.

Audience Analysis

Audience analysis measures include:

- *Quantity of impressions or visitors:* How many people see paid advertisements (impressions) or visitors come to the social media pages or website?
- *User demographics:* What are the demographics of people who engage with the company's digital marketing touchpoints?
- *Geography:* Where are visitors to owned, paid, and earned digital media touchpoints located?

Exhibit 12-7 is an example of some audience measures produced in Google Analytics.

Exhibit 12-7 Audience Analysis

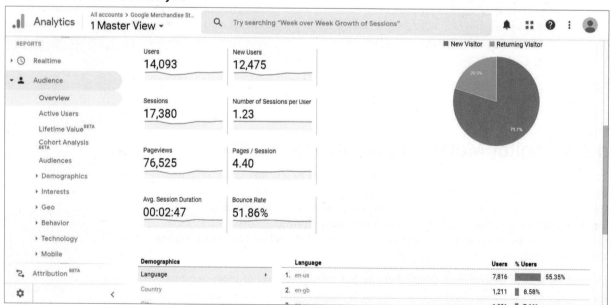

Google Analytics

Acquisition Analysis

Acquisition analysis measures include:

- *Traffic sources:* Which sources are visitors choosing to click on paid advertising or to enter the company social media pages or website?
- *Campaigns:* How are different marketing campaigns driving visitors to the website?

Exhibit 12-8 is an example of some acquisition measures produced in Google Analytics.

Exhibit 12-8 Acquisition Analysis

Google Analytics

Behavior Analysis

Behavior analysis measures include:

- *Pageviews:* This represents the number of sessions during which a particular webpage was viewed.
- *Frequency of engagement:* What is the frequency of how often visitors return to your site within a certain time frame?
- *Site speed:* How quickly are users able to see and interact with the website content?
- *Bounce rate:* What is the rate at which customers are arriving to your site and not clicking on anything on the page they entered?
- *Click-through rate:* What is the rate at which customers are clicking on paid advertising or campaign emails?
- *Site content:* Which pages are visitors coming into and exiting the website? Which pages are the most or least popular?
- *Site search:* What are visitors searching for when on the company website?

Exhibit 12-9 is an example of some behavior measures produced in Google Analytics. The information shows, for example, the number of pages viewed, the bounce rate, and the average time visitors spent on the page.

Exhibit 12-9 Behavior Analysis

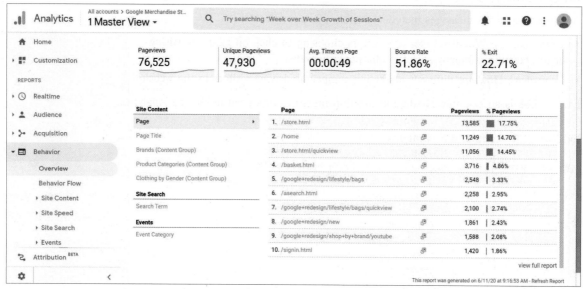

Google Analytics

Conversion Analysis

Conversion analysis measures include:

- *Conversion rate: It is used to assess the effectiveness of the marketing campaign and website design. It is measured as the ratio of visitors who have become customers.*

- *Conversion by traffic source:* What are the origins of visitors entering the site that result in conversions?

Exhibit 12-10 is an example of conversion measures produced in Google Analytics. This report shows conversion measures such as what day of the week orders are occurring, the average order value, and the total revenue.

Exhibit 12-10 Conversion Analysis

Google Analytics

There are also more complex analyses such as A/B testing that can be performed using Google tools (e.g., Google Optimization) and others.

A/B Testing

A/B testing (also known as split testing) enables marketers to experiment with different digital options to identify which ones are likely to be the most effective. For example, they can compare one Treatment (A/Control Group) to another Treatment (B). **Treatment** is the term used to describe the digital marketing intervention being tested. An example of a treatment tested as an intervention could be the color of certain buttons when navigating through the website, images, website layout, and more. Another example of an intervention might be placement of the button at the bottom versus on the right side of the screen, or the use of the same button in two different places on the screen ("Add to Cart" on Amazon).

The results of A/B testing are designed to improve online visitor experiences, and ultimately increase the likelihood of purchasing. Examples of A/B testing might be how to improve Google search page results, revising the layout of the list of movies on Netflix or Prime Video to make it easier to find a good movie, or how to present news on *The New York Times* website to improve readership.

Companies run digital A/B experiments regularly to learn what digital marketing works best. For example, Capital One ran over 80,000 digital A/B experiments in a single year promoting personalized credit card offers.[7] Non-profit organizations, including political campaigns, can also benefit from A/B experiments. When Barack Obama ran for President of the United States, the campaign experimented with variations of media content and the call to action buttons on its campaign landing page. They discovered a black-and-white photo of the Obama family generated more clicks than color images. Another A/B test found that a call to action labeled "Learn More" resulted in more clicks than the same button labeled "Sign Up Now." In fact, the combination of a black-and-white image and a "Learn More" button resulted in 40 percent more sign-ups to learn more about the campaign. These changes translated into an increase equivalent to 2.8 million new email addresses and an additional $60 million in donations.[8] These are all examples of how A/B testing provides an understanding of which content is being received and acted on by website visitors, and more quickly leads to improved conversion.

Multivariate Testing

Companies often want to make several changes from one visitor to another and compare them at the same time. **Multivariate testing** enables companies to test whether changing several different variables on their website at the same time leads to a higher conversion rate. For example, a company might be considering redesigning its website. Prior to the full launch, the marketing team will want to examine several different changes to the image on the website, the text content, and the color scheme. Multiple changes are being considered at the same time from one visitor to another. Multivariate testing is used so companies can examine several different variations at the same time to determine how to best optimize different combinations (e.g., site layout, images) of proposed changes to the website.

Multichannel Attribution

The customer path to purchase is rarely linear and usually involves cross-channel touchpoints. For example, a visitor might view a company Facebook page, and then several days after they might click on an online advertisement where they will be redirected to a company web page. When this happens, companies are interested in understanding whether paid, owned, or earned digital touchpoints are directing customers to the website to make a purchase. Which digital touchpoint has the strongest influence on the customer? Do two digital touchpoints in combination produce a stronger influence on the customer journey? **Multichannel attribution** assesses how, when, and where these various touchpoints influence customers.

There are several different types of attribution models that enable marketers to assess the effectiveness of multiple channels. For example, some attribution models are rule-based, meaning there are rules assigned for allocating credit to which touchpoint is contributing to conversions. Maybe the first click or last click before conversion are considered the most important. Other models depend upon more advanced methods to analyze the data. For example, machine learning examines the data and determines how different touchpoints impact conversion performance. Results from multichannel attribution provide insights that lead to less expensive and more effective interactions with customers.

Many digital marketing technology platforms, in combination with traditional statistics software, perform basic to more advanced analyses. Sophisticated analyses with deeper insights provide improved decision-making information. But less complex metrics discussed earlier are also useful in selecting the best digital marketing strategy.

12.4 How Does A/B Testing Work?

A/B testing enables a company to continuously test and examine how visitors respond to one change versus another. Measurements using A/B testing are useful in understanding which variations perform the best, and ultimately in determining which had the greatest influence on a particular performance metric.

The following is an example of how A/B testing can be used. Suppose customers who are visiting a website to purchase facemasks are randomly assigned to Treatment A or Treatment B. The website layout for both treatments is the same (see Exhibit 12-11). The only difference is the color of the purchase button. Customers in Treatment A see a black "Add to Bag" button, while customers in Treatment B see a blue "Add to Bag" button. Does the color of the purchase button influence whether visitors click the button to add the facemask to the cart?

The hypothesis is that for Treatment A, using the black "Add to Bag" button results in lower clicks, while for Treatment B, using the blue "Add to Bag" button results in higher clicks.

Success will be measured by reporting the number of clicks on the "Add to Bag" button.

Most web analytics software reports a conversion rate for customers who saw Treatment A and customers who saw Treatment B. For instance, a report may indicate that for Treatment A (black button), conversion is 11 percent (+/−1.5 percent) and for Treatment B (blue button), conversion is 15 percent (+/−1.3 percent). That means, on average, 11 percent of users clicked on the black button and 15 percent of users clicked on the blue button. Marketing analysts sometimes refer to the improved conversion as a 4 percent uplift (15 percent − 11 percent). Of course, in addition to conversion rates, the analytics software provides information to enable marketers to optimize other aspects of the customer purchase journey.

Exhibit 12-11 E-Commerce Website for Treatments A and B

Treatment A (**ADD TO BAG** Black Color)

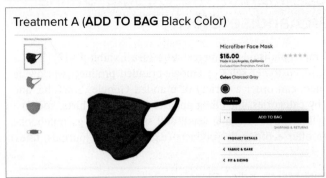

Treatment B (**ADD TO BAG** Blue Color)

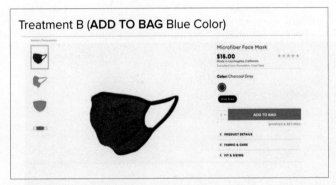

Banana Republic.

Case Study E-Commerce: The Google Online Merchandise Store

Google maintains an official merchandise e-commerce store (see Exhibit 12-12). The store was established to support customer sales of Google-branded products worldwide. In the Google e-store, customers can order a variety of branded Google, YouTube, and Android products organized by categories, including apparel (e.g., hats, shirts, socks), lifestyle (e.g., drinkware, sunglasses, pins, magnet sets), and stationery (e.g., notebooks, pens, and stickers). They also offer ecofriendly products (e.g., tumblers, journals, totes).

Exhibit 12-12 Google Official Merchandise Store

Google

Understanding the Business Problem

As of June 2020, the Google e-commerce store had over $10.7 million in revenue. These sales represented a total of 65,307 transactions, an average order value of $163.59, and an overall conversation rate of 1.40 percent. Over the past two years, however, the revenue generated from the e-commerce website has dropped substantially (Exhibit 12-13). Google wants to know why the revenue has dropped.

Understanding the Dataset

Recall that the customer journey is a process consisting of several stages: (1) previous experience the customer might possess, (2) the prepurchase stage when the customer

Exhibit 12-13 E-Commerce Overview for Google Official Merchandise Store

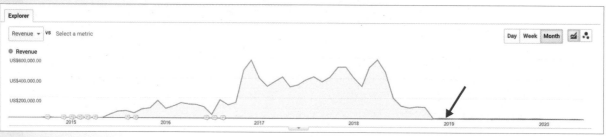

Google Analytics

becomes aware of or searches for the product or service, (3) the purchase stage when the customer selects a product or service and buys it, and (4) the postpurchase stage where the customer uses the product or service and shares information with the company and others. Throughout the purchase journey, customers search for information and interact with companies through various digital touchpoints. Company websites help in building awareness to acquire customers, engage customers and capture their behavior, and hopefully convert visitors to customers through the purchase of products or services. The advantage of an online store over a physical store is that every interaction with the user, through every touchpoint, is tracked. The result of this tracking is that trends are developed and can be analyzed over time. For instance, results indicate where customers originate from (e.g., paid advertising, social media accounts), the demographics of customers (e.g., age, gender), and even the technology they use (e.g., mobile phone, tablet, laptop).

For this case study, data is accessed using a demo Google Analytics account. The data includes incoming user web traffic to the Google Official Merchandise Store. The demo account is current and represents all transactions associated with the Google Merchandise e-commerce store in the past five years. Analysis of the data from the account enables us to understand online purchase behavior and use that knowledge to better market products and services.

When companies choose to use the Google Analytics tool for their own website, how is data collected for online user interactions? Google provides an analytics tool to companies with websites. There is a basic free version of this tool and a more advanced paid version. The free version has limited capabilities, but it is still very useful for companies. Once the Google Analytics account is setup, Google provides a tracking code for a company to install on its site. This tracking code captures every interaction with the user and sends the data to the Google Analytics platform. The tool then organizes the information in meaningful reports. For example, data is collected on the website traffic source, geographic location, type of browser, operating system, device brand name of the users, and more.

Applying the Concepts

After reviewing what Google Analytics reports, which questions do you need to ask to better understand what is occurring on the website? Here are some suggestions:

- What are the top ten products being purchased?
- What are customer profiles?
- What is the customer reach, or how many users started at least one session on the website during a certain time period?
- What are the touchpoints driving the highest sales conversions?
- Where should the company advertise?
- When and why are customers churning, or leaving, the website?

Getting Started with Google Analytics

Google Analytics is an online platform that collects user engagement data from company websites. Google Analytics collects and stores the information, and then aggregates the data and makes it available to companies in a dashboard format that summarizes the information. The purpose of the dashboard is to help companies understand overall website users' profiles, engagement, and conversion. Web data can also be combined with other customer data sources and analyzed using Google Analytics. Reports from Google Analytics can be organized using several criteria, such as data source, date, and other performance metrics. Data stored in the Google Analytics system cannot be altered and reports are "view only."

In the following, we have defined a few commonly used terms employed by Google Analytics. This will help you better understand the dashboard reports. The terms include:

- **Session:** A session starts when the user lands on a page and it expires after 30 minutes of user inactivity. The time limit can be adjusted as needed in the admin section of Google Analytics. If a user leaves the page and returns later, this is considered a new session.

- **Channel:** A channel is the mechanism in which the user found the website. Some common types of channels are:

  a. *Organic:* User lands on the website through unpaid search results such as Google, Yahoo, Bing, or Baidu.

  b. *Social:* User lands on the page from a social media page link on Twitter, LinkedIn, or Facebook.

  c. *Direct:* User enters the website directly by typing the specific website URL into a browser.

  d. *Paid search:* User comes through a paid search campaign, such as Google Ads.

  e. *Display:* User lands on the site after clicking on a banner ad on another site, such as a news or blog page.

  f. *Referral:* User enters the website after clicking on a link on another website.

  g. *Affiliates:* A subgroup of referral. Affiliates are websites where a relationship exists, and they will get paid when a purchase is completed.

- **Bounce rate:** The bounce rate is the percentage of single page visits in which the user exits without browsing beyond the initial page. This is a key measure to optimize in website setup. Companies use this metric to improve user engagement when they first land on their page. The objective is to manage bounce rates so the user continues on the company website and ultimately makes a purchase. The bounce rate is calculated by dividing the total bounces by the total page session entrances. For example, assume there are 20 bounced visitors on a page and 100 total sessions on the same page. The bounce rate is $(20/100) \times 100 = 20$ percent. Bounce rates are context dependent, meaning they vary by type of product and other variables. As a rule of thumb, however, bounce rates higher than 60 percent typically indicate that the audience needs are not met with the setup of the site, the quality of the page is not engaging, or the customer found what they were looking for on one page.

- **Conversion rate:** Conversion rate is measured as the number of completed sales transactions divided by the total number of sessions. For example, assume there are four purchases and 300 total sessions. The conversion rate is $(4/300) \times 100 = 1.33$ percent.

To answer the business questions for this case study, you will execute the following steps: (1) Accessing the demo account, (2) reviewing the main dashboard, and (3) reviewing several reports, including the:

- Real-time report
- Audience report
- Acquisition report
- Behavior report
- Conversion report

Step 1: Accessing the Demo Account

A Gmail account is required before registering for the demo account. If you don't have a Gmail account, you can sign up here: https://accounts.google.com/signup.

After logging into the Gmail account, open your web browser and search for: "Google analytics demo account." In the search results, click "Google Analytics Demo Account," as shown in Exhibit 12-14.

Exhibit 12-14 Search Results for Google Analytics Demo Account

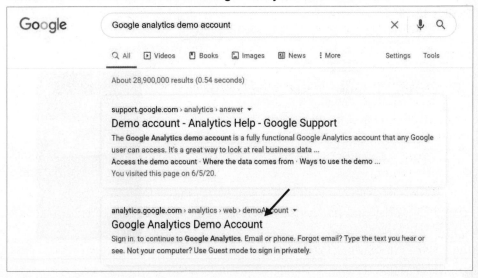

Google

Under the section "Access the Demo Account," click on the "ACCESS DEMO ACCOUNT" hyperlink (Exhibit 12-15). This will load a new page in the Google Analytics platform for the Google Official Merchandise Store.

Exhibit 12-15 Accessing the Google Analytics Demo Account

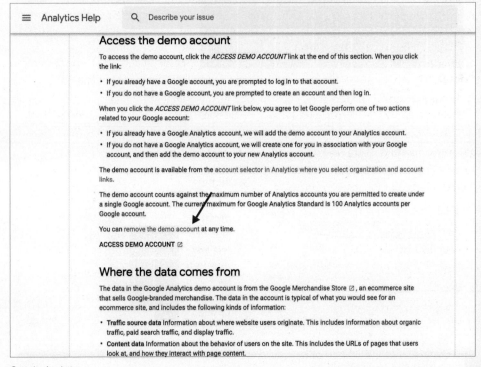

Google Analytics

Step 2: Reviewing the Main Dashboard

The Google Analytics Demo Site will now load. Click on "Home" at the top left side of the screen (Exhibit 12-16). The dashboard in Exhibit 12-16 shows data for website visitors, revenue, conversion rates, and the number of sessions over the past seven days.

Exhibit 12-16

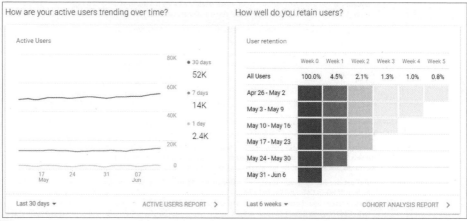

Google Analytics

It also shows the details of real-time users and main traffic channels that bring users to the website, heat maps of users' geographic locations, and the times and days of the week users access the site.

Now, scroll down in the main dashboard and find top products information (Exhibit 12-17). Look at the bottom right corner and find the block titled "What are your top selling products?" Review the default results based on the last seven days. The view can also be changed to show a different time frame. To change the date range, click on "Last 7 days" at the bottom of the chart, and select "Custom" to change the values from January 1, 2020 to the current date, as shown in Exhibit 12-17. Click "Apply." Note, your values will be different from the ones below given the real-time nature of the analysis.

Exhibit 12-17

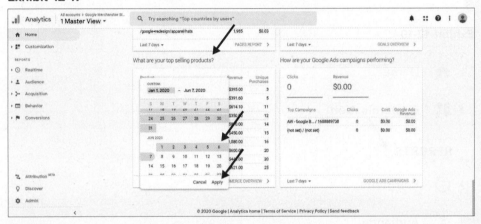

Google Analytics

Applying the time filter will change the table values shown in Exhibit 12-18. The resulting table shows the top products sold by revenue covering the period

Exhibit 12-18

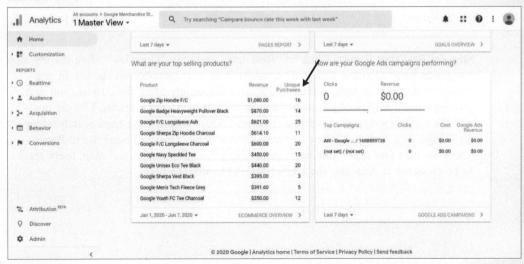

Google Analytics

January 2020 to the current date (our current date is June 7, 2020). The top three products by revenue for our time frame are Google zip hoodie, Google badge heavyweight pullover Black, and Google long sleeve (Exhibit 12-18). Remember, your top products will be different based on the time frame selected, because many items are purchased based on seasonal weather considerations.

Consider changing the date to prior years and see how the top ten products change. The product portfolio on the Google Merchandise Store has been evolving and changing over time. Note your initial observations about products that have been in the top ten over the past two years.

Step 3: Reviewing the Reports

Next, examine "Reports" using the navigation panel on the left side (Exhibit 12-19). Click on each of the reports and explore the information it provides.

Exhibit 12-19

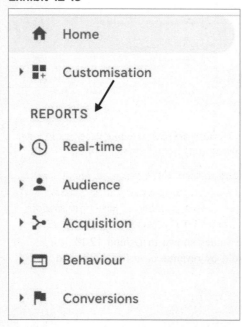

Google Analytics

Step 3a: Real-Time Report. Click on "Real-time" and then "Overview" using the left side navigation panel (Exhibit 12-20). The results show user behavior on the site in real time. At this point in time, a total of 33 users are mainly using the desktop and are arriving from a variety of channels, such as Google.com search results, Google mail, and the support.google.com website (Exhibit 12-20). Visitors have used search terms on Google.com such as "Infant Charcoal Onesie" and "Google Phone Stand Bamboo." There are also four users looking at bags. Using the "Top Locations" map, users seem to be clustered in Asia and the United States (Exhibit 12-20).

Exhibit 12-20

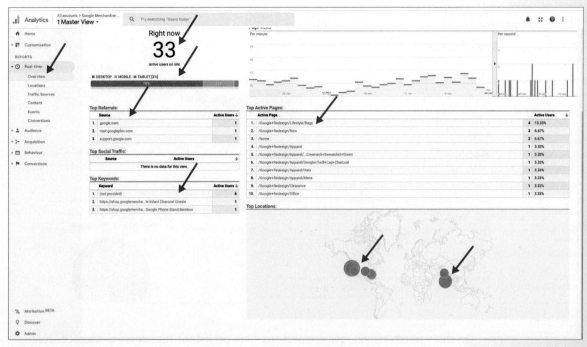

Google Analytics

Step 3b: Audience Reports. The Audience report uncovers users characteristics like age, gender, interest, location, and technology used, as well as users' engagement.

Click on "Audience" and then "Overview" using the left side navigation panel (Exhibit 12-21). This report shows the number of returning users and new users, number of sessions, total number of web pages viewed, number of pages per session, and bounce rate. For the past seven days, there are 79.7% new users and a 51.72% bounce rate (Exhibit 12-21).

Exhibit 12-21

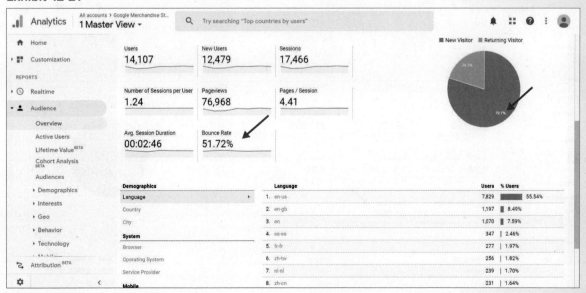

Google Analytics

Exhibit 12-22

Google Analytics

Do these trends remain consistent if the time period for the report is changed from seven days to another specified time period? Using the date filter on the right top corner (Exhibit 12-22), update the date range from January 1, 2020 to your current date (our current date is June 7, 2020) using the Custom option. Click "Apply." Examine how the trends change and make notes on the patterns you identify.

In Exhibit 12-23, the results indicate there are 84% new users and a slightly lower bounce rate (48.06%), compared to the 7-day average that was examined previously. Furthermore, 53.42% of the web visitors' language is U.S. English.

Now, let's dive deeper into the geographic location of visitors, the browser used, and the operating system on Mobile.

Exhibit 12-23

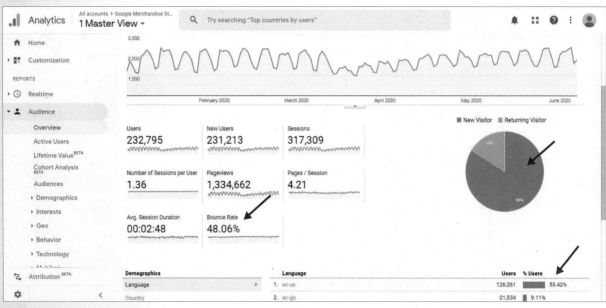

Google Analytics

First, we will explore the geographic locations of the users. Still in the "Overview" under the "Audience" report, click on "Country" under the "Demographics" section (Exhibit 12-24). We see in Exhibit 12-24 that the users mainly come from the United States, India, the United Kingdom, and Canada. At this point, you can also explore the users' City under "Demographics," as well as the Browser and Operating System using the links under "System." What noteworthy patterns do you notice? What marketing strategies could these patterns suggest?

Exhibit 12-24

Google Analytics

Next, under the "Audience" report, click on "Active Users" using the left side navigation panel (Exhibit 12-25). This report helps assess the "website reach" as measured by how many users started at least one session on the website during the specified time period. At the top of the Active Users chart, check the box for "7 Day Active Users," "14 Day Active Users," and "28 Day Active Users" to visually represent the incremental increase

Exhibit 12-25

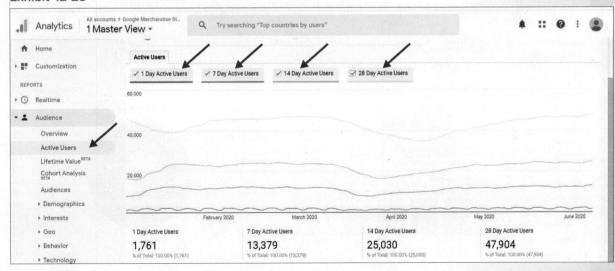

Google Analytics

Exhibit 12-26

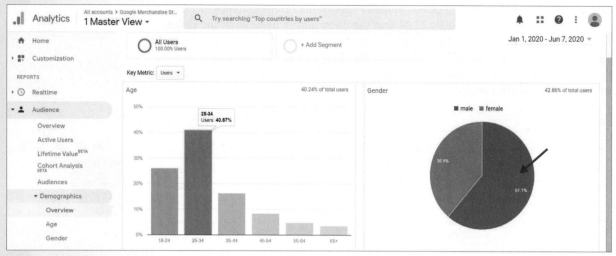

Google Analytics

in reach, as shown in Exhibit 12-25. We anticipate that the trend is healthy, which indicates a growing market over time. This is visible in Exhibit 12-25.

Still under the "Audience" report, click on "Demographics" and then click on "Overview" using the left side navigation panel (Exhibit 12-26). For the period between January 1, 2020 and June 7, 2020 there were 40.87% of the users between the ages of 25 and 34 with 61.1% of users being male. Now review the demographics overview report. Are the correct users being targeted through messages, design, and the digital marketing campaign? Note: Demographics reports will not display any data if the web traffic is low because no meaningful segments can be created with a low number of users.

Is the bounce rate the same across the different age groups? What about gender? To examine these questions, you need to change the key metric under the Demographics Overview from users to bounce rate. To do so, click on the drop-down menu next to "Key Metric" and select "Bounce Rate," as shown in Exhibit 12-27.

Exhibit 12-27

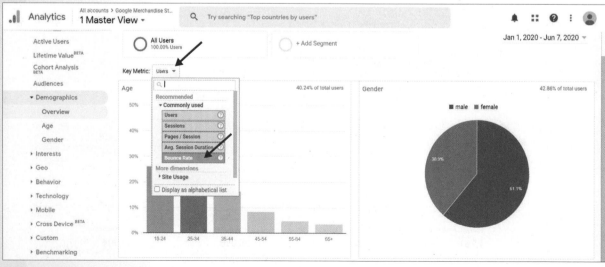

Google Analytics

Exhibit 12-28

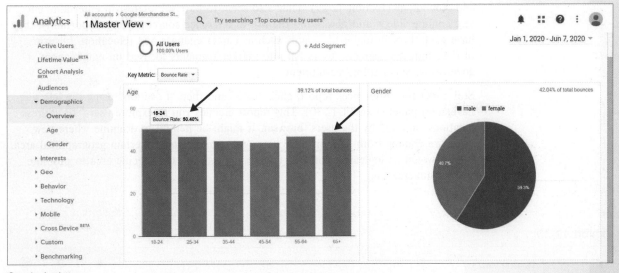

Google Analytics

Exhibit 12-28 indicates that users 18–24 and 65+ tend to have a slightly higher bounce rate compared to the other age groups. That means they exit after the landing page slightly more often than other age groups.

Still under the "Audience" report, click on "Interest" using the left side navigation panel (Exhibit 12-29). Then, click on "Overview" to discover what the users' interests are across the internet. Understanding users' interests will help identify more specific cross-selling and up-selling opportunities for more specific target customer segments. It will also help decide on which affiliate websites to advertise certain products.

Exhibit 12-29

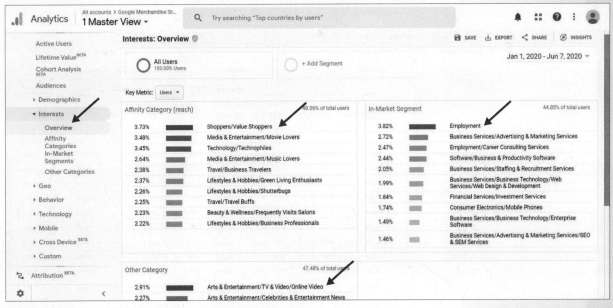

Google Analytics

Users from January 1, 2020 to June 7, 2020 seem to enjoy value shopping, movies, and technology (Exhibit 12-29). They also seem to have an interest in entertainment (e.g., online videos and news) and the use of reference sources. More importantly, they have gone through major life events such as career changes and relocation. In terms of their industry segment, users fall into market segments focused on employment, advertising, and staffing/recruitment.

Still under the "Audience" report, click "Geo" and then "Location" using the left side navigation panel (Exhibit 12-30). This report enables you to explore users' IP address locations captured by the users' browser. It might be helpful to examine where new users are coming from. If more new users are coming from a certain geographical area, then it would be logical to consider advertising more in the specific area to promote the e-commerce site.

Exhibit 12-30

Google Analytics

Exhibit 12-30 shows how Japan has higher revenue compared to other countries with a similar number of users. This type of analysis can help identify markets that are underreached and preferred locations in which to market products and invest in potential loyalty programs.

Note other interesting patterns. For instance, Italy has a fairly high bounce rate. Why are users in Italy leaving the site at a higher rate after viewing a single page compared to other countries? Should the page be translated into Italian? Should product selections be personalized to local trends?

To help answer these questions, we must review the data by examining cities in Italy. Click on Italy in the world heat map or in the list of countries, as shown in Exhibit 12-30.

You can click on any region on the map to open the cities where the users are coming from. For Italy, the highest number of the users are logging into the site from Milan (Exhibit 12-31). Most of the cities have a high bounce rate and had no revenue generated from January 1, 2020 to June 7, 2020. What other patterns do you notice?

Exhibit 12-31

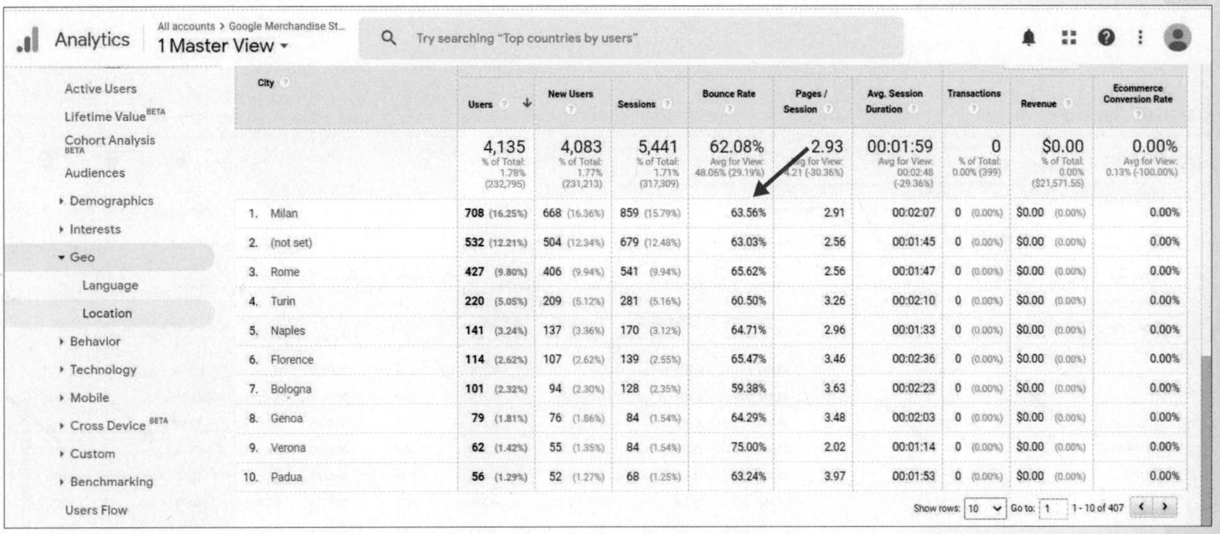

City	Users	New Users	Sessions	Bounce Rate	Pages / Session	Avg. Session Duration	Transactions	Revenue	Ecommerce Conversion Rate
	4,135 % of Total: 1.78% (232,795)	4,083 % of Total: 1.77% (231,213)	5,441 % of Total: 1.71% (317,909)	62.08% Avg for View: 48.06% (29.19%)	2.93 Avg for View: 4.21 (-30.36%)	00:01:59 Avg for View: 00:02:48 (-29.36%)	0 % of Total: 0.00% (399)	$0.00 % of Total: 0.00% ($21,571.55)	0.00% Avg for View: 0.13% (-100.00%)
1. Milan	708 (16.25%)	668 (16.36%)	859 (15.79%)	63.56%	2.91	00:02:07	0 (0.00%)	$0.00 (0.00%)	0.00%
2. (not set)	532 (12.21%)	504 (12.34%)	679 (12.48%)	63.03%	2.56	00:01:45	0 (0.00%)	$0.00 (0.00%)	0.00%
3. Rome	427 (9.80%)	406 (9.94%)	541 (9.94%)	65.62%	2.56	00:01:47	0 (0.00%)	$0.00 (0.00%)	0.00%
4. Turin	220 (5.05%)	209 (5.12%)	281 (5.16%)	60.50%	3.26	00:02:10	0 (0.00%)	$0.00 (0.00%)	0.00%
5. Naples	141 (3.24%)	137 (3.36%)	170 (3.12%)	64.71%	2.96	00:01:33	0 (0.00%)	$0.00 (0.00%)	0.00%
6. Florence	114 (2.62%)	107 (2.62%)	139 (2.55%)	65.47%	3.46	00:02:36	0 (0.00%)	$0.00 (0.00%)	0.00%
7. Bologna	101 (2.32%)	94 (2.30%)	128 (2.35%)	59.38%	3.63	00:02:23	0 (0.00%)	$0.00 (0.00%)	0.00%
8. Genoa	79 (1.81%)	76 (1.86%)	84 (1.54%)	64.29%	3.48	00:02:03	0 (0.00%)	$0.00 (0.00%)	0.00%
9. Verona	62 (1.42%)	55 (1.35%)	84 (1.54%)	75.00%	2.02	00:01:14	0 (0.00%)	$0.00 (0.00%)	0.00%
10. Padua	56 (1.29%)	52 (1.27%)	68 (1.25%)	63.24%	3.97	00:01:53	0 (0.00%)	$0.00 (0.00%)	0.00%

Google Analytics

Still under the "Audience" report, click on "Behavior" using the left side navigation panel to develop an understanding of new versus returning website visitors (Exhibit 12-32). Now, click on "New vs Returning." Check the boxes next to "New Visitor" and "Returning Visitor" and then click "Plot Rows" (Exhibit 12-32). This will display on the graph new visitors versus returning visitors. Notice that higher transactions and revenues are associated with new visitors to the website (Exhibit 12-32). However, they also have a higher bounce rate. This is a useful report to compare over time and ensure that new and returning user ratios align with the marketing strategy.

Still under the "Audience" report, click on "Technology" and then "Browser & OS" using the left side navigation panel (Exhibit 12-33). Using this report, identify the technology applied by the user to access the website. Under the "Primary Dimension" menu, click "Operating System" to view results by operating system type. Notice that 0.79 percent of conversions occur using the iOS platform on the iPhone and iPod Touch. Upon further examination, it is evident that $14,873 of the revenue from January 1, 2020 to June 7, 2020 has been generated on iOS (Exhibit 12-33). It is important to ensure that the website is mobile friendly for all the major mobile devices.

Exhibit 12-32

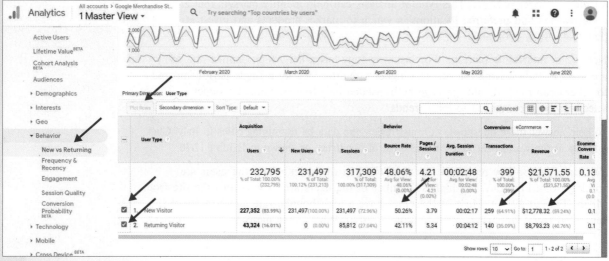

Google Analytics

Exhibit 12-33

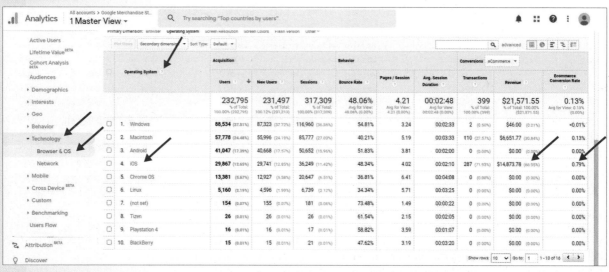

Google Analytics

Other questions you can answer by examining the technology types could include: Are users migrating from desktop to mobile? What are the common devices used to access the website? Learning details of the technology used to access the site will help us optimize experiences for the technology commonly used.

Step 3c: Acquisition Reports. Next, click on "Acquisition" and then "Overview" using the left-hand navigation panel (Exhibit 12-34). This report will compare the site performance across the different marketing touchpoints. From the report, you can identify which touchpoints brought quality users to the site. The report can also be used to show where advertising might be most effective for acquiring new users. After a user lands on a website, the tracking script is able to collect attributes including traffic source, which identifies where the user navigated from.

Exhibit 12-34

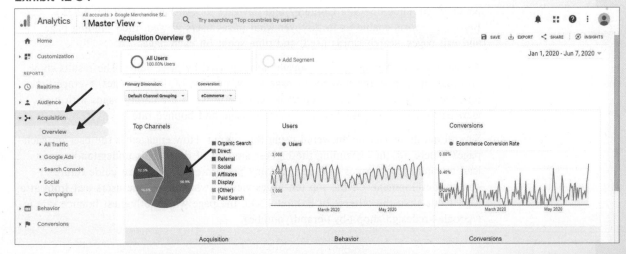

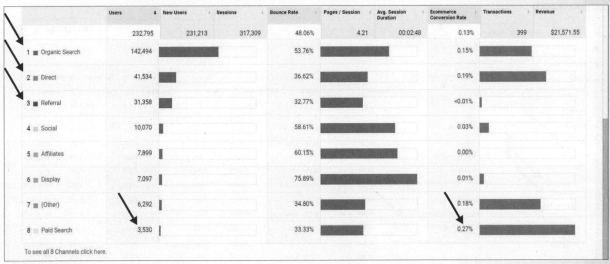

Google Analytics

As shown in Exhibit 12-34, the majority of users are arriving to the site through organic searches (i.e., unpaid search results such as Google, Yahoo, Bing, or Baidu), direct channel (i.e., typing address into URL), and referral (i.e., directed traffic from another website). The quality of the traffic can be measured using bounce rate and conversion rate. Review Exhibit 12-34 and consider how the company might use this information to acquire new customers, influence customer behavior, and convert visitors into customers.

Continuing with Exhibit 12-34, review the bounce rate. The Referral group has the lowest bounce rate. That means people in this group are navigating on the website beyond a single page. The problem is that this group also has the lowest conversion rate. What else can you learn about referral traffic to convert users into a purchasing customer? The Direct channel has a lower bounce rate than organic search and a higher conversion rate. Another interesting observation is the paid advertising channel has the highest conversion rate (0.27) and the lowest bounce rate. However, only 3,530 users arrived to the site via paid search. One possible recommendation would be to invest more in paid advertising to drive high-quality traffic to the website, because this group is more likely to have higher conversion and a lower bounce rate.

Step 3d: Behavior Reports. Next, click on "Behavior" using the left-hand navigation panel. Then, click on "Site Content" and navigate to "All Pages" (Exhibit 12-35). Behavior reports enable us to discover what pages users viewed, their landing page and exit pages, search words used, and time spent on each page.

As can be seen in Exhibit 12-35, results are reported by page name. The results show information such as the number of page views, number of unique pages, average time on page, and page value. This report is very useful when evaluating pages with high view performance against the time spent on page and bounce rate.

Several questions can be answered using this output. How engaged is the user on each page? Where are they spending the highest amount of time? This understanding can lead to ranking web pages as best and worst performers so they can guide future content development. Of the top ten pages viewed, what is the one users exit from at a higher rate than the others? In Exhibit 12-35, the page with the highest bounce rate is (/google+redesign/shop+by+brand/youtube).

Exhibit 12-35

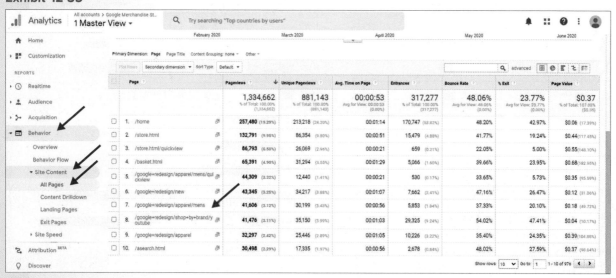

Google Analytics

Click the pop-out window button to go to the page link (/google+redesign/shop+by +brand/youtube), given that it has the highest exit rate for the time frame between January 1, 2020 and June 7, 2020. The landing page in Exhibit 12-36 will open. Study the page carefully to identify some reasons why the user is exiting the site upon landing on this page. Is the product display optimal? What types of products are presented? What can the company do to reduce the exit rate? What can be learned from pages with the lowest exit rates? Answering these types of questions is essential in creating a better user experience for visitors.

Step 3e: Conversion Reports. Using the Conversions report, you can track the website goals and compare this to the business objectives. Is the goal to maximize sales? Maximize brand exposure? Increase the number of loyal customers? Optimize advertising? Maximize the conversion rate? Minimize the bounce rate? - or a combination of several or all of these.

Google Analytics enables you to measure your success in achieving your business goals and manage them over time. We will review one of the conversion reports that is helpful in measuring performance.

Exhibit 12-36

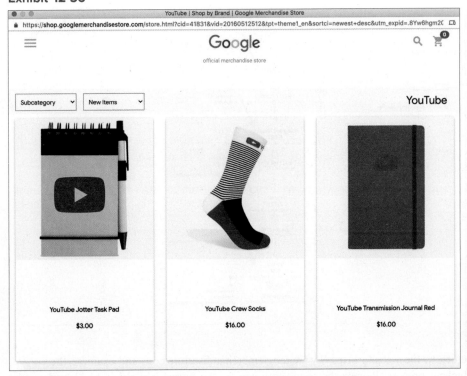

Google Analytics

Click on "Conversions" using the left side navigation panel. Now click on "Goals" and then "Funnel Visualization," and scroll down to view the funnel in Exhibit 12-37. This report shows the funnel in the checkout process (e.g., cart, billing and shipping, payment). Identify where the users are leaving the site at the checkout process. This information could suggest website layout issues or possibly slow processing times that need attention to optimize the checkout process.

Notice how in Exhibit 12-37 under Cart, only 18.02% users proceed from the cart to billing and shipping. Of those who make it to the billing and shipping stage, about 48.27% proceed to payment. However, from payment information to review order, there is a significant loss of users, with only 24.77% moving on to the review order stage. Once the user reviews the page, you can see that 60.98% complete the purchase process. Each of these processes requires deeper examination to better understand why users are leaving the checkout process. Once we have a better understanding, we can then make recommendations regarding improvements.

The following are some possible solutions to address these issues:

- *What can be done to improve Cart to the Billing and Shipping process?* In addition to the current Google email checkout option, the company could consider the use of a guest checkout process to reduce the burden on the user to sign up for a new account.

- *What can be done to improve the Payment to order Review process?* The company could offer easier payment options using a Google Pay account that is already linked to Gmail, because a considerable amount of purchases in the dataset from January 1, 2020 to June 7, 2020 took place on iOS, the company might consider enabling Apple Pay for a seamless integrated payment.

Exhibit 12-37

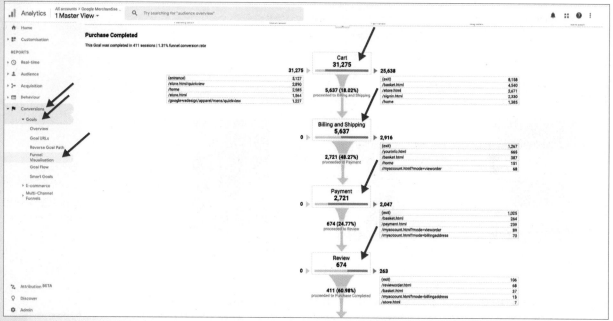

Google Analytics

Return to the website https://www.googlemerchandisestore.com and examine the checkout process. Review the page setup against the funnel in Exhibit 12-37, and provide other improvement ideas based on your observations. Note that tools often make changes to improve functionality and that some options might be available now that were not available at the time this case was written.

Insights Learned from Applying the Concepts

A wealth of information is available for business decision making when using Google Analytics. This platform and other similar tools provide an understanding of search and shopping patterns that can guide informative marketing campaigns and design choices for the website.

Many marketing problems can be solved with digital marketing analytics. In this case, what insights were revealed? Recall several of the initial questions in the case:

- What is the customer reach or how many users started at least one session on the website during a certain time period?
- What are the touchpoints driving the highest sales conversions?
- Where should the company advertise?
- When and why are customers churning, or leaving the website?

Insights discovered from using Google Analytics can be used to enhance the customer purchase journey. The information can be applied to create awareness, stimulate engagement, and convert visitors into customers. For example, now that there is an understanding of users' interests and profiles, marketers can identify more specific cross-selling and up-selling opportunities. They can also use this information to determine affiliate websites on which to advertise certain products. Finally, knowing the technology being used to enter the website makes it possible to reconsider methods of payment to increase customer conversion rate.

Now, that you have a basic understanding of Google Analytics, it might be useful to study it for the Google Analytics Individual Qualification (GAIQ) test. You can earn

Exhibit 12-38

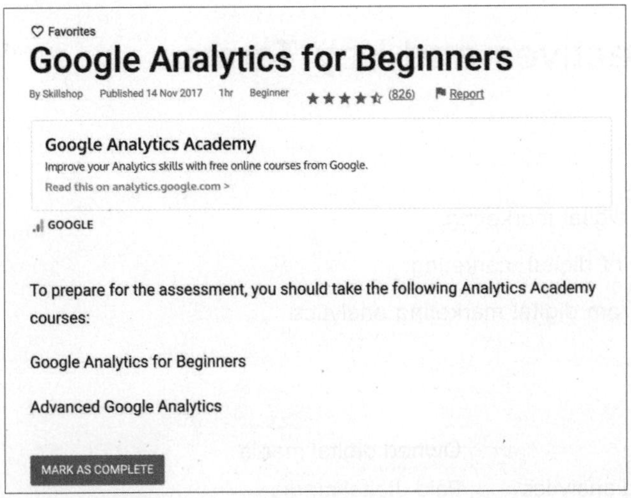

Google Analytics

> ♡ Favorites
>
> # Google Analytics for Beginners
>
> By Skillshop   Published 14 Nov 2017   1hr   Beginner   ★★★★☆ (826)   ⚑ Report
>
> ---
>
> **Google Analytics Academy**
> Improve your Analytics skills with free online courses from Google.
> Read this on analytics.google.com >
>
> ---
>
> ▁▂▃ GOOGLE
>
> ---
>
> To prepare for the assessment, you should take the following Analytics Academy
> courses:
>
> Google Analytics for Beginners
>
> Advanced Google Analytics
>
> [MARK AS COMPLETE]

Google Analytics

a Google Analytics Certification by following the instructions in Exhibit 12-38. This will provide a good signal to employers that you are committed to your career advancement in the field of Marketing Analytics.

A Final Note

We enjoyed writing these chapters for you and hope you enjoyed your learning journey with us. The skills you have developed in this textbook are in high demand in the marketplace. We are confident that as you apply these skills in your future organization, you will be contributing to its competitive positioning in the market.

We believe analytics will continue to shape the future of marketing for many years. For that reason, we are excited that you are on the forefront of this change.

Summary of Learning Objectives and Key Terms

LEARNING OBJECTIVES

Objective 12.1 Define digital marketing.

Objective 12.2 Understand the importance of digital marketing.

Objective 12.3 Investigate different use cases of digital marketing.

Objective 12.4 Evaluate and interpret results from digital marketing analytics.

KEY TERMS

Amazon effect	Digital marketing	Owned digital media
A/B testing	Digital marketing analytics	Paid digital media
Bounce rate	Earned digital media	Session
Channel	Multichannel attribution	Treatment
Conversion rate	Multivariate testing	

Discussion and Review Questions

1. Define digital marketing.

2. How can marketers use digital marketing analytics?

3. What are the three categories of digital marketing media touchpoints?

4. List several examples of touchpoints for each digital marketing media.

5. What are some basic and complex measurements associated with digital marketing analytics?

6. Describe A/B testing and explain its purpose.

Critical Thinking and Marketing Applications

1. Consider the data in the Google Analytics reports. What external data might be helpful to combine with this data to drive more insights?

2. Exhibit 12-28 indicates which age groups are exiting the landing page at a slightly higher rate. Brainstorm some ideas that might be helpful to keep them engaged longer on our website.

References

1. Tessa Roberts, "5 Natural Language Processing Examples: How NLP Is Used," Bloomreach, September 2019, https://www.bloomreach.com/en/blog/2019/09/natural-language-processing.html; The Daily Egg, "The 15 Second Rule: 3 Reasons Why Users Leave a Website," Crazy Egg, May 25, 2020, https://www.crazyegg.com/blog/why-users-leave-a-website; and Jakob Nielsen, "How Long Do Users Stay on Web Pages?" Nielsen Norman Group, September 11, 2011, https://www.nngroup.com/articles/how-long-do-users-stay-on-web-pages.

2. Dan Alaimo, "87% of Shoppers Now Begin Product Searches Online," *Retail Dive*, August 15, 2018, https://www.retaildive.com/news/87-of-shoppers-now-begin-product-searches-online/530139; Heike Young, "Nine Stats About the Retail Customer Journey in 2019," Salesforce blog, April 9, 2019, https://www.salesforce.com/blog/2019/04/customer-retail-statistics.html; and Blake Morgan, "50 Retail Innovation Stats that Prove the Power of Customer Experience," *Forbes*, May 21, 2019, https://www.forbes.com/sites/blakemorgan/2019/05/21/50-retail-innovation-stats-power-customer-experience.

3. Paige Cooper, "140+ Social Media Statistics that Matter to Marketers in 2020," Hootsuite, February 20, 2020, https://blog.hootsuite.com/social-media-statistics-for-social-media-managers.

4. Rob Roy, "How Sprint Won the Race for Customer Satisfaction," Adobe, https://www.adobe.com/customer-success-stories/sprint-case-study.html.

5. "Nissan Case Study," Adobe, https://www.adobe.com/customer-success-stories/nissan-case-study.html.

6. Travis Trembath, "How the PGA TOUR Drives Fan Engagement," Adobe, https://www.adobe.com/customer-success-stories/pga-tour-case-study.html.

7. "Doing Business the Digital Way: How Capital One Fundamentally Disrupted the Financial Services Industry," Capgemini Consulting, July 2017, https://www.capgemini.com/wp-content/uploads/2017/07/capital-one-doing-business-the-digital-way_0.pdf.

8. Dan Stroker, "How Obama Raised $60 Million by Running a Simple Experiment," Optimizely, November 29, 2011, https://blog.optimizely.com/2010/11/29/how-obama-raised-60-million-by-running-a-simple-experiment.

GLOSSARY

A/B testing A/B testing (also known as split testing) enables marketers to experiment with different digital options to identify which ones are likely to be the most effective.

activation functions Activation functions consist of mathematical calculations that are performed within the hidden and output layers of the neural network. These functions enable the model to detect non-linear relationships.

agglomerative clustering Agglomerative cluster (a bottom-up approach) is where each observation is initially considered to be a separate cluster. A linkage method is used to merge smaller clusters into larger clusters.

aggregation Aggregation refers to the summing of data according to the unit of analysis desired. For example, summing all weekly data into quarterly data.

Amazon effect The Amazon effect refers to the often-disruptive influence e-commerce and digital market-places have had on traditional brick-and-mortar retailers.

Apriori algorithm The Apriori algorithm identifies combinations of items in datasets that are associated with each other.

artificial intelligence Artificial intelligence (AI) is a branch of computer science that is designed to mimic human-like intelligence for certain tasks, such as discovering patterns in data, recognizing objects from an image, understanding the meaning of text, and processing voice commands.

association rule An association rule helps define relationships in a transaction dataset using if-then statements.

Automated Machine Learning (AutoML) A mainly supervised approach that explores and selects models using different algorithms and compares their predictive performance.

average linkage Average linkage is a method in hierarchical clustering, and is defined by the group average of observations from one cluster to all observations from another cluster.

backpropogation Backpropagation transmits the total loss back into the neural network to understand the amount of loss from each neuron.

backward elimination Backward elimination is a quantitative approach to identify the independent variable to include in a model. It starts with all the independent variables in the model first and each one is deleted one

at a time if they are not significant. The process stops when all variables in the model are significant.

bagging Bagging is short for "Bootstrap Aggregating." There are two main steps in bagging. Step 1 generates multiple random smaller samples from the larger sample. The second step in bagging is to execute a model on each sample and then combine the results.

bag of words The bag of words technique counts the occurrence of words in a document while ignoring the order or the grammar of words.

balance Balance refers to how objects or shapes are distributed to correctly use space. There are three different types of balance: symmetrical, asymmetrical, and radial.

betweenness centrality Betweenness centrality measures centrality based on the number of times a node is on the shortest path between other nodes. This measure helps identify individuals who influence the flow of information in a social network.

bias Bias is the constant value given to the weighted input of each node. Bias is learned by the model and helps to create flexibility and the best model fit for the data.

big data Big data is the term typically used to describe massive amounts of data. It is a relative term that requires special tools to manage and analyze.

binary Binary categorical data can have only two values—for example, yes or no. This can be represented in different ways such as 1 or 0 or "True" and "False." Binary data is commonly used for classification in predictive modeling.

boosting Boosting helps reduce error in the model. Boosting achieves this by observing the error records in a model and then oversampling misclassified records in the next model created.

bounce rate The bounce rate is the percentage of single page visits in which the user exits without browsing beyond the initial page.

categorical data Categorical data exists when values represent a group of categories. Categorical variables can be one of three types: binary, nominal, or ordinal.

categorical variables A categorical variable is when the data represents one of a limited number of categories. Geographic location (e.g., Northeast, Southeast, Northwest, Southwest, Midwest) is an example of a categorical variable.

channel A channel is the mechanism in which the user found the website.

closeness centrality Closeness centrality measures the proximity of a node to all other nodes in the network. The measure is calculated for each node based on its sum of shortest paths.

cluster analysis In cluster analysis, groups are created based upon similarities to determine if any observations have a considerable distance to other clusters.

cognitive analytics Cognitive analytics uses advanced analytics capabilities to draw conclusions and develop insights hidden in data without being explicitly programmed.

collaborative filtering Collaborative filtering uses the idea of identifying relevant items for a specific user from a large set of items by taking into consideration the preferences of many similar users. Collaborative filtering is based on data such as what a user has bought in the past, which items a user liked, and what the other similar customers have viewed and bought.

complete linkage Complete linkage is a method in hierarchical clustering, and is defined by the maximum distance between observations in two different clusters.

computer vision Computer vision refers to the ability of a machine to extract meaning from image pixels such as faces, scenes, or objects.

confidence Confidence measures the conditional probability of the consequent actually occurring given that the antecedent occurs. It is calculated as the count of purchases consisting of both items in the association rule divided by the total number of times the antecedent item is purchased.

connections Connections within a neural network transmit information from one neuron (node) to another. Each network consists of connected neurons and each connection is weighted.

continuous data Continuous data includes values with decimals: 1, 1.4, 3.75, . . .

conversion rate Conversion rate is measured as the number of completed sales transactions divided by the total number of sessions.

conviction Conviction is the ratio of the expected frequency that the antecedent occurs without the consequent if items were separate, and then divided by the frequency of incorrect predictions.

corpus A corpus refers to a collection of a large body of text that is ready to be preprocessed.

correlation Correlation estimates the relationship between two or more numerical variables.

database A database contains collected data from company operations.

data lake A data lake (often included in Hadoop systems) is a storage repository that holds a large amount of data in its native format. It is typically used to investigate data patterns and to archive data for future use.

data management Data management as a process is the lifecycle management of data from acquisition to disposal.

data mart A data mart is a subset of the data warehouse that provides a specific value to a group of users. For example, a marketing data mart would be limited to data on customers, sales, products, and similar marketing metrics. There are two types of data marts: dependent and independent.

data quality Data quality refers to attributes such as timeliness, completeness, accuracy, consistency, and format of the dataset.

data visualization Data visualization combines data analysis with computer graphics to efficiently identify trends, patterns, relationships, and outliers. Data visualization encodes quantitative values into graphical formats so data can be presented visually.

data warehouse A data warehouse contains historical data from various databases throughout a company and provides a structured environment for high-speed querying. A data warehouse consists of data from different functional areas of the firm such as customer data, accounting data, and human resources data.

deep learning Deep learning uses an algorithm to build neural network models that classify or predict target variables. They are often used for speech recognition and image identification.

degree centrality Degree centrality measures centrality based on the number of edges that are connected to a node.

density Density measures the extent to which the edges are connected in the network and indicates how fast the information is transmitted.

dependent (target) variable (Y) The variable being predicted is referred to as the dependent (target) variable (Y).

dependent variable (also target or outcome) The dependent variable is the target variable (y). Its outcome is impacted by other variables.

descriptive analytics Descriptive analytics are a set of techniques used to explain or quantify the past.

design elements Design elements are visual attributes describing various elements of a display. These building blocks of design can be represented by seven elements: color, form, line, shape, space, texture, and typography.

deviation Deviation analysis shows changes (departures) compared to another standard or value of reference.

differential market basket analysis Differential market basket analysis is the use of market basket analysis techniques across stores, locations, seasons, days of the week, and so forth.

digital marketing Digital marketing is the use of marketing touchpoints that are executed electronically through a digital channel to communicate and interact with current and potential customers and partners

digital marketing analytics Digital marketing analytics enables marketers to monitor, understand, and evaluate the performance of digital marketing initiatives.

dimension Dimensions consist of qualitative or categorical information and usually identify variable names.

directed network A directed network relationship is typically depicted using a line with a directional arrow from one node to another.

discrete data Discrete data is measured in whole numbers (integers): 1, 2, 3, . . .

distribution of node degrees The distribution of node degrees measures the degree of relationship (or connectedness) among the nodes.

divisive clustering Divisive clustering (a top-down approach) is where all records are initially assigned to a single cluster. Then, a step-by-step process follows in which the most dissimilar observations (records) are sequentially separated from the initial cluster.

dummy coding Dummy coding involves creating a dichotomous value from a categorical value.

E

earned digital media Communication or exposure not initiated or posted by the company is called earned digital media.

edges Edges are the links and relationships between nodes.

edge weight Edge weight is the strength of the relationship between two nodes. The thicker the line, the higher the exchange between the two nodes.

egocentric network An egocentric network is an individual network such as a social media network on Facebook or LinkedIn.

eigenvector centrality Eigenvector centrality measures the number of links from a node and the number of connections those nodes have. Eigenvector centrality, also referred to as relational centrality, shows whether a node is well-connected to other nodes, who in turn are also well-connected.

emphasis Involves placing emphasis on important insights to attract the viewer's attention.

ensemble model An ensemble model combines the most favorable elements from all models into a single model.

Euclidean The Euclidean distance is measured as the true straight line distance between two points.

exploratory data analysis Exploratory data analysis provides a summary of the main characteristics within the data. The purpose is to determine what is going on by exploring data trends, types, and values.

external sources of data External sources of data are from outside a business, generally related to the economy, supply chain partners, competitors, weather, or customer-generated social media feedback, for instance.

F

feature Feature is another name for variable.

feature selection Feature selection refers to identifying the optimal subset of features (independent variables) to explain a target variable. Feature selection can be done quantitatively or qualitatively.

forward propagation Forward propagation is the process whereby data from the input layer moves forward through the network.

forward selection Forward selection is a quantitative approach to identify the independent variable to include in a model. A separate regression model is created for each predictor and then variables are added one by one to determine which variables improve the model prediction.

FP-growth algorithm The FP-growth algorithm is used to calculate frequently co-occurring items in a transaction dataset.

frequency distribution Frequency distributions indicate how many observations fall within a certain interval, and the bars do not overlap or touch each other.

G

gain theta Gain theta parameter is similar to confidence. Higher values indicate a stronger relationship between the items.

graph A graph is a visualization that enables viewers to understand the relationship between nodes and the importance of nodes.

H

Hadoop Hadoop is an open-source software that helps distributed computers solve problems of big data computation. Hadoop divides the big data processing over multiple computers, allowing it to handle massive amounts of data simultaneously at a reduced cost.

hidden layer The hidden layer sits in between the input and output layers. Calculations are performed in the hidden layer to produce weights from the input layer.

hierarchical clustering Hierarchical clustering produces solutions in which the data is grouped into a hierarchy of clusters. This method is a widely used method for identifying subgroups to use in market segmentation.

hue Hue is the name of the color, such as red, blue, or green.

independent (predictor or feature) variable (X) The variables used to make the prediction are called independent variables (X) (also referred to as predictors or features).

independent variable The independent variable is the predictor or feature variable (x). This variable could potentially influence or drive the dependent or outcome variable(s).

influencer Influencers are individuals who initiate or actively engage others in conversation and are often well-connected to others in the network.

input layer The data is entered into the neural network analysis in the input layer.

inputs Inputs are values representing features (variables) from the dataset that pass information to the next layer via connections.

integer An integer is a whole number.

internal sources data Internal sources of data typically consist of customer sales and service data.

interval Interval data has an equal distance between data points and does not include an absolute zero.

inverse document frequency (IDF) The inverse document frequency (IDF) measures the frequency of a term (or word) over all the documents.

Jaccard's Jaccard's measures the similarity between two observations based on how dissimilar two observations are from each other.

k-means clustering K-means clustering uses the mean value for each cluster and minimizes the distance to individual observations.

knowledge discovery applications Knowledge discovery applications allow users to upload data to find data trends and patterns without being explicitly programmed.

laplace Laplace K parameter is a confidence estimator that uses support in its estimation. It decreases as support of the antecedent decreases. It ranges from between 0 and 1 with higher values indicating a stronger relationship between the items.

Latent Dirichlet Allocation (LDA) Latent Dirichlet Allocation (LDA) is a popular algorithm for topic modeling. LDA identifies important words in the text and groups them into topics.

learning rate Learning rate determines the speed at which the model can arrive at the most accurate solution. The learning rate consists of positive values that generally range between 0 and 1.

learning weight Learning weight determines the amount of adjustment made to the weights in the network.

lemmatization Lemmatization reduces the word to its lemma form while considering the context of the word, such as the part of speech and meaning.

lift Lift enables us to evaluate the strength of the association. In a lift ratio, we divide the confidence with a benchmark score that is called expected confidence.

linear regression Linear regression is a type of modeling that shows a relationship between the independent and dependent variables. It is represented by a straight line that best fits the data.

link prediction In link prediction, the objective is to predict new links between unconnected nodes. Link prediction uses a variety of methods such as similarity and machine learning algorithms.

Louvain communities Louvain communities measure non-overlapping communities, or groups of closely connected nodes, in the network.

machine learning Machine learning is a statistical method of learning that can be trained without human intervention to understand and identify relationships between previously established variables.

Manhattan Manhattan is where the distance between two points is not straight. It is a path with right turns as if you are walking a grid in a city. It is also referred to as the 'City Block' distance measure.

market basket analysis Market basket analysis, sometimes referred to by marketers as association discovery, uses purchase transaction data to identify associations between products or combinations of products and services that occur together frequently.

marketing analytics Marketing analytics uses data, statistics, mathematics, and technology to solve marketing business problems.

matching Matching measures the similarity between two observations with values that represent the minimum differences between two points.

Mean Absolute Error (MAE) Mean Absolute Error (MAE) measures the absolute difference between the predicted and actual values of the model.

Mean Absolute Percentage Error (MAPE) Mean Absolute Percentage Error (MAPE) is the percentage absolute difference the prediction is, on average, from the actual target.

measure When data is quantitative or numerical, it is considered a measure.

multichannel attribution Multichannel attribution assesses how, when, and where these various touchpoints influence customers.

multicollinearity Multicollinearity is a situation where the predictor variables are highly correlated with each other.

multiple regression Multiple regression is used to determine whether two or more independent variables are good predictors of the single dependent variable.

multivariate testing Multivariate testing enables companies to test whether changing several different variables on their website at the same time leads to a higher conversion rate.

n-grams N-grams is a simple technique that captures the set of co-occurring or continuous sequences of n-items from a large set of text.

natural language processing (NLP) Natural language processing (NLP) is a branch of artificial intelligence (AI) used to identify patterns by reading and understanding meaning from human language.

neural networks Neural networks are algorithms that are trained to recognize patterns in data that are non-linear.

neurons (nodes) They receive input from an external source or from other nodes to calculate an output. Each input has a weight (w) based on its relative importance to other inputs. The hidden nodes apply an activation function to convert inputs into an output.

nodes A node is an entity (e.g., people or product) that is also known as a vertex.

nominal Nominal categorical data consist of characteristics that have no meaningful order.

nominal comparison Nominal comparisons display different quantitative values of subcategories that are not in a specific order and do not share a particular relationship.

normalization Normalization helps bring all variables into the same scale. To normalize a variable, we scale it by subtracting the variable from the mean and then dividing it by the standard deviation.

ordinal Ordinal categorical data represent meaningful values with a natural order but the intervals between scale points may be uneven.

ordinary least squares (OLS) The ordinary least squares (OLS) regression method commonly referred to as linear regression minimizes the sum of squared errors.

outlier A value that is at a considerable distance from any of the other data clusters.

output layer In the output layer, the model arrives at a prediction.

outputs The output is the resulting prediction from the model. It is calculated as:
Output = sum (weights × inputs) + bias

overfitting Overfitting occurs from an overly complex model where the results are limited to the data being used and are not generalizable—which means future relationships cannot be inferred, and results will be inconsistent when using other data.

owned digital media Owned digital media is managed by the company and includes touchpoints such as email marketing, social media pages, and company websites.

paid digital media Exposure that the company pays others to provide is referred to as paid digital media.

part to whole Part to whole relationships consist of categories measured as fractions or ratios.

Piatetsky-Shapiro (p-s) The Piatetsky-Shapiro criteria is used for selecting rules. When examining the items, values between 0 and 1 reflect stronger relationships where negative values reflect no relationship.

power calculation A power calculation helps determine that outcomes will be estimated from a sample with a sufficient level of precision.

predictive analytics Predictive analytics is used to build models based on the past to explain the future.

prescriptive analytics Prescriptive analytics identifies the best optimal course of action or decision.

primary data Primary data is collected for a specific purpose. For example, companies conduct primary research with surveys, focus groups, interviews, observations, and experiments to address problems or answer distinct questions.

principles of design Principles of design are foundational rules to apply when creating visualizations. The six basic principles of design—balance, emphasis, proportion, rhythm, variety, and unity.

proportion Proportion refers to the size of each object in the visualization relative to its importance or numerical value.

**R² ** R² measures the amount of variance in the dependent variable that is predicted by the independent variable(s). The R² value ranges between 0 and 1, and the closer the value is to 1, the better the prediction by the regression model. When the value is near 0, the regression model is not a good predictor of the dependent variable.

rankings Rankings demonstrate a data point's position based upon importance, preference, or achievement.

ratio Ratio values can have an absolute zero point and can be discussed in terms of multiples when comparing one point to another.

regression modeling Regression modeling captures the strength of a relationship between a single numerical dependent or target variable, and one or more (numerical or categorical) predictor variables.

relational database A relational database is a type of database management system (DBMS). It is a collection of interrelated data items organized using software programs to manipulate and access data.

residuals Residuals represent the difference between the observed and predicted value of the dependent variable.

rhythm Rhythm ensures a perception of seamless, visually appealing transition between design elements.

Root Mean Squared Error (RMSE) Root Mean Squared Error (RMSE) indicates how different the residuals are from zero.

sample size A sample size is a portion of data from the entire population.

saturation Saturation is a measure of the intensity or dullness of the color. Colors are highly saturated when they appear pure, whereas desaturated colors look dull.

secondary data Secondary data relies on existing data that has been collected for another purpose.

sentiment analysis Sentiment analysis is a measure of emotions, attitudes, and beliefs.

sentiment polarity Sentiment polarity includes text that contains contradictory or different opinions.

session Starts when the user lands on a page and it expires after a set time of user inactivity.

silhouette score The silhouette score is another way to identify the optimal number of clusters for the data. Is calculated after the cluster algorithm has assigned each observation to a cluster.

simple linear regression Simple linear regression is used when the focus is limited to a single, numeric dependent variable and a single independent variable.

single linkage Single linkage is one method in hierarchical clustering, and is defined by the shortest distance from an object in a cluster to an object from another cluster.

singleton A singleton is a node that is unconnected to all others in the network.

smart data Smart data represents data that is valuable and can be effectively used.

SMART principles SMART principles are used as a goal-setting technique. The acronym stands for specific, measurable, attainable, relevant, and timely.

social network analysis Social network analysis identifies relationships, influencers, information dissemination patterns, and behaviors among connections in a network.

stemming Stemming is the process of removing prefixes or suffixes of words, thus reducing words to a simple or root form.

stepwise selection Stepwise selection is a quantitative approach to identify the independent variable to include in a model. Stepwise selection follows forward selection by adding a variable at each step, but also includes removing variables that no longer meet the threshold. The stepwise selection stops when the remaining predictors in a model satisfy the threshold to remain in the model.

stop words Stop words are uninformative, such as "the" and "and."

streaming data Streaming data is the continuous transfer of data from numerous sources in different formats.

structured data Structured data is made up of records that are organized in rows and columns. This type of data can be stored in a database or spreadsheet format.

Structured Query Language (SQL) Structured querying language (SQL) is the language developed by IBM and is used to access and update data stored in the database.

supervised learning In supervised learning, the target variable of interest is known and is available in a historical dataset.

supervised model A supervised model is one that consists of a defined target variable.

support Support measures the frequency of the specific association rule. Support shows the number of transactions that include the items of interest divided by the total number of transactions.

term-document matrix (TDM) The term-document matrix (TDM) uses rows and columns to separate the text

term frequency (TF) The term frequency (TF) measures the number of times a term (or word) occurs in a document.

testing data (also known as holdout data) A testing dataset is used to evaluate the final selection algorithm on a dataset unique from the training and validation datasets.

testing dataset A testing dataset is used to evaluate the final selection algorithm on a dataset unique from the training and validation datasets.

text classification Text classification creates categories or groups that are associated with the content.

time series Time series visuals demonstrate how values change over time.

tokenization Tokenization is the process of taking the entire text data corpus and separating it into smaller, more manageable sections.

tokens A token is a smaller section of the entire text data corpus and is known as the basic unit of analysis in the text analytics process.

topic modeling Topic modeling enables the analyst to discover hidden thematic structures in the text.

training data The training dataset is the data used to build the algorithm and "learn" the relationship between the predictors and the target variable.

training dataset The training dataset is the data used to build the algorithm and "learn" the relationship between the predictors and the target variable.

treatment Treatment is the term used to describe the digital marketing intervention being tested.

U

undirected network When no arrow is directed toward a node, there is either a two-way direction or the relationship is referred to as undirected.

unit of analysis A unit of analysis describes the what, when, and who of the analysis.

unity Unity is achieved when there is a harmonious appearance and the design elements appear to belong together.

unstructured data Unstructured data does not have a predefined structure and does not fit well into a table format (within rows and columns).

unsupervised learning Unsupervised learning has no previously defined target variable. The goal of unsupervised learning is to model the underlying structure and distribution in the data to discover and confirm patterns in the data.

unsupervised model An unsupervised model is one that does not consist of a defined target variable.

V

validation data The validation data is used to assess how well the regression model estimates the target variable when compared to the actual values.

validation dataset The validation dataset is used to assess how well the algorithm estimates the target variable, and helps select the model that most accurately predicts the target value of interest.

value Value means the data is useful for making accurate business decisions.

value (color) Value is the lightness or darkness of the color. The color changes from a high value color when adding white to the hue or to a low value color when adding black to the hue.

variables Variables are characteristics or features that pertain to a person, place, or object. Marketing analysts explore relationships between variables to improve decision making.

variety (data) Variety refers to the variety of the dataset. Holistic and diverse data provides a better understanding of customers and market situations.

variety (visualization) Variety in the type of visualizations used (e.g., bar graph, line chart, map, etc.); promotes engagement in the presentation, and helps viewers process the information into long-term memory.

velocity Velocity refers to the rapid pace in which data is being collected or is available.

veracity Veracity refers to the messy data that could have missing values, inconsistencies in the unit of measurement, erroneous information, or lack of reliability.

volume Volume refers to large amounts of data per time unit.

W

Ward's method Ward's method applies a measure of the sum of squares within the clusters summed over all variables.

weights Weights determine how important each neuron is. Features that are important in predicting the output have larger weights.

word cloud A word cloud provides a high-level understanding of frequently used terms.

Note: Page numbers in *italics* represent exhibits.

owned digital marketing media, 410–412, *411*

paid digital marketing media, 412–413, *412–413*

in practice, 408–414

Digital marketing media

earned, 413–414, *414*

owned, 410–412, *411*

paid, 412–413, *412–413*

Dimensions, 114

Direct channel, 424

Directed network relationship, 380, *380*

Disch, William, 70–71

Discovery questions, for business problem identification, 9–10

Discrete data, 14

Dish Network, 339

Disney, 188, 235

Display channel, 424

Distances, measurement with hierarchical clustering, 273–275, *274–275*

Distribution channels, 11–12

Distribution of node degrees, 381, *381*

Divisive clustering, 273

DMway, 232

Domino's Pizza, 339–340

dotdata Enterprise, 232

Drewes, Peter, 31, 37–38, 40, 42, 43

Dummy coding, 46, 151

Dunkin', 5, 407

E

Earned digital marketing media, 413–414, *414*

Earned digital media, 407

eBay, 29

E-commerce, 422–441

Edges, 379

Edge weight, 379

Effect size, 44

Egocentric network, 380

Eigenvector centrality, *382,* 382–383

Elbow chart, 272, *272*

Emphasis, as principle of design, 99

Enron, 413

Ensemble models

approaches to, 239

bagging, *239,* 239–240

boosting, 240, *240*

creation of, 238–239

defined, 238

Enterprise Resource Planning (ERP), 35

Error term (e), 144

ESPN, 69

Ethics, 240

Euclidean distance, 273, *274*

Expected confidence, 310

Expected customer experience, 313

Expedia, 3

Exploratory data analysis

cognitive analytics. *See* Cognitive analytics

defined, 66

importance of, 66–67

External sources of data, 71

Extract, Transform, and Load (ETL)

functions of, 36, *36*

traditional, 36

using Hadoop, 36

Extraction, data, 36

F

Facebook, 21, 31, 72, 234, 373, 380, 384, 415, 424

Farmers Insurance, 236

Features, 19–20, 33, 43–44, 46, 142. *See also* Variables

Feature selection, 153, *153*

FedEx, 105

Feedback, 70

Filters pane, Tableau, 119

Ford, 339

Foreign keys, 33

Form, as design element, 101

Format, data quality measurement, 41–42

Forward propagation, neural networks, 190

Forward selection, 154

FP-growth algorithm, 326

Frequency bar chart, 344, *344*

Frequency distributions, 107–109

G

Gain theta parameter, 330

"Garbage in, garbage out" statement, 39, 40, 237

General Data Protection Regulation (GDPR), 195, 196, 241, 313

General Electric, 30

Geographic location, as categorical variable, 46